Most people have three things in common when they buy a car.

"Edmund's® arms you with more facts. In addition to reviews and specs, new-car buyers will find each car's invoice price, sticker price, destination charge and dealer holdback (profit the dealer makes even if the car sells at invoice)."

—Kristin Davis, **Kiplinger's Personal Finance Magazine,** December, 1997

"Never pay retail. Buy only at wholesale or below. When buying a car, it is <u>imperative</u> that you know the dealer's cost. Refer to Edmund's® ... price guides for current dealer cost information. Armed with this information, you can determine the price that provides the dealer with a <u>minimum</u> 'win' profit."

—Lisa Murr Chapman, **The Savvy Woman's Guide to Cars** (New York, NY: Bantam Books, 1995)

"Edmund's®...is jam-packed with valuable information on virtually every new and used vehicle model as well as tips and safety information."

—Glenn Fannick, **Dow Jones Business Directory** (http://bd.dowjones.com), April 20, 1998

"The Edmund's® car buying guide print version...is an excellent product for consumers to use...(and is) one of the best auto information sources."

—Paul Maghielse, **The Motley Fool** (http://www.fool.com/car/step5car.htm), March 8, 1998

"Another resource of general auto pricing information can be found in bookstores, called the Edmund's® New Car Price Books. *Make sure you get their latest quarterly edition..."*

—Darrell Parrish, **The Car Buyer's Art** (Bellflower, CA: Book Express, 1998)

"Using the percent factor to figure dealer cost is not as accurate as using specific information published in Edmund's® New Car Prices.*"*

—Mark Eskeldson, **What Car Dealers Don't Want You to Know** (Fair Oaks, CA: Technews Publishing, 1997)

"Edmund's® Automobile Buyers Guides are among the most respected new car books around...they're well-written, too, even entertaining. You'll also find detailed pricing information, as well as information about how dealers structure their prices. Ever heard of "dealer holdback"? You can use this kind of knowledge in bargaining for a great price."

—**Houston Chronicle,** January 23, 1998

"Wouldn't it be nice if you could know beforehand the dealer's cost for the new vehicle you just fell in love with? Wouldn't it be even nicer if you knew how much to offer him over his costs, a price he would just barely be able to accept? Well you are in luck. You can find out exactly what the car cost the dealership ... in Edmund's® auto books."

—Burke Leon, **The Insider's Guide to Buying A New or Used Car** (Cincinnati, OH: Betterway Books, 1997)

"If you really want the nitty-gritty, you're going to have to ... (get) ... Edmund's® New Car Prices. *This little book is a gold mine for the curious car buyer... It is an automobile fancier's delight, a straightforward, meaty compendium of raw facts. Buy the book, follow the steps outlined ... and you will determine the exact cost of just about any car."*

—Remar Sutton, **Don't Get Taken Every Time** (New York, NY: Penguin Books, 1997)

Perfect Partners

USED CARS: PRICES & RATINGS

For over 30 years, Edmund's® has guided smart consumers through the complex used car marketplace. By providing you with the latest trade-in and market value, you are able to determine a fair price for your car before negotiations begin.

Whether buying, selling, or trading, Edmund's® *Used Cars: Prices & Ratings* gives all the information you need to get your very best deal.

- Prices Most American and Imported Used Cars, Pickup Trucks, Vans, and Sport Utilities
- Shows Summary Ratings for Most Used Vehicles
- Listings Cover Models Over Last 10 Years
- Price any Vehicle Quickly and Accurately
- Adjust Value for Optional Engines, Equipment and Mileage

$8.99
CANADA
$11.99

For information on all Edmund's® Automotive Books, call 914-962-6297

1999

Edmund's®

NEW TRUCKS

PRICES & REVIEWS

"THE ORIGINAL CONSUMER PRICE AUTHORITY"

Cover photo:
1999 Honda Odyssey

ISBN: 0-87759-644-1
ISSN: 1089-8735

TABLE OF CONTENTS

SUMMER 1999 **VOL S3302-9909**

Special offer from 1-800-CAR-CLUB - details on page 3

1999 Oldsmobile Bravada

Edmund's®

Edmund Publications Corp.
P.O. Box 18827 • Beverly Hills, CA 90209-4827

President: Peter Steinlauf *Vice President:* Lev R. Stark

Since 1966, Edmund's has been providing consumers with the information they need to get the best price on a new car. This edition of New Car Prices continues the tradition of listing most of the cars available on the market today, including pricing data for dealer invoice price and Manufacturer's Suggested Retail Price (MSRP) on each model and its options. For each model, we also provide detailed lists of standard equipment and specifications. Helpful articles will allow you to make an educated decision about your purchase.

What's New For 1999?

The first annual Edmund's "Most Wanted List" appears in this edition of *New Trucks: Prices and Reviews*. Our editorial staff gathered in September of 1998 to hash over the roster of 1999 models available to the public. We picked our favorites in a variety of price and size classes; keep in mind that we're a group of men and women that enjoy driving. You will be able to find out which new models our staff covets by checking our Most Wanted article. Also, we've indicated our favorites throughout the book with a Most Wanted graphic that overlays photography for each winner.

How did we select the Edmund's Most Wanted? Only 1999 models were eligible, and at least one member

of our editorial team had to have driven the vehicle. We awarded Most Wanted status to those cars and trucks that the majority of our staffers would park in their own garage. On some nominations there was unanimous agreement, but on others we engaged in long discussions that occasionally involved shouting, cursing, and, in one instance, a near brawl. The resulting Edmund's Most Wanted List is, in our collective opinion, the best of what's available on the market today.

We've also added bumper bash crash test results, as conducted by the Insurance Institute for Highway Safety (IIHS). See our crash test article for a complete listing of results from the IIHS and the National Highway and Traffic Safety Administration (NHTSA). If a vehicle isn't listed, it's because neither organization had tested the vehicle before April 1999.

Why Are Some Models Missing From This Book?

With printing costs escalating and more new models on the market than ever before, we had to decide if we were going to raise the price of the guide or find a way to cut the number of pages in the book. We opted for the latter, removing vehicles that have a base price over $55,000. We also cut commercial cargo van models from the listings and trimmed our spec table to save space in the guide. The end result is that the price stays the same and our book still covers most of the vehicles on the market today. For pricing on those expensive models that are missing, such as the AM General Hummer, Land Rover Range Rover and Lexus LX470, please visit our website at http://www.edmunds.com. Buyers looking for information on cargo vans can get it on our website as well.

How Do I Use This Guide?

If you're new to Edmund's, or are new to the car buying experience, here is how to use this guide. Your first step should be to visit a car dealership. Take a pad of paper with you, and write down all pertinent information from the window sticker of the car you like. Then, go home and snuggle up with your Edmund's guide to start figuring out how to get the best deal on the car of your dreams.

Read the articles on **dealer holdbacks**, **buying your next new automobile**, and **leasing tips**. Then study the make and model that you're interested in. You'll find a representative photo of the vehicle, followed by a synopsis of "What's New for 1999." Then, a short review provides our opinion of the car, followed by safety data. An extensive listing of standard equipment for each trim level comes next, telling you what items are included in the base price of the vehicle. The first paragraph pertains to the base model, and if more than one trim level is available, successive paragraphs will explain what additional features the additional trim levels include over the base model.

"Generally, you can haggle about 25% off dealer-installed accessories with little effort."

Next is the meat of this guide: the pricing data. Each vehicle has base invoice price and base MSRP listed for each trim level, and the destination charge, which is the cost of shipping the vehicle from the factory to the dealer. Don't forget to add the destination charge, which is non-negotiable, when pricing a vehicle. Following the base prices and destination charge is a listing of all the optional equipment available on the vehicle from the factory. Along the left margin you'll find a factory code for each option. The dealer invoice price and the MSRP are listed near the right margin. Some option listings have short descriptions that tell you, for example, what might be included in a particular option package, or what trim level the option is available on, or that you must purchase the power lock group to get the power sunroof. Options are listed alphanumerically by option code.

You'll notice that some imported makes do not have options listings. This is because the automaker includes the most popular accessories as standard equipment on a particular trim level, and any additional items that you might like to add to the vehicle will have to be purchased from and installed by the dealer, or are installed at the port of entry. For example, more expensive Hondas might be equipped with power door locks and power windows standard from the factory. Air conditioning is sometimes a dealer add-on, and each dealer may price the item differently. Generally, you can haggle about 25% off dealer-installed accessories with little effort.

Looking for the exact specifications of your dream car? Check the back of this book, where you'll find charts displaying the length of the vehicle, the curb weight of the vehicle, and how much horsepower the base engine makes, among others. This format allows you to easily locate and compare specifications between different models and trim levels.

Supply and Demand

Now that you've priced the vehicle you're interested in, and you've read the articles about how to get the best deal, you're ready to go back to the dealership and buy your new car armed with the knowledge and information that is crucial to getting a good deal. Keep in mind that the laws of supply and demand apply to automobiles as much as they apply to any other material commodity. If a vehicle is in great demand and short supply, don't expect to get much of a discount. On the other hand, inflated inventories and tough competition mean that deals are readily available on models that aren't selling well. If a rebate is available on the car or truck you're shopping for, that's an indicator that the dealer will slash the price to the bone to get the car off the lot.

If you've got to be the first on your block with a hot new model, you'll pay for the privilege. In fact, dealers sometimes demand profit above the MSRP on ultra hot models, and they expect to get it. Meanwhile, it is not uncommon for older, stale models to sell below invoice, thanks to hefty incentive programs and rebates, particularly at year-end clearance time. All things considered equal, Edmund's feels that a profit amounting to 3% over invoice to the dealer is fair on a new vehicle.

Write to Us

New Trucks: Prices and Reviews has even more to offer, from step-by-step cost worksheets that you can use right at the dealership, to lists of warranty coverage, to pages of crash test data. Edmund's strives to give you precise, accurate information so that you can make your very best deal, and we invite your comments. Please send correspondence to:

Edmund Publications Corporation
P.O. Box 18827
Beverly Hills, CA 90209-4827
Attn: Automotive Editors

or send e-mail to:
editor@edmunds.com

We wish you luck in your hunt for a new vehicle. Use the information contained within to your advantage!

NOTE: All information and prices published herein are gathered from sources which, in the editor's opinion, are considered reliable, but under no circumstances is the reader to assume that this information is official or final. All prices are represented as approximations only, in US dollars, and are rounded to the highest whole dollar amount over 50 cents. Unless otherwise noted, all prices are effective as of 4/1/99, but are subject to change without notice. The publisher does not assume responsibility for errors of omission or interpretation. The computerized consumer pricing services advertised herein are not operated by nor are they are the responsibility of the publisher. The publisher assumes no responsibility for claims made by advertisers regarding their products or services.

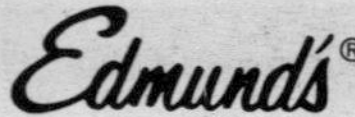

STEP-BY-STEP COST WORKSHEET

MAKE: EXTERIOR COLOR:

MODEL: INTERIOR COLOR:

TRIM LEVEL: ENGINE SIZE/TYPE:

ITEMS	INVOICE
Basic Vehicle Price:	
Optional Equipment:	
1.	
2.	
3.	
4.	
5.	
6.	
7.	
8.	
9.	
10.	
11.	
12.	
13.	
14.	
15.	
TOTAL	
SUBTRACT Holdback Amount (if ordering car)	
SUBTRACT Rebates and/or Incentives	
ADD 3% Fair Profit	
ADD Destination Charge	
ADD Advertising Fees (1% of MSRP maximum)	
ADD Documentation and D&H fees ($100 maximum)	
SUBTRACT Trade-In Value or Cash Down Payment	
or	
ADD Difference Between Trade Value and Loan Balance	
FINAL Price for Purchase or Capitalized Cost for Lease	
ADD Sales Taxes (and Registration fees, if applicable in your region)	
TOTAL COST	

HOW TO BUY YOUR NEXT NEW AUTOMOBILE

Every automobile buyer has but one thought in mind — to save money by getting a good deal. Your goal should be to pay 3% over the dealer's invoice, not the 10-15% the dealer wants you to pay. Use the following guide to help you plan your purchase:

Step 1 Know what type of vehicle you need, and study the different models available.

Step 2 Test-drive, as extensively as possible, each model you're interested in. Pay special attention to safety features, design, comfort, braking, handling, acceleration, ride quality, ease of entry and exit, etc.

Step 3 Check insurance rates on the models you're interested in to make sure the premiums fall within your budget.

Step 4 Contact several financial institutions to obtain loan rate information. Later on, you can compare their arrangement with the dealer's financing plan.

Step 5 Find the exact vehicle you want, and copy all of the contents of the window sticker onto a pad of paper. Then, use the information in this book to determine dealer invoice (if ordering the vehicle from the factory, just use the book to determine what the order will cost when you place it):

a) Total the dealer invoice column for the model and equipment you want using the cost worksheet on the opposite page.

b) Subtract any applicable customer rebates and dealer incentives.

c) If ordering the vehicle, find the holdback amount on page 513, and subtract this amount as well. If the dealer orders the vehicle, he won't pay floorplanning (the charge to stock the vehicle), or advertising, which the holdback is designed to subsidize.

d) Add 3% fair profit. Keep in mind that hot-selling models in high demand and short supply will command additional profit, sometimes in excess of MSRP.

e) Add the destination charge, which is non-negotiable. Also expect to be charged advertising fees. You should negotiate advertising fees, and pay no more than 1% of the vehicle's MSRP.

f) Some dealers charge a Delivery & Handling (D&H) fee. Negotiate this fee. It's just added profit.

Step 6 Shop this price around to several different dealerships. The dealer who meets or comes closest to your target price should get your business. Be sure that the dealer's price quote will be your final cost. Get it in writing!

Step 7 If your present vehicle will be used as a trade-in, negotiate the highest possible value for it. Try not to accept a value that is less than Edmund's® trade-in value for your car (consult Edmund's® *Used Cars; Prices and Ratings* book). When trading in your vehicle, you should deduct the trade value from the cost of the new vehicle. If you owe the bank more money than the trade-in is worth to the dealer, you are upside-down on your trade and must add the difference between what you owe and the trade value to the cost of the new vehicle. If you're making a cash down payment, either with or without a trade-in, be sure to deduct this amount from the cost of the new vehicle as well.

Step 8 To the final vehicle cost, add dealer preparation charges (a.k.a., D&H fee), documentation fees, applicable state and/or local sales taxes and, in some areas, license plate charges.

Step 9 When talking to the finance manager as you close the deal, he or she will try to sell you rustproofing, undercoating, protection packages, dealer-added options, and an extended warranty or service contract. Forget about this stuff. Dealers charge a substantial markup on these usually useless items to fatten the profit margin on your deal.

Step 10 Enjoy your new vehicle, knowing that you did everything possible to get the best deal.

See our Frequently Asked Questions section on Page 517 for more information on cars and car buying.

EDMUND'S® MOST WANTED

by Christian Wardlaw, B. Grant Whitmore, Greg Anderson, Ingrid Palmer, John Clor and Karl Brauer
Automotive Editors, Edmund Publications

Our staff members get the same question over and over: What's the best car or truck? There are many ways to answer this question, starting with quizzing the inquiring mind about their needs and wants in a vehicle.

Still, it seems readers want to know what cars and trucks we'd buy given the resources. So our editorial staff gathered to hash over the roster of 1999 models available to the public. We picked our favorites in a variety of price and size classes: keep in mind that we're a group of men and women that enjoys driving. Our staff of writers ranges in age from the mid-twenties to the mid-forties. Half of us have kids; one of us has two large dogs. We camp, hike, bike, surf and coach hockey. We enjoy long road trips. We need vehicles that fit this kind of lifestyle.

How did we select the Edmund's® Most Wanted? Only 1999 models were eligible, and at least one member of our editorial team had to have driven the vehicle. Nominations were accepted, and votes were counted. Majority rule determined the winner. On some occasions there was unanimous agreement, such as our election of the Honda Accord for best midsize under $25,000. On others we engaged in long discussions that occasionally involved shouting and cursing, such as when deciding if the Acura 3.2TL or the Saab 9-5 should be our selection for best midsize $25,000 to $40,000. And in one instance, a near brawl ensued over a Chevrolet/GMC Suburban vs. Toyota Land Cruiser debate for best fullsize SUV.

But we survived, we're all still friends, and the resulting Edmund's® Most Wanted List is, in our collective opinion, the best of what's available on the market today.

EDMUND'S® MOST WANTED

CARS: $10,000-$25,000

SUBCOMPACT: Honda Civic Hatchback

Shoppers in the lowest cost segment of the new car market are looking for value and reliability, and nothing comes close to matching the Honda Civic hatchback in either department. With room for four adults, a folding rear seat to increase cargo capacity and funky styling to lend personality to the car, the Civic is perfect for everyone from a college freshman to a high-mileage commuter to a retired couple looking for wheels to tow behind the Winnebago. Cheap and relentlessly reliable, the Civic is also fun to drive. Starting prices are about $11,000 for a bare-bones CX, while another $1,500 buys DX trim with wheel covers, a stereo, a rear wiper and a cargo cover.

COMPACT: Volkswagen New Beetle

Honestly, who's gonna buy the Acura Integra, BMW 318ti, Chevrolet Cavalier Z24, Dodge Avenger, Ford Escort ZX2, Honda Civic, Hyundai Tiburon, Mercury Cougar, Mitsubishi Eclipse, Plymouth Neon, Pontiac Sunfire, or Saturn SC when the lovable Bug is available? Well, those who hate the New Beetle's retro style. But with three versions available (115-hp gas, 90-hp diesel and soon, 150-hp turbo) in a wide variety of colors, VW is building a Beetle for just about everyone. Better still, as the months wear on dealers should stop price-gouging customers looking for a taste of the 1960s poured atop solid 1990s engineering. Now all we need is a convertible.

MIDSIZE: Honda Accord V6 Sedan

There's a reason the Accord has enjoyed immense popularity during the past decade; it's a perfect family car. And with the most recent edition, interior volume is capacious enough to actually haul a good-sized family in comfort. The Accord is more than roomy; with a powerful V6 under the hood it gets out of its own way in a hurry. Simplicity is another hallmark of this Honda, and reliability is legendary. Finally, Accords hold their value like the Titanic does water. Aside from rather dull sheetmetal, it's very hard to go wrong with this Honda.

FULLSIZE: Ford Crown Victoria (twin – Mercury Grand Marquis)

These are the last body-on-frame rear-wheel drive sedans on the market. Favored by police departments, cab companies and Floridians in large numbers, the Crown Vic (and its twin, the Mercury Grand Marquis) have survived for a reason – they're the best at what they do. A strong 4.6-liter V8 engine delivers smooth power. Six adults can occupy the cabin with little discomfort. Interstate travel is effortless, and these big Fords are among the few passenger cars that can tow something larger than a Sea Doo. Looking for a budget Lincoln? Just add leather.

WAGON: Subaru Legacy Outback

With all-wheel drive, a gutsy powertrain, a roomy interior and a well-deserved reputation for quality, this selection was a no-brainer. Look past the faux-SUV styling cues and you'll find a competent wagon that can crawl over terrain that the neighbor's Taurus can't. Tidy exterior packaging blends with an airy cabin to provide the Outback with a light and lively feel. A cold weather package provides seat warmers, heated exterior mirrors and a wiper deicer. While this design is aging rapidly (particularly the dashboard's ergonomics), no wagon under $25,000 beats the Outback for everyday practicality with a splash of panache.

SPORT SEDAN: Ford SVT Contour

Check out that sticker price. Can you believe it? This fully-loaded sedan provides 0-60 blasts measuring just 7.5 seconds, hauls itself down from the same speed in a shade over 130 feet, and holds a corner as well as a Chevy Camaro – all for $23,000. And the sound as that hot-rodded V6 winds up is pure bliss to the enthusiast. Limited production means exclusivity, even if it looks little different from Hertz specials in the airport parking lot. With a power boost, a roomier back seat and expanded color availability for 1999, the SVT Contour is better than ever.

SPORT COUPE: Honda Prelude

To drive the Prelude is to love the Prelude. Sure, it's somewhat dowdy three-box styling and odd, oversized headlights may be off-putting, but the cops don't notice this Honda nearly as much as they do a be-spoilered Mitsubishi Eclipse. Fire up the rev-happy, 200-horsepower, 2.2-liter, VTEC four-banger and head for the hills. You'll never be the same. This is a driver's car first and foremost, blended with Honda reliability and a no-nonsense interior environment. Add a small back seat good for toting passengers in a pinch, and you've got a perfect sport coupe recipe.

CONVERTIBLE: Mazda Miata

Two seats, a quick dropping top, flawless handling, an eager motor, a snick-snick gearbox, astounding Bose audio and Jag Junior styling all conspire to make the Mazda Miata irresistible. This car boosts energy better than a MET-RX and Viagra malted. It will put a smile on your face, as well as a burn if you forget the sunblock. And if the weather isn't cooperating, the Miata is still a fine companion with the top raised. This year's fresh design includes more power, a glass rear window with defogger, improved handling and other refinements. So what are you waiting for?

SPORTS CAR: Chevrolet Camaro Z28 (twins – Pontiac Firebird Formula and Trans Am)

Pure muscle characterizes this trio from General Motors. A 305-horsepower rip-snorting 5.7-liter V8 is housed beneath the long, low hood, optimally connected to a six-speed manual transmission. Power is transmitted to rear wheels that can smoke the tires with little provocation. Interiors are dank and cheaply outfitted, the price you pay for such inexpensive performance. Exteriors are sleek on the Camaro and in-your-face on the Firebird. Neither car would ever qualify as sophisticated or refined. But the charm here lies in brute force, not finesse. Sadly, GM is considering killing these slow-selling pony cars. Get 'em while you can.

CARS: $25,001-$40,000

COMPACT: BMW 323i

If you truly consider yourself an automotive enthusiast, then a BMW 3-Series is automatically on your "must drive" list. These cars are *that* good. And every time BMW improves the breed, as it has done in the case of the new 323i, it serves only to raise the bar a little higher for everybody else. Don't let the European "323" designation fool you: Underhood is a silky-smooth, 24-valve 2.5-liter that puts the power of 170 horses to the pavement. Thanks to variable valve timing and 10.5:1 compression, this dual overhead cam inline six can propel the 323i to 60 mph in about seven seconds. Make ours a five-speed manual, please, with the optional Sport Suspension and 16-inch alloy wheels wearing 225/50 rubber. Behind the wheel, this car is a model of communication with its driver. And with freshened sheetmetal that looks as if it were hewn from a single hunk of metal, you won't find a more purposeful looking compact at any price.

MIDSIZE: Saab 9-5

There were plenty of reasons to find favor with the all-new Saab 9-5: distinctive styling, improved body rigidity, new fully independent suspension, innovative safety features – even theft-resistant door locks. But when an ingenious, asymmetrically turbocharged 3.0-liter V6 was added as a mid-year option, it became clear that Saab was positioning this new model as a showcase for innovation. Indeed, by integrating a low-pressure turbo on the front cylinder bank and feeding compressed air to the rest of the V6, the 3.0-liter generates 200 horsepower, with some 229 pounds-feet of torque spread across a nice, fat band from a down-low 2,500 rpm all the way up to 4,000. If the sedan's this neat, we can't wait for the 9-5 Wagon (which debuted at the Paris Motor Show) to arrive Stateside this spring.

FULLSIZE: Chrysler LHS (close relative – Chrysler 300M)

Ask car-watchers what automotive designs catch their eye on the road today, and you'll likely hear mention of the Chrysler LHS (or its stunning sister, the Chrysler 300M). One glance will tell you these cars are meant to define cutting-edge style and grace. For our money, these smoothly sculpted models are a refreshing departure from typical cookie-cutter GM and over-oval-esque Ford sheetmetal. The idea of resurrecting a glorious nameplate and placing it on a modern interpretation that doesn't quite live up to the legend is a topic for another time and place. But at least the lines of an LHS attempt to establish a heritage of daring LH-based designs true to their concept car roots. The feature-laden LHS boasts raw curb appeal, a cavernous interior, roomy trunk and a smooth ride, all motivated by a 253-horsepower 3.5-liter V6. What more could you ask for in a full-size Mopar? All right, who said a V8-powered rear-driver?

WAGON: Audi A4 Avant 2.8

When "American Family Trucksters" like those of *Vacation* fame gave way to the birth of the minivan and SUV, the American station wagon segment was as dead as old Aunt Edna. It took more than a decade for us to learn that driving a minivan is like driving … well, a van, and that driving an SUV is like driving a truck. Then marketers invented the word "carlike" to describe their vans, trucks and SUVs, and suddenly the idea of a car-based wagon became almost refreshing. Problem is, when wagon variants are spun off some of today's clean-looking front-drive cars, the results are sometimes visually disturbing. It is rare, indeed, when a wagon is actually more stylish than its sedan sibling, which is what makes the ruggedly handsome Audi A4 Avant a stand-alone among few peers. Powered by Audi's190-horse five-valve 2.8-liter V6, the Avant Quattro automatic can reach 60 mph in a little better than eight seconds. There's even an enhanced performance package that includes a lower, firmer suspension, thicker rear stabilizer bar and 205/55 tires on 16-inch alloy wheels. All this makes driving an A4 Avant sport wagon like driving ... well, a roomier A4 2.8 sport sedan. The Avant is a perfect cure for a family suffering from the minivan blahs.

SPORT SEDAN: Audi A4 2.8

Looking for a small sport sedan that blends performance and luxury in an unmistakably European package but don't have the bread to plunk down for a Bimmer or Benz? Look no further than Audi's little A4 with the 2.8-liter V6. The look is contemporary, the finish superb, the performance satisfying – and the feel oh-so German! Slam the door on this baby bank vault, buckle into your leather bucket and the A4 will straighten a twisty section of tarmac like few Asian and even fewer domestic sport sedans can – and at a price that will distance itself from its Teutonic counterparts.

SPORT COUPE: Ford SVT Mustang Cobra

The mating of a sophisticated dual overhead cam V8 engine with a compliant chassis in the 1996 Cobra helped the Ford Special Vehicle Team add a new page to Mustang performance history. But Ford's hottest factory Mustang has always been saddled with the limited handling ability of a live rear axle – a setup that was quick to bare the Cobra's pony car roots when driven at the limit. What's more, Mustang fans have remained very vocal that the Cobra's hand-assembled 4.6-liter V8 needs more oats than the 305 ponies it makes all-too-high in the rev range. It took a while, but the folks at Team Mustang finally listened. The 1999 SVT Cobra is not only the first-ever Mustang to leave the factory with a true independent rear suspension, but it also packs 320 more useable horses to boot. Add a first-ever traction control system and other improvements such as increased seat travel, wrap it in fresh new sheetmetal (save for the greenhouse) and hold the line on price, and the new Cobra is sure to be a hit with the performance crowd. Ford expects to build only about 5,000 Cobra Coupes and 3,000 Convertibles this year. As always, they are available only through one of the roughly 700 specially trained and certified SVT dealers across the United States and Canada.

CONVERTIBLE: BMW Z3 2.8

Two seats, flawless handling, a snick-snick gearbox – sure we said those things about the Miata, but there's one huge difference that sets BMW's mini-roadster light years apart from any other two-seater on the planet: the velvety torque of BMW's 2.8-liter inline six-cylinder engine. Yeah, we know that the Miata boasts Jag Junior styling and feels light as a feather, while the Z3's bodywork actually looks out of proportion to some and feels as thick and beefy as any BMW made to date. But even the upscale Mercedes-Benz SLK runabout can't play in the 2.8 Z3's sandbox. With the wind in your hair, a six-second 0-60 sprint in a car this size plants a smile on your face that no four-cylinder car can match.

SPORTS CAR: Chevrolet Corvette

Bet you wish you had a nickel for every time you read some auto editor write, "This is the best 'Vette yet." Us, too. It seems each time this classic American sports car has gone in for a remake over the last few decades, reviewers come back with that same old saw. But, like the boy who cried wolf, we're here to tell you that this time, it is *really* true. Without getting into a discussion of age, let's just say that we're including our experience with big blocks, LT1 small blocks, pace cars, LT5-powered ZR-1s, anniversary editions, second-generation LT1s – you name 'em. And toss in countless hours sampling rides at Bloomington Gold and Corvettes at Carlisle. Granted, the new, 345-horsepower LS1 V8 is not the most awe-inspiring 'Vette powerplant ever made. But its smoothness almost belies its pushrod architecture. And its delivery of power – when experienced in concert with this car's improved shift action, steering, brakes, suspension, rigidity, comfort, ergonomics and features – positions the new Corvette as a well-thought-out performance package that has obviously benefited from its own market experience. It may look a lot like the old 'Vette, but one drive will convince you there's never been a more capable Corvette built than the C5.

CARS: $40,001-$55,000

MIDSIZE: Mercedes-Benz E430

Near the top of the E-class food chain sits the V8-powered E430. Equipped with 275 horsepower, door-mounted side air bags, and a leather interior, this midsize sedan offers performance, safety, and luxury. There's also a BabySmart system that keeps the airbags from injuring young children and a Brake Assist system that keeps adults from injuring themselves. Of course, you could always opt for the E300DT that costs less and offers better mileage. But whom are we kidding? This is America, home of the V8.

FULLSIZE: Lexus LS400

Is it too confusing to call this the Cadillac of Lexuses? O.K., then we'll just say that for those interested in the pinnacle of luxury sedans, without spending over $55,000, this is it. I mean come on, a climate control system that automatically re-circulates the airflow when a pollution sensor detects high levels of exhaust in the outside air? How about a touch screen display that controls everything from the radio to the GPS system? The LS isn't just about gadgets, either. A new V8 with variable valve timing puts out 290 horsepower and scoots this luxury liner to 60 mph in less than 6.5 seconds. No, it won't give you BMW-type passion when traveling through twisties. But it might make you forget about that upcoming gridlock on your commute home.

WAGON: Volvo V70 AWD R

So you want to transport your family in comfort and safety without worrying about a rollover or getting 12 mpg? Then scrap those SUV plans and head down to your local Volvo dealer. In addition to the safety, comfort, and handling characteristics that are standard with all Volvos, you'll get the reassurance of all-wheel drive and the thrill of 236 turbocharged horsepower. These wagons offer almost everything the prudent parent could want. Side air bags? Check. Strengthened B-pillars? Check. Cutting edge style? Hmm, did we mention the side air bags are standard? When it comes to safe, non-SUVs, this one's the winner.

SPORT COUPE: BMW M3

Touted by some magazines as the "best handling car in the world," BMW's M3 is a tour de force that earns the company's "ultimate driving machine" title more appropriately than any other Bavarian product. At over $40,000 before you even add on the sunroof option, some might wonder if this is just an expensive and glorified version of a 328is. We have only one response for these misguided souls, "Drive It!" If you've got a pulse and even an ounce of automotive enthusiasm, you'll know what we're talking about.

SPORT SEDAN: BMW 540i

The V8 rear-drive sports sedan class is heating up with the top entries coming from upstart Lexus (GS400) and the always-impressive BMW (540i). After a recent shootout between these two titans, we found ourselves more than surprised by the overall competency of the GS. However, for pure smiles-per-mile, you simply can't beat the BMW 5-series. It offers every luxury option a mere mortal could need combined with the sort of driving experience we all want; smooth, safe, and thrillng at the same time. If you've got the cash, this is your car.

CONVERTIBLE: Mercedes-Benz SLK230

While the Boxster wins our pure sports car award in this price range, if you're looking for a car that offers all the benefits of top-down fun *and* all the practical advantages of a coupe, Mercedes' SLK230 delivers. With the touch of a button, the SLK's retractable, metal roof folds up and tucks itself neatly behind the two comfortable (and optionally heated) seats. Last year's model was a kick even with the standard automatic-only transmission. Now that manual shift is an option, the SLK is a joy to be seen in and drive. Additionally, since it's a Mercedes, features like front and side airbags, integrated rollbars, and even BabySmart technology are all standard equipment. Fun, practical, and safe, the SLK offers convertible fans the most while giving up the least.

SPORTS CAR: Porsche Boxster

We don't mean to belittle the recent efforts of BMW or Mercedes in the area of pure sports cars, but when it comes to making a high-performance two-seater for less than $55,000, Porsche's Boxster is way out in front. Sure, the SLK's got that mechanical folding roof and the Z3 looks like it was carved from a solid piece of billet aluminum. But with a mid-engine design, almost 10 cubic feet of storage space, and the fastest closing automatic top in the business (12 seconds) this German 'bahnstormer takes affordable performance to a new level. It pulls better slalom numbers than a *new* 911 and, at 201 horsepower, is no slouch on the straightaways. Look for a more powerful version to be available sometime this year.

TRUCKS: $10,000 - $25,000

COMPACT PICKUP: Dodge Dakota

The compact pickup segment is loaded with competent trucks. The Ford Ranger / Mazda B-Series twins are available with four-door extended cabs, the Toyota Tacoma is as reliable as a Swiss watch, and even the GM S-Series pickups offer substantial power for the money. But the pickup we most want in our garage is the Dodge Dakota. The Dakota provides a comfortable ride, a roomy cab, heavy-duty towing and hauling capacity, and capable performance both on and off the road. While it still doesn't offer more than two doors, its body is tight and rattle-free, and a quad-cab is coming soon. Plus, the R/T image truck appeals to our enthusiast roots. The R/T is a limited production sport truck, available only with rear driven wheels and a torque beast 5.9-liter V8 engine. A lowered suspension, fat wheels and tires, and gobs of power make the Dakota R/T as much fun to drive as many sport coupes.

FULLSIZE PICKUP: Ford F-250 Super Duty

Let's see...how much truck can we squeeze under the $25,000 mark? Well, a number of Ford F-250 Super Duty models equipped with a 6.8-liter V10 engine fit in quite nicely. Possibilities range from a 2WD SuperCab with Lariat trim to a 2WD Crew Cab XLT to a 4WD SuperCab in basic XL guise. The V10's 275 horsepower and 410 foot-pounds of torque are quite adequate at moving the truck's bulk up to speed in short order, or for hauling around massive pieces of farm equipment. The interior is not as refined as what you'll find in other full-sized trucks, but we're talking about performance here, not luxury. And for under $25,000, the F-250 Super Duty brings a lot of beef to the table.

MINIVAN: Dodge Caravan (twins – Chrysler Town & Country SX and Plymouth Voyager)

The minivan market makes up approximately eight percent of the U.S. new vehicle market, and Chrysler owns half of that share. The company invented the idea of a family room on wheels, and they've been able to stay one step ahead of the competition for the past 14 years. But times are changing, and minivans are getting better all the time – to put it bluntly, the competition is no longer a step behind. Except, of course, when it comes to value. The Caravan may not offer as much behind-the-seat storage space as its longer sibling with the Grand prefix, but this is one minivan that won't break the bank. It drives like a car, it can haul the entire family, and with a properly optioned SE model (with the 3.3-liter engine and

Sport Option Package, which includes a firmer suspension, alloy wheels, fog lights and monochromatic trim), the Caravan is the most fun-to-drive minivan you can buy at this price.

FULLSIZE VAN: Ford Econoline E-150

An available V10 powers this big van from Ford, but that's not the only reason this is our choice for the Most Wanted full-size van. The only competition comes from Dodge, whose van was engineered before the first wave of disco, and General Motors, in the form of the Chevrolet Express and the GMC Savana. GM's vans are of a newer design, but lack a quality feel inside, have pushrod engines, and are more ponderous in everyday driving. Full-size vans fell out of favor with families when the minivan was introduced, and few find their way into suburban driveways anymore. The Ford Econoline is the best of this small group, and can be had at prices that rival Ford's own Windstar. For your money, wouldn't you rather have more space and utility?

MINI SUV: Suzuki Grand Vitara

When the conservatively-named Vitara and Grand Vitara replaced the Sidekick, we were afraid that part of the truck's scrappy character would be lost. Thankfully, Suzuki only made things better: noise, vibration and harshness are way down while comfort, practicality and rugged capability are improved. Off road, the Grand Vitara's rigid body-on-ladderbox frame construction proves more than capable at handling trails, while on-road performance is improved due to less body roll and noise, more standard equipment and better visibility. The Grand Vitara's V6 offers buyers something that has never before appeared in this segment: power. Suzuki has infused the Grand Vitara with a 2.5-liter DOHC V6 engine that makes 155 horsepower and 160 foot-pounds of torque. If that doesn't make you seriously consider owning a small sport-ute, nothing will.

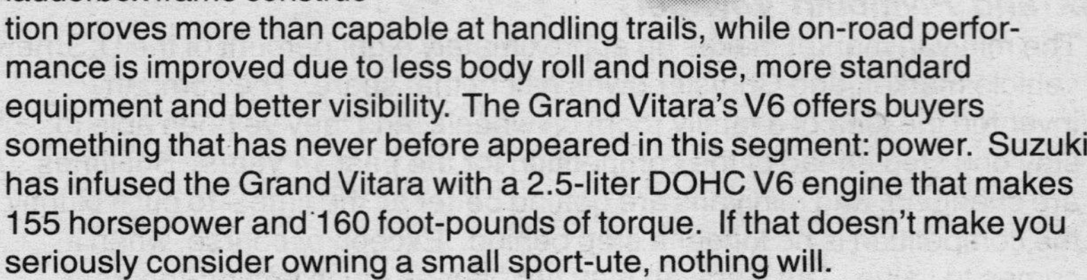

COMPACT SUV: Jeep Cherokee

Nothing beats a Jeep. That's true in every classification of vehicle the company makes, as we name all three Jeep models to our Most Wanted List of trucks. The Cherokee hasn't been improved much for 1999, but it still does everything right. Offering room for four adults, optional antilock brakes, exceptional ground clearance for its class, and an available 190-horsepower 4.0-liter engine, the Cherokee is fun on the road and off. Cherokee is available any way you want it: with two or four doors, in sparse SE trim or luxurious "Limited" trim complete with seat heaters. Just don't ask for a split-folding rear seat.

BEST OFFROAD: Jeep Wrangler

It doesn't take a leap of faith or imagination to choose the Jeep Wrangler as the best off-road vehicle for this price class. Our staff voted unanimously for the icon that continues to impress us year after year. The Wrangler is unbeatable when it comes to scrambling over rough terrain. But the off-road experience is only part of this truck's natural goodness. The interior is designed with the minimalist styling approach, and everything about it is utilitarian. The Quadra-Coil suspension makes the Wrangler stable on the road, so it can be used as an every day commuter. For 1999, Jeep has done away with the sliding heater controls in favor of dials, making the Wrangler that much more user friendly. Our favorite Wrangler is the Sport model with the hardtop and 4.0-liter inline six-cylinder motor.

TRUCKS: $25,000 +

FULLSIZE PICKUP: Ford F-150 Lightning

Ford claims that lightning *can* strike twice, and after driving the new Ford F-150 Lightning pickup, we agree. The three year wait for Ford's return to the sport pickup segment was well worth it, as the Lightning goes beyond a big engine and racing stripes. With a 5.4-liter SVT supercharged Triton V8, the Lightning produces a neck-snapping 340 horsepower. This truck has the ability to tow 5,000 pounds of widgets without breaking a sweat as well as attack corners like it was meant to be a sports coupe. It outperforms its competitors, is reasonably priced, and, suited up inside with white-on-black gauges, we couldn't resist.

MINIVAN: Honda Odyssey EX

Honda is poised to sell 60,000 of its all-new Odyssey minivans this year—and that's a minimal estimate for the largest Honda ever built. For '99, our minivan of choice touts a class-leading 3.5-liter 24-valve VTEC V6 engine that makes 210 horsepower @ 5,200 rpm and 229 foot-pounds of torque @ 4,300 rpm. It also comes with standard dual sliding doors that can be opened automatically, providing both practicality and gee-whiz appeal. With its popular third row seat that folds into the floor and its second row split seats that can be joined to make a bench, the Odyssey will take families into the minivan millenium.

COMPACT SUV: Jeep Grand Cherokee

With all the hype preceding the debut of the all-new 1999 Grand Cherokee, it would have been easy to be disappointed once behind the wheel. Instead, we found that Jeep took a really good sport-ute and made it even better. On-road driving feels more car-like than ever, the optional 235-horsepower V8 engine makes plenty of power, the slick-shifting automatic transmission chooses the right gear every time, and the truck simply kicked butt when put to the off-road test on a Jeep playground. All this coupled with subtle, appreciated enhancements, like moving the spare tire under the cargo area to create more cargo room, makes the Grand Cherokee the compact SUV we'd most like to see parked in our driveways this year.

FULLSIZE SUV / BEST OFFROAD: Toyota Land Cruiser

Though the Ford Expedition and GMC Suburban came close, they couldn't win out over the all-new Land Cruiser, with its 4.7-liter V8 engine and unbelievably smooth ride. Touting 9.8 inches of minimum ground clearance, a quiet, commodious cabin, and flashy passing power, the Land Cruiser is a tough beast to beat. Other pluses include third row seats that are easy to fold out, plenty of interior lighting for late-night map reading, and an engine so smooth it felt like it wasn't even running when stopped at lights. All in all, the Cruiser is the perfect family truckster that can also climb a mountain if it needs to.

1999 Honda Odyssey

By B. Grant Whitmore
photography courtesy of Honda Motors Co.

PROS:
Excellent visibility, good power, spacious interior, and ingenious seating options.

CONS:
The transmission exhibits hesitation when shifting under medium acceleration. Power window and lock buttons are not illuminated at night.

We see them all the time: minivans loaded to the gills with kids, pets and housing supplies, hurtling down the freeway toward some unknown suburban destination for a soccer match, piano recital or doctor's appointment. Does anyone ever look at the minivan and think to him or herself, "Boy, I sure wish I had one of those things for toting my kids around?" Maybe some people do, but I bet most of us have been leaning toward sport-utility vehicles when it comes time to make a decision to buy a family car. In fact, Edmund's knows that people have been buying more sport-utes than minivans, because we've figured out how to read monthly sales charts.

Most people on Edmund's staff would probably buy an SUV before a minivan, too. Strangely, though, the most vehement minivan detractor on our staff has decided that one minivan in particular suits his lifestyle more than a sport-utility vehicle. What changed his mind? What caused him to admit that he may, in fact, be a dork? The completely redesigned Honda Odyssey, that's what. Our intrepid writer had the chance to spend a week with the Odyssey over the Thanksgiving holiday, followed immediately by a full-size SUV comparison test. While the SUVs were impressive and their coolness factor incomparable, the Odyssey offered his brood greater utility than the largest multi-passenger, ground-pounding, sport-utes on the market.

The Odyssey is totally new this year, gaining an increased wheelbase, greater interior volume, and sliding rear passenger doors. The Odyssey's motor also got a huge power jump during the redesign: a 60-horsepower and 70-foot-pounds torque increase that totally transforms the Odyssey. These are considerable improvements for a minivan that was cited as too small and underpowered since its introduction in 1995. As we've said before, Honda only makes mistakes one time; the new Odyssey stands poised to redefine what it takes to compete for family car dollars.

Before you sport-ute defenders out there start composing your emails, let me explain. The editor who's judgment you question does not need a vehicle for four-wheeling – he would rather hike through the great outdoors than drive over it. He also doesn't need a vehicle for driving in foul weather – he lives in Southern California. What he does need is a vehicle that can handle his wife, two large dogs, three small cats, and a whole lot of gear, for routine trips to the family cabin and to his parent's house during the holidays. Could an SUV do the job? You bet. He and his family have done the drive plenty of times in Navigators, Explorers, Mountaineers and Rodeos. None of those trucks, however, was as perfectly suited to the job as the new Odyssey.

Just looking at the Odyssey lets you know that it is purpose-built for moving large quantities of people and their stuff great distances in comfort. A mere 201 inches separates the tip of the front bumper from the tail of the rear bumper on the Odyssey. Yet this minivan offers 15 more cubic feet

"... nothing, not even the vaunted Chrysler minivans, offers as much interior versatility as the Honda Odyssey."

of total cargo space (163.3 cubic feet with folded and stowed rear and second-row seats) than the 219-inch, road-hogging Suburban. Sure, the Odyssey may seat only seven people, as opposed to the Suburban's nine, but, unless you are the captain of a softball team, you probably don't need to drive nine people around on a regular basis.

Where the Odyssey differs from sport-utes, and other minivan competition for that matter, is the ease with which the Odyssey's people- and cargo-carrying capacities can be exploited. Dual power sliding rear doors on EX models make entry to the second-row seats simple and convenient. A low floor makes it easy for toddlers and puppies to clamber aboard without banging their shins. Variable seating locations mean that the middle seats can be positioned as captain's chairs or a bench seat by merely sliding the modular units along a lateral track. The rear seat can be used to hold three additional passengers, or can be folded flat with the floor for cargo hauling by simply pulling on two straps and pushing it downward. In our opinion, nothing, not even the vaunted Chrysler minivans, offers as much interior versatility as the Honda Odyssey.

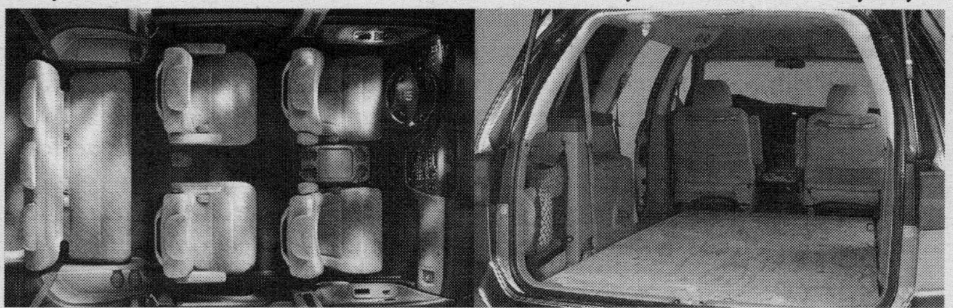

The Odyssey does not cater solely to passengers and cargo; drivers are also treated to a number of controls and features that will make their experience on the open road a pleasurable one. Peering out of the windshield of the Odyssey is like watching the world go by on an Imax screen. The Odyssey's windshield seems impossibly large, offering the most amazing forward visibility some of us have ever enjoyed. To capitalize on this, the front seats sit relatively high, giving owners that king-of-the-road feeling that so many sport-ute buyers crave. An eight-way power driver's seat (standard on the EX) makes it easy to find a comfortable seating position, and well-positioned center console controls mean that even short drivers won't have to lean to the right to change the interior temperature or activate the rear window defroster. Steering wheel-mounted cruise control and stereo buttons further enhance a driver's ability to operate the Odyssey with eyes on the road. An abundance of cubbyholes makes it easy

"... although it was seamless during regular around-town driving, the Odyssey suffered somewhat during hill climbing."

for drivers to stow cell phones, chewing gum and road maps, and the cupholders had no difficulty accepting a large Mountain Dew. Our drivers found the Odyssey to be a comfortable, if not terribly invigorating, place to spend the afternoon.

The driving experience in the Odyssey may lack excitement, but it is by no means bad. The powerful 3.5-liter V6 under the hood is derived from the same engine found in the ultra-smooth Honda Accord. In this application the motor gains a half-liter of displacement and makes 210 horsepower @ 5200 rpm and 229 foot-pounds of torque @ 4300 rpm, giving the Odyssey very good acceleration and passing ability. This is particularly impressive because the Odyssey now qualifies as a Low Emissions Vehicle (LEV) as classified by the California Air Resources Board (CARB).

Transferring the power from the engine to the front wheels is Honda's ubiquitous four-speed automatic transaxle that also sees duty on the Accord. We found that the shift quality was typically good, providing a strong kickdown when passing was necessary, and although it was seamless during regular around-town driving, the Odyssey suffered somewhat during hill climbing. In particular, the Odyssey's transaxle was hesitant to shift from overdrive into third gear when traveling uphill at freeway speeds. With the cruise control set, the minivan would begin to lose power, hesitate for a second, then shift with an abrupt jerk into third gear, finally giving us enough oomph to regain our lost speed. While not an earth-shattering defect, it was annoying enough to turn off the cruise control on hilly sections of road. We

found that jabbing the throttle when the engine started to bog reduced the transaxle's tendency to lag.

The Odyssey rides on a four-wheel, double-wishbone suspension; it's the first minivan to ever use this type of setup. This improves the Odyssey's handling characteristics by reducing the amount of bump the rear of the vehicle experiences when traversing uneven pavement. It also helps give the Odyssey fairly neutral handling, keeping this tall five-door vehicle from leaning too hard around tight corners.

Was our odyssey with the Odyssey perfect? Well, no. We wish the power door lock and window switches were backlit; we found them difficult to find and operate at night. We also wish the seat upholstery were more upscale — crushed velour looks low rent in this otherwise tastefully appointed cabin. As previously mentioned, we can't help but want the Odyssey's transaxle to have better shift quality.

Nevertheless, the Odyssey is a nearly perfect family vehicle. While a full-blown comparison test may be in order to confirm this, we are fairly certain that the Honda Odyssey is the best minivan on the market in the United States right now. There is a downside to that, however. Honda is planning to build only 60,000 Odysseys this year. Demand is expected to be high, so plan on paying sticker for quite awhile. ▪

Vehicle Tested: *1999 Honda Odyssey EX*
Base Price of Test Vehicle: *$26,215 (including destination charge)*
Options on Test Vehicle: *None*
Price of Test Vehicle: *$26,215 (including destination charge)*

Abbreviations

8V	8-valve
12V	12-valve
16V	16-valve
24V	24-valve
2WD	two-wheel drive
4WD	four-wheel drive
4WS	four-wheel steering
ABS	antilock braking system
A/C	air conditioning
ALR	automatic locking retractor
Amp	ampere
AS	all-season
ASR	automatic slip regulation
AT	automatic
Auto	automatic
AWD	all-wheel drive
BSW	black sidewall
Cass	cassette
CD	compact disc
CFC	chloroflourocarbon
Cntrls	controls
Cntry	country
Conv	convertible
Cpe	coupe
CPI	cross-port injection
Cu. Ft.	cubic foot (feet)
Cyl.	cylinder
Diff.	differential
DOHC	dual overhead cam
Dr	door
DRL	daytime running light(s)
DRW	dual rear wheels
DSC	dynamic stability control
Dsl	diesel
EDL	electronic differential lock
EFI	electronic fuel injection
ELR	emergency locking retractor
EQ	equalizer
ETR	electronically-tuned radio
Ext.	extended
FWD	front-wheel drive
Gal	gallon(s)
GAWR	gross axle weight rating
GVW	gross vehicle weight
GVWR	gross vehicle weight rating
GPS	global positioning satellite
Hbk	hatchback
HD	heavy duty
HO	high output
Hp	horsepower
HUD	heads-up display
HVAC	heating, ventilation and air conditioning
I-4	inline four
I-5	inline five
I-6	inline six
ICCS	integrated chassis control system
IROC	International Race of Champions
L	liter
LB	longbed
Lb(s)	pound(s)
Lbs.-ft	pounds-feet
LCD	liquid crystal display
LED	light emitting diode
LH	left hand
LWB	long wheelbase
M&S	mud and snow
Mpg	miles per gallon
Mph	miles per hour
MPI	multi-port injection
MSRP	manufacturer's suggested retail price
N/A	not available OR not applicable
NC	no charge
NHTSA	National Highway and Traffic Safety Administration
NVH	noise, vibration and harshness
OD	overdrive
OHC	overhead cam

OHV	overhead valve	**SRW**	single rear wheels
Opt	option OR optional	**Std**	standard
OWL	outline white-letter	**Susp**	suspension
Pass	passenger	**SUV**	sport utility vehicle
Pkg	package	**SWB**	short wheelbase
PRNDL	Park, Reverse, Neutral, Drive, Low	**TDI**	turbocharged direct injection
r/l	right and left	**TOD**	torque on demand
RBL	raised black-letter	**Turbodsl**	turbodiesel
Reg	regular	**V6**	V-type six
RH	right hand	**V8**	V-type eight
Rpm	revolutions per minute	**V10**	V-type ten
RWD	rear-wheel drive	**V12**	V-type twelve
SB	shortbed	**VR**	v-rated
SBR	steel-belted radial	**VSC**	vehicle skid contrl
Sdn	sedan	**VTEC and**	variable valve timing lift electronic control
SFI	sequential fuel injection	**W/T**	work truck
SLA	short/long arm	**Wgn.**	wagon
SMPI	sequential multi-port injection	**WOL**	white outline-letter
SOHC	single overhead cam	**WS**	work series
SPI	sequential port injection	**WSW**	white sidewall
Sprchgd	supercharged	**X-cab**	extended cab

1999 SLX

1999 Acura SLX

What's New?

The SLX is carried over unchanged from a year ago.

Review

Corporate sharing is all the rage these days. Manufacturers are scrambling to fill the holes in their lineups by slapping their badges on vehicles they buy from other makers. Even highly regarded firms like Acura are not above climbing into a cozy relationship with another marque; witness the Acura SLX. Based on Isuzu's competent Trooper, the Acura is a marginally spruced-up version of the same truck. This isn't necessarily a bad thing, but it does seem dishonest. Imagine the embarrassment of the SLX owner who thinks they bought something special only to find that they are driving an Isuzu?

The SLX has a 3.5-liter, dual-overhead-cam engine that produces 215 horsepower at 5,400 rpm and 230 foot-pounds of torque at 3,000 rpm. It delivers capable acceleration in a vehicle this large, and this vehicle is definitely large. Markedly wider and taller than most of its competitors, the SLX has a rear cargo capacity capable of hauling several sheets of plywood.

Last year's revisions included a more powerful engine, as well as the Torque On Demand (TOD) drive system, which replaced conventional four-high mode for better performance on paved or slippery roads. While improved under the skin the interior design is starting to show its age. A recently revised instrument panel includes a digital odometer and trip meter.

The Acura SLX is priced the same as a fully loaded Isuzu Trooper. The SLX has a softer ride that results in improved on-road manners, but it still handles like a tall truck. Off-road capability is equal to the ground-pounding Trooper, but large bumps may cause the suspension to bottom out; the price you pay for that luxurious highway ride. Of course, very few SLXs will ever find their way off-road, unless the gravel driveway of the local polo club counts.

Luxurious sport-utes of today are like the sports cars so prevalent in the mid-eighties. Designed for function but purchased for prestige, they are seldom driven to their full potential. With this in mind, the SLX is a fine vehicle, delivering the prestige and comfort that Acura owners have come to expect from their cars. If you are looking for a large, luxurious sport-utility vehicle, and you aren't prone to whipsawing the steering wheel back and forth during your daily commute, this truck might just be your best option.

Safety Data

Side Airbag: *Not Available*
4-Wheel ABS: *Standard*
Driver Crash Test Grade: *Average*
Side Impact Crash Test Front: *Not Available*
Crash Offset: *Not Available*
Integrated Child Seat(s): *Not Available*
Traction Control: *Not Available*
Passenger Crash Test Grade: *Average*
Side Impact Crash Test Rear: *Not Available*

Standard Equipment

SLX (4A): 3.5L V6 DOHC SMPI 24-valve engine; 4-speed electronic overdrive automatic transmission with lock-up; 80-amp battery; engine oil cooler; 75-amp alternator; driver selectable program transmission; part-time 4 wheel drive, auto locking hub control and electronic shift, 4.3 axle ratio; stainless steel exhaust; front independent double wishbone suspension with anti-roll bar, front torsion springs, front torsion bar, rigid rear axle multi-link suspension with anti-roll bar, rear coil springs; power re-circulating ball steering with engine speed-sensing assist; 4 wheel disc brakes with 4 wheel antilock braking system; 22.5 gal. capacity fuel tank; front and rear mud flaps, skid plates; split swing-out rear cargo door; class II trailering; front power sliding glass sunroof with sunshade; front and rear body-colored bumpers with front and rear tow hooks, rear step; rocker panel extensions, body-colored fender flares; monotone paint; aero-composite halogen headlamps; additional exterior lights include cornering lights, front fog/driving lights, center high mounted stop light; driver's and passenger's power remote body-colored heated electric folding outside mirrors; front and rear 16" x 7" silver alloy wheels; P245/70SR16 BSW M&S front and rear tires; outside rear mounted full-size conventional alloy spare wheel; air conditioning, rear heat ducts; premium AM/FM stereo with seek-scan, cassette, single CD, 6 speakers, and window grid diversity antenna; cruise control; power door locks with 2 stage unlock, remote keyless entry, child safety rear door locks, remote fuel release; 1 power accessory outlet; instrumentation display includes tachometer, water temp gauge, in-dash clock, compass, exterior temp, trip odometer; warning indicators include oil pressure, battery, lights on, key in ignition, low fuel, door ajar, brake fluid; dual airbags; ignition disable, security system; deep tinted windows, power front windows with driver's 1-touch down, power rear windows, fixed 1/4 vent windows; variable intermittent front windshield wipers, rear window defroster; seating capacity of 5, heated front bucket seats with adjustable headrests, driver's and passenger's armrests, driver's seat includes 6-way power seat, passenger's seat includes 4-way power seat with 6-way direction control; 60-40 folding rear bench seat with reclining adjustable headrests, center armrest; front height adjustable seatbelts; leather seats, leatherette door trim insert, full cloth headliner, full carpet floor covering, wood trim; interior lights include dome light with fade, front reading lights, 4 door curb lights; leather-wrapped steering wheel with tilt adjustment; dual illuminated vanity mirrors; day-night rearview mirror; full floor console, locking glove box with light, front and rear cupholders, instrument panel bin, 2 seat back storage pockets, driver's and passenger's door bins, rear underseat tray; carpeted cargo floor, plastic trunk lid, cargo net, cargo tie downs, cargo light, cargo concealed storage; chrome grille, chrome side window moldings, black front windshield molding, black rear window molding and chrome door handles.

Base Prices

9C427WF34	SLX (4A)	32522	36300
Destination Charge:		455	455

Accessories

NOTE: Accessories are dealer installed. Contact a dealer for accessory availability.

1999 ESCALADE

1999 Cadillac Escalade

What's New?

The new Cadillac Escalade is really more a 1999 GMC Yukon Denali than it is a Cadillac. (And GMC's Yukon Denali is really more Yukon than anything else-except, perhaps, a Chevrolet Tahoe, but that's another story.) Regardless of its origins, think of the Escalade as a big, four-wheel-drive Cadillac limo for well-heeled, outdoorsy types. Loaded with luxury touches and every possible convenience (even GM's OnStar mobile communications system), Escalade comes in four special colors and lacks only one thing: an options list. Why? It's got it all.

Review

Cadillac dealers weren't too happy watching thousands of new luxury sport/utility customers walk into rival Lincoln showrooms and snap up the big Navigator SUV. General Motors had been working on a new, full-size Cadillac sport/utility project, but it was still a ways off, and those Caddy dealers were getting mighty antsy. So GM brand managers came up with an idea to clone GMC's new-for-'99 premium SUV, the Yukon Denali, and rebadge it as Cadillac to give those dealers something to sell until GM's next big SUV project is ready.

Enter the 1999 Cadillac Escalade. The first truck-based vehicle in Cadillac's 96-year history, Escalade is meant to combine the best features of a luxury car with those of an all-weather, all-terrain vehicle. Exterior styling differs from the donor Denali by the use of a more distinct grille with bright chrome bezel and the Cadillac wreath-and-crest logo affixed smack dab in the middle.

Reflector-optic halogen headlamps and recessed projector-beam fog lamps reside in a smooth-style front fascia. Body-color cladding and integrated running boards spruce up the flanks, with textured body-color door handles, outside rearview mirrors and color-keyed rails on the flush roof rack completing the monotone look. Out back, a functional step bumper conceals a standard trailer hitch.

The Escalade's interior features upper and lower consoles packed with storage cubbies and other conveniences such as reading lamps, cupholders, a rear power point and audio controls. Instrumentation is backlit in blue with white pointers and includes a tachometer. Luxury touches abound, with Zebrano wood trim, leather-trimmed front and rear heated seats, and a premium Bose sound system with six-CD changer and single-CD in-dash player. GM's OnStar mobile communications system is standard, as are dual front next-generation airbags and keyless remote entry with an adjustable, shock-sensing anti-theft system.

Powering all this opulence is 5.7-liter pushrod V8 packing 255 horsepower. The Vortec 5700 puts its 330 foot-pounds of torque to the ground via a four-speed automatic transmission and the AutoTrac full-time four-wheel-drive system. When activated, the AutoTrac transfer case will automatically shift from two-wheel drive to 4WD when it senses wheel slippage. Escalade rides on unique six-spoke chromed aluminum wheels wearing Firestone 265/70R-16 touring tires designed especially for sport/utility applications on- and off-road in both wet and dry conditions.

The Escalade provides a "look-at-me" driving experience around town and a king-of-the-road feel out on the highway. There's no question that the big Caddy SUV has gobs of curb appeal, but understand that it is all riding atop a 10-year-old pickup truck design, with all the flaws inherent to its humble underpinnings. The steering is vague, brakes are on the numb side and the ride quality is not as highly tuned as the price tag. What's worse, use of standard GM interior plastics is not in keeping with the Escalade's image.

If you need to be the first one on your block with the latest the luxo-SUV world has to offer, there's no doubt the Escalade is made for you. But if you happen to think, as we do, that the price walk from an optioned-out GMC Yukon to the dolled-up Cadillac Escalade is rather steep, then maybe you should be shopping elsewhere. For our money, the Escalade model will lose much of its luster every time you see a GMC Yukon Denali pass by. We prefer to wait and see what the next-generation big luxury SUV GM is working on will be like.

Safety Data

Side Airbag: *Not Available*
4-Wheel ABS: *Standard*
Driver Crash Test Grade: *Good*
Side Impact Crash Test Front: *Not Available*
Crash Offset: *Not Available*
Integrated Child Seat(s): *Not Available*
Traction Control: *Not Available*
Passenger Crash Test Grade: *Good*
Side Impact Crash Test Rear: *Not Available*

Standard Equipment

ESCALADE (4A): 5.7L V8 OHV SMPI 16-valve engine; 4-speed electronic overdrive automatic transmission with lock-up; 600-amp battery with run down protection; engine oil cooler; 140-amp alternator; transmission oil cooler; part-time 4-wheel drive, auto locking hub control with electronic shift, limited slip differential, 3.73 axle ratio; stainless steel exhaust with chrome tip; front independent torsion suspension with anti-roll bar, front torsion springs, front torsion bar, premium front shocks, rigid rear axle suspension with anti-roll bar, rear leaf springs, premium rear shocks; power re-circulating ball steering with vehicle speed-sensing assist; front disc/rear drum brakes with 4 wheel antilock braking system; 29.5. gal capacity fuel tank; front license plate bracket, running boards; tailgate cargo door; HD trailering, trailer harness, trailer hitch; roof rack; front and rear body-colored bumpers, rear tow hooks, rear step; body-colored bodyside cladding, body-colored fender flares; monotone paint; aero-composite halogen fully automatic headlamps with daytime running lights; additional exterior lights include front fog/driving lights, center high mounted stop light, underhood light; driver's and passenger's power remote body-colored heated folding outside mirrors; front and rear 16" x 7" chrome alloy wheels; P265/70SR16 BSW AS front and rear tires; underbody mounted full-size temporary steel spare wheel; air conditioning, rear air conditioning with separate controls, rear heat ducts; AM/FM stereo with clock, seek-scan, cassette, 6 premium speakers, amplifier, automatic equalizer, theft deterrent, and fixed antenna, rear audio controls; OnStar navigation system, cruise control; power door locks, remote keyless entry, child safety rear door locks, power remote hatch/trunk release; 4 power accessory outlets, retained accessory power, garage door opener; instrumentation display includes tachometer, oil pressure gauge, water temp gauge, volt gauge, compass, exterior temperature, trip odometer; warning indicators include battery, lights on, key in ignition, door ajar; dual airbags; ignition disable, panic alarm, security system; deep tinted windows, power front windows with driver's 1-touch down, power rear windows, fixed 1/4 vent windows; variable intermittent front windshield wipers, flip-up rear window, rear window wiper, rear window defroster; seating capacity of 5, heated front bucket seats with adjustable tilt headrests, center armrest with storage, driver's seat includes 4-way power seat with 8-way direction control and power lumbar support, passenger's seat

CODE	DESCRIPTION	INVOICE	MSRP

includes 4-way power seat with 8-way direction control and power lumbar support; heated 60-40 folding rear split-bench seat with tilt headrests, center armrest with storage; front and rear height adjustable seatbelts; leather seats, leather door trim insert, full cloth headliner, full carpet floor covering with carpeted floor mats, deluxe sound insulation, wood trim, leather-wrapped gear shift knob; interior lights include dome light with fade, front and rear reading lights, 4 door curb lights, illuminated entry; sport steering wheel with tilt adjustment; dual illuminated vanity mirrors, dual auxiliary visors; auto-dimming day-night rearview mirror; full floor console, full overhead console with storage, glove box with light, front and rear cupholders, 2 seat back storage pockets, driver's and passenger's door bins; carpeted cargo floor, carpeted trunk lid, cargo cover, cargo net, cargo light; chrome grille, black side window moldings, black front windshield molding, black rear window molding and body-colored door handles.

Base Prices

6VR69	Escalade (4A)	42131	45875
Destination Charge:		650	650

Accessories

NOTE: Escalade is not available with factory options. All accessories are standard.

1999 ASTRO

1999 Chevrolet Astro

What's New?

A new, all-wheel-drive active transfer case replaces the previous AWD system, and includes a new control module and service light. There are two new interior roof consoles: one with storage is optional on base model, another with trip computer is standard on LS and LT trim. A new LT stripe design comes in three new colors. Dealer-installed running boards are available, as are new optional aluminum wheels. Three exterior paint colors are added for '99, while depowered airbags finally arrive this year. Finally, the outside mirrors are redesigned, available heated and with or without electrochromic glare reduction.

Review

Models that have been around for a while can still deliver impressive value-and valor. That's true of the long-lived Astro van, a staple in Chevy's lineup since 1985. This hard-working passenger/cargo hauler, sporting a conventionally boxy shape, has, if anything, mellowed with age.

No, you don't get the curvaceous contours or the ergonomics of a Chrysler mini or a Ford Windstar. What you do acquire is a highly practical carrier that can be equipped to suit just about any family, trimmed in any of three levels. Depending on configuration, Astros can seat up to eight passengers and haul as much as three tons.

Out on the road, rolling hour after hour, is where the Astro demonstrates its true worth. Taller than its likely rivals, Astros are admittedly more truck-like in temperament, but deliver a pleasant highway ride with competent handling for long journeys. Seats are a little short, but comfortable, in both the front and center positions. Unfortunately, overly small front footwells drop the comfort level a notch, especially after long stints behind the wheel. A 190-horsepower 4.3-liter V6 is standard, putting power through a smooth-shifting four-speed electronically controlled automatic transmission to drive the rear wheels.

Dual depowered airbags and antilock brakes are standard. You get only one body choice: the extended-length version. The lower-priced rear-drive rendition is the ticket for hauling plenty of weight. All-wheel-drive costs more and delivers improved wet-pavement traction, but slurps up more fuel along the route.

This year, Chevy adds a state-of-the-art all-wheel-drive transfer case to replace the old AWD system. It operates in two-wheel-drive until the system senses rear-wheel slippage. It then immediately transfers torque between the front and rear axles to help regain traction and optimize control. Also new are interior roof consoles, redesigned outside mirrors, and new optional aluminum wheels.

Three new paint colors are available for 1999, while the LT model gets a redesigned stripe, itself available in three new colors. And dealers can now install optional running boards in six colors. Solid and substantial, Astros remain tempting-if dated-choices, whether for hauling passenger or cargo. If you need a small van with big van capacity and versatility, the Astro should be on your shopping list.

Safety Data

Side Airbag: *Not Available*
Integrated Child Seat(s): *Not Available*
4-Wheel ABS: *Standard*
Traction Control: *Not Available*
Driver Crash Test Grade: *Average*
Passenger Crash Test Grade: *Average*
Side Impact Crash Test Front: *Not Available*
Side Impact Crash Test Rear: *Not Available*
Crash Offset: *Poor*

Standard Equipment

BASE RWD PASSENGER VAN (4A): 4.3L V6 OHV SMPI 12-valve engine; 4-speed electronic overdrive automatic transmission with lock-up; 600-amp battery; engine oil cooler, HD radiator; 100-amp alternator; HD transmission oil cooler; rear wheel drive, 3.23 axle ratio; partial stainless steel exhaust; front independent suspension with anti-roll bar, front coil springs, rigid rear axle suspension with rear leaf springs; power re-circulating ball steering with engine speed-sensing assist; front disc/rear drum brakes with 4 wheel antilock braking system; 25 gal capacity fuel tank; front license plate bracket; 3 doors with sliding right rear passenger door, split swing-out rear cargo door; trailer harness; front and rear body-colored bumpers with rear step; monotone paint; sealed beam halogen headlamps with daytime running lights; additional exterior lights include center high mounted stop light; driver's and passenger's manual black folding outside mirrors; front and rear 15" x 6" painted styled steel wheels; P215/75SR15 BSW AS front and rear tires; underbody mounted compact steel spare wheel; air conditioning, rear heat ducts; AM/FM stereo with clock, seek-scan, 6 speakers, and fixed antenna; child safety rear door locks; 4 power accessory outlets; instrumentation display includes oil pressure gauge, water temp gauge, volt gauge, trip odometer; warning indicators include battery, lights on, key in ignition; dual airbags; tinted windows, vented rear windows, fixed 1/4 vent windows; variable intermittent front windshield wipers; seating capacity of 5, front bucket seats with fixed headrests, driver's seat includes 4-way direction control, passenger's seat includes 4-way direction control; removable 2nd row bench seat with adjustable rear headrest; front height adjustable seatbelts; vinyl seats, cloth door trim insert, full cloth headliner, full carpet floor covering, deluxe sound insulation; interior lights include dome light; vanity mirrors, dual auxiliary visors; day-night rearview mirror; engine cover console with storage, locking glove box with light, front and rear cupholders, driver's and passenger's door bins; carpeted cargo floor, plastic trunk lid, cargo light; colored grille, black side window moldings, black front windshield molding, black rear window molding and black door handles.

BASE AWD PASSENGER VAN (4A) (in addition to or instead of BASE RWD PASSENGER VAN (4A) equipment): Full-time 4 wheel drive, 3.42 axle ratio; front independent torsion suspension with anti-roll bar, front torsion springs and front torsion bar.

Base Prices

Code	Description	Invoice	MSRP
CM11006-ZW9	Base RWD Passenger Van (4A)	18962	20952
CL11006-ZW9	Base AWD Passenger Van (4A)	21043	23252
	Destination Charge:	595	595

CODE	DESCRIPTION	INVOICE	MSRP
	Accessories		
—	Custom Cloth Seat Trim	NC	NC
—	Leather Seat Trim	817	950
1SA	Preferred Equipment Group 1SA *Includes Base Decor package.*	NC	NC
1SC	Preferred Equipment Group 1SC	2869	3336
	Manufacturer Discount	(1817)	(2113)
	Net Price *Includes LS Decor package: cargo convenience net, convenience group: tilt steering wheel, speed control; power convenience group: power windows, power door lock system; deep tinted solar-ray glass, eight person seating: front and rear color-keyed floor mats; seat package: seat map pocket, inboard/outboard armrests, manual lumbar; electric remote black mirrors, front passenger storage compartment, ETR AM/FM stereo with cassette and seek/scan, black luggage carrier, remote keyless entry: key fob remote release, illuminated entry; overhead console with electronics: compass and exterior temp instrumentation; chrome grille, aero-composite headlamps, custom cloth seat trim, carpet trunk lid trim, rear quarter vent window and styled steel chrome appearance wheels.*	1052	1223
1SE	Preferred Equipment Group 1SE *Includes LT Decor package: cargo convenience net, convenience group: tilt steering wheel, speed control; power convenience group: power windows, power door lock system; deep tinted solar-ray glass, eight person seating: front and rear color-keyed floor mats; seat package: seat map pocket, inboard/outboard armrests, manual lumbar; electric remote black mirrors, front passenger storage compartment, ETR AM/FM stereo with cassette and seek/scan, black luggage carrier, remote keyless entry: key fob remote release, illuminated entry; overhead console with electronics: compass and exterior temp instrumentation; chrome grille, aero-composite headlamps, custom cloth seat trim, carpet trunk lid trim, rear quarter vent window, brushed aluminum wheels, black leather-wrapped steering wheel, body side accent stripe, dual illuminated visor vanity mirrors, front and rear reading lights, dual door curb/courtesy lights, power windows and premium cloth seat trim.*	4400	5116
AG1	6-Way Power Driver's Seat	206	240
AG2	6-Way Power Passenger's Seat *Deletes underseat storage compartment.*	206	240
AJ1	Deep Tinted Solar-Ray Glass	249	290
AN0	Seat Package *Includes inboard/outboard armrests and manually adjustable lumbar support and seat map pocket.*	144	168
AN6	Seat Lumbar Support *Only on middle seating. REQUIRES ZP7.*	86	100
AP9	Cargo Convenience Net	26	30
AU0	Remote Keyless Entry *Includes key fob remote release and illuminated entry. REQUIRES AU3.*	129	150
AU3	Power Door Lock System	192	223
B37	Front and Rear Color-Keyed Floor Mats *REQUIRES ZP7.*	59	69

CODE	DESCRIPTION	INVOICE	MSRP
B37	Front and Rear Color-Keyed Floor Mats *REQUIRES 1SA.*	40	47
B74	Body Side Molding	104	121
BVE	Running Boards *NOT AVAILABLE with B74.*	344	400
C36	Rear Heater	176	205
C49	Electric Rear Window Defogger *REQUIRES E54.*	132	154
C69	Front and Rear Air Conditioning *Includes 105-amp alternator.*	450	523
C95	Reading Lamps *NOT AVAILABLE with DK6.*	28	33
D48	Electric Remote Black Mirrors	84	98
DK6	Overhead Console *Includes illuminated driver's and passenger's sunshade mirrors. Does not include electronics. NOT AVAILABLE with C95.*	137	159
DK6	Overhead Console *Does not include electronics.*	71	83
DK8	Overhead Console with Electronics *Includes compass and exterior temp instrumentation.*	192	223
E54	Cargo Dutch Doors *Includes rear window wiper/washer. REQUIRES 1SA and AU3.*	313	364
E54	Cargo Dutch Doors *Includes rear window wiper/washer. REQUIRES 1SC or 1SE.*	262	305
FE2	Touring Suspension Package (RWD) *Includes front and rear gas shock absorbers, 4:1 ratio power assist steering and P235/65R15 touring WOL tires.*	263	306
G80	Locking Differential	217	252
GT4	3.73 Axle Ratio	NC	NC
GU5	3.23 Axle Ratio (RWD)	NC	NC
GU6	3.42 Axle Ratio	NC	NC
NG1	Emissions *Includes Connecticut, Washington D.C, Delaware, Massachusetts, Maryland, New Hampshire, New Jersey, New York, Pennsylvania, Rhode Island and Virginia.*	146	170
NP5	Black Leather Wrapped Steering Wheel *REQUIRES 1SC.*	46	54
PA6	Wheels: Styled Steel Painted Silver *REQUIRES 1SA.*	79	92
PC2	Wheels: Styled Steel Chrome Appearance *REQUIRES 1SE. NOT AVAILABLE with FE2.*	(22)	(25)
PC2	Wheels: Styled Steel Chrome Appearance *REQUIRES 1SA or 1SC.*	292	340
PF3	Wheels: Aluminum Brushed *REQUIRES 1SA.*	314	365
QCM	Tires: P215/75R15 AS WOL *Includes compact spare.*	76	88

CODE	DESCRIPTION	INVOICE	MSRP
TL1	Uplevel Grille *Includes aero-composite headlamps.*	129	150
UG1	3 Channel Garage Door Opener *REQUIRES DK8.*	99	115
UK6	Rear Seat Audio Controls *REQUIRES (1SC or 1SE) and (ULO or UPO). NOT AVAILABLE with UNO.*	108	125
ULO	Radio: AM/FM Stereo with Cassette and Automatic Tone Control *Includes digital clock, theft lock and speed compensated volume.*	138	160
UM6	Radio: AM/FM Stereo with Cassette and Seek/Scan *Includes digital clock.*	126	147
UNO	Radio: AM/FM Stereo with CD *Includes seek and scan, automatic tone control, digital clock, theft lock and speed compensated volume.*	224	260
UPO	Radio: AM/FM Stereo with CD and Cassette *Includes seek and scan, automatic tone control, digital clock, cassette with search and repeat, theft lock and speed compensated volume.*	310	360
V10	Cold Climate Package *Includes coolant protection and engine block heater.*	40	46
V54	Black Luggage Carrier	108	126
YF5	California Emissions	146	170
Z82	Trailering Special Equipment *Includes platform trailer hitch and 8-lead wiring harness.*	266	309
ZP7	Seven Person Seating *Includes 4 high back buckets with seat back recliner and 3-passenger bench and seat package: seat map pocket, inboard/outboard armrests and manual lumbar adjustment.*	494	574
ZP7	Seven Person Seating *Includes 4 high back buckets with seat back recliner and 3-passenger bench and seat package: seat map pocket, inboard/outboard armrests and manual lumbar adjustment. REQUIRES 1SE.*	NC	NC
ZP7	Seven Person Seating *Includes 4 high back buckets with seat back recliner and 3-passenger bench and seat package: seat map pocket, inboard/outboard armrests and manual lumbar adjustment. REQUIRES 1SC.*	273	318
ZP8	Eight Person Seating *Includes 2 high back reclining bucket seats and 2 3-passenger bench seats. REQUIRES ZP7.*	340	395
ZQ2	Power Convenience Group *Includes power windows and power door lock system.*	408	474
ZQ3	Convenience Group *Includes speed control.*	329	383
ZY2	Two-Tone Appearance Paint *REQUIRES BVE.*	NC	NC

1999 BLAZER

1999 Chevrolet Blazer

What's New?

Blazer gets automatic transmission improvements, new exterior colors and larger outside mirrors, while four-wheel-drive versions can be equipped with GM's AutoTrac active transfer case. Inside, there's new power-seating features, upgraded sound system options and available redundant radio controls in the steering wheel. On the safety side, the '99 Blazer now offers a vehicle content theft alarm, flash-to-pass headlamp feature, and a liftgate ajar warning lamp. What's more, a new TrailBlazer trim package is available on four-door versions, featuring monochrome paint with gold accents, unique aluminum wheels, touring suspension and leather-lined interior.

Review

Back in 1982, Chevrolet rolled out the S-10 Blazer, the first modern compact sport-utility vehicle. Seventeen years later, the Blazer remains a strong seller in one of the hottest automotive markets. Take only one good look and it's easy to see why the Blazer has such lasting appeal.

Powered by a stout 4.3-liter, 190-horsepower V6 and available with several suspension choices, the Blazer can be tailored to specific needs, as either two-wheel or four-wheel drive, with two doors or four. The four-door is the most popular by far, easily the model of choice with families on the go.

There are accommodations for as many as six passengers in the bigger Blazer, if they don't mind squeezing. There's lots of cargo space too, with the spare tire mounted underneath the cargo floor on four-door models. Chevy claims that with the rear seat folded, a washing machine box will fit into the cargo bay. We actually tried it with a test vehicle, and they aren't fibbing. Sadly, the Blazer's interior is marred by acres of chintzy plastic and precious little rear foot room in front of a rather low and mushy seat. Adult rear-seat riders are likely to complain loudly.

Off road is not where the Blazer shines brightest, despite the availability of a ZR2 super-duty suspension package. Offered only on two-door 4WD models, the ZR2 Blazer has a special chassis with a four-inch wider track, huge 31-inch tires, specially tuned Bilstein 46mm shocks, drivetrain refinements, an underbody shield package and LS trim. Regular Blazers are capable enough for two-track dirt, but serious off-road adventures would be better handled by something with a little more wheel travel. It's not a major shortcoming, being that most families don't spend much time off road – if any – in their sport-utes.

On the other hand, as a road-going hauler the Blazer is quite capable. All 4x4 models come standard with GM's Insta-Trac shift-on-the-fly 4WD system, or can be equipped with the new-for-'99 AutoTrac pushbutton electronic transfer case. AutoTrac automatically senses wheel slippage and sends power to the axle with the most traction, which makes those old full-time all-wheel-drive systems obsolete. This setup takes the guesswork out of sure-footed travel over wet or snowy pavement.

GM's PassLock anti-theft system, automatic headlight control and four-wheel disc brakes are all standard. Heated exterior mirrors and an electrochromic rearview mirror are standard on LT models, and optional on the LS. Three new colors debut: Victory Red, Sunset Gold and Meadow Green Metallic.

For 1999, Chevrolet has added power-seat enhancements, sound system upgrades with optional steering wheel radio controls and CD changer. There's also a new headlamp flash-to-pass feature, a liftgate ajar warning lamp and a vehicle content theft deterrent system on Blazers equipped with remote keyless entry. An all-new model, the TrailBlazer, is based on a four-door LT and then adds a monochrome exterior theme with gold accents, special alloy wheels, the Z85 Touring Suspension and two-tone leather-trimmed interior.

When the current Blazer debuted for the 1995 model year, it won the North American Truck of the Year award. Smart styling, a powerful drivetrain and reasonable pricing made it an instant hit. Lately, however, the competition has again raised the bar on the Blazer. The segment-leading Ford Explorer finally got a new V6 in 1997 that is more refined and powerful than the Blazer's V6, and it's sister, the Mercury Mountaineer, has an available V8. That same year, Jeep updated the Cherokee, offering nearly as much interior space as the Blazer and 4WD for around $20,000. For 1998, the Dodge Durango came to market as an instant success, and Jeep has now gone back and redesigned its Grand Cherokee for '99. Simply put, with all the new product in the compact-SUV world, this Chevy isn't the value it used to be.

Safety Data

Side Airbag: *Not Available*
4-Wheel ABS: *Standard*
Driver Crash Test Grade: *Average*
Side Impact Crash Test Front: *Excellent*
Crash Offset: *Poor*
Integrated Child Seat(s): *Not Available*
Traction Control: *Not Available*
Passenger Crash Test Grade: *Good*
Side Impact Crash Test Rear: *Excellent*

Standard Equipment

BASE 2WD 2-DOOR (5M): 4.3L V6 OHV SMPI 12-valve engine; 5-speed overdrive manual transmission; 525-amp battery with run down protection; engine oil cooler; 100-amp alternator; transmission oil cooler; rear wheel drive, 3.08 axle ratio; stainless steel exhaust; front independent suspension with antiroll bar, front coil springs, rigid rear axle suspension with antiroll bar, rear leaf springs; power re-circulating ball steering; 4 wheel disc brakes with 4 wheel antilock braking system; 19 gal. capacity fuel tank; front license plate bracket; tailgate rear cargo door; trailer harness; front chrome bumper with black rub strip, rear body-colored bumper with rear step; monotone paint; aero-composite halogen fully automatic headlamps with daytime running lights; additional exterior lights include center high mounted stop light, underhood light; driver's and passenger's manual black folding outside mirrors; front and rear 15" x 7" painted styled steel wheels; P205/75SR15 BSW AS front and rear tires; inside mounted full-size temporary steel spare wheel; air conditioning, rear heat ducts; AM/FM stereo with clock, seek-scan, 4 speakers, and fixed antenna; power rear window remote release; 1 power accessory outlet, retained accessory power; instrumentation display includes oil pressure gauge, water temp gauge, volt gauge, trip odometer; warning indicators include battery, lights on, key in ignition; dual airbags; ignition disable; deep tinted windows, vented rear windows, fixed 1/4 vent windows; variable intermittent front windshield wipers, flip-up rear window; seating capacity of 5, front bucket seats with fixed headrests, center armrest with storage, driver's seat includes 4-way direction control with lumbar support, passenger's seat includes 4-way direction control with lumbar support and easy entry; 50-50 folding rear split-bench seat with adjustable headrests; cloth seats, cloth door trim insert, full cloth headliner, full carpet floor covering with carpeted floor mats;

interior lights include dome light; passenger's side vanity mirror; day-night rearview mirror; full floor console, glove box with light, front and rear cupholders, instrument panel bin, interior concealed storage, driver's and passenger's door bins; carpeted cargo floor, cargo tie downs, cargo light; chrome grille, black side window moldings, black front windshield molding, black rear window molding and black door handles.

BASE 2WD 4-DOOR (4A) (in addition to or instead of BASE 2WD 2-DOOR (5M) equipment): Four-speed electronic overdrive automatic transmission with lock-up; 18 gal. capacity fuel tank; underbody mounted full-size temporary steel spare wheel; child safety rear door locks; manual rear windows; seating capacity of 6, 60-40 split-bench front seat with fixed headrests; 60-40 folding rear split-bench seat with adjustable headrests; 2 seat back storage pockets and rear door bins.

LS 2WD 4-DOOR (4A): REQUIRES Preferred Equipment Group 1SC for trim and content.

LT 2WD 4-DOOR (4A): REQUIRES Preferred Equipment Group 1SD for trim and content.

TRAILBLAZER 2WD 4-DOOR (4A): REQUIRES Preferred Equipment Group 1SE for trim and content.

BASE 4WD 2-DOOR (5M)/BASE 4WD 4-DOOR (4A) (in addition to or instead of BASE 2WD 2-DOOR (5M)/ BASE 2WD 4-DOOR (4A) equipment): Part-time 4 wheel drive, auto locking hub control with electronic shift; front torsion springs, front torsion bar and rear tow hooks.

LS 4WD 4-DOOR (4A): REQUIRES Preferred Equipment Group 1SC for trim and content.

LT 4WD 4-DOOR (4A): REQUIRES Preferred Equipment Group 1SD for trim and content.

TRAILBLAZER 4WD 4-DOOR (4A): REQUIRES Preferred Equipment Group 1SE for trim and content.

Base Prices

Code	Description	Invoice	MSRP
CS10516-E55	Base 2WD 2-Door (5M)	16715	18470
CT10516-E55	Base 4WD 2-Door (5M)	19430	21470
CS10506-E55	Base 2WD 4-Door (4A)	21331	23570
CT10506-E55	Base 4WD 4-Door (4A)	23141	25570
CS10506-YC5	LS 2WD 4-Door (4A)	24589	27170
CT10506-YC5	LS 4WD 4-Door (4A)	26399	29170
CS10506-YC6	LT 2WD 4-Door (4A)	26580	29370
CT10506-YC6	LT 4WD 4-Door (4A)	28390	31370
CS10506-CTB	Trailblazer 2WD 4-Door (4A)	27666	30570
CT10506-CTB	Trailblazer 4WD 4-Door (4A)	29657	32770
Destination Charge:		525	525

Accessories

Code	Description	Invoice	MSRP
—	Leather Seat Trim (4-Door Except Base)	NC	NC
1SA	Preferred Equipment Group 1SA (Base) *Includes vehicle with standard equipment. NOT AVAILABLE with M30.*	NC	NC
1SB	Preferred Equipment Group 1SB (Base 2-Door) *Includes ETR AM/FM stereo with seek, scan and cassette, black luggage carrier, touring suspension package, P235/70R15 AS BSW tires, full-size spare, reclining*	860	1000

CODE	DESCRIPTION	INVOICE	MSRP
	high back bucket seats, tachometer, power door locks, power windows with driver's one-touch down; heated power mirrors, manual tilt steering wheel and speed control.		
1SB	**Preferred Equipment Group 1SB (Base 4-Door)**	553	643
	Manufacturer Discount	(295)	(343)
	Net Price	258	300
	Includes convenience group: manual tilt steering wheel, speed control; black luggage carrier, ETR AM/FM stereo with cassette, seek and scan. NOT AVAILABLE with UL5.		
1SC	**Preferred Equipment Group 1SC (LS 4-Door)**	(1204)	(1400)
	REQUIRED on all LS models. Includes manual tilt steering wheel, speed control, black luggage carrier, custom overhead console with compass/temperature display, power windows with driver's one-touch down, power door locks, electric remote heated outside mirrors, electric rear window release, rear window defogger and wiper/washer, LS Decor and exterior appearance package with colored bodyside moldings, instrument panel storage delete, cargo net and cover, 3 accessory outlets, leather-wrapped steering wheel, high back reclining bucket seats, floor console, premium ride suspension package: premium smooth ride suspension and tachometer.		
1SC	**Preferred Equipment Group 1SC (Base 2-Door)**	1720	2000
	Includes LS Decor: black luggage carrier, P235/70R15 AS BSW tires, full-size spare, reclining high back bucket seats, tachometer, power door locks, power windows with driver's one-touch down, heated power mirrors, manual tilt steering wheel, speed control, dual illuminated visor vanity mirrors, instrument panel storage delete, 3 accessory outlets, leather-wrapped steering wheel, cargo net, remote keyless entry with trunk release, illuminated entry, keyfob remote release, 6-way power driver's seat and custom overhead console with compass/temp/trip computer.		
1SD	**Preferred Equipment Group 1SD (LT)**	(1204)	(1400)
	REQUIRED on all LT models. Includes LT Decor: manual tilt steering wheel, speed control, black luggage carrier, power windows with driver's one-touch down, power door locks, electric rear window release, rear window defogger, rear wiper/washer, premium smooth ride suspension, tachometer, automatic air conditioning, deluxe overhead console, fog lamps, remote keyless entry with keyfob, illuminated entry, alarm system, bodyside stripe, cargo net, cargo cover, leather-wrapped steering wheel, colored bodyside moldings, 3 accessory outlets, leather seat trim, electric remote control heated outside mirrors, 8-way power driver's and passenger's seats and floor console.		
1SE	**Preferred Equipment Group 1SE (Trailblazer)**	(1204)	(1400)
	REQUIRED on all Trailblazer models. Includes Trailblazer decor: automatic air conditioning, deluxe overhead console, manual tilt steering wheel, speed control, power windows with driver's one-touch down, power door locks, fog lamps, black luggage carrier, electrochromic inside rearview mirror, electrochromic remote control heated outside mirrors, ETR AM/FM stereo with cassette, seek and scan, split folding rear seat, 8-way power driver's and passenger's seats, floor console, touring suspension package with firm ride suspension, tachometer, leather-wrapped steering wheel, leather seat trim, body color front bumper, body color grille and alloy wheels.		
AG1	**6-Way Power Driver's/Passenger's Seats (4-Door - LS/LT)**	206	240
AM6	**60/40 Split Front Reclining Bench Seat (LS 4-Door)**	NC	NC
	Includes storage armrest and dual cupholders. NOT AVAILABLE with U1Z, AV5, UQ3.		
ANL	**Fog Lamps (Base/LS)**	99	115

CODE	DESCRIPTION	INVOICE	MSRP
AU0	Remote Keyless Entry (Base/LS) *Includes keyfob remote release, illuminated entry and alarm system.*	146	170
AV5	High Back Reclining Bucket Seats (LS 4-Door) *Includes floor console. NOT AVAILABLE with AM6.*	NC	NC
CF5	Electric Tilt and Sliding Sunroof (2-Door/4-Door - LS/LT/Trailblazer) *Includes mini console.*	645	750
DK8	Deluxe Overhead Console (LS) *Includes Homelink 3-channel programmable, operates garage doors, lights and other devices. Also includes enhanced electronic display: trip computer, compass and exterior temperature. REQUIRES AV5.*	112	130
G80	Locking Differential *REQUIRES GU6 or GT4.*	232	270
GT4	3.73 Axle Ratio (4WD) *REQUIRES ZW7. NOT AVAILABLE with GU6, ZQ1.*	NC	NC
GU6	3.42 Axle Ratio *REQUIRES M30 or G80. NOT AVAILABLE with ZR2, GT4.*	NC	NC
KA1	Driver's and Passenger's Heated Seats (LT/Trailblazer) *REQUIRES Leather Trim.*	215	250
M30	Transmission: 4-Speed Automatic with Overdrive (2-Door) *Includes brake-transmission shift interlock. NOT AVAILABLE with 1SA.*	860	1000
N60	Wheels: Aluminum Argent (2WD 4-Door)	241	280
N90	Wheels: Cast Aluminum (4WD 4-Door)	241	280
NP8	Autotrac Active Transfer Case (4WD - Base/LS)	194	225
P16	Spare Tire and Wheel Carrier (4WD 2-Door) *Includes cover. NOT AVAILABLE with PNV.*	137	159
PNV	Spare Tire Carrier Not Desired (4WD 2-Door) *NOT AVAILABLE with QEB, P16.*	NC	NC
QBF	Tires: P235/70R15 AS BSW (Base 4-Door) *Includes spare P235/70R15 AS BSW SBR tire. NOT AVAILABLE with QBG, QCA, ZQ1, QEB.*	165	192
QBG	Tires: P235/70R15 AS WOL SBR (Base 4-Door) *Includes spare P235/70R15 AS WOL SBR tire. NOT AVAILABLE with QCA, QEB.*	280	325
QBG	Tires: P235/70R15 AS WOL SBR (2WD) *Includes spare P235/70R15 AS WOL SBR tire. NOT AVAILABLE with QCA, ZQ1, QEB.*	114	133
QBG	Tires: P235/70R15 M&S WOL *Includes spare P235/70R15 AS WOL SBR tire. REQUIRES 1SA or 1SB or 1SC. NOT AVAILABLE with QCA, QEB, ZR2.*	114	133
QCA	Tires: P205/75R15 AS WOL (2WD 4-Door) *Includes spare P205/75R15 AS WOL SBR tire. NOT AVAILABLE with ZW7, QBG.*	104	121
QEB	Tires: P235/75R15 AT WOL (4WD) *Includes spare P235/75R15 AT WOL tire. REQUIRES 1SC or 1SD and P16. NOT AVAILABLE with PNV, QBG, ZR2, ZQ1.*	144	168
QEB	Tires: P235/75R15 AT WOL (4WD Base 4-Door) *Includes spare P235/75R15 AT WOL tire. NOT AVAILABLE with QBG, ZW7.*	310	360
RYJ	Rear Compartment Shade (Base 4-Door)	59	69
U16	Tachometer (Base 4-Door)	51	59

CODE	DESCRIPTION	INVOICE	MSRP
U1Z	Remote 6 Disc CD Changer *REQUIRES 1SC or 1SD. NOT AVAILABLE with UPO, AM6.*	340	395
UA1	690 CCA HD Delco Freedom Battery	48	56
UK3	Redundant Steering Wheel Audio Controls (4-Door - Except Base)	108	125
ULO	Radio: AM/FM Stereo with Cassette (2-Door) *Includes auto tone control, digital clock, theft lock and speed compensated volume. REQUIRES 1SC. NOT AVAILABLE with UPO.*	NC	NC
UM6	Radio: AM/FM Stereo with Cassette (Base 4-Door) *Includes digital clock and enhanced performance speaker system. NOT AVAILABLE with UL5.*	105	122
UNO	Radio: AM/FM Stereo with CD and Auto. Tone Control (4-Door Except Base) *Includes digital clock, theft lock and speed compensated volume. NOT AVAILABLE with UPO, U1Z.*	86	100
UPO	Radio: AM/FM Stereo with Cassette and CD (2-Door) *Includes auto tone control, digital clock, theft lock and speed compensated volume. REQUIRES 1SC, M30. NOT AVAILABLE with U1Z, UQ3.*	86	100
UPO	Radio: AM/FM Stereo with Cassette and CD (2-Door) *Includes auto tone control, digital clock, theft lock and speed compensated volume. REQUIRES 1SC, M30. NOT AVAILABLE with U1Z, UQ3.*	86	100
UPO	Radio: AM/FM Stereo with Cassette and CD (4-Door - LS/LT) *Includes auto tone control, digital clock, theft lock and speed compensated volume. NOT AVAILABLE with UQ3, U1Z.*	172	200
UPO	Radio: AM/FM Stereo with Cassette and CD (LS 4-Door) *Includes auto tone control, digital clock, theft lock and speed compensated volume. NOT AVAILABLE with UQ3, U1Z.*	89	100
UQ3	Bose Premium Sound System *REQUIRES (1SC, 1SD or 1SE) and (ULO or UNO). NOT AVAILABLE with UPO, AM6.*	426	495
V10	Cold Climate Package *Includes 690-cca HD Delco freedom battery and engine block heater.*	77	89
V54	Black Luggage Carrier (4-Door) *REQUIRES 1SA.*	108	126
Z82	HD Trailering Special Equipment *Includes weight distribution hitch platform. REQUIRES M30. NOT AVAILABLE with ZR2.*	181	210
Z85	Touring Suspension Package (Base 4-Door) *Includes GVWR 5000 lbs, GAWF/GAWR 2500/2800 lbs and firm ride suspension. REQUIRES QBG or QEB. NOT AVAILABLE with QCA, ZW7.*	169	197
ZM5	Shield Package (4WD) *Includes shield/skid plates for: transfer case, front differential, fuel tank and steering linkage.*	108	126
ZM8	Convenience Group (Base 4-Door) *Includes electric rear window release, rear window defogger and wiper/washer.*	277	322
ZQ1	Smooth Ride Suspension Package (4-Door Except Base) *Includes GAWF/GAWR 2500/2700 lbs and GVWR 5000 lbs. NOT AVAILABLE with QBG, QEB, GT4.*	(236)	(275)

CODE	DESCRIPTION	INVOICE	MSRP
ZQ3	Convenience Group (Base 4-Door) *Includes manual tilt steering wheel and speed control. REQUIRES 1SA.*	340	395
ZQ6	Convenience Group (Base 4-Door) *Includes power windows with driver's one-touch down, power door locks, electric remote heated outside mirrors.*	641	745
ZR2	Wide Stance Sport Performance Package (4WD 2-Door) *Includes 5000 lbs GVWR, GAWF/GAWR 2500/2700, unique revised frame for wide tread, unique strengthened front differential gears and drive axles, unique rear axle with 8.5" ring gear, larger wheel bearings and longer, larger diameter axle shafts, unique rear suspension with revised multilleaf springs and added rear axle track bar, unique (28mm vs 25mm diameter) front stabilizer bar, 46mm Bilstein gas pressurized shock absorbers, modified jack and spare tire stowage winch, shield package, extra wide wheel flares, firm ride suspension, 31 x 10.5R15 AT BSW tires and spare 31x10.5R15 BSW tire. Body is 3" higher than normal. REQUIRES 1SC, GT4 and G80. NOT AVAILABLE with GU6, QBG, QEB, Z82.*	1720	2000
ZW7	Premium Ride Suspension Package (Base 4-Door) *Includes GAWF/GAWR 2500/2700 lbs, GVWR 5000 lbs and premium smooth ride suspension. REQUIRES QBG. NOT AVAILABLE with QCA, QEB.*	169	197
ZY7	Custom Two-Tone Paint (4-Door - LS/LT) *Includes chrome grille.*	194	225

1999 C/K PICKUP

1999 Chevrolet K1500

What's New?

A few new colors are added to Chevrolet's popular pickup as it is slowly phased out.

Review

General Motors' best-selling vehicles, as truck loyalists know full well, are the full-size pickups: half-, 3/4- and one-tonners with a reputation as reliable workhorses. Ford's similar-sized F-Series grabs the higher sales totals each year, but faithful Chevrolet buyers are seldom swayed. The pickup that feels right at home to a Chevy fan tends to send prickles up the spine of a Ford fan, and vice versa. Each is likely to declare the other's truck to be harder riding or anemic in acceleration, even if an impartial observer discerns little difference between the two.

Most truck fans know by now that an all-new Chevrolet pickup is in showrooms. Dubbed Silverado, this model is available as 1500 and 2500 light-duty models, with the heavy-duty 2500 and 3500 trucks following soon. So, it's not surprising that few changes are on tap for the 1999 C/K pickup. In fact, the only changes from the 1998 models are the addition of three new colors. Why introduce 1999 C/K's with the Silverado sharing floor space at the dealer? Well, it seems that Chevrolet was running into Corporate Average Fuel Economy (CAFE) problems in mid-1998. In order to get around this, Chevrolet began to sell the 1999 models early. Problem solved, for now.

Four-wheel antilock braking is standard fare, and models under 8,600 lbs. GVWR have an airbag installed in the steering wheel hub. Correctly fitted, a C/K pickup can tow as much as 10,000 pounds. Long-life engine components extend service intervals up to 100,000 miles on some items. For luxury-oriented truckers, a C/K can be trimmed in leather when the top Silverado trim package is specified.

When selecting a full-size Chevy truck, you have to face the usual bewildering selection of models, which vary by wheelbase, cargo-bed size, cab design, and Sportside or Fleetside bed styling. Don't stop yet: you also have to choose from five engine sizes (including two diesels), and decide whether you want two- or four-wheel drive. Then, you still have the dizzying single-option list to ponder.

We get tired just thinking about all those possibilities, but they come with the territory when you're heading into big-pickup range. Truck customers don't want the same hauler that everybody else is buying. They want one tailored to their own specific needs, and Chevrolet provides these customers with myriad possibilities to create that special, one-of-a-kind truck.

1999 C/K 1500 PICKUP

Safety Data

Side Airbag: *Not Available*
4-Wheel ABS: *Standard*
Driver Crash Test Grade: *Good*
Side Impact Crash Test Front: *Not Available*
Crash Offset: *Not Available*
Integrated Child Seat(s): *Not Available*
Traction Control: *Not Available*
Passenger Crash Test Grade: *Average*
Side Impact Crash Test Rear: *Not Available*

Standard Equipment

C1500 LS EXTENDED CAB SHORTBED: 5.0L V8 OHV SMPI 16-valve engine; 4-speed electronic overdrive automatic transmission with lock-up; 600-amp HD battery; 100-amp alternator; rear wheel drive, 3.42 axle ratio; stainless steel exhaust; front independent suspension with anti-roll bar, front coil springs, rigid rear axle suspension with rear leaf springs; power re-circulating ball steering with engine speed-sensing assist; front disc/rear drum brakes with 4 wheel antilock braking system; 25 gal capacity fuel tank; 3rd door access; trailer harness; regular pickup box; front and rear chrome bumpers with black rub strip and chrome bumper insert, rear step bumper; black bodyside molding with chrome bodyside insert, chrome wheel well molding; monotone paint; aero-composite halogen headlamps with daytime running lights; additional exterior lights include center high mounted stop light, pickup cargo box light, underhood light; driver and passenger power remote black folding outside mirrors; front and rear 15" x 7" painted styled steel wheels with hub wheel covers with trim rings; P235/75SR15 BSW AS front and rear tires; underbody mounted full-size conventional steel spare wheel; air conditioning; AM/FM stereo, clock, seek-scan, cassette, 4 speakers, and fixed antenna; cruise control; 3 power accessory outlets; instrumentation display includes tachometer, oil pressure gauge, water temp gauge, volt gauge, trip odometer; warning indicators include battery,

CODE	DESCRIPTION	INVOICE	MSRP

lights on, key in ignition, door ajar; driver side airbag, passenger side cancellable airbag; ignition disable; tinted windows, power front windows with driver 1-touch down, vented rear windows; variable intermittent front windshield wipers; seating capacity of 6, 60-40 split-bench front seat with adjustable headrests, center armrest with storage, driver seat includes 4-way direction control, power lumbar support, easy entry, passenger seat includes 4-way direction control power lumbar support, easy entry; full folding rear bench seat with adjustable rear headrest; front height adjustable seatbelts; premium cloth seats, cloth door trim insert, full cloth headliner, full carpet floor covering with rubber floor mats, cabback insulator; interior lights include dome light, front reading lights, 2 door curb lights; leather-wrapped sport steering wheel with tilt adjustment; passenger side vanity mirror; day-night rearview mirror; glove box with light, front cupholder, 2 seat back storage pockets, driver and passenger door bins; chrome grille, black side windows moldings, black front windshield molding, black rear window molding and black door handles.

K1500 LS EXTENDED CAB SHORTBED (in addition to or instead of C1500 LS EXTENDED CAB SHORTBED equipment): Engine oil cooler; part-time 4 wheel drive, auto locking hub control and manual shift, 3.73 axle ratio; front independent torsion suspension with anti-roll bar, front torsion springs, front torsion bar, rigid rear axle suspension with rear leaf springs; front and rear chrome bumpers with black rub strip, front chrome bumper insert, rear tow hooks, rear step bumper; front and rear 16" x 6.5" painted styled steel wheels with hub wheel covers with trim rings.

Base Prices

CODE	DESCRIPTION	INVOICE	MSRP
CC10753	C1500 LS X-Cab Shortbed (4A)	19885	22726
CK10753	K1500 LS X-Cab Shortbed (4A)	22642	25876
Destination Charge:		625	625

Accessories

CODE	DESCRIPTION	INVOICE	MSRP
—	Leather Seat Trim	860	1000
1SB	Preferred Equipment Group 1SB *Includes vehicle with standard equipment.*	NC	NC
1SC	Preferred Equipment Group 1SC *Includes remote keyless entry, 10" electrochromic ISRV mirror: 8 point compass, power driver's seat, leather seat trim and LS premium decor with leather.*	1320	1535
A28	Sliding Rear Window *NOT AVAILABLE with (C49) electric rear window defogger.*	99	115
A95	Reclining High Back Bucket Seats *Includes power lumbar, floor console and overhead console.*	232	270
AG9	Power Driver's Seat	206	240
AJ1	Deep Tinted Solar Ray Glass *REQUIRES (1SB) or (1SC).*	92	107
AJ1	Deep Tinted Solar Ray Glass *REQUIRES (C49) electric rear window defogger.*	62	72
AU0	Remote Keyless Entry	129	150
BG9	Full Rubber Color-Keyed Flooring *Replaces carpeting and floor mats.*	(44)	(51)
BZY	Under Rail Bedliner	194	225
C49	Electric Rear Window Defogger *NOT AVAILABLE with (A28) sliding rear window.*	132	154
C5S	GVWR: 6,600 Lbs (K1500 LS X-Cab SB) *REQUIRES (F44) HD chassis equipment.*	NC	NC

CODE	DESCRIPTION	INVOICE	MSRP
DD7	10" Electrochromic ISRV Mirror *Includes 8 point compass.*	125	145
DF2	Stainless Steel Camper Type Mirrors *7.5" width x 10.5" height.*	(39)	(45)
EF1	Rear Bumper Delete *Vehicles registered in certain states must have a rear bumper to be operated on their roads. Consult your local laws.*	(172)	(200)
F44	HD Chassis Equipment (K1500 LS X-Cab SB) *Includes larger brakes, stronger U-joint and heavy duty rear springs.*	198	230
F51	HD Front and Rear Shock Absorbers	34	40
F60	HD Front Springs (K1500 LS X-Cab SB)	54	63
FG5	46 MM Bilstein Shocks (C1500 LS X-Cab SB)	194	225
G80	Locking Differential	217	252
GT4	3.73 Axle Ratio *Engine oil cooler comparable to KC4 is standard and engine oil cooling.*	116	135
K47	High Capacity Air Cleaner	22	25
KC4	Engine Oil Cooler	116	135
KNP	HD Auxiliary Transmission Cooler *REQUIRES (L31) engine.*	83	96
L31	Engine: Vortec 5700 V8 SFI	602	700
N83	Wheels: Chrome (C1500 LS X-Cab SB) *Includes spare wheel not matching.*	215	250
N90	Wheels: Aluminum (C1500 LS X-Cab SB) *Includes spare wheel not matching.*	292	340
NC7	Federal Emission Override *For vehicles that will be registered or leased in California, Connecticut, Washington D.C, Delaware, Massachusetts, Maryland, New Hampshire, New Jersey, New York, Pennsylvania, Rhode Island and Virginia but sold by retailers outside those states. REQUIRES (YF5) California emissions.*	NC	NC
NP1	Electronic Shift Transfer Case (K1500 LS X-Cab SB) *With 2 speeds.*	129	150
NZZ	Off Road Skid Plates (K1500 LS X-Cab SB) *Includes fuel tank shield and front differential and transfer case shields.*	82	95
PF4	Wheels: Aluminum (K1500 LS X-Cab SB) *Includes spare wheel not matching.*	344	400
TP2	Auxiliary Battery	115	134
UL0	Radio: AM/FM Stereo with Cassette and Automatic Tone Control *Includes electronically tuned radio, digital clock, theft lock, speed compensated volume and enhanced performance speaker system.*	77	90
UN0	Radio: AM/FM Stereo with Automatic Tone Control and CD *Includes electronically tuned radio, digital clock, theft lock, speed compensated volume and enhanced performance speaker system.*	163	190
UP0	Radio: AM/FM Stereo with Automatic Tone Control, CD and Cass *Includes electronically tuned radio, digital clock, search and repeat, theft lock, speed compensated volume and enhanced performance speaker system.*	249	290
V10	Cold Climate Package *Includes engine block heater.*	28	33

CODE	DESCRIPTION	INVOICE	MSRP
V76	2 Front Tow Hooks (C1500 LS X-Cab SB)	33	38
XBN	Tires: Front LT245/75R16C AT BSW (K1500 LS X-Cab SB) *REQUIRES (YBN) tires: rear LT245/75R16C AT BSW and (ZBN) tire: spare LT245/75R16C AT BSW.*	19	22
XBX	Tires: Front LT245/75R16C AT WOL (K1500 LS X-Cab SB) *REQUIRES (YBX) tires: rear LT245/75R16C AT WOL and (ZBX) tire: spare LT245/75R16C AT WOL.*	62	72
XFN	Tires: Front P235/75R15N AS with L (C1500 LS X-Cab SB) *REQUIRES (YFN) tires: rear P235/75R15N AS WOL and (ZFN) tires: spare P235/75R15N AS WOL.*	43	50
XGB	Tires: Front P245/75R16 AT WOL (K1500 LS X-Cab SB) *REQUIRES (YGB) tires: rear P245/75R16 AT WOL and (ZGB) tire: spare P245/75R16 AT WOL.*	43	50
XGC	Tires: Front P265/75R16C AT BSW (K1500 LS X-Cab SB) *REQUIRES (PF4) wheels and (YGC) tires: rear P265/75R16C AT BSW and (ZGC) tire: spare P265/75R16C AT BSW.*	46	54
XGD	Tires: Front P265/75R16C AT WOL (K1500 LS X-Cab SB) *REQUIRES (PF4) wheels and (YGD) tires: rear P265/75R16C AT WOL and (ZGD) tire: spare P265/75R16C AT WOL.*	89	104
YBN	Tires: Rear LT245/75R16C AT BSW (K1500 LS X-Cab SB) *REQUIRES (ZBN) tire: spare LT245/75R16C AT BSW.*	19	22
YBX	Tires: Rear LT245/75R16C AT WOL (K1500 LS X-Cab SB) *REQUIRES (ZBX) tire: spare LT245/75R16C AT WOL.*	62	72
YF5	California Emissions *Automatically added to vehicles shipped to and/or sold to retailers in California. Out-of-state retailers must order on vehicles to be registered or leased in California.*	146	170
YFN	Tires: Rear P235/75R15N AS with L (C1500 LS X-Cab SB) *REQUIRES (ZFN) tires: spare P235/75R15N AS WOL.*	43	50
YGB	Tires: Rear P245/75R16 AT WOL (K1500 LS X-Cab SB) *REQUIRES (ZGB) tire: spare P245/75R16 AT WOL.*	43	50
YGC	Tires: Rear P265/75R16C AT BSW (K1500 LS X-Cab SB) *REQUIRES (PF4) wheels and (ZGC) tire: spare P265/75R16C AT BSW.*	46	54
YGD	Tires: Rear P265/75R16C AT WOL (K1500 LS X-Cab SB) *REQUIRES (PF4) wheels and (ZGD) tire: spare P265/75R16C AT WOL.*	89	104
Z71	Off-Road Package (K1500 LS X-Cab SB) *Includes off road skid plates. REQUIRES XGC or XGD or XBN or XBX.*	232	270
Z82	Trailering Special Equipment (K1500 LS X-Cab SB) *Includes trailer hitch platform and engine oil cooler.*	292	339
Z82	Trailering Special Equipment (K1500 LS X-Cab SB) *Includes trailer hitch platform.*	175	204
ZBN	Tire: Spare LT245/75R16C AT BSW (K1500 LS X-Cab SB)	9	11
ZBX	Tire: Spare LT245/75R16C AT WOL (K1500 LS X-Cab SB)	31	36
ZFN	Tire: Spare P235/75R15N AS WOL (C1500 LS X-Cab SB)	22	25
ZGB	Tire: Spare P245/75R16 AT WOL (K1500 LS X-Cab SB)	22	25
ZGC	Tire: Spare P265/75R16C AT BSW (K1500 LS X-Cab SB) *REQUIRES (PF4) wheels.*	23	27

CODE	DESCRIPTION	INVOICE	MSRP
ZGD	Tire: Spare P265/75R16C AT WOL (K1500 LS X-Cab SB) *REQUIRES (PF4) wheels.*	45	52
ZY2	Conventional Two-Tone Paint	163	190

1999 C/K 2500 PICKUP

Safety Data

Side Airbag: *Not Available*
4-Wheel ABS: *Standard*
Driver Crash Test Grade: *Good*
Side Impact Crash Test Front: *Not Available*
Crash Offset: *Not Available*
Integrated Child Seat(s): *Not Available*
Traction Control: *Not Available*
Passenger Crash Test Grade: *Average*
Side Impact Crash Test Rear: *Not Available*

Standard Equipment

BASE 2WD REGULAR CAB LB (5M): 5.7L V8 OHV SMPI 16-valve engine; 5-speed overdrive manual transmission; 600-amp HD battery; engine oil cooler; 100-amp alternator; rear wheel drive, 3.73 axle ratio; stainless steel exhaust; front independent suspension with anti-roll bar, front coil springs, rigid rear axle suspension with rear leaf springs; power re-circulating ball steering with vehicle speed-sensing assist; front disc/rear drum brakes with 4 wheel antilock braking system; 34 gal capacity fuel tank; trailer harness; front chrome bumper, rear black bumper with rear step; monotone paint; sealed beam halogen headlamps with daytime running lights; additional exterior lights include center high mounted stop light, pickup cargo box light, underhood light; driver's and passenger's manual black folding outside mirrors; front and rear 16" x 6.5" painted styled steel wheels; LT245/75SR16 BSW AS front and rear tires; underbody mounted full-size conventional steel spare wheel; AM/FM stereo with clock, seek-scan, 4 speakers, and fixed antenna; 3 power accessory outlets; instrumentation display includes tachometer, oil pressure gauge, water temp gauge, volt gauge, trip odometer; warning indicators include battery, lights on, key in ignition, door ajar; ignition disable; tinted windows; variable intermittent front windshield wipers; seating capacity of 3, bench front seat with adjustable headrests, driver's seat includes 2-way direction control, passenger's seat includes 2-way direction control; front height adjustable seatbelts; vinyl seats, full cloth headliner, full vinyl floor covering, cabback insulator; interior lights include dome light, front reading lights; sport steering wheel; passenger's side vanity mirror; day-night rearview mirror; glove box with light, front cupholder, dashboard storage, driver's and passenger's door bins; black grille, black side window moldings, black front windshield molding, black rear window molding and black door handles.

BASE 2WD EXTENDED CAB LB (5M) (in addition to or instead of BASE 2WD REGULAR CAB LB (5M) equipment): Vented rear windows; seating capacity of 6, 60-40 split-bench front seat with adjustable headrests, driver's seat includes 4-way direction control with easy entry, passenger's seat includes 4-way direction control with easy entry; full folding rear bench seat with adjustable headrests.

BASE 2WD CREW CAB SB (4A) (in addition to or instead of BASE 2WD EXTENDED CAB LB (5M) equipment): Four-speed electronic overdrive automatic transmission with lock-up; transmission oil cooler; 26 gal capacity fuel tank; rear heat ducts; manual rear windows; bench front seat with adjustable headrests, driver's seat includes 2-way direction control, passenger's seat includes 2-way direction control; reclining rear bench seat with adjustable headrests; driver's and passenger's door bins and rear door bins.

BASE 4WD REGULAR CAB LB HD (5M) (in addition to or instead of BASE 2WD REGULAR CAB LB (5M) equipment): Part-time 4 wheel drive, auto locking hub control with manual shift; front independent torsion suspension with anti-roll bar, front torsion springs, front torsion bar; rear tow hooks and black fender flares.

CODE	DESCRIPTION	INVOICE	MSRP

BASE 4WD EXTENDED CAB SB/LB HD(5M) (in addition to or instead of BASE 2WD EXTENDED CAB LB (5M) equipment): Part-time 4 wheel drive, auto locking hub control with manual shift; front independent torsion suspension with anti-roll bar, front torsion springs, front torsion bar; rear tow hooks, black fender flares and 25 gal (35 gal/LB) capacity fuel tank.

BASE 4WD CREW CAB SB (4A) (in addition to or instead of BASE 2WD CREW CAB SB (4A) equipment): Part-time 4 wheel drive, auto locking hub control with manual shift; front independent torsion suspension with anti-roll bar, front torsion springs, front torsion bar; rear tow hooks and black fender flares.

Base Prices

Code	Description	Invoice	MSRP
CC20903	Base 2WD Regular Cab LB (5M)	16727	19118
CC20953	Base 2WD Extended Cab LB (5M)	18131	20722
CC20743	Base 2WD Crew Cab SB (4A)	20213	23102
CK20903	Base HD 4WD Regular Cab LB (5M)	19138	21873
CK20753	Base HD 4WD X-Cab SB (5M)	20849	23828
CK20953	Base HD 4WD X-Cab LB (5M)	20960	23955
CK20743	Base 4WD Crew Cab SB (4A)	22991	26276
Destination Charge:		640	640

Accessories

Code	Description	Invoice	MSRP
—	**Cloth Seat Trim (4WD - Reg Cab/X-Cab)**	NC	NC
1SA	**Preferred Equipment Group 1SA (Crew Cab)** *Includes Base Decor package. NOT AVAILABLE with R9B.*	NC	NC
1SA	**Preferred Equipment Group 1SA (Reg Cab/X-Cab)** *Includes Base Decor package. NOT AVAILABLE with UL5.*	NC	NC
1SA	**Preferred Equipment Group 1SA with R9A (Reg Cab/X-Cab)** *Includes Base Decor package. NOT AVAILABLE with R9B, YG6, UL5.*	(430)	(500)
1SA	**Preferred Equipment Group 1SA with R9A and R9B (Reg Cab/X-Cab)** *Includes Base Decor package. NOT AVAILABLE with YG6, UL5.*	(602)	(700)
1SA	**Preferred Equipment Group 1SA with R9B (Reg Cab/X-Cab)** *Includes Base Decor package. NOT AVAILABLE with R9A.*	(172)	(200)
1SB	**Preferred Equipment Group 1SB (Reg Cab/X-Cab)**	2611	3036
	Manufacturer Discount	(645)	(750)
	Net Price *Includes LS Decor: dual exterior power remote mirrors, chrome deluxe front bumper with rub strip, rally wheel trim, cloth with lower carpet door trim, deluxe sound insulation, 2 door curb/courtesy lights, air conditioning, ETR AM/FM stereo with cassette, seek and scan, convenience group: speed control, tilt wheel; power door locks, leather-wrapped steering wheel, power windows with driver's one-touch down, appearance package: composite halogen headlamps, chrome grille, dual note horn; custom cloth seat trim, seatback storage pockets (2), LS badging, carpet floor covering, front floor mats and rear floor mats. NOT AVAILABLE with APC, BNP.*	1966	2286
1SB	**Preferred Equipment Group 1SB (Crew Cab)** *Includes LS Decor: dual exterior power remote mirrors, chrome deluxe front bumper with rub strip, rally wheel trim, cloth with lower carpet door trim, deluxe sound insulation, 2 door curb/courtesy lights, air conditioning, ETR AM/FM stereo with*	3156	3670

CODE	DESCRIPTION	INVOICE	MSRP
	cassette, seek and scan, convenience group: speed control, tilt wheel; power door locks, leather-wrapped steering wheel, power windows with driver's one-touch down, appearance package: composite halogen headlamps, chrome grille, dual note horn; custom cloth seat trim, seatback storage pockets (2), LS badging, carpet floor covering, front floor mats and rear floor mats.		
1SC	**Preferred Equipment Group 1SC (Reg Cab)**	3874	4505
	Manufacturer Discount	(645)	(750)
	Net Price	3229	3755
	Includes LS premium decor with leather: air conditioning, power windows with driver's one-touch down, power door locks, convenience group: speed control, tilt wheel; carpet floor covering, front floor mats, leather-wrapped steering wheel, behind seat storage tray, seatback storage pockets (2), cloth with lower carpet door trim, deluxe sound insulation, 2 door curb/courtesy lights, dual remote power black mirrors, chrome deluxe front bumper with rub strip, rear chrome step bumper with rub strip, appearance package: composite halogen headlamps, chrome grille, dual note horn; LS badging, rally wheel trim, ETR AM/FM stereo with cassette, remote keyless entry, 10" electrochromic ISRV mirror, 8 point compass, 60/40 reclining split-bench seat and leather seat trim. NOT AVAILABLE with A95, APC, BNP.		
1SC	**Preferred Equipment Group 1SC (Crew Cab)**	4524	5260
	Includes LS premium decor with leather: dual exterior power remote mirrors, chrome deluxe front bumper with rub strip, rally wheel trim, cloth with lower carpet door trim, deluxe sound insulation, 2 door curb/courtesy lights, air conditioning, ETR AM/FM stereo with cassette, convenience group: speed control, tilt wheel; power door locks, leather-wrapped steering wheel, power windows with driver's one-touch down, appearance package: composite halogen headlamps, chrome grille, dual note horn; seatback storage pockets (2), LS badging, carpet floor covering, front floor mats, rear floor mats, remote keyless entry, power driver's seat and leather seat trim.		
1SC	**Preferred Equipment Group 1SC (X-Cab)**	3931	4571
	Manufacturer Discount	(645)	(750)
	Net Price	3286	3821
	Includes LS premium decor with leather: air conditioning, power windows with driver's one-touch down, power door locks, convenience group: speed control, tilt wheel; carpet floor covering, front floor mats, leather-wrapped steering wheel, behind seat storage tray, seatback storage pockets (2), cloth with lower carpet door trim, deluxe sound insulation, 2 door curb/courtesy lights, dual remote power black mirrors, chrome deluxe front bumper with rub strip, rear chrome step bumper with rub strip, appearance package: composite halogen headlamps, chrome grille, dual note horn; LS badging, rally wheel trim, ETR AM/FM stereo with cassette, remote keyless entry, 10" electrochromic ISRV mirror, 8 point compass, 60/40 reclining split-bench seat and leather seat trim. NOT AVAILABLE with APC, BNP.		
A28	**Sliding Rear Window**	99	115
	NOT AVAILABLE with C49.		
A52	**Leather Bench Seat (Reg Cab)**	860	1000
	REQUIRES 1SB. NOT AVAILABLE with 1SC.		
A52	**Leather Bench Seat (Crew Cab)**	946	1100
	REQUIRES 1SB. NOT AVAILABLE with 1SC.		

CODE	DESCRIPTION	INVOICE	MSRP
A95	Reclining Leather High Back Bucket Seats (X-Cab) *Includes power lumbar and overhead console. REQUIRES 1SC.*	232	270
A95	Reclining Leather High Back Bucket Seats (X-Cab) *Includes power lumbar and overhead console. REQUIRES 1SB.*	1092	1270
A95	Reclining Leather High Back Bucket Seats (Crew Cab) *Includes power lumbar and overhead console. REQUIRES 1SC.*	278	323
A95	Reclining Leather High Back Bucket Seats (Crew Cab) *Includes power lumbar and overhead console. REQUIRES 1SB.*	1310	1523
A95	Reclining Cloth High Back Bucket Seats (X-Cab) *Includes power lumbar and overhead console. REQUIRES 1SB.*	232	270
A95	Reclining Cloth High Back Bucket Seats (Crew Cab) *Includes power lumbar and overhead console. REQUIRES 1SB.*	364	423
A95	Reclining Cloth High Back Bucket Seats (Reg Cab) *Includes power lumbar and floor console. NOT AVAILABLE with 1SC.*	332	386
AE7	60/40 Reclining Cloth Split-Bench Seat (Crew Cab) *Includes storage armrest and power lumbar. NOT AVAILABLE with 1SC.*	86	100
AE7	60/40 Reclining Cloth Split-Bench Seat (X-Cab) *Includes storage armrest and power lumbar. REQUIRES 1SA or 1SB. NOT AVAILABLE with 1SC.*	NC	NC
AE7	60/40 Reclining Cloth Split-Bench Seat (Reg Cab) *Includes storage armrest and power lumbar. NOT AVAILABLE with 1SC.*	150	174
AE7	60/40 Reclining Leather Split-Bench Seat (X-Cab) *NOT AVAILABLE with 1SA, 1SC.*	860	1000
AE7	60/40 Reclining Leather Split-Bench Seat (Crew Cab) *REQUIRES 1SB. NOT AVAILABLE with 1SC.*	1032	1200
AE7	60/40 Reclining Leather Split-Bench Seat (Reg Cab) *Includes storage armrest and power lumbar. NOT AVAILABLE with 1SA, 1SC.*	1010	1174
AG9	Power Driver's Seat *REQUIRES AE7 or A95. NOT AVAILABLE with APC.*	206	240
AJ1	Deep Tinted Solar-Ray Glass (X-Cab) *REQUIRES 1SB or 1SC.*	92	107
AJ1	Deep Tinted Solar-Ray Glass (X-Cab) *Includes light tint glass rear window. REQUIRES C49.*	62	72
AJ1	Deep Tinted Solar-Ray Glass (Crew Cab) *Includes light tint glass rear window when ordered with C49.*	185	215
AJ1	Deep Tinted Solar-Ray Glass (Reg Cab) *REQUIRES A28.*	30	35
AJ1	Deep Tinted Solar-Ray Glass (Crew Cab) *REQUIRES A28.*	155	180
AU0	Remote Keyless Entry	129	150
AU3	Power Door Locks (Crew Cab)	192	223
AU3	Power Door Locks (Reg Cab/X-Cab)	134	156
B30	Carpet Floor Covering (Reg Cab)	30	35
B30	Carpet Floor Covering (X-Cab)	44	51
B32	Front Floor Mats (Reg Cab/X-Cab) *REQUIRES B30.*	17	20

CODE	DESCRIPTION	INVOICE	MSRP
B33	Rear Floor Mats (X-Cab)	14	16
	REQUIRES B30. NOT AVAILABLE with YG4.		
B85	Bright Bodyside and Wheel Opening Moldings (2WD - Reg Cab/X-Cab)	92	107
B85	Bright Bodyside Moldings (4WD - Reg Cab/X-Cab)	65	76
BG9	Full Rubber Color-Keyed Flooring (Reg Cab)	(30)	(35)
	Replaces carpeting and floor mats.		
BG9	Full Rubber Color-Keyed Flooring (X-Cab)	(44)	(51)
	Replaces carpeting and floor mats.		
BZY	Under Rail Bedliner	194	225
	NOT AVAILABLE with KL6.		
C49	Electric Rear Window Defogger	132	154
	REQUIRES R9A. NOT AVAILABLE with A28.		
C60	Air Conditioning	692	805
	NOT AVAILABLE with YG6.		
DD7	10" Electrochromic ISRV Mirror (Reg Cab/X-Cab)	125	145
	Includes 8 point compass.		
DF2	Stainless Steel Camper Type Mirrors	(39)	(45)
	7.5" W x 10.5" H. REQUIRES 1SB or 1SC.		
DF2	Stainless Steel Camper Type Mirrors	46	53
	7.5" W x 10.5" H.		
EF1	Rear Bumper Delete Provisions (Reg Cab/X-Cab)	(172)	(200)
	Vehicles registered in certain states must have a rear bumper to be operated on their roads. Consult your local laws. REQUIRES 1SB or 1SC. NOT AVAILABLE with Z82.		
EF1	Rear Bumper Delete Provisions	(112)	(130)
	Vehicles registered in certain states must have a rear bumper to be operated on their roads. Consult your local laws. NOT AVAILABLE with Z82, R9B, 8E8.		
F60	HD Front Springs (4WD)	54	63
G80	Locking Differential	217	252
GT5	4.10 Axle Ratio	NC	NC
	Includes engine oil cooler. NOT AVAILABLE with KL6.		
K47	High Capacity Air Cleaner	22	25
KL5	Alternative Fuel Conversion (Reg Cab/X-Cab)	108	125
	LPG and CNG conversion ready. REQUIRES MT1. NOT AVAILABLE with L29, L65.		
KL6	Natural Gas Provisions (Reg Cab/X-Cab)	4988	5800
	Includes alternative fuel conversion. REQUIRES MT1. NOT AVAILABLE with L29, L65, GT5, BZY.		
L29	Engine: Vortec 7400 V8 SFI	516	600
	REQUIRES F60. NOT AVAILABLE with KL5, VYU, KL6.		
L65	Engine: 6.5L V8 Turbo Diesel	2460	2860
	Includes HD auxiliary battery and engine block heater. REQUIRES F60. NOT AVAILABLE with KL5, TP2, V10, VYU, KL6.		
MT1	Transmission: 4-Speed Automatic OD HD (Reg Cab/X-Cab)	856	995
	Includes PRNDL in instrument panel.		
MW3	Transmission: 5-Speed Manual OD HD (Crew Cab)	(856)	(995)
	Includes deleted PRNDL in instrument panel and deleted auxiliary transmission cooler. REQUIRES L29. NOT AVAILABLE with UP0.		

CODE	DESCRIPTION	INVOICE	MSRP
NP1	Electronic Shift Transfer Case (4WD) *Includes 2 speeds. REQUIRES MT1 and R9A.*	129	150
NZZ	Skid Plate Package (4WD) *Includes fuel tank shield, front differential and transfer case shields.*	82	95
P06	Rally Wheel Trim	52	60
R9A	Comfort and Convenience Package *Includes air conditioning, convenience group: speed control, tilt wheel and ETR AM/FM stereo with cassette. NOT AVAILABLE with YG6, UL5.*	1150	1337
R9B	Bright Appearance Package (4WD - Reg Cab/X-Cab) *Includes bright bodyside moldings, appearance package: composite halogen headlamps, chrome grille, dual note horn; chrome deluxe front bumper with rub strip and rally wheel trim.*	389	452
R9B	Bright Appearance Package (Crew Cab) *Includes appearance package: composite halogen headlamps, chrome grille, dual note horn and rally wheel trim. NOT AVAILABLE with EF1.*	301	350
R9B	Bright Appearance Package (2WD - Reg Cab/X-Cab) *Includes bright bodyside and wheel opening moldings, appearance package: composite halogen headlamps, chrome grille, dual note horn; chrome deluxe front bumper with rub strip and rally wheel trim.*	415	483
TP2	Auxiliary Battery *NOT AVAILABLE with L65.*	115	134
U01	Roof Marker Lamps	47	55
UL0	Radio: AM/FM Stereo with Cassette *Includes digital clock, automatic tone control, theft lock, speed compensated volume and enhanced speaker system. REQUIRES 1SB or 1SC. NOT AVAILABLE with UN0, UP0.*	77	90
UL5	Radio Delete *Includes clock delete. NOT AVAILABLE with 1SA, R9A.*	(247)	(287)
UM6	Radio: AM/FM Stereo with Cassette *Includes digital clock. NOT AVAILABLE with UL5.*	126	147
UN0	Radio: AM/FM Stereo and CD *Includes digital clock, automatic tone control, theft lock, speed compensated volume and enhanced performance speaker system. REQUIRES 1SB or 1SC. NOT AVAILABLE with UL0, UP0.*	163	190
UP0	Radio: AM/FM Stereo with Cassette and CD *Includes digital clock, automatic tone control, search and repeat on cassette, theft lock, speed compensated volume and enhanced performance speaker system. REQUIRES MT1 and (1SB or 1SC). NOT AVAILABLE with UL0, UN0.*	249	290
V10	Cold Climate Package *Includes engine block heater. NOT AVAILABLE with L65.*	28	33
V22	Appearance Package *Includes composite halogen headlamps, chrome grille and dual note horn.*	164	191
V76	Recovery Hooks (2WD)	33	38
VB3	Chrome Rear Step Bumper (4WD) *REQUIRES VG3. NOT AVAILABLE with EF1.*	85	99
VB3	Chrome Rear Step Bumper with Rub Strip (2WD) *REQUIRES VG3. NOT AVAILABLE with EF1.*	85	99

CODE	DESCRIPTION	INVOICE	MSRP
VG3	Chrome Deluxe Front Bumper with Rub Strip (Reg Cab/X-Cab)	22	26
VYU	Snow Plow Prep Package (4WD - Reg Cab/X-Cab) *Includes HD front springs. NOT AVAILABLE with L29, L65.*	101	118
XGK	Tires: Front LT245/75R16E AT BSW (4WD) *REQUIRES YGK.*	19	23
YG4	Rear Seat Delete (X-Cab) *NOT AVAILABLE with A95.*	(374)	(435)
YG6	Air Conditioning Not Desired *NOT AVAILABLE with R9A.*	NC	NC
YGK	Tires: Rear LT245/75R16E AT BSW	19	23
Z82	HD Trailering Special Equipment (Reg Cab/X-Cab) *Includes trailer hitch platform. REQUIRES GT5. NOT AVAILABLE with EF1.*	257	299
Z82	HD Trailering Special Equipment *Includes trailer hitch platform. NOT AVAILABLE with EF1.*	141	164
ZQ3	Convenience Group *Includes speed control and tilt wheel.*	331	385

1999 C/K 3500 PICKUP

Safety Data

Side Airbag: *Not Available*
4-Wheel ABS: *Standard*
Driver Crash Test Grade: *Not Available*
Side Impact Crash Test Front: *Not Available*
Crash Offset: *Not Available*
Integrated Child Seat(s): *Not Available*
Traction Control: *Not Available*
Passenger Crash Test Grade: *Not Available*
Side Impact Crash Test Rear: *Not Available*

Standard Equipment

BASE 2WD REGULAR CAB LB SRW (5M): 5.7L V8 OHV SMPI 16-valve engine; 5-speed overdrive manual transmission; 600-amp HD battery; engine oil cooler; 100-amp alternator; rear wheel drive, 4.1 axle ratio; stainless steel exhaust; front independent suspension with anti-roll bar, front coil springs, rigid rear axle suspension with rear leaf springs; power re-circulating ball steering with vehicle speed-sensing assist; front disc/rear drum brakes with 4 wheel antilock braking system; 34 gal capacity fuel tank; trailer harness; front chrome bumper, rear black bumper with rear step; monotone paint; sealed beam halogen headlamps with daytime running lights; additional exterior lights include center high mounted stop light, pickup cargo box light, underhood light; driver's and passenger's manual black folding outside mirrors; front and rear 16" x 6.5" painted styled steel wheels; LT245/75SR16 BSW AS front and rear tires; underbody mounted full-size conventional steel spare wheel; AM/FM stereo with clock, seek-scan, 4 speakers, and fixed antenna; 3 power accessory outlets; instrumentation display includes tachometer, oil pressure gauge, water temp gauge, volt gauge, trip odometer; warning indicators include battery, lights on, key in ignition, door ajar; ignition disable; tinted windows; variable intermittent front windshield wipers; seating capacity of 3, bench front seat with adjustable headrests, driver's seat includes 2-way direction control, passenger's seat includes 2-way direction control; front height adjustable seatbelts; vinyl seats, full cloth headliner, full vinyl floor covering, cabback insulator; interior lights include dome light, front reading lights; sport steering wheel; passenger's side vanity mirror; day-night rearview mirror; glove box with light, front cupholder, dashboard storage, driver's and passenger's door bins; black grille, black side window moldings, black front windshield molding, black rear window molding and black door handles.

CODE	DESCRIPTION	INVOICE	MSRP

BASE 2WD EXTENDED CAB LB DRW (5M) (in addition to or instead of BASE 2WD REGULAR CAB LB SRW (5M) equipment): Additional exterior lights include cab clearance lights; front and rear 16" x 6" painted steel wheels; vented rear windows; seating capacity of 6, 60-40 split-bench front seat with adjustable headrests, driver's seat includes 4-way direction control with easy entry, passenger's seat includes 4-way direction control with easy entry and full folding rear bench seat with adjustable headrests.

BASE 2WD CREW CAB LB SRW (5M) (in addition to or instead of BASE 2WD EXTENDED CAB LB DRW (5M) equipment): Rear heat ducts; manual rear windows; bench front seat with adjustable headrests, driver's seat includes 2-way direction control, passenger's seat includes 2-way direction control; reclining rear bench seat with adjustable headrests and rear door bins.

BASE 4WD REGULAR CAB LB SRW (5M) (in addition to or instead of BASE 2WD REGULAR CAB LB SRW (5M) equipment): Part-time 4 wheel drive, auto locking hub control with manual shift; front independent torsion suspension with anti-roll bar, front torsion springs, front torsion bar; rear tow hooks and black fender flares.

BASE 4WD EXTENDED CAB LB DRW (5M) (in addition to or instead of BASE 2WD EXTENDED CAB LB DRW (5M) equipment): Part-time 4 wheel drive, auto locking hub control with manual shift; front independent torsion suspension with anti-roll bar, front torsion springs, front torsion bar; rear tow hooks and black fender flares.

BASE 4WD CREW CAB LB SRW (5M) (in addition to or instead of BASE 2WD CREW CAB LB SRW (5M) equipment): Part-time 4 wheel drive, auto locking hub control with manual shift; front independent torsion suspension with HD anti-roll bar, front torsion springs, front torsion bar; rear tow hooks; black fender flares; front and rear 16" x 6.5" painted styled steel wheels and child safety rear door locks.

BASE 4WD CREW CAB SB SRW(5M) (in addition to or instead of BASE 4WD CREW CAB LB SRW (5M) equipment): 7.4L V8 OHV SMPI 16-valve engine; 26 gal capacity fuel tank and front and rear 16" x 6" painted steel wheels.

Base Prices

CODE	DESCRIPTION	INVOICE	MSRP
CC30903-E63	Base 2WD Regular Cab LB SRW (5M)	17251	19715
CC30953-E63	Base 2WD Extended Cab LB DRW (5M)	20249	23142
CC30943-E63	Base 2WD Crew Cab LB SRW (5M)	19989	22845
CC30743-E63	Base 2WD Crew Cab SB SRW (5M)	21285	24326
CK30903-E63	Base 4WD Regular Cab LB SRW (5M)	19876	22715
CK30953-E63	Base 4WD Extended Cab LB DRW (5M)	21930	25953
CK30943-E63	Base 4WD Crew Cab LB SRW (5M)	22767	26019
CK30743-E63	Base 4WD Crew Cab SB SRW (5M)	24063	27500
Destination Charge:		640	640

Accessories

CODE	DESCRIPTION	INVOICE	MSRP
—	Cloth Seat Trim *NOT AVAILABLE with A95.*	NC	NC
—	Leather Seat Trim (Crew Cab) *REQUIRES 1SB. NOT AVAILABLE with 1SC.*	946	1100
—	Leather Seat Trim (Reg Cab/X-cab) *REQUIRES 1SB. NOT AVAILABLE with 1SC, A95.*	860	1000

CODE	DESCRIPTION	INVOICE	MSRP
1SA	Preferred Equipment Group 1SA	NC	NC
	Includes Base Decor package.		
1SA	Preferred Equipment Group 1SA with R9A and R9B (Reg Cab/X-Cab)	(602)	(700)
	Includes Base Decor package. REQUIRES R9A and R9B.		
1SB	Preferred Equipment Group 1SB (SRW - Reg Cab/X-Cab)	2611	3036
	Manufacturer Discount	(645)	(750)
	Net Price	1966	2286
	Includes LS Decor: LS badging, AM/FM stereo with cassette, leather-wrapped steering wheel, seatback storage tray, remote electric black OSRV mirrors, appearance package: chrome grille, composite halogen headlamps, rally wheel trim; custom cloth seat trim, air conditioning, convenience group: tilt wheel, speed control; power door locks and chrome rear step bumper. NOT AVAILABLE with R05, C7A, XYK, YYK, ZYK, XYL, YYL, ZYL, XHR, YHR, ZHR, XHP, YHP, ZHP, APC, BNP.		
1SB	Preferred Equipment Group 1SB (Crew Cab)	3156	3670
	Includes LS Decor: LS badging, AM/FM stereo with cassette, leather-wrapped steering wheel, seatback storage tray, remote electric black OSRV mirrors, appearance package: chrome grille, composite halogen headlamps, rally wheel trim; custom cloth seat trim, air conditioning, convenience group: tilt wheel, speed control and power door locks. NOT AVAILABLE with A95.		
1SB	Preferred Equipment Group 1SB with R05 (Reg Cab/X-Cab)	2526	2937
	Manufacturer Discount	(645)	(750)
	Net Price	1881	2187
	Includes LS Decor: LS badging, AM/FM stereo with cassette, leather-wrapped steering wheel, seatback storage tray, remote electric black OSRV mirrors, appearance package: chrome grille, composite halogen headlamps, rally wheel trim; custom cloth seat trim, air conditioning, convenience group: tilt wheel, speed control; power door locks and chrome rear step bumper. NOT AVAILABLE with KL5, XGK, YGK, ZGK, APC, BNP. REQUIRES R05.		
1SC	Preferred Equipment Group 1SC (Crew Cab)	4524	5260
	Includes LS Decor: LS badging, AM/FM stereo with cassette, leather-wrapped steering wheel, seatback storage tray, remote electric black OSRV mirrors, appearance package: chrome grille, composite halogen headlamps, rally wheel trim, custom cloth seat trim, air conditioning, convenience group: speed control, tilt wheel; power door locks, remote keyless entry, power driver's seat and reclining 60/40 split bench seat. NOT AVAILABLE with A95.		
1SC	Preferred Equipment Group 1SC (SRW Reg Cab)	3874	4505
	Manufacturer Discount	(645)	(750)
	Net Price	3229	3755
	Includes LS Decor: LS badging, AM/FM stereo with cassette, leather-wrapped steering wheel, seatback storage tray, remote electric black OSRV mirrors, appearance package: chrome grille, composite halogen headlamps, rally wheel trim; carpet floor covering, power door locks, chrome rear step bumper, front floor mats, remote keyless entry, 10" electrochromic ISRV mirror: 8 point compass, reclining 60/40 split bench seat and convenience group: tilt wheel, speed control. NOT AVAILABLE with R05, A95, APC, BNP.		

CODE	DESCRIPTION	INVOICE	MSRP
1SC	**Preferred Equipment Group 1SC (X-Cab)**	3846	4472
	Manufacturer Discount	(645)	(750)
	Net Price	3201	3722
	Includes LS Decor: LS badging, AM/FM stereo with cassette, leather-wrapped steering wheel, seatback storage tray, remote electric black OSRV mirrors, appearance package: chrome grille, composite halogen headlamps, rally wheel trim; carpet floor covering, power door locks, chrome rear step bumper, front floor mats, remote keyless entry, 10" electrochromic ISRV mirror: 8 point compass, reclining 60/40 split bench seat and convenience group: tilt wheel, speed control. NOT AVAILABLE with APC.		
1SC	**Preferred Equipment Group 1SC with R05 (Reg Cab)**	3789	4406
	Manufacturer Discount	(645)	(750)
	Net Price	3144	3656
	Includes LS Decor: LS badging, AM/FM stereo with cassette, leather-wrapped steering wheel, seatback storage tray, remote electric black OSRV mirrors, appearance package: chrome grille, composite halogen headlamps, rally wheel trim; carpet floor covering, power door locks, chrome rear step bumper, front floor mats, remote keyless entry, 10" electrochromic ISRV mirror: 8 point compass, reclining 60/40 split bench seat and convenience group: tilt wheel, speed control. NOT AVAILABLE with A95, APC, BNP. REQUIRES R05.		
A28	**Sliding Rear Window**	99	115
	NOT AVAILABLE with C49.		
A95	**High Back Reclining Bucket Seats (Crew Cab)**	364	423
	Includes power lumbar, floor console and overhead console. REQUIRES 1SB. NOT AVAILABLE with 1SC.		
A95	**High Back Reclining Bucket Seats (Crew Cab)**	278	323
	Includes power lumbar, floor console and overhead console. REQUIRES 1SC. NOT AVAILABLE with 1SB.		
A95	**High Back Reclining Bucket Seats (Reg Cab)**	332	386
	Includes power lumbar and floor console. NOT AVAILABLE with 1SC.		
A95	**High Back Reclining Bucket Seats (Reg Cab)**	332	386
	Includes power lumbar, floor console and overhead console. REQUIRES 1SB. NOT AVAILABLE with 1SC.		
A95	**High Back Reclining Bucket Seats (Crew Cab)**	278	323
	Includes power lumbar, floor console and overhead console. REQUIRES 1SC. NOT AVAILABLE with 1SB.		
A95	**High Back Reclining Bucket Seats (X-Cab)**	232	270
	Includes power lumbar, seatback storage pockets, floor console and overhead console. REQUIRES 1SC.		
A95	**Reclining High Back Bucket Seats (Crew Cab)**	364	423
	Includes power lumbar, floor console and overhead console. REQUIRES 1SB. NOT AVAILABLE with 1SC.		
AE7	**Reclining 60/40 Split Bench Seat (Crew Cab)**	86	100
	Includes storage armrest and power lumbar. REQUIRES 1SB or 1SC.		
AE7	**Reclining 60/40 Split Bench Seat (Reg Cab)**	150	174
	Includes storage armrest and power lumbar. NOT AVAILABLE with A95.		

CODE	DESCRIPTION	INVOICE	MSRP
AG9	Power Driver's Seat *REQUIRES A95 or 1SB or 1SC.*	206	240
AJ1	Deep Tinted Solar-Ray Glass (Crew Cab) *Includes light tinted rear window when (A28) sliding rear window is specified.*	185	215
AJ1	Deep Tinted Solar-Ray Glass (Reg Cab) *REQUIRES A28.*	30	35
AJ1	Deep Tinted Solar-Ray Glass (Crew Cab) *Includes light tinted rear window. REQUIRES A28.*	155	180
AJ1	Deep Tinted Solar-Ray Glass (X-Cab) *REQUIRES 1SB or 1SC.*	92	107
AJ1	Deep Tinted Solar-Ray Glass (X-Cab) *The rear window is light tint glass. REQUIRES C49.*	62	72
AU0	Remote Keyless Entry	129	150
AU3	Power Door Locks (Crew Cab)	192	223
AU3	Power Door Locks (Reg Cab/X-Cab)	135	156
B30	Carpet Floor Covering (Reg Cab)	30	35
B30	Carpet Floor Covering (X-Cab)	44	51
B32	Front Floor Mats (Reg Cab/X-Cab)	17	20
B33	Rear Floor Mats (X-Cab) *NOT AVAILABLE with YG4.*	14	16
B85	Bright Exterior Moldings (2WD Reg Cab/X-Cab) *Includes bodyside and wheel opening moldings. NOT AVAILABLE with R05.*	92	107
B85	Bright Exterior Moldings (4WD - Reg Cab/X-Cab) *NOT AVAILABLE with R05.*	65	76
BG9	Full Rubber Color-Keyed Flooring (X-Cab) *Replaces carpeting and floor mats.*	(44)	(51)
BG9	Full Rubber Color-Keyed Flooring (Reg Cab) *Replaces carpeting and floor mats.*	(30)	(35)
BZY	Under Rail Bedliner	194	225
C49	Electric Rear Window Defogger *REQUIRES R9A. NOT AVAILABLE with A28, AJ1, YG6.*	132	154
C60	Air Conditioning *NOT AVAILABLE with YG6.*	692	805
C7A	GVWR: 10,000 Lbs *REQUIRES R05 and (XYK or XYL or XHR or XHP). NOT AVAILABLE with XGK, 1SB, YGK, ZGK, KL5.*	NC	NC
DD7	10" Electrochromic ISRV Mirror (Reg Cab/X-Cab) *Includes 8 point compass.*	125	145
DF2	Stainless Steel Camper Type Mirrors *Exterior stainless steel 7.5"W x 10.5"H mirrors.*	46	53
DF2	Stainless Steel Camper Type Mirrors *7.5"W x 10.5"H stainless steel. REQUIRES 1SB or 1SC.*	(39)	(45)
EF1	Rear Bumper Delete Provisions *Vehicles registered in certain states and must have a rear bumper to be operated on their roads. Consult your local laws. REQUIRES 1SB or 1SC. NOT AVAILABLE with Z82.*	(172)	(200)

CODE	DESCRIPTION	INVOICE	MSRP
EF1	Rear Bumper Delete Provisions *Vehicles registered in certain states and must have a rear bumper to be operated on their roads. Consult your local laws. NOT AVAILABLE with Z82, VB3, R9B.*	(112)	(130)
F60	HD Front Springs (4WD)	54	63
G80	Locking Differential	217	252
HC4	4.56 Axle Ratio *Includes locking differential. REQUIRES C7A and L29 or MT1. NOT AVAILABLE with L65, KL5, VYU, XGK, YGK, ZGK, R9B.*	217	252
K47	High Capacity Air Cleaner	22	25
KL5	Alternative Fuel Compatible Engine (Reg Cab/X-Cab) *LPG and CNG conversion ready. REQUIRES MT1. NOT AVAILABLE with L29, L65, C7A, R05.*	108	125
L29	Engine: Vortec 7400 V8 SFI (All Except SB Crew Cab) *NOT AVAILABLE with KL5, L65, VYU.*	516	600
L65	Engine: 6.5L V8 Turbo Diesel *Includes engine block heater and HD auxiliary battery. NOT AVAILABLE with KL5, TP2, HC4, L29, V10, VYU.*	2460	2860
MT1	Transmission: 4-Speed Automatic OD HD	856	995
NC7	Federal Emission Override *For vehicles that will be registered or leased in California, Connecticut, Washington D.C, Delaware, Massachusetts, Maryland, New Hampshire, New Jersey, New York, Pennsylvania, Rhode Island and Virginia but sold by retailers outside those states.*	NC	NC
NZZ	Skid Plate Package (4WD) *Includes fuel tank shield, front differential and transfer case shields.*	82	95
P06	Rally Wheel Trim *NOT AVAILABLE with R05.*	52	60
R05	Dual Rear Wheels (4WD Crew Cab) *Includes tailgate lamps and roof marker lamps. NOT AVAILABLE with XGK, YGK, ZGK.*	737	857
R05	Dual Rear Wheels (4WD SRW Reg Cab) *Includes tailgate lamps and roof marker lamps. NOT AVAILABLE with B85, KL5, XGK, YGK, ZGK, R9B.*	821	955
R05	Dual Rear Wheels (2WD SRW Reg Cab) *Includes roof marker lamps. NOT AVAILABLE with KL5, YGK, ZGK, R9B, B85, P06, BNP.*	821	955
R9A	Comfort and Convenience Package *Includes air conditioning and convenience group: tilt wheel, cruise control. NOT AVAILABLE with YG6, UL5.*	1150	1337
R9B	Bright Appearance Package (4WD Reg Cab) *Includes bright exterior moldings, appearance package: chrome grille, composite halogen headlamps, chrome rear step bumper, chrome deluxe front bumper with rub strip and rally wheel trim. NOT AVAILABLE with R05, ZHP, YHP, ZHR, YHR, ZYL, YYL, ZYK, YYK, XHP, XHR, XYL, XYK.*	389	452
R9B	Bright Appearance Package (Crew Cab) *Includes appearance package: chrome grille, composite halogen headlamps and rally wheel trim. NOT AVAILABLE with C7A, HC4, XHP, XYK, YHP, YHR, YYK, ZHP, ZHR, ZYK.*	301	350

CODE	DESCRIPTION	INVOICE	MSRP
R9B	Bright Appearance Package (2WD Reg Cab) *Includes bright exterior moldings, appearance package: chrome grille, composite halogen headlamps, chrome rear step bumper, deluxe chrome front bumper and rally wheel trim. NOT AVAILABLE with R05, EF1.*	416	483
R9B	Bright Appearance Package with R05 (Reg Cab/X-Cab) *Includes appearance package: chrome grille, composite halogen headlamps, chrome rear step bumper and rally wheel trim. NOT AVAILABLE with EF1. REQUIRES R05.*	323	376
TP2	Auxiliary Battery *NOT AVAILABLE with L65.*	115	134
U01	Roof Marker Lamps	47	55
ULO	Radio: AM/FM Stereo with Cassette and Automatic Tone Control *Includes digital clock, theft lock, speed compensated volume and enhanced performance speaker system. REQUIRES 1SB or 1SC. NOT AVAILABLE with UN0, UP0.*	77	90
UL5	Radio Delete *NOT AVAILABLE with UM6, R9A, 1SB or 1SC.*	(247)	(287)
UM6	Radio: AM/FM Stereo with Cassette *Includes digital clock. NOT AVAILABLE with UL5.*	126	147
UN0	Radio: AM/FM Stereo with CD and Automatic Tone Control *Includes digital clock, theft lock, speed compensated volume and enhanced performance speaker system. REQUIRES 1SB or 1SC. NOT AVAILABLE with ULO, UP0.*	163	190
UP0	Radio: AM/FM Stereo with CD and Cassette *Includes digital clock, search and repeat cassette, automatic tone control, theft lock, speed compensated volume and enhanced performance speaker system. REQUIRES 1SB or 1SC and MT1. NOT AVAILABLE with ULO, UN0.*	249	290
V10	Cold Climate Package *Includes engine block heater. NOT AVAILABLE with L65.*	28	33
V22	Appearance Package *Includes chrome grille and composite halogen headlamps. NOT AVAILABLE with 1SB, 1SC.*	164	191
V76	Recovery Hooks (2WD)	33	38
VB3	Chrome Rear Step Bumper (Reg Cab/X-Cab) *Includes rubber step pad. NOT AVAILABLE with EF1.*	85	99
VB3	Deluxe Chrome Rear Bumper (2WD Crew Cab) *Includes rub strip. NOT AVAILABLE with EF1.*	85	99
VG3	Deluxe Chrome Front Bumper (2WD - Reg Cab/X-Cab) *Includes rubber strip.*	22	26
VG3	Deluxe Chrome Front Bumper with Rub Strip (4WD - Reg Cab/X-Cab)	22	26
VYU	Snow Plow Prep Package (4WD - Reg Cab/X-Cab) *Includes HD front springs. NOT AVAILABLE with L29, L65, HC4.*	101	118
XGK	Tires: Front LT245/75R16E AT BSW (4WD) *REQUIRES YGK and ZGK. NOT AVAILABLE with 1SB, XYK, YYK, ZYK, XYL, YYL, ZYL, XHR, YHR, ZHR, XHP, YHP, ZHP, R05, C7A, HC4.*	19	23
XHP	Tires: Front LT225/75R16/D AS BSW (SRW Crew Cab) *REQUIRES YHP and R05. NOT AVAILABLE with XYK, YYK, ZYK, YGK, ZGK, R9B.*	(58)	(68)

CODE	DESCRIPTION	INVOICE	MSRP
XHP	Tires: Front LT225/75R16D AS BSW (4WD - Reg Cab/X-Cab) *REQUIRES YHP and R05 and ZHP. NOT AVAILABLE with XYK, YYK, ZYK, XYL, YYL, ZYL, XHR, ZHR, XGK, YGK, ZGK, KL5, R9B, 1SB.*	(58)	(68)
XHR	Tires: Front LT225/75R16D AT BSW (4WD - X-Cab/Crew Cab) *REQUIRES YHR and ZHR. NOT AVAILABLE with XYK, YYK, ZYK, XYL, YYL, ZYL.*	19	22
XHR	Tires: Front LT225/75R16D AT BSW (4WD Reg Cab) *REQUIRES YHR and R05 and ZHR. NOT AVAILABLE with XYK, YYK, ZYK, XYL, YYL, ZYL, XHP, YHP, ZHP, XGK, YGK, ZGK, KL5, R9B, 1SB.*	(40)	(46)
XYK	Tires: Front LT215/85R16D Highway BSW (4WD X-Cab/SB Crew Cab) *REQUIRES YYK and ZYK. NOT AVAILABLE with XYL, YYL, ZYL, XHR, YHR, ZHR.*	122	142
XYK	Tires: Front LT215/85R16D Highway BSW (4WD Reg Cab/LB Crew Cab) *REQUIRES YYK and R05 and ZYK. NOT AVAILABLE with XYL, YYL, ZYL, XHR, YHR, ZHR, XHP, YHP, ZHP, XGK, YGK, ZGK, KL5, R9B, 1SB.*	64	74
XYL	Tires: Front LT215/85R16D AT BSW (4WD X-Cab/SB Crew Cab) *REQUIRES F60 and YYL and ZYL. NOT AVAILABLE with XYK, YYK, ZYK, XHR, YHR, ZHR.*	170	198
XYL	Tires: Front LT215/85R16D AT BSW (4WD Reg Cab/LB Crew Cab) *REQUIRES F60 and YYL and R05 and ZYL. NOT AVAILABLE with XYK, YYK, ZYK, XHR, YHR, ZHR, XHP, YHP, ZHP, XGK, YGK, ZGK, KL5, R9B, 1SB.*	112	130
YG4	Rear Seat Delete (X-Cab) *NOT AVAILABLE with B33 or A95.*	(374)	(435)
YG6	Air Conditioning Not Desired *NOT AVAILABLE with 1SB, 1SC, R9A, C49.*	NC	NC
YGK	Tires: Rear LT245/75R16E AT BSW (4WD) *REQUIRES ZGK or 4HH. NOT AVAILABLE with 1SB, XYK, YYK, ZYK, XYL, YYL, ZYL, XHR, YHR, ZHR, XHP, YHP, ZHP, R05, C7A, HC4.*	19	23
YHP	Tires: Rear LT225/75R16D AS BSW (4WD Reg Cab/LB Crew Cab) *REQUIRES R05 and ZHP or C7A. NOT AVAILABLE with XYK, YYK, ZYK, XYL, YYL, ZYL, XHR, YHR, ZHR, XGK, YGK, ZGK, KL5, R9B, 1SB.*	370	430
YHR	Tires: Rear LT225/75R16D AT BSW (4WD Reg Cab/LB Crew Cab) *REQUIRES R05 and ZHR or C7A. NOT AVAILABLE with XYK, YYK, ZYK, XYL, YYL, ZYL, YHP, ZHP, XGK, YGK, ZGK, KL5, R9B, 1SB.*	408	474
YHR	Tires: Rear LT225/75R16D AT BSW (4WD X-Cab/SB Crew Cab) *REQUIRES ZHR. NOT AVAILABLE with XYK, YYK, ZYK, XYL, YYL, ZYL.*	38	44
YYK	Tires: Rear LT215/85R16D Highway BSW (4WD X-Cab/SB Crew Cab) *REQUIRES ZYK. NOT AVAILABLE with XYL, YYL, ZYL, XHR, YHR, ZHR.*	244	284
YYK	Tires: Rear LT215/85R16D Highway BSW (4WD Reg Cab/LB Crew Cab) *REQUIRES R05 and ZYK or C7A. NOT AVAILABLE with XYL, YYL, ZYL, XHR, YHR, ZHR, XHP, YHP, ZHP, XGK, YGK, ZGK, KL5, R9B, 1SB.*	614	714
YYL	Tires: Rear LT215/85R16D AT BSW (4WD X-Cab/SB Crew Cab) *REQUIRES F60 and ZYL. NOT AVAILABLE with XYK, YYK, ZYK, XHR, YHR, ZHR.*	341	396
YYL	Tires: Rear LT215/85R16D AT BSW (4WD Reg Cab/LB Crew Cab) *REQUIRES F60 and R05 and ZYL. NOT AVAILABLE with XYK, YYK, ZYK, XHR, YHR, ZHR, XHP, YHP, ZHP, XGK, ZGK, KL5, YGK, R9B, 1SB.*	710	826
Z82	HD Trailering Special Equipment *Includes trailer hitch platform. NOT AVAILABLE with EF1.*	141	164

CODE	DESCRIPTION	INVOICE	MSRP
ZGK	Tire: Spare LT245/75R16E BSW AT *Includes tire carrier. NOT AVAILABLE with XYK, YYK, ZYK, XYL, YYL, ZYL, XHR, YHR, ZHR, XHP, YHP, ZHP, R05, C7A, HC4.*	9	11
ZHP	Tire: Spare LT225/75R16D AS BSW (4WD Reg Cab/LB Crew Cab) *Includes tire carrier. REQUIRES R05. NOT AVAILABLE with XYK, YYK, ZYK, XYL, YYL, ZYL, XHR, YHR, ZHR, XGK, YGK, ZGK, KL5, R9B, 1SB.*	(29)	(34)
ZHR	Tire: Spare LT225/75R16D AT BSW (4WD Reg Cab/LB Crew Cab) *Includes tire carrier. REQUIRES R05. NOT AVAILABLE with XYK, YYK, ZYK, XYL, YYL, ZYL, XHP, YHP, ZHP, XGK, YGK, ZGK, KL5, R9B, 1SB.*	(20)	(23)
ZHR	Tire: Spare LT225/75R16D AT BSW (4WD X-Cab/SB Crew Cab) *Includes tire carrier. NOT AVAILABLE with XYK, YYK, ZYK, XYL, YYL, ZYL.*	9	11
ZQ3	Convenience Group *Includes tilt wheel and cruise control. NOT AVAILABLE with 1SB or 1SC.*	331	385
ZYK	Tire: Spare LT215/85R16D Highway BSW (4WD Reg Cab/LB Crew Cab) *Includes tire carrier. REQUIRES R05. NOT AVAILABLE with XYL, YYL, ZYL, XHR, YHR, ZHR, XHP, YHP, ZHP, XGK, YGK, ZGK, KL5, R9B, 1SB.*	32	37
ZYK	Tire: Spare LT215/85R16D Highway BSW (4WD X-Cab/SB Crew Cab) *Includes tire carrier. NOT AVAILABLE with XYL, YYL, ZYL, XHR, YHR, ZHR.*	61	71
ZYL	Tire: Spare LT215/85R16D AT BSW (4WD Reg Cab/LB Crew Cab) *Includes tire carrier. REQUIRES F60 and R05. NOT AVAILABLE with XYK, YYK, ZYK, XHR, YHR, ZHR, XHP, YHP, ZHP, XGK, ZGK, YGK, KL5, R9B, 1SB.*	56	65
ZYL	Tires: Spare LT215/85R16D AT BSW (4WD X-Cab/SB Crew Cab) *Includes tire carrier. REQUIRES F60. NOT AVAILABLE with XYK, YYK, ZYK, XHR, YHR, ZHR.*	85	99

1999 EXPRESS

1999 Chevrolet Express

What's New?

The Chevy Express line of full-size vans is available in a variety of configurations, including the G1500 (1/2-ton), G2500 (3/4-ton) and G3500 (1-ton) series. Two wheelbases (135-inches and 155-inches) are available on 2500 and 3500 models. For '99, all Express vans get automatic transmission enhancements to increase durability and improve sealing, plus de-powered dual front airbags. There are also two new exterior paint colors and one new interior shade for the 1999 model year.

Review

When Chevy dealers received a brand-new, full-size van to sell in 1996, it marked the first time in 25 years that GM completely redesigned its big vans. The Chevy Express comes standard with lots of cargo space, dual airbags and four-wheel antilock brakes. And it can be equipped with a variety of powerful engines. With this modern new design, Chevrolet is stealing some of Ford's thunder in the full-size van market.

Converters prefer the rugged full-frame construction of full-size vans, because they are easy to modify and can handle a lot of add-ons without degrading stability, ride and handling. Because most full-size vans are bought for conversion into rolling motel rooms, engineers decided to put the Chevy Express on this type of platform. Regular-length models carry 267 cubic feet of cargo, and extended-length vans can haul 317 cubic feet of stuff. Trick rear doors open 180 degrees to make loading and unloading easier. Up to 15 passengers can ride in the extended-length model, making it perfect for use as an airport shuttle. Other seating options include five-, eight- and 12-passenger arrangements. And G3500s can tow up to 10,000 pounds when properly equipped.

For convenience, the full-size spare is stored underneath the cargo floor. A 31-gallon fuel tank keeps this thirsty vehicle from frequent fill-ups, but topping off an empty tank will quickly empty your wallet. Engine choices are sourced from the Chevrolet family of Vortec gasoline motors, or if you prefer, a turbocharged diesel can be installed under the hood. Available are the Vortec 4300 V6, the 5000, 5700, and 7400 V8s, and a 6.5-liter Turbo-diesel V8. Standard side cargo doors are a 60/40 panel arrangement, but a traditional slider is a no-cost option on 135-inch wheelbase vans.

Child safety locks are standard on the rear and side doors. Handy assist handles help folks climb in and out. Front and rear air conditioning is optional. Last year, all vans got a standard theft deterrent system, and new seat belt comfort guides. For 1999, both the passenger-side and driver-side mini-module style airbag are the depowered type.

Exterior styling is an interesting mix of corporate Chevrolet, Astro Van and old Lumina Minivan. We'll admit the high, rear pillar-mounted taillights are odd looking, but at least they're functional. They can easily be seen even if the van is operated with the rear doors open. Low-mounted bumpers and moldings make the Chevy Express look much taller than it is. An attractively sculpted body side gives the van's smooth, slab-sided flanks a dose of character, as does the quad-lamp grille arrangement. Two new Chevy Express paint choices arrive for 1999, and one new interior color.

Overall, Chevrolet's latest rendition of the traditional full-size van appears to be right on target, giving Ford's Econoline the first real competition it has faced in years.

Safety Data

Side Airbag: *Not Available*
4-Wheel ABS: *Standard*
Driver Crash Test Grade: *Not Available*
Side Impact Crash Test Front: *Not Available*
Crash Offset: *Not Available*
Integrated Child Seat(s): *Not Available*
Traction Control: *Not Available*
Passenger Crash Test Grade: *Not Available*
Side Impact Crash Test Rear: *Not Available*

Standard Equipment

G1500 PASSENGER VAN LD (4A): 4.3L V6 OHV SMPI 12-valve engine; 4-speed electronic overdrive automatic transmission with lock-up; 600-amp HD battery; 100-amp alternator; rear wheel drive, 3.42 axle ratio; stainless steel exhaust; front independent suspension with anti-roll bar, front coil springs, rigid rear axle suspension with HD rear leaf springs; power re-circulating ball steering with vehicle speed-sensing assist; front disc/rear drum brakes with 4 wheel antilock braking system; 31 gal. capacity fuel tank; 3 doors with split swing-out right rear passenger's door, split swing-out rear cargo door; trailer harness; front and rear argent bumpers with rear step; monotone paint; sealed beam halogen headlamps with daytime running lights; additional exterior lights include center high mounted stop light; driver's and passenger's manual black folding outside mirrors; front and rear 15" x 6" silver styled steel wheels; P235/75SR15 BSW AS front and rear tires; underbody mounted full-size conventional steel spare wheel; air conditioning; AM/FM stereo with clock, seek-scan, 4 speakers, and fixed antenna; child safety rear door locks; 2 power accessory outlets; instrumentation display includes oil pressure gauge, water temp gauge, volt gauge, trip odometer; warning indicators include battery, lights on, key in ignition; dual airbags; ignition disable; tinted windows, vented rear windows, fixed 1/4 vent windows; variable intermittent front windshield wipers, vented rear window; seating capacity of 8, front bucket seats with fixed headrests, driver's seat includes 4-way direction control, passenger's seat includes 4-way direction control; 2nd row bench seat with adjustable headrests; 3rd row removable bench seat with adjustable headrests; vinyl seats, cloth door trim insert, full cloth headliner, full vinyl floor covering; interior lights include dome light; day-night rearview mirror; engine cover console with storage, glove box, front cupholder, instrument panel covered bin, 2 seat back storage pockets, driver's and passenger's door bins; vinyl cargo floor, plastic trunk lid, cargo light; black grille, black side window moldings, black front windshield molding, black rear window molding and black door handles.

G2500/G3500 PASSENGER VAN HD (4A) (in addition to or instead of G1500 PASSENGER VAN LD (4A) equipment): 5.7L V8 OHV SMPI 16-valve engine; 124-amp alternator; 3.73 axle ratio; front and rear 16" x 6.5" silver styled steel wheels and seating capacity of 12.

G2500/G3500 EXTENDED PASSENGER VAN HD (4A) (in addition to or instead of G2500/G3500 PASSENGER VAN HD (4A) equipment): Colored grille.

CODE	DESCRIPTION	INVOICE	MSRP

Base Prices

CODE	DESCRIPTION	INVOICE	MSRP
CG11406	Base G1500 Passenger Van (4A)	20186	23070
CG21406	Base G2500 Passenger Van (4A)	22374	25570
CG21706	Base G2500 Passenger Van Ext. (4A)	23161	26470
CG31406	Base G3500 Passenger Van (4A)	22623	25859
CG31706	Base G3500 Passenger Van Ext. (4A)	23450	26804
Destination Charge:		615	615

Accessories

CODE	DESCRIPTION	INVOICE	MSRP
1SA	**Option Package 1SA** *Includes vehicle with standard equipment.*	NC	NC
1SB	**Option Package 1SB** *Includes Convenience Package: cruise control, tilt steering wheel; and Power Convenience Package: power windows, power door locks.*	739	859
1SC	**Option Package ISC** *Includes LS Decor: chrome front and rear bumpers with front step pad and rear entry assist step, chrome grille, composite headlights, gray bodyside moldings, wheel trim rings, auxiliary lighting package: stepwell lights, reading lights, underhood light; full floor carpet, cloth seat trim, inboard seat armrests, cloth door panel inserts; Convenience Package: cruise control, tilt steering wheel; and Power Convenience Package: power windows, power door locks.*	1423	1655
1SD	**Option Package 1SD (G2500 Ext./G3500 Ext.)** *Includes LS Decor: chrome front and rear bumpers with front step pad and rear entry assist step, chrome grille, composite headlights, gray bodyside moldings, wheel trim rings, auxiliary lighting package: stepwell lights, reading lights, underhood light; full floor carpet, cloth seat trim, inboard seat armrests, cloth door panel inserts; Convenience Package: cruise control, tilt steering wheel; and Power Convenience Package: power windows, power door locks; dual air conditioning with rear heater, deep tinted glass, remote keyless entry, dual power exterior mirrors, dual illuminated visor vanity mirrors, leather-wrapped steering wheel.*	2101	2443
1SD	**Option Package 1SD (G2500/G3500)** *Includes LS Decor: chrome front and rear bumpers with front step pad and rear entry assist step, chrome grille, composite headlights, gray bodyside moldings, wheel trim rings, auxiliary lighting package: stepwell lights, reading lights, underhood light; full floor carpet, cloth seat trim, inboard seat armrests, cloth door panel inserts; Convenience Package: cruise control, tilt steering wheel; and Power Convenience Package: power windows, power door locks; dual air conditioning with rear heater, deep tinted glass, remote keyless entry, dual power exterior mirrors, dual illuminated visor vanity mirrors, leather-wrapped steering wheel.*	2792	3247
1SD	**Option Package 1SD (G1500)** *Includes LS Decor: chrome front and rear bumpers with front step pad and rear entry assist step, chrome grille, composite headlights, gray bodyside moldings, wheel trim rings, auxiliary lighting package: stepwell lights, reading lights, underhood light; full floor carpet, cloth seat trim, inboard seat armrests, cloth door panel inserts; Convenience Package: cruise control, tilt steering wheel; and Power Convenience*	2841	3303

CODE	DESCRIPTION	INVOICE	MSRP
	Package: power windows, power door locks; dual air conditioning with rear heater, deep tinted glass, remote keyless entry, dual power exterior mirrors, dual illuminated visor vanity mirrors, leather-wrapped steering wheel.		
AG1	Power Driver's Seat *Includes 6-way adjustment. REQUIRES 1SC or 1SD.*	206	240
AG2	Power Passenger's Seat *Includes 6-way adjustment. REQUIRES 1SC or 1SD.*	206	240
AJ1	Deep Tinted Glass *NOT AVAILABLE with 1SD.*	335	390
AU0	Remote Keyless Entry *REQUIRES 1SC.*	129	150
B30	Carpeting *NOT AVAILABLE with 1SC or 1SD.*	126	147
C36	Rear Heater *NOT AVAILABLE with C69.*	206	240
C69	Rear Air Conditioning (G2500/G3500) *Includes rear heater and 124-amp alternator. NOT AVAILABLE with 1SD.*	691	804
C69	Rear Air Conditioning (G1500) *Includes rear heater and 124-amp alternator. NOT AVAILABLE with 1SD.*	740	860
C69	Rear Air Conditioning (G2500 Ext./G3500 Ext.) *Includes rear heater and 124-amp alternator.*	NC	NC
DE5	Power Exterior Mirrors *Includes defogger. REQUIRES ZQ2 or 1SB or 1SC.*	97	118
DH6	Visor Vanity Mirrors *Include illumination. REQUIRES 1SC.*	65	75
G80	Locking Differential *NOT AVAILABLE with GU6 on G3500.*	217	252
GT4	Rear Axle Ratio: 3.73 *NOT AVAILABLE with L30.*	NC	NC
GT5	Rear Axle Ratio: 4.10 (G2500/G3500)	NC	NC
GU6	Rear Axle Ratio: 3.42 (G1500/G3500) *REQUIRES L29 on G3500. NOT AVAILABLE with G80 on G3500.*	NC	NC
KL5	Alternative Fuel Conversion (G2500/G3500) *REQUIRES L31.*	108	125
KW2	Alternator: 124-amp (G1500) *NOT AVAILABLE with C69.*	52	60
L29	Engine: Vortec 7400 V8 (G3500)	516	600
L30	Engine: Vortec 5000 V8 (G1500) *REQUIRES GU6.*	426	495
L31	Engine: Vortec 5700 V8 (G1500)	1027	1195
L65	Engine: 6.5L Turbo Diesel V8 (G2500/G3500)	2460	2860
N83	Chrome Wheels (G1500) *REQUIRES 1SC or 1SD.*	215	250
N83	Chrome Wheels (G1500) *NOT AVAILABLE with 1SC or 1SD.*	267	310
N90	Cast Aluminum Wheels (G1500) *NOT AVAILABLE with 1SC or 1SD.*	267	310

CODE	DESCRIPTION	INVOICE	MSRP
N90	Cast Aluminum Wheels (G1500) *REQUIRES 1SC or 1SD.*	215	250
NP5	Leather-Wrapped Steering Wheel *NOT AVAILABLE with 1SD.*	52	60
P06	Wheel Trim Rings *Includes chrome center cap. NOT AVAILABLE with 1SC or 1SD.*	52	60
TR9	Auxiliary Lighting Package *Includes stepwell lights, reading lights, underhood light. NOT AVAILABLE with 1SC or 1SD.*	138	160
U75	Power Antenna	73	85
UL0	Radio: Uplevel AM/FM with Cassette *Includes seek/scan, digital clock, 8 speakers, automatic tone control, power antenna. REQUIRES 1SB or 1SC or 1SD.*	380	442
UM6	Radio: AM/FM with Cassette *Includes seek/scan, digital clock, 4 speakers.*	126	147
UN0	Radio: Uplevel AM/FM with CD *Includes seek/scan, digital clock, 8 speakers, automatic tone control, power antenna. REQUIRES 1SB or 1SC or 1SD.*	466	542
UP0	Radio: Uplevel AM/FM with Cassette and CD *Includes seek/scan, digital clock, 8 speakers, automatic tone control, power antenna. REQUIRES 1SB or 1SC or 1SD.*	552	642
V10	Cold Climate Package *NOT AVAILABLE with L65.*	41	48
VK3	Front License Plate Bracket	NC	NC
XHB	Tires: P235/75R15 AS WSW (G1500)	86	100
XHM	Tires: P235/75R15 AS WOL (G1500)	108	125
YA2	Sliding Side Cargo Door	NC	NC
YF5	California Emissions	NC	NC
Z82	Trailering Package *Includes platform trailer hitch and 8-wire harness.*	267	310
ZP3	Seating: 15-Passenger (G3500 Ext.)	319	371
ZP5	Seating: 5-Passenger (G1500)	(319)	(371)
ZP8	Seating: 8-Passenger (G2500/G3500)	(319)	(371)
ZQ2	Power Convenience Package *Includes power windows and power door locks. NOT AVAILABLE with 1SB, 1SC, 1SD.*	408	474
ZQ3	Convenience Package *Includes cruise control and tilt steering wheel. NOT AVAILABLE with 1SB, 1SC, 1SD.*	331	385
ZX9	Spare Tire Delete (G1500) *NOT AVAILABLE with XHB or XHM.*	(122)	(142)
ZX9	Spare Tire Delete (G1500) *REQUIRES XHB.*	(139)	(162)
ZX9	Spare Tire Delete (G1500) *REQUIRES XHM.*	(144)	(167)
ZX9	Spare Tire Delete (G2500)	(232)	(270)
ZX9	Spare Tire Delete (G3500)	(256)	(298)

1999 S-10

1999 Chevrolet S-10

What's New?

An all-new sport package called the Xtreme replaces the old SS model. All S-10s get automatic transmission enhancements to improve sealing and durability and larger outside mirrors with an optional power heated mirror. Other changes for '99 include a content theft alarm, headlamp flash-to-pass feature, three new exterior paint choices and the availability of GM's AutoTrac electronic push-button transfer case on select four-wheel-drive models.

Review

Like most of today's compact trucks, Chevrolet's S-Series has been growing more car-like, especially since its last redesign in 1994. That's the trend, and Chevy has done a good job of transforming its small-scale pickups into everyday vehicles, without blurring their identity as practical machines. Riding smoother and handling better, they gained plenty in performance and overall refinement, ranking closer to their main competition, Ford's similar-size Ranger. Grasp the S-10's long manual-transmission gearshift lever and it's easy to imagine you're piloting a big rig, while enjoying the blissful comforts of a compact.

Four-cylinder models need that manual shift to gain top performance, but the two V6 engine options are strong with either manual or automatic transmissions. For maximum output, the optional 180-horsepower L35 Vortec 4300 V6 is the engine to select (190 horsepower in 4WD models). But the slightly less- energetic LF6 Vortec 4300 V6 is no slouch, thanks to 175 horses and 180 pounds-feet of torque.

Extended cab models can be equipped with a handy access panel that opens wide to allow for easier access to the rear of the cab. Located on the driver's side, this optional third door deletes one of the extended cab's jump seats, but makes it much easier to load cargo, a friend, or your pal Spot into the S-10. But be warned, the third door makes for aggravating rattles on broken pavement.

Two- and four-wheel-drive trucks come in several configurations, with a short or long bed, a Fleetside box or Sportside box, and a short or extended wheelbase available. Ride comfort varies from car-smooth to strictly firm, depending on the choice of suspensions and tires.

Headroom is ample and seats are supportive, but the driver sits low, facing a tall steering wheel and cowl. In theory, three people fit across an S-Series bench seat, but only someone as slim as TV's Ally

McBeal could fit comfortably in the space allotted. Surprisingly, the extended cab's rear jump seats are comfortable enough for short trips, as long as only one adult occupies the space behind the front seats.

The full complement of gauges is excellent and easy to read, but the upright dashboard is constructed of cheap- and brittle-looking plastic. Despite a low-height windshield-not unlike the Ranger's-visibility is super, helped by huge mirrors. Dual airbags and daytime running lamps are standard, as well as a theft deterrent system four-wheel ABS. Off-roaders will want the burly ZR2 package with its wider track and taller ride height, featuring special wheel flares, tough suspension components and aggressive rubber.

New this year is the Xtreme package, which can be had as a regular or extended cab, with a Fleetside or Sportside box, a four- or six-cylinder engine, manual or automatic transmission, and in base or LS trim. Riding on a special ZQ8 suspension that is lowered two full inches, the two-wheel-drive only Xtreme aims to be a factory sport truck that can be custom-tailored to meet a variety of needs and budgets. No matter how you configure it, Xtreme stands out from the crowd with body-color grille and bumpers, front air dam with fog lamps, full ground effects with wheel flares and unique 16-inch aluminum wheels wearing P235/55 blackwall tires. While we'd pick an extended cab LS Sportside with the V6 and a five-speed, this truck rides sports-car firm and handles superbly any way you package it.

Like many Chevrolets, the S-10 is loaded with value, but we've never quite warmed up to it. Occasional squeaks and rattles and the low-buck interior don't provide the feeling of brawny quality that we've experienced in the S-10's major competitor, Ford's Ranger. With further refinement in this year's S-10, maybe more test drives will help win us over.

Safety Data

Side Airbag: *Not Available*
4-Wheel ABS: *Standard*
Driver Crash Test Grade: *Poor*
Side Impact Crash Test Front: *Average*
Crash Offset: *Marginal*
Integrated Child Seat(s): *Not Available*
Traction Control: *Not Available*
Passenger Crash Test Grade: *Average*
Side Impact Crash Test Rear: *Not Available*

Standard Equipment

BASE 2WD REGULAR CAB SB/LB (5M): 2.2L I4 OHV SMPI 8-valve engine; 5-speed overdrive manual transmission; 525-amp battery with run down protection; 100-amp alternator; rear wheel drive, 3.73 axle ratio; stainless steel exhaust; comfort ride suspension (firm ride suspension - LB), front independent suspension with antiroll bar, front coil springs, rigid rear axle suspension with rear leaf springs; power re-circulating ball steering; front disc/rear drum brakes with 4 wheel antilock braking system; 19 gal. capacity fuel tank; front license plate bracket; front and rear black bumpers with rear step; monotone paint; aero-composite halogen fully automatic headlamps with daytime running lights, delay-off feature; additional exterior lights include center high mounted stop light; driver's and passenger's manual black folding outside mirrors; front and rear 15" x 7" silver styled steel wheels; P205/75SR15 BSW AS front and rear tires; underbody mounted compact steel spare wheel; AM/FM stereo with clock, seek-scan, 4 speakers, and fixed antenna; 1 power accessory outlet, retained accessory power; instrumentation display includes oil pressure gauge, water temp gauge, volt gauge, trip odometer; warning indicators include battery, lights on, key in ignition; driver's side front airbag, passenger's side cancelable front airbag; ignition disable; tinted windows; variable intermittent front windshield wipers; seating capacity of 3, bench front seat with fixed headrests, driver's seat includes 2-way direction control, passenger's seat includes 2-way direction control; vinyl seats, full cloth headliner, full vinyl floor covering, cabback insulator; interior lights include dome light; passenger's side vanity mirror; day-night rearview mirror; glove box with light, front cupholder, instrument panel bin, driver's and passenger's door bins; vinyl cargo floor, cargo concealed storage; black grille, black side window moldings, black front windshield molding, black rear window molding and black door handles.

CODE	DESCRIPTION	INVOICE	MSRP

LS 2WD REGULAR CAB SB/LB (5M) (in addition to or instead of BASE 2WD REGULAR CAB SB/LB (5M) equipment): Front and rear body-colored bumpers with rear step; 3 power accessory outlets, retained accessory power; center armrest with storage, driver's seat includes 4-way direction control, passenger's seat includes 4-way direction control; cloth seats, cloth door trim insert, full carpet floor covering; interior lights include front reading lights; vanity mirrors and carpeted cargo floor.

LS 2WD EXTENDED CAB SB (5M) (in addition to or instead of LS 2WD REGULAR CAB SB/LB (5M) equipment): 4.1 axle ratio; vented rear windows; seating capacity of 5, 60-40 split-bench front seat with fixed headrests, center armrest with storage, driver's seat includes 4-way direction control, passenger's seat includes 4-way direction control with easy entry; 50-50 side facing rear jump seats; front and rear cupholders and 2 seat back storage pockets.

BASE 4WD REGULAR CAB SB (5M) (in addition to or instead of BASE 2WD REGULAR SB (5M) equipment): 4.3L V6 OHV SMPI 12-valve engine; engine oil cooler; transmission oil cooler; part-time 4 wheel drive, auto locking hub control with manual shift, 3.08 axle ratio; front torsion springs, front torsion bar; 4 wheel disc brakes with 4 wheel antilock braking system and rear tow hooks.

BASE 4WD REGULAR CAB LB (5M) (in addition to or instead of BASE 2WD REGULAR CAB LB (5M) equipment): 4.3L V6 OHV SMPI 12-valve engine; engine oil cooler; transmission oil cooler; part-time 4 wheel drive, auto locking hub control with manual shift, 3.42 axle ratio; front torsion springs, front torsion bar; 4 wheel disc brakes with 4 wheel antilock braking system and rear tow hooks.

LS 4WD REGULAR CAB SB (5M) (in addition to or instead of LS 2WD REGULAR CAB SB (5M) equipment): 4.3L V6 OHV SMPI 12-valve engine; engine oil cooler; transmission oil cooler; part-time 4 wheel drive, auto locking hub control with manual shift, 3.08 axle ratio; front torsion springs, front torsion bar; 4 wheel disc brakes with 4 wheel antilock braking system, rear tow hooks; seating capacity of 2, front bucket seats with fixed headrests, center armrest with storage, driver's seat includes 4-way direction control with lumbar support and full floor console.

LS 4WD REGULAR CAB LB (5M) (in addition to or instead of LS 2WD REGULAR CAB LB (5M) equipment): 4.3L V6 OHV SMPI 12-valve engine; engine oil cooler; transmission oil cooler; part-time 4 wheel drive, auto locking hub control with manual shift, 3.42 axle ratio; front torsion springs, front torsion bar; 4 wheel disc brakes with 4 wheel antilock braking system, rear tow hooks; seating capacity of 2, front bucket seats with fixed headrests, center armrest with storage, driver's seat includes 4-way direction control with lumbar support and full floor console.

LS 4WD EXTENDED CAB SB (5M) (in addition to or instead of LS 2WD EXTENDED CAB SB (5M) equipment): 4.3L V6 OHV SMPI 12-valve engine; engine oil cooler; transmission oil cooler; part-time 4 wheel drive, auto locking hub control with manual shift, 3.08 axle ratio; front torsion springs, front torsion bar; 4 wheel disc brakes with 4 wheel antilock braking system, rear tow hooks; seating capacity of 4, front bucket seats with fixed headrests, center armrest with storage, driver's seat includes 4-way direction control with lumbar support and full floor console.

Base Prices

CODE	DESCRIPTION	INVOICE	MSRP
CS10603-E63	Base 2WD Regular Cab SB (5M)	11520	12190
CS10803-E63	Base 2WD Regular Cab LB (5M)	12147	12854
CS10603-E63-YC3	LS 2WD Regular Cab SB (5M)	12101	13371
CS10803-E63-YC3	LS 2WD Regular Cab LB (5M)	12418	13722
CS10653-E63-YC3	LS 2WD Extended Cab SB (5M)	13957	15422
CT10603-E63	Base 4WD Regular Cab SB (5M)	15813	16733
CT10803-E63	Base 4WD Regular Cab LB (5M)	16126	17065
CT10603-E63-YC3	LS 4WD Regular Cab SB (5M)	16221	17924

CODE	DESCRIPTION	INVOICE	MSRP
CT10803-E63-YC3	LS 4WD Regular Cab LB (5M)	16608	18351
CT10653-E63-YC3	LS 4WD Extended Cab SB	17941	19824
Destination Charge:		520	520

Accessories

CODE	DESCRIPTION	INVOICE	MSRP
—	Custom Cloth Seat Trim (Base)	NC	NC
1SA	**Preferred Equipment Group 1SA (Base 2WD Reg Cab SB)**	(430)	(500)
	Includes solid smooth ride suspension, P205/75R15 AS BSW tires, fleetside box, ETR AM/FM stereo with seek/scan, front bench seat, rear step bumper, air conditioning not desired and solid paint. NOT AVAILABLE with UN0, VF7, ZQ6, M30, ZQ8, GU4, GU6, M50, G80, UM6, R6G, U16, ZM6, N90.		
1SA	**Preferred Equipment Group 1SA (Base 4WD Reg Cab)**	815	948
	Manufacturer Discount	(344)	(400)
	Net Price	471	548
	Includes engine: Vortec 4300 SFI V6: engine oil cooler, transmission oil cooler, increased capacity suspension package: GAWR: 2800/2800, GVWR: 5,150 lbs, P235/75R15 AT WOL tires, fleetside box, ETR AM/FM stereo with seek/scan, front bench seat, air conditioning, rear step bumper and solid paint. NOT AVAILABLE with R6G, VF7, ZQ6, UM6.		
1SA	**Preferred Equipment Group 1SA (Base 2WD Reg Cab LB)**	1630	1895
	Manufacturer Discount	(86)	(100)
	Net Price	1544	1795
	Includes engine: Vortec 4300 SFI V6, increased capacity suspension package: GAWR: 2500/2700, GVWR: 4,900 lbs, P205/75R15 AS BSW tires, fleetside box, ETR AM/FM stereo with seek/scan, front bench seat, air conditioning, rear step bumper and solid paint. NOT AVAILABLE with R6G, VF7, U16, ZQ6, G80, UM6.		
1SB	**Preferred Equipment Group 1SB (LS 2WD - Reg Cab SB/X-Cab)**	1060	1232
	Manufacturer Discount	(731)	(850)
	Net Price	329	382
	Includes engine: Vortec 2200 I4 SFI, transmission: 5-speed manual, P205/75R15 AS BSW tires, fleetside box, deluxe reclining split bench seat, custom cloth seat trim, floor mats, aluminum wheels and solid paint. NOT AVAILABLE with GU4, GU6, G80, R6G, UL0, UP0, UN0, ZQ8.		
1SB	**Preferred Equipment Group 1SB (LS 4WD Reg Cab LB)**	1281	1490
	Manufacturer Discount	(860)	(1000)
	Net Price	421	490
	Includes LS Decor package, engine: Vortec 4300 SFI V6: engine oil cooler, transmission oil cooler, increased capacity suspension package: GAWR: 2800/2800, GVWR: 5,150 lbs, P235/75R15 AT WOL tires, bright aluminium wheels, fleetside box, high back reclining bucket seats, floor console, air conditioning, convenience group: tilt wheel, cruise control; floor mats and solid paint. NOT AVAILABLE with R6G, UL0, UN0, UP0.		

CODE	DESCRIPTION	INVOICE	MSRP
1SB	**Preferred Equipment Group 1SB (LS 4WD X-Cab)**	1858	2160
	Manufacturer Discount	(860)	(1000)
	Net Price	998	1160
	Includes LS Decor package, engine: Vortec 4300 SFI V6: engine oil cooler, transmission oil cooler, increased capacity suspension package: GAWR: 2800/2800, GVWR: 5,150 lbs, P235/75R15 AT WOL tires, bright aluminium wheels, fleetside box, high back reclining bucket seats, floor console, air conditioning, third door, convenience group: tilt wheel, cruise control; deep tinted glass, floor mats and solid paint. NOT AVAILABLE with R6G, ZCA, QCA, ZCE, ULO, UNO, UPO.		
1SB	**Preferred Equipment Group 1SB (LS 2WD Reg Cab LB)**	1901	2211
	Includes LS Decor package, engine: Vortec 4300 SFI V6: engine oil cooler, transmission oil cooler, increased capacity suspension package: GAWR: 2500/2700, P205/75R15 AS BSW tires, bright aluminium wheels, fleetside box, high back reclining bucket seats, floor console, air conditioning, convenience group: tilt wheel, cruise control; floor mats and solid paint. NOT AVAILABLE with R6G, ANL, B32.		
1SB	**Preferred Equipment Group 1SB (LS 4WD X-Cab)**	1981	2303
	Manufacturer Discount	(860)	(1000)
	Net Price	1121	1303
	Includes LS Decor package, engine: Vortec 4300 SFI V6: engine oil cooler, transmission oil cooler, increased capacity suspension package: GAWR: 2800/2800, GVWR: 5,150 lbs, P235/75R15 AT WOL tires, bright aluminium wheels, fleetside box, high back reclining bucket seats, floor console, air conditioning, third door, convenience group: tilt wheel, cruise control; deep tinted glass, floor mats and solid paint. NOT AVAILABLE with UNO, UPO, R6G, QCA, ZCE, ZCA, ULO, QBF.		
1SC	**Preferred Equipment Group 1SC (LS 4WD Reg Cab SB)**	4364	5075
	Manufacturer Discount	(946)	(1100)
	Net Price	3418	3975
	Includes LS Decor package, Wide Stance ZR2 sport performance package: front tread 61.2"/rear tread 59.1", 28mm front stabilizer bar, 46mm gas Bilstein shock absorbers, firm ride suspension, shield package, extra wide wheel flares, engine: Vortec 4300 V6 SFI (L35), engine oil cooler, transmission oil cooler, transmission: 5-speed manual with overdrive, 3.73 axle ratio, locking differential, GVWR: 4,650 lbs, 31 x 10.5R15 AT BSW tires, fleetside box, ETR AM/FM stereo with seek/scan and cassette, high back reclining bucket seats, floor console, tachometer, floor mats, sliding rear window, leather-wrapped steering wheel, bright aluminium wheels and solid paint. NOT AVAILABLE with QBF, QEB, ZBF, ZEB, YC5, ANL, ZY7, ZM6, AM6, R6G, ZCA, UM6, QCA, ZCE, UNO, UPO.		
1SC	**Preferred Equipment Group 1SC (LS 4WD X-Cab)**	4653	5410
	Manufacturer Discount	(946)	(1100)
	Net Price	3707	4310
	Includes LS Decor package, Wide Stance ZR2 sport performance pkg.: front tread 61.2"/rear tread 59.1", 28mm front stabilizer bar, 46mm gas Bilstein shock absorbers, firm ride suspension, shield package, extra wide wheel flares, 3.73 axle ratio, engine: Vortec 4300 V6 SFI (L35), engine oil cooler, GVWR: 4,900 lbs, 31 x 10.5R15 AT BSW tires, bright aluminium wheels, fleetside box, ETR AM/FM stereo with seek/scan and cassette, high back reclining bucket seats, floor console,		

CODE	DESCRIPTION	INVOICE	MSRP
	air conditioning, third door, convenience group: tilt wheel, cruise control; leather-wrapped steering wheel, deep tinted glass, sliding rear window, floor mats and solid paint. NOT AVAILABLE with ANL, YC5, ZM5, ZY7, QBF, ZBF, ZEB, AM6, ZM6, UN0, UP0, R6G, UM6, QCA, ZCE, GU6, ZCA, QEB.		
1SD	**Preferred Equipment Group 1SD (Base 2WD Reg Cab SB)**	2537	2950
	Manufacturer Discount	(524)	(609)
	Net Price	2013	2341
	Includes Xtreme sport appearance package: sport suspension package: 16" x 8" unique aluminum wheels, P235/55R16 AS BSW tires, integral fog lamps, air conditioning, tachometer, leather-wrapped steering wheel, body colored front and rear bumpers, wheel flares, body color grille, engine: Vortec 2200 I4 SFI, transmission: 5-speed manual, 3.73 axle ratio, GVWR: 4,200 lbs, fleetside box, ETR AM/FM stereo with seek/scan, front bench seat and solid paint. NOT AVAILABLE with A28, AJ1, VF7, R6G, ZQ6, M30, GU4, GU6, M50, G80, UM6.		
1SE	**Preferred Equipment Group 1SE (LS 2WD - Reg Cab SB/X-Cab)**	2663	3097
	Manufacturer Discount	(645)	(750)
	Net Price	2018	2347
	Includes Xtreme sport appearance package: sport suspension package: 16" x 8" unique aluminum wheels, P235/55R16 AS BSW tires, integral fog lamps, air conditioning, tachometer, leather-wrapped steering wheel, body colored front and rear bumpers, wheel flares, body color grille, engine: Vortec 2200 I4 SFI, transmission: 5-speed manual, 3.73 axle ratio, GVWR: 4,200 lbs, fleetside box, ETR AM/FM stereo with seek/scan and cassette, deluxe reclining front split bench seat, floor mats and solid paint. NOT AVAILABLE with ANL, YC5, QCA, ZCA, ZCE, ZY7, R6G, UL0, UN0, UP0, ZQ8, L35, GU4, GU6, G80, 9J6.		
1SF	**Preferred Equipment Group 1SF (Base)**	(194)	(226)
	Includes fleetside box, rear step bumper and radio delete. REQUIRES C60 or R6G. NOT AVAILABLE with UN0, ZQ3.		
1SG	**Preferred Equipment Group 1SG**	NC	NC
	Includes fleetside box. REQUIRES C60 or R6G. NOT AVAILABLE with YC5, AM6, L35, N90.		
A28	**Sliding Rear Window**	103	120
	NOT AVAILABLE with 1SD.		
AJ1	**Deep Tinted Glass (LS X-Cab)**	99	115
AJ1	**Deep Tinted Glass (2WD Reg Cab)**	64	75
	NOT AVAILABLE with 1SD.		
AM6	**Deluxe Reclining Split Bench Seat (LS)**	(215)	(250)
	Includes center storage armrest. REQUIRES M30. NOT AVAILABLE with UP0, M50, 1SG, 1SC.		
ANL	**Fog Lamps (LS 2WD - Reg Cab SB/X-Cab)**	99	115
	Includes air dam. NOT AVAILABLE with 1SB, 1SC, 1SE.		
AV5	**High Back Reclining Bucket Seats (Base 2WD)**	250	291
	Includes driver's side manual lumbar and floor console. NOT AVAILABLE with 1SA, 1SD, AM6.		
AV5	**High Back Reclining Bucket Seats (4WD)**	NC	NC
	Includes driver's side manual lumbar and floor console. NOT AVAILABLE with 1SA.		

CODE	DESCRIPTION	INVOICE	MSRP
B32	Floor Mats *NOT AVAILABLE with 1SB, 1SC, 1SE.*	22	25
C5A	GVWR: 4,900 Lbs.	NC	NC
C60	Air Conditioning *NOT AVAILABLE with R6G.*	692	805
E24	Third Door (LS X-Cab)	322	375
G80	Locking Differential *REQUIRES (M50 and GU4) or (M30 and GU6) or L35. NOT AVAILABLE with 1SD, 1SA, 1SB, 1SE.*	232	270
GT5	4.10 Axle Ratio (2WD Reg Cab) *NOT AVAILABLE with 1SA, 1SD, 1SB, L35, M50, 1SE, GU6, GU4, C5A.*	NC	NC
GU4	3.08 Axle Ratio (2WD Reg Cab) *NOT AVAILABLE with 1SA, 1SD, 1SB, GU6, 1SE.*	NC	NC
GU6	3.42 Axle Ratio *NOT AVAILABLE with 1SA, 1SD, M50, 1SB, GU4, 1SE, 1SC.*	NC	NC
L35	Engine: Vortec 4300 V6 SFI (LS 2WD Reg Cab LB/4WD) *Includes engine oil cooler and transmission oil cooler. REQUIRES C5A and (M30 or M50) or (GU6 and G80). NOT AVAILABLE with 1SD, 1SG.*	223	259
L35	Engine: Vortec 4300 V6 SFI (LS 2WD Except LB) *Includes engine oil cooler and transmission oil cooler. REQUIRES (M30 and GU4) or (M50 and GU4) or (M30 and GU6) or C5A or G80. NOT AVAILABLE with 1SB, 1SA.*	1160	1349
LF6	Engine: Vortec 4300 V6 SFI (2WD) *REQUIRES (M30 and GU4) or (M50 and GU4) or (M30 and GU6) or C5A. NOT AVAILABLE with 1SA, 1SD, 1SE, L35.*	937	1090
M30	Transmission: Electronic 4-Speed Automatic *Includes brake-transmission shift interlock. REQUIRES GU6 or GU4. NOT AVAILABLE with 1SA, 1SD, M50.*	920	1070
M50	Transmission: 5-Speed Manual with Overdrive (All Except LS 4WD X-Cab) *REQUIRES GU4. NOT AVAILABLE with 1SA, 1SD, GU6, UP0, M30, AM6.*	NC	NC
N60	Wheels: Cast Aluminum (LS 2WD) *REQUIRES YC5. NOT AVAILABLE with 1SB, 1SE.*	241	280
N90	Wheels: Cast Aluminum (LS 4WD) *REQUIRES 1SB or 1SC. NOT AVAILABLE with PA3, 1SG.*	NC	NC
N90	Wheels: Cast Aluminum (LS 4WD) *NOT AVAILABLE with 1SA, PA3, 1SB, 1SC.*	241	280
NC7	Federal Emission Override *For vehicles that will be registered or leased in California, Connecticut, Washington D.C, Delaware, Massachusetts, Maryland, New Hampshire, New Jersey, New York, Pennsylvania, Rhode Island and Virginia but sold by dealers outside those states.*	NC	NC
NP5	Leather Wrapped Steering Wheel (LS) *NOT AVAILABLE with 1SB.*	46	54
PA3	Wheels: Bright Aluminium (4WD) *Includes medium gray accent. NOT AVAILABLE with YC5, N90.*	241	280
QBF	Tires: P235/75R15 AS BSW (4WD) *Includes front, rear and compact spare. REQUIRES 1SB. NOT AVAILABLE with ZM6, QEB, ZEB, 1SC, ZCA, QCA, ZCE.*	(123)	(143)

CODE	DESCRIPTION	INVOICE	MSRP
QBF	Tires: P235/75R15 AS BSW (4WD) *Includes front, rear and compact spare. REQUIRES 1SG. NOT AVAILABLE with QEB, ZEB, ZCE, QCA, ZCA, ZM6, 1SC, 1SB.*	165	192
QCA	Tires: P205/75R15 WL AS SBR (2WD) *NOT AVAILABLE with ZCE, ZQ8, 1SE, ZBF, ZEB, QBF, QEB, ZM6, 1SB, 1SC.*	104	121
QCA	Tires: P205/75R15 WL AS SBR (2WD) *NOT AVAILABLE with ZCE, ZQ8, 1SE.*	104	121
QEB	Tires: P235/75R15 AT WOL (4WD) *Includes front, rear and compact spare. REQUIRES ZM6 or 1SB. NOT AVAILABLE with ZCE, QBF, ZBF, QCA, ZCA, 1SC.*	288	335
R6G	Air Conditioning Not Desired *NOT AVAILABLE with 1SD, 1SB, 1SE, C60, 1SA, 1SC.*	NC	NC
U16	Tachometer (LS) *NOT AVAILABLE with 1SA.*	51	59
ULO	Radio: AM/FM Stereo with Cassette (LS) *Includes auto tone control, digital clock, theft lock, speed compensated volume and enhanced performance speakers. NOT AVAILABLE with UM6, UNO, UPO, 1SG, 1SC.*	69	80
ULO	Radio: AM/FM Stereo with Cassette (LS) *Includes auto tone control, digital clock, theft lock, speed compensated volume and enhanced performance speakers. NOT AVAILABLE with UM6, UNO, UPO, 1SB, 1SE.*	174	202
UM6	Radio: AM/FM Stereo with Cassette (Base) *Includes seek-scan and digital clock. REQUIRES 1SF. NOT AVAILABLE with UNO, 1SA, 1SD.*	299	348
UM6	Radio: AM/FM Stereo with Cassette *Includes seek-scan and digital clock. NOT AVAILABLE with UNO, 1SF, ULO, UPO, 1SC.*	105	122
UM7	Radio: AM/FM Stereo *Includes digital clock. NOT AVAILABLE with 1SA, 1SD, UM6, UNO.*	194	226
UNO	Radio: AM/FM Stereo with CD *Includes seek-scan, auto tone control, digital clock, theft lock, speed compensated volume and enhanced performance speakers. REQUIRES 1SA or 1SB or 1SD or 1SG. NOT AVAILABLE with UM6, 1SF, ULO, UPO, 1SE, 1SC.*	260	302
UNO	Radio: AM/FM Stereo with CD (LS 4WD - Reg Cab SB/X-Cab) *Includes seek-scan, auto tone control, digital clock, theft lock, speed compensated volume and enhanced performance speakers. REQUIRES 1SC. NOT AVAILABLE with ULO, UPO, UM6, 1SB, 1SG.*	86	100
UNO	Radio: AM/FM Stereo with CD (LS Reg Cab) *Includes seek-scan, auto tone control, digital clock, theft lock, speed compensated volume and enhanced performance speakers. REQUIRES 1SB or 1SE. NOT AVAILABLE with ULO, UM6, UPO, 1SG, 1SC.*	155	180
UPO	Radio: AM/FM Stereo with Cassette and CD (LS 4WD - Reg Cab SB/X-Cab) *Includes seek-scan, auto tone control, digital clock, theft lock, speed compensated volume and enhanced performance speakers. REQUIRES 1SC, M30. NOT AVAILABLE with ULO, UNO, AM6, UM6, 1SB, 1SG.*	172	200

CODE	DESCRIPTION	INVOICE	MSRP
UP0	**Radio: AM/FM Stereo with Cassette and CD (LS - Reg Cab SB/X-Cab)** *Includes seek-scan, auto tone control, digital clock, theft lock, speed compensated volume and enhanced performance speakers. REQUIRES (1SB or 1SE) and M30. NOT AVAILABLE with UL0, UM6, UN0, M50, 1SG, AM6, 1SC.*	241	280
UP0	**Radio: AM/FM Stereo with Cassette and CD (LS 2WD Reg Cab)** *Includes seek-scan, auto tone control, digital clock, theft lock, speed compensated volume and enhanced performance speakers. REQUIRES M30. NOT AVAILABLE with UL0, UM6, UN0, M50, 1SB, 1SE, AM6, 1SC.*	346	402
V10	**Cold Climate Package** *Includes engine block heater. NOT AVAILABLE with 8U4.*	77	89
VF7	**Rear Step Bumper Delete (Base)** *NOT AVAILABLE with 1SA, 1SD.*	NC	NC
YC5	**Exterior Appearance Package (LS)** *Includes full chrome grille and front and rear chrome bumpers. REQUIRES 1SB or 1SC or 1SE. NOT AVAILABLE with ZQ8, 1SG, PA3.*	254	295
YC5	**Exterior Appearance Package (LS)** *Includes full chrome grille and front and rear chrome bumpers. NOT AVAILABLE with 1SE, ZQ8, 1SB, 1SC, PA3.*	494	575
Z85	**Increased Capacity Suspension Package (Base Reg Cab SB)** *Includes firm ride. Primary road use for paved/gravel. REQUIRES GU6. NOT AVAILABLE with ZQ8, 1SD, 1SE, ZCE, QCA, ZCA, ZM6, 1SC, ZEB.*	55	64
ZBF	**Tire: Spare P235/75R15 AS BW SBR (4WD)** *Includes steel wheel. REQUIRES QBF. NOT AVAILABLE with QEB, ZCE, ZEB, QCA, ZCA, ZM6, 1SC.*	82	95
ZCA	**Tire: Spare P205/75R15 AS WL SBR (2WD Reg Cab SB)** *Includes steel wheel. REQUIRES QCA. NOT AVAILABLE with ZQ8, ZCE, 1SE, QBF, QEB, ZEB, ZBF, ZM6, 1SB, 1SC.*	82	95
ZCE	**Tire: Spare P205/75R15 AS BW SBR** *Includes steel wheel. NOT AVAILABLE with QCA, ZCA, ZQ8, 1SE, QEB, ZBF, ZEB, QBF, ZM6, 1SB, 1SC.*	82	95
ZEB	**Tire: Spare P235/75R15 AT WOL SBR (4WD)** *Includes steel wheel. REQUIRES QEB. NOT AVAILABLE with QBF, ZBF, ZCE, QCA, ZCA, 1SC, ZM6.*	82	95
ZEB	**Tire: Spare P235/75R15 AT WOL SBR (LS 4WD X-Cab)** *Includes steel wheel. REQUIRES QEB. NOT AVAILABLE with QBF, ZBF, 1SC, ZCA.*	NC	NC
ZM5	**Shield Package (4WD)** *NOT AVAILABLE with 1SC.*	108	126
ZM6	**On-Off Road Suspension Package (4WD SB)** *Includes very firm ride suspension and P235/75R15 AT WOL tires. NOT AVAILABLE with 1SA, QBF, QCA, ZBF, ZCA, ZCE, 1SC.*	598	695
ZQ3	**Convenience Group** *Includes tilt wheel and cruise control. NOT AVAILABLE with 1SF.*	340	395
ZQ6	**Power Convenience Group** *Includes power door locks, power windows, remote keyless entry, panic alarm and illuminated entry. NOT AVAILABLE with 1SA, 1SD.*	684	795

CODE	DESCRIPTION	INVOICE	MSRP
ZQ8	Sport Suspension Package (2WD Except LB) *Includes 2" lowered ride height, monotube upgraded shock absorbers, antiroll bars and P235/55R16 AS BSW tires. Primary road use: paved. For light duty trailering. NOT AVAILABLE with 1SA, QCA, ZCA, ZCE, YC5, 1SB, 1SE.*	605	703
ZQ8	Sport Suspension Package (LS 2WD Except LB) *Includes 2" lowered ride height, monotube upgraded shock absorbers, antiroll bars and P235/55R16 AS BSW tires. Primary road use: paved. For light duty trailering. REQUIRES 1SB. NOT AVAILABLE with QCA, ZCA, ZCE, YC5, 1SE, 1SG.*	391	455
ZY7	Custom Two-Tone Paint (LS) *NOT AVAILABLE with 1SE, 1SC.*	194	225

1999 SILVERADO

1999 Chevrolet Silverado

What's New?

Chevrolet has redesigned the decade-old C/K pickup and given the truck an actual name. Major structural, power, braking and interior enhancements characterize the new Silverado. Styling is evolutionary rather than revolutionary, inside and out.

Review

Imagine the pressure on engineers and designers when they undertook the task of completely revising the best-selling model General Motors produces. Success would insure that GM could continue to reap large benefits from a booming truck industry. Failure would reduce market share, profits and credibility. Making matters worse, the existing platform was already a hot seller. How to fix something that wasn't broken?

They started by asking Chevy truck customers what they wanted in a new full-size pickup. More power, better handling, more interior room, better fuel economy and a stronger chassis were the answers. What they most certainly did not want was cartoonish or sissified styling, like the Dodge and Ford stores were selling.

So Chevrolet gave the customer what they asked for. Looking at the new Silverado, some might be hard-pressed to discern differences between it and the old C/K model. Inside the trucks look even more identical in appearance, unfortunately. But under the skin, GM has served up a heaping pile of massive improvement.

A new three-section frame is stiffer, lighter and easier to assemble than that of the C/K. It contributes to better impact absorbing, a smoother ride and quieter interior noise volumes. Payload capacity is up as well. A new family of Vortec V8 engines makes more power and torque over a flatter curve, though the 4300 V6 and turbo-diesel 6.5-liter V8 carry over with minor enhancements. Transmission modifications mean the gearchangers should prove more durable, and a tow-haul mode improves performance under heavy loads.

Revised steering, suspension and braking systems make driving the Silverado a joy. Four-wheel disc antilock brakes are standard, steering feel has been tightened up thanks in part to the inclusion of power rack-and-pinion gear on models under 6,400 GVWR, the turning circle is smaller and a wider rear track contributes to greater stability. Optional is Adjustable Electronic Ride Control, the first selective damping system ever offered on a pickup.

Inside Silverado buyers will find logically laid out switchgear, though the plastics still have the same Fisher Price feel to them as the knobs and panels in the previous truck. The cabin is very roomy, particularly on extended cab models. A standard third door on the latter makes entry and exit to the rear bench seat easy, and if front passengers are willing to sacrifice a bit of leg room, the back of the extended cab is actually quite comfortable. Front seatbelts are mounted to the seats themselves so rear passengers don't need to chop through a web of fabric to get in and out. Oddly, a fourth door is unavailable on the Silverado, a major oversight now that Dodge, Ford and Toyota all offer this added convenience.

We've only been able to briefly skim over the major changes Chevrolet made to its full-sized truck in the space alloted here. Electrical system improvements, changes to the manufacturing process and myriad minor modifications all mean the new Silverado is among the most technologically-advanced pickups on the market. The bar has been raised with the introduction of the Chevy Silverado, and GM bean counters needn't worry about their bonuses at year's end. This truck will be a huge success.

1999 SILVERADO 1500

Safety Data

Side Airbag: *Not Available*
4-Wheel ABS: *Standard*
Driver Crash Test Grade: *Not Available*
Side Impact Crash Test Front: *Not Available*
Crash Offset: *Not Available*
Integrated Child Seat(s): *Not Available*
Traction Control: *Not Available*
Passenger Crash Test Grade: *Not Available*
Side Impact Crash Test Rear: *Not Available*

Standard Equipment

BASE 2WD REGULAR CAB (5M): 4.3L V6 OHV SMPI 12-valve engine; 5-speed overdrive manual transmission; 600-amp HD battery; 105-amp alternator; rear wheel drive, 3.08 axle ratio; stainless steel exhaust; front independent suspension with anti-roll bar, front coil springs, rigid rear axle suspension with rear leaf springs; power rack-and-pinion steering with vehicle speed-sensing assist; 4 wheel disc brakes with 4 wheel antilock braking system; 26 gal (34 gal/LB) capacity fuel tank; trailer harness; front chrome bumper with black rub strip, rear argent bumper with black rub strip and rear step; monotone paint; aero-composite halogen fully automatic headlamps with daytime running lights; additional exterior lights include center high mounted stop light, pickup cargo box light, underhood light; driver's and passenger's manual black folding outside mirrors; front and rear 16" x 6.5" silver styled steel wheels; P235/75SR16 BSW AS front and rear tires; underbody mounted full-size conventional steel spare wheel; AM/FM stereo with clock, seek-scan, 4 speakers, and fixed antenna; 3 power accessory outlets; instrumentation display includes tachometer, oil pressure gauge, water temp gauge, volt gauge, trip odometer; warning indicators include oil pressure, water temp warning, battery, low oil level, low coolant, lights on, key in ignition, low fuel, door ajar, service interval; driver's side airbag, passenger's side cancelable airbag; ignition disable; tinted windows; variable intermittent front windshield wipers; seating capacity of 3, 40-20-40 split-bench front seat with adjustable headrests, driver's seat includes 4-way direction control, passenger's seat includes 2-way direction control; vinyl seats, full cloth headliner, full vinyl floor covering, cabback insulator; interior lights include dome light, front reading lights; sport steering wheel with tilt adjustment; passenger side vanity mirror; day-night rearview mirror; glove box with light, front cupholder, driver's and passenger's door bins; black grille, black side window moldings, black front windshield molding, black rear window molding and black door handles.

BASE 2WD EXTENDED CAB SB (5M) (in addition to or instead of BASE 2WD REGULAR CAB (5M) equipment): Rear heat ducts; vented rear windows; seating capacity of 6 and full folding rear bench seat with adjustable headrest.

BASE 2WD EXTENDED CAB LB (5M) (in addition to or instead of BASE 2WD EXTENDED CAB SB (5M) equipment): 4.8L V8 OHV SMPI 16-valve engine and 34 gal capacity fuel tank.

BASE 4WD REGULAR CAB (5M) (in addition to or instead of BASE 2WD REGULAR CAB (5M) equipment): Part-time 4 wheel drive, auto locking hub control and manual shift, 3.73 axle ratio; front independent torsion suspension with anti-roll bar, front torsion springs, front torsion bar; power re-circulating ball steering with vehicle speed-sensing assist; P245/75R16 AT BSW front and rear tires and rear tow hooks.

BASE 4WD EXTENDED CAB (5M)(in addition to or instead of BASE 4WD REGULAR CAB (5M) equipment): 4.8L V8 OHV SMPI 16-valve engine; rear heat ducts; vented rear windows; seating capacity of 6 and full folding rear bench seat with adjustable headrest.

LS 2WD REGULAR CAB (5M) (in addition to or instead of BASE 2WD REGULAR CAB (5M) equipment): Front and rear chrome bumpers with black rub strip; body-colored bodyside molding with chrome bodyside insert; driver's and passenger's power remote chrome folding outside mirrors; air conditioning; AM/FM stereo with clock, seek-scan, single CD, 6 performance speakers, automatic equalizer, theft deterrent, and fixed antenna; cruise control; power door locks with 2 stage unlock, remote keyless entry; retained accessory power; ignition disable, panic alarm, security system; power front windows with driver 1-touch down; center armrest with storage, driver's seat includes 4-way direction control with lumbar support, passenger's seat includes 4-way direction control with lumbar support; premium cloth seats, cloth door trim insert, full carpet floor covering with rubber floor mats; interior lights include illuminated entry; leather-wrapped sport steering wheel with tilt adjustment and chrome grille.

LS 2WD EXTENDED CAB SB (5M) (in addition to or instead of LS 2WD REGULAR CAB (5M) equipment): Rear heat ducts; vented rear windows; seating capacity of 6; full folding rear bench seat with adjustable headrest and mini overhead console with storage.

LS 2WD EXTENDED CAB LB (5M) (in addition to or instead of LS 2WD EXTENDED CAB SB (5M) equipment):): 4.8L V8 OHV SMPI 16-valve engine and 34 gal capacity fuel tank.

LS 4WD REGULAR CAB (5M) (in addition to or instead of LS 2WD REGULAR CAB (5M) equipment): Part-time 4 wheel drive, auto locking hub control and manual shift, 3.73 axle ratio; front independent torsion suspension with anti-roll bar, front torsion springs, front torsion bar; power re-circulating ball steering with vehicle speed-sensing assist; P245/75R16 AT BSW front and rear tires and rear tow hooks.

LS 4WD EXTENDED CAB (5M) (in addition to or instead of LS 4WD REGULAR CAB (5M) equipment): 4.8L V8 OHV SMPI 16-valve engine; rear heat ducts; vented rear windows; seating capacity of 6 and full folding rear bench seat with adjustable headrest.

CODE	DESCRIPTION	INVOICE	MSRP

LT 2WD EXTENDED CAB (4A) (in addition to or instead of LS 2WD EXTENDED CAB (5M) equipment): 5.3L V8 OHV SMPI 16-valve engine; 4-speed electronic overdrive automatic transmission with lock-up; 3.42 axle ratio; additional exterior lights include front fog/driving lights; driver's and passenger's power remote chrome heated folding outside mirrors; instrumentation display includes compass; deep tinted windows; AM/FM stereo with clock, seek-scan, cassette, single CD, 6 performance speakers, automatic equalizer, theft deterrent, and fixed antenna; seating capacity of 5, front heated driver's and passenger's bucket seats with adjustable headrests, driver's and passenger's armrests, driver's seat includes 6-way power seat with power lumbar support, passenger's seat includes 6-way power seat with power lumbar support; leather seats; memory on driver's seat with 2 memory setting(s); auto-dimming day-night rearview mirror; full floor console and full overhead console with storage.

LT 4WD EXTENDED CAB (4A) (in addition to or instead of LT 2WD EXTENDED CAB (4A) equipment): Part-time 4 wheel drive, auto locking hub control and automatic shift (AutoTrac), 3.73 axle ratio; front independent torsion suspension with anti-roll bar, front torsion springs, front torsion bar; power re-circulating ball steering with vehicle speed-sensing assist; P245/75R16 AT BSW front and rear tires and rear tow hooks.

Base Prices

CODE	DESCRIPTION	INVOICE	MSRP
CC15703	Base 2WD Regular Cab SB (5M)	13896	15355
CC15903	Base 2WD Regular Cab LB (5M)	14168	15655
CK15703	Base 4WD Regular Cab SB (5M)	16715	18470
CK15903	Base 4WD Regular Cab LB (5M)	16987	18770
CC15753	Base 2WD Extended Cab SB (5M)	17150	19600
CC15953	Base 2WD Extended Cab LB (5M)	17933	20495
CK15753	Base 4WD Extended Cab SB (5M)	20383	23295
CK15953	Base 4WD Extended Cab LB (5M)	20646	23595
CC15703	LS 2WD Regular Cab SB (5M)	17036	19470
CC15903	LS 2WD Regular Cab LB (5M)	17299	19770
CK15703	LS 4WD Regular Cab SB (5M)	19749	22570
CK15903	LS 4WD Regular Cab LB (5M)	20011	22870
CC15753	LS 2WD Extended Cab SB (5M)	19443	22220
CC15953	LS 2WD Extended Cab LB (5M)	20226	23115
CK15753	LS 4WD Extended Cab SB (5M)	22676	25915
CK15953	LS 4WD Extended Cab LB (5M)	22938	26215
CC15753	LT 2WD Extended Cab SB (4A)	24263	27729
CC15953	LT 2WD Extended Cab LB (4A)	24525	28029
CK15753	LT 4WD Extended Cab SB (4A)	27072	30939
CK15953	LT 4WD Extended Cab LB (4A)	27334	31239
Destination Charge:		640	640

Accessories

CODE	DESCRIPTION	INVOICE	MSRP
—	Cloth Seat Trim (Base)	NC	NC
1SA	Preferred Equipment Group 1SA (Base) *Includes vehicle with standard equipment.*	NC	NC
1SB	Preferred Equipment Group 1SB (LS) *Includes vehicle with standard equipment.*	NC	NC

CODE	DESCRIPTION	INVOICE	MSRP
1SC	Preferred Equipment Group 1SC (LT) *Includes vehicle with standard equipment.*	NC	NC
A28	Sliding Rear Window *NOT AVAILABLE with C49.*	108	125
A95	Reclining Bucket Seats (LS Regular Cab) *Includes inboard armrests, manual lumbar and floor console.*	258	300
A95	Reclining Bucket Seats (LS X-Cab) *Includes inboard armrests, manual lumbar and floor console.*	323	375
AE7	Leather Seat Trim (LS X-Cab) *Includes 6-way power driver's/passenger's seats. REQUIRES M30.*	1273	1480
AG2	6-Way Power Driver's/Passenger's Seats (LS X-Cab)	413	480
AJ1	Deep Tinted Solar Ray Glass (X-Cab Except LT)	92	107
AJ1	Deep Tinted Solar Ray Glass (Regular Cab Except LT) *REQUIRES A28 or C49.*	43	50
BG9	Color-Keyed Rubber Floor Covering (LS X-Cab) *Replaces carpeting and floor mats.*	(77)	(90)
BG9	Color-Keyed Rubber Floor Covering (LS Regular Cab) *Replaces carpeting and floor mats.*	(47)	(55)
C49	Electric Rear Window Defogger (All Except LT) *REQUIRES C60. NOT AVAILABLE with A28.*	151	175
C60	Air Conditioning (Base)	710	825
DD7	10" Electrochromic ISRV Mirror (LS) *Includes 8 point compass.*	125	145
DF2	Camper Type Mirrors (Base) *Retractable with wide field of vision.*	52	60
DF2	Camper Type Mirrors (All Except Base) *Retractable with wide field of vision. NOT AVAILABLE with DL8.*	(33)	(38)
DL8	Electrochromic OSRV with Heater (LS) *REQUIRES C49. NOT AVAILABLE with DF2.*	36	42
G80	Locking Differential *REQUIRES GT4 or GU6.*	245	285
GT4	3.73 Axle Ratio (4WD/2WD LB Except LT) *REQUIRES M30 or LM7 or LR4.*	NC	NC
GT5	3.73 Axle Ratio (4WD) *REQUIRES LM7 or LR4.*	NC	NC
GU6	3.42 Axle Ratio (2WD)	NC	NC
K05	Engine Block Heater	30	35
K34	Cruise Control (Base)	206	240
K47	High Capacity Air Cleaner	22	25
LM7	Engine: Vortec 5300 SFI V8 (X-Cab 4WD/2WD X-Cab LB Except LT) *REQUIRES M30.*	602	700
LM7	Engine: Vortec 5300 SFI V8 (Reg Cab/2WD X-Cab SB Except LT) *REQUIRES (GT4 or GU6) and/or M30.*	1114	1295
LR4	Engine: Vortec 4800 SFI V8 (Reg Cab/X-Cab SB Except LT) *REQUIRES GT4 or GU6.*	512	595
M30	Transmission: 4-Speed Automatic (All Except LT)	856	995

CODE	DESCRIPTION	INVOICE	MSRP
NP8	Autotrac Active Transfer Case (LS 4WD) *REQUIRES M30.*	323	375
NZZ	Skid Plate Package (4WD) *Includes front differential and transfer case shields.*	82	95
PF9	Wheels: 16" Cast Aluminum (LS)	77	90
QBN	Tires: LT245/75R16C On/Off Road BSW (4WD) *REQUIRES Z85 or Z71.*	138	160
QBX	Tires: LT245/75R16C On/Off Road OWL (4WD) *REQUIRES Z85 or Z71.*	245	285
QCC	Tires: P255/70R16 AS BSW (2WD Except LT) *REQUIRES Z85 or ZX3.*	146	170
QCJ	Tires: P255/70R16 AS WOL (2WD Except LT) *REQUIRES Z85 or ZX3.*	254	295
QCJ	Tires: P255/70R16 AS WOL (LT 2WD)	108	125
QGA	Tires: P245/75R16 BSW AT (4WD)	90	105
QGB	Tires: P245/75R16 AT WOL (4WD)	198	230
QGC	Tires: P265/75R16 AT BSW (4WD Except Base) *REQUIRES (Z71 or Z85) and PF9.*	206	240
QGD	Tires: P265/75R16 AT WOL (4WD Except Base) *REQUIRES (Z71 or Z85) and PF9.*	314	365
QNG	Tires: P235/75R16 AS WOL (2WD Except LT)	108	125
QNL	Tires: P245/75R16 AS OWL (4WD)	108	125
R9D	Exterior Appearance Package (All Except LB) *Includes black bodyside moldings, chrome grille, chrome wheels and chrome rear step bumper. REQUIRES E62.*	538	625
R9D	Exterior Appearance Package *Includes black bodyside moldings, chrome grille, chrome wheels and chrome rear step bumper.*	452	525
R9E	Floor Covering Package (Base X-Cab) *Includes floor carpeting with rubber mats.*	77	90
R9E	Floor Covering Package (Base Reg Cab) *Includes floor carpeting with rubber mats.*	47	55
T96	Fog Lamps (LS)	120	140
UL5	Radio Delete (Base) *Stowage tray, base speaker system and antenna remain. NOT AVAILABLE with UM6.*	(215)	(250)
UM6	Radio: AM/FM Stereo with Cassette and Seek/Scan (Base Reg Cab) *Includes digital clock. NOT AVAILABLE with UL5.*	129	150
UM6	Radio: AM/FM Stereo with Cassette and Seek/Scan (Base X-Cab) *Includes digital clock. NOT AVAILABLE with UL5.*	146	170
UP0	Radio: AM/FM Stereo with CD and Cassette (LS) *Includes digital clock, automatic tone control, search and repeat, theft lock, speed compensated volume and enhanced performance speaker system. REQUIRES A95 and NP8 and M30.*	86	100

CODE	DESCRIPTION	INVOICE	MSRP
UV8	Cellular Telephone Wiring Provisions *Includes wiring for remote mircrophone and cellular phone.*	43	50
V76	Tow Hooks (2WD)	33	38
VB3	Chrome Rear Step Bumper (Base) *NOT AVAILABLE with VF7.*	86	100
VF7	Rear Bumper Delete Provisions (LS) *Vehicles registered in certain states must have a rear bumper to be operated on their roads. Consult your local laws. NOT AVAILABLE with Z82.*	(172)	(200)
VF7	Rear Bumper Delete Provisions (Base) *Vehicles registered in certain states must have a rear bumper to be operated on their roads. Consult your local laws.*	(86)	(100)
VYU	Snow Plow Prep Package (4WD Reg Cab SB) *Includes electrical connections and 130-amp alternator. REQUIRES M30.*	245	285
VYU	Snow Plow Prep Package (4WD Reg Cab SB) *Includes electrical connections and 130-amp alternator. REQUIRES (1SA and Z82) or 1SA or (1SB and Z82) or 1SB.*	163	190
YF5	California Emissions	146	170
Z71	Off-Road Package (LS 4WD) *Includes 46mm shocks, off-road jounce bumpers, stabilizer bars, Z71 decal and high capacity air cleaner. REQUIRES LM7 or LR4.*	297	345
Z82	Trailering Special Equipment *Includes 7-lead wiring harness and HD auxiliary transmission cooler. REQUIRES M30. NOT AVAILABLE with VF7, L35 or Z83.*	245	285
Z85	Firm Ride Suspension (2WD Except LT) *Includes monotube 36mm shocks. NOT AVAILABLE with Z71.*	82	95
ZX3	Smooth Ride Suspension (LT 2WD) *Includes 2-position electronic control for shock setting and smooth road/trailering.*	280	325
ZX3	Smooth Ride Suspension (2WD Except LT) *Includes 2-position electronic control for shock setting and smooth road/trailering. REQUIRES LM7 or LR4.*	361	420
ZY2	Two Tone Paint Application (LS)	194	225

1999 SILVERADO 2500

Safety Data

Side Airbag: *Not Available*
4-Wheel ABS: *Standard*
Driver Crash Test Grade: *Not Available*
Side Impact Crash Test Front: *Not Available*
Crash Offset: *Not Available*
Integrated Child Seat(s): *Not Available*
Traction Control: *Not Available*
Passenger Crash Test Grade: *Not Available*
Side Impact Crash Test Rear: *Not Available*

Standard Equipment

BASE 2WD REGULAR CAB LB (4A): 5.3L V8 OHV SMPI 16-valve engine; 4-speed electronic overdrive automatic transmission with lock-up; 600-amp HD battery; 105-amp alternator; rear wheel drive, 3.73 axle ratio; stainless steel exhaust; front independent suspension with anti-roll bar, front coil springs, rigid rear axle suspension with rear leaf springs; power re-circulating ball steering with vehicle speed-sensing assist; 4 wheel disc brakes with 4 wheel antilock braking system; 34 gal capacity fuel tank; trailer harness; front chrome bumper with black rub strip, rear argent bumper with black rub strip and rear step; monotone paint; aero-composite halogen fully automatic headlamps with daytime running lights; additional exterior lights include center high mounted stop light, pickup cargo box light, underhood light; driver's and passenger's manual black folding outside mirrors; front and rear 16" x 6.5" silver styled steel wheels; LT225/75SR16 BSW AS front and rear tires; underbody mounted full-size conventional steel spare wheel; AM/FM stereo with clock, seek-scan, 4 speakers, and fixed antenna; 3 power accessory outlets; instrumentation display includes tachometer, oil pressure gauge, water temp gauge, volt gauge, trip odometer; warning indicators include oil pressure, water temp warning, battery, low oil level, low coolant, lights on, key in ignition, low fuel, low washer fluid, door ajar, service interval; driver's side airbag, passenger's side cancellable airbag; ignition disable; tinted windows; variable intermittent front windshield wipers; seating capacity of 3, 40-20-40 split-bench front seat with adjustable headrests, driver's seat includes 4-way direction control, passenger's seat includes 2-way direction control; vinyl seats, full cloth headliner, full vinyl floor covering, cabback insulator; interior lights include dome light, front reading lights; sport steering wheel with tilt adjustment; passenger's side vanity mirror; day-night rearview mirror; glove box with light, front cupholder, driver's and passenger's door bins; black grille, black side window moldings, black front windshield molding, black rear window molding and black door handles.

BASE 2WD EXTENDED CAB SB (4A) (in addition to or instead of BASE 2WD REGULAR CAB LB (4A) equipment): 3.42 axle ratio; 26 gal capacity fuel tank; rear heat ducts; vented rear windows; seating capacity of 6, 40-20-40 split-bench front seat with adjustable headrests and full folding rear bench seat with adjustable rear headrest.

BASE 2WD EXTENDED CAB LB (5M) (in addition to or instead of BASE 2WD EXTENDED CAB SB (4A) equipment): 6.0L V8 OHV SMPI 16-valve engine; 5-speed overdrive manual transmission; 3.73 axle ratio and 34 gal capacity fuel tank.

BASE 4WD REGULAR CAB LB (4A) (in addition to or instead of BASE 2WD REGULAR CAB LB (4A) equipment): Part-time 4 wheel drive, auto locking hub control and manual shift; front independent torsion suspension with anti-roll bar, front torsion springs, front torsion bar and rear tow hooks.

BASE 4WD EXTENDED CAB (4A) (in addition to or instead of BASE 4WD REGULAR CAB LB (4A) equipment): 26 gal capacity fuel tank; rear heat ducts; vented rear windows; seating capacity of 6, 40-20-40 split-bench front seat with adjustable headrests and full folding rear bench seat with adjustable rear headrest.

LS 2WD REGULAR CAB LB (4A): (in addition to or instead of BASE 2WD REGULAR CAB LB (4A): equipment): Front and rear chrome bumpers with black rub strip, rear step bumper; colored bodyside molding with chrome bodyside insert, colored fender flares; driver's and passenger's power remote chrome folding outside mirrors; air conditioning; AM/FM stereo with clock, seek-scan, single CD, 6 performance speakers, automatic equalizer, theft deterrent, and fixed antenna; cruise control; power door locks with 2 stage unlock, remote keyless entry; retained accessory power; ignition disable, panic alarm, security system; power front windows with driver 1-touch down; center armrest with storage, driver's seat includes 4-way direction control with lumbar support, passenger's seat includes 4-way direction control with lumbar support; premium cloth seats, cloth door trim insert, full carpet floor covering with rubber floor mats; interior lights include front reading lights, illuminated entry; leather-wrapped sport steering wheel with tilt adjustment and chrome grille.

LS 2WD EXTENDED CAB SB (4A) (in addition to or instead of LS 2WD REGULAR CAB LB (4A) equipment: 3.42 axle ratio; 26 gal capacity fuel tank; rear heat ducts; vented rear windows; seating capacity of 6, 40-20-40 split-bench front seat with adjustable headrests, full folding rear bench seat with adjustable rear headrest and mini overhead console with storage.

CODE	DESCRIPTION	INVOICE	MSRP

LS 2WD EXTENDED CAB LB (5M) (in addition to or instead of LS 2WD EXTENDED CAB SB (4A) equipment): 6.0L V8 OHV SMPI 16-valve engine; 5-speed overdrive manual transmission; rear wheel drive, 3.73 axle ratio; 34 gal capacity fuel tank.

LS 4WD REGULAR CAB LB (4A) (in addition to or instead of LS 2WD REGULAR CAB LB (4A) equipment): Part-time 4 wheel drive, auto locking hub control and manual shift; front independent torsion suspension with anti-roll bar, front torsion springs, front torsion bar, rear tow hooks rear step; AM/FM stereo with clock, seek-scan, single CD, 4 performance speakers, automatic equalizer, theft deterrent, and fixed antenna.

LS 4WD EXTENDED CAB (4A) (in addition to or instead of LS 4WD REGULAR CAB LB (4A) equipment): 26 gal capacity fuel tank; vented rear windows; seating capacity of 6; full folding rear bench seat with adjustable rear headrest and mini overhead console with storage.

LT 2WD EXTENDED CAB SB (4A) (in addition to or instead of LS 2WD EXTENDED CAB SB (4A) equipment): Additional exterior lights include front fog/driving lights; power remote chrome driver's heated outside folding mirror; AM/FM stereo with clock, seek-scan, cassette, single CD, 6 performance speakers, automatic equalizer, theft deterrent, and fixed antenna; instrumentation display includes compass; deep tinted glass; seating capacity of 5, heated driver's and passenger's bucket seats with adjustable headrests, driver's and passenger's armrests, driver's seat includes 6-way power seat with power lumbar support, passenger's seat includes 6-way power seat with power lumbar support; leather seats; memory on driver's seat with 2 memory setting(s); auto-dimming day-night rearview mirror; full floor console and full overhead console with storage.

LT 2WD EXTENDED CAB LB (5M) (in addition to or instead of LT 2WD EXTENDED CAB SB (4A) equipment): 6.0L V8 OHV SMPI 16-valve engine; transmission oil cooler; 3.73 axle ratio; 34 gal capacity fuel tank and driver's and passenger's power remote chrome heated folding outside mirrors.

LT 4WD EXTENDED CAB (4A) (in addition to or instead of LT 2WD EXTENDED CAB LB (5M) equipment): 4-speed electronic overdrive automatic transmission with lock-up; part-time 4 wheel drive, auto locking hub control and electronic shift (AutoTrac), 3.73 axle ratio; front independent torsion suspension with anti-roll bar, front torsion springs, front torsion bar; 26 gal capacity fuel tank; rear tow hooks and rear window defroster.

Base Prices

CODE	DESCRIPTION	INVOICE	MSRP
CC25903	Base 2WD Regular Cab LB (4A)	17637	20156
CC25903	Base 2WD Regular Cab LB HD (4A)	17504	20005
CK25903	Base 4WD Regular Cab LB (5M)	20211	23105
CC25753	Base 2WD Extended Cab SB (4A)	19780	22606
CC25953	Base 2WD Extended Cab LB (5M)	19911	22755
CK25753	Base 4WD Extended Cab SB (5M)	22361	25555
CK25953	Base 4WD Extended Cab LB (5M)	22623	25855
CC25903-LS	LS 2WD Regular Cab LB (5M)	19929	22776
CC25903-LS	LS 2WD Regular Cab LB HD (5M)	19797	22625
CK25903-LS	LS 4WD Regular Cab LB (5M)	22509	25725
CC25753-LS	LS 2WD Extended Cab SB (4A)	22073	25226
CC25953-LS	LS 2WD Extended Cab LB (5M)	22203	25375
CK25753-LS	LS 4WD Extended Cab SB (5M)	24653	28175
CK25953-LS	LS 4WD Extended Cab LB (5M)	24916	28475

CODE	DESCRIPTION	INVOICE	MSRP
CC25753-LT	LT 2WD Extended Cab SB (4A)	24658	28181
CC25953-LT	LT 2WD Extended Cab LB (4A)	25659	29324
CK25753-LT	LT 4WD Extended Cab SB (4A)	28437	32499
CK25953-LT	LT 4WD Extended Cab LB (4A)	28699	32799
Destination Charge:		640	640

Accessories

CODE	DESCRIPTION	INVOICE	MSRP
—	Cloth Seat Trim (Base)	NC	NC
1SA	Preferred Equipment Group 1SA (Base) *Includes vehicle with standard equipment.*	NC	NC
1SB	Preferred Equipment Group 1SB (LS) *Includes vehicle with standard equipment.*	NC	NC
1SC	Preferred Equipment Group 1SC (LT) *Includes vehicle with standard equipment.*	NC	NC
A28	Sliding Rear Window *NOT AVAILABLE with C49.*	108	125
A95	Reclining Bucket Seats (LS X-Cab) *Includes inboard armrests and manual lumbar and overhead console.*	323	375
A95	Reclining Bucket Seats (LS Reg Cab) *Includes inboard armrests and manual lumbar and overhead console.*	258	300
A95	Reclining Bucket Seats with Leather (LS X-Cab 4WD SB) *Includes 6-way power driver's/passenger's seats.*	1593	1855
A95	Reclining Bucket Seats with Leather (LS Except X-Cab 4WD SB) *Includes 6-way power driver's/passenger's seats.*	1595	1855
AE7	Reclining Split Bench Seats with Leather (LS Reg Cab) *Includes 6-way power driver's/passenger's seats.*	1273	1480
AG2	6-Way Power Driver's/Passenger's Seats (LS)	413	480
AJ1	Deep Tinted Solar Ray Glass (Regular Cab) *REQUIRES A28 or C49.*	43	50
AJ1	Deep Tinted Solar Ray Glass (X-Cab Except LT)	92	107
AU3	Power Door Locks (Base)	139	162
BG9	Color-Keyed Rubber Floor Covering (LS Reg Cab) *Replaces carpeting and floor mats.*	(77)	(90)
BG9	Color-Keyed Rubber Floor Covering (LS X-Cab) *Replaces carpeting and floor mats.*	(47)	(55)
C49	Electric Rear Window Defogger (All Except LT) *REQUIRES C60. NOT AVAILABLE with A28.*	151	175
C60	Front Air Conditioning (Base)	710	825
DD7	10" Electrochromic ISRV Mirror (LS) *Includes 8 point compass.*	125	145
DF2	Camper Type Mirrors (All Except Base) *Retractable with wide field of vision. NOT AVAILABLE with DL8.*	(33)	(38)
DF2	Camper Type Mirrors (Base) *Retractable with wide field of vision.*	52	60
DL8	Electrochromic OSRV with Heater (LS) *REQUIRES C49. NOT AVAILABLE with DF2.*	36	42

CODE	DESCRIPTION	INVOICE	MSRP
G80	Locking Differential *REQUIRES GT4 or GT5.*	245	285
GT4	3.73 Axle Ratio *NOT AVAILABLE with GT5.*	NC	NC
GT5	4.10 Axle Ratio *REQUIRES LQ4. NOT AVAILABLE with GT4.*	NC	NC
K05	Engine Block Heater	30	35
K34	Cruise Control (Base)	206	240
K47	High Capacity Air Cleaner	22	25
KC4	Engine Oil Cooling (2WD X-Cab LB/4WD) *REQUIRES (Z82 and LQ4) or (VYU and LQ4).*	NC	NC
KC4	Engine Oil Cooling (All Except 2WD X-Cab LB/4WD) *REQUIRES LQ4.*	116	135
LQ4	Engine: Vortec 6000 V8 SFI (All Except 2WD X-Cab LB/4WD) *Includes high capacity air cleaner. REQUIRES (MT1 and Z82).*	430	500
LQ4	Engine: Vortec 6000 V8 SFI (2WD X-Cab LB/4WD) *Includes high capacity air cleaner. REQUIRES C6P.*	NC	NC
MT1	Transmission: 4-Speed Automatic (LT) *Includes transmission oil cooler.*	NC	NC
MT1	Transmission: 4-Speed Automatic (All Except LT) *Includes transmission oil cooler.*	856	995
MW3	Transmission: 5-Speed Manual (2WD X-Cab LB)	NC	NC
NP8	Autotrac Active Transfer Case (LS 4WD) *REQUIRES MT1.*	323	375
NZZ	Skid Plate Package (4WD) *Includes front differential and transfer case shields.*	82	95
PYO	Wheels: Forged Polished Aluminum (LS)	77	90
QIW	Tires: LT245/75R16E AT BSW (All Except 2WD X-Cab LB)	241	280
QIW	Tires: LT245/75R16E AT BSW (2WD X-Cab LB) *REQUIRES C6P.*	47	55
QIZ	Tires: LT245/75R16E AS BSW (2WD X-Cab LB) *REQUIRES C6P.*	NC	NC
QIZ	Tires: LT245/75R16E AS BSW (All Except 2WD X-Cab LB)	194	225
R9D	Exterior Appearance Package (Base) *Includes body side molding, chrome rear step bumper, chrome grille and chrome wheels. NOT AVAILABLE with VF7.*	538	625
R9E	Floor Covering Package (Base Reg Cab) *Includes floor carpeting with rubber mats.*	47	55
R9E	Floor Covering Package (Base X-Cab) *Includes floor carpeting with rubber mats.*	77	90
T96	Front Fog Lamps (LS)	120	140
TP2	Auxiliary Battery	116	135
UL5	Radio Delete (Base) *Stowage tray, base speaker system and antenna remain. NOT AVAILABLE with UM6.*	(215)	(250)
UM6	Radio: AM/FM Stereo with Cassette and Seek/Scan (Base X-Cab) *Includes digital clock. NOT AVAILABLE with UL5.*	129	150

CODE	DESCRIPTION	INVOICE	MSRP
UM6	Radio: AM/FM Stereo with Cassette and Seek/Scan (Base Reg Cab) *Includes digital clock. NOT AVAILABLE with UL5.*	146	170
UPO	Radio: AM/FM Stereo with Auto. Tone Control, CD and Cassette (LS X-Cab) *Includes digital clock, theft lock, speed compensated volume and enhanced performance speaker system. REQUIRES A95 NP8.*	86	100
UV8	Cellular Telephone Wiring Provisions *Includes wiring for remote microphone and cellular phone.*	43	50
UY2	Wiring Provisions *Camper and fifth wheel provisions.*	22	25
V76	Tow Hooks (2WD)	33	38
VB3	Chrome Rear Step Bumper (Base) *NOT AVAILABLE with VF7.*	86	100
VF7	Rear Bumper Delete Provisions (Base) *Vehicles registered in certain states must have a rear bumper to be operated on their roads. Consult your local laws.*	(86)	(100)
VF7	Rear Bumper Delete Provisions (LS) *Vehicles registered in certain states must have a rear bumper to be operated on their roads. Consult your local laws.*	(172)	(200)
VYU	Snow Plow Prep Package (All Except LT) *Includes increased cooling and electrical connections and HD radiator. REQUIRES Z82.*	163	190
VYU	Snow Plow Prep Package (All Except LT) *Includes increased cooling and electrical connections and HD radiator. REQUIRES LQ4. NOT AVAILABLE with LM7 or Z82.*	280	325
VYU	Snow Plow Prep Package (All Except LT) *Includes increased cooling and electrical connections and HD radiator. REQUIRES LM7.*	245	285
YF5	California Emissions	146	170
Z82	HD Trailering Special Equipment *Includes 7-lead wiring harness and transmission oil cooler. NOT AVAILABLE with VF7.*	244	285
Z82	HD Trailering Special Equipment *Includes 7-lead wiring harness and transmission oil cooler. REQUIRES LQ4 or MT1.*	280	325
Z85	Firm Ride Suspension *Includes monotube 36mm shocks. REQUIRES QIW or QIZ.*	82	95
ZY2	Two Tone Paint Application (LS)	194	225

1999 SUBURBAN

1999 Chevrolet Suburban

What's New?

A couple of new colors are the only modifications to the Suburban as Chevrolet prepares a redesigned model for 2000.

Review

In some sections of the country, wise middle-class folks have been tooling around for several years in mile-long Suburbans, whether or not they have great need for all that expanse behind the driver's seat. These days, throughout the suburban reaches of Houston and Dallas, among other spots, the Chevrolet and GMC Suburban have become de facto status-flaunting vehicles, pushing prices beyond the reach of the common man.

Yes, those who formerly wheeled about town in a Cadillac, and wouldn't feel quite right in a pickup truck, appear to have twirled their affections toward the biggest passenger vehicles in the General Motors repertoire. Chevrolet, in fact, considers the Suburban "as suited to the country club as to a roughneck oil field."

Mechanically, you get the same layout in the smaller Chevrolet Tahoe, but that vehicle is only available with Chevy's Vortec 5700 V8 engine. Select a Suburban and you can accept that motor, with 255 horsepower. Or, with the 3/4-ton C/K 2500 series you can go all the way, opting for the mammoth Vortec 7400 V8, whipping out 290 strutting horses and a mean 410 foot-pounds of ground-tromping torque. Oh, there's also an optional turbo-diesel. Both the half- and 3/4-ton versions come with either two- or four-wheel drive, and all have four-wheel anti-lock braking.

Last year Chevrolet introduced a new four-wheel drive system to the Suburban. Called Autotrac, it automatically shifts from 2WD to 4WD when wheel slippage is detected, just like Ford's Control-Trac system in the similarly gargantuan Expedition. Some may wonder why Chevrolet introduced the 1999 Suburban so early. Evidently, GM was running into a problem with Corporate Average Fuel Economy for model year 1998. By cutting 1998 production of this fuel-sucking SUV, they've put the problem off one more year. To celebrate, Chevy makes a couple of new colors available.

Buyers beware that Chevrolet is preparing to introduce a completely new Suburban for the 2000 model year. Based upon the rigid new Silverado pickup platform, the redesigned 'Burban will be much improved inside and out. Wait for the new truck if you can.

Today's Suburban can seat up to nine occupants and tow as much as five tons, when properly equipped. For families that need plenty of room for youngsters, or for retirees who need loads of power to haul a travel trailer, a Suburban can make good sense. Chevrolet is combating competition from Ford's new Expedition, but for heavy-duty use and maximum space, Chevrolet and GMC are still the only serious games in town for a mammoth "truck wagon."

Safety Data

Side Airbag: *Not Available*
4-Wheel ABS: *Standard*
Driver Crash Test Grade: *Good*
Side Impact Crash Test Front: *Not Available*
Crash Offset: *Not Available*
Integrated Child Seat(s): *Not Available*
Traction Control: *Not Available*
Passenger Crash Test Grade: *Good*
Side Impact Crash Test Rear: *Not Available*

Standard Equipment

1500 BASE 2WD (4A): 5.7L V8 OHV SMPI 16-valve engine; 4-speed electronic overdrive automatic transmission with lock-up; 600-amp HD battery; 100-amp alternator; rear wheel drive, 3.42 axle ratio; stainless steel exhaust; front independent suspension with HD anti-roll bar, front coil springs, HD front shocks, rigid rear axle suspension with anti-roll bar, rear leaf springs, HD rear shocks; power re-circulating ball steering with vehicle speed-sensing assist; front disc/rear drum brakes with 4 wheel antilock braking system; 42 gal. capacity fuel tank; split swing-out rear cargo door; trailer harness; front and rear chrome bumpers with black rub strip, front chrome bumper insert, rear step; black bodyside molding with chrome bodyside insert, chrome wheel well molding; monotone paint; sealed beam halogen headlamps with daytime running lights; additional exterior lights include center high mounted stop light, underhood light; driver's and passenger's manual black folding outside mirrors; front and rear 15" x 7" painted styled steel wheels; P235/75SR15 BSW AS front and rear tires; inside mounted full-size conventional steel spare wheel; rear heat ducts; AM/FM stereo with clock, seek-scan, 4 speakers, and fixed antenna; power door locks, child safety rear door locks, power remote hatch/trunk release; 3 power accessory outlets; instrumentation display includes tachometer, oil pressure gauge, water temp gauge, volt gauge, trip odometer; warning indicators include battery, lights on, key in ignition, door ajar; dual airbags; ignition disable; tinted windows, manual rear windows, fixed 1/4 vent windows; variable intermittent front windshield wipers; seating capacity of 3, bench front seat with adjustable headrests, driver's seat includes 2-way direction control, passenger's seat includes 2-way direction control; front height adjustable seatbelts; vinyl seats, full cloth headliner, full vinyl floor covering; interior lights include dome light, front reading lights; sport steering wheel; passenger's side vanity mirror; day-night rearview mirror; glove box with light, front cupholder, instrument panel bin, driver's and passenger's door bins, rear door bins; vinyl cargo floor, cargo tie downs, cargo light; black grille, black side window moldings, black front windshield molding, black rear window molding and black door handles.

2500 BASE 2WD (4A) (in addition to or instead of 1500 BASE 2WD (4A) equipment): HD 4-speed electronic overdrive automatic transmission with lock-up; HD transmission oil cooler; 3.73 axle ratio; front and rear 16" x 6.5" painted styled steel wheels; vinyl trunk lid and colored grille.

1500 BASE 4WD (4A) (in addition to or instead of 1500 BASE 2WD (4A) equipment): Part-time 4 wheel drive, auto locking hub control with manual shift, 3.42 axle ratio; front independent torsion suspension with HD anti-roll bar, front torsion springs, front torsion bar; front tow hooks and interior lights include illuminated entry.

2500 BASE 4WD (4A) (in addition to or instead of 2500 BASE 2WD (4A) equipment): HD 4-speed electronic overdrive automatic transmission with lock-up; HD transmission oil cooler; part-time 4 wheel drive, auto locking hub control with manual shift, 4.1 axle ratio; front independent torsion suspension with HD anti-roll bar, front torsion springs, front torsion bar; front tow hooks and interior lights include illuminated entry.

CODE	DESCRIPTION	INVOICE	MSRP

Base Prices

CODE	DESCRIPTION	INVOICE	MSRP
CC10906	1500 2WD (4A)	22466	25675
CK10906	1500 4WD (4A)	24741	28275
CC20906	2500 2WD (4A)	23848	27259
CK20906	2500 4WD (4A)	26123	29859
Destination Charge:		685	685

Accessories

CODE	DESCRIPTION	INVOICE	MSRP
1SA	**Preferred Equipment Group 1SA** *Includes Base Decor. REQUIRES (YG6 or C69) and (YG4 or AT5).*	NC	NC
1SB	**Preferred Equipment Group 1SB (1500)** *Includes LS Decor: convenience group: tilt wheel, speed control; interior trim, automatic dimming rearview mirror, compass, exterior temperature display, 60/40 split-bench seat, rear bench seat, center folding bench seat, adjustable shoulder belt system, color-keyed cloth spare tire cover, leather-wrapped steering wheel, dual illuminated visor vanity mirrors, roof rack, chrome grille, aero-composite headlamps, exterior power remote mirrors, interior measurements, interior cargo measurements, electric rear window defogger, deep tinted solar-ray glass, power windows, custom cloth seat trim, front and rear air conditioning, AM/FM stereo with seek, scan, automatic tone control and cassette, auxiliary rear passenger heater, remote keyless entry with keyfob remote release, illuminated entry and power driver's seat. NOT AVAILABLE with L65, QIZ, MT1, QIW.*	6379	7418
1SB	**Preferred Equipment Group 1SB** *Includes LS Decor: convenience group: tilt wheel, speed control; interior trim, automatic dimming rearview mirror, compass, exterior temperature display, 60/40 split-bench seat, rear bench seat, center folding bench seat, adjustable shoulder belt system, color-keyed cloth spare tire cover, leather-wrapped steering wheel, dual illuminated visor vanity mirrors, roof rack, chrome grille, aero-composite headlamps, exterior power remote mirrors, interior measurements, interior cargo measurements, electric rear window defogger, deep tinted solar-ray glass, power windows, custom cloth seat trim, front and rear air conditioning, AM/FM stereo with seek, scan, automatic tone control and cassette, auxiliary rear passenger heater, remote keyless entry with keyfob remote release, illuminated entry and power driver's seat. REQUIRES L65 (1500). NOT AVAILABLE with QHM, QBN, QBX, QGB.*	6164	7168
1SC	**Preferred Equipment Group 1SC (1500)** *Includes LT Decor: convenience group: tilt wheel, speed control; interior trim, automatic dimming rearview mirror, compass, exterior temperature display, 60/40 split-bench seat, rear bench seat, center folding bench seat, adjustable shoulder belt system, color-keyed cloth spare tire cover, leather-wrapped steering wheel, dual illuminated visor vanity mirrors, roof rack, chrome grille, aero-composite headlamps, exterior power remote mirrors, interior measurements, interior cargo measurements, electric rear window defogger, deep tinted solar-ray glass, power windows, custom cloth seat trim, front and rear air conditioning, AM/FM stereo with seek, scan, automatic tone control, cassette and CD, auxiliary rear passenger heater, remote*	7884	9168

CODE	DESCRIPTION	INVOICE	MSRP
	keyless entry with keyfob remote release, illuminated entry, leather seat trim and power driver's seat.		
1SC	**Preferred Equipment Group 1SC**	7669	8918
	Includes LT Decor: convenience group: tilt wheel, speed control; interior trim, automatic dimming rearview mirror, compass, exterior temperature display, 60/40 split-bench seat, rear bench seat, center folding bench seat, adjustable shoulder belt system, color-keyed cloth spare tire cover, leather-wrapped steering wheel, dual illuminated visor vanity mirrors, roof rack, chrome grille, aero-composite headlamps, exterior power remote mirrors, interior measurements, interior cargo measurements, electric rear window defogger, deep tinted solar-ray glass, power windows, custom cloth seat trim, front and rear air conditioning, AM/FM stereo with seek, scan, automatic tone control, cassette and CD, auxiliary rear passenger heater, remote keyless entry with keyfob remote release, illuminated entry, leather seat trim and power driver's seat. REQUIRES L65 (1500).		
A95	**Reclining High Back Bucket Seats**	249	290
	Includes power lumbar, center console and roof console. NOT AVAILABLE with 1SA.		
AJ1	**Deep Tinted Solar-Ray Glass**	262	305
AS3	**Rear Bench Seat**	1017	1182
	Includes cloth covered rear quarter trim and center folding bench seat with adjustable shoulder belt system. NOT AVAILABLE with YG4.		
AT5	**Center Folding Bench Seat**	544	632
	Includes adjustable shoulder belt system. NOT AVAILABLE with YG4.		
B39	**Front and Rear Carpeted Floor Mats**	133	155
	Includes carpeted/vinyl reversible rear cargo mat. NOT AVAILABLE with 1SA, YG4.		
B71	**Wheel Flare Moldings (1500 4WD)**	155	180
BVE	**Black Side Step Running Boards**	280	325
	Supports 600 lbs. REQUIRES A95.		
C36	**Auxiliary Rear Passenger Heater**	176	205
	Includes cloth covered rear quarter panel. REQUIRES 1SA.		
C49	**Electric Rear Window Defogger**	132	154
	REQUIRES 1SA or C69.		
C60	**Air Conditioning**	727	845
	NOT AVAILABLE with YG6.		
C69	**Front and Rear Air Conditioning**	1200	1395
	Includes dual controls and cloth covered rear quarter trim. NOT AVAILABLE with YG6.		
DF2	**Stainless Steel Camper Type Mirrors - 7.5" x 10.5"**	(39)	(45)
	NOT AVAILABLE with ZM9, 1SA.		
DF2	**Stainless Steel Camper Type Mirrors - 7.5" x 10.5"**	46	53
	REQUIRES 1SA.		
F60	**HD Front Springs (4WD)**	54	63
	NOT AVAILABLE with L65 (1500).		
G80	**Locking Differential**	217	252
GT4	**3.73 Axle Ratio**	116	135
	Includes engine oil cooler. NOT AVAILABLE with L65 (1500), L31 (2500), MT1, Z82, KC4, QIZ, QIW, TP3.		
GT5	**4.10 Axle Ratio (2500)**	NC	NC
	Includes engine oil cooler.		

CODE	DESCRIPTION	INVOICE	MSRP
K47	High Capacity Air Cleaner	22	25
KC4	Engine Oil Cooler (1500) *NOT AVAILABLE with L65, GT4, MT1, QIZ, QIW.*	116	135
KNP	HD Auxiliary Transmission Oil Cooler (1500)	83	96
L29	Engine: Vortec 7400 V8 SFI (2500) *NOT AVAILABLE with TP3.*	516	600
L65	Engine: 6.5L V8 Turbo Diesel *Includes front bumper guards, engine oil cooler and wheels: 16" steel. REQUIRES MT1 or B71. NOT AVAILABLE with V10, TP3, GT4, KC4, QHM, Z82, N90, QBX, PF4, QBN, QGB, F60.*	2460	2860
MT1	Transmission: HD 4-Speed Automatic with Overdrive (1500) *Includes HD auxiliary transmission oil cooler. NOT AVAILABLE with GT4, KC4, N90, V10, Z82, QHM, PF4, QBX, QBN, QGB, TP3.*	NC	NC
N90	Wheels: Aluminum (1500 2WD) *Includes not matching spare. NOT AVAILABLE with P06, L65, MT1, QIZ.*	267	310
NP8	Autotrac Active Transfer Case (4WD) *NOT AVAILABLE with 1SA.*	344	400
NZZ	Skid Plate Package (4WD) *Includes fuel tank shield, front differential shield and transfer case shield.*	202	235
P06	Rally Wheel Trim *REQUIRES 1SA. NOT AVAILABLE with N90, PF4.*	52	60
PF4	Wheels: 16" x 7" Aluminum (1500 4WD) *Includes not matching spare. NOT AVAILABLE with P06, L65, MT1, QIZ, QIW.*	267	310
QBN	Tires: LT245/75R16C On/Off Road BSW SBR (1500 4WD) *NOT AVAILABLE with L65, QIZ, MT1, 1SB, 1SC, QBX, QGB, QIW.*	47	55
QBX	Tires: LT245/75R16C On/Off Road OWL (1500 4WD) *NOT AVAILABLE with L65, QIZ, MT1, 1SB, 1SC, QBN, QGB, QIW.*	155	180
QGB	Tires: P245/75R16 AT WOL SBR (1500 4WD) *NOT AVAILABLE with L65, QIZ, MT1, 1SB, 1SC, QBX, QBN, QIW.*	120	140
QHM	Tires: P235/75R15 AS WOL (1500 2WD) *NOT AVAILABLE with L65, QIZ, MT1, 1SB, 1SC.*	155	180
QIW	Tires: LT245/75R16E AT BW SBR (2500 4WD) *REQUIRES L65. NOT AVAILABLE with QBX, V10, KC4, PF4, GT4, 1SB, 1SC, QBN, QIZ, QGB.*	194	229
QIW	Tires: LT245/75R16E AT BW SBR (2500 4WD) *REQUIRES L65.*	47	55
QIZ	Tires: LT245/75R/16E AS BSW (2500 4WD) *REQUIRES L65.*	NC	NC
TP3	Dual Batteries (4WD) *REQUIRES ZM9. NOT AVAILABLE with L65, L29, MT1, GT4.*	48	56
U01	Roof Marker Lamps (5)	47	55
UL5	Radio Delete *REQUIRES 1SA. NOT AVAILABLE with UM6.*	(247)	(287)
UM6	Radio: AM/FM Stereo with Cassette *Includes digital clock. REQUIRES 1SA. NOT AVAILABLE with UL5.*	126	147

CODE	DESCRIPTION	INVOICE	MSRP
UN0	**Radio: AM/FM Stereo with CD and Automatic Tone Control** *Includes theft lock, speed compensated volume, digital clock and enhanced performance speaker system. NOT AVAILABLE with 1SA.*	86	100
UP0	**Radio: AM/FM Stereo with Cassette and CD** *Includes automatic tone control, theft lock, cassette with search and repeat, speed compensated volume, digital clock and enhanced performance speaker system. REQUIRES 1SB. NOT AVAILABLE with UN0.*	172	200
V10	**Cold Climate Package** *Includes engine block heater. NOT AVAILABLE with L65, MT1, QIZ, QIW.*	28	33
V76	**Tow Hooks (Front) (2WD)**	33	38
V96	**Trailering Hitch Ball and Mount** *REQUIRES Z82.*	26	30
YG4	**Center and Rear Seat Not Desired** *REQUIRES 1SA. NOT AVAILABLE with AT5.*	NC	NC
YG4	**Third Seat Delete** *REQUIRES 1SC. NOT AVAILABLE with ZM9, B39.*	(875)	(1018)
YG4	**Third Seat Delete** *REQUIRES 1SB. NOT AVAILABLE with B39.*	(531)	(618)
YG6	**Air Conditioning Not Desired** *NOT AVAILABLE with C69, ZP6.*	NC	NC
Z82	**HD Trailering Special Equipment (1500)** *Includes trailer hitch platform, HD oil cooler, HD auxiliary transmission cooler. REQUIRES GU6. NOT AVAILABLE with L65.*	383	445
Z82	**HD Trailering Special Equipment** *Includes trailer hitch platform, HD oil cooler, HD auxiliary transmission cooler. REQUIRES L65 (1500).*	184	214
Z82	**HD Trailering Special Equipment (1500)** *Includes trailer hitch platform, HD oil cooler, HD auxiliary transmission cooler. REQUIRES GU6. NOT AVAILABLE with L65.*	267	310
ZM9	**Comfort and Security Package** *Includes heated driver's and passenger's seats, power passenger's seat, front and rear carpeted floor mats, carpeted/vinyl reversible rear cargo mat, dual heated electrochromic exterior mirrors, Homelink 3 channel transmitter and 46mm Bilstein shocks. REQUIRES A95 and 1SC. NOT AVAILABLE with YG4, DF2.*	1075	1250
ZP6	**Rear Window Equipment** *Includes electric rear window defogger and rear window wiper/washer. REQUIRES 1SA. NOT AVAILABLE with YG6.*	240	279
ZP6	**Rear Window Equipment** *Includes electric rear window defogger and rear window wiper/washer. NOT AVAILABLE with 1SA.*	NC	NC
ZQ3	**Convenience Group** *Includes tilt wheel and speed control. REQUIRES 1SA.*	329	383
ZY2	**Conventional Two-Tone Paint**	172	200

1999 TAHOE

1999 Chevrolet Tahoe

What's New?

The standard cargo net is deleted, and new colors are added as Tahoe cruises into final model year in current guise.

Review

Compact sport-utility vehicles get most of the attention nowadays, but for folks with big families-or scads of goods to lug around-they're just not spacious enough inside. Chevrolet offers a solution to this problem with the Tahoe, based on the full-size C/K pickup platform but garageable in either two- or four-door body styles.

At a glance, the four-door Tahoe and larger Suburban look nearly identical, but a Tahoe measures 20 inches shorter. Beneath the hood sits a Vortec 5700 V8, rated for 255 horsepower. Two-door 4WD Tahoes with LS or LT trim can be equipped with a 6.5-liter turbodiesel V8 instead of the Vortec 5700.

From the driver's seat forward, Tahoes are virtually identical to Chevy's full-size C/K pickups. Space is massive up front. Capable of towing as much as 7,000 pounds, four-door Tahoes seat either five or six passengers, and an underbody-mounted spare tire helps boost cargo space.

On the Interstate, the Tahoe rides nicely, but the wide body takes some getting used to if you're accustomed to compacts. Turning onto smaller roads, it suddenly feels more like a truck. Easy to control either way, this sizable machine is reasonably maneuverable, if driven with discretion. The V8 is strong, and the four-speed automatic transmission shifts neatly.

Think about the "entry assist" running boards if your regular riders aren't so nimble. They help. So do the robust grab bars that ease entry into the rear seats. Rear cargo doors are standard, but a lift glass tailgate version is available.

In 1998, Chevrolet introduced an optional automatic four-wheel drive system that shifts between 2WD and 4WD as conditions warrant. No longer is it necessary to push a button on the dashboard to actively engage four-wheel traction. For 1999, the cargo net has been deleted from the standard equipment list, and new colors have been added to the paint chart. Why did Chevrolet begin producing the 1999 Tahoe early? Seems there was a little problem with meeting 1998 Corporate Average Fuel Economy standards, so by switching to a 1999 model year designation, GM bought itself a little time to make up for the lousy fuel economy the Tahoe tends to get.

Because Chevrolet targets customers with an income of $85,000 a year, luxury conveniences are part of upscale Tahoe packages. The typical prospect is a 40-year-old man who currently drives a Chevy Blazer and is attracted to a vehicle's size and power. Those attributes the Tahoe has in abundance, as does its little-different GMC Yukon counterpart.

With the introduction of the Ford Expedition a few years ago, Chevrolet lost its dominance of the full-size SUV market. Further complicating matters, the Tahoe is based on a decade-old platform, while the slightly larger, slightly less expensive Expedition is derived from more modern F-Series underpinnings. The Ford's edge will shrink by 2000, when a completely redesigned Tahoe based on the all-new Chevrolet Silverado pickup debuts. Buyers might want to wait for a while, because the new truck will be much improved. However, we doubt a 2-door Tahoe will make the cut for the next millennium, so snap one up now while you have the chance. This single remaining full-size 2-door SUV likely has a limited future.

Safety Data

Side Airbag: *Not Available*
4-Wheel ABS: *Standard*
Driver Crash Test Grade: *Good*
Side Impact Crash Test Front: *Not Available*
Crash Offset: *Not Available*
Integrated Child Seat(s): *Not Available*
Traction Control: *Not Available*
Passenger Crash Test Grade: *Good*
Side Impact Crash Test Rear: *Not Available*

Standard Equipment

TAHOE 2WD 2-DOOR: 5.7L V8 OHV SMPI 16-valve engine; 4-speed electronic overdrive automatic transmission with lock-up; 600-amp HD battery; 100-amp alternator; rear wheel drive, 3.08 axle ratio; stainless steel exhaust; front independent suspension with HD anti-roll bar, front coil springs, front shocks, rear suspension with rear leaf springs, rear shocks; power re-circulating ball steering with vehicle speed-sensing assist; front disc/rear drum brakes with 4 wheel anti-lock braking system; 30 gal capacity fuel tank; split swing-out rear cargo door; trailer harness; front and rear chrome bumpers with black rub strip, chrome bumper insert, rear step bumper; black bodyside molding with chrome bodyside insert, chrome wheel well molding; monotone paint; sealed beam halogen headlamps with daytime running lights; additional exterior lights include center high mounted stop light, underhood light; driver and passenger manual black folding outside mirrors; front and rear 15" x 7" silver styled steel wheels with hub wheel covers; P235/75SR15 BSW AS front and rear tires; inside mounted full-size conventional steel spare wheel; rear heat ducts; AM/FM stereo with clock, seek-scan, 4 speakers and fixed antenna; power door locks; 3 power accessory outlets; analog instrumentation display includes tachometer gauge, oil pressure gauge, water temp gauge, volt gauge, PRNDL in instrument panel, trip odometer; warning indicators include battery, lights on, key in ignition, door ajar; dual airbags; ignition disable; tinted windows, fixed rear windows; variable intermittent front windshield wipers; seating capacity of 5, front bucket seats with tilt adjustable headrests, driver seat includes 4-way direction control with easy entry feature, passenger seat includes 4-way direction control with easy entry feature; full folding rear bench seat with adjustable rear headrest; front height adjustable seatbelts; vinyl seats, full cloth headliner, full vinyl floor covering; interior lights include dome light, front and rear reading lights; sport steering wheel; passenger side vanity mirror; day-night rearview mirror; glove box with light, front cupholder, interior concealed storage, driver and passenger door bins; vinyl cargo floor, cargo light; colored grille, black side window moldings, black front windshield molding, black rear window molding, black door handles.

4WD 2-DOOR (in addition to or instead of 2WD 2-DOOR equipment): Part-time 4 wheel drive, auto locking hub control and manual shift, 3.42 axle ratio; front suspension with anti-roll bar, front torsion springs, front torsion bar; tow hooks; front and rear 16" x 6.5" wheels.

2WD 4-DOOR (in addition to or instead of 2WD 2-DOOR equipment): Rear wheel drive; front coil springs; roof rack; aero-composite headlamps; front and rear 15" x 7" alloy wheels; underbody mounted full-size temporary spare wheel; air conditioning; AM/FM stereo with cassette, 8 performance speakers, automatic equalizer, theft deterrent; cruise control; child safety rear door locks; compass; deep tinted windows, power front windows with driver 1-touch down, power rear windows; rear window defroster; seating capacity of 6, 60-40 split-bench front seat with center armrest with storage, driver seat includes power lumbar support, passenger seat includes power lumbar support; 60-40 folding rear split-bench seat with center storage armrest; front and rear height adjustable seatbelts; premium cloth seats, cloth door trim insert, carpet floor covering with rubber floor mats, deluxe sound insulation; interior lights include 4 door curb lights; leather-wrapped steering wheel; illuminated driver's side vanity mirror; dual auxiliary visors; auto-dimming rearview mirror; 2 seat back storage pockets; carpeted cargo floor, cargo cover; chrome grille.

4WD 4-DOOR (in addition to or instead of 2WD 4-DOOR equipment): Part-time 4 wheel drive with auto locking hub control and manual shift; front torsion springs, front torsion bar, rear anti-roll bar; tow hooks.

Base Prices

Code	Description	Invoice	MSRP
CC10516	2WD 2-door	21018	24020
CK10516	4WD 2-door	23293	26620
CC10706	2WD 4-door	26093	29820
CK10706	4WD 4-door	28368	32420
Destination Charge:		640	640

Accessories

Code	Description	Invoice	MSRP
1SA	**Preferred Equipment Group 1SA (2WD)** *Includes Base Decor Package. REQUIRES YG6 or C60. NOT AVAILABLE with UNO, UPO, A95, DF2, ZM9, F60.*	NC	NC
1SA	**Preferred Equipment Group 1SA (4WD)** *Includes Base Decor Package. REQUIRES YG6 or C60. NOT AVAILABLE with Z71, UNO, UPO, A95, BYP, DF2, ZM9, F60.*	NC	NC
1SB	**Preferred Equipment Group 1SB (2WD 4-door)** *Includes LS Decor Package, AM/FM stereo with seek-scan and cassette, remote keyless entry, 6-way power driver's seat. NOT AVAILABLE with A95, ZM9, UM6, C69, AJ1, B85.*	NC	NC
1SB	**Preferred Equipment Group 1SB (4WD 2-door)** *Includes LS Decor Package, ETR AM/FM stereo with cassette, seek-scan; remote keyless entry, 6-way power driver's seat. NOT AVAILABLE with YG6, UM6, A95, P06, DF2, ZM9.*	3757	4369
1SB	**Preferred Equipment Group 1SB (4WD 4-door)** *Includes LS Decor Package, AM/FM stereo with seek-scan and cassette, remote keyless entry, 6-way power driver's seat. NOT AVAILABLE with A95, ZM9.*	NC	NC
1SB	**Preferred Equipment Group 1SB (2WD 2-door)** *Includes LS Decor Package, ETR AM/FM stereo with cassette, seek-scan; remote keyless entry, 6-way power driver's seat. NOT AVAILABLE with YG6, UM6, A95, P06, DF2, ZM9.*	3757	4369
1SC	**Preferred Equipment Group 1SC (2WD 2-door)** *Includes remote keyless entry, 6-way power driver's seat, LT Decor Package: up-level door trim panels, leather seat trim, ETR AM/FM stereo with CD and cassette, 60/40 split-bench seat. NOT AVAILABLE with YG6, UM6, UNO, A95, P06, DF2.*	4918	5719

CODE	DESCRIPTION	INVOICE	MSRP
1SC	**Preferred Equipment Group 1SC (4WD 2-door)** *Includes remote keyless entry, 6-way power driver's seat, LT Decor Package: up-level door trim panels, leather seat trim, ETR AM/FM stereo with CD and cassette, 60/40 split-bench seat. NOT AVAILABLE with YG6, UM6, UN0, A95, P06, DF2.*	4918	5719
1SC	**Preferred Equipment Group 1SC (2WD 4-door)** *Includes remote keyless entry, 6-way power driver's seat, LT Decor Package: up-level door trim panels, leather seat trim, ETR AM/FM stereo with CD and cassette, 60/40 split bench seat. NOT AVAILABLE with A95, UM6, UN0, C69, AJ1, B85.*	1161	1350
1SC	**Preferred Equipment Group 1SC (4WD 4-door)** *Includes remote keyless entry, 6-way power driver's seat, LT Decor Package: up-level door trim panels, leather seat trim, ETR AM/FM stereo with CD and cassette, 60/40 split bench seat. NOT AVAILABLE with A95, UN0.*	1161	1350
A95	**Custom Cloth High-Back Bucket Seats** *Includes power lumbar, floor console and overhead console. NOT AVAILABLE with (1SA) Preferred Equipment Group 1SA, 1SC, 1SB.*	204	237
AG9	**6-Way Power Driver's Seat (2WD 2-door)** *REQUIRES A95. NOT AVAILABLE with 1SB, 1SC.*	206	240
AJ1	**Deep Tinted Glass (4-door)** *Rear doors, quarter glass and cargo doors. NOT AVAILABLE with 1SB, 1SC.*	262	305
AJ1	**Deep Tinted Glass (2-door)** *NOT AVAILABLE with 1SB, 1SC.*	185	215
B39	**Floor Mats (4-door)** *Carpeted front and rear. NOT AVAILABLE with ZM9.*	133	155
B71	**Wheel Flare Moldings (4WD 2-door)** *NOT AVAILABLE with BYP.*	155	180
BVE	**Black Side Step Running Boards** *Supports 600 lbs. Dealer installed. NOT AVAILABLE with NZZ.*	280	325
BYP	**Sport Package (4WD 2-door)** *Includes black front air dam, black mirrors, wheel flare moldings, dark argent grille, dark argent bumpers with rub strip, sport decals, conventional two-tone paint. NOT AVAILABLE with 1SA, L56, QBN, QBX, QGD, DF2.*	260	302
C49	**Electric Rear Window Defogger (2-door)** *REQUIRES 1SA and C60. NOT AVAILABLE with YG6.*	132	154
C60	**Air Conditioning (2-door)** *NOT AVAILABLE with YG6.*	727	845
C69	**Front & Rear Air Conditioning (4-door)** *Includes dual controls.*	473	550
DF2	**Camper Type Mirrors (2-door)** *7.5" x 10.5" stainless steel. NOT AVAILABLE with 1SB, 1SC.*	46	53
DF2	**Camper Type Mirrors (2-door)** *7.5" x 10.5" stainless steel. NOT AVAILABLE with 1SA, BYP.*	(39)	(45)
F60	**HD Front Springs (2-door)** *NOT AVAILABLE with 1SA, L56, Z82.*	54	63
G80	**Locking Differential** *REQUIRES GU6.*	217	252
GT4	**3.73 Axle Ratio** *NOT AVAILABLE with KC4, Z82.*	116	135

CODE	DESCRIPTION	INVOICE	MSRP
GU6	3.42 Axle Ratio (2WD)	NC	NC
K47	High Capacity Air Cleaner *NOT AVAILABLE with L56.*	22	25
KC4	Engine Oil Cooler *NOT AVAILABLE with L56, GT4, Z82.*	116	135
KNP	HD Auxiliary Transmission Cooler *REQUIRES GU6. NOT AVAILABLE with Z82.*	83	96
L56	Engine: 6.5L V8 Turbo Diesel (4WD 2-door) *Includes 4-speed HD automatic transmission: HD auxiliary transmission cooler, GVWR 6450 lbs., HD auxiliary battery. NOT AVAILABLE with KC4, K47, V10, BYP, F60, Z82, YF5.*	2460	2860
N90	Wheels: Aluminum (2WD 2-door) *Includes steel spare. NOT AVAILABLE with P06.*	267	310
NC7	Federal Emission Override *For vehicles that will be registered or leased in California, New York, Massachusetts or Connecticut, but sold by retailers outside those states. REQUIRES YF5.*	NC	NC
NP8	Autotrac Transfer Case (4WD) *REQUIRES (1SA and ZQ3) or 1SB or 1SC.*	344	400
NZZ	Skid Plate Package (4WD 4-door) *Includes fuel tank, front differential and transfer case shields.*	82	95
NZZ	Skid Plate Package (4WD 2-door) *Includes fuel tank, front differential and transfer case shields.*	194	225
P06	Rally Wheel Trim (2-door) *NOT AVAILABLE with 1SB, 1SC, N90, PF4.*	52	60
PF4	Wheels: Aluminum (4WD 2-door) *Includes steel spare. NOT AVAILABLE with P06.*	267	310
QBN	Tires: LT245/75R16C AT BSW SBR (4WD 2-door) *NOT AVAILABLE with QBX, QGC, QGD, BYP.*	47	55
QBX	Tires: LT245/75R16C AT WOL SBR (4WD 2-door) *NOT AVAILABLE with QBN, QGC, QGD, BYP.*	155	180
QFN	Tires: LT235/75R15 AS WOL SBR (2WD)	120	140
QGB	Tires: P245/75R16 AT WOL (4WD 4-door)	120	140
QGC	Tires: P265/75R16 AT BSW SBR (4WD 2-door) *REQUIRES (1SA and PF4) or 1SB or 1SC. NOT AVAILABLE with QBN, QBX, QGD.*	163	190
QGD	Tires: P265/75R16 AT WOL SBR (4WD 2-door) *REQUIRES (1SA and PF4) or 1SB or 1SC. NOT AVAILABLE with QBN, QBX, QGC, BYP.*	271	315
UL5	Radio: Delete (2-door) *REQUIRES 1SA.*	(247)	(287)
UM6	Radio: AM/FM Stereo with Cassette (2-door) *Includes digital clock. NOT AVAILABLE with 1SB, 1SC.*	126	147
UN0	Radio: AM/FM Stereo with CD *Includes digital clock, theft lock, automatic tone control, speed compensated volume and enhanced performance speaker system. NOT AVAILABLE with 1SA, 1SC, UP0.*	86	100

CODE	DESCRIPTION	INVOICE	MSRP
UP0	**Radio: AM/FM Stereo with CD & Cassette** *Includes seek/scan, digital clock, theft lock, automatic tone control, speed compensated volume and enhanced performance speaker system. NOT AVAILABLE with 1SA, 1SC, UN0.*	172	200
V10	**Cold Climate Package** *Includes engine block heater. NOT AVAILABLE with L56.*	28	33
V76	**Tow Hooks (Front) (2WD)**	33	38
YF3	**Limited Package (2WD 4-Door)** *Includes highback bucket seats, carpet floor mats, rear air conditioning, locking differential, engine oil cooler, transmission aoil cooler, upgraded power disc brakes, upgraded suspension, P255/70R16 tires, unique wheels, ground effects, high gloss black painted front bumper, grille and rear bumper, fog lamps, pinstripes and two-toned custom leather seats.*	2034	2365
YF5	**California Emissions** *Required for all vehicles to be registered in the State of California. NOT AVAILABLE with L56.*	146	170
YG6	**Air Conditioning Not Desired (2-door)** *NOT AVAILABLE with 1SB, 1SC, C60, C49.*	NC	NC
Z71	**On/Off Road Chassis Equipment (4WD 2-door)** *Includes skid plate package, Bilstein shock absorbers. REQUIRES QBN or QBX or QGC or QGD. NOT AVAILABLE with 1SA.*	344	400
Z82	**HD Trailering Equipment with GT4** *Includes trailer hitch platform, wiring harness, HD auxiliary transmission cooler. REQUIRES GT4. NOT AVAILABLE with L56, KC4, Z82.*	267	310
Z82	**HD Trailering Equipment with GU4 (2WD 2-door)** *Includes trailer hitch platform, wiring harness, engine oil cooler. REQUIRES GU4.*	300	349
Z82	**HD Trailering Equipment with GU6** *Includes trailer hitch platform, wiring harness, engine oil cooler, HD auxiliary transmission cooler. REQUIRES GU6. NOT AVAILABLE with L56, GT4, Z82.*	383	445
Z82	**HD Trailering Equipment with L56 (4WD 2-door)** *Includes trailer hitch platform and wiring harness. REQUIRES L56. NOT AVAILABLE with F60.*	184	214
ZM9	**Comfort & Convenience Package (4-door)** *Includes carpeted floor mats, carpeted/vinyl reversible cargo mat, electrochromic rearview mirror, heated seats, Bilstein shocks with premium ride, integrated Homelink transmitter, dual illuminated visor vanity mirrors, front and rear air conditioning. REQUIRES A95. NOT AVAILABLE with 1SB.*	1462	1700
ZM9	**Comfort & Convenience Package (2-door)** *Includes carpeted floor mats, carpeted/vinyl reversible cargo mat, electrochromic rearview mirror, heated seats, Bilstein shocks with premium ride, integrated Homelink transmitter, heated mirrors. REQUIRES A95. NOT AVAILABLE with 1SA, 1SB, Z71, BYP.*	783	910
ZM9	**Comfort and Convenience Package (2WD 4-Door)** *Includes carpeted floor mats, carpeted/vinyl reversible cargo mat, electrochromic rearview mirror, heated seats, Bilstein shocks with premium ride, integrated Homelink transmitter, dual illuminated visor vanity mirrors, front and rear air conditioning. REQUIRES A95 and YF3.*	900	1047

CODE	DESCRIPTION	INVOICE	MSRP
ZP6	Rear Window Equipment (2-door) *Includes rear window wiper/washer, electric rear window defogger. REQUIRES 1SB or 1SC.*	NC	NC
ZP6	Rear Window Equipment (2-door) *Includes rear window wiper/washer, electric rear window defogger. REQUIRES 1SA.*	240	279
ZQ3	Convenience Group (2-door) *Includes speed control, tilt steering.*	329	383
ZY2	Conventional Two-Tone Paint *NOT AVAILABLE with BYP.*	172	200

1999 TRACKER

1999 Chevrolet Tracker

What's New?

The redesigned-for-1999 Tracker, available in either two-door convertible or four-door hardtop versions and in two- or four-wheel drive, features sporty new looks, more power, improved ride and handling and a roomier, more comfortable interior.

Review

The all-new Tracker has finally arrived, with a fresh look and revamped interior that are sure to make it more attractive to folks cross-shopping the Kia Sportage, Toyota RAV4 and Honda CR-V mini-utes. Only the name and a handful of components carry over from the previous-generation Tracker, and the many improvements are evident throughout.

With its lower roofline, sloping hood and sculpted flanks, Tracker's design is far more stylish than its predecessor, whether you choose the two-door softtop model or four-door hardtop. Better still, Tracker's all-new interiors are more comfortable and feature better ergonomics, including a reworked instrument panel that houses full instrumentation.

Unlike many of today's unibody mini-SUVs built off car platforms, Tracker boasts full ladder-type frame construction. Track width has been increased for '99 by nearly 2.5 inches for a wider stance, with

MacPherson-strut front suspension and an all-new five-link rear setup locating its rigid axle. Even the steering has been improved, dropping the old recirculating-ball system in favor of a modern rack-and-pinion unit.

The result is improved ride and handling, with better stability and more substantial road feel. Sure, when driven hard the Tracker still exhibits plenty of understeer, but it is more predictable and less twitchy than last year's version. Power front disc brakes with rear drums bring things to a halt, while four-wheel ABS is optional. A new, "shift-on-the-fly" four-wheel-drive system with automatic locking front hubs is now standard on all 4WD models.

Four-door Trackers can be equipped with power windows, door locks and mirrors, while child security rear door locks are standard. Rear seating is surprisingly comfortable for two adults. Improving the way the rear seat is stowed not only provides a nearly flat load floor, but about two-and-a-half more square feet of cargo room as well. There are a wide variety of optional features to equip your four-door Tracker nearly as well as some popular compacts.

The two-door convertibles are more than six inches longer than last year, providing an additional 1.3 square feet of cargo floor area with the rear seat stowed. All have an improved, two-piece "easy opening" top that opens up the front section, rear section or both to the sun. Dealer-installed "Exterior Accessory Packages" can also be added to custom-tailor your Tracker for more serious on- or off-road duty, if you so desire.

New this year is a 2.0-liter, 16-valve DOHC four-cylinder engine that is standard on the four-door and optional on convertibles. It puts out 127 horsepower at 6,000 rpm and 134 foot-pounds of torque at 3,000 revs through a five-speed manual or optional four-speed automatic transmission. The base motor on the two-door is a 1.6-liter inline four available only with the stick shift - but the little motor's 97 tortured ponies and mere 100 foot-pounds of torque demand that you opt for the bigger engine mated to the five-speed.

Sorry, but the V6 that is available in the Chevy's Suzuki twin, the Vitara, cannot be had in the Tracker at any price. That's too bad, because even with its more powerful engine, the Tracker is woefully wheezy while under hard acceleration — buzzing and complaining well before redline.

Power-hungry drivers aside, there's no denying that fun-in-the-sun motoring takes on fresh meaning behind the wheel of a little Tracker convertible — even more so with the go-anywhere attitude afforded by four-wheel drive. And more practical-minded folks will no doubt appreciate the blend of good utility and fuel economy afforded by a Tracker four-door. Indeed, if you're looking for a mini-SUV for city driving chores and short weekend excursions, the new-and-improved Tracker's blend of features and value deserves a look.

Safety Data

Side Airbag: *Not Available*
4-Wheel ABS: *Optional*
Driver Crash Test Grade: *Not Available*
Side Impact Crash Test Front: *Not Available*
Crash Offset: *Acceptable*
Integrated Child Seat(s): *Not Available*
Traction Control: *Not Available*
Passenger Crash Test Grade: *Not Available*
Side Impact Crash Test Rear: *Not Available*

Standard Equipment

2WD CONVERTIBLE (5M): 1.6L I4 SOHC MPI 16-valve engine; 5-speed overdrive manual transmission; rear wheel drive, 5.12 axle ratio; stainless steel exhaust; front independent strut suspension with anti-roll bar, front coil springs, rigid rear axle multi-link suspension with rear coil springs; power rack-and-pinion steering; front disc/rear drum brakes; 14.8 gal. capacity fuel tank; skid plates; conventional rear cargo door; manual convertible roof with roll-over protection; front and rear black bumpers with front and rear tow hooks, rear step; monotone paint; aero-composite halogen auto on headlamps with daytime running lights; additional exterior lights include center high mounted stop light; driver's and passenger's manual black outside mirrors; front and rear 15" x 5.5" silver styled steel wheels; P195/75SR15 BSW AS front and rear tires; outside rear mounted full-size conventional steel spare wheel; rear heat ducts; AM/FM stereo with clock, seek-scan, 4 speakers, and manual retractable antenna; fuel filler door; 2 power accessory outlets; instrumentation display includes tachometer, water temp gauge, trip odometer; warning indicators include oil pressure, battery, lights on, key in ignition; dual airbags; tinted windows; variable intermittent front windshield wipers; seating capacity of 4, front bucket seats with adjustable headrests, driver's seat includes 4-way direction control with easy entry, passenger's seat includes 4-way direction control with easy entry; full folding rear bench seat with adjustable headrests; front height adjustable seatbelts; cloth seats, cloth door trim insert, full carpet floor covering; interior lights include dome light, front reading lights; dual auxiliary visors, passenger's side vanity mirror; day-night rearview mirror; partial floor console, locking glove box, front and rear cupholders, instrument panel bin, 2 seat back storage pockets, driver's and passenger's door bins; carpeted cargo floor, plastic trunk lid; body-colored grille, black front windshield molding and black door handles.

4WD CONVERTIBLE (5M) (in addition to or instead of 4WD CONVERTIBLE (5M) equipment): Part-time 4 wheel drive, auto locking hub control with manual shift, 5.12 axle ratio and black bodyside molding.

2WD 4-DOOR (5M) (in addition to or instead of 2WD CONVERTIBLE (5M) equipment): 2.0L I4 DOHC MPI 16-valve engine; 4.62 axle ratio; 17.4 gal. capacity fuel tank; black bodyside molding; child safety rear door locks; manual rear windows, fixed 1/4 vent windows; rear window defroster; seating capacity of 5, front bucket seats with adjustable headrests, driver's seat includes 4-way direction control, passenger's seat includes 4-way direction control; 60-40 folding rear bench seat with adjustable headrests; full cloth headliner, full carpet floor covering with carpeted floor mats; cargo light and body-colored side window moldings.

4WD 4-DOOR (5M) (in addition to or instead of 2WD 4-DOOR (5M) equipment): Part-time 4 wheel drive, auto locking hub control with manual shift.

Base Prices

Code	Description	Invoice	MSRP
CE10367	2WD Convertible (5M)	12844	13635
CJ10367	4WD Convertible (5M)	13880	14735
CE10305	2WD 4-Door (5M)	13975	14835
CJ10305	4WD 4-Door (5M)	15011	15935
Destination Charge:		360	360

Accessories

Code	Description	Invoice	MSRP
1SA	**Preferred Equipment Group 1SA** *Includes vehicle with standard equipment. NOT AVAILABLE with UNO.*	NC	NC
1SB	**Preferred Equipment Group 1SB (Convertible)** *Includes air conditioning, ETR AM/FM stereo with cassette, seek and scan, front and rear carpeted floor mats. NOT AVAILABLE with R6G, UL5.*	1064	1195
1SB	**Preferred Equipment Group 1SB (4-Door)** *Includes air conditioning, 15" alloy wheels, steel spare, ETR AM/FM stereo with cassette, seek and scan. NOT AVAILABLE with R6G, UL5.*	1353	1520
B58	**Front and Rear Carpeted Floor Mats (Convertible)**	36	40
BNN	**Lockable Cargo Storage Compartment (Convertible)**	111	125
C25	**Rear Window Wiper/Washer (4-Door)**	111	125
C60	**Air Conditioning** *NOT AVAILABLE with R6G.*	832	935
JM4	**4-Wheel Antilock Brakes**	530	595
K34	**Cruise Control with Resume Speed**	156	175

CODE	DESCRIPTION	INVOICE	MSRP
L34	Engine: 2.0L 4 Cylinder DOHC MPI (Convertible) *Includes 4.62 axle ratio. NOT AVAILABLE with 1SA.*	356	400
MX0	Transmission: 4 Speed Automatic with Overdrive *REQUIRES L34. NOT AVAILABLE with 1SA.*	890	1000
N33	Tilt Steering Wheel *NOT AVAILABLE with 1SA.*	129	145
NY7	Front Differential Skid Plate (4WD) *Includes transfer case.*	67	75
P17	Black Vinyl Spare Tire Cover	44	50
QA4	Wheels: 15" Alloy *Includes spare steel wheel.*	325	365
R6G	Air Conditioning Not Desired *NOT AVAILABLE with C60.*	NC	NC
UL0	Radio: AM/FM Stereo with Cassette *Includes tone select, digital clock and 4 speakers. NOT AVAILABLE with UN0, UL5.*	196	220
UL5	Radio Delete *NOT AVAILABLE with 1SB, UL0, UN0.*	(272)	(306)
UN0	Radio: AM/FM Stereo with CD *Includes tone select, digital clock and 4 speakers. REQUIRES 1SB. NOT AVAILABLE with UL0, UL5, 1SA.*	89	100
UN0	Radio: AM/FM Stereo with CD *Includes tone select, digital clock and 4 speakers. REQUIRES 1SA. NOT AVAILABLE with UL0, UL5, 1SB.*	285	320
V54	Black Luggage Carrier (4-Door)	112	126
Z05	Power Convenience Package (4-Door) *Includes power windows, power door locks, keyless entry and power mirrors.*	650	730

1999 VENTURE

1999 Chevrolet Venture

What's New?

Venture gets some performance and safety enhancements. Other changes include additional seating choices, four new exterior and two new interior colors, as well as fatter standard tires. What's more, there's a newly badged LT model that packages an upgraded audio system with a touring suspension, traction control and captain's seats with available leather.

Review

It should be no surprise that Venture has surpassed previous Chevrolet minivan sales records, given the limited appeal of its mini-vac shaped, plastic-bodied predecessor, the Lumina Minivan. What is noteworthy is the Venture's competitive edge in today's hotly contested minivan market. Developed in concert with GM's European Opel division, Venture enters its third model year wearing conservative yet modern sheetmetal capped by a toothy chrome grille. Looks aside, this minivan's strong suit is versatility, which has helped it gain a couple of "Best Buy" accolades from the motoring media as well as our own nod as an outstanding entry in this ever-evolving segment. Its success can be measured by a number of functional family features, including an available driver-side sliding door, optional passenger-side power sliding door, available modular seating, optional integrated child seats, standard four-wheel antilock brakes and optional traction control - even the ability to pull a 3,500 pound trailer load.

Three versions are available, in Base, LS or new-for-'99 LT trim. Choose a 112-inch wheelbase in three- or four-door bodystyles, or the 120-inch wheelbase as a four-door only. All Ventures come equipped with a 3.4-liter V6 that makes 185 horsepower, up from last year's 180, and a healthy 210 foot-pounds of torque. Designed to satisfy consumers on either side of the Atlantic Ocean, the Venture treats drivers with a communicative chassis, sharp steering, and almost nimble handling, all while providing room inside for up to eight passengers and a good amount of their belongings.

While the additional power is welcome, two other upgrades combine for improved driveability. The move to GM's 4T65-E fully electronically controlled four-speed automatic transmission with overdrive better matches shifting smoothness to engine performance. And going from P205s to P215/70R-15 tires as standard equipment provides a bigger footprint and better roadholding.

Other updates this year include making the rear window defogger standard and adding heated outside rearview mirrors. To help sweeten cabin air, a charcoal air filter is now part of the ventilation system. And four new metallic paints, in shades of blue, green, red and silver, join two leather interiors in neutral or gray on the color palette. Some carryover features worth noting are the optional dual-mode audio unit which allows rear passengers to listen to a CD via headphones while front passengers catch traffic reports on the radio, and a load-leveling suspension complete with auxiliary air hose.

Seating can be configured in several ways, beginning with the standard seven places among the front buckets, second-row 60/40 and third- row 50/50 split bench seats. New this year is an optional eight-seat setup that - thanks to the use of flip-and-fold modular buckets that weigh just 38 pounds each - can be easily removed or re-arranged to handle 32 different combinations of passengers and cargo. Not to be outdone by cubbyhole-happy Chrysler, Chevy's Venture can be outfitted with as many as 17 cup and drink box holders, as well as up to 26 storage compartments, including underseat stowage and a removable CD/cassette bin that can be locked inside the glove box.

Last year, while Chrysler was bragging that it pioneered the four-door minivan and Ford was dodging talk about doors to play up how well its Windstar scored in government crash tests, Chevrolet made the Venture the first of its ilk to receive standard side-impact airbags for both front passengers. Solidly in Venture's court, we had teased Chevy to offer an LTZ model with body-color grille. Well, GM responded with a Venture LT package, complete with custom leather seating, upgraded sound system, rear air and audio controls, a touring suspension and traction control. Not bad, but how about adding the "Z" part of that equation next time and giving us a lower stance, a sporty wheel/tire package and a throaty exhaust note? Oh, and we'd still like that body-color grille.

Yes, we like the Venture, and whether you prefer the Chevy flavor or the Pontiac (Montana) and Oldsmobile (Silhouette) versions of the same van, we think any of the three finally have the credentials to go toe-to-toe with Chrysler, Ford and import minivans.

Safety Data

Side Airbag: *Standard*
4-Wheel ABS: *Standard*
Driver Crash Test Grade: *Good*
Side Impact Crash Test Front: *Excellent*
Crash Offset: *Poor*
Integrated Child Seat(s): *Optional*
Traction Control: *Optional (LS); Standard (LT)*
Passenger Crash Test Grade: *Average*
Side Impact Crash Test Rear: *Excellent*

Standard Equipment

BASE 3-DOOR (4A): 3.4L V6 OHV SMPI 12-valve engine; 4-speed electronic overdrive automatic transmission with lock-up; 600-amp battery with run down protection; 105-amp alternator; front wheel drive, 3.29 axle ratio; stainless steel exhaust; comfort ride suspension, front independent strut suspension with anti-roll bar, front coil springs, rear non-independent suspension with anti-roll bar, rear coil springs; power rack-and-pinion steering with vehicle speed-sensing assist; front disc/rear drum brakes with 4 wheel antilock braking system; 20 gal capacity fuel tank; 3 doors with sliding right rear passenger door, liftback rear cargo door; front and rear body-colored bumpers with front black rub strip and rear step; black bodyside molding; monotone paint; aero-composite halogen fully automatic headlamps with daytime running lights, delay-off feature; additional exterior lights include center high mounted stop light, underhood light; driver's and passenger's power remote black heated folding outside mirrors; front and rear 15" x 6" steel wheels; P215/70SR15 BSW AS front and rear tires; underbody mounted compact steel spare wheel; air conditioning, air filter; AM/FM stereo with clock, seek-scan, 4 speakers, and window grid antenna; power door locks, child safety rear door locks, remote hatch/trunk release; 3 power accessory outlets; instrumentation display includes oil pressure gauge, water temp gauge, volt gauge, trip odometer; warning indicators include oil pressure, water temp warning, battery, low oil level, low coolant, lights on, key in ignition, low fuel; dual airbags, seat mounted side airbags; ignition disable; tinted windows, vented rear windows, manual 1/4 vent windows; variable intermittent front windshield wipers, fixed interval rear wiper, rear window defroster; seating capacity of 7, front bucket seats with adjustable headrests, driver's and passenger's armrests, driver's seat includes 6-way direction control, passenger's seat includes 4-way direction control; removable 40-60 folding split-bench reclining 2nd row seat; 3rd row removable 50-50 folding split-bench reclining seat; front height adjustable seatbelts; cloth seats, cloth door trim insert, full cloth headliner, full carpet floor covering with carpeted floor mats; interior lights include dome light, front reading lights; steering wheel with tilt adjustment; vanity mirrors; day-night rearview mirror; mini overhead console with storage, locking glove box with light, front and rear cupholders, instrument panel covered bin, dashboard storage, 2 seat back storage pockets, driver's and passenger's door bins, front underseat tray; carpeted cargo floor, plastic trunk lid, cargo tie downs, cargo light; chrome grille, black side window molding, black front windshield molding, black rear window molding and black door handles.

BASE 4-DOOR (4A) (in addition to or instead of BASE 3-DOOR (4A) equipment): Four doors with sliding right and left rear passenger doors, 25 gal capacity fuel tank (extended) and cargo net.

Base Prices

Code	Description	Invoice	MSRP
1UN06	Base 3-Door (4A)	18819	20795
1UN16	Base 4-Door (4A)	19996	22095
1UM16	Base Extended 4-Door (4A)	20901	23095
Destination Charge:		580	580

Accessories

Code	Description	Invoice	MSRP
—	**Leather Seat Trim (4-Door)** *REQUIRES ZP7 and 1SD.*	748	870
1SA	**Preferred Equipment Group 1SA** *Includes vehicle with standard equipment.*	NC	NC
1SB	**Preferred Equipment Group 1SB** *Includes deep tinted glass, power windows with driver's side express down, remote keyless entry and speed control with resume speed.*	860	1000
1SC	**Preferred Equipment Group 1SC (4-Door)** *Includes deep tinted glass, power windows with driver's side express down, remote keyless entry, speed control with resume speed, LS trim package: driver's and passenger's lumbar, adjustable headrests, custom cloth seat trim, custom interior panel trim, liftgate cargo net, rear vent power window; wheels: 15" cast aluminum, ETR AM/FM stereo with cassette and seek-scan, luggage carrier, overhead roof console: electronic driver information center and dual illuminated visor vanity mirrors. REQUIRES ZP7 or ZP8.*	1720	2000
1SD	**Preferred Equipment Group 1SD (4-Door Extended)** *Includes speed control with resume speed, deep tinted glass, power windows with driver's side express down, remote keyless entry, wheels: 15" cast aluminum, luggage carrier, overhead roof console: electronic driver information center, dual illuminated visor vanity mirrors, LT Decor package: custom cloth seat trim, 7 passenger seating with 2nd row captains chairs, driver's and passenger's lumbar, adjustable headrests, liftgate cargo net, rear vent power window; ETR AM/FM stereo with cassette and CD, front and rear air conditioning, 6-way power driver's/passenger's seats with front underseat tray delete, power sliding passenger's side door, panic alarm, rear seat audio controls with jacks, security system, touring suspension group: tires: P215/70R15 touring and traction control.*	3784	4400
ABB	**7 Passenger Seating with Rear Buckets (4-Door)** *REQUIRES ZP7 and 1SC.*	241	280

CODE	DESCRIPTION	INVOICE	MSRP
ABD	7 Passenger Seating with 2nd Row Captains (4-Door) *Includes 3rd row 50/50 split-bench seating. REQUIRES ZP7. NOT AVAILABLE with 1SA or 1SB.*	241	280
AG1	6-Way Power Driver's Seat (4-Door) *NOT AVAILABLE with 1SA or 1SB.*	232	270
AJ1	Deep Tinted Glass (4-Door) *Does not include front passenger windows. NOT AVAILABLE with ACG, AB7.*	236	275
AN2	Integral Child Seat (4-Door) *REQUIRES ABB or ZP8.*	108	125
AN5	Dual Integrated Child Seats (4-Door) *REQUIRES ABB or ZP8.*	194	225
C34	Front and Rear Air Conditioning (4-Door Extended) *NOT AVAILABLE with 1SA.*	409	475
E58	Power Sliding Passenger's Side Door (3-Door) *Includes panic alarm. NOT AVAILABLE with 1SA.*	387	450
E58	Power Sliding Passenger's Side Door (4-Door) *Includes rear vent power window and panic alarm.*	430	500
FE3	Touring Suspension Group (4-Door) *Includes load leveling suspension with auxiliary air inflator and tires: P215/70R15 touring. REQUIRES P42 and 1SC.*	181	210
FE3	Touring Suspension Group (4-Door Extended) *Includes load leveling suspension with auxiliary air inflator and tires: P215/70R15 touring. REQUIRES 1SC.*	211	245
FE3	Touring Suspension Group (4-Door Regular Length) *Includes load leveling suspension with auxiliary air inflator and tires: P215/70R15 touring. REQUIRES 1SC.*	245	285
FE3	Touring Suspension Group (4-Door Extended) *Includes load leveling suspension. Does not include auxiliary air inflator and tires: P215/70R15 touring. NOT AVAILABLE with 1SA or 1SB.*	168	195
K05	Engine Block Heater	30	35
NG1	Emissions *Includes Connecticut, Washington D.C, Delaware, Massachusetts, Maryland, New Hampshire, New Jersey, New York, Pennsylvania, Rhode Island and Virginia. Automatically added to vehicles shipped to and/or sold to retailers in the applicable states.*	146	170
NW9	Traction Control (4-Door) *REQUIRES 1SC.*	168	195
P42	Tires: Self Sealing (4-Door Regular Length)	194	225
P42	Tires: Self Sealing (4-Door Extended) *NOT AVAILABLE with 1SA or 1SB.*	129	150
UA6	Security System (4-Door) *REQUIRES 1SC.*	52	60
UK6	Rear Seat Audio Controls with Jacks (4-Door) *REQUIRES 1SC.*	125	145
UL0	Radio: AM/FM Stereo with Cassette *Includes digital clock, automatic tone control, theft lock and premium front and rear coaxial speakers.*	232	270

CODE	DESCRIPTION	INVOICE	MSRP
UM6	Radio: AM/FM Stereo with Cassette (Base) *Includes digital clock.*	142	165
UN0	Radio: AM/FM Stereo with CD (4-Door) *Includes digital clock, automatic tone control, theft lock, speed compensated volume and premium front and rear coaxial speakers.*	86	100
UN0	Radio: AM/FM Stereo with CD *Includes digital clock, automatic tone control, theft lock, speed compensated volume and premium front and rear coaxial speakers. NOT AVAILABLE with 1SC.*	318	370
UN7	Radio: AM/FM Stereo with Cassette and CD *Includes seek and scan, cassette tape with auto reverse, auto-tone control, digital clock, theft lock, speed compensated volume, remote CD player and premium front and rear coaxial speakers. REQUIRES 1SC or 1SD.*	172	200
UN7	Radio: AM/FM Stereo with Cassette and CD *Includes seek and scan, cassette tape with auto reverse, auto-tone control, digital clock, theft lock, speed compensated volume, remote CD player and premium front and rear coaxial speakers. NOT AVAILABLE with 1SC or 1SD.*	404	470
V54	Luggage Carrier *REQUIRES 1SB.*	151	175
V92	Trailering Provisions (4-Door) *Includes HD engine oil cooler and transmission oil cooler. REQUIRES FE3 and 1SC or 1SD.*	129	150
XPU	Tires: P215/70R15 Touring (4-Door) *REQUIRES 1SC.*	129	150
YF5	California Emissions *Automatically added to vehicles shipped to and/or sold to retailers in California.*	146	170
ZP7	7 Passenger Seating *Includes 2nd row 60/40 split bench and 3rd row 50/50 split bench. NOT AVAILABLE with ZP8 or 1SD.*	288	335
ZP8	8 Passenger Seating (4-Door) *Includes 3 bucket seats in 2nd row and 3rd row 50/50 split bench seating. REQUIRES 1SC or 1SD.*	241	280

1999 TOWN & COUNTRY

1999 Chrysler Town & Country

What's New?

The top-of-the-line trim level is now called "Limited," and it offers more standard equipment (hence less options) than any other Chrysler minivan. Leather upgrades, steering wheel mounted stereo controls, and a center armrest in the rear bench are new this year, and the exterior features such details as 16-inch 15-spoke chrome wheels and chrome door handles.

Review

Elegance and expressiveness. Grace and grandeur. These are the words that describe Chrysler's posh rendition of the Dodge/Plymouth minivan.

Oh sure, you get the same fresh shape and interior space in a lower-priced Caravan or Voyager, the same car-like ride and handling qualities, the same practical virtues as a people and cargo hauler. What Chrysler adds to that mix is luxury, and plenty of it - and that's enough to attract a fair share of extra customers to the Chrysler end of the minivan spectrum. In fact, Chrysler has sold hundreds of thousands of these luxury vans since 1990.

In the past, Town & Country customers have had three distinct models to choose from: the LX model, an "ultimate" LXi that promises features ordinarily found only on luxury cars, and the short-wheelbase (113.3-inch) SX version. This year, the highest trim level is called "Limited." Don't let the name fool you: they'll make enough to go around.

All-wheel drive is available on the T&C. Since these minivans only have 5" of ground clearance, they aren't meant for serious off-road adventure. They do, however, give drivers the security of knowing that their traction is improved when driving on slippery surfaces. They also make piloting the extended-length minivans a little more fun by evening out the weight distribution and providing some rear-wheel motive power. Chrysler's AWD minivans also include standard rear disc brakes rather than drums.

All Chrysler minivans feature seven-passenger seating, with an "Easy-Out" rollaway back seat. A recently revised 3.8-liter V-6 offers 180 horsepower and 227 foot-pounds of torque. This engine is standard in the Limited, and optional in its mates, which otherwise come with a 3.3-liter engine. Both engines drive a four-speed automatic transmission, which delivers neat and smooth gearchanges. Minivanners who do lots of highway cruising and Interstate hopping might be happier with the bigger engine, which lets the T&C pass and merge into traffic with greater confidence and briskness.

Extras in the new Limited edition include dual zone control heat/air conditioning, eight-way leather trimmed driver and passenger seats, plus a memory for both the seats and outside mirrors. A body-colored roof rack is standard on the Limited, and optional on the others. If you want luxury and spaciousness, but you just can't abide the thought of a boxy Volvo wagon or lethargic Audi A6, drop by your local Chrysler store and try the Town & Country on for size.

Safety Data

Side Airbag: *Not Available*
4-Wheel ABS: *Standard*
Driver Crash Test Grade: *Average*
Side Impact Crash Test Front: *Excellent*
Crash Offset: *Poor*
Integrated Child Seat(s): *Optional*
Traction Control: *Opt. (LX/SX); Std. (Limited)*
Passenger Crash Test Grade: *Average*
Side Impact Crash Test Rear: *Average*

Standard Equipment

SX FWD (4A): 3.3L V6 OHV SMPI 12-valve engine, flexible fuel capable; 4-speed electronic overdrive automatic transmission with lock-up; 500-amp battery; 120-amp HD alternator; front wheel drive, 3.61 axle ratio; stainless steel exhaust; front independent strut suspension with anti-roll bar, front coil springs, rear non-independent suspension with rear leaf springs; power rack-and-pinion steering; front disc/rear drum brakes with 4 wheel antilock braking system; 20 gal capacity fuel tank; rear lip spoiler; sliding left rear passenger door, sliding right rear passenger door, liftback rear cargo door; roof rack; front and rear body-colored bumpers with rear step; body-colored bodyside molding with chrome bodyside insert; monotone paint; aero-composite halogen headlamps with delay-off feature; additional exterior lights include front fog/driving lights, center high mounted stop light; driver's and passenger's power remote black folding outside mirrors; front and rear 16" x 6.5" silver alloy wheels; P215/65TR16 BSW AS front and rear tires; underbody mounted full-size temporary steel spare wheel; dual zone front air conditioning; AM/FM stereo with clock, seek-scan, cassette, CD changer pre-wiring, in-dash CD pre-wiring, 4 speakers, and fixed antenna; cruise control with steering wheel controls; power door locks, remote keyless entry, child safety rear door locks, power remote hatch/trunk release; 2 power accessory outlets, driver's foot rest; instrumentation display includes tachometer, water temp gauge, compass, exterior temp, trip computer, trip odometer; warning indicators include oil pressure, water temp, battery, lights on, key in ignition, low fuel, low washer fluid, door ajar, trunk ajar; dual airbags; panic alarm; deep tinted windows, power front windows with driver's 1-touch down, fixed rear windows, power 1/4 vent windows; variable intermittent front windshield wipers with heated wipers, variable intermittent rear wiper, rear window defroster; seating capacity of 7, front bucket seats with adjustable headrests, driver's and passenger's armrests, driver's seat includes 4-way direction control with lumbar support, passenger's seat includes 4-way direction control; removable reclining 2nd row bucket seat with adjustable headrests; removable full folding bench 3rd row seat with adjustable headrests; front and rear height adjustable seatbelts; premium cloth seats, cloth door trim insert, full cloth headliner, full carpet floor covering with carpeted floor mats, deluxe sound insulation, wood trim; interior lights include dome light with fade, front reading lights, 2 door curb lights, illuminated entry; leather-wrapped steering wheel with tilt adjustment; dual illuminated vanity mirrors, dual auxiliary visors; day-night rearview mirror; full overhead console with storage, glove box with light, front and rear cupholders, instrument panel covered bin, 1 seat back storage pocket, driver's and passenger's door bins, front underseat tray; carpeted cargo floor, plastic trunk lid, cargo light; chrome grille, black side window moldings, black front windshield molding, black rear window molding and body-colored door handles.

LX FWD (4A) (in addition to or instead of SX FWD (4A) equipment): Front and rear body-colored bumpers with chrome bumper insert; underbody mounted compact steel spare wheel.

LX AWD (4A) (in addition to or instead of LX FWD (4A) equipment): 3.8L V6 OHV SMPI 12-valve engine; 600-amp battery; full-time 4 wheel drive, 3.45 axle ratio; auto-leveling suspension and rigid rear axle suspension with rear leaf springs.

CODE	DESCRIPTION	INVOICE	MSRP

LIMITED FWD (4A) (in addition to or instead of LX FWD (4A) equipment): Traction control; auto-leveling suspension; roof rack; chrome bodyside insert, body-colored bodyside cladding; aero-composite halogen fully automatic headlamps with delay-off feature; driver's and passenger's power remote black heated folding outside mirrors; underbody mounted full-size temporary steel spare wheel; dual zone front air conditioning, rear air conditioning with separate controls, rear heater; premium AM stereo/FM stereo with clock, seek-scan, cassette, single CD, 10 premium speakers, amplifier, graphic equalizer, and fixed antenna, radio steering wheel controls; garage door opener; panic alarm, security system; heated front bucket seats; driver's seat includes 6-way power seat with lumbar support, passenger's seat includes 6-way power seat; leather seats, leatherette door trim insert; memory on driver's seat with 2 memory setting(s) includes settings for exterior mirrors; interior lights include rear reading lights; auto-dimming day-night rearview mirror and chrome door handles.

LIMITED AWD (4A) (in addition to or instead of LIMITED FWD (4A) equipment): Full-time 4 wheel drive, 3.45 axle ratio and rigid rear axle suspension with rear leaf springs.

Base Prices

CODE	DESCRIPTION	INVOICE	MSRP
NSYP52	SX FWD (4A)	24849	27385
NSYP53	LX FWD (4A)	25091	27660
NSCP53	LX AWD (4A)	27885	30835
NSYS53	Limited FWD (4A)	30463	33765
NSCS53	Limited AWD (4A)	32553	36140
Destination Charge:		580	580

Accessories

CODE	DESCRIPTION	INVOICE	MSRP
25H	Quick Order Package 25H (SX) *Includes vehicle with standard equipment. REQUIRES EGM and DGB.*	NC	NC
25R	Quick Order Package 25R (LX FWD) *Includes vehicle with standard equipment. REQUIRES EGM and DGB and (AAB or 4XN).*	NC	NC
28H	Quick Order Package 28H (SX) *Includes vehicle with standard equipment. REQUIRES EGA and DGB and NAE.*	NC	NC
28R	Quick Order Package 28R (LX FWD) *Includes vehicle with standard equipment. REQUIRES EGA and DGB and NAE and (AAB or 4XN).*	NC	NC
29H	Quick Order Package 29H (SX) *Includes vehicle with standard equipment. REQUIRES EGH and DGB.*	NC	NC
29R	Quick Order Package 29R (LX) *Includes vehicle with standard equipment. REQUIRES EGH and DGB and (AAB or 4XN).*	NC	NC
29Y	Quick Order Package 29Y (LX AWD) *Includes steering wheel mounted audio controls, LXi badging, body color lower bodyside cladding, climate group III: rear air conditioning and heater; universal garage door opener, power heated exterior mirrors, AM/FM stereo with CD, cassette, EQ, 10/200w Infinity speakers, roof rack, low back leather bucket seats, 8-way power driver's seat, driver's seat and exterior mirrors memory, security alarm, full size spare tire, seat side lockable storage compartment, window surround stripe, traction control and 16" aluminum wheels. REQUIRES EGH and DGB.*	3009	3540

CODE	DESCRIPTION	INVOICE	MSRP
29Y	Quick Order Package 29Y (LX FWD) *Includes LXi badging, climate group III: rear air conditioning and heater; steering wheel mounted audio controls, body color lower bodyside cladding, universal garage door opener, power heated exterior mirrors, AM/FM stereo with CD, cassette, EQ, 10/200w Infinity speakers, roof rack, low back leather bucket seats, 8-way power driver's seat, driver's seat and exterior mirrors memory, security alarm, full size spare tire, seat side lockable storage compartment, window surround stripe, traction control and 16" aluminum wheels. REQUIRES EGH and DGB.*	3158	3715
29Z	Quick Order Package 29Z (Limited) *Includes vehicle with standard equipment. REQUIRES EGH and DGB.*	NC	NC
4XN	Rear Air Conditioning Bypass (LX)	NC	NC
AA2	Convenience Group VI (SX/LX) *Includes headlamp off time delay, illuminated entry, keyless entry, speed sensitive power locks, power fold-away mirrors, speed control, tilt steering column, power quarter vent windows, driver's one-touch power windows and security alarm. NOT AVAILABLE with 29Y.*	204	240
AAB	Climate Group III (LX) *Includes dual zone temperature control and rear air conditioning and heater. NOT AVAILABLE with 4XN.*	383	450
AAP	Loading Group (LX FWD) *Includes full size spare tire and HD suspension. REQUIRES AGA. NOT AVAILABLE with 29Y.*	94	110
AAP	Loading Group (LX FWD) *Includes full size spare tire and HD suspension. NOT AVAILABLE with 29Y.*	153	180
AGA	Wheels/Handling Group (LX FWD) *Includes front and rear stabilizer bars, HD suspension, P215/65R16 AS touring tires and 16" aluminum wheels. REQUIRES 25R or 28R or 29R.*	434	510
AGA	Wheels/Handling Group (LX FWD) *Includes front and rear stabilizer bars, HD suspension and P215/65R16 AS touring tires. REQUIRES 29Y.*	81	95
AGA	Wheels/Handling Group (LX FWD) *Includes front and rear stabilizer bars and P215/65R16 AS touring tires. REQUIRES 29Y and AHT.*	21	25
AGA	Wheels/Handling Group (LX FWD) *Includes front and rear stabilizer bars, P215/65R16 AS touring tires and wheels: 16" aluminum. REQUIRES (25R or 28R or 29R) and AHT.*	374	440
AHT	Trailer Tow Group (LX FWD/Limted FWD) *Includes heavy-duty front disc/rear drum brakes, HD transmission oil cooler, HD suspension and trailer tow wiring harness. REQUIRES 29Y.*	208	245
AHT	Trailer Tow Group (LX FWD) *Includes heavy-duty front disc/rear drum brakes, 600-amp maintenance free battery, HD transmission oil cooler, full size spare tire, HD suspension and trailer tow wiring harness. REQUIRES 25R or 28R or 29R.*	302	355
AHT	Trailer Tow Group (LX AWD) *Includes 600-amp maintenance free battery, HD transmission oil cooler, full size spare tire and trailer tow wiring harness. REQUIRES 29R.*	242	285

CODE	DESCRIPTION	INVOICE	MSRP
AHT	Trailer Tow Group (AWD)	149	175
	Includes 600-amp maintenance free battery, HD transmission oil cooler and trailer tow wiring harness. REQUIRES 29Y.		
AWS	Smoker's Group	17	20
	Includes front and rear ash receiver and cigar lighter.		
BNM	Traction Control (SX/LX FWD)	149	175
CMA	Heated Front Seats (LX)	213	250
CYT	7 Passenger Quad Buckets with Child Seats	106	125
DGB	Transmission: 4-Speed Automatic	NC	NC
EGA	Engine: 3.3L V6 MPI (SX/LX FWD)	NC	NC
EGH	Engine: 3.8L MPI V6 (LX AWD/Limited)	NC	NC
	Includes traction control.		
EGH	Engine: 3.8L V6 MPI (SX/LX FWD)	434	510
	Manufacturer Discount	(43)	(50)
	Net Price	391	460
	Includes traction control.		
EGH	Engine: 3.8L V6 MPI with 29Y (LX FWD)	285	335
EGM	Engine: 3.3L V6 FFV (SX/LX FWD)	NC	NC
HL	Low Back Leather Bucket Seats (SX/LX)	757	890
	REQUIRES AAB.		
MWG	Roof Rack (LX)	166	195
NAE	California Emissions	NC	NC
	Automatically coded.		
NBN	Northeastern States Emissions	NC	NC
	Includes Connecticut, Delaware, Maryland, New Hampshire, New Jersey, Pennsylvania, Rhode Island, Virginia and District of Columbia. Also available in border states of these states. Not available in Massachusetts or New York.		
NHK	Engine Block Heater	30	35
PH2	Candy Apple Red Metallic Clear Coat	170	200
PWP	Golden White Pearl Tri-Coat	170	200
RAZ	Radio: AM/FM Stereo with CD, Cassette and EQ (SX/LX)	264	310
	Includes steering wheel controls and ten 200-watt Infinity speakers.		
SER	Load Leveling and Height Control (FWD)	247	290
TBB	Tire: Full Size Spare (LX)	94	110
WNW	Wheels: 16" Aluminum (LX)	353	415
YCF	Border State Emissions (California)	NC	NC

1999 CARAVAN

1999 Dodge Caravan

What's New?

A revised front fascia is common to all models.

Review

If there is a perfect family vehicle in existence, it is one of Chrysler's minivans. What's the data say? The average American has two kids and spends a little more than $20,000 on a new car or truck. The Dodge Caravan/Grand Caravan fits into this scenario better than Velveeta in a grilled cheese sandwich.

The Caravan rides on a 113.3-inch wheelbase, and the Grand Caravan adds six inches to that and 13 extra inches of overall length. That extra length is noticed in the Grand Caravan's rear seat legroom, which allows rear passengers to stretch out their legs an extra three and four inches (second row and third row, respectively). The vehicles are identical in width and height, but the longer-wheelbase Grand Caravan offers more cargo room at 147.7 cubic feet, compared to the Caravan's 126.7 cubic feet. The big Grand Caravan also offers standard seven-passenger seating, but the third row is optional on the Caravan.

The Caravan line offers several thoughtful details; the most important are the easy-out rolling seats and the innovative driver-side sliding door—a first in the minivan class (that has since been copied by everyone else). Easy-out seats are a snap to release and remove, though lifting the seat from the rear of the van still requires two sets of biceps. Optional on the base Caravan and standard on everything else, the driver's side sliding door offers the convenience of loading kids and cargo from either side of the Caravan.

A 150-horsepower 16-valve dual-cam four (coupled with a three-speed automatic) serves as the base engine of the Caravan, but these sizeable vans benefit from a little extra oomph. The 3.0-liter V6, borrowed from Mitsubishi Motors, is standard on the Grand Caravan, and offers the same horsepower as the 2.4-liter but with an extra nine foot-pounds of torque. A 3.3-liter V6, standard on SE and LE trim, is a step in the right direction, but our favorite motor is the 3.8-liter unit, which outputs 180 horsepower and 227 foot-pounds of torque. The 3.8-liter engine (standard on AWD versions of the Grand Caravan and the Grand Caravan ES model, optional on the Caravan and Grand Caravan LE), comes with a four-speed automatic transmission which provides shifts that are neat and smooth.

Light steering response gives these minivans an undeniably car-like feel, with an exceptionally smooth ride. Highly maneuverable and easy to control, the minivan delivers just a hint that you could exceed its capabilities, as when rounding a sharp curve. The Sport package features specially tuned shocks and springs.

The Dodge brand of Chrysler minivans offers affordable transportation in just about any conceivable configuration. Buyers can choose from two different sizes, five usable doors, four engine choices, three rows of seats, two distinct suspensions, all-wheel drive capability, and a partridge in a pear tree. So mix and match to your own specific needs.

Safety Data

Side Airbag: *Not Available*
4-Wheel ABS: *Optional (Base); Standard (LE/SE)*
Driver Crash Test Grade: *Average*
Side Impact Crash Test Front: *Excellent*
Crash Offset: *Poor*
Integrated Child Seat(s): *Optional*
Traction Control: *Opt. (LE); N/A (Base/SE)*
Passenger Crash Test Grade: *Average*
Side Impact Crash Test Rear: *Average*

Standard Equipment

CARAVAN BASE [3A]: 2.4L DOHC 16-valve four cylinder engine, 3-speed automatic transmission, 3.19 axle ratio, front wheel drive, power rack and pinion steering, power front disc/rear drum brakes, strut-type front suspension with gas-charged shocks, coil springs, assymetrical lower control arms and link-type stabilizer bar; single-leaf spring rear suspension with tubular beam axle, track bar and gas-charged shocks; 14" steel wheels with full wheel covers, P205/75R14 AS BSW tires, compact spare tire, tinted glass, bodyside molding, variable intermittent windshield wipers, rear window wiper/ washer, dual manual exterior mirrors, dual front airbags, 5-passenger seating, AM/FM stereo with digital clock and 4 speakers, gauges include fuel, coolant temp., trip odometer; warning indicators include low fuel, low washer fluid, check engine, liftgate ajar, door ajar, low voltage, seat belt unfastened; message center warnings for airbags, ABS, engine temp., oil pressure; chimes for headlights-on, key-in-ignition; dashboard storage bin, rear seatback grocery bag hooks, full carpeting, front and rear dome lighting, cargo light, courtesy lights, map lights, liftgate flood lighting, dual front and rear accessory power outlets, visor mirrors.

CARAVAN SE [4A] (in addition to or instead of CARAVAN BASE [3A] equipment): 3.3L V6 engine, 4-speed automatic transmission, four-wheel antilock brakes, 3.62 axle ratio, 15" steel wheels with full wheel covers, P215/65R15 AS BSW tires, wide bodyside molding, left side sliding door, dual power exterior mirrors, 7-passenger seating, air conditioning, rear window defroster, windshield wiper de-icer, tachometer, tilt steering wheel, cruise control, AM/FM stereo with cassette player and 4 speakers, rear floor silencer, front seat cargo net, underseat locking storage bin.

CARAVAN LE [4A] (in addition to or instead of CARAVAN SE [4A] equipment): Bodyside paint stripe, lower body cladding, deep tinted glass, remote keyless entry, illuminated entry, headlights-off delay, low-back front bucket seats, power driver's seat with 8-way adjustment and manual lumbar, premium cloth upholstery, covered console storage, overhead console with trip computer, dual-zone climate control, power door locks, power windows, power quarter vent windows, AM/FM stereo with cassette, CD changer controls, Infinity sound system; floor mats, deluxe sound insulation, illuminated visor vanity mirrors, door courtesy lights, reading lights, illuminated ignition ring, glovebox light, ashtray light.

Base Prices

Code	Description	Invoice	MSRP
NSKL52	Base [3A]	16374	18005
NSKH52	SE [4A]	19784	21880
NSKP52	LE [4A]	23146	25700
Destination Charge:		580	580

CODE	DESCRIPTION	INVOICE	MSRP

Accessories

CODE	DESCRIPTION	INVOICE	MSRP
***	Paint: Candy Apple Red (SE/LE)	170	200
	*REQUIRES 2*E or 2*N on SE models.*		
2*B	SE Quick Order Package 2*B (SE)	NC	NC
	Includes vehicle with standard equipment.		
2*D	SE Quick Order Package 2*D (SE)	854	1005
	Manufacturer Discount	(255)	(300)
	Net Price	599	705
	Includes power door locks, power windows, power quarter vent windows, floor mats, illuminated visor vanity mirrors, deluxe insulation, light group (ashtray light, glovebox light, illuminated ignition ring, storage bin light).		
2*E	SE Sport Quick Order Package 2*E (SE)	1879	2210
	Manufacturer Discount	(489)	(575)
	Net Price	1390	1635
	Includes power door locks, power windows, power quarter vent windows, floor mats, illuminated visor vanity mirrors, deluxe insulation, light group (ashtray light, glovebox light, illuminated ignition ring, storage bin light), 16" steel wheels with full wheel covers, P215/65R16 AS touring tires, rear fascia scuff pad, heavy-duty suspension, fog lights, body color moldings, rear spoiler, deep tinted glass, leather-wrapped steering wheel.		
2*K	LE Quick Order Package 2*K (LE)	NC	NC
	Includes vehicle with standard equipment.		
2*N	SE Sport Quick Order Package 2*N (SE)	3086	3630
	Manufacturer Discount	(574)	(675)
	Net Price	2512	2955
	Includes power door locks, power windows, power quarter vent windows, floor mats, illuminated visor vanity mirrors, deluxe insulation, light group (ashtray light, glovebox light, illuminated ignition ring, storage bin light), 16" steel wheels with full wheel covers, P215/65R16 AS touring tires, rear fascia scuff pad, heavy-duty suspension, fog lights, body color moldings, rear spoiler, deep tinted glass, leather-wrapped steering wheel, overhead console with trip computer, readling lights, power driver's seat with 8-way adjustment and manual lumbar, quad bucket seating with premium cloth upholstery.		
2*S	Base Quick Order Package 2*S (Base)	NC	NC
	Includes vehicle with standard equipment. REQUIRES EDZ.		
2*T	Base Quick Order Package 2*T (Base)	1084	1275
	Manufacturer Discount	(646)	(760)
	Net Price	438	515
	Includes air conditioning, front seat cargo net, rear floor silencer, 7-passenger seating, undeseat locking storage.		
4XA	Air Conditioning Bypass (Base)	NC	NC
	*REQUIRES 2*S.*		
AAA	Climate Group 2 (SE)	383	450
	*Includes front air conditioning and deep tinted glass. NOT AVAILABLE with 2*E or 2*N.*		

CODE	DESCRIPTION	INVOICE	MSRP
AAA	Climate Group 2 (Base) *Includes air conditioning and deep tinted glass. REQUIRES 2*T.*	383	450
AAC	Convenience Group 1 (Base) *Includes power exterior mirrors, tilt steering wheel, cruise control. REQUIRES 2*T.*	370	435
AAE	Convenience Group 2 (SE) *Includes power exterior mirrors, tilt steering wheel, cruise control, power door locks. REQUIRES 2*B.*	268	315
AAE	Convenience Group 2 (Base) *Includes power exterior mirrors, tilt steering wheel, cruise control, power door locks. REQUIRES 2*T.*	638	750
AAF	Convenience Group 3 (Base) *Includes power exterior mirrors, tilt steering wheel, cruise control, power door locks, power windows, power quarter vent windows.*	952	1120
AAF	Convenience Group 3 (SE) *Includes power exterior mirrors, tilt steering wheel, cruise control, power door locks, power windows, power quarter vent windows.*	582	685
AAG	Convenience Group 4 (SE) *Includes remote keyless entry, illuminated entry and headlight-off delay. NOT AVAILABLE with 2*B.*	204	240
AAH	Convenience Group 5 (SE) *Includes remote keyless entry, illuminated entry, headlight-off delay, security alarm. NOT AVAILABLE with 2*B.*	332	390
AAH	Convenience Group 5 (LE) *Includes remote keyless entry, illuminated entry, headlight-off delay, security alarm.*	128	150
AAP	Loading & Towing Group 2 (LE) *Includes heavy-duty suspension and fullsize spare.*	153	180
AAP	Loading & Towing Group 2 (SE) *Includes heavy-duty suspension and fullsize spare. REQUIRES 2*B or 2*D.*	153	180
AHT	Trailer Tow Group (LE) *Includes 125-amp alternator, 600-amp battery, heavy-duty brakes, heavy-duty transmission oil cooler, heavy-duty suspension, trailer wiring harness, fullsize spare.*	357	420
AWS	Smoker's Group *Includes cigar lighter and three ashtrays.*	17	20
BGF	Antilock Brakes (Base)	480	565
BNM	Traction Control (LE) *NOT AVAILABLE with EGH.*	149	175
CLE	Floor Mats (SE) *REQUIRES 2*B.*	77	90
CYE	Seating: 7-Passenger (Base) *REQUIRES 2*S.*	319	375
CYK	Seating: 7-Passenger with Integrated Child Seats (Base)	200	235
CYR	Seating: 7-Passenger with Integrated Child Seats (SE) *NOT AVAILABLE with 2*N.*	191	225
CYS	Seating: 7-Passenger Quad Command Group (SE/LE) *Includes premium cloth upholstery. NOT AVAILABLE with 2*B or 2*N on SE models.*	570	670
CYT	Seating: 7-Pass. Quad Command Grp. w/Integrated Child Safety Seats (LE) *Includes premium cloth upholstery.*	676	795

CODE	DESCRIPTION	INVOICE	MSRP
CYT	Seating: 7-Pass. Quad Command Group with Integrated Child Seats (SE) *Includes premium cloth upholstery. REQUIRES 2*N.*	106	125
CYT	Seating: 7-Pass. Quad Command Group with Integrated Child Seats (SE) *Includes premium cloth upholstery. NOT AVAILABLE with 2*B or 2*N.*	676	795
DGA	Transmission: 3-Speed Automatic (Base) *REQUIRES EDZ.*	NC	NC
DGB	Transmission: 4-Speed Automatic (SE/LE)	NC	NC
DGB	Transmission: 4-Speed Automatic (Base) *NOT AVAILABLE with EDZ.*	170	200
EDZ	Engine: 2.4L DOHC I4 (Base) *REQUIRES 2*S and DGA.*	NC	NC
EDZ	Engine: 2.4L DOHC I4 (Base) *REQUIRES 2*T and DGA.*	(438)	(515)
EFA	Engine: 3.0L V6 (Base) *NOT AVAILABLE with NAE.*	655	770
EGA	Engine: 3.3L V6 (Base) *REQUIRES 2*T and NAE.*	825	970
EGA	Engine: 3.3L V6 (SE/LE) *REQUIRES NAE.*	NC	NC
EGH	Engine: 3.8L V6 (LE)	434	510
	Manufacturer Discount	(43)	(50)
	Net Price *Includes traction control.*	391	460
EGH	Engine: 3.8L V6 (SE) *REQUIRES 2*N.*	285	335
EGM	Engine: 3.3L FFV V6 (Base) *REQUIRES 2*T. NOT AVAILABLE with NAE.*	825	970
EGM	Engine: 3.3L FFV V6 (SE/LE) *NOT AVAILABLE with NAE.*	NC	NC
GFA	Rear Window Defroster (Base) *Includes windshield wiper de-icer. NOT AVAILABLE with AAA, AAC, AAE.*	166	195
GFA	Rear Window Defroster (Base) *Includes windshield wiper de-icer. REQUIRES 2*T and (AAA or AAC or AAE).*	196	230
GKD	Left Side Sliding Door (Base) *REQUIRES 2*T.*	506	595
HAA	Climate Group 1 (Base) *Includes air conditioning. REQUIRES 2*S.*	731	860
HL*	Leather Seats (LE) *REQUIRES CYS and AAB.*	757	890
MDA	Front License Plate Bracket	NC	NC
MWG	Luggage Rack (Base/SE/LE) *Painted black.*	166	195
NAE	Emissions: California	NC	NC
NBN	Emissions: Northeast States	NC	NC
NHK	Engine Block Heater	30	35
PH2	Candy Apple Red Metallic Clear Coat *NOT AVAILABLE with 25B, 25D, 28B, 28D, 26B.*	170	200

CODE	DESCRIPTION	INVOICE	MSRP
RAS	Radio: AM/FM with Cassette (Base) *REQUIRES 2*T.*	153	180
RAZ	Radio: AM/FM with Cassette and CD (SE) *Includes equalizer.*	276	325
RAZ	Radio: AM/FM with Cassette and CD (LE) *Includes equalizer.*	264	310
RBR	Radio: AM/FM with CD (Base) *REQUIRES 2*T.*	276	325
RCE	Radio: Infinity Sound System (SE) *Includes 10 Infinity loudspeakers and 200-watt amplifier. REQUIRES RAZ. NOT AVAILABLE with 2*B.*	336	395
SER	Load Leveling Suspension (LE)	247	290
TBB	Tire: Full Size Spare *NOT AVAILABLE with 2*S, AWA, AAP, AHT.*	94	110
WJB	Aluminum Wheels (SE) *15-inch wheels.*	353	415
WNG	Aluminum Wheels (SE) *16-inch wheels. REQUIRES 2*E or 2*N.*	225	265
WNG	Aluminum Wheels (LE) *16-inch wheels.*	353	415
YCF	Emissions: Border States	NC	NC

1999 DAKOTA

1999 Dodge Dakota

What's New?

Solar Yellow paint is now available for those who want their pickups to get noticed. Other un-pickup-like refinements include an express down feature for the driver's window, extra storage space for cassettes or CDs, and remote radio controls on the steering wheel.

Review

The Dakota was completely redesigned inside and out in 1997, and since then changes have been kept to a minimum. That's because Dodge got it right the first time. The Dakota is an exceptional truck on and off the road. The steering is communicative, the brake pedal provides excellent feel and feedback, the ride is surprisingly quiet, the cab is roomy, and the Dakota is altogether a very likeable truck.

An R/T edition is available for anyone who prefers the ride height of a truck to the natural handling of a sports car. The R/T gets the 5.9-liter Magnum V8 with 250 horsepower and 335 foot-pounds of torque, sport bucket seats, a sport-tuned suspension, attractive wheels, and various R/T decals. Though it's a blast to drive, who really needs to haul things fast?

Inside the Dakota, user- friendly controls and displays pass the same work-glove ease-of-operation test that the bigger Dodge Ram does. Seats are king-of-the-road high, and extremely comfortable. Club Cab models will carry up to six people, but the rear seat is an extremely tight squeeze, meant for smaller folks.

The Club Cab offers no third door option. Seems odd from the company that pioneered the fourth sliding door on minivans and has a Quad Cab full-size Ram pickup. To get this convenience, you've got to buy a different truck. Dodge had the chance to build the perfect compact pickup, but we'll have to wait until the 2000 Quad Cab arrives to see if they've succeeded.

Still, the Dakota is a nice piece of work. Base, Sport, SLT and R/T models are available. Regular cab 2WD models feature a 2.5-liter inline four-cylinder engine that provides 120 horsepower. Club Cab and 4WD models get a 3.9-liter V6 good for 175 horsepower and 225 foot-pounds of torque. Optional on all models (except R/T) is a 5.2-liter V8 engine that makes 230 horsepower and 300 foot-pounds of torque at 3,200 rpm and sucks gas like it's going out of style. Crammed into a regular cab shortbed with 2WD, the V8 transforms the Dakota into a storming sport truck.

Overall, the Dakota is quite a nice package. Want the best-looking, best-performing compact pickup on the market? Look no further.

Safety Data

Side Airbag: *Not Available*
4-Wheel ABS: *Optional*
Driver Crash Test Grade: *Good*
Side Impact Crash Test Front: *Excellent*
Crash Offset: *Poor*
Integrated Child Seat(s): *Not Available*
Traction Control: *Not Available*
Passenger Crash Test Grade: *Good*
Side Impact Crash Test Rear: *Not Available*

Standard Equipment

REGULAR CAB 2WD (5M): 2.5L I4 OHV SMPI 8-valve engine; 5-speed overdrive manual transmission; 600-amp battery; 117-amp alternator; rear wheel drive, 3.55 axle ratio; stainless steel exhaust; HD ride suspension, front independent suspension with anti-roll bar, front coil springs, HD front shocks, rigid rear axle suspension with leaf springs, HD rear shocks; power rack-and-pinion steering; front disc/rear drum brakes with rear wheel antilock braking system; 15 gal capacity fuel tank; regular pickup box; front and rear argent bumpers with black rub strip, rear step bumper; monotone paint; aero-composite halogen headlamps; additional exterior lights include center high mounted stop light; driver's and passenger's manual black outside mirrors; front and rear 15" x 7" silver styled steel wheels; P215/75SR15 BSW AS front and rear tires; underbody mounted full-size conventional steel spare wheel; AM/FM stereo with clock, seek-scan, cassette, 4 speakers, and fixed antenna; 1 power accessory outlet; instrumentation display includes tachometer, oil pressure gauge, water temp gauge, volt gauge, trip odometer; warning indicators include battery, lights on, key in ignition, low fuel, low washer fluid; driver's side airbag, passenger's side cancelable airbag; tinted windows; variable intermittent front windshield wipers; seating capacity of 3, bench front seat with fixed headrests, driver's seat includes 2-way direction control, passenger's seat includes 2-way direction control; front height adjustable seatbelts; vinyl seats, full cloth headliner, full vinyl floor covering, cabback insulator; interior lights include dome light; sport steering wheel; passenger side vanity mirror; day-night rearview mirror; glove box, front cupholder; vinyl cargo floor; black grille, black side window moldings, black front windshield molding, black rear window molding and black door handles.

CLUB CAB 2WD (5M) (in addition to or instead of REGULAR CAB 2WD (5M) equipment): 3.9 axle ratio; deep tinted windows, vented rear windows; seating capacity of 6, 40-20-40 split-bench front seat with fixed headrests, center armrest with storage, driver's seat includes 4-way direction control with lumbar support, passenger's seat includes 4-way direction control; full folding rear split-bench seat; premium cloth seats, full carpet floor covering, and carpeted cargo floor.

REGULAR CAB 4WD (5M) (in addition to or instead of REGULAR CAB 2WD (5M) equipment): 3.9L V6 OHV SMPI 12-valve engine; part-time 4 wheel drive, auto locking hub control and manual shift, 3.55 axle ratio; front torsion springs, front torsion bar and power re-circulating ball steering.

CLUB CAB 4WD (5M) (in addition to or instead of CLUB CAB 2WD (5M) equipment): 3.9L V6 OHV SMPI 12-valve engine; part-time 4 wheel drive, auto locking hub control and manual shift, 3.55 axle ratio; front torsion springs, front torsion bar and power re-circulating ball steering.

Base Prices

Code	Description	Invoice	MSRP
AN1L61	Regular Cab 2WD SB (5M)	12167	13360
AN1L62	Regular Cab 2WD LB (5M)	12572	13820
AN5L61	Regular Cab 4WD SB (5M)	15254	16840
AN1L31	Club Cab 2WD SB (5M)	15003	16555
AN5L31	Club Cab 4WD SB (5M)	17863	19765
Destination Charge:		510	510

Accessories

Code	Description	Invoice	MSRP
21B	Quick Order Package 21B (Club Cab 2WD)	880	1035
	Manufacturer Discount	(880)	(1035)
	Net Price	NC	NC
	Includes cloth door trim panel with map pocket, 22 gallon fuel tank, Sport Appearance Group: sport badging on door, front and rear body color fascias, body color grille and wheels: 15" x 7" 5-spoke aluminum; and tires: P215/75R15 RWL AS. REQUIRES 4XA and EPE and DDK.		
21B	Quick Order Package 21B (Regular Cab 2WD)	1390	1635
	Manufacturer Discount	(553)	(650)
	Net Price	837	985
	Includes front seat area carpet, cloth door trim panel with map pocket, 40/20/40 cloth split bench seat, Sport Appearance Group: sport badging on door, front and rear body color fascias, body color grille and wheels: 15" x 7" 5-spoke aluminum; tires: P215/75R15 RWL AS and 3.55 axle ratio. REQUIRES 4XA and EPE and DDK.		
21W	Quick Order Package 21W (Regular Cab 2WD)	NC	NC
	Includes vehicle with standard equipment. REQUIRES 4XA and EPE and DDK.		
23B	Quick Order Package 23B (Regular Cab 4WD)	1543	1815
	Manufacturer Discount	(553)	(650)
	Net Price	990	1165
	Includes front seat area carpet, cloth door trim panel with map pocket, cloth 40/20/40 split bench seat, Sport Appearance Group: sport badging on door, front and rear		

CODE	DESCRIPTION	INVOICE	MSRP
	body color fascias, body color grille and wheels: 15" x 7" 5-spoke aluminum; tires: P235/75R15 AS OWL and 3.55 axle ratio. REQUIRES 4XA and EHC and DDQ.		
23B	**Quick Order Package 23B (Regular Cab 2WD)**	1390	1635
	Manufacturer Discount	(553)	(650)
	Net Price	837	985
	Includes front seat area carpet, cloth door trim panel with map pocket, 40/20/40 cloth split bench seat, Sport Appearance Group: sport badging on door, front and rear body color fascias, body color grille and wheels: 15" x 7" 5-spoke aluminum; tires: P215/75R15 RWL AS and 3.21 axle ratio. REQUIRES 4XA and EHC and DDQ.		
23B	**Quick Order Package 23B (Club Cab 4WD)**	1020	1200
	Manufacturer Discount	(1020)	(1200)
	Net Price	NC	NC
	Includes cloth door trim panel with map pocket, 22 gallon fuel tank, Sport Appearance Group: sport badging on door, front and rear body color fascias, body color grille and wheels: 15" x 7" 5-spoke aluminum; tires: P235/75R15 AS OWL and 3.55 axle ratio. REQUIRES 4XA and EHC and DDQ.		
23B	**Quick Order Package 23B (Club Cab 2WD)**	880	1035
	Manufacturer Discount	(880)	(1035)
	Net Price	NC	NC
	Includes cloth door trim panel with map pocket, 22 gallon fuel tank, Sport Appearance Group: sport badging on door, front and rear body color fascias, body color grille and wheels: 15" x 7" 5-spoke aluminum; tires: P215/75R15 RWL AS, 3.21 axle ratio and payload: 1450 lbs. REQUIRES 4XA and EHC and DDQ.		
23G	**Quick Order Package 23G (Regular Cab 2WD)**	2627	3090
	Manufacturer Discount	(638)	(750)
	Net Price	1989	2340
	Includes air conditioning, front seat area carpet, deluxe convenience group: speed control, tilt steering column; cloth door trim panel with map pocket, front floor mats, 22 gallon fuel tank, light group: cargo lamp, glove box lamp, underhood lamp, auxiliary 12v power outlet, mini overhead console, SLT Decor Group: liftgate and door badging, front bright bumper, bright grille, bright rear bumper with step pads, wheels: 15" x 7" 5-spoke aluminum; cloth 40/20/40 split bench seat, tires: P215/75R15 RWL AS and 3.21 axle ratio. REQUIRES EHC and DDQ.		
23G	**Quick Order Package 23G (Club Cab 2WD)**	2036	2395
	Manufacturer Discount	(1105)	(1300)
	Net Price	931	1095
	Includes air conditioning, cloth door trim panel with map pocket, front floor mats, 22 gallon fuel tank, light group: cargo lamp, glove box lamp, underhood lamp, auxiliary 12v power outlet, mini overhead console; SLT Decor Group: liftgate and door badging, front bright bumper, bright grille, bright rear bumper with step pads, wheels: 15" x 7" 5-spoke aluminum; tilt steering column, tires: P215/75R15 RWL AS, warning lamp shift indicator, 3.21 axle ratio and payload: 1450 lbs. REQUIRES EHC and DDQ.		

CODE	DESCRIPTION	INVOICE	MSRP
23G	Quick Order Package 23G (Club Cab 4WD)	2189	2575
	Manufacturer Discount	(1105)	(1300)
	Net Price	1084	1275
	Includes deluxe convenience group: speed control, tilt steering column; cloth door trim panel with map pocket, front floor mats, 22 gallon fuel tank, light group: cargo lamp, glove box lamp, underhood lamp, auxiliary 12v power outlet, mini overhead console, SLT Decor Group: liftgate and door badging, front bright bumper, bright grille, bright rear bumper with step pads, wheels: 15" x 7" 5-spoke aluminum; tilt steering column, tires: P235/75R15 AS OWL and 3.55 axle ratio. REQUIRES EHC and DDQ.		
23G	Quick Order Package 23G (Regular Cab 4WD)	2780	3270
	Manufacturer Discount	(638)	(750)
	Net Price	2142	2520
	Includes air conditioning, front seat area carpet, deluxe convenience group: speed control, tilt steering column; cloth door trim panel with map pocket, front floor mats, 22 gallon fuel tank, light group: cargo lamp, glove box lamp, underhood lamp, auxiliary 12v power outlet, mini overhead console, SLT Decor Group: liftgate and door badging, front bright bumper, bright grille, bright rear bumper with step pads, wheels: 15" x 7" 5-spoke aluminum; cloth 40/20/40 split bench seat, tires: P235/75R15 AS OWL and 3.55 axle ratio. REQUIRES EHC and DDQ.		
23W	Quick Order Package 23W (Regular Cab 2WD)	NC	NC
	Includes vehicle with standard equipment. REQUIRES (4XA and EHC and DDQ).		
24B	Quick Order Package 24B (Regular Cab 4WD)	1543	1815
	Manufacturer Discount	(553)	(650)
	Net Price	990	1165
	Includes front seat area carpet, cloth door trim panel with map pocket, cloth 40/20/40 split bench seat, Sport Appearance Group: sport badging on door, front and rear body color fascias, body color grille and wheels: 15" x 7" 5-spoke aluminum; tires: P235/75R15 AS OWL and 3.92 axle ratio. REQUIRES 4XA and EHC and DGB.		
24B	Quick Order Package 24B (Club Cab 2WD)	880	1035
	Manufacturer Discount	(880)	(1035)
	Net Price	NC	NC
	Includes cloth door trim panel with map pocket, 22 gallon fuel tank, Sport Appearance Group: sport badging on door, front and rear body color fascias, body color grille and wheels: 15" x 7" 5-spoke aluminum; tires: P215/75R15 RWL AS, 3.55 axle ratio and payload: 1450 lbs. REQUIRES 4XA and EHC and DGB.		
24B	Quick Order Package 24B (Club Cab 4WD)	1020	1200
	Manufacturer Discount	(1020)	(1200)
	Net Price	NC	NC
	Includes cloth door trim panel with map pocket, 22 gallon fuel tank, Sport Appearance Group: sport badging on door, front and rear body color fascias, body color grille and wheels: 15" x 7" 5-spoke aluminum and tires: P235/75R15 AS OWL. REQUIRES 4XA and EHC and DGB.		

CODE	DESCRIPTION	INVOICE	MSRP
24B	**Quick Order Package 24B (Regular Cab 2WD)**	1390	1635
	Manufacturer Discount	(553)	(650)
	Net Price	837	985
	Includes front seat area carpet, cloth door trim panel with map pocket, 40/20/40 cloth split bench seat, Sport Appearance Group: sport badging on door, front and rear body color fascias, body color grille and wheels: 15" x 7" 5-spoke aluminum; tires: P215/75R15 RWL AS and 3.55 axle ratio. REQUIRES 4XA and EHC and DGB.		
24G	**Quick Order Package 24G (Club Cab 2WD)**	2036	2395
	Manufacturer Discount	(935)	(1100)
	Net Price	1101	1295
	Includes air conditioning, cloth door trim panel with map pocket, front floor mats, 22 gallon fuel tank, light group: cargo lamp, glove box lamp, underhood lamp, auxiliary 12v power outlet, mini overhead console; SLT Decor Group: liftgate and door badging, front bright bumper, bright grille, bright rear bumper with step pads, wheels: 15" x 7" 5-spoke aluminum; tilt steering column, tires: P215/75R15 RWL AS, warning lamp shift indicator, payload: 1450 lbs and 3.55 axle ratio. REQUIRES EHC and DGB.		
24G	**Quick Order Package 24G (Regular Cab 4WD)**	2780	3270
	Manufacturer Discount	(638)	(750)
	Net Price	2142	2520
	Includes air conditioning, front seat area carpet, deluxe convenience group: speed control, tilt steering column; cloth door trim panel with map pocket, front floor mats, 22 gallon fuel tank, light group: cargo lamp, glove box lamp, underhood lamp, auxiliary 12v power outlet, mini overhead console; SLT Decor Group: liftgate and door badging, front bright bumper, bright grille, bright rear bumper with step pads, wheels: 15" x 7" 5-spoke aluminum; cloth 40/20/40 split bench seat, and tires: P235/75R15 AS OWL. REQUIRES EHC and DGB.		
24G	**Quick Order Package 24G (Regular Cab 2WD)**	2627	3090
	Manufacturer Discount	(638)	(750)
	Net Price	1989	2340
	Includes air conditioning, front seat area carpet, deluxe convenience group: speed control, tilt steering column; cloth door trim panel with map pocket, front floor mats, 22 gallon fuel tank, light group: cargo lamp, glove box lamp, underhood lamp, auxiliary 12v power outlet, mini overhead console; SLT Decor Group: liftgate and door badging, front bright bumper, bright grille, bright rear bumper with step pads, wheels: 15" x 7" 5-spoke aluminum; 40/20/40 cloth split bench seat, tires: P215/75R15 RWL AS and 3.55 axle ratio. REQUIRES EHC and DGB.		
24G	**Quick Order Package 24G (Club Cab 4WD)**	2189	2575
	Manufacturer Discount	(1105)	(1300)
	Net Price	1084	1275
	Includes deluxe convenience group: speed control, tilt steering column; cloth door trim panel with map pocket, front floor mats, 22 gallon fuel tank, light group: cargo lamp, glove box lamp, underhood lamp, auxiliary 12v power outlet, mini overhead console; SLT Decor Group: liftgate and door badging, front bright bumper, bright grille, bright rear bumper with step pads, wheels: 15" x 7" 5-spoke aluminum; tires: P235/75R15 AS OWL and 3.92 axle ratio. REQUIRES EHC and DGB.		

CODE	DESCRIPTION	INVOICE	MSRP
24W	**Quick Order Package 24W (Regular Cab 2WD)**	NC	NC
	Includes vehicle with standard equipment. REQUIRES 4XA and EHC and DGB.		
25B	**Quick Order Package 25B (Regular Cab 4WD)**	1543	1815
	Manufacturer Discount	(553)	(650)
	Net Price	990	1165
	Includes front seat area carpet, cloth door trim panel with map pocket, cloth 40/20/40 split bench seat, Sport Appearance Group: sport badging on door, front and rear body color fascias, body color grille and wheels: 15" x 7" 5-spoke aluminum; tires: P235/75R15 AS OWL and 3.55 axle ratio. REQUIRES 4XA and ELF and DDC.		
25B	**Quick Order Package 25B (Club Cab 2WD)**	880	1035
	Manufacturer Discount	(880)	(1035)
	Net Price	NC	NC
	Includes cloth door trim panel with map pocket, 22 gallon fuel tank, Sport Appearance Group: sport badging on door, front and rear body color fascias, body color grille and wheels: 15" x 7" 5-spoke aluminum; tires: P215/75R15 RWL AS, 3.55 axle ratio and payload: 1450 lbs. REQUIRES 4XA and ELF and DDC.		
25B	**Quick Order Package 25B (Club Cab 4WD)**	1020	1200
	Manufacturer Discount	(1020)	(1200)
	Net Price	NC	NC
	Includes cloth door trim panel with map pocket, 22 gallon fuel tank, Sport Appearance Group: sport badging on door, front and rear body color fascias, body color grille and wheels: 15" x 7" 5-spoke aluminum; P235/75R15 AS OWL and 3.55 axle ratio. REQUIRES 4XA and ELF and DDC.		
25B	**Quick Order Package 25B (Regular Cab 2WD)**	1390	1635
	Manufacturer Discount	(553)	(650)
	Net Price	837	985
	Includes front seat area carpet, cloth door trim panel with map pocket, 40/20/40 cloth split bench seat, Sport Appearance Group: sport badging on door, front and rear body color fascias, body color grille and wheels: 15" x 7" 5-spoke aluminum; tires: P215/75R15 RWL AS and 3.55 axle ratio. REQUIRES 4XA and ELF and DDC.		
25G	**Quick Order Package 25G (Club Cab 4WD)**	2189	2575
	Manufacturer Discount	(1105)	(1300)
	Net Price	1084	1275
	Includes deluxe convenience group: speed control, tilt steering column; cloth door trim panel with map pocket, front floor mats, 22 gallon fuel tank, light group: cargo lamp, glove box lamp, underhood lamp, auxiliary 12v power outlet, mini overhead console; SLT Decor Group: liftgate and door badging, front bright bumper, bright grille, bright rear bumper with step pads, wheels: 15" x 7" 5-spoke aluminum; tires: P235/75R15 AS OWL and 3.55 axle ratio. REQUIRES ELF and DDC.		
25G	**Quick Order Package 25G (Regular Cab 2WD)**	2627	3090
	Manufacturer Discount	(638)	(750)
	Net Price	1989	2340
	Includes air conditioning, front seat area carpet, deluxe convenience group: speed control, tilt steering column; cloth door trim panel with map pocket, front floor mats, 22 gallon fuel tank, light group: cargo lamp, glove box lamp, underhood lamp, auxiliary 12v power outlet, mini overhead console; SLT Decor Group: liftgate and		

CODE	DESCRIPTION	INVOICE	MSRP
	door badging, front bright bumper, bright grille, bright rear bumper with step pads, wheels: 15" x 7" 5-spoke aluminum; 40/20/40 cloth split bench seat, tires: P215/75R15 RWL AS and 3.55 axle ratio. REQUIRES ELF and DDC.		
25G	Quick Order Package 25G (Regular Cab 4WD)	2780	3270
	Manufacturer Discount	(638)	(750)
	Net Price	2142	2520
	Includes air conditioning, front seat area carpet, deluxe convenience group: speed control, tilt steering column; cloth door trim panel with map pocket, front floor mats, 22 gallon fuel tank, light group: cargo lamp, glove box lamp, underhood lamp, auxiliary 12v power outlet, mini overhead console; SLT Decor Group: liftgate and door badging, front bright bumper, bright grille, bright rear bumper with step pads, wheels: 15" x 7" 5-spoke aluminum; cloth 40/20/40 split bench seat, tires: P235/75R15 AS OWL and 3.55 axle ratio. REQUIRES ELF and DDC.		
25G	Quick Order Package 25G (Club Cab 2WD)	2036	2395
	Manufacturer Discount	(935)	(1100)
	Net Price	1101	1295
	Includes air conditioning, cloth door trim panel with map pocket, front floor mats, 22 gallon fuel tank, light group: cargo lamp, glove box lamp, underhood lamp, auxiliary 12v power outlet, mini overhead console; SLT Decor Group: liftgate and door badging, front bright bumper, bright grille, bright rear bumper with step pads, wheels: 15" x 7" 5-spoke aluminum; tilt steering column, tires: P215/75R15 RWL AS, warning lamp shift indicator, 3.55 axle ratio and payload: 1450 lbs. REQUIRES ELF and DDC.		
26B	Quick Order Package 26B (Club Cab 4WD)	1020	1200
	Manufacturer Discount	(1020)	(1200)
	Net Price	NC	NC
	Includes cloth door trim panel with map pocket, 22 gallon fuel tank, Sport Appearance Group: sport badging on door, front and rear body color fascias, body color grille and wheels: 15" x 7" 5-spoke aluminum; tires: P235/75R15 AS OWL and 3.55 axle ratio. REQUIRES 4XA and ELF and DGB.		
26B	Quick Order Package 26B (Regular Cab 2WD)	1390	1635
	Manufacturer Discount	(553)	(650)
	Net Price	837	985
	Includes front seat area carpet, cloth door trim panel with map pocket, 40/20/40 cloth split bench seat, Sport Appearance Group: sport badging on door, front and rear body color fascias, body color grille and wheels: 15" x 7" 5-spoke aluminum; tires: P215/75R15 RWL AS and 3.55 axle ratio. REQUIRES 4XA and ELF and DGB.		
26B	Quick Order Package 26B (Club Cab 2WD)	880	1035
	Manufacturer Discount	(880)	(1035)
	Net Price	NC	NC
	Includes cloth door trim panel with map pocket, 22 gallon fuel tank, Sport Appearance Group: sport badging on door, front and rear body color fascias, body color grille and wheels: 15" x 7" 5-spoke aluminum; tires: P215/75R15 RWL AS, 3.55 axle ratio and payload: 1450 lbs. REQUIRES 4XA and ELF and DGB.		

CODE	DESCRIPTION	INVOICE	MSRP
26B	Quick Order Package 26B (Regular Cab 4WD)	1543	1815
	Manufacturer Discount	(553)	(650)
	Net Price	990	1165
	Includes front seat area carpet, cloth door trim panel with map pocket, cloth 40/20/40 split bench seat, Sport Appearance Group: sport badging on door, front and rear body color fascias, body color grille and wheels: 15" x 7" 5-spoke aluminum;tires: P235/75R15 AS OWL and 3.55 axle ratio. REQUIRES 4XA and ELF and DGB.		
26G	Quick Order Package 26G (Club Cab 2WD)	2036	2395
	Manufacturer Discount	(1105)	(1300)
	Net Price	931	1095
	Includes air conditioning, cloth door trim panel with map pocket, front floor mats, 22 gallon fuel tank, light group: cargo lamp, glove box lamp, underhood lamp, auxiliary 12v power outlet, mini overhead console; SLT Decor Group: liftgate and door badging, front bright bumper, bright grille, bright rear bumper with step pads, wheels: 15" x 7" 5-spoke aluminum; tilt steering column, tires: P215/75R15 RWL AS, warning lamp shift indicator, payload: 1450 lbs and 3.55 axle ratio. REQUIRES ELF and DGB.		
26G	Quick Order Package 26G (Club Cab 4WD)	2189	2575
	Manufacturer Discount	(1105)	(1300)
	Net Price	1084	1275
	Includes deluxe convenience group: speed control, tilt steering column; cloth door trim panel with map pocket, front floor mats, 22 gallon fuel tank, light group: cargo lamp, glove box lamp, underhood lamp, auxiliary 12v power outlet, mini overhead console; SLT Decor Group: liftgate and door badging, front bright bumper, bright grille, bright rear bumper with step pads; wheels: 15" x 7" 5-spoke aluminum; tires: P235/75R15XL AS OWL and 3.55 axle ratio. REQUIRES ELF and DGB.		
26G	Quick Order Package 26G (Regular Cab 2WD)	2627	3090
	Manufacturer Discount	(638)	(750)
	Net Price	1989	2340
	Includes air conditioning, front seat area carpet, deluxe convenience group: speed control, tilt steering column; cloth door trim panel with map pocket, front floor mats, 22 gallon fuel tank, light group: cargo lamp, glove box lamp, underhood lamp, auxiliary 12v power outlet, mini overhead console; SLT Decor Group: liftgate and door badging, front bright bumper, bright grille, bright rear bumper with step pads, wheels: 15" x 7" 5-spoke aluminum; 40/20/40 cloth split bench seat, tires: P215/75R15 RWL AS and 3.55 axle ratio. REQUIRES ELF and DGB.		
26G	Quick Order Package 26G (Regular Cab 4WD)	2780	3270
	Manufacturer Discount	(638)	(750)
	Net Price	2142	2520
	Includes air conditioning, front seat area carpet, deluxe convenience group: speed control, tilt steering column; cloth door trim panel with map pocket, front floor mats, 22 gallon fuel tank, light group: cargo lamp, glove box lamp, underhood lamp, auxiliary 12v power outlet, mini overhead console; SLT Decor Group: liftgate and door badging, front bright bumper, bright grille, bright rear bumper with step pads, wheels: 15" x 7" 5-spoke aluminum; cloth 40/20/40 split bench seat, tires: P235/75R15 AS OWL and 3.55 axle ratio. REQUIRES ELF and DGB.		

CODE	DESCRIPTION	INVOICE	MSRP
28B	Quick Order Package 28B (Regular Cab 2WD)	1390	1635
	Manufacturer Discount	(553)	(650)
	Net Price	837	985
	Includes front seat area carpet, cloth door trim panel with map pocket, 40/20/40 cloth split bench seat, Sport Appearance Group: sport badging on door, front and rear body color fascias, body color grille and wheels: 15" x 7" 5-spoke aluminum and tires: P215/75R15 RWL AS. REQUIRES EML and DGB and 4XA and ASU.		
28B	Quick Order Package 28B (Club Cab 2WD)	880	1035
	Manufacturer Discount	(880)	(1035)
	Net Price	NC	NC
	Includes cloth door trim panel with map pocket, 22 gallon fuel tank, Sport Appearance Group: sport badging on door, front and rear body color fascias, body color grille and wheels: 15" x 7" 5-spoke aluminum and tires: P215/75R15 RWL AS. REQUIRES EML and DGB and 4XA and ASU.		
4XA	Air Conditioning Bypass	NC	NC
ADA	Light Group	132	155
	Includes ash tray lamp and courtesy lamps, cargo lamp, glove box lamp, underhood lamp and auxiliary 12v power outlet. NOT AVAILABLE with AJL.		
ADH	HD Electrical Group	102	120
	Includes 136-amp alternator and 750-amp maintenance free battery.		
ADJ	HD Service Group	153	180
	Includes 22-gallon fuel tank heavy-duty engine cooling, heavy duty electrical group: 750-amp maintenance free battery and 136-amp alternator. REQUIRES AGU.		
ADJ	HD Service Group	251	295
	Includes 22-gallon fuel tank heavy-duty engine cooling, heavy duty electrical group: 750-amp maintenance free battery and 136-amp alternator. REQUIRES DGB.		
ADJ	HD Service Group	200	235
	Includes 22-gallon fuel tank heavy-duty engine cooling, heavy duty electrical group: 750-amp maintenance free battery and 136-amp alternator.		
ADJ	HD Service Group	204	240
	Includes 22-gallon fuel tank heavy-duty engine cooling, heavy duty electrical group: 750-amp maintenance free battery and 136-amp alternator. REQUIRES (AGU and DGB) or (ASU and DGB).		
ADL	Skid Plate Group (4WD)	111	130
	Includes fuel tank skid plate shield and front suspension skid plate.		
AGB	Tire and Handling Group (Club Cab 2WD)	332	390
	Includes front and rear stabilizer bars, tires: P255/65R15 BSW and wheels: 15" x 8" aluminum. REQUIRES 23B or 24B or 25B or 26B or 28B or 23G or 24G or 25G or 26G.		
AGB	Tire and Handling Group (Regular Cab 2WD)	310	365
	Includes front and rear stabilizer bars, tires: P255/65R15 BSW and wheels: 15" x 8" aluminum. REQUIRES 23B or 24B or 25B or 26B or 28B.		
AGB	Tire and Handling Group (Regular Cab 4WD)	340	400
	Includes front and rear stabilizer bars, tires: P255/65R15 BSW and wheels: 15" x 8" aluminum.		

CODE	DESCRIPTION	INVOICE	MSRP
AGU	Sport Plus Group (Club Cab 4WD)	1254	1475
	Manufacturer Discount	(502)	(590)
	Net Price	752	885
	Includes air conditioning, fog lamps, 22-gallon fuel tank, tire and handling group: 15" x 8" aluminum and tires: P255/65R15 BSW.		
AGU	Sport Plus Group (Regular Cab 2WD)	1271	1495
	Manufacturer Discount	(298)	(350)
	Net Price	973	1145
	Includes air conditioning, fog lamps, 22-gallon fuel tank, tire and handling group: 15" x 8" aluminum and tires: P255/65R15 BSW. REQUIRES 25B or 26B.		
AGU	Sport Plus Group (Regular Cab 4WD)	1301	1530
	Manufacturer Discount	(298)	(350)
	Net Price	1003	1180
	Includes air conditioning, fog lamps, 22-gallon fuel tank, tire and handling group: 15" x 8" aluminum and tires: P255/65R15 BSW. REQUIRES 25B or 26B.		
AGU	Sport Plus Group (Club Cab 2WD)	1245	1465
	Manufacturer Discount	(298)	(350)
	Net Price	947	1115
	Includes 22-gallon fuel tank, tire and handling group: wheels: 15" x 8" aluminum and tires: P255/65R15 BSW. REQUIRES 25B or 26B.		
AHC	Trailer Tow Group (Regular Cab 2WD LB/Regular Cab 4WD)	234	275
	Includes trailer hitch receiver (class IV) and 7-lead wiring harness. REQUIRES ADJ.		
AJB	Security Alarm	128	150
	REQUIRES ATK.		
AJK	Deluxe Convenience Group	332	390
	Includes speed control and tilt steering column. REQUIRES 23D or 24D or 25D or 26D. NOT AVAILABLE with 21B, EPE, 23G, 24G, 25G, 26G.		
AJL	Power Overhead Convenience Group	667	785
	Includes overhead console: compass/temperature display, map/reading lights, auto day/night mirror; power convenience group: keyless entry, power locks and power windows with driver's one touch down.		
AJL	Power Overhead Convenience Group	157	185
	Includes overhead console: compass/temperature display, map/reading lights, auto day/night mirror; power convenience group: keyless entry, power locks and power windows with driver's one touch down. REQUIRES ATK.		
AJL	Power Overhead Convenience Group	642	755
	Includes overhead console: compass/temperature display, map/reading lights, auto day/night mirror; power convenience group: keyless entry, power locks and power windows with driver's one touch down. REQUIRES ADA or (ADA and AGU) or AGU.		
AJP	Power Convenience Group	485	570
	Includes keyless entry, power locks and power windows with driver's one touch down.		
APD	Two Tone Lower Paint	166	195
	*REQUIRES 6D**		
ASU	R/T Sport Group (Club Cab 2WD)	1934	2275
	Includes "Dakota" R/T tailgate and front door badge, seat track cover, left sun visor and right sun visor with mirror, body colored front and rear bumpers, extra HD front		

CODE	DESCRIPTION	INVOICE	MSRP
	and rear shock absorbers, cloth door trim panel with map pockets, deluxe convenience group: speed control and tilt steering column; deluxe insulation group, cloth high-back bucket seats with floor console, HD rear stabilizer bar, leather-wrapped steering wheel, sport suspension, tires: P225/55R17 BSW, wheelflares and wheels: 17" x 9" aluminum.		
ASU	R/T Sport Group (Regular Cab 2WD SB)	1981	2330
	Includes "Dakota" front door R/T badge, left sun visor and right sun visor with mirror, front and rear body colored bumpers and extra HD front and rear shock absorbers and door trim panel with map pockets, 22-gallon fuel tank, deluxe insulation group, cloth high-back bucket seats with floor console, HD rear stabilizer bar, leather-wrapped steering wheel, sport suspension, tires: P225/55R17 BSW, wheelflares and wheels: 17" x 9" aluminum.		
ATK	SLT Plus Decor Group (Club Cab 2WD)	935	1100
	Manufacturer Discount	(383)	(450)
	Net Price	552	650
	Includes power mirrors, power convenience group: keyless entry, power locks and power windows with driver's one touch down.		
ATK	SLT Plus Decor Group (Regular Cab 2WD)	914	1075
	Manufacturer Discount	(383)	(450)
	Net Price	531	625
	Includes power mirrors, power convenience group: keyless entry, power locks and power windows with driver's one touch down.		
ATK	SLT Plus Decor Group (Regular Cab 4WD)	944	1110
	Manufacturer Discount	(213)	(250)
	Net Price	731	860
	Includes tire and handling group: wheels: 15" x 8" aluminum and tires: P255/65R15 BSW; power convenience group: keyless entry, power locks and power windows with driver's one touch down.		
BGK	4-Wheel Antilock Brakes	298	350
CLA	Front Floor Mats	26	30
DDC	Transmission: 5-Speed Manual	NC	NC
	REQUIRES ELF.		
DDK	Transmission: HD 5-Speed Manual	(170)	(200)
	REQUIRES EPE. NOT AVAILABLE with ASP on Club Cab 4WD.		
DDQ	Transmission: 5-Speed Manual	NC	NC
	REQUIRES EHC.		
DGB	Transmission: 4-Speed Automatic	829	975
	REQUIRES EHC or ELF.		
DHC	Full Time Transfer Case (4WD)	336	395
	NOT AVAILABLE with EHC.		
DMD	3.55 Axle Ratio	34	40
DMH	3.92 Axle Ratio	34	40
	REQUIRES DSA and (25B or 25G or 25D).		
DSA	Anti-Spin Differential Axle	242	285
EHC	Engine: 3.9L SMPI V6 Magnum (4WD)	NC	NC

CODE	DESCRIPTION	INVOICE	MSRP
EHC	Engine: 3.9L SMPI V6 Magnum (2WD X-Cab)	476	560
	Manufacturer Discount	(476)	(560)
	Net Price	NC	NC
EHC	Engine: 3.9L SMPI V6 Magnum (2WD Reg Cab)	476	560
ELF	Engine: 5.2L SMPI V8 Magnum (4WD)	502	590
ELF	Engine: 5.2L SMPI V8 Magnum (2WD)	927	1090
	Manufacturer Discount	(476)	(560)
	Net Price	451	530
EML	Engine: 5.9L SMPI V8 Magnum (Regular Cab 2WD SB/Club Cab 2WD) *REQUIRES ASU.*	1432	1685
EPE	Engine: 2.5L SMPI I4 Magnum (2WD)	(170)	(200)
G1	Cloth Bench Seat (Regular Cab) *REQUIRES 2*W.*	47	55
GFD	Sliding Rear Window	98	115
GT4	6" x 9" Power Fold Away Mirrors *REQUIRES ATK. NOT AVAILABLE with GUR.*	17	20
GT4	6" x 9" Power Fold Away Mirrors *NOT AVAILABLE with GUR.*	136	160
GUR	Power Mirrors	119	140
HAA	Air Conditioning *NOT AVAILABLE with 4XA.*	680	800
JPS	6-Way Power Driver's Seat (Club Cab)	272	320
K17	Bodyside Molding	64	75
LNJ	Fog Lamps *REQUIRES ADA.*	102	120
M5	Cloth High-Back Bucket Seats *Includes floor console. REQUIRES 2*G.*	170	200
NAE	CA/CT/MA/NY Emissions *Automatically coded.*	NC	NC
NBN	Northeastern States Emissions	NC	NC
NFB	22 Gallon Fuel Tank	47	55
NHK	Engine Block Heater	30	35
NMC	HD Engine Cooling *Includes HD auxiliary transmission oil cooler. NOT AVAILABLE with EPE.*	51	60
NMC	HD Engine Cooling *Includes HD auxiliary transmission oil cooler. REQUIRES DGB.*	102	120
RAZ	Radio: AM/FM Stereo with CD, Cassette and EQ *Includes Infinity speaker system.*	561	660
RBN	Radio: AM/FM Stereo with Cassette *Includes Infinity speaker system.*	255	300
RBR	Radio: AM/FM Stereo with CD *Includes Infinity speaker system.*	408	480
RDZ	Steering Wheel Mounted Audio Controls *REQUIRES RAZ or (AJK and AJP) or SCG.*	64	75
SCG	Leather-Wrapped Steering Wheel *NOT AVAILABLE with 21B.*	43	50
SUA	Tilt Steering Column	119	140

CODE	DESCRIPTION	INVOICE	MSRP
TS1	Tires: P235/75R15XL AS BSW *NOT AVAILABLE with AGB or ASU.*	55	65
TS1	Tires: P235/75R15XL AS BSW (2WD)	162	190
YCF	Border State Emissions (California)	NC	NC
Z1D	Payload: 2000 Lbs (2WD) *Includes 10" x 2.5" rear drum brakes and tires: P235/75R15 AS BSW.*	157	185
Z5B	Payload 1800 Lbs (Club Cab 4WD) *Includes 10" x 2.5" rear drum brakes. REQUIRES 23B or 24B or (25B and DSA) or 26B or 23D or 23G or 24D or 24G or (25D and DSA) or (25G and DSA) or 26D or 26G.*	34	40
Z5C	Payload: 2000 Lbs. (Regular Cab 4WD) *Includes 10" x 2.5" rear drum brakes. REQUIRES (25B and DSA) or 26B or 23B or 24B.*	47	55

1999 DURANGO

1999 Dodge Durango

What's New?

Two-wheel drive models finally show up for true flatlander use, and all Durangos gain a rear power outlet. Also available are steering wheel-mounted radio controls, heated mirrors, and two new colors: Bright Platinum Metallic and Patriot Blue.

Review

As the most recent addition to the Dodge truck lineup, the Durango makes quite an entry. Offering the most cargo space in its class, along with a standard Magnum V8 engine, eight-passenger seating, and three-and-a-half tons of towing capacity, the Durango is one of the most versatile sport-utility vehicles on the market.

Remember the Ramcharger? Neither do we, with the help of the Dodge Durango. Based on the Dakota platform, the Durango is Dodge's best-ever attack on the booming sport-utility segment. And from the looks of things, the Dodge boys have done their homework. Though 80 percent of its parts are shared, the Durango's frame is actually three times stiffer than its Dakota sibling.

Competing directly with the sales king Ford Explorer is no easy task. But the Durango can seat up to eight passengers, which is one set of triplets more than the Explorer. It can tow up to 7,300 lbs., which is a full ton more than the Explorer. The Durango has a minimum of 7.9 inches of ground clearance, and feels plenty capable off the pavement. With the rear seats folded, it can swallow up to 88 cubic feet of cargo. Big, strong, and utilitarian; sounds like a winning formula.

The Durango is larger than anything else in its class, which explains the expansive interior. Yet it's noticeably smaller than the Chevrolet Tahoe or Ford Expedition giants, so we can't call it full-sized. But the niche is filled. Need more room than an Explorer, Blazer or Cherokee? Don't want to fork over the price of an Expedition? Take a good look at the Dodge Durango — it's the only option.

There are two engines to choose from: a 5.2-liter V8 with 230 horsepower and 300 foot-pounds of torque or a massive 5.9-liter V8 with 245 horsepower and 335 foot-pounds of torque. The massive engine is our favorite, but fuel conservation is not one of that motor's strong points. For the environmentally concerned, go with the 5.2-liter V8. It's not as thirsty, and performance doesn't lag far behind anything else in this class.

A two-wheel drive model is available for 1999, meaning that even more buyers are likely to defect from the competition's ranks. With fresh new styling, superior versatility, and an attractive base price, the newest Dodge makes a statement all its own. It says, "Buy me."

Safety Data

Side Airbag: *Not Available*
4-Wheel ABS: *Optional*
Driver Crash Test Grade: *Poor*
Side Impact Crash Test Front: *Not Available*
Crash Offset: *Not Available*
Integrated Child Seat(s): *Not Available*
Traction Control: *Not Available*
Passenger Crash Test Grade: *Average*
Side Impact Crash Test Rear: *Not Available*

Standard Equipment

2WD (4A): 5.2 V8 OHV SMPI 16-valve engine; 4-speed electronic overdrive automatic transmission with lock-up; 600-amp battery; 117-amp alternator; rear wheel drive, 3.55 axle ratio; stainless steel exhaust; front independent suspension with anti-roll bar, front torsion springs, front torsion bar, HD front shocks, rigid rear axle suspension with anti-roll bar, rear leaf springs, HD rear shocks; power re-circulating ball steering; front disc/rear drum brakes with rear wheel antilock braking system; 25 gal capacity fuel tank; liftback rear cargo door; roof rack; front and rear body-colored bumpers with rear step; monotone paint; aero-composite halogen headlamps; additional exterior lights include center high mounted stop light, underhood light; driver's and passenger's power remote black outside mirrors; front and rear 15" x 7" silver alloy wheels; P235/75SR15 BSW AS front and rear tires; underbody mounted full-size temporary steel spare wheel; air conditioning, rear heat ducts; AM/FM stereo with clock, seek-scan, cassette, 4 speakers, and fixed antenna; cruise control with steering wheel controls; power door locks, remote keyless entry, child safety rear door locks, power remote hatch/trunk release; 2 power accessory outlets; instrumentation display includes tachometer, oil pressure gauge, water temp gauge, trip odometer; warning indicators include oil pressure, battery, lights on, key in ignition, low fuel, low washer fluid, door ajar, trunk ajar; driver's side airbag, passenger's side cancellable airbag; panic alarm; deep tinted windows, power front windows with driver's 1-touch down, power rear windows, fixed 1/4 vent windows; variable intermittent front windshield wipers, fixed interval rear wiper, rear window defroster; seating capacity of 5, front bucket seats with fixed headrests, center armrest with storage, driver's seat includes 4-way direction control with lumbar support, passenger's seat includes 4-way direction control; 60-40 folding rear split-bench seat with fixed rear headrest, center armrest; front and rear height adjustable seatbelts; cloth seats, vinyl door trim insert, full cloth headliner, full carpet floor covering, deluxe sound insulation; interior lights include dome light, front reading lights, illuminated entry; sport steering wheel with tilt adjustment; vanity mirrors; day-night rearview mirror; full floor console, locking glove box with light, front cupholder, 2 seat back storage pockets; carpeted cargo floor, carpeted trunk lid, cargo tie downs, cargo light, cargo concealed storage; body-colored grille, black side window moldings, black front windshield molding, black rear window molding and black door handles.

4WD (4A) (in addition to or instead of 2WD (4A) equipment): Part-time 4 wheel drive and auto locking hub control with manual shift.

Base Prices

Code	Description	Invoice	MSRP
DN1L74	2WD (4A)	23528	26055
DN5L74	4WD (4A)	25313	28055
Destination Charge:		525	525

Accessories

Code	Description	Invoice	MSRP
26D	Quick Order Package 26D	NC	NC
	Includes 3.55 axle ratio. REQUIRES ELF and DGB.		
26F	Quick Order Package 26F (4WD)	2576	3030
	Manufacturer Discount	(255)	(300)
	Net Price	2321	2730
	Includes steering wheel radio controls, front and rear floor mats, fog lamps, body colored bodyside moldings, overhead convenience group: overhead console with instrumentation, automatic dimming rearview mirror, dual sunvisors with illuminated mirrors; AM/FM stereo with CD, cassette and EQ, Infinity speaker system, 6-way power driver's seat, leather high-back bucket seats, security group, tires: 31 X 10.5 R15 AS OWL: wheels: 15" x 8" cast aluminum, wheel flares and 3.92 axle ratio. REQUIRES ELF and DGB.		
26F	Quick Order Package 26F (2WD)	2359	2775
	Manufacturer Discount	(255)	(300)
	Net Price	2104	2475
	Includes steering wheel radio controls, front and rear floor mats, fog lamps, body colored bodyside moldings, overhead convenience group: overhead console with instrumentation, automatic dimming rearview mirror, dual sunvisors with illuminated mirrors; AM/FM stereo with CD, cassette, EQ, Infinity speaker system, 6-way power driver's seat, leather high-back bucket seats, security group, and 3.55 axle ratio.		
28D	Quick Order Package 28D	NC	NC
	Includes 3.55 axle ratio. REQUIRES EML and DGB.		
28F	Quick Order Package 28F (4WD)	2576	3030
	Manufacturer Discount	(255)	(300)
	Net Price	2321	2730
	Includes steering wheel radio controls, front and rear floor mats, fog lamps, body colored bodyside moldings, overhead convenience group: overhead console with instrumentation, automatic dimming rearview mirror, dual sunvisors with illuminated mirrors; AM/FM stereo with CD, cassette, EQ, Infinity speaker system, 6-way power driver's seat, leather high-back bucket seats, security group, tires: 31 X 10.5 R15 AS OWL: wheels: 15" x 8" cast aluminum, wheel flares and 3.92 axle ratio. REQUIRES EML and DGB.		

CODE	DESCRIPTION	INVOICE	MSRP
28F	Quick Order Package 28F (2WD)	2359	2775
	Manufacturer Discount	(255)	(300)
	Net Price	2104	2475
	Includes steering wheel radio controls, front and rear floor mats, fog lamps, body colored bodyside moldings, overhead convenience group: overhead console with instrumentation, automatic dimming rearview mirror, dual sunvisors with illuminated mirrors; AM/FM stereo with CD, cassette, EQ, Infinity speaker system, 6-way power driver's seat, leather high-back bucket seats, security group, and 3.55 axle ratio.		
4XN	Rear Air Conditioning Bypass	NC	NC
ADJ	HD Service Group	204	240
	Includes HD engine cooling, HD electrical group: HD 136-amp alternator and 750-amp maintenance free battery.		
ADL	Skid Plate Group (4WD)	77	90
	Includes fuel tank and transfer case skid plate shields.		
AFH	Overhead Convenience Group	349	410
	Includes overhead console with instrumentation, automatic dimming rearview mirror and dual sunvisors with illuminated mirrors.		
AHC	Trailer Tow Group	234	275
	Includes trailer hitch receiver (Class IV). REQUIRES ADJ.		
AJB	Security Group	128	150
	Includes panic alarm.		
BGK	4-Wheel Antilock Brakes	336	395
CFP	Third Row Seat	468	550
	With leather, the third row bench seat is vinyl. NOT AVAILABLE with EHC.		
CLE	Front and Rear Floor Mats	43	50
DGB	Transmission: 4-Speed Automatic	NC	NC
DHC	Full Time Transfer Case (4WD)	336	395
	NOT AVAILABLE with EHC.		
DMH	3.92 Axle Ratio	34	40
	REQUIRES 26D or 28D.		
DSA	Anti-Spin Differential Axle	242	285
ELF	Engine: 5.2L SMPI V8	NC	NC
EML	Engine: 5.9L SMPI V8	506	595
GTS	Dual Power Heated Foldaway Mirrors	64	75
HBA	Rear Air Conditioning w/o Heater	458	550
	REQUIRES 26F or 28F. NOT AVAILABLE with 4XN, ADJ, 24D, 26D, 28D.		
HBA	Rear Air Conditioning w/o Heater	366	430
	REQUIRES 24D or 26D or 28D. NOT AVAILABLE with 4XN, 26F or 28F .		
JPS	6-Way Power Driver's Seat	272	320
K17	Black Bodyside Molding	68	80
LNJ	Fog Lamps	204	240
	REQUIRES HBA.		
LNJ	Fog Lamps	102	120
	NOT AVAILABLE with HBA.		
NAE	CA/CT/MA/NY Emissions	NC	NC
NHK	Engine Block Heater	30	35
RAZ	Radio: AM/FM Stereo with CD, Cassette and EQ	255	300

DESCRIPTION		INVOICE	MSRP
	Infinity Speaker System	281	330
	Tires: P235/75R15 AS BSW (2WD)	213	250
	Includes matching spare wheel and wheel flares.		
TUT	Tires: 31 x 10.5R15 AS OWL (4WD)	395	465
	Includes 15" x 8" cast aluminum wheels and wheel flares. REQUIRES 26D or 28D.		
V9	40/20/40 Cloth Bench Seat	NC	NC
	Includes center armrest and console delete.		
YCF	Border State Emissions (California)	NC	NC
	For states that border California only: Arizona, Nevada and Oregon.		

1999 GRAND CARAVAN

1999 Dodge Grand Caravan

What's New?

A revised front fascia is common to all models. The Grand Caravan ES gets an AutoStick transmission, 17-inch wheels and tires, and steering wheel-mounted radio controls.

Review

If there is a perfect family vehicle in existence, it is one of Chrysler's minivans. What's the data say? The average American has two kids and spends a little more than $20,000 on a new car or truck. The Dodge Caravan/Grand Caravan fits into this scenario better than Velveeta in a grilled cheese sandwich.

The Caravan rides on a 113.3-inch wheelbase, and the Grand Caravan adds six inches to that and 13 extra inches of overall length. That extra length is noticed in the Grand Caravan's rear seat legroom, which allows rear passengers to stretch out their legs an extra three and four inches (second row and third row, respectively). The vehicles are identical in width and height, but the longer-wheelbase Grand Caravan offers more cargo room at 147.7 cubic feet, compared to the Caravan's 126.7 cubic feet. The big Grand Caravan also offers standard seven-passenger seating, but the third extra row is optional on the Caravan.

The Caravan line offers several thoughtful details, but the most important are the easy-out rolling seats and the innovative driver-side sliding door—a first in the minivan class that has since been copied by everyone. Easy-out seats are a snap to release and remove, though lifting the seat from the rear of the van still requires two sets of biceps. Optional on base Caravan and standard on everything else, the driver's side sliding door offers the convenience of loading kids and cargo from either side of the Caravan.

A 150-horsepower 16-valve dual-cam four (coupled with a three-speed automatic) serves as the base engine of the Caravan, but these sizeable vans benefit from a little extra oomph. The 3.0-liter V6, borrowed from Mitsubishi Motors, is standard on the Grand Caravan, and offers the same horsepower as the 2.4-liter but with an extra nine foot-pounds of torque. A 3.3-liter V6, standard on SE and LE trim, is a step in the right direction, but our favorite motor is the 3.8-liter unit, which outputs 180 horsepower and 227 foot-pounds of torque. The 3.8-liter engine (standard on AWD versions of the Grand Caravan and the Grand Caravan ES model, optional on the Caravan and Grand Caravan LE), comes with a four-speed automatic transmission which provides shifts that are neat and smooth.

Light steering response gives these minivans an undeniably car-like feel, with an exceptionally smooth ride. Highly maneuverable and easy to control, the minivan delivers just a hint that you could exceed its capabilities, as when rounding a sharp curve. The Sport package features specially tuned shocks and springs.

The Dodge brand of Chrysler minivans offers affordable transportation in just about any conceivable configuration. Buyers can choose from two different sizes, five usable doors, four engine choices, three rows of seats, two distinct suspensions, all-wheel drive capability, and a partridge in a pear tree. So mix and match to your own specific needs.

Safety Data

Side Airbag: *Not Available*
4-Wheel ABS: *Opt. (Base); Std. (SE/LE/ES)*
Driver Crash Test Grade: *Average*
Side Impact Crash Test Front: *Excellent*
Crash Offset: *Poor*
Integrated Child Seat(s): *Optional*
Traction Control: *N/A (Base/SE); Opt. (LE); Std. (ES)*
Passenger Crash Test Grade: *Average*
Side Impact Crash Test Rear: *Average*

Standard Equipment

BASE FWD (4A): 3.3L V6 OHV SMPI 12-valve engine; 4-speed electronic overdrive automatic transmission with lock-up; 600-amp battery; 90-amp alternator; front wheel drive, 3.61 axle ratio; stainless steel exhaust; front independent strut suspension with anti-roll bar, front coil springs, rear non-independent suspension with rear leaf springs; power rack-and-pinion steering; front disc/rear drum brakes; 20 gal capacity fuel tank; rear lip spoiler; 4 doors with sliding left rear passenger's door, sliding right rear passenger's door, liftback rear cargo door; front and rear colored bumpers with rear step; colored bodyside molding; monotone paint; aero-composite halogen headlamps; additional exterior lights include center high mounted stop light; driver's and passenger's manual black folding outside mirrors; front and rear 14" x 6" steel wheels; P205/75SR14 BSW AS front and rear tires; underbody mounted compact steel spare wheel; AM/FM stereo with clock, seek-scan, 4 speakers, and fixed antenna; child safety rear door locks; 2 power accessory outlets, driver's foot rest; instrumentation display includes water temp gauge, trip odometer; warning indicators include oil pressure, water temp warning, battery, lights on, key in ignition, low fuel, low washer fluid, door ajar, trunk ajar; dual airbags; tinted windows, fixed rear windows, manual 1/4 vent windows; variable intermittent front windshield wipers, variable intermittent rear wiper; seating capacity of 7, front bucket seats with fixed headrests, driver's and passenger's armrests, driver's seat includes 4-way direction control, passenger's seat includes 4-way direction control; removable 2nd row bench seat with adjustable rear headrests; 3rd row removable full folding bench seat with adjustable headrests; front and 2nd row height adjustable seatbelts; cloth seats, vinyl door trim insert, full cloth headliner, full carpet floor covering; interior lights include dome light, front reading lights; driver side vanity mirror; day-night rearview mirror; glove box, front and rear cupholders, instrument panel bin; carpeted cargo floor, plastic trunk lid, cargo light; body-colored grille, black side window moldings, black front windshield molding, black rear window molding and black door handles.

SE FWD (4A) (in addition to or instead of BASE FWD (4A) equipment): 500-amp battery; front disc/rear drum brakes with 4 wheel antilock braking system; driver's and passenger's power remote black heated folding outside mirrors; front and rear 15" x 6.5" steel wheels; AM/FM stereo with clock, seek-scan, cassette, 4 speakers, and fixed antenna; cruise control with steering wheel controls; instrumentation display includes tachometer; variable intermittent front windshield wipers with heated wipers, variable intermittent rear wiper, rear window defroster; removable full folding 2nd row bench seat with reclining adjustable rear headrest; 3rd row removable full folding bench seat with reclining adjustable 3rd row headrest; cloth door trim insert; steering wheel with tilt adjustment and body-colored door handles.

SE AWD (4A) (in addition to or instead of SE FWD (4A) equipment): 3.8L V6 OHV SMPI 12-valve engine; 600-amp battery; 120-amp alternator; full-time 4 wheel drive; auto-leveling, rear semi-independent suspension with rear leaf springs; vinyl trunk lid and black door handles.

LE FWD (4A) (in addition to or instead of SE FWD (4A) equipment): Colored bodyside cladding; monotone paint with bodyside accent stripe; aero-composite halogen headlamps with delay-off feature; dual zone front air conditioning; premium AM/FM stereo with clock, seek-scan, cassette, CD changer pre-wiring, in-dash CD pre-wiring, 10 premium speakers, amplifier, graphic equalizer, and fixed antenna; power door locks, remote keyless entry; instrumentation display includes compass, exterior temp; panic alarm; power front windows with driver's 1-touch down, power 1/4 vent windows; driver's seat includes 6-way power seat with lumbar support; premium cloth seats, carpeted floor mats, deluxe sound insulation; interior lights include front and rear reading lights, 2 door curb lights, illuminated entry; dual illuminated vanity mirrors, dual auxiliary visors; full overhead console with storage, glove box with light; instrument panel covered bin, 1 seat back storage pocket and front underseat tray.

LE AWD (4A) (in addition to or instead of LE FWD (4A) equipment): 3.8L V6 OHV SMPI 12-valve engine; 600-amp battery; 120-amp alternator; full-time 4 wheel drive, auto-leveling; rear semi-independent suspension with rear leaf springs.

ES FWD (4A) (in addition to or instead of LE FWD (4A) equipment): 3.8L V6 OHV SMPI 12-valve engine; 4-speed electronic overdrive automatic transmission with lock-up and manual shift capability (AutoStick); front wheel drive, traction control, 3.45 axle ratio; rear wing spoiler; additional exterior lights include front fog/driving; front and rear 17" x 6.5" silver alloy wheels; underbody mounted full-size temporary steel spare wheel; radio steering wheel controls; garage door opener; leather-wrapped steering wheel with tilt adjustment; auto-dimming day-night rearview mirror.

ES AWD (4A) (in addition to or instead of ES FWD (4A) equipment): 600-amp battery; full-time 4 wheel drive, 3.61 axle ratio; auto-leveling; rear semi-independent suspension with rear leaf springs; front and rear 16" x 6.5" silver alloy wheels and underbody mounted compact steel spare wheel.

Base Prices

Code	Description	Invoice	MSRP
NSKL53	Base FWD (4A)	19188	21140
NSKH53	SE FWD (4A)	20715	22875
NSDH53	SE AWD (4A)	23500	26040
NSKP53	LE FWD (4A)	24077	26695
NSDP53	LE AWD (4A)	26871	29870
NSKX53	ES FWD (4A)	26021	28905
NSDX53	ES AWD (4A)	28314	31510
Destination Charge:		580	580

CODE	DESCRIPTION	INVOICE	MSRP

Accessories

CODE	DESCRIPTION	INVOICE	MSRP
25B	**Quick Order Package 25B (SE FWD)**	NC	NC
	Includes vehicle with standard equipment. REQUIRES EGM and DGB.		
25D	**Quick Order Package 25D (SE FWD)**	854	1005
	Manufacturer Discount	(255)	(300)
	Net Price	599	705
	Includes front and rear floor mats, deluxe insulation group, light group: illuminated glove box, illuminated ignition and illuminated ash tray; dual illuminated visor vanity mirrors; power windows with driver's 1 touch down and speed sensitive power door locks. REQUIRES EGM and DGB.		
25E	**Quick Order Package 25E Sport (SE FWD)**	1879	2210
	Manufacturer Discount	(489)	(575)
	Net Price	1390	1635
	Includes front and rear floor mats, fog lamps, deluxe insulation group, light group: illuminated glove box, illuminated ignition and illuminated ash tray; speed sensitive power door locks, dual illuminated visor vanity mirrors, body colored bodyside moldings, rear fascia scuff pad, body colored rear spoiler, front and rear stabilizer bars, leather-wrapped steering wheel, HD suspension, tires: P215/65R16 AS SBR, 16" wheel covers and power windows with driver's 1 touch down. REQUIRES EGM and DGB.		
25K	**Quick Order Package 25K (LE FWD)**	NC	NC
	Includes vehicle with standard equipment. REQUIRES EGM and DGB.		
25N	**Quick Order Package 25N Sport (SE FWD)**	3086	3630
	Manufacturer Discount	(574)	(675)
	Net Price	2512	2955
	Includes overhead console, front and rear floor mats, fog lamps, deluxe insulation group, door courtesy lamps, rear reading lamps, light group: illuminated glove box, illuminated ignition and illuminated ash tray; speed sensitive power door locks, dual illuminated visor vanity mirrors, body colored bodyside moldings, rear fascia scuff pad, 8-way power driver's seat, 7-passenger quad buckets, premium cloth low back bucket seats: 8-way power driver's seat, body colored rear spoiler, front and rear stabilizer bars, leather-wrapped steering wheel, HD suspension, tires: P215/65R16 AS SBR, 16" wheel covers and power windows with driver's 1 touch down. REQUIRES EGM and DGB.		
25S	**Quick Order Package 26S (Base)**	NC	NC
	Includes vehicle with standard equipment. REQUIRES 4XA and (EGM and DGB).		
25T	**Quick Order Package 26T (Base)**	765	900
	Manufacturer Discount	(646)	(760)
	Net Price	119	140
	Includes air conditioning, under seat lockable drawer, rear floor silencer pad and front seat cargo net. REQUIRES EGM and DGB.		

CODE	DESCRIPTION	INVOICE	MSRP
26T	Quick Order Package 26T (Base FWD)	1084	1275
	Manufacturer Discount	(646)	(760)
	Net Price	438	515
	Includes air conditioning, front seat cargo net, under seat lockable drawer, 7 passenger seating and rear floor silencer. REQUIRES EFA and DGB. NOT AVAILABLE with 4XA, NAE, EDZ, EGA, DGA, EGM.		
28B	Quick Order Package 28B (SE FWD)	NC	NC
	Includes vehicle with standard equipment. REQUIRES EGA and DGB and NAE.		
28D	Quick Order Package 28D (SE FWD)	854	1005
	Manufacturer Discount	(255)	(300)
	Net Price	599	705
	Includes front and rear floor mats, deluxe insulation group, light group: illuminated glove box, illuminated ignition and illuminated ash tray; dual illuminated visor vanity mirrors, power windows with driver's 1 touch down and speed sensitive power door locks. REQUIRES EGA and DGB and NAE.		
28E	Quick Order Package 28E Sport (SE FWD)	1879	2210
	Manufacturer Discount	(489)	(575)
	Net Price	1390	1635
	Includes front and rear floor mats, fog lamps, deluxe insulation group, light group: illuminated glove box, illuminated ignition and illuminated ash tray; speed sensitive power door locks, dual illuminated visor vanity mirrors, body colored bodyside moldings, rear fascia scuff pad, body colored rear spoiler, front and rear stabilizer bars, leather-wrapped steering wheel, HD suspension, tires: P215/65R16 AS SBR, 16" wheel covers and power windows with driver's 1 touch down. REQUIRES EGA and DGB and NAE.		
28K	Quick Order Package 28K (LE FWD)	NC	NC
	Includes vehicle with standard equipment. REQUIRES EGA and DGB and NAE.		
28N	Quick Order Package 28N Sport (SE FWD)	3086	3630
	Manufacturer Discount	(574)	(675)
	Net Price	2512	2955
	Includes overhead console with trip computer, front and rear floor mats, fog lamps, deluxe insulation group, door courtesy lamps, rear reading lamps, light group: illuminated glove box, illuminated ignition and illuminated ash tray; speed sensitive power door locks, dual illuminated visor vanity mirrors, body colored bodyside moldings, rear fascia scuff pad, 8-way power driver's seat, 7-passenger quad buckets, premium cloth low back bucket seats: 8-way power driver's seat, body colored rear spoiler, front and rear stabilizer bars, leather-wrapped steering wheel, HD suspension, tires: P215/65R16 AS SBR, 16" wheel covers and power windows with driver's 1 touch down. REQUIRES EGA and DGB and NAE .		
28S	Quick Order Package 28S (Base)	NC	NC
	Includes vehicle with standard equipment. REQUIRES EGA and DGB and NAE and 4XA.		
28T	Quick Order Package 28T (Base)	765	900
	Manufacturer Discount	(646)	(760)
	Net Price	119	140
	Includes air conditioning, under seat lockable drawer, rear floor silencer pad and front seat cargo net. REQUIRES NAE and EGA and DGB.		

CODE	DESCRIPTION	INVOICE	MSRP
29D	**Quick Order Package 29D (SE AWD)**	854	1005
	Manufacturer Discount	(255)	(300)
	Net Price	599	705
	Includes front and rear floor mats, deluxe insulation group, light group: illuminated glove box, illuminated ignition and illuminated ash tray; power door locks, illuminated visor vanity mirrors, power windows quarter vent and power windows with driver's one touch down. REQUIRES (EGH and DGB) and (AAB or 4XN).		
29K	**Quick Order Package 29K (LE FWD/LE AWD)**	NC	NC
	Includes vehicle with standard equipment. REQUIRES (EGH and DGB) or (EGH and DGB) and (AAB or 4XN).		
29M	**Quick Order Package 29M (SE FWD/SE AWD)**	NC	NC
	Includes vehicle with standard equipment. REQUIRES (EGH and DGB) or (EGH and DGB) and (AAB or 4XN).		
29N	**Quick Order Package 29N (SE FWD)**	3086	3630
	Manufacturer Discount	(574)	(675)
	Net Price	2512	2955
	Includes overhead console with trip computer, front and rear floor mats, fog lamps, deluxe insulation group, door courtesy lamps, rear reading lamps, light group: illuminated glove box, illuminated ignition and illuminated ash tray; speed sensitive power door locks, dual illuminated visor vanity mirrors, body colored bodyside moldings, rear fascia scuff pad, 8-way power driver's seat, 7-passenger quad buckets, premium cloth low back bucket seats: 8-way power driver's seat, body colored rear spoiler, front and rear stabilizer bars, leather-wrapped steering wheel, HD suspension, tires: P215/65R16 AS SBR, 16" wheel covers and power windows with driver's 1 touch down. REQUIRES EGH and DGB.		
4XA	**Air Conditioning Bypass (Base)**	NC	NC
4XN	**Rear Air Conditioning Bypass (All Except ES AWD)**	NC	NC
AAA	**Climate Group II (Base/SE FWD/SE AWD)**	383	450
	Includes sunscreen glass and windshield wiper de-icer. REQUIRES 25T or 28T for FWD models.		
AAB	**Climate Group III (LE FWD/LE AWD)**	438	515
	NOT AVAILABLE with 4XN.		
AAB	**Climate Group III (LE FWD/ES FWD/ES AWD)**	383	450
	REQUIRES AHT on LE FWD. NOT AVAILABLE with 4XN.		
AAB	**Climate Group III (SE FWD)**	1020	1200
	Includes rear air conditioning and heater, overhead console, air conditioning with dual temp control, deluxe insulation group and rear reading lamps.		
AAB	**Climate Group III (SE FWD/SE AWD)**	1024	1205
	Includes air conditioning with dual temp control and rear reading lamps. REQUIRES 25D or 28D on SE FWD.		
AAB	**Climate Group III (SE FWD)**	969	1140
	Includes rear air conditioning and heater, air conditioning with dual temp control, overhead console with trip computer and rear reading lamps. REQUIRES AHT.		
AAB	**Climate Group III with Sport (SE FWD)**	587	690
	Includes rear air conditioning and heater, overhead console with trip computer, air conditioning with dual temp control and rear reading lamps.		

CODE	DESCRIPTION	INVOICE	MSRP
AAB	Climate Group III with Sport (SE FWD) *Includes rear air conditioning and heater and air conditioning with dual temp control.*	421	495
AAC	Convenience Group I (Base) *Includes speed control, tilt steering column and power fold-away mirrors.*	370	435
AAE	Convenience Group II (SE FWD) *Includes power fold-away mirrors, speed control and tilt steering column and speed sensitive power door locks.*	268	315
AAE	Convenience Group II (Base) *Includes speed control, tilt steering column, power fold-away mirrors and speed sensitive power door locks.*	638	750
AAF	Convenience Group III (Base) *Includes speed control, tilt steering column, power fold-away mirrors, speed sensitive power door locks and power windows with driver's 1 touch down.*	952	1120
AAF	Convenience Group III (SE FWD) *Includes power fold-away mirrors, speed control and tilt steering column and speed sensitive power door locks and power windows with driver's 1 touch down.*	582	685
AAG	Convenience Group IV (SE FWD/SE AWD) *Includes power fold-away mirrors, speed control and tilt steering column, speed sensitive power door locks, power windows with driver's 1 touch down, and remote keyless and illuminated entry.*	204	240
AAH	Convenience Group V (LE/ES) *Includes power fold-away mirrors, speed control and tilt steering column, speed sensitive power door locks, power windows with driver's 1 touch down, remote keyless and illuminated entry and vehicle theft alarm.*	128	150
AAH	Convenience Group V (SE FWD/SE AWD) *Includes convenience group IV.*	332	390
AAP	Loading and Towing Group II (SE FWD/LE FWD) *Includes HD suspension.*	153	180
AAP	Loading and Towing Group II (LE FWD) *Includes HD suspension. REQUIRES AGA.*	94	110
AGA	Wheels/Handling Group (LE FWD) *Includes wheels: 16" aluminum (silver).*	434	510
AGA	Wheels/Handling Group (LE FWD) *Includes wheels: 16" aluminum (silver). REQUIRES AHT.*	374	440
AHT	Trailer Tow Group (SE FWD/LE FWD) *Includes front disc/rear drum heavy duty brakes, 600-amp maintenance free battery, HD transmission oil cooler, HD suspension and trailer tow wiring harness.*	357	420
AHT	Trailer Tow Group (SE FWD/SE AWD/LE AWD) *Includes front disc/rear drum heavy duty brakes, HD transmission oil cooler and trailer tow wiring harness. REQUIRES AAB.*	242	285
AHT	Trailer Tow Group (SE AWD/LE AWD) *Includes 600-amp maintenance free battery, HD transmission oil cooler, HD radiator and trailer tow wiring harness.*	298	350
AHT	Trailer Tow Group (ES FWD/ES AWD) *Includes front disc/rear drum heavy duty brakes, HD transmission oil cooler and trailer tow wiring harness.*	149	175

CODE	DESCRIPTION	INVOICE	MSRP
AWS	Smoker's Group	17	20
	Includes front and rear ash receivers and cigar lighter.		
BGF	Antilock Brakes (Base)	480	565
BNM	Traction Control (LE FWD)	149	175
CMA	Heated Front Seats (ES FWD/ES AWD)	213	250
	REQUIRES HL. NOT AVAILABLE with CYT.		
CYK	7 Passenger Seating with Child Seats (Base)	200	235
	Includes 2 child seats.		
CYR	7 Passenger Deluxe with Child Seats (SE FWD/SE AWD)	191	225
	Includes 2 child seats.		
CYS	7 Passenger Quad Buckets (All Except ES AWD)	570	670
CYT	7 Passenger Quad Buckets with Child Seats (SE FWD)	106	125
	Includes 2 child seats. REQUIRES 25N or 28N or 29N.		
CYT	7 Passenger Quad Buckets with Child Seats (All Except ES AWD/SE FWD)	676	795
	Includes 2 child seats. REQUIRES 25E or 28E or 25D or 28D.		
DGB	Transmission: 4-Speed Automatic	NC	NC
EGA	Engine: 3.3L MPI V6 (All Except AWD and ES)	NC	NC
EGH	Engine: 3.8L MPI V6 (AWD and ES)	NC	NC
EGH	Engine: 3.8L MPI V6 (LE FWD)	434	510
	Manufacturer Discount	(43)	(50)
	Net Price	391	460
	Includes traction control.		
EGH	Engine: 3.8L MPI V6 (FWD SE)	285	335
EGM	Engine: 3.3L FFV V6 (All Except AWD and ES)	NC	NC
GFA	Rear Window Defroster (Base)	166	195
	Includes windshield wiper de-icer.		
GFA	Rear Window Defroster (Base)	196	230
	Includes windshield wiper de-icer. REQUIRES AAC or AAE or AAF.		
HAA	Air Conditioning (Base)	731	860
	NOT AVAILABLE with 4XA.		
HL	Leather Low Back Bucket Seats (LE FWD/LE AWD)	757	890
	REQUIRES CYS and AAB.		
HL	Leather Low Back Bucket Seats (ES FWD/ES AWD)	1058	1245
	REQUIRES AAB or (CYS and AAB).		
MWG	Roof Rack (All Except ES FWD/ES AWD)	166	195
MWP	Body Colored Roof Rack (ES FWD/ES AWD)	204	240
NAE	CA/CT/MA/NY Emissions	NC	NC
	Automatically coded.		
NBN	Northeastern States Emissions	NC	NC
	Includes Connecticut, Delaware, Maryland, New Hampshire, New Jersey, Pennsylvania, Rhode Island, Virginia and District of Columbia. Also available in border states of these states. NOT AVAILABLE in Massachusetts or New York.		
NHK	Engine Block Heater	30	35
PH2	Candy Apple Red Metallic Clear Coat (All Except Base)	170	200
PWP	Golden White Pearl Tri-Coat (ES FWD/ES AWD)	170	200
RAS	Radio: AM/FM Stereo with Cassette (Base)	153	180

CODE	DESCRIPTION	INVOICE	MSRP
RAZ	Radio: AM/FM Stereo with CD, Cassette and EQ (SE FWD/SE AWD) *Includes 4 speakers.*	276	325
RAZ	Radio: AM/FM Stereo with CD, Cassette and EQ (LE FWD/LE AWD)	264	310
RBR	Radio: AM/FM Stereo with CD (Base)	276	325
RCE	10 Speaker Infinity Sound System (SE FWD/SE AWD) *200 watts. REQUIRES RAZ.*	336	395
WJB	Wheels: 15" Aluminum (SE FWD/SE AWD)	353	415
WNG	Wheels: 16" Aluminum (silver) (SE FWD)	225	265
WNG	Wheels: 16" Aluminum (silver) (LE FWD/LE AWD)	353	415
YCF	Border State Emissions (California)	NC	NC

1999 RAM PICKUP

1999 Dodge Ram Pickup

What's New?

The Sport model gets a new front bumper, fascia, grille, headlamps, graphics, and Solar Yellow exterior color just to make sure it won't go unnoticed in traffic. All Rams get an express down feature for the power windows, a new headlamp switch, and four-wheel ABS is standard on vehicles over 10,000-lb. GVW.

Review

The Dodge boys had to know they had a winner when their bold Ram pickup debuted in 1994. Few trucks have turned as many heads, or prompted so much comment. Whether decked out in Sport trim or wearing conventional chrome on its chest-thumping grille, this is macho mentality sculpted in steel.

Under the hood, the goods range from modest to mammoth. For the practical-minded, there's a mild-mannered 3.9-liter V6 that makes 175 horsepower. Then there's a Cummins diesel with 460 foot-pounds of torque whose throbbing note and power make a guy want to grab his Stetson and haul on out.

Those who'd like a little more muscle have a pair of V8s to choose from. Whoa! You're still not satisfied? Like TV's Tim the Tool Man, you want "more power?" Say no more. Just check the option list and you can barrel homeward with an 8.0-liter V10, blasting out 300 horses, and a locomotive-like 450 foot-pounds of torque. The Magnum V10 is available only in heavy-duty 2500 and 3500 series pickups.

One first-season criticism centered on space. Only the regular cab was available, seating three on a bench. Dodge claimed its cab was the most spacious in the industry, but that was little consolation to potential buyers who needed to carry extra people. So Dodge introduced a Club Cab that seated six adults, even if access to the rear wasn't so easy. Then Club Cab models received standard rear-quarter window glass. Last year, the rules changed again. Dodge now offers a Ram Quad Cab, which means rear-access doors on either side of the cab. And for 1999, all extended-cab models get some storage space under the rear seats.

Inside, the Ram is fully modernized, with ergonomics that match the utility of the rest of the truck. The passenger-side airbag comes with a cutoff switch, so it's perfectly safe to strap in a child seat up front. With any engine, tromping the gas produces a reassuring roar — a reverberation of vitality. Otherwise, it's fairly quiet. Ride and handling are so competent that you almost forget you're in a full-size pickup, though occupants will notice plenty of bumps. Visibility is excellent, and controls are first-rate. Automatic-transmission shifts are firm, but not harsh, and the column-mounted gearshift operates easily. For such a bulky vehicle, the Ram is surprisingly agile and reasonably surefooted, but think twice before making any quick maneuvers.

Demand for the Ram is still strong. When pickup owners try to sleep on the idea of buying a new truck, they count Rams.

1999 RAM 1500

Safety Data

Side Airbag: *Not Available*
4-Wheel ABS: *Optional*
Driver Crash Test Grade: *Good*
Side Impact Crash Test Front: *Not Available*
Crash Offset: *Not Available*
Integrated Child Seat(s): *Not Available*
Traction Control: *Not Available*
Passenger Crash Test Grade: *Good*
Side Impact Crash Test Rear: *Not Available*

Standard Equipment

WS 2WD REGULAR CAB (5M): 3.9L V6 OHV SMPI 12-valve engine; 5-speed overdrive manual transmission; 600-amp battery; 117-amp alternator; rear wheel drive, 3.21 axle ratio; stainless steel exhaust; front independent suspension with anti-roll bar, front coil springs, HD front shocks, rigid rear axle suspension with rear leaf springs, HD rear shocks; power re-circulating ball steering with vehicle speed-sensing assist; front disc/rear drum brakes with rear wheel antilock braking system; 26 gal (35 gal/LB) capacity fuel tank; front and rear black bumper with black rub strip; monotone paint; aero-composite halogen headlamps; additional exterior lights include center high mounted stop light; driver's and passenger's manual black folding outside mirrors; front and rear 16" x 7" steel wheels with black hub caps; P225/75SR16 BSW AS front and rear tires; underbody mounted full-size conventional steel spare wheel; 2 power accessory outlets; instrumentation display includes oil pressure gauge, water temp gauge, volt gauge, trip odometer; warning indicators include low oil level, lights on, key in ignition; driver's side airbag, passenger's side cancelable airbag; tinted windows; variable intermittent front windshield wipers; seating capacity of 3, front bench seat with fixed headrests, driver's seat includes 2-way direction control, passenger's seat includes 2-way direction control; front height adjustable seatbelts; vinyl seats, full cloth headliner, full vinyl floor covering, cabback insulator; interior lights include dome light; day-night rearview mirror; glove box, front cupholder, instrument panel bin, driver's and passenger's door bins; cargo concealed storage; chrome grille, black side window moldings, black front windshield molding, black rear window molding and black door handles.

ST 2WD REGULAR CAB (5M) (in addition to or instead of WS 2WD REGULAR CAB (5M) equipment): Front and rear argent bumpers with black rub strip, rear step; front and rear 16" x 7" silver styled steel wheels; additional exterior lights include cargo lamp; AM/FM stereo with digital clock, cassette and 4 speakers; 40-20-40 split-bench front seat with fixed headrests, center armrest with storage, driver's seat includes 4-way direction control and passenger's seat includes 4-way direction control.

ST 2WD CLUB CAB (5M) (in addition to or instead of ST 2WD REGULAR CAB (5M) equipment): 5.2L V8 OHV SMPI 16-valve engine; deep tinted windows, vented rear windows; seating capacity of 6, driver's seat includes 4-way direction control with easy entry, passenger's seat includes 4-way direction control with easy entry, additional access doors (Quad Cab only) and full folding rear bench seat.

ST 4WD REGULAR CAB (5M) (in addition to or instead of ST 2WD REGULAR CAB (5M) equipment): 5.2L V8 OHV SMPI 16-valve engine, part-time 4 wheel drive, auto locking hub control and manual shift, 3.55 axle ratio; front non-independent suspension with anti-roll bar, front coil springs, HD front shocks and cargo concealed storage.

ST 4WD CLUB CAB (5M) (in addition to or instead of ST 4WD REGULAR CAB (5M) equipment): Deep tinted windows, vented rear windows; seating capacity of 6, driver's seat includes 4-way direction control with easy entry, passenger's seat includes 4-way direction control with easy entry, additional access doors (Quad Cab only) and full folding rear bench seat.

Base Prices

Code	Description	Invoice	MSRP
BR1E61	WS 2WD Regular Cab SB (5M)	13510	14795
BR1E62	WS 2WD Regular Cab LB (5M)	13747	15065
BR1L61	ST 2WD Regular Cab SB (5M)	14579	16575
BR1L62	ST 2WD Regular Cab LB (5M)	14821	16860
BE1L31	ST 2WD Club Cab SB (5M)	16841	19195
BE1L32	ST 2WD Club Cab LB (5M)	17079	19475
BE1L33	ST 2WD Quad Cab SB (5M)	17527	19990
BE1L34	ST 2WD Quad Cab LB (5M)	17765	20270
BR6L61	ST 4WD Regular Cab SB (5M)	17646	20130
BR6L62	ST 4WD Regular Cab LB (5M)	17935	20470
BE6L31	ST 4WD Club Cab SB (5M)	19652	22455
BE6L32	ST 4WD Club Cab LB (5M)	19932	22785
BE6L33	ST 4WD Quad Cab SB (5M)	20328	23250
BE6L34	ST 4WD Quad Cab LB (5M)	20608	23580
Destination Charge:		640	640

Accessories

Code	Description	Invoice	MSRP
—	Regional Discount: TX/OK/LA/AZ/NM (Reg Cab 4WD) *REQUIRES 23A or 24A and HAA.*	(684)	(805)
21A	Quick Order Package 21A (Reg Cab 2WD Except WS) *Includes 3.21 axle ratio. REQUIRES (HAA or 4XA) and EHC and DDC.*	NC	NC
21W	Quick Order Package 21W (WS) *Includes 3.21 axle ratio. REQUIRES (HAA or 4XA) and EHC and DDC.*	NC	NC
22A	Quick Order Package 22A (Reg Cab 2WD Except WS) *Includes 3.55 axle ratio. REQUIRES (HAA or 4XA) and EHC and DGB.*	NC	NC

CODE	DESCRIPTION	INVOICE	MSRP
22W	**Quick Order Package 22W (WS)**	NC	NC
	Includes 3.55 axle ratio. REQUIRES (HAA or 4XA) and EHC and DGB.		
23A	**Quick Order Package 23A (All Except WS)**	NC	NC
	Includes vehicle with standard equipment. REQUIRES (HAA or 4XA) and ELF and DDC.		
23G	**Quick Order Package 23G (Reg Cab 2WD Except WS)**	2644	3110
	Manufacturer Discount	(595)	(700)
	Net Price	2049	2410
	Includes air conditioning, deluxe convenience group: tilt steering column, speed control; instrument cluster with tachometer, light group: mini overhead console, glove box light, map/reading lights, underhood lamp; power heated foldaway mirrors, bodyside molding, power convenience group: power door locks, power windows with driver's 1 touch down; SLT Decor group: front floor mats, right sun visor mirror, leather-wrapped steering wheel, premium cloth 40/20/40 split bench seat, black tailgate applique, carpeted floor covering, hood insulation, power fold-away heated mirrors, body-side molding and front bumper sight shields; P245/75R16 BSW AS tires, 16" x 7" cast aluminum wheels and 3.55 axle ratio. REQUIRES EML and DGB.		
23G	**Quick Order Package 23G (All Except Reg Cab 2WD)**	2533	2980
	Manufacturer Discount	(595)	(700)
	Net Price	1938	2280
	Includes air conditioning, deluxe convenience group: tilt steering column, speed control; instrument cluster with tachometer, light group: mini overhead console, glove box light, map/reading lights, underhood lamp; power heated foldaway mirrors, bodyside molding, power convenience group: power door locks, power windows with driver's 1 touch down; SLT Decor group: front floor mats, right sun visor mirror, leather-wrapped steering wheel, premium cloth 40/20/40 split bench seat, black tailgate applique, carpeted floor covering, hood insulation, power fold-away heated mirrors, body-side molding and front bumper sight shields; 16" x 7" cast aluminum wheels and 3.55 axle ratio. REQUIRES ELF and DDC.		
24A	**Quick Order Package 24A (Reg Cab 2WD Except WS)**	NC	NC
	Includes 3.55 axle ratio. REQUIRES (HAA or 4XA) and ELF and DGB.		
24G	**Quick Order Package 24G (Reg Cab 2WD Except WS)**	2644	3110
	Manufacturer Discount	(595)	(700)
	Net Price	2049	2410
	Includes air conditioning, deluxe convenience group: tilt steering column, speed control; instrument cluster with tachometer, light group: mini overhead console, glove box light, map/reading lights, underhood lamp; power heated foldaway mirrors, bodyside molding, power convenience group: power door locks, power windows with driver's 1 touch down; SLT Decor group: front floor mats, right sun visor mirror, leather-wrapped steering wheel, premium cloth 40/20/40 split bench seat, black tailgate applique, carpeted floor covering, hood insulation, power fold-away heated mirrors, body-side molding and front bumper sight shields; P245/75R16 BSW AS tires, 16" x 7" cast aluminum wheels and 3.55 axle ratio. REQUIRES ELF and DGB.		

CODE	DESCRIPTION	INVOICE	MSRP
24G	**Quick Order Package 24G (All Except Reg Cab 2WD)**	2533	2980
	Manufacturer Discount	(595)	(700)
	Net Price	1938	2280
	Includes air conditioning, deluxe convenience group: tilt steering column, speed control; instrument cluster with tachometer, light group: mini overhead console, glove box light, map/reading lights, underhood lamp; power heated foldaway mirrors, bodyside molding, power convenience group: power door locks, power windows with driver's 1 touch down; SLT Decor group: front floor mats, right sun visor mirror, leather-wrapped steering wheel, premium cloth 40/20/40 split bench seat, black tailgate applique, carpeted floor covering, hood insulation, power fold-away heated mirrors, body-side molding and front bumper sight shields; 16" x 7" cast aluminum wheels and 3.55 axle ratio. REQUIRES ELF and DGB.		
26A	**Quick Order Package 26A (Reg Cab 2WD Except WS)**	NC	NC
	Includes 3.55 axle ratio. REQUIRES (HAA or 4XA) and EML and DGB.		
26G	**Quick Order Package 26G (Reg Cab 2WD Except WS)**	2644	3110
	Manufacturer Discount	(595)	(700)
	Net Price	2049	2410
	Includes air conditioning, deluxe convenience group: tilt steering column, speed control; instrument cluster with tachometer, light group: mini overhead console, glove box light, map/reading lights, underhood lamp; power heated foldaway mirrors, bodyside molding, power convenience group: power door locks, power windows with driver's 1 touch down; SLT Decor group: front floor mats, right sun visor mirror, leather-wrapped steering wheel, premium cloth 40/20/40 split bench seat, black tailgate applique, carpeted floor covering, hood insulation, power fold-away heated mirrors, body-side molding and front bumper sight shields; P245/75R16 BSW AS tires, 16" x 7" cast aluminum wheels and 3.55 axle ratio. REQUIRES EML and DGB.		
26G	**Quick Order Package 26G (All Except Reg Cab 2WD)**	2533	2980
	Manufacturer Discount	(595)	(700)
	Net Price	1938	2280
	Includes air conditioning, deluxe convenience group: tilt steering column, speed control; instrument cluster with tachometer, light group: mini overhead console, glove box light, map/reading lights, underhood lamp; power heated foldaway mirrors, bodyside molding, power convenience group: power door locks, power windows with driver's 1 touch down; SLT Decor group: front floor mats, right sun visor mirror, leather-wrapped steering wheel, premium cloth 40/20/40 split bench seat, black tailgate applique, carpeted floor covering, hood insulation, power fold-away heated mirrors, body-side molding and front bumper sight shields; 16" x 7" cast aluminum wheels and 3.55 axle ratio. REQUIRES EML and DGB.		
4XA	**Air Conditioning Bypass**	NC	NC
4XM	**No Rear Bumper (WS)**	NC	NC
	NOT AVAILABLE with MBD.		
ADA	**Light Group (All Except WS)**	102	120
	Includes passenger assist handles, deluxe headliner and ignition key light with time delay, glove box light, underhood lamp and map/reading lights.		

CODE	DESCRIPTION	INVOICE	MSRP
ADJ	HD Service Group (4WD) *Includes 136-amp alternator, 750-amp maintenance free battery and transfer case skid plate. REQUIRES DDC.*	221	260
ADJ	HD Service Group (2WD Except WS) *Includes 136-amp alternator, 750-amp maintenance free battery and HD engine cooler: auxiliary transmission oil cooler. REQUIRES DGB.*	293	345
ADJ	HD Service Group (4WD) *Includes 136-amp alternator, 750-amp maintenance free battery, HD engine cooler: auxiliary transmission oil cooler and transfer case skid plate. REQUIRES DGB.*	332	390
ADJ	HD Service Group (2WD Except WS) *Includes 136-amp alternator and 750-amp maintenance free battery. REQUIRES DDC.*	183	215
AGG	Sport Appearance Group (2WD Except WS) *Includes 'Sport' badge, '1500 V8' badge on door, quad halogen headlamps, instrument cluster with tach, fog lamps, color keyed grille and bodyside moldings delete. REQUIRES 2*G.*	429	505
AGG	Sport Appearance Group (4WD) *Includes 'Sport' badge, '1500 V8' badge on door, quad halogen headlamps, instrument cluster with tach, 16" x 7" cast aluminum wheels, rear body color bumper, fog lamps and color keyed grille. REQUIRES 2*G.*	672	790
AHC	Trailer Tow Group (All Except WS) *Includes HD flasher, 7 lead harness and trailer hitch receiver (class IV). REQUIRES ADJ.*	208	245
AHH	Light Duty Snow Plow Prep Group (4WD)	72	85
	Manufacturer Discount	(72)	(85)
	Net Price *Recommended front clear lights and extra duty front suspension. REQUIRES ADJ and AHC and ELF. NOT AVAILABLE with 26A, 26G.*	NC	NC
AJD	Leather Interior Group (Club Cab 4WD/Quad Cab 4WD) *Includes leather 40/20/40 split bench seat, 8-way power driver's seat, travel convenience group: overhead console with trip computer, automatic dimming rearview mirror and illuminated visor vanity mirrors. REQUIRES 2*G.*	1352	1590
AJD	Leather Interior Group (Reg Cab 2WD Except WS) *Includes leather 40/20/40 split bench seat, 8-way power driver's seat, travel convenience group: overhead console with trip computer, automatic dimming rearview mirror and illuminated visor vanity mirrors. REQUIRES 2*G.*	1233	1450
AJK	Deluxe Convenience Group (All Except WS) *Includes speed control and tilt steering column.*	332	390
AMR	Behind Seat Storage (WS) *Includes storage tray and cab-back stowage.*	81	95
APD	Lower Two-Tone Paint (All Except WS)	166	195
AWK	Travel Convenience Group (All Except WS) *Includes overhead console with trip computer, automatic dimming rearview mirror and illuminated visor vanity mirrors. REQUIRES 2*G.*	293	345

CODE	DESCRIPTION	INVOICE	MSRP
AYB	Wheel Plus Group (4WD)	523	615
	Manufacturer Discount	(230)	(270)
	Net Price	293	345
	Includes 16" x 7" chrome wheels, P245/75R16 AS OWL tires and sliding rear window. REQUIRES 23A or 24A.		
AYB	Wheel Plus Group (2WD Except WS)	633	745
	Manufacturer Discount	(340)	(400)
	Net Price	293	345
	Includes 16" x 7" chrome wheels, P245/75R16 AS OWL tires and sliding rear window. REQUIRES ELF or EHC or 23A or 24A.		
AZB	Regional Savings Package: AL/AR/FL/GA/MS/NC/SC/TN (All Except WS)	553	650
	Manufacturer Discount	(425)	(500)
	Net Price	128	150
	REQUIRES HAA.		
BGK	4-Wheel Antilock Brakes	425	500
CF8	Rear Seat Delete (Quad Cab)	NC	NC
	REQUIRES TY.		
CKE	Carpet Floor Covering (All Except WS)	94	110
CKJ	Black Vinyl Floor Covering (All Except WS)	NC	NC
	*NOT AVAILABLE with CUE. REQUIRES 2*G.*		
CUE	Rear Underseat Compartment Storage (Quad Cab)	47	55
	NOT AVAILABLE with CKJ.		
D3	Deluxe Cloth and Vinyl Bench Seat (WS)	94	110
	NOT AVAILABLE with D2.		
DDC	Transmission: 5-Speed Manual	NC	NC
DGB	Transmission: 4-Speed Automatic	808	950
DMD	3.55 Axle Ratio (2WD)	43	50
DMH	3.92 Axle Ratio (2WD Except WS)	43	50
	REQUIRES DSA.		
DSA	Anti-Spin Differential Axle	242	285
	REQUIRES DMD or DMH.		
EHC	Engine: 3.9L SMPI V6 Magnum (Reg Cab 2WD)	NC	NC
ELF	Engine: 5.2L SMPI V8 Magnum (All Except Reg Cab 2WD)	NC	NC
	NOT AVAILABLE with 26A.		
ELF	Engine: 5.2L SMPI V8 Magnum (Reg Cab 2WD Except WS)	502	590
EML	Engine: 5.9L SMPI V8 Magnum (Regular Cab Except WS)	1007	1185
	REQUIRES DGB.		
EML	Engine: 5.9L SMPI V8 Magnum (Club Cab/Quad Cab)	506	595
	REQUIRES DGB.		
GFD	Sliding Rear Window	119	140
GPC	Wide Mount 7"x10" Dual Bright Mirrors (All Except WS)	43	50
GPC	Wide Mount 7"x10" Dual Bright Mirrors (All Except WS)	NC	NC
	*REQUIRES 2*G.*		
GTS	Power Heated Foldaway Mirrors (All Except WS)	123	145
	REQUIRES HAA.		
GXM	Remote Keyless Entry (All Except WS)	162	190
	*REQUIRES 2*G.*		

CODE	DESCRIPTION	INVOICE	MSRP
HAA	Air Conditioning *NOT AVAILABLE with 4XA.*	684	805
JAY	Instrument Cluster with Tachometer (All Except WS)	68	80
JPS	6-Way Power Driver's Seat (Regular Cab Except WS) *REQUIRES 2*G.*	272	320
JPV	8-Way Power Driver's Seat (Club Cab/Quad Cab) *REQUIRES 2*G.*	306	360
LNC	Cab Clearance Lamps	68	80
LNJ	Fog Lamps (All Except WS) *REQUIRES 2*G.*	119	140
LPE	Cargo Lamp (WS)	34	40
LSA	Security Alarm (All Except WS) *REQUIRES GXM and AWK and 2*G.*	128	150
MBD	Rear Argent Bumper (WS) *NOT AVAILABLE with 4XM.*	115	135
NAE	California Emissions *Automatically coded. NOT AVAILABLE with YCF.*	NC	NC
NHK	Engine Block Heater	34	40
NMC	HD Engine Cooler (All Except WS) *Includes auxiliary transmission oil cooler.*	111	130
RAS	Radio: AM/FM Stereo with Cassette (WS)	340	400
RAZ	Radio: AM/FM Stereo with CD, Cassette and EQ (All Except WS) *REQUIRES 2*G.*	587	690
RBN	Radio: AM/FM Stereo with Cassette and CD Changer Control (All Except WS) *REQUIRES 2*G.*	285	335
RBR	Radio: AM/FM Stereo with CD (All Except WS) *REQUIRES 2*G.*	434	510
RDZ	Steering Wheel Mounted Audio Controls (All Except WS) *REQUIRES RAZ and GXM and 2*G.*	64	75
REG	Regional Discount: TX/OK/LA/AZ/NM (Regular Cab 2WD Except WS) *REQUIRES (21A or 22A) and HAA.*	(1296)	(1525)
REG	Regional Discount: TX/OK/LA/AZ/NM (All Except Regular Cab 2WD) *REQUIRES (23A or 24A) and HAA.*	(684)	(805)
S9	Deluxe Cloth 40/20/40 Split Bench Seat (All Except WS) *NOT AVAILABLE with TY.*	94	110
TXW	Tires: P265/75R16 OWL AT (4WD) *REQUIRES 2*G.*	353	415
TY	HD Vinyl 40/20/40 Front Bench Seat (Quad Cab) *NOT AVAILABLE with S9.*	NC	NC
TYU	Tires: P245/75R16 BSW AS (2WD Except WS) *NOT AVAILABLE with AYB, TYX.*	111	130
TYV	Tires: P245/75R16C AS OWL (2WD Except WS) *REQUIRES 2*G.*	111	130
TYX	Tires: P245/75R16 BSW AT (4WD Except Regular Cab) *NOT AVAILABLE with AYB.*	128	150
TYX	Tires: P245/75R16 BSW AT (Regular Cab 4WD)	238	280

CODE	DESCRIPTION	INVOICE	MSRP
TYZ	Tires: P245/75R16 OWL AT (4WD) *REQUIRES 2*G.*	234	275
WDX	Wheels: 16" x 7" Forged Aluminum (All Except WS) *REQUIRES 2*G.*	NC	NC
YCF	Border State Emissions (California) *NOT AVAILABLE with NAE.*	NC	NC

1999 RAM 2500

Safety Data

Side Airbag: *Not Available*
4-Wheel ABS: *Optional*
Driver Crash Test Grade: *Good*
Side Impact Crash Test Front: *Not Available*
Crash Offset: *Not Available*
Integrated Child Seat(s): *Not Available*
Traction Control: *Not Available*
Passenger Crash Test Grade: *Good*
Side Impact Crash Test Rear: *Not Available*

Standard Equipment

ST 2WD REGULAR CAB (5M): 5.9L V8 OHV SMPI 16-valve engine; 5-speed overdrive manual transmission; 600-amp battery; 117-amp alternator; rear wheel drive, 3.54 axle ratio; stainless steel exhaust; front independent suspension with anti-roll bar, front coil springs, HD front shocks, rigid rear axle suspension with rear leaf springs, HD rear shocks; power re-circulating ball steering with vehicle speed-sensing assist; front disc/rear drum brakes with rear wheel antilock braking system; 35 gal capacity fuel tank; front and rear chrome bumpers with black rub strip, rear step; monotone paint; aero-composite halogen headlamps; additional exterior lights include center high mounted stop light, pickup cargo box light; driver's and passenger's manual black folding outside mirrors; front and rear 16" x 6.5" silver styled steel wheels; LT245/75SR16 BSW AS front and rear tires; underbody mounted full-size conventional steel spare wheel; AM/FM stereo with clock, seek-scan, cassette, 4 speakers, and fixed antenna; 2 power accessory outlets; instrumentation display includes oil pressure gauge, water temp gauge, volt gauge, trip odometer; warning indicators include low oil level, lights on, key in ignition; driver's side airbag, passenger's side cancelable airbag; tinted windows; variable intermittent front windshield wipers; seating capacity of 3, 40-20-40 split-bench front seat with fixed headrests, center armrest with storage, driver's seat includes 4-way direction control, passenger's seat includes 4-way direction control; front height adjustable seatbelts; vinyl seats, full cloth headliner, full vinyl floor covering, cabback insulator; interior lights include dome light; day-night rearview mirror; glove box, front cupholder, instrument panel bin; cargo concealed storage; chrome grille, black side window moldings, black front windshield molding, black rear window molding and black door handles.

ST 2WD CLUB/QUAD CAB (5M) (in addition to or instead of ST 2WD REGULAR CAB (5M) equipment): 34 gal capacity fuel tank; deep tinted windows, vented rear windows; seating capacity of 6, 40-20-40 split-bench front seat with fixed headrests, center armrest with storage, driver's seat includes 4-way direction control with easy entry, passenger's seat includes 4-way direction control with easy entry and full folding rear bench seat.

ST 4WD REGULAR CAB (5M) (in addition to or instead of ST 2WD REGULAR CAB (5M) equipment): Part-time 4 wheel drive, auto locking hub control with manual shift; front non-independent suspension with anti-roll bar, front coil springs, HD front shocks and tinted windows.

ST 4WD CLUB/QUAD CAB (5M) (in addition to or instead of ST 2WD CLUB/QUAD CAB (5M) equipment): Part-time 4 wheel drive, auto locking hub control with manual shift; front non-independent suspension with anti-roll bar, front coil springs, HD front shocks and tinted windows.

CODE	DESCRIPTION	INVOICE	MSRP

Base Prices

CODE	DESCRIPTION	INVOICE	MSRP
BR2L62	ST 2WD Regular Cab LB (5M)	17341	19825
BE2L31	ST 2WD Club Cab SB (5M)	18299	20910
BE2L32	ST 2WD Club Cab LB (5M)	18460	21100
BE2L33	ST 2WD Quad Cab SB (5M)	19069	21805
BE2L34	ST 2WD Quad Cab LB (5M)	19231	21995
BR7L62	ST 4WD Regular Cab LB (5M)	19953	22845
BE7L31	ST 4WD Club Cab SB (5M)	21097	24155
BE7L32	ST 4WD Club Cab LB (5M)	21258	24345
BE7L33	ST 4WD Quad Cab SB (5M)	21858	25050
BE7L34	ST 4WD Quad Cab LB (5M)	22019	25240
Destination Charge:		640	640

Accessories

CODE	DESCRIPTION	INVOICE	MSRP
25A	Quick Order Package 25A	NC	NC
	Includes vehicle with standard equipment. REQUIRES (HAA or 4XA) and EML and DDP.		
25G	Quick Order Package 25G	2516	2960
	Manufacturer Discount	(595)	(700)
	Net Price	1921	2260
	Includes air conditioning, deluxe convenience group: speed control, tilt steering column; instrument cluster with tachometer, light group: mini overhead console, glove box lamp, map/courtesy lamp, underhood lamp, passenger assist handles; power convenience group: power door locks, power windows with driver's one touch down; SLT Decor group: black tailgate applique, carpet floor covering, body side molding, front floor mats, power heated foldaway mirrors, right sun visor mirror, front bumper sight shields, leather-wrapped steering wheel, premium cloth 40/20/40 split bench seat; and 16" x 6.5" chrome wheels. REQUIRES EML and DDP.		
26A	Quick Order Package 26A	NC	NC
	Includes vehicle with standard equipment. REQUIRES (HAA or 4XA) and EML and DGB.		
26G	Quick Order Package 26G	2516	2960
	Manufacturer Discount	(595)	(700)
	Net Price	1921	2260
	Includes air conditioning, deluxe convenience group: speed control, tilt steering column; instrument cluster with tachometer, light group: mini overhead console, glove box lamp, map/courtesy lamp, underhood lamp, passenger assist handles; power convenience group: power door locks, power windows with driver's one touch down; SLT Decor group: black tailgate applique, carpet floor covering, body side molding, front floor mats, power heated foldaway mirrors, right sun visor mirror, front bumper sight shields, leather-wrapped steering wheel, premium cloth 40/20/40 split bench seat; and 16" x 6.5" chrome wheels. REQUIRES EML and DGB.		
27A	Quick Order Package 27A	NC	NC
	Includes vehicle with standard equipment. REQUIRES (HAA or 4XA) and DDX and EWA.		

CODE	DESCRIPTION	INVOICE	MSRP
27G	Quick Order Package 27G	2516	2960
	Manufacturer Discount	(595)	(700)
	Net Price	1921	2260
	Includes air conditioning, deluxe convenience group: speed control, tilt steering column; instrument cluster with tachometer, light group: mini overhead console, glove box lamp, map/courtesy lamp, underhood lamp, passenger assist handles; power convenience group: power door locks, power windows with driver's one touch down; SLT Decor group: black tailgate applique, carpet floor covering, body side molding, front floor mats, power heated foldaway mirrors, right sun visor mirror, front bumper sight shields, leather-wrapped steering wheel, premium cloth 40/20/40 split bench seat; and 16" x 6.5" chrome wheels. REQUIRES DDX and EWA.		
28A	Quick Order Package 28A	NC	NC
	Includes vehicle with standard equipment. REQUIRES (HAA or 4XA) and DGB and EWA.		
28G	Quick Order Package 28G	2516	2960
	Manufacturer Discount	(595)	(700)
	Net Price	1921	2260
	Includes air conditioning, deluxe convenience group: speed control, tilt steering column; instrument cluster with tachometer, light group: mini overhead console, glove box lamp, map/courtesy lamp, underhood lamp, passenger assist handles; power convenience group: power door locks, power windows with driver's one touch down; SLT Decor group: black tailgate applique, carpet floor covering, body side molding, front floor mats, power heated foldaway mirrors, right sun visor mirror, front bumper sight shields, leather-wrapped steering wheel, premium cloth 40/20/40 split bench seat; and 16" x 6.5" chrome wheels. REQUIRES DGB and EWA.		
2CA	Quick Order Package 2CA	NC	NC
	Includes vehicle with standard equipment. REQUIRES (HAA or 4XA) and DGB and ETC.		
2CG	Quick Order Package 2CG	2516	2960
	Manufacturer Discount	(595)	(700)
	Net Price	1921	2260
	Includes air conditioning, deluxe convenience group: speed control, tilt steering column; instrument cluster with tachometer, light group: mini overhead console, glove box lamp, map/courtesy lamp, underhood lamp, passenger assist handles; power convenience group: power door locks, power windows with driver's one touch down; SLT Decor group: black tailgate applique, carpet floor covering, body side molding, front floor mats, power heated foldaway mirrors, right sun visor mirror, front bumper sight shields, leather-wrapped steering wheel, premium cloth 40/20/40 split bench seat; and 16" x 6.5" chrome wheels. REQUIRES DGB and ETC.		
2GA	Quick Order Package 2GA	NC	NC
	Includes vehicle with standard equipment. REQUIRES (HAA or 4XA) and DDX and ETC.		
2GG	Quick Order Package 2GG	2516	2960
	Manufacturer Discount	(595)	(700)
	Net Price	1921	2260
	Includes air conditioning, deluxe convenience group: speed control, tilt steering column; instrument cluster with tachometer, light group: mini overhead console, glove		

CODE	DESCRIPTION	INVOICE	MSRP
	box lamp, map/courtesy lamp, underhood lamp, passenger assist handles; power convenience group: power door locks, power windows with driver's one touch down; SLT Decor group: black tailgate applique, carpet floor covering, body side molding, front floor mats, power heated foldaway mirrors, right sun visor mirror, front bumper sight shields, leather-wrapped steering wheel, premium cloth 40/20/40 split bench seat; and 16" x 6.5" chrome wheels. REQUIRES DDX and ETC.		
2HA	**Quick Order Package 2HA**	NC	NC
	Includes 3.54 axle ratio. REQUIRES (HAA or 4XA), ETC and DEE. NOT AVAILABLE with EML, EWA, DDP, DGB, DDX, ADJ, AHD.		
2HG	**Quick Order Package 2HG**	2156	2960
	Manufacturer Discount	(595)	(700)
	Net Price	1561	2260
	Includes air conditioning, deluxe convenience group: speed control, tilt steering column; instrument cluster with tachometer, light group: mini overhead console, glove box lamp, map/courtesy lamp, underhood lamp, passenger assist handles; power convenience group: power door locks, power windows with driver's one touch down; SLT Decor group: black tailgate applique, carpet floor covering, body side molding, front floor mats, power heated foldaway mirrors, right sun visor mirror, front bumper sight shields, leather-wrapped steering wheel, premium cloth 40/20/40 split bench seat; and 16" x 6.5" chrome wheels. REQUIRES DEE and ETC.		
4XA	**Air Conditioning Bypass**	NC	NC
	NOT AVAILABLE with HAA.		
ADA	**Light Group**	102	120
	Includes passenger assist handles, deluxe headliner, ignition time delay lamp, glove box lamp, map/courtesy lamp and underhood lamp.		
ADJ	**HD Service Group (4WD)**	281	330
	Includes 136-amp alternator, 750-amp maintenance free battery, HD engine cooling and transfer case skid plate shield.		
ADJ	**HD Service Group (2WD)**	242	285
	Includes 136-amp alternator and 750-amp maintenance free battery.		
ADJ	**HD Service Group (4WD)**	332	390
	Includes 136-amp alternator, 750-amp maintenance free battery, HD engine cooling and transfer case skid plate shield. REQUIRES DGB.		
ADJ	**HD Service Group (2WD)**	293	345
	Includes 136 amp alternator, 750-amp maintenance free battery and HD engine cooling: auxiliary transmission oil cooler. REQUIRES DGB.		
AGG	**Sport Appearance Group (4WD)**	455	640
	*Includes 1500 V8 door badge, sport badge, front and rear body color bumpers, instrument cluster with tachometer, quad halogen headlamps, fog lamps, body color grille, LT245/75R16 OWL on/off road tires and bodyside moldings delete. REQUIRES 2*G.*		
AGG	**Sport Appearance Group (2WD)**	425	500
	*Includes 1500 V8 door badge, sport badge, front and rear body color bumpers, instrument cluster with tachometer, quad halogen headlamps, fog lamps, body color grille, LT245/75R16 OWL on/off road tires and bodyside moldings delete. REQUIRES 2*G.*		

CODE	DESCRIPTION	INVOICE	MSRP
AHC	Trailer Tow Group	234	275
	Includes HD flasher and trailer hitch receiver (class IV). REQUIRES ADJ.		
AHD	HD Snow Plow Prep Group (4WD)	157	185
	Manufacturer Discount	(72)	(85)
	Net Price	85	100
	Includes computer selected springs, auto trans oil overheat light and shift-on-the-fly transfer case. Front clearance lights (LNC) are recommended. REQUIRES ADJ, AHC and EML.		
AHJ	Auxiliary Rear Suspension Group	81	95
	Includes rear stabilizer bar and auxiliary springs. REQUIRES NMC.		
AJD	Leather Interior Group (Club/Quad Cab)	1352	1590
	*Includes leather 40/20/40 split bench seat, 8-way power driver's seat, travel convenience group: overhead console, trip computer and auto day/night rear-view mirror. REQUIRES 2*G.*		
AJD	Leather Interior Group (Regular Cab)	1233	1450
	*Includes leather 40/20/40 split bench seat, 6-way power driver's seat, travel convenience group: overhead console, trip computer and auto day/night rear-view mirror. REQUIRES 2*G.*		
AJK	Deluxe Convenience Group	332	390
	Includes speed control and tilt steering column.		
APD	Two Tone Lower Paint	166	195
AWK	Travel Convenience Group	293	345
	*Includes overhead console, trip computer and auto day/night rear-view mirror. REQUIRES 2*G.*		
BGK	4-Wheel Antilock Brakes	298	350
CF8	Rear Seat Delete (Quad Cab)	NC	NC
	*REQUIRES TY and 2*A. NOT AVAILABLE with S9.*		
CKE	Carpet Floor Covering	94	110
CKJ	Black Vinyl Floor Covering	NC	NC
	*REQUIRES 2*G. NOT AVAILABLE with CUE.*		
CUE	Rear Underseat Compartment Storage (Quad Cab)	51	60
	*REQUIRES 2*G. NOT AVAILABLE with CKJ.*		
DDP	Transmission: 5-Speed Manual	NC	NC
DDX	Transmission: HD 5-Speed Manual	NC	NC
DEE	Transmission: HD 6-Speed Manual	298	350
	REQUIRES ETC.		
DGB	Transmission: 4-Speed Automatic	829	975
DHG	Shift-On-The-Fly Transfer Case (4WD)	85	100
DMF	4.10 Axle Ratio	43	50
	NOT AVAILABLE with 28A, 28G.		
DSA	Anti-Spin Differential Axle	242	285
EML	Engine: 5.9L SMPI V8 Magnum	NC	NC
	REQUIRES DDP or DGB.		
ETC	Engine: 5.9L Cummins 24V Diesel	3931	4625
	Includes evaporative control system delete, heavy duty insulation group, warning lights for low fuel, low oil, water in fuel, wait to start, antilock brakes, HD service		

CODE	DESCRIPTION	INVOICE	MSRP
	group: 136-amp alternator, 750-amp maintenance free battery and dual 750-amp batteries. REQUIRES DGB or DDX.		
EWA	Engine: 8.0L Magnum MPI V10	400	470
	Includes 750-amp maintenance free battery.		
GFD	Sliding Rear Window	119	140
GPC	Wide Mount 7"x10" Dual Bright Mirrors	43	50
GPC	Wide Mount 7"x10" Dual Bright Mirrors	NC	NC
	*REQUIRES 2*G.*		
GTS	Power Heated Foldaway Mirrors	123	145
	REQUIRES HAA.		
GXM	Remote Keyless Entry	162	190
	*REQUIRES 2*G.*		
HAA	Air Conditioning	684	805
	NOT AVAILABLE with 4XA.		
JAY	Instrument Cluster with Tachometer	68	80
JPS	6-Way Power Driver's Seat (Regular Cab)	272	320
	*REQUIRES 2*G.*		
JPV	8-Way Power Driver's Seat (Club Cab/Quad Cab)	306	360
	*REQUIRES 2*G.*		
K17	Body Side Molding	89	105
LNC	Clearance Lamps	68	80
LNJ	Fog Lamps	119	140
	*REQUIRES 2*G.*		
LSA	Security Alarm	128	150
	*REQUIRES 2*G, GXM and AWK.*		
MXB	Front Air Dam	21	25
	NOT AVAILABLE with AGG.		
NAE	California Emissions	NC	NC
	Automatically coded. NOT AVAILABLE with YCF.		
NHK	Engine Block Heater	77	90
NMC	HD Engine Cooling	60	70
NMC	HD Engine Cooling	111	130
	REQUIRES DGB.		
RAZ	Radio: AM/FM Stereo with CD, Cassette and EQ	587	690
	*REQUIRES 2*G.*		
RBN	Radio: AM/FM Stereo with Cassette and CD Changer Control	285	335
	*REQUIRES 2*G.*		
RBR	Radio: AM/FM Stereo with CD	434	510
	*REQUIRES 2*G.*		
RDZ	Steering Wheel Mounted Audio Controls	64	75
	*REQUIRES 2*G, RAZ and GXM.*		
S9	Deluxe Cloth 40/20/40 Split Bench Seat	94	110
TY	HD Vinyl Bench Seat (Quad Cab)	NC	NC
	REQUIRES CF8.		
TY1	Tires: LT245/75R16-E BSW On/Off Road	119	140
	NOT AVAILABLE with AGG.		

CODE	DESCRIPTION	INVOICE	MSRP
TY2	Tires: LT245/75R16-E OWL On/Off Road *REQUIRES 2*G.*	225	265
TYN	Tires: LT245/75R16E AS OWL *REQUIRES 2*G. NOT AVAILABLE with AGG and TY2.*	106	125
WDC	Wheels: 16" x 6.5" Chrome	276	325
YCF	Border State Emissions (California) *NOT AVAILABLE with NAE.*	NC	NC

1999 RAM 3500

Safety Data

Side Airbag: *Not Available*
4-Wheel ABS: *Standard*
Driver Crash Test Grade: *Good*
Side Impact Crash Test Front: *Not Available*
Crash Offset: *Not Available*
Integrated Child Seat(s): *Not Available*
Traction Control: *Not Available*
Passenger Crash Test Grade: *Good*
Side Impact Crash Test Rear: *Not Available*

Standard Equipment

ST 2WD REGULAR CAB DRW (5M): 5.9L V8 OHV SMPI 16-valve engine; 5-speed overdrive manual transmission; 750-amp HD battery; 136-amp HD alternator; rear wheel drive, 3.54 axle ratio; stainless steel exhaust; front independent suspension with anti-roll bar, front coil springs, HD front shocks, rigid rear axle suspension with rear leaf springs, HD rear shocks; power re-circulating ball steering with vehicle speed-sensing assist; front disc/rear drum brakes with 4 wheel antilock braking system; 35 gal capacity fuel tank; front and rear chrome bumpers with black rub strip, rear step; monotone paint; aero-composite halogen headlamps; additional exterior lights include cab clearance lights, center high mounted stop light, pickup cargo box light; driver's and passenger's power remote black heated folding outside mirrors; front and rear 16" x 6" chrome steel wheels; LT215/85SR16 BSW AS front and rear tires; underbody mounted full-size conventional steel spare wheel; AM/FM stereo with clock, seek-scan, cassette, 4 speakers, and fixed antenna; 2 power accessory outlets; instrumentation display includes oil pressure gauge, water temp gauge, volt gauge, trip odometer; warning indicators include low oil level, lights on, key in ignition; driver's side airbag, passenger's side cancelable airbag; tinted windows; variable intermittent front windshield wipers; seating capacity of 3, 40-20-40 split-bench front seat with fixed headrests, center armrest with storage, driver's seat includes 4-way direction control, passenger's seat includes 4-way direction control; front height adjustable seatbelts; vinyl seats, full cloth headliner, full vinyl floor covering, cabback insulator; interior lights include dome light; day-night rearview mirror; glove box, front cupholder, instrument panel bin, driver's and passenger's door bins; cargo concealed storage; chrome grille, black side window moldings, black front windshield molding, black rear window molding and black door handles.

ST 2WD QUAD CAB DRW (5M) (in addition to or instead of ST 2WD REGULAR CAB DRW (5M) equipment): HD radiator; deep tinted windows, vented rear windows; seating capacity of 6, 40-20-40 split-bench front seat with fixed headrests, center armrest with storage, driver's seat includes 4-way direction control with easy entry, passenger's seat includes 4-way direction control with easy entry and full folding rear bench seat.

ST 4WD REGULAR CAB DRW (5M) (in addition to or instead of ST 2WD REGULAR CAB DRW (5M) equipment): Part-time 4 wheel drive, auto locking hub control with manual shift, 3.54 axle ratio; front non-independent suspension with anti-roll bar, front coil springs, HD front shocks and skid plates.

CODE	DESCRIPTION	INVOICE	MSRP

ST 4WD QUAD CAB DRW (5M) (in addition to or instead of ST 2WD QUAD CAB DRW equipment): Part-time 4 wheel drive, auto locking hub control with manual shift, 3.54 axle ratio; front non-independent suspension with anti-roll bar, front coil springs, HD front shocks and skid plates.

Base Prices

BR3L62	ST 2WD Regular Cab DRW (5M)	18863	21615
BE3L34	ST 2WD Quad Cab DRW (5M)	21411	24595
BR8L62	ST 4WD Regular Cab DRW (5M)	21466	24625
BE8L34	ST 4WD Quad Cab DRW (5M)	23787	27320
Destination Charge:		640	640

Accessories

25A	**Quick Order Package 25A**	NC	NC
	Includes 3.54 axle ratio. REQUIRES EMM and DDP and 4XA.		
25G	**Quick Order Package 25G**	2117	2490
	Manufacturer Discount	(595)	(700)
	Net Price	1522	1790
	Includes air conditioning, deluxe convenience group: speed control, tilt steering; carpet floor covering, instrument cluster with tachometer, light group: overhead console, glove box light, front map lights, underhood lamp; power convenience group: power door locks, power windows with driver's 1 touch down; SLT Decor group: SLT applique on tailgate, front bumper sight shields, front floor mats, right sun visor mirror, leather-wrapped steering wheel, bodyside molding, premium cloth 40/20/40 split bench seat and 3.54 axle ratio. REQUIRES EMM and DDP.		
26A	**Quick Order Package 26A**	NC	NC
	Includes 3.54 axle ratio. REQUIRES EMM and DGB and 4XA.		
26G	**Quick Order Package 26G**	2117	2490
	Manufacturer Discount	(595)	(700)
	Net Price	1522	1790
	Includes air conditioning, deluxe convenience group: speed control, tilt steering; carpet floor covering, instrument cluster with tachometer, light group: overhead console, glove box light, front map lights, underhood lamp; power convenience group: power door locks, power windows with driver's 1 touch down; SLT Decor group: SLT applique on tailgate, front bumper sight shields, front floor mats, right sun visor mirror, leather-wrapped steering wheel, bodyside molding, premium cloth 40/20/40 split bench seat and 3.54 axle ratio. REQUIRES EMM and DGB.		
27A	**Quick Order Package 27A**	NC	NC
	Includes 3.54 axle ratio. REQUIRES EWA and DDX and 4XA. NOT AVAILABLE with AHD.		
27G	**Quick Order Package 27G**	2117	2490
	Manufacturer Discount	(595)	(700)
	Net Price	1522	1790
	Includes air conditioning, deluxe convenience group: speed control, tilt steering; carpet floor covering, instrument cluster with tachometer, light group: overhead console, glove box light, front map lights, underhood lamp; power convenience group: power door locks, power windows with driver's 1 touch down; SLT Decor		

CODE	DESCRIPTION	INVOICE	MSRP
	group: SLT applique on tailgate, front bumper sight shields, front floor mats, right sun visor mirror, leather-wrapped steering wheel, bodyside molding, premium cloth 40/20/40 split bench seat and 3.54 axle ratio. REQUIRES EWA and DDX.		
28A	**Quick Order Package 28A**	NC	NC
	Includes 3.54 axle ratio. REQUIRES EWA and DGB and 4XA. NOT AVAILABLE with AHD.		
28G	**Quick Order Package 28G**	2117	2490
	Manufacturer Discount	(595)	(700)
	Net Price	1522	1790
	Includes air conditioning, deluxe convenience group: speed control, tilt steering; carpet floor covering, instrument cluster with tachometer, light group: overhead console, glove box light, front map lights, underhood lamp; power convenience group: power door locks, power windows with driver's 1 touch down; SLT Decor group: SLT applique on tailgate, front bumper sight shields, front floor mats, right sun visor mirror, leather-wrapped steering wheel, bodyside molding, premium cloth 40/20/40 split bench seat and 3.54 axle ratio. REQUIRES EWA and DGB.		
2CA	**Quick Order Package 2CA**	NC	NC
	Includes 3.54 axle ratio. REQUIRES ETC and DGB and 4XA.		
2CG	**Quick Order Package 2CG**	2117	2490
	Manufacturer Discount	(595)	(700)
	Net Price	1522	1790
	Includes air conditioning, deluxe convenience group: speed control, tilt steering; carpet floor covering, instrument cluster with tachometer, light group: overhead console, glove box light, front map lights, underhood lamp; power convenience group: power door locks, power windows with driver's 1 touch down; SLT Decor group: SLT applique on tailgate, front bumper sight shields, front floor mats, right sun visor mirror, leather-wrapped steering wheel, bodyside molding, premium cloth 40/20/40 split bench seat and 3.54 axle ratio. REQUIRES ETC and DGB.		
2EA	**Quick Order Package 2EA**	NC	NC
	Includes 3.54 axle ratio. REQUIRES NAE and EML and DDP and 4XA.		
2EG	**Quick Order Package 2EG**	2117	2490
	Manufacturer Discount	(595)	(700)
	Net Price	1522	1790
	Includes air conditioning, deluxe convenience group: speed control, tilt steering; carpet floor covering, instrument cluster with tachometer, light group: overhead console, glove box light, front map lights, underhood lamp; power convenience group: power door locks, power windows with driver's 1 touch down; SLT Decor group: SLT applique on tailgate, front bumper sight shields, front floor mats, right sun visor mirror, leather-wrapped steering wheel, bodyside molding, premium cloth 40/20/40 split bench seat and 3.54 axle ratio. REQUIRES NAE and EML and DDP.		
2FA	**Quick Order Package 2FA**	NC	NC
	Includes 3.54 axle ratio. REQUIRES NAE and EML and DGB and 4XA.		
2FG	**Quick Order Package 2FG**	2117	2490
	Manufacturer Discount	(595)	(700)
	Net Price	1522	1790
	Includes air conditioning, deluxe convenience group: speed control, tilt steering; carpet floor covering, instrument cluster with tachometer, light group: overhead		

CODE	DESCRIPTION	INVOICE	MSRP
	console, glove box light, front map lights, underhood lamp; power convenience group: power door locks, power windows with driver's 1 touch down; SLT Decor group: SLT applique on tailgate, front bumper sight shields, front floor mats, right sun visor mirror, leather-wrapped steering wheel, bodyside molding, premium cloth 40/20/40 split bench seat and 3.54 axle ratio. REQUIRES NAE and EML and DGB.		
2GA	Quick Order Package 2GA	NC	NC
	Includes 3.54 axle ratio. REQUIRES ETC and DDX and 4XA.		
2GG	Quick Order Package 2GG	2117	2490
	Manufacturer Discount	(595)	(700)
	Net Price	1522	1790
	Includes air conditioning, deluxe convenience group: speed control, tilt steering; carpet floor covering, instrument cluster with tachometer, light group: overhead console, glove box light, front map lights, underhood lamp; power convenience group: power door locks, power windows with driver's 1 touch down; SLT Decor group: SLT applique on tailgate, front bumper sight shields, front floor mats, right sun visor mirror, leather-wrapped steering wheel, bodyside molding, premium cloth 40/20/40 split bench seat and 3.54 axle ratio. REQUIRES ETC and DDX.		
2HA	Quick Order Package 2HA	NC	NC
	Includes 3.54 axle ratio. REQUIRES DEE and ETC. NOT AVAILABLE with EMM, EML, EWA, DDP, DGB, DDX, AHD.		
2HG	Quick Order Package 2HG	2117	2490
	Manufacturer Discount	(595)	(700)
	Net Price	1522	1790
	Includes air conditioning, deluxe convenience group: speed control, tilt steering; carpet floor covering, instrument cluster with tachometer, light group: overhead console, glove box light, front map lights, underhood lamp; power convenience group: power door locks, power windows with driver's 1 touch down; SLT Decor group: SLT applique on tailgate, front bumper sight shields, front floor mats, right sun visor mirror, leather-wrapped steering wheel, bodyside molding, premium cloth 40/20/40 split bench seat and 3.54 axle ratio. REQUIRES DEE and ETC.		
4XA	Air Conditioning Bypass	NC	NC
ADA	Light Group	102	120
	Includes passenger assist handles, deluxe headliner, time delay ignition lamp, glove box light, front map lights and underhood lamp.		
AGG	Sport Appearance Group	319	375
	*Includes 3500 V8 door badging, halogen quad headlamps, body colored front and rear bumpers, fog lamps and body color grille. REQUIRES 2*G.*		
AHC	Trailer Tow Group	234	275
	Includes adaptor plug, HD flasher and trailer hitch receiver.		
AHD	Snow Plow Prep Package (4WD)	72	85
	Manufacturer Discount	(72)	(85)
	Net Price	NC	NC
	Includes HD shift on-the-fly transfer case, computer selected springs and auto trans oil overheat light. REQUIRES AHC and EMM.		
AHJ	Auxiliary Rear Suspension Group	81	95
	Includes rear stabilizer bar and auxiliary rear springs.		

CODE	DESCRIPTION	INVOICE	MSRP
AJD	Leather Interior Group (Quad Cab) *Includes leather 40/20/40 split bench seat, 8-way power driver's seat, travel convenience group: overhead console with trip computer, automatic dimming rearview mirror and dual illuminated visor vanity mirrors. REQUIRES 2*G.*	1352	1590
AJD	Leather Interior Group (Regular Cab) *Includes leather 40/20/40 split bench seat, 6-way power driver's seat, travel convenience group: overhead console with trip computer, automatic dimming rearview mirror and dual illuminated visor vanity mirrors. REQUIRES 2*G.*	1233	1450
AJK	Deluxe Convenience Group *Includes speed control and tilt steering.*	332	390
AWK	Travel Convenience Group *Includes overhead console with trip computer, automatic dimming rearview mirror and dual illuminated visor vanity mirrors. REQUIRES 2*G.*	293	345
CF8	Rear Seat Delete (Quad Cab) *NOT AVAILABLE with S9.*	NC	NC
CKE	Carpet Floor Covering	94	110
CKJ	Black Vinyl Floor Covering *NOT AVAILABLE with CUE. REQUIRES 2*G.*	NC	NC
CUE	Rear Underseat Compartment Storage (Quad Cab) *NOT AVAILABLE with CKJ. REQUIRES 2*G.*	51	60
DDP	Transmission: 5-Speed Manual	NC	NC
DDX	Transmission: HD 5-Speed Manual	NC	NC
DEE	Transmission: 6-Speed Manual With Overdrive *REQUIRES ETC.*	298	350
DGB	Transmission: 4-Speed Automatic *Includes HD auxiliary transmission oil cooler.*	829	975
DMF	4.10 Axle Ratio *REQUIRES DSA.*	43	50
DSA	Anti-Spin Differential Axle	242	285
EML	Engine: 5.9L SMPI V8 Magnum *REQUIRES NAE.*	NC	NC
EMM	Engine: 5.9L SMPI V8 Magnum	NC	NC
ETC	Engine: 5.9L Cummins 24V Diesel *Includes evaporative control system delete, 136-amp alternator, 750-amp maintenance free battery, HD engine cooling, warning lights for low fuel, low oil, water in fuel, wait to start, antilock brakes, deluxe insulation group and dual 750-amp batteries.*	3931	4625
EWA	Engine: 8.0L Magnum MPI V10 *Includes evaporative control system, 136-amp alternator, 750-amp maintenance free battery and HD engine cooling.*	400	470
GFD	Sliding Rear Window	119	140
GPC	Wide Mount 7"x10" Dual Bright Mirrors *NOT AVAILABLE with GP8.*	NC	NC
GXM	Remote Keyless Entry *REQUIRES 2*G.*	162	190
HAA	Air Conditioning *NOT AVAILABLE with 4XA.*	684	805

CODE	DESCRIPTION	INVOICE	MSRP
JAY	Instrument Cluster with Tachometer	68	80
JPS	6-Way Power Driver's Seat (Regular Cab) *REQUIRES 2*G.*	272	320
JPV	8-Way Power Driver's Seat (Quad Cab) *REQUIRES 2*G.*	306	360
K17	Bodyside Molding	89	105
LNJ	Fog Lamps *REQUIRES 2*G.*	119	140
LSA	Security Alarm *REQUIRES 2*G, GXM and AWK.*	128	150
MXB	Front Air Dam *NOT AVAILABLE with AGG.*	21	25
NAE	California Emissions *Automatically coded.*	NC	NC
NHK	Engine Block Heater	77	90
RAZ	Radio: AM/FM Stereo with CD, Cassette and EQ *REQUIRES 2*G.*	587	690
RBN	Radio: AM/FM Stereo with Cassette and CD Changer Control *REQUIRES 2*G.*	285	335
RBR	Radio: AM/FM Stereo with CD *REQUIRES 2*G.*	434	510
RDZ	Steering Wheel Radio Controls *REQUIRES 2*G, RAZ and GXM.*	64	75
S9	Deluxe Cloth 40/20/40 Split Bench Seat	94	110
TV2	Tires: LT215/85R16E On/Off RD BSW	170	200
TY	HD Vinyl 40/20/40 Front Bench Seat (Quad Cab) *REQUIRES CF8.*	NC	NC
YCF	Border State Emissions (California)	NC	NC

1999 RAM WAGON

1999 Dodge Ram Wagon

What's New?

Seat track travel has increased substantially, and the remote keyless entry has been improved. For fleet customers, Ram Wagons have an available 5.2-liter Compressed Natural Gas V8 engine.

Review

Dodge's full-size vans haven't changed all that much through nearly three decades of existence. Squint your eyes and focus away from the front end (which was redesigned last year), and the latest big Rams could almost be mistaken for 1971 models. But this does not matter to Dodge fans. Dodge's brawny haulers have earned an enviable reputation over the years, proving their worth against rivals from Ford and General Motors. Like those makes, Dodge offers a bewildering selection of models, in three capacities with payloads as great as 4,264 pounds — not to mention the dazzlingly long list of options to be considered. Wagons can be equipped to carry as many as 15 passengers.

All Rams have four-wheel anti-lock braking. The base engine in the 1500 and 2500 series is a 3.9-liter V6, but most buyers would be better off with a V8 (standard in the 3500 series). With 295 pound-feet of torque on tap, the 5.2-liter V8 yields a rewarding combination of strength and economy, but no Ram vehicle ranks miserly at the gas pump.

For demanding applications, whether in cargo-carrying or passenger-seating, the 5.9-liter V8, packing 335 foot-pounds of twisting force, might be a better bet. To compensate for thirsty engine choices, Dodge includes a 35-gallon gas tank on all Ram Wagons.

In 1998, Ram Wagons were redesigned to catch up with some of the technology that has appeared since the vehicles were introduced decades ago. One-third of the components were new, including a new instrument panel, retuned suspension, new brakes, and transformed body panels. Most noticeable is an updated front end, and a less intrusive forward position for the V8 engines. This year, changes are few. The seat travel has been increased by 32 percent, and the remote keyless entry is improved. For fleet customers, a 5.2-liter Compressed Natural Gas V8 engine is available, which substantially reduces emissions.

Plenty of RV converters turn out fancied-up variants of the Dodge Ram, but even the stock models can be fitted with a few comforts and conveniences to make driving pleasant, if not exactly posh. Wagons can have a power driver's seat, for instance, and you can even get a CD player with a graphic equalizer and Infinity speakers. An upscale SLT Wagon Package includes cupholders, seat map pockets, and cloth trim panels. Standard gear includes dual side doors, tinted windows, power steering, and a front stabilizer bar.

The Ram Wagon is packed full of value and is a reasonable alternative to the full-size offerings from Ford and Chevy for those on a strict budget. When searching in this market segment, price is often the only thing separating somewhat unequal competitors.

Safety Data

Side Airbag: *Not Available*
4-Wheel ABS: *Optional*
Driver Crash Test Grade: *Not Available*
Side Impact Crash Test Front: *Not Available*
Crash Offset: *Not Available*
Integrated Child Seat(s): *Not Available*
Traction Control: *Not Available*
Passenger Crash Test Grade: *Not Available*
Side Impact Crash Test Rear: *Not Available*

Standard Equipment

1500 (3A): 3.9L V6 OHV SMPI 12-valve engine; 3-speed automatic transmission; 600-amp battery; 136-amp alternator; rear wheel drive, 3.55 axle ratio; stainless steel exhaust; front independent suspension with anti-roll bar, front coil springs, HD front shocks, rigid rear axle suspension with rear leaf springs, HD rear shocks; power rack-and-pinion steering; front disc/rear drum brakes with rear wheel antilock braking system; 32 gal capacity fuel tank; 3 doors with split swing-out right rear passenger's door, conventional rear cargo door; front and rear chrome bumpers with black rub strip; monotone paint; aero-composite halogen headlamps; additional exterior lights include center high mounted stop light, underhood light; driver's and passenger's manual black folding outside mirrors; front and rear 15" x 7" silver styled steel wheels; P235/75SR15 BSW AS front and rear tires; underbody mounted full-size temporary steel spare wheel; air conditioning; AM/FM stereo with clock, seek-scan, cassette, 6 speakers, and fixed antenna; 2 power accessory outlets; instrumentation display includes oil pressure gauge, water temp gauge, volt gauge, trip odometer; warning indicators include oil pressure, battery, lights on, key in ignition, low washer fluid; dual airbags; tinted windows, vented rear windows; variable intermittent front windshield wipers, vented rear window; seating capacity of 8, front bucket seats with fixed headrests, driver's and passenger's armrests, driver's seat includes 4-way direction control, passenger's seat includes 4-way direction control; removable 2nd row bench seat; removable 3rd row bench seat; front height adjustable seatbelts with front pretensioners; premium cloth seats, vinyl door trim insert, full cloth headliner, full carpet floor covering, deluxe sound insulation; interior lights include dome light, front reading lights; sport steering wheel with tilt adjustment; day-night rearview mirror; engine cover console with storage, locking glove box with light, front cupholder; chrome grille, black side window moldings, black front windshield molding, black rear window molding and black door handles.

2500 (4A) (in addition to or instead of 1500 (3A) equipment): 5.2L V8 OHV SMPI 16-valve engine; 4-speed electronic overdrive automatic transmission with lock-up; 3.92 axle ratio; 36 gal capacity fuel tank; front and rear 16" x 6.5" silver steel wheels; underbody mounted full-size conventional steel spare wheel and cargo light.

3500 MAXI-WAGON (4A) (in addition to or instead of 2500 (4A) equipment): HD radiator; transmission oil cooler; seating capacity of 15; premium cloth seats, cloth door trim, full vinyl floor covering and deluxe sound insulation.

Base Prices

CODE	DESCRIPTION	INVOICE	MSRP
AB1L51	1500 (3A)	18954	20880
AB2L52	2500 (4A)	20296	23195
AB3L53	3500 Maxi-Wagon (4A)	22595	25900
Destination Charge:		630	630

CODE	DESCRIPTION	INVOICE	MSRP

Accessories

CODE	DESCRIPTION	INVOICE	MSRP
22C	**Quick Order Package 22C (1500)** *Includes 3.55 axle ratio. REQUIRES EHC and DGA. NOT AVAILABLE with ELF.*	NC	NC
26B	**Quick Order Package 26B (3500)** *Includes vehicle with standard equipment. REQUIRES ELF and DGB.*	NC	NC
26C	**Quick Order Package 26C (2500)** *Includes vehicle with standard equipment. REQUIRES ELF and DGB.*	NC	NC
28B	**Quick Order Package 28B (3500)** *Includes vehicle with standard equipment. REQUIRES EML and DGB.*	NC	NC
28C	**Quick Order Package 28C (2500)** *Includes vehicle with standard equipment. REQUIRES EML and DGB.*	NC	NC
AHC	**Trailer Tow Group (1500/2500)** *Includes 750-amp maintenance free battery, auxiliary transmission oil cooler and HD engine cooler. NOT AVAILABLE with EHC.*	191	225
AHC	**Trailer Tow Group (3500)** *Includes 136-amp alternator, heavy duty engine cooler and auxiliary transmission oil cooler. NOT AVAILABLE with ELN.*	81	95
AJK	**Deluxe Convenience Group** *Includes speed control.*	217	255
AJP	**Power Convenience Group** *Includes illuminated entry, power door locks and power windows.*	608	715
ASP	**Premium Decor Group (1500/2500)** *Includes front door trim panels, electric horns, dashliner insulation, right illuminated visor mirror, lower bodyside and rear molding, power convenience group: illuminated entry, power door locks and power windows.*	1012	1190
ASP	**Premium Decor Group (3500)** *Includes carpet cargo compartment, front seat area carpet, front door trim panels, electric horns, dashliner insulation, illuminated passenger's visor mirror, lower bodyside and rear molding, power convenience group: illuminated entry, power door locks and power windows.*	1148	1350
ATF	**CNG Conversion Group (3500)**	NC	NC
BCQ	**750-Amp Maintenance Free Battery**	51	60
BGK	**4-Wheel Antilock Brakes**	298	350
CKE	**Front Seat Area Carpet (3500)** *REQUIRES CKN.*	51	60
CKN	**Carpet Cargo Compartment (3500)**	85	100
CKZ	**Black Rubber Floor Covering (1500/2500)**	NC	NC
CTJ	**Front Door Trim Panels** *REQUIRES AJP or ASP.*	43	50
CYH	**12 Passenger Seating (2500)**	242	285
CYH	**12 Passenger Seating (3500)**	(242)	(285)
DGA	**Transmission: 3-Speed Automatic (1500)** *NOT AVAILABLE with ELF.*	NC	NC
DGB	**Transmission: 4 Speed Automatic (1500)** *NOT AVAILABLE with EHC.*	255	300

CODE	DESCRIPTION	INVOICE	MSRP
DGB	Transmission: 4-Speed Automatic (2500/3500)	NC	NC
DMF	4.10 Axle Ratio (2500)	NC	NC
DMH	3.92 Axle Ratio (1500)	34	40
DSA	Anti-Spin Differential Axle	242	285
	NOT AVAILABLE with Z3F, DMH.		
EHC	Engine: 3.9L SMPI V6 Magnum (1500)	NC	NC
ELF	Engine: 5.2L SMPI V8 Magnum (1500)	502	590
ELF	Engine: 5.2L SMPI V8 Magnum (2500/3500)	NC	NC
ELN	Engine: 5.2L SMPI V8 CNG (3500)	3608	4245
	Includes CNG Fuel system badge, inside mount spare tire and spare tire cover.		
EML	Engine: 5.9L SMPI V8 Magnum (2500/3500)	421	495
GAE	Sunscreen Glass	366	430
GFA	Rear Window Defroster	153	180
	NOT AVAILABLE with GLC.		
GKC	Sliding Side Door with Vented Glass	NC	NC
GLC	Dual Rear Hinged Doors with Vented Glass	NC	NC
	NOT AVAILABLE with GFA.		
GPS	Dual 6" x 9" Black Power Mirrors	136	160
HBB	Rear A/C and Heater (2500)	765	900
	Includes 750-amp maintenance free battery. REQUIRES ELF or EML.		
HBB	Rear Air Conditioning and Heater (3500)	718	845
	Manufacturer Discount	(425)	(500)
	Net Price	293	345
	REQUIRES AHC.		
HD	HD Vinyl Seat Trim	NC	NC
JPS	6-Way Power Driver's Seat	255	300
	NOT AVAILABLE with HD.		
LSA	Security Alarm	128	150
	REQUIRES AJP or ASP.		
MBF	Bright Rear Step Bumper	81	95
NAE	California Emissions	NC	NC
	Automatically coded.		
NHB	Auxiliary Transmission Oil Cooler (1500/2500)	72	85
	REQUIRES NMC (2500).		
NHK	Engine Block Heater	43	50
NMC	HD Engine Cooler (1500/2500)	72	85
	REQUIRES NHB (2500).		
RAZ	Radio: AM/FM Stereo with Cassette, CD and EQ	565	665
	Includes Infinity speaker system.		
RBN	Radio: AM/FM Stereo Cassette with CD Changer Control	281	330
	Includes Infinity speaker system.		
RBR	Radio: AM/FM Stereo with CD	412	485
	Includes Infinity speaker system.		
RCE	Infinity Speaker System	149	175
	NOT AVAILABLE with RAL.		
TSF	Tires: P235/75R15 AS OWL (1500)	106	125
TWY	Tires: LT225/75R16D OWL AS (2500)	106	125

CODE	DESCRIPTION	INVOICE	MSRP
WDC	Wheels: 16" x 6.5" Chrome (2500/3500)	340	400
WJC	Wheels: 15" Aluminum (1500) *NOT AVAILABLE with WJM.*	128	150
WJM	Wheels: 15" x 7" Chrome (1500) *NOT AVAILABLE with WJC.*	128	150
YCF	Border State Emissions (California)	NC	NC
Z3F	GVWR: 9,200 Lbs (3500) *Includes 4.10 axle ratio. REQUIRES EML.*	221	260

1999 ECONOLINE

1999 Ford Econoline Wagon

What's New?

An all-new alphanumeric vehicle badging system is being applied to all Econoline Wagon models. This will replace the past Club Wagon badge. Four-wheel disc brakes with ABS are now standard on all E-350 Super Duty vans. The 4R70W electronic four-speed automatic is now standard on all E-150 models. Improved "fail-safe" cooling is now a feature on all Econoline gasoline engines.

Review

Tough and roomy, rugged and reliable, Ford's full-size vans have a favorable, well-earned reputation that reaches way back to the Sixties. Ford calls the Econoline the U.S. industry's only family of body-on-frame passenger wagons, adding that the Econoline leads in sales to aftermarket conversions—the folks who turn no-frills vans into alluring recreational vehicles.

All Econoline vans ride on a 138-inch wheelbase. All of Ford's full-size vans have four-wheel anti-lock brakes and dual air bags. These features, their large size, and better than average crash test scores, make the Ford vans some of the safest vehicles on the road.

Driving an Econoline, despite its passenger seating, differs little from piloting a delivery vehicle, so it's not a logical choice for everyday motoring—though quite a few families happily employ their Wagons exactly that way. The virtues of sitting tall with a panoramic view of the road ahead can outweigh many a minor inconvenience—such as the difficulty of squeezing these biggies into urban parking spots and compact garages. Handling is light, seats are acceptably comfortable, and Wagons don't ride badly at all, considering the old-fashioned suspension configurations they employ.

As with most full-size vans the Econoline features a wide choice of powerplants. Exclusive to Ford, however, is the industry's first SOHC engines found in a van. The three SOHC engines include a 4.6-liter V-8 producing 215 horsepower, a 5.4-liter V-8 producing 235 horsepower, and 6.8-liter V-10 that produces 265 horsepower and a massive 410 ft./lbs. of torque.

Full-size vans fell out of favor with families when the minivan was introduced. Few find their way into suburban driveways anymore. The Ford Econoline is one of the best, and can be had at prices that rival Ford's own Windstar. For your money, wouldn't you rather have more space and utility?

1999 E-150 WAGON

Safety Data

Side Airbag: *Not Available*
4-Wheel ABS: *Standard*
Driver Crash Test Grade: *Good*
Side Impact Crash Test Front: *Not Available*
Crash Offset: *Not Available*
Integrated Child Seat(s): *Not Available*
Traction Control: *Not Available*
Passenger Crash Test Grade: *Good*
Side Impact Crash Test Rear: *Not Available*

Standard Equipment

E-150 XL WAGON (4A): 4.2L V6 OHV SMPI 12-valve engine; 4-speed electronic overdrive automatic transmission with lock-up; 72-amp battery; 95-amp alternator; rear wheel drive, 3.55 axle ratio; stainless steel exhaust; front independent suspension with front coil springs, rigid rear axle suspension with rear leaf springs; power re-circulating ball steering; front disc/rear drum brakes with 4 wheel antilock braking system; 35 gal capacity fuel tank; 3 doors with split swing-out right rear passenger door, split swing-out rear cargo door; front and rear argent bumpers; monotone paint; sealed beam halogen headlamps; additional exterior lights include center high mounted stop light; driver's and passenger's manual black folding outside mirrors; front and rear 15" x 6" steel wheels; P235/75SR15 BSW AS front and rear tires; underbody mounted full-size conventional steel spare wheel; air conditioning; AM/FM stereo with clock, seek-scan, 4 speakers, and fixed antenna; 2 power accessory outlets; instrumentation display includes oil pressure gauge, water temp gauge, volt gauge, trip odometer; warning indicators include water temp warning, battery; dual airbags; tinted windows, vented rear windows, fixed 1/4 vent windows; variable intermittent front windshield wipers; seating capacity of 8, front bucket seats with fixed headrests, driver's seat includes 2-way direction control, passenger's seat includes 2-way direction control; 2nd row bench seat; 3rd row bench seat; front height adjustable seatbelts with front pretensioners; vinyl seats, full cloth headliner, full vinyl floor covering; interior lights include dome light; passenger side vanity mirror; day-night rearview mirror; engine cover console with storage, front cupholder, dashboard storage; vinyl cargo floor, cargo light; black grille, black side window moldings, black front windshield molding, black rear window molding and black door handles.

E-150 XLT WAGON (4A) (in addition to or instead of E-150 XL WAGON (4A) equipment): Front anti-roll bar, HD front shocks, HD rear shocks; class I trailer harness; front and rear chrome bumpers; aero-composite halogen headlamps; AM/FM stereo with clock, seek-scan, 6 speakers, and fixed antenna; warning indicators include lights on; front captain seats with fixed headrests, driver's and passenger's armrests, driver's seat includes 4-way direction control, passenger's seat includes 4-way direction control; cloth seats, cloth door trim, full carpet floor covering, deluxe sound insulation; interior lights include front reading lights, illuminated entry; driver's and passenger's door bins; carpeted cargo floor, plastic trunk lid and chrome grille.

Base Prices

CODE	DESCRIPTION	INVOICE	MSRP
E11	E-150 XL Wagon	19403	22250
E11	E-150 XLT Wagon	21026	24160
Destination Charge:		615	615

Accessories

CODE	DESCRIPTION	INVOICE	MSRP
18A	Exterior Upgrade Package (XL) *Includes chrome front and rear bumpers, chrome grille, aero-composite halogen headlamps and full wheel covers. NOT AVAILABLE with 769.*	285	335

CODE	DESCRIPTION	INVOICE	MSRP
18G	**Interior Upgrade Package (XL)** *Includes XLT side/rear cargo door trim panels and dash absorber, cloth trim, illuminated entry and headlights-on audible alert/chime.*	522	615
415	**Deluxe Engine Console Cover (XL)** *Includes stowage area and 2 cupholders.*	128	150
419	**Dual Illuminated Sunvisors (XLT)**	43	50
41H	**Engine Block Heater** *Recommended when minimum temperature is -10F or below.*	30	35
52N	**Convenience Group (XL)** *Includes speed control and tilt steering.*	328	385
534	**Trailer Towing Package (Class I) (XL)** *Includes trailer wiring harness. REQUIRES 684.*	128	150
534	**Trailer Towing Package (Class I) (XL)** *Includes trailer wiring harness, HD front and rear shock absorbers.*	196	230
535	**Trailer Towing Package (Class II/III/IV) (XLT)** *Includes electric brake controller tap-in capability, trailer wiring harness (blade-style female connector) with bumper bracket and relay system for backup/B+/running lights, HD front and rear shock absorbers and HD alternator.*	162	190
535	**Trailer Towing Package (Class II/III/IV) (XLT)** *Includes electric brake controller tap-in capability, trailer wiring harness (blade-style female connector) with bumper bracket and relay system for backup/B+/running lights, HD front and rear shock absorbers and HD alternator. REQUIRES 99W.*	93	110
548	**Bright Swing-Out Recreational Mirrors** *Deletes power mirrors when equipped. NOT AVAILABLE with 77C.*	51	60
574	**High Capacity Front and Rear Air Conditioning (XL)** *Includes auxiliary rear heater and overhead ducts and front air conditioning.*	702	825
588	**Radio: Premium AM/FM Stereo with Cassette (XLT)** *Includes clock and 6 speakers.*	64	75
589	**Radio: AM/FM Stereo with Cassette and Clock (XL)** *Includes 4 speakers.*	132	155
58K	**Radio: AM/FM Stereo with Clock, Cassette and CD (XLT)** *Includes in-dash single disc CD player, cassette tape player and 6 speakers. NOT AVAILABLE with 588.*	235	275
60S	**Sliding Side Cargo Door** *Upgrade from standard 60/40 hinged door.*	NC	NC
633	**HD 130-Amp Alternator (XL)**	68	80
634	**HD 78 AH/Auxiliary 75 AH Batteries (XLT)** *Includes deep-cycle non-starting auxiliary battery.*	123	145
645	**Wheels: 15" x 7" Bright Cast Aluminum (XLT)** *Includes 15" steel spare.*	263	310
684	**Handling Package (XL)** *Includes front stabilizer bar, HD front and rear shock absorbers.*	68	80
700A	**Preferred Equipment Package 700A (XL)** *Includes front air conditioning, engine: 4.2L EFI V6, transmission: 4 speed auto with overdrive, tires: P235/75R15 XL AS BSW, 8 passenger seating and AM/FM stereo with clock.*	NC	NC

CODE	DESCRIPTION	INVOICE	MSRP
705A	Preferred Equipment Package 705A (XLT)	1428	1680
	Includes high capacity front and rear air conditioning, HD alternator, deluxe engine console cover, AM/FM stereo with cassette and clock, power sail mount mirrors, convenience group: speed control, tilt steering; engine: 4.2L EFI V6, transmission: 4 speed auto with overdrive, tires: P235/75R15 XL AS BSW, 8 passenger seating, power convenience group: power door locks, power windows; carpet door trim, handling package: front stabilizer bar, HD front and rear shock absorbers; trailer towing package (class I).		
768	Chrome Rear Step Bumper	119	140
	REQUIRES 18A. NOT AVAILABLE with 769.		
769	Light Charcoal Rear Step Bumper (XL)	102	120
77C	Chateau Appearance Package (XLT)	876	1030
	Includes rear door badge, 15" x 7" bright cast aluminum wheels, lower accent two-tone paint and 7 passenger seating with 4 captain chairs and 1 bench seat. REQUIRES 924.		
903	Power Convenience Group (XL)	421	495
	Includes XLT door trim panels and memory lock module with sliding cargo door, power windows and carpet door trim.		
90P	Power Driver's Seat (XLT)	332	390
	Includes manual lumbar.		
924	Privacy Glass	391	460
948	Remote Keyless Entry with Panic Alarm	170	200
	REQUIRES 18G.		
99L	Engine: 5.4L EFI V8 (E-150)	1186	1495
99W	Engine: 4.6L EFI V8 (E-150)	591	695
C2	Cloth Trim (XL)	NC	NC
XH9	Limited Slip Differential	229	270

1999 E-350 SUPER DUTY WAGON

Safety Data

Side Airbag: *Not Available*
4-Wheel ABS: *Standard*
Driver Crash Test Grade: *Good*
Side Impact Crash Test Front: *Not Available*
Crash Offset: *Not Available*
Integrated Child Seat(s): *Not Available*
Traction Control: *Not Available*
Passenger Crash Test Grade: *Good*
Side Impact Crash Test Rear: *Not Available*

Standard Equipment

E-350 XL WAGON (4A): 5.4L V8 SOHC SMPI 16-valve engine; 4-speed electronic overdrive automatic transmission with lock-up; 72-amp battery; 95-amp alternator; rear wheel drive, 3.55 axle ratio; stainless steel exhaust; front independent suspension with anti-roll bar, front coil springs, HD front shocks, rigid rear axle suspension with rear leaf springs, HD rear shocks; power re-circulating ball steering; 4 wheel disc brakes with 4 wheel antilock braking system; 35 gal capacity fuel tank; 3 doors with split swing-out right rear passenger door, split swing-out rear cargo door; class I trailer harness; front and rear argent bumpers; monotone paint; sealed beam halogen headlamps; additional exterior lights include center high mounted stop light; driver's and passenger's manual black folding outside mirrors; front and rear

CODE	DESCRIPTION	INVOICE	MSRP

16" x 7" steel wheels; LT225/75SR16 BSW AS front and rear tires; underbody mounted full-size conventional steel spare wheel; air conditioning; AM/FM stereo, clock with seek-scan, 4 speakers, and fixed antenna; 2 power accessory outlets; instrumentation display includes oil pressure gauge, water temp gauge, volt gauge, trip odometer; warning indicators include oil pressure, water temp warning; dual airbags; tinted windows, vented rear windows, fixed 1/4 vent windows; variable intermittent front windshield wipers; seating capacity of 12; front bucket seats with fixed headrests, driver's seat includes 2-way direction control, passenger's seat includes 2-way direction control; 2nd row bench seat; 3rd row bench seat; front height adjustable seatbelts with front pretensioners; vinyl seats, full cloth headliner, full vinyl floor covering; interior lights include dome light; passenger side vanity mirror; day-night rearview mirror; engine cover console with storage, front cupholder, dashboard storage; vinyl cargo floor, cargo light; black grille, black side window moldings, black front windshield molding, black rear window molding and black door handles.

E-350 XL EXTENDED WAGON (4A) (in addition to or instead of E-350 XL WAGON (4A) equipment): Seating capacity of 15.

E-350 XLT WAGON (4A) (in addition to or instead of E-350 XL WAGON (4A) equipment): Front and rear chrome bumpers; aero-composite halogen headlamps; AM/FM stereo with clock, seek-scan, 6 speakers, and fixed antenna; warning indicators include lights on; power front windows; front captain seats with fixed headrests, driver's and passenger's armrests, driver's seat includes 4-way direction control, passenger's seat includes 4-way direction control; cloth seats, cloth door trim, full carpet floor covering, deluxe sound insulation; interior lights include front reading lights, illuminated entry; driver's and passenger's door bins; carpeted cargo floor, plastic trunk lid and chrome grille.

E-350 XLT EXTENDED WAGON (4A) (in addition to or instead of E-350 XLT WAGON (4A) equipment): Seating capacity of 15.

Base Prices

CODE	DESCRIPTION	INVOICE	MSRP
E31	XL	21898	25185
S31	XL Extended	23275	26805
E31	XLT	23415	26970
S31	XLT Extended	24099	27775
Destination Charge:		615	615

Accessories

CODE	DESCRIPTION	INVOICE	MSRP
18A	**Exterior Upgrade Package (XL)** *Includes chrome front and rear bumpers, chrome grille, aero-composite halogen headlamps and full wheel covers. NOT AVAILABLE with 769.*	285	335
18G	**Interior Upgrade Package (XL)** *Includes XLT side/rear cargo door trim panels and dash absorber, cloth trim, illuminated entry and headlights-on audible alert/chime.*	522	615
216	**8-Passenger Seating with Vinyl Trim (XL)** *Includes two standard buckets and two 3-passenger bench seats.*	(162)	(190)
218	**12-Passenger Vinyl Seating (XL Extended)** *Includes two standard buckets, two 3-passenger benches and one 4-passenger bench.*	(119)	(140)
21E	**8 Passenger Seating with Cloth Trim (XLT)** *Includes dual captain chairs and two 3-passenger bench seats.*	(162)	(190)
21M	**12 Passenger Seating (XLT Extended)** *Includes dual captain chairs, two 3-passenger benches and one 4-passenger bench.*	(118)	(140)

CODE	DESCRIPTION	INVOICE	MSRP
415	**Deluxe Engine Console Cover (XL)** *Includes stowage area and 2 cupholders.*	128	150
419	**Dual Illuminated Sunvisors (XLT)**	43	50
41H	**Engine Block Heater** *Recommended when minimum temperature is -10F or below.*	30	35
52N	**Convenience Group (XL)** *Includes tilt steering and speed control.*	328	385
535	**Trailer Towing Package (Class II/III/IV)** *Includes electric brake controller tap-in capability, blade-style female connector with bumper bracket and relay system for backup/B+/running lightst and trailer towing package (class I) with front stabilizer bar.*	93	110
548	**Bright Swing-Out Recreational Mirrors** *Deletes power mirrors when equipped. NOT AVAILABLE with 77C.*	51	60
574	**High Capacity Front and Rear Air Conditioning (XL)** *Includes auxiliary heater, overhead ducts and 130-amp HD alternator.*	702	825
588	**Radio: Premium AM/FM Stereo with Cassette (XLT)** *Includes clock and 6 speakers.*	64	75
589	**Radio: AM/FM Stereo with Cassette with Clock (XL)** *Includes 4 speakers.*	132	155
58K	**Radio: AM/FM Stereo with Clock, Cassette and CD (XLT)** *Includes in-dash single disc CD player, cassette tape player and 6 speakers. NOT AVAILABLE with 588.*	235	275
60S	**Sliding Side Cargo Door** *Upgrade from standard 60/40 hinged door.*	NC	NC
633	**130-Amp HD Alternator (XL)**	68	80
634	**HD 78-Amp with Auxiliary 75-Amp Batteries (XLT)** *Deep-cycle non-starting.*	123	145
63A	**Dual System Alternator (XLT)** *Includes two 110-amp alternators. REQUIRES 99F.*	493	580
710A	**Preferred Equipment Package 710A (XL)** *Includes front air conditioning, engine: 5.4L EFI V8, transmission: electronic 4 speed automatic, tires: LT 225/75R16E AS BSW, 12-passenger vinyl seating, handling package: front stabilizer bar, HD front and rear shock absorbers; trailer towing package (class I), AM/FM stereo with clock and 3.55 axle ratio.*	NC	NC
713A	**Preferred Equipment Package 713A (XLT)** *Includes full wheel covers, high capacity front and rear air conditioning, 130-amp HD alternator, deluxe engine console cover, AM/FM stereo with cassette and clock, power sail mount mirrors, convenience group: tilt steering, speed control, engine: 5.4L EFI V8, transmission: electronic 4 speed automatic, 12 passenger seating, power convenience group: power windows, power door locks; handling package: front stabilizer bar, HD front and rear shock absorbers and trailer towing package (class I).*	1428	1680
721A	**Preferred Equipment Package 721A (XL Extended)** *Includes high capacity front and rear air conditioning, 130-amp HD alternatorr, engine: 5.4L EFI V8, transmission: electronic 4 speed automatic, tires: LT245/75R16E AS BSW, 15-passenger seating, handling package: front stabilizer bar, HD*	702	825

CODE	DESCRIPTION	INVOICE	MSRP
	front and rear shock absorbers; trailer towing package (class I) and AM/FM stereo with clock.		
723A	Preferred Equipment Package 723A (XLT Extended)	1428	1680
	Includes high capacity front and rear air conditioning, 130-amp HD alternator, deluxe engine console cover, AM/FM stereo with cassette and clock, power sail mount mirrors, convenience group: tilt steering, speed control; engine: 5.4L EFI V8, transmission: electronic 4 speed automatic, tires: LT 245/75R16E AS BSW, 15-passenger seating, power convenience group: power windows, power door locks; handling package: front stabilizer bar, HD front and rear shock absorbers and trailer towing package (class I).		
768	Chrome Rear Step Bumper	119	140
	REQUIRES 18A. NOT AVAILABLE with 769.		
769	Light Charcoal Rear Step Bumper (XL)	102	120
77C	Chateau Appearance Package (XLT)	702	825
	Includes 16" full wheel covers and rear door badge, 7-passenger cloth quad captain's chairs and lower accent two-tone paint. REQUIRES 924.		
87N	Natural Gas Fuel System (Bi-Fuel) (XL Extended/XLT Extended)	6217	7315
87P	Propane Fuel System (Bi-Fuel)	4679	5505
903	Power Convenience Group (All Except XLT Extended)	421	495
	Includes XLT door trim panels and memory lock module with sliding cargo door and power door locks.		
90P	Power Driver's Seat (XLT)	332	390
	Includes manual LH/RH lumbar.		
924	Privacy Glass	391	460
948	Remote Keyless Entry with Panic Alarm	170	200
	REQUIRES 18G.		
961	Auxiliary Idle Control	170	200
	REQUIRES 99F.		
99F	Engine: 7.3L V8 Turbo Diesel	4174	4910
	Power Stroke diesel.		
99M	Engine: 5.4L Natural Gas	5308	6245
	Includes standard NG fuel cylinders (15.4 gallons total capacity) and interior mounted spare. REQUIRES 216 or 21E.		
99S	Engine: 6.8L EFI V8	595	700
	Includes 3.73 axle ratio.		
99Z	Engine: 5.4L Bi-Fuel Prep	128	150
	Includes 4.10 axle ratio. REQUIRES 87P or 87N.		
C2	Cloth Trim (XL)	NC	NC
T38	Tires: LT245/75R16E AS BSW (XL/XLT)	119	140
X32	4.10 Axle Ratio	38	45
XC2	Limited Slip Differential	229	270
	REQUIRES X32.		
XC4	Limited Slip Differential	229	270
	REQUIRES 99S.		
XC9	Limited Slip Differential	229	270

1999 EXPEDITION

1999 Ford Expedition

What's New?

Power output is improved for both Triton V8 engines on Ford's full-size sport-ute. Package content is added for both XLT and Eddie Bauer trim levels. Power adjustable accelerator and brake pedals have been added to the option list to make it easier for the vertically challenged to reach the stop and go pedals. An updated Command Trac four-wheel drive system allows automatic four-wheel drive operation when required. Spruce Green, Harvest Gold, Tropic Green and Deep Wedgewood Blue replace Light Prairie Tan, Vermont Green, Light Denim Blue and Pacific Green on the color chart.

Review

After allowing GM to dominate the full-size SUV arena for years, Ford introduced a vehicle in 1997 that had its sights squarely aimed at the Chevy Tahoe, GMC Yukon, and the Suburban sold at both Chevy and GMC dealerships. Ford boasts that its Expedition is superior to the GM full-size sport/utes in every way. We've had the chance to drive many of these brute-utes since its introduction, and here is what we found out.

Larger than the Tahoe and Yukon, the Expedition can seat nine people with its optional third-row bench seat; the Tahoe and Yukon can only seat six. Unlike the Suburban, which may have difficulty fitting into a standard garage, the Expedition can be accommodated in most residential garages. The Expedition also has the best payload and towing capacity in its class: 2,000-lbs. and 8000-lbs. respectively.

On the road the Expedition is well mannered. It's obvious that this is not a car, but compared to the old Bronco, the Expedition rides like a limousine. Interior ergonomics are first rate and will be familiar to anyone who has spent time in the current F-150. From the front seat forward the Expedition is nearly identical to the pickup. That's a good thing; we love the cab of the F-150 with its easy-to-use climate and stereo controls, steering wheel-mounted cruise control, abundance of cupholders, and great storage space.

Ford has put a lot of time and money into making this truck the next sales leader in their already dominant light-truck lineup. We came away impressed and think you will too. The Expedition comes standard with dual airbags, antilock brakes, and fold-flat second row seats; features that we feel are important in this increasingly competitive segment. Our few gripes stem from the powertrain. Ford has boosted output for both the 4.6 and 5.4-liter engines, making them somewhat more competitive against the awesome Vortec powerplants found in GM's full-size trucks. One option that we think everyone should investigate is the lighted running boards. The Expedition towers above the ground, and entering and exiting this truck will take its toll on most passengers after a few days.

Ford has shuffled several of the packages on the 1999 Expedition, and has added a number of features to the standard equipment lists of the Eddie Bauer and XLT. Ford has rolled the contents of the former Popular Equipment Group into the Comfort and Convenience Group. The group now includes 16-inch wheels, privacy glass, removable fold-flat third seat, and captain's chairs with floor console.

The Ford Expedition is a nice balance between comfort and function, and its ability to seat nine people makes it popular with large families and those who have to haul stuff around. Nevertheless, we can't overlook the new Dodge Durango and the outstanding Chevrolet Tahoe and GMC Yukon when discussing big trucks. In the last few years, the mid- and full-size sport-ute market has gotten very competitive and the choices are much more difficult to make.

Safety Data

Side Airbag: *Not Available*
4-Wheel ABS: *Standard*
Driver Crash Test Grade: *Good*
Side Impact Crash Test Front: *Not Available*
Crash Offset: *Not Available*
Integrated Child Seat(s): *Not Available*
Traction Control: *Not Available*
Passenger Crash Test Grade: *Good*
Side Impact Crash Test Rear: *Not Available*

Standard Equipment

XLT 2WD (4A): 4.6L V8 SOHC SMPI 16-valve engine; 4-speed electronic overdrive automatic transmission with lock-up; 72-amp battery with run down protection; 130-amp alternator; rear wheel drive, 3.31 axle ratio; stainless steel exhaust; front independent suspension with anti-roll bar, front coil springs, rigid rear axle multi-link suspension with anti-roll bar, rear coil springs; power re-circulating ball steering with vehicle speed-sensing assist, steering cooler; 4 wheel disc brakes with 4 wheel antilock braking system; 26 gal capacity fuel tank; liftback rear cargo door; class II trailering, trailer harness; roof rack; front and rear chrome bumpers with front body-colored rub strip, rear black rub strip and rear step; body-colored bodyside molding with chrome bodyside insert; monotone paint; aero-composite halogen headlamps; additional exterior lights include center high mounted stop light, underhood light; driver's and passenger's power remote chrome folding outside mirrors; front and rear 16" x 7" silver styled steel wheels; P255/70SR16 BSW AS front and rear tires; underbody mounted full-size temporary steel spare wheel; air conditioning, rear heat ducts; premium AM/FM stereo with clock, seek-scan, cassette, 4 speakers, automatic equalizer, and fixed antenna; cruise control with steering wheel controls; power door locks, remote keyless entry, child safety rear door locks, power remote hatch/trunk release; 2 power accessory outlets, driver's foot rest, retained accessory power; instrumentation display includes tachometer, oil pressure gauge, water temp gauge, volt gauge, trip odometer; warning indicators include oil pressure, water temp warning, battery, lights on, key in ignition, low fuel, low washer fluid, door ajar, brake fluid; dual airbags; ignition disable, panic alarm; tinted windows, power front windows with driver's 1-touch down, power rear windows, fixed 1/4 vent windows; variable intermittent front windshield wipers, flip-up rear window, fixed interval rear wiper, rear window defroster; seating capacity of 6, 40-60 split-bench front seat with fixed headrests, center armrest with storage, driver's seat includes 4-way power seat with 8-way direction control and lumbar support, passenger's seat includes 4-way direction control; 60-40 folding rear split-bench seat with reclining adjustable rear headrest, center armrest with storage; front and rear height adjustable seatbelts; cloth seats, cloth door trim, full cloth headliner, full carpet floor covering with carpeted floor mats; interior lights include dome light, front reading lights, 2 door curb lights, illuminated entry; steering wheel with tilt adjustment; dual auxiliary visors, passenger side vanity mirror; day-night rearview mirror; glove box with light, front and rear cupholders, instrument panel bin, dashboard storage, driver's and passenger's door bins, rear door bins; carpeted cargo floor, plastic trunk lid, cargo tie downs, cargo light, cargo concealed storage; chrome grille, black side window moldings, black front windshield molding, black rear window molding and body-colored door handles.

CODE	DESCRIPTION	INVOICE	MSRP

XLT 4WD (4A) (in addition to or instead of XLT 2WD (4A) equipment): Part-time 4 wheel drive, auto locking hub control and electronic shift, 3.55 axle ratio; front independent suspension with anti-roll bar, front torsion springs and 30 gal capacity fuel tank.

EDDIE BAUER 2WD (4A) (in addition to or instead of XLT 2WD equipment): Running boards; front and rear chrome bumpers with body-colored rear rub strip; body-colored bodyside molding, rocker panel extensions, colored wheel well molding; monotone paint with bodyside accent stripe; aero-composite halogen fully automatic headlamps with delay-off feature; additional exterior lights include front fog/driving lights; driver's and passenger's power remote body-colored folding outside mirrors; air conditioning with climate control, rear air conditioning with separate controls, rear heater; premium AM/FM stereo with clock, seek-scan, cassette, 7 premium speakers, automatic equalizer, and fixed antenna rear controls; 3 power accessory outlets; instrumentation display includes compass, trip computer; deep tinted windows; power 1/4 vent windows; seating capacity of 8, front captain seats with fixed headrests, driver's and passenger's armrests, passenger's seat includes 4-way direction control with lumbar support; 3rd row removable full folding bench seat; leather seats and door trim; interior lights include front and rear reading lights, illuminated entry; leather-wrapped steering wheel with tilt adjustment; dual illuminated vanity mirrors, dual auxiliary visors; full floor console, full overhead console with storage; 2 seat back storage pockets and body-colored grille.

EDDIE BAUER 4WD (4A)(in addition to or instead of EDDIE BAUER 2WD (4A) equipment): 5.4L V8 SOHC SMPI 16-valve engine; part-time 4 wheel drive, auto locking hub control and electronic shift, 3.55 axle ratio; front independent suspension with anti-roll bar, front torsion springs; 30 gal capacity fuel tank; rear tow hooks and front and rear 17" x 7" silver alloy wheels.

Base Prices

CODE	DESCRIPTION	INVOICE	MSRP
U17	XLT 2WD (4A)	25687	29355
U18	XLT 4WD (4A)	28012	32090
U17	Eddie Bauer 2WD (4A)	30677	35225
U18	Eddie Bauer 4WD (4A)	33885	39000
Destination Charge:		640	640

Accessories

CODE	DESCRIPTION	INVOICE	MSRP
—	Auxiliary Air Conditioning Delete (Eddie Bauer) *REQUIRES 43M.*	(600)	(705)
—	Cloth Captain's Chairs Delete (XLT) *REQUIRES 66A.*	(328)	(385)
—	Power Signal Mirrors Delete (Eddie Bauer) *REQUIRES 54H.*	(81)	(95)
1	Leather Captain's Chairs (XLT) *Includes 3rd row seat and floor console.*	1105	1300
17P	Power Adjustable Pedals System *Allows fore/aft travel for brake and gas pedals.*	102	120
186	Illuminated Running Boards (XLT)	370	435
413	Skid Plate Package (4WD) *Includes skid plates for front differential/suspension, fuel tank and transfer case.*	89	105
41H	Engine Block Heater	30	35
43M	Power Moonroof with Sunshade (Eddie Bauer) *Includes mini overhead console and deletes rear auxiliary heater/air conditioner.*	680	800

CODE	DESCRIPTION	INVOICE	MSRP
44E	Transmission: Electronic 4 Speed with OD (Eddie Bauer 4WD) *NOT AVAILABLE with XH7, XH9.*	NC	NC
535	Trailer Towing Group (Class III) (2WD) *Includes super engine cooling, auxiliary transmission oil cooler, rear load leveling and 30 gallon fuel tank.*	748	880
535	Trailer Towing Group (Class III) (4WD) *Includes super engine cooling, auxiliary transmission oil cooler and rear load leveling.*	332	390
53T	Tow Hooks (XLT 4WD)	34	40
54H	Heated Mirrors	43	50
595	Fog Lamps (XLT)	93	110
647	Wheels: 17" Cast Aluminum (XLT 4WD) *REQUIRES 99L and XH6. NOT AVAILABLE with 66A.*	370	435
647	Wheels: 17" Cast Aluminum (XLT 4WD) *REQUIRES 66A, 99L and XH6.*	158	185
66A	Comfort/Convenience Group (XLT)	2176	2560
	Manufacturer Discount	(544)	(640)
	Net Price *Includes cloth captain's chairs, floor console, six way power driver's seat, manual passenger lumbar, third row bench seat, auxiliary heater/air conditioner (rear), privacy glass and dual illuminated visor vanity mirrors.*	1632	1920
685A	Preferred Equipment Package 685A (XLT) *Includes vehicle with standard equipment.*	NC	NC
687A	Preferred Equipment Package 687A (Eddie Bauer)	404	475
	Manufacturer Discount	(404)	(475)
	Net Price *Includes leather captain's chairs, floor console, 6 disc CD changer, electronic automatic temperature control, fog lamps, Ford Mach cassette audio system, power signal mirror, power flip-out quarter windows, illuminated running boards and third row bench seat.*	NC	NC
68P	Four Corner Load Leveling Suspension (4WD)	692	815
875	Third Row Bench Seat (XLT) *Includes removable seat that folds flat with rollers. Available in matching front seat material.*	544	640
87D	3rd Row Bench Seat Delete (XLT)	(544)	(640)
90H	Heated Front Seats (Eddie Bauer)	247	290
91P	6 Disc CD Changer (XLT)	404	475
99L	Engine: 5.4L SOHC (All Except Eddie Bauer 4WD) *Includes super engine cooling. REQUIRES XH6. NOT AVAILABLE with XH7, XH9.*	565	665
T5N	Tires: P265/70R17 AT OWL (XLT 4WD)	323	380
T65	Tires: P255/70R16 AT OWL (XLT 2WD)	196	230
XH6	Limited Slip Differential *Includes 3.55 axle ratio. REQUIRES 99L. NOT AVAILABLE with XH7, XH9.*	217	255
XH7	Limited Slip Differential (2WD)	217	255
XH9	Limited Slip Differential (XLT 4WD)	217	255

1999 EXPLORER

1999 Ford Explorer

What's New?

The Explorer gets exterior revisions including new fog lamps, rocker panel moldings, wheel moldings, running boards and wheels. Harvest Gold, Chestnut, Deep Wedgewood, Spruce Green and Tropic Green replaces Light Prairie Tan, Desert Violet, Light Denim Blue, Pacific Green and Evergreen Frost on the color chart. New options include a reverse sensing system and rear load leveling. Side impact airbags are also newly available.

Review

Since its introduction in 1991, the Ford Explorer has resided at the top of the sport utility sales heap. With good reason, the Explorer combines style, comfort and room in a go-anywhere package. The modern day Country Squire, some have called it, after the segment leading station wagon of the 1950s.

We think that there's a good reason for this. Simply stated, the Explorer is a roomier and more refined vehicle than the competition at Chrysler and General Motors. The interior instills a feeling of quality that is missing from the Chevrolet Blazer and the Dodge Durango. An organically sweeping dashboard houses radio controls that can actually be operated without a magnifying glass. Materials in the Explorer look and feel rich. Rear seat comfort surpasses Chevy, and entry/exit is easier than Jeep. Explorers offer more cargo capacity than most rivals do, and five passengers can ride with ease. Exterior styling is a subjective matter, but we think that the Explorer is an attractive SUV.

The Explorer's standard 4.0-liter V6 is the puniest engine found in a domestic sport-ute. Acceleration is fine from a standstill, but step on the gas at 50 mph and not much happens. That's not good news when there's a need to pass or merge. Ford also offers an OHV 5.0-liter V8 engine that used to power the 1994-95 Mustang GT. While the acceleration with the 5.0-liter motor is improved over the base V6, it gives up a lot in fuel consumption. Fortunately, Ford introduced an optional SOHC V6 in 1997 that offers nearly as much power as the V8, for less money while offering greater fuel efficiency. We recommend this engine over the other two engine choices due to its great power and affordable price.

The Explorer gets exterior changes this year that include new quarter panel sheetmetal, body moldings, badging and running boards. New options include a reverse sensing system, rear load leveling, automatic ride control and side impact air bags.

Unlike the current Nissan Pathfinder, Explorers retain a distinctly truck-like character, which could be a bonus or a demerit. They're tough and solid, and easy to maneuver, though steering is a little slow and ponderous, and the body leans through tight corners. Braking is excellent, and the suspension has a compliant attitude, but Ford's Explorer can bounce around, making occupants regret the Denver omelet they had for breakfast.

Ford has a philosophy of building vehicles that everyone can be happy with. Sure, the Jeep Grand Cherokee feels sportier, and the Dodge Durango looks cooler, but the Explorer has just the right amount of class and ruggedness to make it America's best-selling off-roader. If you are thinking about buying an sport-ute, chances are you've already checked out the Explorer. If you haven't, do yourself a favor and find out why there are so many of these trucks on the road.

Safety Data

Side Airbag: *Optional*
4-Wheel ABS: *Standard*
Driver Crash Test Grade: *Good*
Side Impact Crash Test Front: *Excellent*
Crash Offset: *Acceptable*
Integrated Child Seat(s): *Not Available*
Traction Control: *Not Available*
Passenger Crash Test Grade: *Good*
Side Impact Crash Test Rear: *Excellent*

Standard Equipment

SPORT 2WD (5M): 4.0L V6 OHV SMPI 12-valve engine; 5-speed overdrive manual transmission; 72-amp battery with run down protection; HD radiator; 95-amp alternator; rear wheel drive, 3.27 axle ratio; steel exhaust; front independent suspension with anti-roll bar, front torsion springs, front torsion bar, HD front shocks, rigid rear axle suspension with anti-roll bar, rear leaf springs, HD rear shocks; power rack-and-pinion steering, power steering cooler; 4 wheel disc brakes with 4 wheel antilock braking system; 17.5 gal capacity fuel tank; liftback rear cargo door; roof rack; front and rear argent bumpers with black rub strip, rear step; body-colored bodyside molding, rocker panel extensions, black fender flares; monotone paint; aero-composite halogen headlamps; additional exterior lights include center high mounted stop light; driver's and passenger's power remote black folding outside mirrors; front and rear 15" x 7" silver alloy wheels; P235/70SR15 OWL AT front and rear tires; underbody mounted full-size temporary steel spare wheel; air conditioning, rear heat ducts; AM/FM stereo with clock, seek-scan, cassette, 4 speakers, and fixed antenna; power door locks with 2 stage unlock, power remote hatch/trunk release; 2 power accessory outlets, retained accessory power; instrumentation display includes tachometer, oil pressure gauge, water temp gauge, volt gauge, trip odometer; warning indicators include oil pressure, battery, lights on, key in ignition, door ajar; dual airbags; ignition disable; deep tinted windows, power front windows with driver's 1-touch down, vented rear windows, fixed 1/4 vent windows; variable intermittent front windshield wipers, flip-up rear window, fixed interval rear wiper, rear window defroster; seating capacity of 4, front captain seats with fixed headrests, driver's seat includes 4-way direction control, passenger's seat includes 4-way direction control; 50-50 folding rear bench seat with tilt rear headrest; front height adjustable seatbelts; vinyl seats, vinyl door trim, full cloth headliner, full carpet floor covering, deluxe sound insulation; interior lights include dome light with fade, front reading lights, illuminated entry; dual illuminated vanity mirrors, dual auxiliary visors; day-night rearview mirror; full floor console, glove box with light; carpeted cargo floor, vinyl trunk lid, cargo tie downs, cargo light; body-colored grille, black side window moldings, black front windshield molding, black rear window molding and body-colored door handles.

SPORT 4WD (5M) (in addition to or instead of SPORT 2WD (5M) equipment): Part-time 4 wheel drive, auto locking hub control with electronic shift and skid plates.

XL 2WD (5M) (in addition to or instead of SPORT 2WD (5M) equipment): 21 gal capacity fuel tank; driver's and passenger's manual black folding outside mirrors; underbody mounted full-size conventional steel spare wheel; child safety rear door locks; tinted windows, manual rear windows; seating capacity of 5, front bucket seats with fixed headrests; 60-40 folding rear bench seat with tilt rear headrest and chrome grille.

XL 4WD (5M) (in addition to or instead of XL 2WD (5M) equipment): Part-time 4 wheel drive, auto locking hub control with electronic shift, 3.55 axle ratio and skid plates.

XLT 2WD (5A) (in addition to or instead of XL 2WD (5M) equipment): 5-speed electronic overdrive automatic transmission; 3.73 axle ratio; front and rear chrome bumpers with black rub strip; body-colored bodyside molding with chrome bodyside insert; monotone paint with bodyside accent stripe; additional exterior lights include front fog/driving lights; driver's and passenger's power remote black folding outside mirrors; underbody mounted full-size temporary steel spare wheel; AM/FM stereo with clock, seek-scan, single CD, 4 speakers, and fixed antenna; cruise control with steering wheel controls; power door locks with 2 stage unlock, remote keyless entry; instrumentation display includes compass, exterior temp; ignition disable, panic alarm, security system; deep tinted windows, power front windows with driver 1-touch down, power rear windows; front sport seats with fixed headrests, center armrest with storage, driver's seat includes 4-way power seat with 8-way direction control and lumbar support, passenger's seat includes 4-way direction control with lumbar support; premium cloth seats; carpeted floor mats; interior lights include front and rear reading lights; leather-wrapped steering wheel with tilt adjustment; full floor console, full overhead console with storage, front cupholder and driver's and passenger's door bins.

XLT 4WD (5A) (in addition to or instead of XLT 2WD (5A) equipment): Part-time 4 wheel drive, auto locking hub control with electronic shift and skid plates.

XLT AWD (4A) (in addition to or instead of XLT 4WD (5A) equipment): 5.0L V8 OHV SMPI 16-valve engine; 4-speed electronic overdrive automatic transmission with lock-up; full-time 4 wheel drive and limited slip differential.

EDDIE BAUER 2WD (5A) (in addition to or instead of XLT 2WD (5A) equipment): 4.0L V6 SOHC SMPI 12-valve engine; transmission oil cooler; 4.1 axle ratio; running boards; front and rear bumpers with body-colored rub strip, front chrome bumper, rear body-colored bumper; body-colored fender flares; two-tone paint; aero-composite halogen fully automatic headlamps with delay-off feature; front and rear 16" x 7" chrome alloy wheels; air conditioning with climate control, rear heat ducts; AM/FM stereo with clock, seek-scan, single CD, 4 speakers, amplifier, and fixed antenna; garage door opener; instrumentation display systems monitor; passenger's seat includes 4-way power seat with 8-way direction control and lumbar support; auto-dimming day-night rearview mirror; instrument panel bin and cargo cover.

EDDIE BAUER 4WD (5A) (in addition to or instead of EDDIE BAUER 2WD (5A) equipment): Part-time 4 wheel drive, auto locking hub control with electronic shift and skid plates.

EDDIE BAUER AWD (4A) (in addition to or instead of EDDIE BAUER 4WD (5A) equipment): 5.0L V8 OHV SMPI 16-valve engine; 4-speed electronic overdrive automatic transmission with lock-up; 3.73 axle ratio; full-time 4 wheel drive and limited slip differential.

LIMITED 2WD (5A) (in addition to or instead of EDDIE BAUER 2WD (5A) equipment): Front and rear body-colored bumpers with body-colored rub strip; monotone paint with bodyside accent stripe; driver's and passenger's power remote black heated folding outside mirrors; power retractable antenna; instrumentation display includes trip computer; warning indicators include low fuel, low washer fluid, trunk ajar, service interval; heated front premium bucket seats with adjustable headrests; memory on driver's seat with 3 memory setting(s) and body-colored grille.

LIMITED 4WD (5A) (in addition to or instead of LIMITED 2WD (5A) equipment): Part-time 4 wheel drive, auto locking hub control with electronic shift; automatic ride control and auto-leveling front independent suspension with anti-roll bar.

CODE	DESCRIPTION	INVOICE	MSRP

LIMITED AWD (4A) (in addition to or instead of LIMITED 4WD (5A) equipment): 5.0L V8 OHV SMPI 16-valve engine; 4-speed electronic overdrive automatic transmission with lock-up; 3.73 axle ratio; full-time 4 wheel drive and limited slip differential.

Base Prices

CODE	DESCRIPTION	INVOICE	MSRP
U22	Sport 2-Door 2WD (5M)	18267	20065
U24	Sport 2-Door 4WD (5M)	20889	23045
U32	XL 2WD (5M)	19948	21975
U34	XL 4WD (5M)	21603	23855
U32	XLT 2WD (5M)	24330	27000
U34	XLT 4WD (5A)	26100	28965
U35	XLT AWD (4A)	26759	29715
U32	Eddie Bauer 2WD (5A)	28295	31460
U34	Eddie Bauer 4WD (5A)	30024	33425
U35	Eddie Bauer AWD (4A)	30389	33840
U32	Limited 2WD (5A)	28911	32160
U34	Limited 4WD (5A)	30640	34125
U35	Limited AWD (4A)	31005	34540
Destination Charge:		525	525

Accessories

CODE	DESCRIPTION	INVOICE	MSRP
182	Side Step Bar (Sport)	251	295
186	Running Boards (XL/XLT)	336	395
	Deletes rocker moldings.		
21A	Front Side Airbags	332	390
21H	Heated Front Seats (Eddie Bauer)	206	245
41H	Engine Block Heater	30	35
	Includes 400-watt single element.		
439	Power Moonroof (All Except XL)	680	800
	Includes overhead console. REQUIRES (94A and 47P) (Sport).		
44D	Transmission: 5-Speed Automatic with Overdrive (Sport/XL)	905	1065
44U	Transmission: 4-Speed Auto with Overdrive (XLT/Eddie Bauer/Limited)	NC	NC
47E	XLT Sport Group (XLT)	931	1095
	Manufacturer Discount	(255)	(300)
	Net Price	676	795
	Includes body color grille, platinum wheel lip moldings and front and rear bumpers, P255/70R16 OWL AT tires, 16" aluminum wheels, unique door mounted XLT badging and side step bars. REQUIRES 99E or 99P.		
47P	Premium Sport Package (Sport)	1275	1500
	Manufacturer Discount	(425)	(500)
	Net Price	850	1000
	Includes fog lamps, medium platinum colored wheellip moldings, front and rear bumpers and side step bar and tow hooks (rear). REQUIRES 55T.		

CODE	DESCRIPTION	INVOICE	MSRP
534	Trailer Tow Prep Package	302	355
	Includes super engine cooling, wiring harness, limited slip axle and HD flasher. Recommended for towing trailers.		
55G	Convenience Group (XL)	638	750
	Includes cargo cover, privacy glass, remote keyless entry: keyfob trunk release, panic alarm and speed control.		
55T	Convenience Group (Sport)	638	750
	Includes cargo cover, floor mats, remote keyless entry: keyfob trunk release, panic alarm; speed control and leather-wrapped tilt steering wheel.		
58K	Radio: AM/FM Stereo with CD, Cassette and Clock (Sport/XL/XLT)	111	130
	80 watt. Includes 4 speakers. REQUIRES 94A (Sport) or 773 (XL).		
58K	Radio: AM/FM Stereo with CD, Cassette and Clock (Sport/XL)	196	230
	80 watt. Includes 4 speakers.		
58Z	Radio: AM/FM Stereo with Clock and CD (XL)	85	100
	Includes 4 speakers and 24-watt amplifier. NOT AVAILABLE with 58K.		
59B	Electrochromic Mirror/Autolamp (XLT)	158	185
	Includes automatic day/night mirror and automatic headlamps.		
67H	Homelink with Travelnote (XLT)	182	216
68L	Rear Load Leveling (All 4WD/AWD Except Sport/XL)	298	350
	REQUIRES F (XLT/Eddie Bauer).		
76R	Reverse Sensing System (All Except XL)	208	245
	REQUIRES 94A and 47P (Sport).		
773	XLS Package (XL)	2831	3330
	Manufacturer Discount	(1020)	(1200)
	Net Price	1811	2130
	Includes unique cloth captain's chairs, removable storage bag, side step bar, wheellip moldings, fog lamps, color-keyed bodyside molding/grille, ETR AM/FM stereo with clock and CD, 15" chrome steel wheels, power windows, power door locks, power mirrors, luggage rack and P235/75R15SL AT OWL tires.		
86D	XL Appearance Group (XL)	1556	1830
	Manufacturer Discount	(595)	(700)
	Net Price	961	1130
	Includes cloth captain's chairs, floor console, power windows, power door locks, power mirrors, luggage rack, 15" cast aluminum deep dish wheels, P235/75R15SL AT OWL tires and color-keyed bodyside molding and grille.		
87K	Skid Plates (4WD/AWD)	89	105
916	Ford MACH Audio System (Sport/XLT)	565	665
	Includes cassette, CD, 290 watts (peak power), clock, sub woofer, amplifier and digital signal processor. REQUIRES 94A (Sport).		
91P	6 Disc CD Changer (All Except XL)	314	370
	REQUIRES 94A (Sport).		
931A	Preferred Equipment Package 931A (Sport)	NC	NC
	Includes engine: 4.0L OHV EFI V6, transmission: 5-speed manual with overdrive, air conditioning, cloth captain's chairs: floor console, AM/FM stereo with cassette and clock, privacy glass, luggage rack, tires: P235/75R15SL AT OWL, power windows, power door locks, power mirrors, rear wiper/washer/defroster, securilock passive anti-theft system, wheels: deep dish cast aluminum and 3.27 axle ratio.		

CODE	DESCRIPTION	INVOICE	MSRP
940A	**Preferred Equipment Package 940A (XL)**	NC	NC
	Includes engine: 4.0L OHV EFI V6, air conditioning, AM/FM stereo with cassette and clock, tires: P225/70R15SL BSW AS, rear wiper/washer/defroster, securilock passive anti-theft system, wheels: 15" full face steel and vinyl bucket seats.		
943A	**Preferred Equipment Package 943A (Limited)**	1373	1615
	Manufacturer Discount	(1373)	(1615)
	Net Price	NC	NC
	Includes puddle lamps located on outside rearview mirrors, color-keyed key pad with autolock, securilock passive anti-theft system, high series floor console, fog lamps, privacy glass, overhead console, remote keyless entry, auxiliary steering wheel controls, electronic automatic temperature control, Ford Mach audio system, homelink with travelnote message center, tires: P255/70R16 AT OWL, illuminated running boards, heated front seat, power mirrors, luxury leather bucket seats and wheels: 16" limited cast aluminum.		
945A	**Preferred Equipment Package 945A (XLT)**	905	1065
	Manufacturer Discount	(905)	(1065)
	Net Price	NC	NC
	Includes puddle lamps located on outside rearview mirrors, key pad/autolock, rear wiper/washer/defroster, securilock passive anti-theft system, cloth sport bucket seats, high series floor console, floor mats, fog lamps, privacy glass, overhead console, tires: P235/75R15SL AT OWL, remote keyless entry, speed control, leather-wrapped tilt steering wheel, wheels: luxury cast aluminum and 3.73 axle ratio.		
946A	**Preferred Equipment Package 946A (Eddie Bauer)**	1373	1615
	Manufacturer Discount	(1373)	(1615)
	Net Price	NC	NC
	Includes puddle lamps located on outside rearview mirrors, color-keyed key pad with autolock, securilock passive anti-theft system, high series floor console, floor mats, fog lamps, privacy glass, overhead console, remote keyless entry, speed control, leather-wrapped tilt steering wheel, auxiliary steering wheel controls, electronic automatic temperature control, Ford Mach audio system, homelink with travelnote message center, tires: P255/70R16 AT OWL, illuminated running boards, leather sport bucket seats and wheels: 16" polished aluminum.		
94A	**Comfort Group (Sport)**	1989	2340
	Manufacturer Discount	(905)	(1065)
	Net Price	1084	1275
	Includes puddle lamps located on outside rearview mirrors, cloth sport bucket seats, ETR AM/FM stereo with clock and CD, high series floor console, dual illuminated visor vanity mirrors, overhead console, electrochromic mirror, and autolamp automatic headlamps. REQUIRES 55T. NOT AVAILABLE with IAE.		
954	**Two-Tone Rocker Paint (XLT)**	102	120
99E	**Engine: 4.0L SOHC V6 (Sport/XL/XLT)**	459	540
	REQUIRES 44D.		
99P	**Engine: 5.0L EFI V8 (XLT 2WD)**	659	775
	REQUIRES 44U and 58K.		
99P	**Engine: 5.0L EFI V8 (Eddie Bauer/Limited (2WD Models Only))**	366	430
	Includes 3.73 axle ratio. REQUIRES 44U.		

CODE	DESCRIPTION	INVOICE	MSRP
F	Leather Sport Bucket Seats (XLT/Eddie Bauer) *Includes driver's and passenger's 6 way power adjustment with manual lumbar support. Deletes floor console.*	808	950
F	Sport Buckets with Leather Surface (Sport) *Includes driver's 6-way power adjustment with manual driver's and passenger's lumbar support.*	557	655
G	Cloth Sport Bucket Seats (XL) *REQUIRES 21A.*	238	280
IAE	Sport Bonus Discount (Sport 2WD) *NOT AVAILABLE with 94A or 47P.*	(506)	(595)
WF	Pearlescent Paint	170	200

1999 F-SERIES PICKUP

1999 Ford F-150

What's New?

The "Standard" trim level is replaced by the "Work" trim level. XLT and Lariat models get standard four-wheel antilock brakes, and the XLT gets standard air conditioning. All SuperCab models get a fourth door and horsepower is improved for engines across the board. Option content is shuffled and simplified as Ford reduces the number of optional features.

Review

When Ford introduced the new family of F-Series trucks in 1996, as a 1997 model, there was an uproar among old-school Blue Oval fans. Gone were their beloved Twin-I-Beam suspensions, pushrod engines, and traditional boxy styling. The new model appeared with a short- and long-arm front suspension, overhead cam engines, and more swoops than a Dairy Queen sundae.

Now that the vehicle has been out for a few years, naysayers have put their fears to rest. The SLA suspension provides excellent on- and off-road articulation giving the most demanding drivers the best ride available in any truck. Overhead cam engines provide capable acceleration and enough power to tow Rhode Island to the West Coast. The swoopy exterior means that parking an F-Series truck in a crowded parking lot may be a bit of a challenge, but the outstanding visibility it gives when off-roading more than makes up for its aerodynamic, car-like shape.

The Ford F-Series' interior is also a breakthrough. All of the Ford's hard edges have been softened, and the interior materials are not something that one would expect to see in a vehicle meant for a hard day's work. When put to the test, however, the Ford's interior can stand up to the rigors thrown at it by the meanest of foreman and orneriest of ranch hands. Until this vehicle came onto the scene, ergonomic and truck were not words that we were likely to use in the same sentence. The positioning of the F-Series' controls, however, makes this vehicle easier to drive than many mid-size sedans.

Our main gripe about the new F-Series is its overly twitchy steering and the tall step-in height on the four-wheel drive model. We're also unimpressed with the F-Series engine choices, especially when compared to the GM pickup engine roster, but Ford has bumped output for both its six- and eight-cylinder engines this year, so maybe they can catch up a bit in the power department.

The 1999 model year sees the addition of a standard fourth door to all SuperCab models and the simplification of the option selection process. The "Work" trim level replaces the "Standard" trim level as the entry-level offering. Ford also makes four-wheel antilock brakes standard on the XLT and Lariat trims.

After driving several F-150s, it appears that Ford has taken a path designed to bring more personal use buyers into the Ford fold without alienating truck buyers who work their pickups hard. Styling, always a subjective point, might turn potential buyers off with its free-flowing forms and smooth contours. We, however, like its clean lines and lack of clutter, particularly around the grille.

Ford should watch out, though, because the redesigned Chevrolet Silverado and GMC Sierra are guaranteed to make a big splash on the sales chart this year. Bigger, faster, and arguably better looking than the F-150, GM's new full-size trucks spell trouble for the Blue Oval.

Safety Data

Side Airbag: *Not Available*
4-Wheel ABS: *Std. (XLT/Lariat); Opt. (WS/XL)*
Driver Crash Test Grade: *Good*
Side Impact Crash Test Front: *Good*
Crash Offset: *Not Available*
Integrated Child Seat(s): *Not Available*
Traction Control: *Not Available*
Passenger Crash Test Grade: *Good*
Side Impact Crash Test Rear: *Not Available*

1999 F-150 PICKUP

Standard Equipment

WORK SERIES 2WD REGULAR CAB (5M): 4.2L V6 OHV SMPI 12-valve engine; 5-speed overdrive manual transmission; 58-amp battery with run down protection; 95-amp alternator; rear wheel drive, 3.08 axle ratio; stainless steel exhaust; front independent suspension with anti-roll bar, front coil springs, rigid rear axle suspension with rear leaf springs; power re-circulating ball steering; front disc/rear drum brakes with rear wheel antilock braking system; 25 gal capacity fuel tank; trailer harness; regular pickup box; front and rear argent bumpers with rear step; monotone paint; aero-composite halogen headlamps; additional exterior lights include center high mounted stop light; driver's and passenger's manual black folding outside mirrors; front and rear 16" x 7" silver steel wheels; P235/70SR16 BSW AS front and rear tires; underbody mounted full-size conventional steel spare wheel; AM/FM stereo with clock, seek-scan, 2 speakers, and fixed antenna; 2 power accessory outlets, driver's foot rest; instrumentation display includes oil pressure gauge, water temp gauge, volt gauge, trip odometer; warning indicators include oil pressure, water temp warning, battery, key in ignition, low fuel, door ajar; driver's side airbag, passenger's side cancellable airbag; ignition disable; tinted windows; variable intermittent front windshield wipers; seating capacity of 3, bench front seat with fixed headrests, seat includes 2-way direction control; height adjustable seatbelts; vinyl seats, vinyl door trim insert, front cloth headliner, full vinyl floor covering, cabback insulator; interior lights include dome light; day-night rearview mirror; glove box, front cupholder, instrument panel bin; vinyl cargo floor; black grille, black side window moldings, black front windshield molding, black rear window molding and black door handles.

WORK SERIES 2WD SUPERCAB (5M) (in addition to or instead of WORK SERIES 2WD REGULAR CAB (5M) equipment): 25.1 gal capacity fuel tank; fixed rear windows; seating capacity of 6 and 60-40 folding rear bench seat.

WORK SERIES 4WD REGULAR CAB (5M) (in addition to or instead of WORK SERIES 2WD REGULAR CAB (5M) equipment): Part-time 4 wheel drive, auto locking hub control and manual shift, 3.31 axle ratio; front independent torsion suspension with anti-roll bar, front torsion springs, front torsion bar; 24.5 gal capacity fuel tank and colored wheel well molding.

WORK SERIES 4WD SUPERCAB (5M) (in addition to or instead of WORK SERIES 4WD REGULAR CAB (5M) equipment): 4.6L V8 SOHC SMPI 16-valve engine; 130-amp HD alternator; 3.55 axle ratio; 25.1 gal capacity fuel tank; tinted windows, fixed rear windows; seating capacity of 6 and 60-40 folding rear bench seat.

XL 2WD REGULAR CAB (5M) (in addition to or instead of WORK SERIES 2WD REGULAR CAB (5M) equipment): Front and rear chrome bumpers with front black rub strip and rear step; underhood light; cloth seats; interior lights include front reading lights; passenger side vanity mirror and chrome grille.

XL 2WD SUPERCAB (5M) (in addition to or instead of XL 2WD REGULAR CAB (5A) equipment): 25.1 gal capacity fuel tank; fixed rear windows; seating capacity of 6 and 60-40 folding rear bench seat.

XL 4WD REGULAR CAB (5M) (in addition to or instead of XL 2WD REGULAR CAB (5M) equipment): Part-time 4 wheel drive, auto locking hub control and manual shift, 3.31 axle ratio; front independent torsion suspension with anti-roll bar, front torsion springs, front torsion bar; 24.5 gal capacity fuel tank and colored wheel well molding.

XL 4WD SUPERCAB (5M) (in addition to or instead of XL 4WD REGULAR CAB (5M) equipment): 4.6L V8 SOHC SMPI 16-valve engine; 130-amp HD alternator; part-time 4 wheel drive, auto locking hub control and manual shift, 3.55 axle ratio; 25.1 gal capacity fuel tank; tinted windows, fixed rear windows; seating capacity of 6 and 60-40 folding rear bench seat.

XLT 2WD REGULAR CAB (5M) (in addition to or instead of XL 2WD REGULAR CAB (5M) equipment): 3.08 axle ratio; front disc/rear drum brakes with 4 wheel antilock braking system; body-colored bodyside molding with chrome bodyside insert; additional exterior lights include pickup cargo box light; driver's and passenger's power remote chrome folding outside mirrors; air conditioning; AM/FM stereo with clock, seek-scan, cassette, 4 speakers, and fixed antenna; cruise control with steering wheel controls; power front windows with driver's 1-touch down; 60-40 split-bench front seat with fixed headrests, center armrest with storage, driver's seat includes 4-way direction control with lumbar support, passenger's seat includes 4-way direction control; interior 2 door curb lights; steering wheel with tilt adjustment; driver's and passenger's door bins; carpeted cargo floor and cargo concealed storage.

XLT 2WD SUPERCAB (5M) (in addition to or instead of XLT 2WD REGULAR CAB (5M) equipment): 25.1 gal capacity fuel tank; deep tinted windows, vented rear windows; seating capacity of 6; 60-40 folding rear bench seat and front and rear cupholders.

XLT 4WD REGULAR CAB (5M) (in addition to or instead of XLT 2WD REGULAR CAB (5M) equipment): Part-time 4 wheel drive, auto locking hub control and manual shift, 3.31 axle ratio; front independent torsion suspension with anti-roll bar, front torsion springs, front torsion bar; 24.5 gal capacity fuel tank, rear tow hooks; additional exterior lights include front fog/driving lights; driver and passenger power remote body-colored folding outside mirrors and body-colored grille.

CODE	DESCRIPTION	INVOICE	MSRP

XLT 4WD SUPERCAB (5M) (in addition to or instead of XLT 4WD REGULAR CAB (5M) equipment): 4.6L V8 SOHC SMPI 16-valve engine; 130-amp HD alternator; 3.55 axle ratio; 25.1 gal capacity fuel tank; tinted windows, fixed rear windows; seating capacity of 6 and 60-40 folding rear bench seat.

LARIAT 2WD REGULAR CAB (4A) (in addition to or instead of XLT 2WD REGULAR CAB (5M) equipment): 4-speed electronic overdrive automatic transmission with lock-up; 130-amp HD alternator; 3.55 axle ratio; driver's and passenger's power remote body-colored folding outside mirrors; premium AM/FM stereo with clock, seek-scan, single CD, 4 speakers, automatic equalizer, and fixed antenna; remote keyless entry; driver seat includes 4-way power seat with 8-way direction control and lumbar support; leather seats, vinyl door trim insert; illuminated entry; leather-wrapped steering wheel with tilt adjustment and body-colored grille.

LARIAT 2WD SUPERCAB (4A) (in addition to or instead of LARIAT 2WD REGULAR CAB (4A) equipment): 25.1 gal capacity fuel tank; deep tinted windows, vented rear windows; seating capacity of 6 and 60-40 folding rear bench seat.

LARIAT 4WD REGULAR CAB (4A) (in addition to or instead of LARIAT 2WD REGULAR CAB (4A) equipment): Part-time 4 wheel drive, auto locking hub control and manual shift; front independent torsion suspension with anti-roll bar, front torsion springs, front torsion bar; 24.5 gal capacity fuel tank and rear tow hooks.

LARIAT 4WD SUPERCAB (4A) (in addition to or instead of LARIAT 4WD REGULAR CAB (4A) equipment): 25.1 gal capacity fuel tank; deep tinted windows, vented rear windows; seating capacity of 6 and 60-40 folding rear bench seat.

Base Prices

CODE	DESCRIPTION	INVOICE	MSRP
F17	Work Series 2WD Regular Cab Styleside SB	13931	15250
F17-8	Work Series 2WD Regular Cab Styleside LB	14185	15540
X17	Work Series 2WD SuperCab Styleside SB	16209	17840
X17-8	Work Series 2WD SuperCab Styleside LB	16464	18130
F18	Work Series 4WD Regular Cab Styleside SB	16764	18470
F18-8	Work Series 4WD Regular Cab Styleside LB	17079	18760
X18	Work Series 4WD SuperCab Styleside SB	19491	21570
X18-8	Work Series 4WD SuperCab Styleside LB	19747	21860
F17	XL 2WD Regular Cab Styleside SB	14298	16220
F17-8	XL 2WD Regular Cab Styleside LB	14553	16520
F07	XL 2WD Regular Cab Flareside SB	15156	17230
X17	XL 2WD SuperCab Styleside SB	16579	18905
X17-8	XL 2WD SuperCab Styleside LB	16834	19205
X07	XL 2WD SuperCab Flareside SB	17437	19915
F18	XL 4WD Regular Cab Styleside SB	17136	19560
F18-8	XL 4WD Regular Cab Styleside LB	17391	19860
F08	XL 4WD Regular Cab Flareside SB	17994	20570
X18	XL 4WD SuperCab Styleside SB	19864	22770
X18-8	XL 4WD SuperCab Styleside LB	20119	23070
X08	XL 4WD SuperCab Flareside SB	20723	23780
F17	XLT 2WD Regular Cab Styleside SB	16715	19065
F17-8	XLT 2WD Regular Cab Styleside LB	16966	19360

CODE	DESCRIPTION	INVOICE	MSRP
F07	XLT 2WD Regular Cab Flareside SB	17574	20075
X17	XLT 2WD SuperCab Styleside SB	19040	21800
X17-8	XLT 2WD SuperCab Styleside LB	19295	22100
X07	XLT 2WD SuperCab Flareside SB	19898	22810
F18	XLT 4WD Regular Cab Styleside SB	19703	22580
F18-8	XLT 4WD Regular Cab Styleside LB	19963	22885
F08	XLT 4WD Regular Cab Flareside SB	20562	23590
X18	XLT 4WD SuperCab Styleside SB	22240	25565
X18-8	XLT 4WD SuperCab Styleside LB	22665	26065
X08	XLT 4WD SuperCab Flareside SB	23269	26775
F17	Lariat 2WD Regular Cab Styleside SB	19572	22425
F17-8	Lariat 2WD Regular Cab Styleside LB	19827	22725
F07	Lariat 2WD Regular Cab Flareside SB	20430	23435
X17	Lariat 2WD SuperCab Styleside SB	21900	25165
X17-8	Lariat 2WD SuperCab Styleside LB	22155	25465
X07	Lariat 2WD SuperCab Flareside SB	22759	26175
F18	Lariat 4WD Regular Cab Styleside SB	22717	26125
F18-8	Lariat 4WD Regular Cab Styleside LB	22972	26425
F08	Lariat 4WD Regular Cab Flareside SB	23575	27135
X18	Lariat 4WD SuperCab Styleside SB	24782	28555
X18-8	Lariat 4WD SuperCab Styleside LB	25037	28855
X08	Lariat 4WD SuperCab Flareside SB	25640	29565
Destination Charge:		640	640

Accessories

CODE	DESCRIPTION	INVOICE	MSRP
—	Special Discount (WS/XL) *REQUIRES 44M and 572.*	(425)	(500)
—	Special Discount (XLT) *REQUIRES 44M.*	(425)	(500)
167	Carpeted Color-Keyed Floor Mats (XL/XLT) *REQUIRES 168. NOT AVAILABLE with 16G.*	43	50
168	Color-Keyed Carpeting (XL)	85	100
16G	Carpet Delete (Lariat) *Replace with black vinyl mat and deletes floor mats.*	(85)	(100)
16G	Carpet Delete (XLT) *Replace with black vinyl mat and deletes floor mats.*	(43)	(50)
18E	Black Cab Steps (Reg Cab 2WD Styleside) *Black platform type.*	213	250
18E	Black Cab Steps (SuperCab 2WD Styleside) *Black platform type.*	255	300
18E	Black Cab Steps (Reg Cab 4WD/Reg Cab 2WD Styleside) *Black tubular type. NOT AVAILABLE with 66P.*	298	350
18E	Black Cab Steps (SuperCab 4WD/X-Cab 2WD Flareside) *Black tubular type.*	340	400

CODE	DESCRIPTION	INVOICE	MSRP
202	Payload Package #2 (WS 2WD Regular Cab) *Includes maximum payload of 1965 lbs and GVWR of 6000 lbs and tires: P255/70R16 SL AS OWL. REQUIRES X19. NOT AVAILABLE with 99W.*	399	470
202	Payload Package #2 (XL/XLT - 2WD Reg Cab) *Includes maximum payload of 1965 lbs, GVWR of 6000 lbs and HD shocks and springs. REQUIRES X19. NOT AVAILABLE with 99L, 44E, 94S, T53, T54, 44U, 99Z, 203.*	229	270
203	Payload Package #3 (2WD Regular Cab LB Except WS) *Includes maximum payload of 2195 lbs and GVWR of 6600 lbs. REQUIRES 99L.*	229	270
203	Payload Package #3 (2WD Regular Cab LB) *Includes maximum payload of 2375 lbs, GVWR of 6600 lbs, wheels: 16" styled steel, HD shocks and springs.*	399	470
215	4x4 Electric Shift-On-The-Fly (XLT 4WD/Lariat 4WD) *REQUIRES (99W or 99L or 99Z) and 44E.*	128	150
413	Transfer Case and Fuel Tank Skid Plates (All Except Regular Cab 4WD SB)	136	160
413	Transfer Case and Fuel Tank Skid Plates (Regular Cab 4WD SB) *Fuel tank skid plate standard on SB.*	68	80
41H	Engine Block Heater *Includes 600-watt element and 72-amp HD battery. Recommended when minimum temperature is -10 degrees F or below.*	77	90
433	Sliding Rear Window	107	125
44E/44U	Transmission: Electronic 4-Speed Auto with Overdrive	846	995
44M	Transmission: 5-Speed Manual (All Except Lariat)	NC	NC
47F	Special Regional Appearance Package (XLT 2WD) *Includes mesh grille insert, color-keyed grille surround and color-keyed mirrors. Available only in the following states/cities: Texas, Oklahoma, Louisiana, New Mexico, Los Angeles, San Francisco, Atlanta, Memphis and Orlando.*	NC	NC
47T	Bonus Discount (XL) *REQUIRES 572. Available only in the following states: Texas, Oklahoma, Louisiana, New Mexico.*	(684)	(805)
47T	Bonus Discount (XLT/Lariat) *Discount on standard air conditioning. Available only in the following states: Texas, Oklahoma, Louisiana, New Mexico.*	(410)	(500)
500A	Preferred Equipment Package 500A (WS) *Includes transmission: 5-speed manual with overdrive, tires: P235/70R16 SL AT BSW, vinyl bench seat, electronic AM/FM stereo with clock radio, argent rear step bumper, securilock and steel wheels.*	NC	NC
502A	Preferred Equipment Package 502A (XL) *Includes tires: P235/70R16 SL AT BSW, cloth bench seat, electronic AM/FM stereo with clock radio, securilock, chrome rear step bumper and styled steel wheels.*	NC	NC
507A	Preferred Equipment Package 507A (XLT) *Includes tires: P235/70R16 SL AT BSW, 40/60 split bench with driver's lumbar, electronic AM/FM stereo with cassette, 4-wheel antilock brakes, air conditioning, color-keyed carpeting, securilock, power convenience group: power door locks, power windows and polished aluminum wheels.*	1003	1180

CODE	DESCRIPTION	INVOICE	MSRP
508A	Preferred Equipment Package 508A (Lariat) *Includes engine: 4.6L EFI V8, transmission: 4 speed automatic transmission with overdrive, 40/60 leather split bench, electronic AM/FM stereo with CD, 4-wheel antilock brakes, air conditioning, color-keyed carpeting, carpeted color-keyed floor mats, power driver's seat, remote keyless entry, illuminated entry, securilock, power convenience group: power door locks, power windows, aero power color-keyed mirrors and 3.55 axle ratio.*	1165	1370
52N	Convenience Group (WS) *Includes speed control and tilt steering.*	328	385
535	Trailer Towing Group *Includes 7-pin trailer wiring harness, HD shocks and HD electrical/cooling package.*	340	400
53C	Snow Plow Prep Package (WS/XL/XLT - 4WD Reg Cab LB) *Includes styled steel wheels and HD shocks. REQUIRES (99L or 99W) and 44E.*	429	505
53T	Tow Hooks (XL 4WD) *Includes 2 cast iron front tow hooks.*	34	40
55R	Off-Road Package (Lariat 4WD Except SuperCab) *Includes off-road decal, skid plates for frame front crossmember, steel wheels, HD shocks, transfer case and fuel tank skid plates. REQUIRES 413.*	667	785
55R	Off-Road Package (XLT 4WD Except SuperCab LB) *Includes off-road decal, skid plates for frame front crossmember, steel wheels, transfer case, fuel tank skid plates and HD shocks. REQUIRES T3P or 413 or 99Z.*	973	1145
572	Air Conditioning (WS/XL/XLT)	684	805
585	Radio: Electronic AM/FM Stereo with CD (XL) *Includes 4 speakers, clock and speed compensated volume control. REQUIRES 572 and 60B. NOT AVAILABLE with 589.*	273	320
585	Radio: Electronic AM/FM Stereo with CD (XLT) *Includes 4 speakers, clock and speed compensated volume control. NOT AVAILABLE with 91P.*	162	190
589	Radio: Electronic AM/FM Stereo with Cassette (XL) *Includes 4 speakers and clock. NOT AVAILABLE with 585.*	111	130
595	Fog Lamps (XL 4WD)	119	140
60B	Convenience Group (XL) *Includes speed control, tilt steering and pickup box security group.*	293	345
60S	STX Graphic Package (XL Styleside) *Includes unique vinyl bodyside and tailgate graphic and an "STX" decal. REQUIRES (T53 and 31P and D9K) or (T3P and 31P and D9K).*	198	295
62N	Nascar Appearance Package (XL/XLT/Lariat) *Includes NASCAR Official Truck on pickup box sides and badge on tailgate, NASCAR logo embroidered on driver's and passenger's head restraints, "Sport" decal delete and bodyside stripe. REQUIRES 94S and M or 94T. NOT AVAILABLE with 99L, 44E, T53, T54, 954, 60S, T3P, T65, 55R, F.*	128	150
63H	HD Electrical/Cooling Package *Includes super engine cooling.*	178	210
653	Optional Tank Configuration *REQUIRES 99Z and 66P. NOT AVAILABLE with 66N.*	115	135
653	Optional Tank Configuration *REQUIRES 99Z and 66N. NOT AVAILABLE with 66P.*	1088	1280

CODE	DESCRIPTION	INVOICE	MSRP
66N	**Natural Gas Bi-Fuel Prep Group (Reg Cab Styleside LB Except Lariat 4WD)** .. *Includes standard single in-bed fuel tank (33.75 gal.) and California catalysts in all states. Engine oil cooler is not included. NOT AVAILABLE with 53C.*	4938	5810
66P	**Propane Bi-Fuel Prep Group (Reg Cab Styleside LB Except Lariat 4WD)** .... *Includes standard single in-bed fuel tank (33.75 gal.) and California catalysts in all states. Engine oil cooler is not included. NOT AVAILABLE with 53C.*	4208	4950
67B	**4-Wheel Antilock Brakes (WS/XL/XLT)**	319	375
86T	**Soft Tonneau Cover (All Except WS)**	128	150
87D	**Rear Seat Delete (WS SuperCab)**	(352)	(415)
904	**Remote Keyless Entry (XLT)** .... *Includes 2 key fobs and illuminated entry.*	128	150
90P	**Power Driver's Seat (XLT)** .... *Includes autolamp. REQUIRES 572 and 52N.*	306	360
91P	**6 Disc CD Changer (Lariat)** .... *Includes premium AM/FM stereo with cassette. REQUIRES H.*	178	210
91P	**6 Disc CD Changer (XLT)** .... *Includes premium AM/FM stereo with cassette. REQUIRES F. NOT AVAILABLE with 585.*	340	400
94S	**Sport Group (XL 2WD)** .... *Includes color-keyed grille insert, color-keyed bumpers, color-keyed exterior mirrors, P255/70R16 AS OWL tires, aluminum wheels, 3.55 rear axle, "Sport" badges, fog lights, tachometer.*	421	495
94S	**Sport Group (XL 4WD)** .... *Includes color-keyed grille insert, color-keyed bumpers, color-keyed exterior mirrors, P255/70R16 AS OWL tires, aluminum wheels, 3.55 rear axle, "Sport" badges, fog lights, tachometer.*	506	595
94T	**Sport Group (XLT)** .... *Includes black grille insert, color-keyed bumpers, color-keyed exterior mirrors, P275/60R17 OWL tires, aluminum wheels, 3.55 rear axle, "Sport" badges, fog lights, tachometer.*	506	595
954	**Two-Tone Lower Paint (XL/XLT/Lariat)** .... *NOT AVAILABLE with 94S, 55R, 94T.*	192	225
99L	**Engine: 5.4L EFI V8 (All Except Lariat or 4WD SuperCab)** .... *Includes 130-amp HD alternator and 3.55 axle ratio. REQUIRES 44E or 44U.*	1202	1415
99L	**Engine: 5.4L EFI V8 (Lariat or 4WD SuperCab)** .... *REQUIRES 44E or 44U. NOT AVAILABLE with 203.*	565	665
99W	**Engine: 4.6L EFI V8 (All Except Lariat or 4WD SuperCab)** .... *Includes 130-amp HD alternator.*	638	750
99Z	**Engine: 5.4L Bi-Fuel Prep (Lariat Regular Cab)**	692	815
99Z	**Engine: 5.4L Bi-Fuel Prep (Regular Cab Except Lariat)**	1233	1450
B3R	**Regional Discount:** .... **Denver, Seattle, Twin-Cities and Chicago (Lariat Except SuperCab LB)** *REQUIRES 55R. NOT AVAILABLE with NAT.*	(417)	(490)
B3R	**Regional Discount:** .... **Denver, Seattle, Twin-Cities and Chicago (XLT Except SuperCab LB)** *REQUIRES 55R. NOT AVAILABLE with NAT.*	(723)	(850)

CODE	DESCRIPTION	INVOICE	MSRP
F	Cloth Captain's Seats (XLT) *Includes driver's lumbar and center console.*	417	490
H	Leather Captain's Seats (Lariat) *Includes driver's lumbar and center console.*	417	490
ITP	Bonus Discount (WS/XL/XLT (Except SuperCa) *Base engine discount. NOT AVAILABLE with 99W, 99L and 99Z.*	(425)	(500)
M	40/60 Split Bench with Driver's Lumbar (XL) *Includes center seat storage.*	221	260
T34	Tires: LT245/75R16D AS BSW (2WD Except Lariat) *Includes 3.55 axle ratio.*	374	440
T34	Tires: LT245/75R16D AS BSW (2WD Lariat) *REQUIRES 203. NOT AVAILABLE with T53.*	77	90
T3P	Tires: LT245/75R16D AT OWL (4WD LB Except Lariat) *Includes 3.55 axle ratio. REQUIRES 53C.*	204	240
T3P	Tires: LT245/75R16D AT OWL (Lariat 4WD)	293	345
T3P	Tires: LT245/75R16D AT OWL (XL 4WD/XLT 4WD)	591	695
T53	Tires: P235/70R16SL AS OWL (XL 2WD/XLT 2WD) *Includes BSW AS spare.*	107	125
T54	Tires: P255/70R16SL AS BSW (2WD - XL/XLT) *REQUIRES 99L. NOT AVAILABLE with 94S, T53, T55, T3P, T65, 94T, 47T.*	144	170
T55	Tires: P255/70R16SL AS OWL (XLT 2WD) *Includes BSW AS spare and 3.55 axle ratio.*	251	295
T65	Tires: P255/70R16SL AT OWL (WS 4WD/XL 4WD/XLT 4WD) *REQUIRES 53C.*	340	400
X19	3.55 Axle Ratio (All Except Lariat) *REQUIRES T34 or T55 or 203 or 66N or 66P or 203. NOT AVAILABLE with T53.*	43	50
XB6	Limited Slip Rear Axle (4WD) *REQUIRES X26. NOT AVAILABLE with 99W.*	272	320
XH9	Limited Slip Rear Axle *REQUIRES X19.*	NC	NC

1999 F-250 PICKUP

Standard Equipment

WORK SERIES 2WD REGULAR CAB (5M): 4.6L V8 SOHC SMPI 16-valve engine; 5-speed overdrive manual transmission; 58-amp battery with run down protection; 130-amp HD alternator; rear wheel drive, 3.73 axle ratio; stainless steel exhaust; firm ride suspension, front independent double wishbone suspension with anti-roll bar, front coil springs, rigid rear axle suspension with rear leaf springs; power re-circulating ball steering; front disc/rear drum brakes with rear wheel antilock braking system; 30 gal capacity fuel tank; regular pickup box; front and rear argent bumpers with rear step; monotone paint; aero-composite halogen headlamps; additional exterior lights include center high mounted stop light; driver's and passenger's manual black folding outside mirrors; front and rear 16" x 7" silver styled steel wheels; P255/70SR16 BSW AS front and rear tires; underbody mounted full-size conventional steel spare wheel; AM/FM stereo with clock, seek-scan, 2 speakers, and fixed antenna; 2 power accessory outlets; instrumentation display includes oil pressure gauge, water temp gauge, volt gauge, trip odometer; warning indicators include oil pressure, water temp, battery, key in ignition, low fuel, door ajar; driver's side airbag, passenger's side cancelable airbag; ignition disable; tinted windows; variable intermittent front windshield wipers; seating capacity of 3, bench front seat with fixed headrests, driver's seat includes 2-way direction control, passenger's seat includes 2-way direction control; front height adjustable seatbelts; vinyl seats, vinyl door trim insert, full cloth headliner, full vinyl floor covering, cabback insulator; interior lights include dome light; day-night rearview mirror; glove box, front cupholder, instrument panel bin, dashboard storage; vinyl cargo floor, cargo tie downs; gray colored grille, black side window moldings, black front windshield molding, black rear window molding and black door handles.

WORK SERIES 2WD SUPERCAB (5M) (in addition to or instead of WORK SERIES 2WD REGULAR CAB STYLESIDE (5M) equipment): 25 gal capacity fuel tank; tinted windows, fixed rear windows; seating capacity of 6 and 60-40 folding rear bench seat.

XL 2WD REGULAR CAB (5M) (in addition to or instead of WORK SERIES 2WD REGULAR CAB STYLESIDE (5M) equipment): Front and rear chrome bumpers, front black rub strip; additional exterior lights include underhood light; cloth seats; interior lights include front reading lights; passenger side vanity mirror and chrome grille.

XL 2WD SUPERCAB (5M) (in addition to or instead of XL 2WD REGULAR CAB STYLESIDE (5M) equipment): 25 gal capacity fuel tank; tinted windows, fixed rear windows; seating capacity of 6 and 60-40 folding rear bench seat.

XLT 2WD REGULAR CAB (5M) (in addition to or instead ofXL 2WD REGULAR CAB STYLESIDE (5M) equipment): Four-wheel disc brakes with rear wheel antilock braking system; body-colored bodyside molding; additional exterior lights include pickup cargo box light; driver's and passenger's power remote chrome folding outside mirrors; AM/FM stereo with clock, seek-scan, cassette, 4 speakers, and fixed antenna; cruise control with steering wheel controls; retained accessory power; instrumentation display includes tachometer; tinted windows, power front windows with driver's 1-touch down; 40-60 split-bench front seat with fixed headrests, center armrest with storage, driver's seat includes 4-way direction control with lumbar support, passenger's seat includes 4-way direction control; full carpet floor covering; interior lights include front reading lights, 2 door curb lights; steering wheel with tilt adjustment; driver's side auxiliary visor; carpeted cargo floor; cargo concealed storage and body-colored door handles.

XLT 2WD SUPERCAB (5M) (in addition to or instead of XLT 2WD REGULAR CAB STYLESIDE (5M) equipment): 25 gal capacity fuel tank; deep tinted windows; vented rear windows; seating capacity of 6, 40-60 split-bench front seat with fixed headrests; 60-40 folding rear bench seat.

LARIAT 2WD REGULAR CAB (5M) (in addition to or instead of XLT 2WD REGULAR CAB STYLESIDE (5M) equipment): Firm ride suspension; body-colored wheel well molding; aero-composite halogen fully automatic headlamps; driver's and passenger's power remote body-colored folding outside mirrors; underbody mounted full-size temporary steel spare wheel; air conditioning; premium AM/FM stereo with clock, seek-scan, single CD, 4 speakers, automatic equalizer, and fixed antenna; power door locks, remote keyless entry; driver's seat includes 4-way power seat with 8-way direction control and lumbar support; leather seats; interior lights include illuminated entry; leather-wrapped steering wheel with tilt adjustment; driver's and passenger's door bins and body-colored grille.

LARIAT 2WD SUPERCAB (5M) (in addition to or instead of LARIAT 2WD REGULAR CAB STYLESIDE (5M) equipment): 25 gal capacity fuel tank; deep tinted windows; vented rear windows; seating capacity of 6 and 60-40 folding rear bench seat.

WORK SERIES 4WD REGULAR CAB (5M) (in addition to or instead of WORK SERIES 2WD REGULAR CAB STYLESIDE (5M) equipment): Part-time 4 wheel drive, auto locking hub control with manual shift; firm ride suspension, front torsion springs, front torsion bar and colored wheel well molding.

WORK SERIES 4WD SUPERCAB (5M) (in addition to or instead of WORK SERIES 4WD REGULAR CAB STYLESIDE (5M) equipment): 25 gal capacity fuel tank; tinted windows, fixed rear windows; seating capacity of 6 and 60-40 folding rear bench seat.

XL 4WD REGULAR CAB (5M) (in addition to or instead of XL 2WD REGULAR CAB STYLESIDE (5M) equipment): Part-time 4 wheel drive, auto locking hub control with manual shift; firm ride suspension, front torsion springs, front torsion bar and colored wheel well molding.

XL 4WD SUPERCAB (5M) (in addition to or instead of XL 4WD REGULAR CAB STYLESIDE (5M) equipment): 25 gal capacity fuel tank; tinted windows, fixed rear windows; seating capacity of 6 and 60-40 folding rear bench seat.

XLT 4WD REGULAR CAB (5M) (in addition to or instead of XLT 2WD REGULAR CAB STYLESIDE (5M) equipment): Part-time 4 wheel drive, auto locking hub control with manual shift; firm ride suspension, front torsion springs, front torsion bar, colored wheel well molding and rear tow hooks.

XLT 4WD SUPERCAB (5M) (in addition to or instead of XLT 4WD REGULAR CAB STYLESIDE (5M) equipment): 25 gal capacity fuel tank; tinted windows, fixed rear windows; seating capacity of 6 and 60-40 folding rear bench seat.

LARIAT 4WD REGULAR CAB (5M) (in addition to or instead of LARIAT 2WD REGULAR CAB STYLESIDE (5M) equipment): Part-time 4 wheel drive, auto locking hub control with manual shift; firm ride suspension, front torsion springs, front torsion bar, body colored wheel well molding and rear tow hooks.

LARIAT 4WD SUPERCAB (5M) (in addition to or instead of LARIAT 4WD REGULAR CAB STYLESIDE (5M) equipment): 25 gal capacity fuel tank; tinted windows, fixed rear windows; seating capacity of 6 and 60-40 folding rear bench seat.

Base Prices

Code	Description	Invoice	MSRP
F27	Work Series 2WD Regular Cab Styleside	15730	17295
X27	Work Series 2WD SuperCab Styleside	18009	19885
F28	Work Series 4WD Regular Cab Styleside	18423	20355
X28	Work Series 4WD SuperCab Styleside	20697	22940
F27	XL 2WD Regular Cab Styleside	16099	18340
X27	XL 2WD SuperCab Styleside	18381	21025
F28	XL 4WD Regular Cab Styleside	18789	21505
X28	XL 4WD SuperCab Styleside	21072	24190
F27	XLT 2WD Regular Cab Styleside	18577	21255
X27	XLT 2WD SuperCab Styleside	20910	24000
F28	XLT 4WD Regular Cab Styleside	21424	24605
X28	XLT 4WD SuperCab Styleside	23681	27260
F27	Lariat 2WD Regular Cab Styleside	20655	23700
X27	Lariat 2WD SuperCab Styleside	22984	26440
F28	Lariat 4WD Regular Cab Styleside	23758	27350
X28	Lariat 4WD SuperCab Styleside	26014	30005
Destination Charge:		640	640

CODE	DESCRIPTION	INVOICE	MSRP
	Accessories		
167	Carpeted Color-Keyed Floor Mats (XL Reg Cab/XLT Reg Cab) *REQUIRES 168. NOT AVAILABLE with 16G.*	26	30
167	Carpeted Color-Keyed Floor Mats (XL X-Cab/XLT X-Cab) *REQUIRES 168. NOT AVAILABLE with 16G.*	43	50
168	Color-Keyed Carpeting (XL)	85	100
16G	Carpet Delete (XLT) *Replaces carpet with black vinyl mat and deletes floor mats. NOT AVAILABLE with 167.*	(43)	(50)
16G	Carpet Delete (Lariat) *Replaces carpet with black vinyl mat and deletes floor mats.*	(85)	(100)
18E	Black Cab Steps (2WD Reg Cab) *Platform type.*	213	250
18E	Black Cab Steps (2WD X-Cab) *Platform type.*	255	300
18E	Black Cab Steps (4WD Reg Cab) *Tubular type.*	298	350
18E	Black Cab Steps (4WD X-Cab) *Tubular type.*	340	400
207	Optional Payload Package #2 (2WD X-Cab) *Includes 7500 lbs GVWR and 2930 lbs payload and HD shocks and springs. NOT AVAILABLE with T55.*	43	50
209	Optional Payload Package #2 (All Except 2WD X-Cab) *Includes 7700 lbs GVWR and 3295 lbs payload and HD shocks and springs. REQUIRES 99L or 99Z or XB6. NOT AVAILABLE with 99M, T55.*	43	50
215	4x4 Electric Shift-On-The-Fly (4WD XLT/4WD Lariat)	128	150
413	Skid Plates (4WD) *Includes transfer case and fuel tank skid plates.*	136	160
41H	Engine Block Heater *Includes 600-watt element. Recommended when minimum temperature is -10 degrees F or below and 72-amp HD battery.*	77	90
433	Sliding Rear Window	107	125
44E	Transmission: Electronic 4 Speed Automatic (WS/XL/XLT)	846	995
44U	Transmission: Electronic 4-Speed Automatic (WS/XL/XLT) *NOT AVAILABLE with 99L, 99M, 653, 99Z, 66N, 66P.*	846	995
510A	Preferred Equipment Package 510A (WS) *Includes engine: 4.6L EFI V8, transmission: 5-speed manual with overdrive, argent styled steel wheels, vinyl bench seat, ETR AM/FM stereo, argent rear step bumper and Securilock.*	NC	NC
512A	Preferred Equipment Package 512A (XL) *Includes engine: 4.6L EFI V8, transmission: 5-speed manual with overdrive, cloth bench seat, ETR AM/FM stereo, Securilock and chrome rear step bumper.*	NC	NC
517A	Preferred Equipment Package 517A (XLT) *Includes engine: 4.6L EFI V8, transmission: 5-speed manual with overdrive, chrome styled steel wheels, cloth 40/60 split bench, ETR AM/FM stereo with cassette, 4-wheel antilock braking system, air conditioning, color-keyed carpeting, Securilock,*	1003	1180

CODE	DESCRIPTION	INVOICE	MSRP
	convenience group: speed control, tilt steering wheel, cargo box light, tailgate lock and power convenience group: power door locks.		
518A	Preferred Equipment Package 518A (Lariat) *Includes engine: 4.6L EFI V8, transmission: 4-speed auto with overdrive, chrome styled steel wheels, 40/60 leather split bench, ETR AM/FM stereo with CD, 4-wheel antilock braking system, air conditioning, color-keyed carpeting, carpeted color-keyed floor mats, power driver's seat, autolamp, remote keyless entry, illuminated entry, Securilock, chrome rear step bumper and convenience group: power door locks.*	1165	1370
52N	Convenience Group (WS) *Includes speed control, tilt steering wheel, cargo box light, tailgate lock*	328	385
535	Trailer Towing Group *Includes 7-pin trailer wiring harness and HD electrical/cooling package: super engine cooling. NOT AVAILABLE with 63H, 653, 66N, 66P.*	340	400
53C	Snow Plow Prep Package (4WD Except Lariat) *Includes front GAWR upgrade to 4150 lb. and LT245/75R16D AT OWL tires. Maximum snowplow weight including permanent attachments is 700 lbs. NOT AVAILABLE with 99Z, 66N, 66P, 653, 63H, 44E.*	387	455
53T	Tow Hooks (XL 4WD) *Includes 2 cast iron front tow hooks.*	34	40
572	Air Conditioning (WS/XL)	684	805
585	Radio: AM/FM Stereo with CD (XL) *Includes clock, 4 speakers and speed compensated volume control. REQUIRES 572 and 60B. NOT AVAILABLE with 589.*	273	320
585	Radio: AM/FM Stereo with CD (XLT) *Includes clock, 4 speakers and speed compensated volume control. NOT AVAILABLE with 91P.*	162	190
589	Radio: AM/FM Stereo with Cassette (XL) *Includes digital clock and 4 speakers. NOT AVAILABLE with 585.*	111	130
595	Fog Lamps (XL)	119	140
60B	Convenience Group (XL) *Includes speed control, tilt steering wheel, cargo box light and tailgate lock.*	293	345
63H	HD Electrical/Cooling Pkg. *Includes HD 72-amp hour battery, super engine cooling and auxiliary automatic transmission oil cooler. NOT AVAILABLE with 535, 99Z, 653, 66N, 66P, 53C.*	128	150
643	Wheels: Chrome Styled Steel (XL) *Includes chrome hub.*	170	200
653	Optional Tank Configuration (2WD Reg Cab) *REQUIRES 66N and 99Z. NOT AVAILABLE with 99L, 44U, 99M, 63H, 535, 66P.*	1088	1280
653	Optional Tank Configuration *REQUIRES 99M. NOT AVAILABLE with 99L, 44U, 99Z, 66N, 66P, 63H, 535.*	931	1095
653	Optional Tank Configuration *REQUIRES 66P and 99Z. NOT AVAILABLE with 99L, 44U, 99M, 63H, 535, 66N, 53C.*	115	135
66N	Natural Gas Fuel System *REQUIRES 99Z. NOT AVAILABLE with 99L, 99M, 44U, 66P, 653, 535, 63H, 53C.*	4938	5810

CODE	DESCRIPTION	INVOICE	MSRP
66P	Propane Fuel System *REQUIRES 99Z. NOT AVAILABLE with 99L, 99M, 44U, 66N, 653, 535, 63H, 53C.*	4208	4950
67B	4-Wheel Antilock Braking System (WS/XL) *Includes 4-wheel disc brakes.*	319	375
86T	Soft Tonneau Cover (XL/XLT/Lariat)	170	200
87D	Rear Seat Delete (WS X-Cab)	(352)	(415)
904	Remote Keyless Entry (XLT) *Includes 2 key fobs and illuminated entry. REQUIRES 517A.*	128	150
90P	Power Driver's Seat (XLT) *Includes autolamp. REQUIRES (44E and 44U) or 517A.*	306	360
91P	Radio: AM/FM Stereo with CD and Cassette (Lariat) *Includes 6 disc CD changer. REQUIRES H.*	178	210
91P	Radio: AM/FM Stereo with CD and Cassette (XLT) *Includes 6 disc CD changer. REQUIRES 572, 52N, 61S (Reg Cab), F (X-Cab). NOT AVAILABLE with 585.*	340	400
954	Two-Tone Lower Paint (XLT/Lariat)	192	225
99L	Engine: 5.4L EFI V8 *Includes a 130-amp HD alternator. REQUIRES 44E. NOT AVAILABLE with 44U, 653, 66N, 66P.*	565	665
99M	Engine: 5.4L Natural Gas (WS/XL) *Available to certified dealers only and with payload package #1. REQUIRES 44E. NOT AVAILABLE with 44U, 66N, 66P, 209.*	4692	5520
99Z	Engine: 5.4L Bi-Fuel Prep *Available to certified dealers only. Includes California catalysts in all states and single in-bed fuel tank. REQUIRES 44E. NOT AVAILABLE with 44U, 63H, 653, 53C.*	692	815
F	Cloth Captain's Seats (XLT) *Includes driver's lumbar and floor console.*	417	490
H	Leather Captain's Chairs (Lariat) *Includes driver's lumbar and floor console.*	417	490
M	Cloth 40/60 Split Bench (XL) *Includes driver's lumbar and seat center storage. Available in medium graphite and medium prairie tan only.*	221	260
M61	Rear Storage Bin Delete (Reg Cab - XLT/Lariat) *NOT AVAILABLE with 91P.*	(51)	(60)
T34	Tires: LT245/75R16D AS BSW (2WD - WS/XL/XLT) *NOT AVAILABLE with T55.*	182	215
T3P	Tires: LT245/75R16D AT OWL (4WD - WS/XL/XLT) *Includes BSW all-terrain spare.*	217	255
T55	Tires: P255/70R16SL AS OWL (XLT 2WD) *Includes BSW all-season spare. NOT AVAILABLE with 209, 207.*	107	125
XB6	Limited Slip Rear Axle	243	285

1999 F-SERIES SUPER DUTY PICKUP

1999 Ford F-250 Super Duty

What's New?

The all-new Super Duty F-Series is a full-size truck developed and built on a separate platform from the under-8,500lb GVWR F150 and F250. For '99 the Super Duty is available in Regular Cab, four-door Super Cab or Crew Cab models.

Review

Commercial/small business demand is one of the fastest growing segments in the expanding truck market. Ford has acknowledged the need to create a special utility vehicle aimed squarely at these customers in creating the new Super Duty F-Series. This line of trucks can be had in one of 44 configurations, 21 of which are new. By using a separate platform from the smaller F-150 and F-250 trucks, Ford hopes to meet all the needs of both the personal-use and commercial-use markets.

The 1999 Super Duty F-Series trucks feature a 5.4-liter Triton V8 making 235 horsepower and a 6.8-liter Triton V10 making 275 horsepower. Both of these powerplants are new to the lineup and compliment the existing 7.3-liter Power Stroke diesel engine. The diesel has also been updated for '99 and makes an impressive 235 horsepower and 500 foot-pounds trailer-towing torque. All three engines offer more horsepower, higher torque and better fuel economy than the engines they replace.

The Super Duty's new body style incorporates a larger cab and an overall length increase of nine inches over last year. The wheelbase is also up by four inches and the cargo area has grown slightly taller and longer. The increased dimensions allow the various cabs to be made larger without compromising load space. Despite its larger size, the Super Duty maintains a confident on- and off-road feel. The new truck features an updated power steering system and enhanced suspension components to improve vehicle ride, handling, responsiveness, and maneuverability. Four-wheel disc antilock brakes are standard on all Super Duty models over 10,000 pounds GVW (ABS is optional on the "smaller" Super Duty trucks).

Inside, the roomier cabs have larger, more comfortable seats and greater seat track travel. In addition, there are many interior convenience features designed for today's stylish business owners. For example, a fold-down armrest and utility bin is designed to house a portable fax machine or laptop computer. In the Crew Cab XLT and Lariat models, a new rear bench seat incorporates a fold-down armrest and a cupholder. For truck owners who don't want to skimp on luxury, leather seating, a leather-wrapped steering wheel, air conditioning and power windows are just some of the many options available.

The Super Duty F-Series isn't for everyone. However, if you need more truck than the regular F-Series can provide, Ford has quite an impressive lineup to peruse.

1999 F-250 SUPER DUTY PICKUP

Safety Data

Side Airbag: *Not Available*
4-Wheel ABS: *Optional*
Driver Crash Test Grade: *Not Available*
Side Impact Crash Test Front: *Not Available*
Crash Offset: *Not Available*
Integrated Child Seat(s): *Not Available*
Traction Control: *Not Available*
Passenger Crash Test Grade: *Not Available*
Side Impact Crash Test Rear: *Not Available*

Standard Equipment

XL 2WD: 5.4L V8 SOHC SMPI 16-valve engine; 5-speed overdrive manual transmission; 72-amp battery with run down protection; 95-amp alternator; rear wheel drive, 4.1 axle ratio; stainless steel exhaust; firm ride suspension, front independent suspension, front coil springs, HD front shocks, rear suspension with rear leaf springs, HD rear shocks; power re-circulating ball steering; 4-wheel disc brakes with rear wheel antilock braking system; 38 gal capacity fuel tank; trailer harness; regular pick-up box; front argent bumper; monotone paint; sealed beam halogen headlamps; additional exterior lights include center high mounted stop light, pickup cargo box light; driver and passenger manual black folding outside mirrors; front and rear 16" x 7" silver styled steel wheels with hub wheel covers; LT235/85SR16 BSW AS front and rear tires; AM/FM stereo, clock, seek-scan, 2 speakers and fixed antenna; 2 power accessory outlets; analog instrumentation display includes tachometer, oil pressure gauge, water temp gauge, volt gauge, trip odometer; warning indicators include oil pressure, water temp warning, battery, key in ignition, low fuel, door ajar; dual airbags; tinted windows; fixed interval front windshield wipers; seating capacity of 3, bench front seat with fixed headrests, driver's seat includes 2-way direction control, passenger's seat includes 2-way direction control; front height adjustable seatbelts; vinyl seats, full cloth headliner, full vinyl floor covering, cabback insulator; interior lights include dome light; day-night rearview mirror; glove box, front cupholder, instrument panel bin, dashboard storage; black grille, black side windows moldings, black front windshield molding, black rear window molding, black door handles, vented rear windows (SuperCab), manual rear windows (Crew Cab), seating capacity of 6 (SuperCab, Crew Cab), full folding rear bench seat (SuperCab, Crew Cab); vinyl cargo floor (Crew Cab).

XL 4WD (in addition to or instead of XL 2WD equipment): Part-time 4-wheel drive, manual locking hub control and manual shift; front leaf springs; 38 gal. capacity fuel tank; rear tow hooks.

XLT 2WD (in addition to or instead of XL 2WD equipment): Front chrome bumper with black rub strip; black bodyside molding with chrome bodyside insert; aero-composite headlamps; additional exterior lights include underhood light; stereo with cassette, 4 speakers; 40-20-40 split-bench front seat with center storage armrest, driver's seat includes 4-way direction control with lumbar support, passenger's seat includes 4-way direction control; cloth seats, vinyl door trim insert, carpet floor covering; interior lights include; passenger side vanity mirror; driver and passenger door bins; cargo concealed storage; chrome grille.

XLT 4WD (in addition to or instead of XLT 2WD equipment): Part-time 4-wheel drive, manual locking hub control and manual shift; front leaf springs; 38 gal. capacity fuel tank; rear tow hooks.

LARIAT 2WD (in addition to or instead of XLT 2WD equipment): Running boards; rear tow hooks; retained accessory power; compass, trip computer; passenger side cancellable airbag; power front

CODE	DESCRIPTION	INVOICE	MSRP

windows with driver 1-touch down; leather seats, carpeted floor mats; dual auxiliary visors; power rear windows (Crew Cab), full overhead console with storage.

LARIAT 4WD (in addition to or instead of LARIAT 4WD equipment): Part-time 4-wheel drive, manual locking hub control and manual shift; front leaf springs; 38 gal. capacity fuel tank.

Base Prices

CODE	DESCRIPTION	INVOICE	MSRP
F20	XL 2WD Regular Cab	17080	19370
F21	XL 4WD Regular Cab	19634	22375
X20	XL 2WD SuperCab SWB	18572	21125
X20-8	XL 2WD SuperCab LWB	18742	21325
X21	XL 4WD SuperCab SWB	21207	24225
X21-8	XL 4WD SuperCab LWB	21377	24425
W20	XL 2WD Crew Cab SWB	20038	22850
W20-8	XL 2WD Crew Cab LWB	20208	23050
W21	XL 4WD Crew Cab SWB	22673	25950
W21-8	XL 4WD Crew Cab LWB	22843	26150
F20	XLT 2WD Regular Cab	18172	20655
F21	XLT 4WD Regular Cab	20888	23850
X20	XLT 2WD SuperCab SWB	19744	22505
X20-8	XLT 2WD SuperCab LWB	19914	22705
X21	XLT 4WD SuperCab SWB	22379	25605
X21-8	XLT 4WD SuperCab LWB	22549	25805
W20	XLT 2WD Crew Cab SWB	21211	24230
W20-8	XLT 2WD Crew Cab LWB	21381	24430
W21	XLT 4WD Crew Cab SWB	24016	27530
W21-8	XLT 4WD Crew Cab LWB	XXXXX	XXXXX
F20	Lariat 2WD Regular Cab	19447	22155
F21	Lariat 4WD Regular Cab	22082	25255
X20	Lariat 2WD SuperCab SWB	20938	23910
X20-8	Lariat 2WD SuperCab LWB	21108	24110
X21	Lariat 4WD SuperCab SWB	23573	27010
X21-8	Lariat 4WD SuperCab LWB	23743	27210
W20	Lariat 2WD Crew Cab SWB	22405	25635
W20-8	Lariat 2WD Crew Cab LWB	22575	25835
W21	Lariat 4WD Crew Cab SWB	25040	28735
W21-8	Lariat 4WD Crew Cab LWB	25210	28935
Destination Charge:		640	640

Accessories

CODE	DESCRIPTION	INVOICE	MSRP
166	Carpet Delete (XLT/Lariat) *Replaces carpet with black floor mat.*	(43)	(50)

CODE	DESCRIPTION	INVOICE	MSRP
17F	XL Decor Group (XL 2WD)	117	135
	Includes locking tailgate, chrome front bumper with lower valance, aero-composite halogen headlamps, and steel wheels with full wheel covers.		
17F	XL Decor Group (XL 4WD)	150	175
	Includes locking tailgate, chrome front bumper with lower valance, front tow hooks, aero-composite halogen headlamps, and steel wheels with full wheel covers.		
18L	Cab Steps (Crew Cab)	272	320
18L	Cab Steps (SuperCab)	314	370
2	Cloth Luxury Captain's Chairs (XLT)	NC	NC
	Includes floor console.		
213	4WD Electric Shift-On-The-Fly (4WD)	128	150
4	Leather Luxury Captain's Chairs (Lariat Crew Cab)	621	730
	Includes floor console.		
4	Leather Luxury Captain's Chairs (Lariat Reg Cab/Lariat SuperCab)	310	365
	Includes floor console.		
41H	Engine Block Heater	30	35
	Recommended when min. temp. is -10 degrees F or below. NOT AVAILABLE with 60X.		
422	California Emissions	144	170
	Required on units for California registration.		
428	High Altitude Principal Use	NC	NC
433	Sliding Rear Window	107	125
446	Transmission: 6-Speed HD Manual with OD	NC	NC
	Includes transmission power take-off provision. REQUIRES 99F. NOT AVAILABLE with 99S, XC2, XC3, 62R, 90G, 68P.		
44E	Transmission: Electronic 4-Speed Automatic	824	970
	Deletes provisions for a power take-off (PTO). NOT AVAILABLE with XC1, XC3.		
512	Spare Tire and Wheel AS	251	295
	Includes underframe crank carrier and steel spare wheel. REQUIRES T46.		
512	Spare Tire and Wheel AS	251	295
	Includes underframe crank carrier and steel spare wheel. REQUIRES T43.		
512	Spare Tire and Wheel AS	251	295
	Includes underframe crank carrier and steel spare wheel. REQUIRES T35.		
515	Spare Tire and Wheel	251	295
	Includes underframe crank carrier and steel spare wheel. REQUIRES T4B.		
515	Spare Tire and Wheel	251	295
	Includes underframe crank carrier and steel spare wheel. REQUIRES T3R.		
515	Spare Tire and Wheel	310	365
	Includes underframe crank carrier and steel spare wheel. REQUIRES T4R.		
515	Spare Tire and Wheel	251	295
	Includes underframe crank carrier and steel spare wheel. REQUIRES T3N.		
529	Leather-Wrapped Steering Wheel (Lariat)	51	60
	Color-keyed.		
52N	Convenience Group	328	385
	Includes speed control and tilt steering wheel.		

CODE	DESCRIPTION	INVOICE	MSRP
531	Trailer Towing Package with Gas Engine *Includes 7-wire harness, trailer brake wiring kit and trailer tow guide. NOT AVAILABLE with XC1, 532, XC2, XC3, 86M.*	162	190
532	Camper Package with Gas Engine (2WD) *Includes slide-in camper certification, front stabilizer bar, rear stabilizer bar, and auxiliary rear springs. NOT AVAILABLE with XC1, 674, XC2, XC3.*	250	295
532	Camper Package with Gas Engine (4WD) *Includes slide-in camper certification, front stabilizer bar, rear stabilizer bar, and auxiliary rear springs. NOT AVAILABLE with XC1, 674, XC2, XC3.*	293	345
53T	Front Tow Hooks (2WD XL/2WD XLT)	34	40
54Q	Power Mirrors (XLT) *NOT AVAILABLE with 54U or 54Y.*	85	100
54U	Manual Trailer Tow Mirrors (XL/XLT) *NOT AVAILABLE with 54Q, 54Y.*	47	55
54Y	Power Trailer Tow Mirrors (XLT/Lariat) *NOT AVAILABLE with 54U or 54Q.*	132	155
552	Passenger Side Air Bag (XL/XLT) *Includes deactivation switch.*	255	300
55R	Off-Road Package (4WD) *Includes off-road 4x4 decal, fuel tank and transfer case skid plates.*	107	125
572	Air Conditioning	684	805
589	Radio: AM/FM Stereo with Cassette and Clock (XL) *Includes 4 speakers. NOT AVAILABLE with 58Y, 58K.*	115	135
58K	Radio: AM/FM Stereo with CD and Cassette (XL) *Includes premium sound with amplifier, 4 speakers, and clock. NOT AVAILABLE with 58Y, 589.*	277	325
58K	Radio: AM/FM Stereo with CD and Cassette (XLT/Lariat) *Includes premium sound with amplifier, 4 speakers, and clock.*	162	190
58Y	Radio Credit Option (XL) *Deletes radio, speakers, antenna, and clock. NOT AVAILABLE with 589, 58K.*	(153)	(180)
592	Roof Clearance Lights	47	55
600A	Preferred Equipment Package 600A (XL) *Includes vehicle with standard equipment.*	NC	NC
607A	Preferred Equipment Package 607A (XLT Crew Cab) *Includes deluxe aluminum wheels, air conditioning, power convenience group: power door locks, power windows, and convenience group with speed control and tilt steering wheel.*	1819	2140
607A	Preferred Equipment Package 607A (XLT Reg Cab/XLT SuperCab) *Includes deluxe aluminum wheels, air conditioning, Power Convenience Group: power door locks, power windows, and convenience group with speed control and tilt steering wheel.*	1593	1875
608A	Preferred Equipment Package 608A (Lariat Crew Cab) *Includes premium aluminum wheels, air conditioning, remote keyless entry, door courtesy lights, Convenience Group: speed control, tilt steering wheel, and leather-wrapped steering wheel.*	2389	2810

CODE	DESCRIPTION	INVOICE	MSRP
608A	Preferred Equipment Package 608A (Lariat Reg Cab/Lariat SuperCab) .... *Includes premium aluminum wheels, air conditioning, remote keyless entry, door courtesy lights, Convenience Group: speed control, tilt steering wheel, and leather-wrapped steering wheel.*	2078	2445
60X	Cold Weather Package Delete .... *Deletes 41H engine block heater and exhaust back pressure valve (faster cab heating). REQUIRES (99F) Engine. NOT AVAILABLE with (99S) engine, (41H) engine block heater.*	(128)	(150)
62R	Transmission Power Take-Off Provision .... *REQUIRES (99S or 99F) and 44E. NOT AVAILABLE with 446.*	213	250
632	HD Battery 78AH .... *NOT AVAILABLE with (99F) engine.*	47	55
64F	Wheels: Deluxe Aluminum (XL) .... *Includes four forged aluminum wheels. REQUIRES (17F) XL Decor Group.*	272	320
64F	Wheels: Deluxe Aluminum (XL) .... *Includes four forged aluminum wheels.*	323	380
674	Heavy Service Suspension Package .... *NOTE: Recommended only on vehicles which will permanently utilize aftermarket equipment such as heavy-duty winches, brush guards or other apparatus which loads the front axle to the specified gross axle weight rating (GAWR). Includes heavy service front springs and auxiliary rear springs. NOT AVAILABLE with (532) camper package with gas engine, or (86M) snow plow package with gas.*	149	175
67B	4-Wheel ABS Brakes	425	500
68P	Decor Group Plus (2WD) .... *Includes XL Decor Group: chrome front bumper with lower valance, front tow hooks, aero-composite halogen headlamps, deluxe aluminum wheels, HD knitted vinyl full bench seat. NOT AVAILABLE with (99F) engine, (446) transmission.*	506	595
68P	Decor Group Plus (XL) .... *Includes XL Decor Group: chrome front bumper with lower valance, front tow hooks, aero-composite halogen headlamps, deluxe aluminum wheels, HD knitted vinyl full bench seat. NOT AVAILABLE with (99F) engine, (446) transmission.*	472	555
768	Chrome Rear Step Bumper (XLT/Lariat) .... *Includes step pad and integral license plate bracket.*	128	150
769	Argent Rear Step Bumper (XL) .... *Includes step pad and integral license plate bracket.*	85	100
86M	Snow Plow Package with Gas (4WD) .... *Maximum 100 lbs. of permanently-attached hardware. Maximum 680 lbs. of removable plow blade and hardware (maximum plow system weight is the sum of these.) The plow and hardware weight limits shown are based upon a vehicle with maximum buildable option content. NOT AVAILABLE with XC1, 674, XC2, XC3.*	251	295
86R	Trailer Hitch Receiver (Class IV) .... *REQUIRES (532) Camper Package with Gas Engine.*	128	150
87B	Rear Fold Down Bench Seat (XL SuperCab)	352	415
903	Power Convenience Group (XLT Crew Cab) .... *Includes power door locks and power windows.*	536	630
903	Power Convenience Group (XLT Reg Cab/XLT SuperCab) .... *Includes power door locks and power windows.*	310	365

CODE	DESCRIPTION	INVOICE	MSRP
90G	Convenience Group (XL Reg Cab) *Includes air conditioning, convenience group with speed control and tilt steering wheel, AM/FM stereo with cassette and clock. NOT AVAILABLE with (99F) engine, (446) transmission.*	1127	1325
90P	6-Way Power Driver's Seat (XLT/Lariat) *REQUIRES (948) remote keyless entry.*	247	290
924	Privacy Glass (XLT/Lariat) *REQUIRES 433.*	85	100
942	Daytime Running Lights	38	45
948	Remote Keyless Entry (XLT) *Includes two step unlock system and door courtesy lights.*	144	170
954	Lower Accent Two-Tone Paint (XLT/Lariat)	192	225
96P	Full Function Auxiliary Idle Control (XL/XLT) *Includes remote capability and an enhanced power take-off interface. APC Module functions: battery charge protection, high idle control, LCD RPM/Voltage readout. Kit includes: auxiliary idle control module, mounting bracket/hardware, wiring harness and instruction booklet. Stationary use only. Kit shipped in box to vehicle operations for "in cab" shipment. REQUIRES (99F and 44E) or (99F and 446). NOT AVAILABLE with 99S.*	178	210
99F	Engine: 7.3L DI Turbo Diesel V8 *Includes dual 78 AH batteries and engine block heater. NOT AVAILABLE with XC2, XC3, 90G, 68P.*	3910	4600
99S	Engine: 6.8L EFI V10 *NOT AVAILABLE with 446, XC1, XC2, 532, 60X, 86M, 428.*	425	500
C	HD Cloth Full Bench Seat (XL Reg Cab) *NOT AVAILABLE with (K) HD knitted vinyl full bench seat.*	136	160
C	HD Cloth Full Bench Seat (XL SuperCab) *NOT AVAILABLE with (K) HD knitted vinyl full bench seat.*	221	260
K	HD Knitted Vinyl Full Bench Seat (XL) *NOT AVAILABLE with (C) HD cloth full bench seat.*	85	100
T3N	Tires: LT235/85R16E AT BSW (4)	93	110
T3R	Tires: LT235/85R16E AT OWL (4)	187	220
T43	Tires: LT265/75R16E AS BSW (4)	144	170
T46	Tires: LT265/75R16E AS OWL (4)	238	280
T4B	Tires: LT265/75R16E AT BSW (4)	238	280
T4R	Tires: LT265/75R16E AT OWL (4)	332	390
X31	3.73 Axle Ratio *NOT AVAILABLE with (XC2) limited slip rear axle.*	NC	NC
X32	4.10 Axle Ratio *NOT AVAILABLE with 99S, 99F, 446, XC1, XC2, XC3, 532, 422, 86M.*	43	50
XC1	Limited Slip Rear Axle with 3.73 *REQUIRES 99F. NOT AVAILABLE with 99S, 44E, 532, 86M.*	243	285
XC2	Limited Slip Rear Axle with 4.10 *NOT AVAILABLE with 99S, 99F, 446, X31, 532, 422, 86M.*	263	310
XC2	Limited Slip Rear Axle with 4.10 *NOT AVAILABLE with 99S, 99F, 446, 44E, X31, XC3, 532, 422, 86M.*	NC	NC

CODE	DESCRIPTION	INVOICE	MSRP
XC3	Limited Slip Rear Axle with 4.30 *REQUIRES 99S. NOT AVAILABLE with 99F, 446, 44E, XC2, 532, 86M.*	285	335

1999 F-350 SUPER DUTY PICKUP

Safety Data

Side Airbag: *Not Available*
4-Wheel ABS: *Std. (DRW); Opt. (SRW)*
Driver Crash Test Grade: *Not Available*
Side Impact Crash Test Front: *Not Available*
Crash Offset: *Not Available*
Integrated Child Seat(s): *Not Available*
Traction Control: *Not Available*
Passenger Crash Test Grade: *Not Available*
Side Impact Crash Test Rear: *Not Available*

Standard Equipment

XL 2WD REGULAR CAB SRW: 5.4L V8 SOHC SMPI 16-valve engine; 5-speed overdrive manual transmission; 72-amp battery with run down protection; 95-amp alternator; rear wheel drive, 3.73 axle ratio; stainless steel exhaust; firm ride suspension, front independent suspension, front coil springs, HD front shocks, rear suspension with rear leaf springs, HD rear shocks; power re-circulating ball steering; 4 wheel disc brakes with rear wheel anti-lock braking system; 38 gal capacity fuel tank; trailer harness; regular pick-up box; front argent bumper; monotone paint; sealed beam halogen headlamps; additional exterior lights include center high mounted stop light, pickup cargo box light; driver and passenger manual black folding outside mirrors; front and rear 16" x 7" silver styled steel wheels with hub wheel covers; LT265/75SR16 BSW AS front and rear tires; AM/FM stereo, clock, seek-scan, 2 speakers and fixed antenna; 2 power accessory outlets; analog instrumentation display includes tachometer, oil pressure gauge, water temp gauge, volt gauge, trip odometer; warning indicators include oil pressure, water temp warning, battery, key in ignition, low fuel, door ajar; driver side airbag; tinted windows; fixed interval front windshield wipers; seating capacity of 3, bench front seat with fixed headrests, driver's seat includes 2-way direction control, passenger's seat includes 2-way direction control; front height adjustable seatbelts; vinyl seats, full cloth headliner, full vinyl floor covering, cabback insulator; interior lights include dome light; day-night rearview mirror; glove box, front cupholder, instrument panel bin, dashboard storage; black grille, black side window moldings, black front windshield molding, black rear window molding, black door handles.

XLT 2WD REGULAR CAB SRW: (in addition to or instead of XL 2WD REGULAR CAB SRW equipment): Front chrome bumper with black rub strip; black bodyside molding with chrome bodyside insert; aero-composite headlamps; additional exterior lights include underhood light; stereo with cassette, 4 speakers; dual airbags; 40-20-40 split-bench front seat with center storage armrest, driver's seat includes 4-way direction control lumbar support, passenger's seat includes 4-way direction control; cloth seats, vinyl door trim insert, carpet floor covering; passenger side vanity mirror; driver and passenger door bins; cargo concealed storage; and chrome grille.

LARIAT 2WD REGULAR CAB SRW (in addition to or instead XLT 2WD REGULAR CAB SRW equipment): Running boards; rear tow hooks; retained accessory power; compass, trip computer; passenger side cancellable airbag; power front windows with driver 1-touch down; carpeted floor mats; leather-wrapped steering wheel; dual auxiliary visors; full overhead console with storage.

DRW (in addition to or instead of 2WD SRW equipment): 4-speed electronic automatic transmission; 4 wheel anti-lock braking system; additional exterior lights include cab clearance lights; front and rear 6" width steel wheels.

CODE	DESCRIPTION	INVOICE	MSRP

CREW CAB (in addition to or instead of 2WD REGULAR CAB equipment): 6.8L V10 engine; 5-speed manual transmission; manual rear windows; power rear windows (Lariat), seating capacity of 6, full folding rear bench seat.

4WD (in addition to or instead of 2WD equipment): 5.4L V8 engine (Regular Cab/SuperCab); 4-speed electronic automatic transmission; part-time 4 wheel drive, manual locking hub control and manual shift; front non-independent suspension with anti-roll bar, front leaf springs; rear tow hooks.

Base Prices

CODE	DESCRIPTION	INVOICE	MSRP
F30	XL 2WD Super Duty Regular Cab SWB SRW	17526	19895
F30	XLT 2WD Super Duty Regular Cab SWB SRW	19005	21635
F30	Lariat 2WD Super Duty Regular Cab SWB SRW	20199	23040
F31	XL 4WD Super Duty Regular Cab SWB SRW	20161	22995
F31	XLT 4WD Super Duty Regular Cab SWB SRW	21640	24735
F31	Lariat 4WD Super Duty Regular Cab SWB SRW	22834	26140
X30	XL 2WD Super Duty SuperCab SWB SRW	19307	21990
X30	XLT 2WD Super Duty SuperCab SWB SRW	20782	23725
X30	Lariat 2WD Super Duty SuperCab SWB SRW	21980	25135
X30-8	XL 2WD Super Duty SuperCab LWB SRW	19477	22190
X30-8	XLT 2WD Super Duty SuperCab LWB SRW	20952	23925
X30-8	Lariat 2WD Super Duty SuperCab LWB SRW	22150	25335
X31	XL 4WD Super Duty SuperCab SWB SRW	21942	25090
X31	XLT 4WD Super Duty SuperCab SWB SRW	23417	26825
X31	Lariat 4WD Super Duty SuperCab SWB SRW	24615	28235
X31-8	XL 4WD Super Duty SuperCab LWB SRW	22112	25290
X31-8	XLT 4WD Super Duty SuperCab LWB SRW	23587	27025
X31-8	Lariat 4WD Super Duty SuperCab LWB SRW	24785	28435
W30	XL 2WD Super Duty Crew Cab SWB SRW	20658	23580
W30	XLT 2WD Super Duty Crew Cab SWB SRW	22132	25315
W30	Lariat 2WD Super Duty Crew Cab SWB SRW	23332	26725
W30-8	XL 2WD Super Duty Crew Cab LWB SRW	20828	23780
W30-8	XLT 2WD Super Duty Crew Cab LWB SRW	22302	25515
W30-8	Lariat 2WD Super Duty Crew Cab LWB SRW	23502	26925
W31	XL 4WD Super Duty Crew Cab SWB SRW	23293	26680
W31	XLT 4WD Super Duty Crew Cab SWB SRW	24564	28175
W31	Lariat 4WD Super Duty Crew Cab SWB SRW	25758	29580
W31-8	XL 4WD Super Duty Crew Cab LWB SRW	23463	26880
W31-8	XLT 4WD Super Duty Crew Cab LWB SRW	24734	28375
W31-8	Lariat 4WD Super Duty Crew Cab LWB SRW	25928	29780
F32	XL 2WD Super Duty Regular Cab SWB DRW	18346	20860
F32	XLT 2WD Super Duty Regular Cab SWB DRW	19821	22595
F32	Lariat 2WD Super Duty Regular Cab SWB DRW	21019	24005
F33	XL 4WD Super Duty Regular Cab SWB DRW	21074	24070
F33	XLT 4WD Super Duty Regular Cab SWB DRW	22549	25805

CODE	DESCRIPTION	INVOICE	MSRP
F33	Lariat 4WD Super Duty Regular Cab LWB DRW	23747	27215
X32	XLT 2WD Super Duty SuperCab LWB DRW	21768	24885
X32	XL 2WD Super Duty SuperCab LWB DRW	20293	23150
X32	Lariat 2WD Super Duty SuperCab LWB DRW	22966	26295
X33	XL 4WD Super Duty SuperCab SWB DRW	23021	26360
X33	XLT 4WD Super Duty SuperCab SWB DRW	24496	28095
X33	Lariat 4WD Super Duty SuperCab SWB DRW	25694	29505
W32	XL 2WD Super Duty Crew Cab SWB DRW	21691	24795
W32	XLT 2WD Super Duty Crew Cab SWB DRW	23170	26535
W32	Lariat 2WD Super Duty Crew Cab SWB DRW	24364	27940
W32-8	XL 2WD Super Duty Crew Cab LWB DRW	21861	24995
W32-8	XLT 2WD Super Duty Crew Cab LWB DRW	23340	26735
W32-8	Lariat 2WD Super Duty Crew Cab LWB DRW	24534	28140
W33	XL 4WD Super Duty Crew Cab SWB DRW	24419	28005
W33	XLT 4WD Super Duty Crew Cab SWB DRW	25690	29500
W33	Lariat 4WD Super Duty Crew Cab SWB DRW	26884	30905
W33-8	XL 4WD Super Duty Crew Cab LWB DRW	24589	28205
W33-8	XLT 4WD Super Duty Crew Cab LWB DRW	25860	29700
W33-8	Lariat 4WD Super Duty Crew Cab LWB DRW	27054	31105
Destination Charge:		640	640

Accessories

CODE	DESCRIPTION	INVOICE	MSRP
166	Carpet Delete (XLT/Lariat) *Replaces carpet with black floormat.*	(43)	(50)
17F	XL Decor Group (XL 2WD DRW) *Includes locking tailgate, chrome front bumper with lower valance, front tow hooks, steel wheels with full wheel covers.*	100	115
17F	XL Decor Group (XL 2WD SRW) *Includes locking tailgate, chrome front bumper with lower valance, front tow hooks, steel wheels with full wheel covers.*	150	175
17F	XL Decor Group (XL 4WD DRW) *Includes locking tailgate and chrome front bumper with lower valance.*	68	75
17F	XL Decor Group (XL 4WD SRW) *Includes locking tailgate, chrome front bumper with lower valance, front tow hooks, steel wheels with full wheel covers.*	117	135
18L	Cab Steps (XL Regular) *Integrated, molded black.*	272	320
18L	Cab Steps (XL SuperCab/XL Crew Cab) *Integrated, molded black.*	314	370
2	Cloth Luxury Captain's Chairs (XLT) *Includes floor console.*	NC	NC
213	4x4 Electric Shift-On-The-Fly (4WD) *Auto-manual locking hubs.*	128	150

CODE	DESCRIPTION	INVOICE	MSRP
4	Leather Luxury Captain's Chairs (Lariat) *Includes floor console.*	NC	NC
4	Leather Luxury Captain's Chairs (Lariat) *Includes floor console.*	NC	NC
41H	Engine Block Heater	30	35
422	California Emissions *Required on all units for California, Massachusetts or New York registration.*	144	170
428	High Altitude Principal Use	NC	NC
433	Sliding Rear Window	107	125
446	Transmission: 6-Speed HD Manual with OD *NOT AVAILABLE with 99S, XD2, XD3, 532, 531.*	NC	NC
44E	Transmission: Electronic 4-Speed Automatic	846	995
512	Spare Tire and Wheel AS (DRW) *Includes underframe crank carrier and spare wheel. REQUIRES T31.*	213	250
512	Spare Tire and Wheel AS (DRW) *Includes underframe crank carrier and spare wheel. REQUIRES T36.*	251	295
512	Spare Tire and Wheel AS (SRW) *Includes underframe crank carrier and spare wheel. REQUIRES T46.*	289	340
512	Spare Tire and Wheel AS (SRW) *Includes underframe crank carrier and spare wheel. REQUIRES T43.*	263	310
512	Spare Tire and Wheel AS *Includes underframe crank carrier and spare wheel. REQUIRES 620A or 627A. NOT AVAILABLE with T36, 515, T3N, T3R.*	229	270
515	Spare Tire and Wheel AT (DRW) *Includes underframe crank carrier and spare wheel. REQUIRES T3N.*	251	295
515	Spare Tire and Wheel AT (DRW) *Includes underframe crank carrier and spare wheel. REQUIRES T3R.*	272	320
515	Spare Tire and Wheel AT (SRW) *Includes underframe crank carrier and spare wheel. REQUIRES T4B.*	289	340
515	Spare Tire and Wheel AT (SRW) *Includes underframe crank carrier and spare wheel. REQUIRES T4R.*	310	365
52N	Convenience Group (XL) *Includes speed control, tilt steering wheel.*	328	385
531	Trailer Towing Group With Gas Engine (SRW) *Includes 7-wire harness, trailer brake wiring kit and trailer tow guide. NOT AVAILABLE with (532) Camper Package with Gas Engine, (446) transmission, (99S) engine.*	162	190
531	Trailer Towing Group with Gas Engine (DRW) *Includes 7-wire harness, trailer brake wiring kit and trailer tow guide. NOT AVAILABLE with (532) Camper Package with Gas Engine, (446) transmission, (99S) engine.*	182	215
532	Camper Package with Gas Engine *Slide-in camper certification. Includes auxiliary rear springs, rear stabilizer bar. NOT AVAILABLE with 674, 531, M67, 446, 99S, 86M, M86.*	293	345
53T	Front Tow Hooks (2WD)	34	40

CODE	DESCRIPTION	INVOICE	MSRP
54Q	Power Mirrors (XLT) *NOT AVAILABLE with (54U) manual trailer tow mirrors, (54Y) power trailer tow mirrors.*	85	100
54U	Manual Trailer Tow Mirrors *NOT AVAILABLE with (54Y) power trailer tow mirrors.*	47	55
54Y	Power Trailer Tow Mirrors (XLT/Lariat) *NOT AVAILABLE with (54U) manual trailer tow mirrors.*	47	55
552	Passenger's Side Airbag *Includes deactivation switch.*	255	300
55R	Off-Road Package (4WD) *Includes transfer case skid plate, fuel tank skid plate and off-road 4x4 decal.*	107	125
572	Air Conditioning	684	805
589	Radio: AM/FM Stereo with Cassette and Clock (XL) *Includes 4 speakers. NOT AVAILABLE with (58Y) radio, (58K) radio.*	115	135
58K	Radio: AM/FM Stereo with CD and Cassette (XL) *Includes premium sound with amplifier, 4 speakers and clock. NOT AVAILABLE with (589) radio, (58Y) radio.*	277	325
58K	Radio: AM/FM Stereo with CD and Cassette (XLT/Lariat) *Includes premium sound with amplifier, 4 speakers and clock.*	162	190
58Y	Radio Credit Option (XL) *Deletes radio and clock. NOT AVAILABLE with (589) radio, (58K) radio.*	(153)	(180)
592	Roof Clearance Lights (SRW)	47	55
60X	Cold Weather Package Delete *REQUIRES (99F) engine.*	(128)	(150)
610A	Preferred Equipment Package 610A (XL) *Includes engine: 5.4L EFI V-8, 5-speed manual with OD, payload package #1, 3.73 axle ratio, tires: LT265/75R16E AS BSW, steel wheels with black center ornament, HD vinyl full bench seat, black vinyl floor covering, ETR AM/FM stereo with clock radio. REQUIRES (44E) transmission or (446) transmission.*	NC	NC
617A	Preferred Equipment Package 617A (XLT Crew Cab) *Includes engine: 5.4L EFI V8, 5-speed manual with OD, 3.73 axle ratio, payload package #1, tires: LT265/75R16E AS BSW, forged deluxe aluminum wheels, cloth 40/20/40 split bench seat, air conditioning, Power Convenience Group: power door locks, power windows, accessory delay, Convenience Group: speed control, tilt steering wheel, ETR AM/FM stereo with cassette, clock radio. REQUIRES (44E) transmission or (446) transmission.*	1819	2140
617A	Preferred Equipment Package 617A (XLT Reg Cab/XLT SuperCab) *Includes engine: 5.4L EFI V8, 5-speed manual with OD, 3.73 axle ratio, payload package #1, tires: LT265/75R16E AS BSW, forged deluxe aluminum wheels, cloth 40/20/40 split bench seat, air conditioning, Power Convenience Group: power door locks, power windows, accessory delay, Convenience Group: speed control, tilt steering wheel, ETR AM/FM stereo with cassette, clock radio. REQUIRES (44E) transmission or (446) transmission.*	1593	1875
618A	Preferred Equipment Package 618A (Lariat Crew Cab) *Includes engine: 5.4L EFI V8, 5-speed manual with OD, 3.73 axle ratio, payload package #1, tires: LT265/75R16E AS BSW, forged deluxe aluminum wheels, cloth 40/20/40 split bench seat, air conditioning, Power Convenience Group: power door*	2078	2445

CODE	DESCRIPTION	INVOICE	MSRP
	locks, power windows, accessory delay, Convenience Group: speed control, tilt steering wheel, leather-wrapped steering wheel, front tow hooks. REQUIRES (44E) transmission or (446) transmission.		
618A	**Preferred Equipment Package 618A (Lariat Reg Cab/Lariat SuperCab)** *Includes engine: 5.4L EFI V8, 5-speed manual with OD, 3.73 axle ratio, payload package #1, tires: LT265/75R16E AS BSW, forged deluxe aluminum wheels, cloth 40/20/40 split bench seat, air conditioning, Power Convenience Group: power door locks, power windows, accessory delay, Convenience Group: speed control, tilt steering wheel, leather-wrapped steering wheel, front tow hooks. REQUIRES (44E) transmission or (446) transmission.*	2389	2810
620A	**Preferred Equipment Package 620A (XL)** *Includes engine: 5.4L EFI V8, 5-speed manual with OD, payload package #1, 3.73 axle ratio, tires: LT265/75R16E AS BSW, steel wheels with black center ornament, HD vinyl full bench seat, black vinyl floor covering, ETR AM/FM stereo with clock radio. REQUIRES (44E) transmission or (446) transmission.*	NC	NC
627A	**Preferred Equipment Package 627A (XLT Crew Cab)** *Includes engine: 5.4L EFI V8, 5-speed manual with OD, 3.73 axle ratio, payload package #1, tires: LT265/75R16E AS BSW, forged deluxe aluminum wheels, cloth 40/20/40 split bench seat, air conditioning, Power Convenience Group: power door locks, power windows, accessory delay, Convenience Group: speed control, tilt steering wheel, ETR AM/FM stereo with cassette, clock radio. REQUIRES (44E) transmission or (446) transmission.*	2041	2400
627A	**Preferred Equipment Package 627A (XLT Reg Cab/XLT SuperCab)** *Includes engine: 5.4L EFI V8, 5-speed manual with OD, 3.73 axle ratio, payload package #1, tires: LT265/75R16E AS BSW, forged deluxe aluminum wheels, cloth 40/20/40 split bench seat, air conditioning, Power Convenience Group: power door locks, power windows, accessory delay, Convenience Group: speed control, tilt steering wheel, ETR AM/FM stereo with cassette, clock radio. REQUIRES (44E) transmission or (446) transmission.*	1815	2135
628A	**Preferred Equipment Package 628A (Lariat Reg Cab/Lariat SuperCab)** *Includes engine: 5.4L EFI V8, 5-speed manual with OD, 3.73 axle ratio, payload package #1, tires: LT265/75R16E AS BSW, forged deluxe aluminum wheels, cloth 40/20/40 split bench seat, air conditioning, Power Convenience Group: power door locks, power windows, accessory delay, Convenience Group: speed control, tilt steering wheel, leather-wrapped steering wheel, front tow hooks. REQUIRES (44E) transmission or (446) transmission.*	2257	2655
628A	**Preferred Equipment Package 630A (Lariat Crew Cab)** *Includes engine: 5.4L EFI V8, 5-speed manual with OD, 3.73 axle ratio, payload package #1, tires: LT265/75R16E AS BSW, forged deluxe aluminum wheels, cloth 40/20/40 split bench seat, air conditioning, Power Convenience Group: power door locks, power windows, accessory delay, Convenience Group: speed control, tilt steering wheel, leather-wrapped steering wheel, front tow hooks. REQUIRES (44E) transmission or (446) transmission.*	2568	3020
62R	**Transmission Power Take-Off Provision** *REQUIRES (44E) transmission and (99S) engine or (99F) engine.*	213	250
632	**HD Battery 78AH**	47	55
649	**Wheels: Polished Aluminum (DRW)**	493	580

CODE	DESCRIPTION	INVOICE	MSRP
64F	Wheels: Forged Deluxe Aluminum (4) (SRW XL) *REQUIRES (17F) XL Decor Group.*	272	320
64F	Wheels: Forged Deluxe Aluminum (4) (SRW XL)	323	380
674	Heavy Service Suspension Package (DRW) *Recommended only on vehicles that will permanently utilize aftermarket equipment such as heavy-duty winches, brush guards or other apparatus which loads the front axle to the specified gross axle weight rating (GAWR). Includes front stabilizer bar, auxiliary rear springs. NOT AVAILABLE with (532) Camper Package with Gas Engine, (86M) Snow Plow Package with gas.*	170	200
674	Heavy Service Suspension Package (SRW) *Recommended only on vehicles which will permanently utilize aftermarket equipment such as heavy-duty winches, brush guards or other apparatus which loads the front axle to the specified gross axle weight rating (GAWR). Includes auxiliary rear springs, front stabilizer bar. NOT AVAILABLE with 532, M53, N53, 86M, M86.*	149	175
67B	4-Wheel ABS Brakes (Models under 10,000 GVWR) *NOTE: ABS is standard on vehicles with GVWR over 10,000.*	425	500
768	Chrome Rear Step Bumper (XLT/Lariat) *Includes step pad and integral license plate bracket.*	128	150
769	Argent Rear Step Bumper (XL) *Includes step pad and integral license plate bracket.*	85	100
86M	Snow Plow Package with Gas (4WD) *NOT AVAILABLE with 674, 532, M99, M53, M67.*	251	295
86R	Trailer Hitch Receiver (Class IV) *REQUIRES (531) Trailer Towing Group with Gas Engine or (532) Camper Package with Gas Engine.*	128	150
87B	Rear Fold Down Bench Seat (XL SuperCab)	352	415
90G	Convenience Group *NOT AVAILABLE with (99F) engine.*	1127	1325
90P	6-Way Power Driver's Seat (XLT/Lariat) *REQUIRES (948) remote keyless entry.*	247	290
924	Privacy Glass (XLT/Lariat) *REQUIRES (433) sliding rear window.*	85	100
948	Remote Keyless Entry (XLT) *Includes two step unlock system, door courtesy lights.*	144	170
954	Lower Accent Two-Tone Paint (XLT/Lariat)	192	225
96P	Full Function Auxiliary Idle Control (XL/XLT) *APC module function includes battery charge protection, high idle control and LCD RPM/voltage readout. Kit includes auxiliary idle control module, mounting bracket/hardware, wiring harness and instruction booklet. Also includes remote capability and an enhanced power take-off interface. Stationary use only and kit is shipped in box to vehicle operations for "in cab" shipment. REQUIRES (99F, 44E and 62R) or (99F and 446) or 62R. NOT AVAILABLE with 532, 531, 86M.*	178	210
99F	Engine: 7.3L DI Turbo Diesel V8 (Crew Cab) *Includes HD battery 78AH, engine block heater. REQUIRES (446) transmission or (44E) transmission.*	3910	4600

CODE	DESCRIPTION	INVOICE	MSRP
99F	Engine: 7.3L DI Turbo Diesel V8 (Reg Cab/SuperCab) *Includes HD battery 78AH. REQUIRES 446 or 44E. NOT AVAILABLE with XD2, XD3, 17D, 90G.*	3910	4600
99S	Engine: 6.8L EFI V10 (Reg Cab/SuperCab) *NOT AVAILABLE with XD2, 446, 532, 531, XF2.*	425	500
C	HD Cloth Full Bench Seat (Reg Cab/SuperCab) *NOT AVAILABLE with (K) HD knitted vinyl full bench seat.*	136	160
C	HD Cloth Full Bench Seat (SuperCab/Crew Cab) *NOT AVAILABLE with (K) HD knitted vinyl full bench seat.*	221	260
K	HD Knitted Cinyl Full Bench Seat (Reg Cab/SuperCab) *NOT AVAILABLE with 87B.*	85	100
K	HD Knitted Vinyl Full Bench Seat (SuperCab/Crew Cab) *REQUIRES 87B on SuperCab.*	128	150
M53	Camper Package with Trailer Tow Package Credit *REQUIRES 532 and 531. NOT AVAILABLE with 674, M67, 86M, M86.*	(119)	(140)
M67	Heavy Service Suspension with Trailer Tow Package Credit *REQUIRES 674 and 531. NOT AVAILABLE with N53, M53, 532, 86M, M86.*	(22)	(25)
M86	Snow Plow Pkg with Trailer Tow Package Credit *REQUIRES 86M and 531. NOT AVAILABLE with M53, M67, 532, 674.*	(97)	(115)
M99	Camper Or Trailer Tow Package Credit with 99F *REQUIRES (99F) engine. NOT AVAILABLE with (86M) Snow Plow Package with Gas.*	(97)	(115)
N53	Camper Package Credit *REQUIRES (532) Camper Package with Gas Engine. NOT AVAILABLE with (M67) heavy service suspension with trailer tow package credit, (674) Heavy Service Suspension Package.*	(43)	(50)
T35	Tires: LT235/85R16E AS BSW (6) (DRW)	93	110
T36	Tires: LT235/85R16E AS OWL (6) (DRW)	221	260
T36	Tires: LT235/85R16E AS OWL (6) (DRW)	128	150
T3N	Tires: LT235/85R16E AT BSW (6) (DRW)	132	155
T3N	Tires: LT235/85R16E AT BSW (6) (DRW)	225	265
T3R	Tires: LT235/85R16E AT OWL (6) (DRW)	352	415
T3R	Tires: LT235/85R16E AT OWL (6) (DRW)	259	305
T46	Tires: LT265/75R16E AS OWL (4) (SRW)	93	110
T4B	Tires: LT265/75R16E AT BSW (4) (SRW)	93	110
T4R	Tires: LT265/75R16E AT OWL (4) (SRW)	187	220
XD1	Limited Slip Rear Axle with 3.73 (SRW)	243	285
XD2	Limited Slip Rear Axle with 4.10 (SRW) *NOT AVAILABLE with 99S, 99F, 446, XD1, XD3.*	243	285
XD3	Limited Slip Rear Axle with 4.30 (SRW) *REQUIRES 99S. NOT AVAILABLE with 99F, XD1, XD2, 446.*	285	335
XF2	Limited Slip Rear Axle with 4.10 (DRW) *NOT AVAILABLE with (99S) engine, (XF3) limited slip rear axle.*	221	260
XF3	Limited Slip Rear Axle with 4.30 (DRW) *NOT AVAILABLE with (99S) engine, (XF3) limited slip rear axle.*	221	260

1999 RANGER

1999 Ford Ranger

What's New?

The Ranger is "Built Ford Tough" according to its ads and we tend to agree. This year's changes include standard 15-inch silver styled wheels, a class III frame-mounted hitch receiver for V6 applications, and a spare tire access lock. All models get dual front cup holders and Dark Graphite has been added to the interior colors option list while Willow Green and Denim Blue have been removed as interior choices. Too bad for you folks who liked the splashy "Splash" model, it has been discontinued. Finally, a 3.0-liter V6 flexible fuel engine is available that is designed specifically for ethanol/gasoline fuel blends.

Review

Whether it's image or utility that attracts you to a compact truck, Ford stands ready to seduce you into its strong-selling Ranger. Trim levels range from the practical XL through the well-trimmed XLT which now has a color-keyed grille, bumpers, wheel lip moldings, and door handles.

With the optional 4.0-liter V6 engine, in particular, acceleration is impressively brisk, whether from a standstill or when merging and passing. Automatic-transmission upshifts are crisp and barely noticed, with just a slight jolt under hard throttle, and downshifts deliver only slightly more harshness. Dash-mounted four-wheel-drive, if installed, is a snap to use.

Well-controlled overall, with good steering feedback, Rangers handle easily, corner capably, maneuver neatly, and stay reasonably stable on curves. Occupants aren't likely to complain about the ride, either, though it can grow bouncy around town. Gas mileage isn't the greatest with the big engine and automatic, as expected.

Ranger sports a worldwide industry first for safety protection. An optional passenger side airbag is available, and it can be disabled with the flick of a switch in the event that a child safety seat is installed in the truck. The Ranger is also the only small truck to be available with a five-speed automatic transmission (not including Ranger's twin, the Mazda B4000). Ford claims that the five-speed automatic allows better acceleration, trailering, and hill climbing by their capable Ranger.

Ford lost its deathgrip on the small truck segment when Dodge introduced the outstanding Dakota in 1997. In a retaliatory effort, Ford gave the 1998 Ranger an unneeded facelift that we think renders the truck less attractive than before. With that facelift came an increase in wheelbase, a larger base engine, a new front suspension, rack-and-pinion steering and a four-door model. Also new for 1998 was the introduction of an electric model. Marketed primarily to fleets, the electric Ranger boasts a top speed of 75 mph and a 700-lb. payload.

Ford has had the best-selling small trucks in the country for years. We think it's because Rangers are all truck, with few pretensions toward any other identity yet capable of being loaded with gadgets like a luxury auto. Fun to drive, sharp looking, and well built, they deliver a solid compact-pickup experience. Even though we're not crazy about the front styling, we're certain that they will continue to be a big hit.

Safety Data

Side Airbag: *Not Available*
4-Wheel ABS: *Standard (XLT 4WD); Optional (All Others)*
Driver Crash Test Grade: *Good*
Side Impact Crash Test Front: *Excellent*
Crash Offset: *Acceptable*
Integrated Child Seat(s): *Not Available*
Traction Control: *Not Available*
Passenger Crash Test Grade: *Good*
Side Impact Crash Test Rear: *Not Available*

Standard Equipment

XL 2WD REGULAR CAB (5M): 2.5L I4 SOHC SMPI 8-valve engine; 5-speed overdrive manual transmission; 540-amp battery with run down protection; 95-amp alternator; rear wheel drive, 3.45 axle ratio; partial stainless steel exhaust; front independent suspension with anti-roll bar, front coil springs, rigid rear axle suspension with rear leaf springs; power rack-and-pinion steering; front disc/ rear drum brakes with rear wheel antilock braking system; 16.5 gal (19.5 gal LB) capacity fuel tank; front and rear mud flaps; front and rear black bumpers with rear step; monotone paint; aero-composite halogen headlamps; additional exterior lights include center high mounted stop light; driver's and passenger's manual black folding outside mirrors; front and rear 14" x 5.5" silver styled steel wheels; P205/75SR14 BSW AS front and rear tires; underbody mounted full-size conventional steel spare wheel; AM/FM stereo with clock, seek-scan, 2 speakers, and fixed antenna; 2 power accessory outlets; instrumentation display includes oil pressure gauge, water temp gauge, volt gauge, trip odometer; warning indicators include battery, lights on, key in ignition, door ajar; driver's side airbag, passenger's side cancelable airbag; tinted windows; variable intermittent front windshield wipers; seating capacity of 3, 60-40 split-bench front seat with fixed headrests, driver's seat includes 2-way direction control, passenger's seat includes 2-way direction control; front height adjustable seatbelts; vinyl seats, full cloth headliner, full vinyl floor covering; interior lights include dome light, illuminated entry; day-night rearview mirror; partial floor console, glove box, front cupholder; black grille, black side window moldings, black front windshield molding, black rear window molding and black door handles.

XL 2WD SUPERCAB (5M) (in addition to or instead of XL 2WD REGULAR CAB (5M) equipment): 3.73 axle ratio; tinted windows, fixed rear windows; seating capacity of 5, center armrest with storage; 50-50 folding rear jump facing side seat and cloth seats.

XL 4WD REGULAR CAB (5M) (in addition to or instead of XL 2WD REGULAR CAB (5M) equipment): 3.0L V6 OHV SMPI 12-valve engine; part-time 4 wheel drive, auto locking hub control and electronic shift, 3.73 axle ratio; front independent suspension with anti-roll bar, front torsion springs, front torsion bar, HD front shocks, rigid rear axle suspension with anti-roll bar, rear leaf springs, HD rear shocks; rear tow hooks; black fender flares; front and rear 15" x 6" silver styled steel wheels; instrumentation display includes tachometer and ignition disable.

XL 4WD SUPERCAB (5M) (in addition to or instead of XL 4WD REGULAR CAB (5M) equipment): Tinted windows, fixed rear windows; seating capacity of 5, center armrest with storage, driver's seat includes 4-way direction control, passenger's seat includes 4-way direction control; 50-50 folding rear jump facing side seat and cloth seats.

CODE	DESCRIPTION	INVOICE	MSRP

XLT 2WD REGULAR CAB (5M) (in addition to or instead of XL 2WD REGULAR CAB (5M) equipment): Trailer harness; front and rear chrome bumpers with rear step; additional exterior lights include pickup cargo box light; front and rear 15" x 6" silver styled steel wheels; air conditioning; AM/FM stereo with clock, seek-scan, cassette, 4 speakers, and fixed antenna; center armrest with storage, driver's seat includes 4-way direction control, passenger's seat includes 4-way direction control; cloth seats, cloth door trim insert; interior lights include front reading lights, illuminated entry; passenger side vanity mirror; driver's and passenger's door bins; cargo concealed storage and chrome grille.

XLT 2WD SUPERCAB (5M) (in addition to or instead of XLT 2WD REGULAR CAB (5M) equipment): 3.73 axle ratio; tinted windows, vented rear windows; seating capacity of 5; 50-50 folding rear jump facing side seat and cargo net.

XLT 4WD REGULAR CAB (5M) (in addition to or instead of XLT 2WD REGULAR CAB (5M) equipment): 3.0L V6 OHV SMPI 12-valve engine; part-time 4 wheel drive, auto locking hub control and electronic shift, 3.73 axle ratio; front independent suspension with anti-roll bar, front torsion springs, HD front shocks, rigid rear axle suspension with anti-roll bar, rear leaf springs, HD rear shocks; front disc/rear drum brakes with 4 wheel antilock braking system; 16.5 gal capacity fuel tank; front and rear chrome bumpers with rear tow hooks; black fender flares; monotone paint with bodyside accent stripe; front and rear 15" x 7" silver alloy wheels; instrumentation display includes tachometer and ignition.

XLT 4WD SUPERCAB (5M) (in addition to or instead of XLT 4WD REGULAR CAB (5M) equipment): Tinted windows, vented rear windows; seating capacity of 5; 50-50 folding rear jump facing side seat and cargo net.

Base Prices

CODE	DESCRIPTION	INVOICE	MSRP
R10	XL 2WD Regular Cab SB (5M)	11198	11785
R10-7	XL 2WD Regular Cab LB (5M)	11630	12255
R11	XL 4WD Regular Cab SB (5M)	14767	15665
R11-7	XL 4WD Regular Cab LB (5M)	15199	16135
R14	XL 2WD SuperCab SB (5M)	13767	15240
R15	XL 4WD SuperCab SB (5M)	15557	17275
R10	XLT 2WD Regular Cab SB (5M)	12553	13860
R10-7	XLT 2WD Regular Cab LB (5M)	13036	14410
R11	XLT 4WD Regular Cab SB (5M)	15909	17675
R11-7	XLT 4WD Regular Cab LB (5M)	16416	18250
R14	XLT 2WD SuperCab SB (5M)	14400	15960
R15	XLT 4WD SuperCab SB (5M)	17405	19375
Destination Charge:		510	510

Accessories

CODE	DESCRIPTION	INVOICE	MSRP
—	Bonus Discount (2WD) *NOT AVAILABLE with 99V or 99X.*	(425)	(500)
173	Flareside Box (All Except LB) *NOT AVAILABLE with T7S (4WD) or T81 (2WD).*	387	455
202	Optional Payload Package #2 (Regular Cab 2WD SB) *Maximum payload 1660 lbs with GVWR 4740 lbs.*	64	75
205	Optional Payload Package #2 (Regular Cab 2WD LB) *Maximum payload 1660 lbs with GVWR 4780 lbs.*	64	75

CODE	DESCRIPTION	INVOICE	MSRP
20B	Optional Payload Package #2 (SuperCab 2WD) *Maximum payload 1660 lbs with GVWR 4740 lbs.*	64	75
20G	Optional Payload Package #2 (Regular Cab 4WD LB) *Maximum payload 1500 lbs with GVWR 5020 lbs.*	64	75
20T	Optional Payload Package #2 (SuperCab 4WD) *Maximum payload 1500 lbs with GVWR 5120 lbs.*	64	75
20W	Optional Payload Package #2 (Regular Cab 4WD SB) *Maximum payload 1500 lbs with GVWR 4980 lbs.*	64	75
433	Sliding Rear Window (XL SuperCab)	107	125
44D	Transmission: 5-Speed Automatic with Overdrive (XLT) *REQUIRES 99X.*	961	1130
44T	Transmission: 4-Speed Automatic with Overdrive *REQUIRES 99V or 99C.*	931	1095
47F	Power Equipment Group (XLT) *Includes power mirrors, power door locks, power windows with driver's one-touch down and remote keyless entry with panic alarm.*	455	535
47P	Convenience Group (XLT) *Includes leather-wrapped tilt steering wheel and speed control.*	336	395
53L	Frame Mounted Trailer Hitch (Class III) (XLT) *REQUIRES 99V or 99X.*	182	215
572	Air Conditioning (XL)	684	805
589	Radio: AM/FM Stereo with Cassette and Clock (XL) *Includes 4 speakers. NOT AVAILABLE with 58Z.*	119	140
58K	Radio: AM/FM Stereo Dual Media (XLT) *Includes CD and cassette player with 80-watt amplifier and clock. NOT AVAILABLE with 58Z.*	196	230
58Z	Radio: AM/FM Stereo with Clock and CD (XLT) *Includes 4 speakers. NOT AVAILABLE with 58K.*	81	95
58Z	Radio: AM/FM Stereo with Clock and CD (XL) *Includes 4 speakers. NOT AVAILABLE with 589.*	200	235
63B	4-Door SuperCab (XLT SuperCab) *REQUIRES 99V or 99X.*	561	660
646	Wheels: 15" Full Face Chrome (XLT 2WD) *REQUIRES T7K.*	170	200
67B	4-Wheel Antilock Brakes (All Except XLT 4WD)	255	300
861A	Preferred Equipment Package 861A (XL) *Includes vehicle with standard equipment.*	NC	NC
864A	Preferred Equipment Package 864A (XLT)	695	805
	Manufacturer Discount	(695)	(805)
	Net Price *Includes vehicle with standard equipment.*	NC	NC
87D	Rear Jump Seat Delete (XLT SuperCab) *REQUIRES 63B.*	(123)	(145)
91R	Off-Road Package (XLT 4WD) *Includes styled manual mirrors, bulge body shocks, P245/75R16 OWL AT tires, 16" 5-spoke cast aluminum wheels, fog lamps, 4x4 off road decal, 4.10 axle ratio, and skid plates.*	336	395

CODE	DESCRIPTION	INVOICE	MSRP
95P	XLT Sport Appearance Group (XLT 4WD) *Includes styled manual mirrors, P245/75R16 OWL AT tires, 16" 5-spoke cast aluminum wheels, color keyed front and rear bumpers, color-keyed grille, color-keyed door handles, fog lamps and sport decal. NOT AVAILABLE with 91R or 173.*	370	435
95P	XLT Sport Appearance Group (XLT 2WD) *Includes styled manual mirrors, P225/70R15 OWL AS tires, 15" deep dish cast aluminum wheels, tachometer, color-keyed front and rear bumpers, color-keyed grille, color-keyed door handles, fog lamps and sport decal. NOT AVAILABLE with 99C.*	421	495
95S	XL Sport Appearance Package (XL 2WD) *Includes 15" styled steel silver wheels, P225/70R15 AS OWL tires, spare tire lock, sport decal, color keyed front and rear bumpers and color-keyed grille.*	421	495
95S	XL Sport Appearance Package (XL 4WD) *Includes platinum wheel-lip moldings, 15" deep dish cast aluminum wheels, P235/75R15 AT OWL tires, spare tire lock, sport decal, color keyed front and rear bumpers and color-keyed grille. NOT AVAILABLE with 173.*	506	595
99C	Engine: 2.5L EFI I4 (2WD)	NC	NC
99V	Engine: 3.0L FFV V6 (All Except 4WD) *Flexible fuel capable and securilock. REQUIRES IAE.*	442	520
99X	Engine: 4.0L EFI V6 (XLT 4WD) *Includes 3.73 axle ratio.*	574	675
99X	Engine: 4.0L EFI V6 (XLT 2WD)	1016	1195
E	60/40 Split Cloth Bench Seat (XL)	247	290
G	Cloth Sport Bucket Seats (XLT) *Includes driver's side manual lumbar and floor console.*	306	360
IAE	Bonus Discount (2WD) *REQUIRES 99V.*	(442)	(520)
T7K	Tires: P225/70R15 AS OWL (XLT 2WD) *Includes P205 temporary spare tire.*	107	125
T7S	Tires: P265/75R15SL AT OWL (XLT 4WD) *Includes P235 temporary spare. REQUIRES 99X.*	93	110
X87	4.10 Axle Ratio (XL) *REQUIRES 44T and 95S. NOT AVAILABLE with XF6.*	NC	NC
XAB	Limited Slip Differential with 4.10 *NOT AVAILABLE with 99C.*	229	270
XF6	Limited Slip Differential with 3.73 *REQUIRES 99U and (44M or 44T).*	229	270
XR5	Limited Slip Differential with 3.55 (XLT) *REQUIRES 99X and (44D or 44M).*	229	270

1999 WINDSTAR

1999 Ford Windstar

What's New?

Ford continues to battle it out with GM and Chrysler in the hotly contested minivan segment. This year the Windstar has been totally redesigned in yet another attempt to dethrone the hot pentastar prospects. The biggest news for '99, in addition to the completely new exterior and interior styling, is a left-hand sliding door. The second and third row seats are now on rollers for easier adjustment/interchangeability and the instrument panel has been redesigned for improved ergonomics. There's also a more powerful and cleaner-burning 3.8-liter V6 plus upgraded suspension, transmission, brakes and air conditioning components. Hot new options include side airbags and a trick reverse sensing system to keep you from banging into those short gas station poles.

Review

This is the Windstar's first major redesign since it was introduced in 1995. It now boasts a bevy of high-tech features like key fob operated, dual-power sliding doors, head and chest side airbags, and a sonar-based reverse sensing system.

Safety has also been addressed in the new Windstar with government crash ratings of five stars in frontal and side impacts. The optional side airbags mean you can carry your family in style, comfort, and confidence.

The 3.8-liter V6 offers a robust 200 horsepower while still meeting the current low-emission vehicle (LEV) and Ultra Low Emission Vehicle (ULEV) standards, meaning it produces 65 percent less hydrocarbon emissions than required for the average vehicle in its class.

An innovative seating design allows the second-row bench seat to be positioned on either the right or left side of the vehicle, meaning the aisle to the third row seat can be set-up based on owner preference. And speaking of preference, the Personal Audio System means that front seat passengers can listen to one type of media (radio, cassette, CD) while rear-seat passengers listen to a totally separate system, complete with volume control, through headphones.

With a list of standard equipment that includes an anti-theft system, power windows, a 26-gallon fuel tank and antilock brakes, the Windstar enters 1999 ready to challenge all comers for minivan supremacy. It should prove an interesting battle.

Safety Data

Side Airbag: *Optional*
4-Wheel ABS: *Standard*
Driver Crash Test Grade: *Excellent*
Side Impact Crash Test Front: *Excellent*
Crash Offset: *Good*
Integrated Child Seat(s): *Not Available*
Traction Control: *N/A (Base); Opt. (LX/SE/SEL)*
Passenger Crash Test Grade: *Excellent*
Side Impact Crash Test Rear: *Excellent*

Standard Equipment

BASE (4A): 3.0L V6 OHV SMPI 12-valve engine; 4-speed electronic overdrive automatic transmission with lock-up; 58-amp battery with run down protection; 130-amp alternator; front wheel drive, 3.98 axle ratio; power rack-and-pinion steering; front disc/rear drum brakes with 4 wheel antilock braking system; 26 gal capacity fuel tank; stainless steel exhaust; front independent strut suspension with anti-roll bar, front strut springs, rear non-independent suspension with rear coil springs; front and rear argent bumpers with rear step; black bodyside molding and rocker panel extensions; monotone paint; aero-composite halogen headlamps; additional exterior lights include center high mounted stop light; driver's and passenger's manual black outside mirrors; front and rear 15" x 6" steel wheels; P215/70SR15 BSW AS front and rear tires; underbody mounted compact steel spare wheel; air filter; AM/FM stereo with clock, seek-scan, 4 speakers, and window grid antenna; child safety rear door locks; 3 power accessory outlets; instrumentation display includes tachometer, water temp gauge, trip odometer; warning indicators include oil pressure, battery, low oil level, lights on, key in ignition, low fuel, low washer fluid, door ajar; dual airbags; ignition disable; tinted windows, fixed rear windows, manual 1/4 vent windows; variable intermittent front windshield wipers, fixed interval rear wiper; seating capacity of 7, front bucket seats with fixed headrests, driver's and passenger's armrests, driver's seat includes 4-way direction control, passenger's seat includes 4-way direction control; removable full folding 2nd row bench seat with adjustable rear headrest; 3rd row removable full folding bench seat with adjustable 3rd row headrest; cloth seats, vinyl door trim insert, full cloth headliner, full carpet floor covering, deluxe sound insulation; carpeted cargo floor; interior lights include dome light with fade; vanity mirrors; day-night rearview mirror; locking glove box, instrument panel bin, driver's and passenger's door bins, vinyl trunk lid; vinyl cargo floor, cargo light; body-colored grille, black side window moldings, black front windshield molding, black rear window molding, black door handles and cargo concealed storage.

LX (4A) (in addition to or instead of BASE (4A) equipment): 3.8L V6 OHV SMPI 12-valve engine; front and rear colored bumpers with rear step; colored bodyside molding and rocker panel extensions; black driver's power remote outside mirror; air conditioning, AM/FM stereo with clock, seek-scan, cassette, 4 speakers, and window grid antenna; cruise control with steering wheel controls; retained accessory power; power front windows; power 1/4 vent windows; rear window defroster; cloth door trim insert; interior lights include rear reading lights; steering wheel with tilt adjustment; locking glove box with light, front and rear cupholders; 2 seat back storage pockets, cargo net and cargo light.

SE (4A) (in addition to or instead of LX (4A) equipment): Manual sliding left-side passenger door, 72-amp battery with run down protection; 3.56 axle ratio; roof rack; front and rear body-colored bumpers with chrome bumper insert; body-colored bodyside molding with chrome bodyside insert; additional exterior lights include cornering lights, underhood light; driver's and passenger's power remote black heated outside mirrors; rear air conditioning with separate controls; power door locks, remote keyless entry; ignition disable, panic alarm; deep tinted windows, power front windows with driver 1-touch down; front bucket seats with adjustable headrests, driver's seat includes 4-way power seat with 8-way direction control and power lumbar support; removeable full folding 2nd row bucket seat with reclining adjustable rear headrest; carpeted floor mats; interior lights include front and rear reading lights, 2 door curb lights, illuminated entry; leather-wrapped steering wheel with tilt adjustment; dual illuminated vanity mirrors, driver side auxiliary visor; full overhead console with storage; front underseat tray; chrome grille and body-colored door handles.

SEL (4A) (in addition to or instead of SE (4A) equipment): Dual power sliding passenger doors, 78-amp battery with run down protection; body-colored bodyside cladding; monotone paint with bodyside accent stripe; aero-composite halogen fully automatic headlamps; additional exterior lights include front fog/driving lights; front and rear 16" x 6" silver alloy wheels; premium AM/FM stereo with clock, seek-scan, cassette, single CD, 4 speakers, and window grid antenna, rear stereo controls; garage door opener; instrumentation display includes compass, exterior temp; passenger's seat includes 4-way power seat with 8-way direction control and power lumbar support; removeable 50-50 folding 2nd row bucket seat with reclining adjustable rear headrest; leather seats, leatherette door trim insert and auto-dimming day-night rearview mirror.

Base Prices

Code	Description	Invoice	MSRP
A51	Base (4A)	18738	20220
A51	LX (4A)	21361	23660
A52	SE (4A)	24736	27495
A53	SEL (4A)	27305	30415
Destination Charge:		580	580

Accessories

Code	Description	Invoice	MSRP
152	Electronics Group (SE)	455	535
	Includes message center, programmable transmitter and autolamp.		
167	Front and Rear Floor Mats (Base/LX)	77	90
184	LH Manual Sliding Door (4 Door) (LX)	298	350
	Includes tires: P215/70R15 BSW.		
184	LH Manual Sliding Door (4 Door) (Base)	425	500
	Includes tires: P215/70R15 BSW. REQUIRES 86A.		
18D	RH/LH Power Sliding Door (SE)	680	800
	Not authorized for delivery or heavy-duty commercial use. NOT AVAILABLE with 18E.		
18E	RH Power Door/LH Manual Door (SE)	383	450
	Not authorized for delivery or heavy-duty commercial use. NOT AVAILABLE with 18D.		
18E	RH Power Door/LH Manual Door (LX)	680	800
	Not authorized for delivery or heavy-duty commercial use. REQUIRES 41N, 948 and 86C.		
2	Leather Seat Trim (SE)	735	865
21L	Quad Buckets (Base/LX)	910	1070
	Includes power driver's seat, high back front and low back second row. REQUIRES 994 and 86C.		
21L	Quad Buckets (SE/SEL)	910	1070
	Manufacturer Discount	(910)	(1070)
	Net Price	NC	NC
	Includes power driver's seat, low back front and low back second row. REQUIRES 86C or 184 or 18E.		
21P	High Back Buckets with Power Driver's Seat (LX)	277	325
	REQUIRES 86C, 184 or 18E.		

CODE	DESCRIPTION	INVOICE	MSRP
21Q	Quad Buckets (LX)	633	745
	Includes 1st row high back buckets, 2nd row low back buckets and 3rd row bench.		
414	Floor Console (All Except Base)	132	155
41N	Full Overhead Console (LX)	43	50
	Includes conversation mirror, dome lamp, provision for power sliding door switch, coin holder, sunglasses holder, garage door opener holder and provision for rear audio controls for personal audio system and reading lamp. REQUIRES 184 or 18E.		
43B	Reverse Sensing System (All Except Base)	208	245
	REQUIRES 184 or 18E.		
51A	Tire: Full Size Spare (SE/SEL)	93	110
52N	Convenience Group (Base)	319	375
	Includes speed control and tilt steering wheel.		
539	Trailer Towing Package (Class II) (All Except Base)	370	435
	Includes HD halfshafts and a high speed ambient temperature package including HD battery, full size spare tire, auxiliary transmission oil cooler and trailer tow electronic package class I.		
54H	Heated Mirrors (LX)	43	50
	REQUIRES 184.		
589	Radio: AM/FM Stereo with Cassette (Base)	144	170
58K	Personal Audio System (LX/SE)	255	300
	Includes premium AM/FM stereo with cassette, in-dash single CD (dual media), 4 speakers and rear seat audio controls.		
60S	Family Security Package (SEL)	234	275
	Includes P225/60R16 BSW tires, remote keyless entry, heated mirrors and perimeter anti-theft system.		
60S	Family Security Package (LX)	498	585
	Includes P215/70R15 BSW tires, traction control, perimeter anti-theft and heated mirrors.		
60S	Family Security Package (SE)	370	435
	Includes remote keyless entry, heated mirrors, traction control and perimeter anti-theft system.		
615	Roof Rack (LX)	149	175
647	Wheels: 16" 5-Spoke Aluminum (SE)	144	170
	Includes tires: P225/60R16 BSW.		
64F	Wheels: 15" Aluminum (LX)	352	415
	REQUIRES 18E.		
65T	Trailer Tow Electronic Package Class I	30	35
	Includes module, wiring and jumper for trailering light hook up. Required for all class I towing applications.		
67E	Enhanced Seating Group (Base)	348	410
	Includes reclining rear seat backs, adjustable rear seat tracks, rear bench seat rollers, 2nd row seat mounted cupholders and map pocket.		
86A	Family Value Group (Base)	914	1075
	Includes manual air conditioning, power convenience group: power windows, power mirrors and electric rear window defroster.		

CODE	DESCRIPTION	INVOICE	MSRP
86C	Comfort Group (LX)	862	1015
	Includes rear window defrost, climate control system, privacy glass, roof rack, mini overhead console and provision for rear radio controls. REQUIRES 184.		
86C	Comfort Group (LX)	820	965
	Includes rear window defrost, climate control system, privacy glass, roof rack, mini overhead console and provision for rear radio radio controls.		
91P	CD Changer Prep (All Except Base)	34	40
	REQUIRES 414.		
924	Privacy Glass (LX)	352	415
	REQUIRES 86A.		
948	Remote Keyless Entry (Base/LX)	149	175
994	Engine: 3.8L SPI V6 (Base)	583	685
	REQUIRES 86A.		
994	Engine: 3.8L SPI V6 (LX)	583	685
	Manufacturer Discount	(583)	(685)
	Net Price	NC	NC
A3D	Side Air Bags	332	390
	REQUIRES 86A on Base.		

1999 ENVOY

1999 GMC Envoy

What's New?

After its debut as General Motors' high-end compact SUV last year, the GMC Envoy gets equipment upgrades for '99. A new mini-module for the driver's airbag allows for steering-wheel radio controls, and the turn-signal stalk now incorporates a flash-to-pass headlamp feature. Heated, eight-way power front seating is improved, thanks to available two-position memory for the driver and power recliners. A liftgate ajar telltale resides in the instrument cluster, and the outside rearview mirrors have been redesigned, featuring electrochromic dimming and power folding capability. GM's advanced AutoTrac active transfer case is now standard, while a new, shift lever-mounted button selects a Tow/Haul mode to optimize transmission shift points. There are three new metallic exterior paint colors: Topaz gold, Meadow green and Indigo blue.

Review

GMC has been positioning itself as the premium truck division for three years running, so it should be no surprise that last year GMC dolled-up a four-door, four-wheel drive Jimmy and packed it full of fancy touches, calling it the Envoy. This year, GMC's upscale compact sport-utility vehicle adds minor feature enhancements to its already staggering list of standard equipment.

Motivated by the same 190-horse Vortec 4.3-liter V6 and four-speed automatic transmission that's found in the Jimmy, the Envoy disguises its rugged underpinnings with full-wrap body cladding, molded wheel flares and a monochrome paint scheme. Envoy also has a unique body-colored front bumper/fascia with upper and lower grilles, chrome accents, round fog lamps and integrated tow hooks. Out back there's a step bumper with integrated trailer hitch, as well as a rear spoiler whose rearward edge incorporates a neon Center High Mounted Stop Lamp (CHMSL), although rear-end styling is hardly distinctive enough to tell it apart from any other GM compact sport-utility.

Envoy features High-Intensity Discharge (HID) headlamps. These lamps emit a true-white light that is brighter, lasts longer and uses less electricity than halogen bulbs. They offer more than two-and-a-half times the light emitted by halogen bulbs and provide a longer, wider beam. Other standard equipment on the Envoy includes Next Generation driver and passenger airbags, the PassLock theft deterrent system, keyless remote entry, electronic climate control, retained accessory power, self-dimming outside heated mirrors and tinted glass behind the B-pillars. There's even a built-in air compressor as part of the standard Premium Luxury Ride suspension package that includes an automatic load-leveling system.

Inside you'll find a variety of luxury touches, including Zebrano wood trim and heated Nuance leather power seating with the "Envoy" badge stitched into the headrests. Designers sought a cockpit theme by putting the gauges on a semicircular cluster and angling the instrument panel 15 degrees toward the driver. The center console can hold a cell phone, while the overhead unit includes a three-button HomeLink transmitter. The standard sound system is none other than GM's Premium Bose unit, with CD player and high-tech Bose Nd speakers for deep bass tones.

For '99, Envoy's four-wheel drive system now employs GM's new AutoTrac two-speed active transfer case, which allows for automatic shifting from all-wheel drive to four-wheel drive when road conditions warrant. (It also allows the Envoy to be towed behind, say, a motor home, without having to disconnect the propshaft.) Plus, there's a new Tow/Haul button on the transmission shift lever that adjusts the shift points in the electronically controlled automatic when the vehicle is heavily loaded or towing a trailer.

GMC packs tons of standard equipment on this sport-ute (among the rare options are a power sunroof and GM's dealer-installed OnStar mobile communications system) and wraps it with a cleanly upscale look. Priced competitively in this segment, the Envoy is one to look at if you are thinking along the lines of a Ford Explorer Limited, or perhaps the Infiniti QX4.

Safety Data

Side Airbag: *Not Available*
4-Wheel ABS: *Standard*
Driver Crash Test Grade: *Average*
Side Impact Crash Test Front: *Excellent*
Crash Offset: *Poor*
Integrated Child Seat(s): *Not Available*
Traction Control: *Not Available*
Passenger Crash Test Grade: *Good*
Side Impact Crash Test Rear: *Excellent*

Standard Equipment

ENVOY (4A): 4.3L V6 OHV SMPI 12-valve engine; 4-speed electronic overdrive automatic transmission with lock-up; 690-amp battery with run down protection; engine block heater, engine oil cooler; 100-amp alternator; transmission oil cooler; part-time 4 wheel drive, auto locking hub control with electronic shift, limited slip differential, 3.73 axle ratio; stainless steel exhaust; comfort ride suspension with auto-leveling, front independent suspension with anti-roll bar, front torsion springs, front torsion bar, premium front shocks, rigid rear axle suspension with anti-roll bar, rear leaf springs, premium rear shocks; power re-circulating ball steering; 4 wheel disc brakes with 4 wheel antilock braking system; 18 gal. capacity fuel tank; front license plate bracket, rear wing spoiler; tailgate rear cargo door; HD trailering, trailer harness, trailer hitch; roof rack; front and rear body-colored bumpers with chrome bumper insert, rear tow hooks, rear step; chrome bodyside insert, body-colored bodyside cladding; monotone paint; aero-composite halogen fully automatic headlamps with daytime running lights; additional exterior lights include front fog/driving lights, center high mounted stop light, underhood light; driver's and passenger's power remote body-colored heated electric folding outside mirrors; front and rear 15" x 7" silver alloy wheels; P235/70SR15 BSW AS front and rear tires; underbody mounted full-size temporary steel spare wheel; air conditioning with climate control, rear heat ducts; premium AM/FM stereo with clock, seek-scan, cassette, 6 premium speakers, premium amplifier, automatic equalizer, theft deterrent, and fixed antenna rear controls; cruise control; power door locks, remote keyless entry, child safety rear door locks, power remote hatch/trunk release, keyfob rear window remote release; cell phone pre-wiring, 4 power accessory outlets, retained accessory power, garage door opener; instrumentation display includes tachometer, oil pressure gauge, water temp gauge, volt gauge, compass, exterior temp, trip computer, trip odometer; warning indicators include battery, lights on, key in ignition, trunk ajar; dual airbags; ignition disable, panic alarm, security system; deep tinted windows, power front windows with driver's 1-touch down, power rear windows, fixed 1/4 vent windows; variable intermittent front windshield wipers, flip-up rear window, fixed interval rear wiper, rear window defroster; seating capacity of 5, heated front bucket seats with adjustable tilt headrests, center armrest with storage, driver's seat includes 4-way power seat with 8-way direction control and power lumbar support,

CODE	DESCRIPTION	INVOICE	MSRP

passenger's seat includes 4-way power seat with 8-way direction control and power lumbar support; 60-40 folding rear bench seat with adjustable rear headrest; leather seats, leather door trim insert, full cloth headliner, full carpet floor covering with carpeted floor mats, wood trim; memory on driver's seat with 2 memory setting(s); interior lights include dome light, front and rear reading lights, illuminated entry; leather-wrapped steering wheel with tilt adjustment; dual illuminated vanity mirrors, dual auxiliary visors; auto-dimming day-night rearview mirror; full floor console, full overhead console with storage, glove box with light, front and rear cupholders, instrument panel bin, 1 seat back storage pocket, driver's and passenger's door bins, rear door bins; carpeted cargo floor, carpeted trunk lid, cargo cover, cargo net, cargo tie downs, cargo light; body-colored grille, black side window moldings, black front windshield molding, black rear window molding and body-colored door handles.

Base Prices

CODE	DESCRIPTION	INVOICE	MSRP
TT10506	Envoy (4A)	30408	33600
Destination Charge:		525	525

Accessories

CODE	DESCRIPTION	INVOICE	MSRP
1SG	Marketing Option Package 1SG *Includes vehicle with standard equipment.*	NC	NC
AG0	2-Position Memory Driver Seat	74	85
AH8	8-Way Power Passenger Seat	219	250
CF5	Power Sliding Sunroof with Express Open *Includes wind deflector.*	645	750
G80	Locking Rear Differential	236	270
GT4	3.73 Axle Ratio *REQUIRES G80.*	NC	NC
NG1	Northeast Emissions *Includes Connecticut, District of Columbia, Delaware, Massachusetts, Maryland, New Hampshire, New Jersey, New York, Pennsylvania, Rhode Island and Virginia. Automatically added to vehicles shipped to and/or sold to retailers in the applicable states. NOT AVAILABLE with YF5.*	146	170
YF5	California Emissions *Automatically added to vehicles shipped to and/or sold to retailers in California. NOT AVAILABLE with NG1.*	146	170

1999 JIMMY

1999 GMC Jimmy

What's New?

There are three new colors and revised outside mirrors, but most changes to the '99 Jimmy are inside. You'll find new power-seating features, redundant radio controls and a mini-module depowered airbag in the steering wheel, as well as a new Bose premium sound system and six-disc CD changer. A vehicle content theft alarm, flash-to-pass headlamp feature, and liftgate ajar warning lamp have also been added. Four-wheel-drive versions get the new AutoTrac active transfer case and four-door models gain a Tow/Haul mode for the transmission. Finally, the optional Z85 Euro-Ride suspension has been retuned.

Review

GMC has the unenviable job of marketing the Jimmy as a luxury SUV, thanks to brand managers who are trying to position GMC products as distinctly upscale from Chevrolet. The problem is the Jimmy is essentially identical to the Chevy Blazer and Oldsmobile Bravada. With few distinguishing characteristics to set it apart from either of its stablemates, Jimmy marketers have their work cut out for them. This leaves only one way to convince buyers that the Jimmy-not the Blazer or Bravada-is the one to buy, and that's slick advertising.

Despite a minor redesign for 1998, four-door styling is on the staid side, but the two-doors carry a fastback profile with a distinctive side-window treatment. A Jimmy is comfortable, easy to handle and fun to drive. Upgraded versions can be luxuriously equipped, but each rugged rendition looks and feels tough. An under-the-floor spare tire on four-door models increases cargo space. Headroom is immense and elbow space excellent. There's room for two in back, maybe three if you enjoy hearing comfort complaints while you drive, but the short seat feels hard and there's no foot room under front seats. Basically, the back seat should be reserved for kiddies.

Though exceptionally sure-footed in a straight line, a Jimmy can feel momentarily top-heavy during a sharp maneuver at speed-but that's because it's easy to forget you're driving a sport-utility. On snow-covered pavement and off road, the four-wheel-drive Jimmy inspires confidence, whether maintaining traction while accelerating, or trying to recapture grip through a turn.

All-wheel drive, formerly an option, is no longer available on the Jimmy, but you won't miss it. The new-for-'99 AutoTrac 4WD push-button electronic two-speed transfer case senses wheel slippage and delivers power to the axle with the most traction automatically. Four-wheel antilock braking helps bring this compact sport-ute to a prompt halt, and all models employ four-wheel discs. Depowered airbags are standard. Acceleration is strong from the standard 4300 Vortec V6, and the smooth, four-speed automatic suffers little lag when downshifting. There's a new Tow/Haul mode button standard on four-door versions that optimizes shift points when your Jimmy is heavily burdened. A five-speed manual transmission is available on two-door models.

Other news this year includes revised power seats, upgraded sound systems, steering wheel radio controls and a vehicle content theft alarm. The headlamp stalk now has a flash-to-pass feature, and a new warning lamp reveals if you haven't properly latched the rear liftgate.

A "Truck Body Computer" controls the PassLock theft deterrent system, automatic headlights, battery rundown protection, retained accessory power, and lockout prevention features. For cold-weather service, buyers of the SLT 4WD can opt for heated front seats, and exterior mirrors can be ordered with a defrost mode, with the electrochromic self-dimming feature now available on the driver's side.

The hardest thing about Jimmy-shopping is deciding what to include. Suspension choices stretch all the way from smooth riding to off-road. Plus there's base (SL) and sport (SLS) two-door, as well as the base (SL), comfort (SLE) and luxury/touring (SLT) four-door trim levels from which to choose. Finally, you've got a huge option list with which to contend. Overdo it, and the price tag can zip skyward in a hurry, though this GMC can offer better value than Oldsmobile's all-wheel-drive Bravada.

Safety Data

Side Airbag: *Not Available*
4-Wheel ABS: *Standard*
Driver Crash Test Grade: *Average*
Side Impact Crash Test Front: *Excellent*
Crash Offset: *Poor*
Integrated Child Seat(s): *Not Available*
Traction Control: *Not Available*
Passenger Crash Test Grade: *Good*
Side Impact Crash Test Rear: *Excellent*

Standard Equipment

SL 2WD 2-DOOR (5M): 4.3L V6 OHV SMPI 12-valve engine; 5-speed overdrive manual transmission; 525-amp battery with run down protection; engine oil cooler; 100-amp alternator; transmission oil cooler; rear wheel drive, 3.42 axle ratio; stainless steel exhaust; comfort ride suspension, front independent suspension with antiroll bar, front coil springs, rigid rear axle suspension with antiroll bar, rear leaf springs; power re-circulating ball steering; 4 wheel disc brakes with 4 wheel antilock braking system; 19 gal. capacity fuel tank; front license plate bracket; tailgate rear cargo door; front and rear body-colored bumpers with rear step; monotone paint; aero-composite halogen fully automatic headlamps with daytime running lights; additional exterior lights include center high mounted stop light, underhood light; driver's and passenger's manual black folding outside mirrors; front and rear 15" x 7" painted steel wheels; P205/75SR15 BSW AS front and rear tires; inside mounted full-size temporary steel spare wheel; air conditioning, rear heat ducts; AM/FM stereo with clock, seek-scan, 4 speakers, and fixed antenna; 1 power accessory outlet, retained accessory power; instrumentation display includes tachometer, oil pressure gauge, water temp gauge, volt gauge, trip odometer; warning indicators include battery, lights on, key in ignition, trunk ajar; dual airbags; ignition disable; deep tinted windows, vented rear windows, fixed 1/4 vent windows; variable intermittent front windshield wipers, flip-up rear window; seating capacity of 5, front bucket seats with adjustable headrests, center armrest with storage, driver's seat includes 4-way direction control with lumbar support, passenger's seat includes 4-way direction control with lumbar support and easy entry; 60-40 folding rear bench seat with adjustable headrests; cloth seats, full cloth headliner, full carpet floor covering with carpeted floor mats; interior lights include dome light, illuminated entry; passenger's side vanity mirror; day-night rearview mirror; full floor console, glove box with light, front and rear cupholders, instrument panel bin, dashboard storage, driver's and passenger's door bins; carpeted cargo floor, carpeted trunk lid, cargo tie downs, cargo light; colored grille, black side window moldings, black front windshield molding, black rear window molding and black door handles.

SL 2WD 4-DOOR (4A) (in addition to or instead of SL 2WD 2-DOOR (5M) equipment): Four-speed electronic overdrive automatic transmission with lock-up; 18 gal. capacity fuel tank; trailer harness; cruise control; child safety rear door locks; manual rear windows; steering wheel with tilt adjustment and 2 seat back storage pockets.

SL 4WD 2-DOOR (5M) (in addition to or instead of SL 2WD 2-DOOR (5M) equipment): Part-time 4 wheel drive, auto locking hub control with electronic shift, 3.42 axle ratio; comfort ride suspension, front independent torsion suspension with antiroll bar, front torsion springs, front torsion bar and rear tow hooks.

SL 4WD 4-DOOR (4A) (in addition to or instead of SL 2WD 4-DOOR (4A) equipment): Part-time 4 wheel drive, auto locking hub control with electronic shift; comfort ride suspension, front independent torsion suspension with antiroll bar, front torsion springs, front torsion bar and rear tow hooks.

SLS - REQUIRES 1SB Package.

SLE - REQUIRES 1SD Package.

SLT - REQUIRES 1SE Package.

Base Prices

Code	Description	Invoice	MSRP
TS10516-R9S	SL 2WD 2-Door (5M)	16773	18534
TT10516-R9S	SL 4WD 2-Door (5M)	19488	21534
TS10506-R9S	SL 2WD 4-Door (4A)	21923	24224
TT10506-R9S	SL 4WD 4-Door (4A)	23733	26224
TS10516-YC3	SLS 2WD 2-Door (4A)	19430	21470
TT10516-YC3	SLS 4WD 2-Door (4A)	22145	24470
TS10506-YC5	SLE 2WD 4-Door (4A)	24589	27170
TT10506-YC5	SLE 4WD 4-Door (4A)	26399	29170
TS10506-YC6	SLT 2WD 4-Door (4A)	26308	29070
TT10506-YC6	SLT 4WD 4-Door (4A)	28118	31070
Destination Charge:		525	525

Accessories

Code	Description	Invoice	MSRP
~~H	**Deluxe Cloth Seat Trim (SLT)** *NOT AVAILABLE with KA1.*	(516)	(600)
1SA	**Marketing Option Package 1SA (SL 2-Door)** *Includes SL Decor package, Euro-ride suspension package: HD springs; P235/70R15 AS BSW SBR tires, ETR AM/FM stereo with seek, scan and cassette and roof mounted black luggage carrier. REQUIRES G80.*	NC	NC
1SB	**Marketing Option Package 1SB (SLS 2-Door)** *Includes SLS Decor package: roof mounted black luggage carrier, body color grille, body side accent stripe, dual illuminated visor vanity mirrors, cloth trim door insert with lower carpet, reading lamp, cargo net, 3 accessory outlets, leather-wrapped steering wheel, rear window convenience package: electric tailgate release, rear window defogger and wiper/washer; custom cloth seat trim, split folding rear seat, transmission: electronic 4-speed automatic with overdrive, Euro ride suspension package: HD springs; ETR AM/FM stereo with seek, scan and CD, overhead console:*	NC	NC

CODE	DESCRIPTION	INVOICE	MSRP
	compass/temperature display; convenience group: tilt steering, speed control; rear window convenience package: electric tailgate release, rear window defogger and wiper/washer and remote keyless entry with vehicle content theft alarm.		
1SC	Marketing Option Package 1SC (SL 4-Door)	NC	NC
	Includes SL Decor package standard equipment.		
1SD	Marketing Option Package 1SD (SLE 4-Door)	(1204)	(1400)
	Includes SLE Decor package: bright grille, dual illuminated visor vanity mirrors, cloth door inserts with lower carpet, front reading lights, cargo cover and net, rear window convenience package: electric tailgate release, rear window defogger and wiper/washer; 3 accessory outlets, leather-wrapped steering wheel, custom cloth seat trim, luxury ride suspension package, P235/70R15 AS BSW SBR tires, power convenience group: power door locks, power windows; heated power exterior mirrors and roof mounted black luggage carrier.		
1SE	Marketing Option Package 1SE (SLT 4-Door)	(1204)	(1400)
	Includes SLT Decor package: luxury ride suspension package, P235/70R15 AS BSW SBR tires, power convenience group: power door locks, power windows; heated power exterior mirrors, roof mounted black luggage carrier, body color moldings, bright grille, dual illuminated visor vanity mirrors, front bucket seats, leather seat trim, leather door trim with lower carpet, front and rear reading lights, dashboard storage delete, cargo cover and net, rear window convenience package: electric tailgate release, rear window defogger and wiper/washer; leather-wrapped steering wheel, 3 accessory outlets, remote keyless entry with vehicle content theft alarm, ETR AM/FM stereo with seek, scan and cassette and overhead console with compass/temperature display.		
AG0	2 Position Memory Driver's Seat (SLT)	73	85
	REQUIRES AH8.		
AG1	6-Way Power Driver's Seat (SLS/SLE)	206	240
AG2	6-Way Power Passenger's Seat (SLS/SLE)	206	240
AH8	8-Way Power Passenger's Seat (SLT)	215	250
ANL	Fog Lamps (SLS 2WD/SLE)	99	115
AU0	Remote Keyless Entry (SLE)	146	170
	Includes 2 transmitters and vehicle content theft alarm.		
CF5	Electric Sliding Glass Sunroof (All Except SL)	645	750
	Includes express open feature and wind deflector. REQUIRES DK8.		
DD0	Power Heated Light Sensitive OSRV Mirror (SLS/SLE)	75	87
	Includes light sensitive rearview mirror.		
DK7	Overhead Console (SLE)	126	147
	Includes compass/temperature display. NOT AVAILABLE with DK8.		
DK8	Deluxe Overhead Console (SLS/SLT)	112	130
	Includes compass/temperature display, trip computer and universal garage door opener.		
DK8	Deluxe Overhead Console (SLE)	238	277
	Includes compass/temperature display, trip computer and universal garage door opener.		
G80	Locking Rear Differential	232	270
	REQUIRES GU6 or GT4. NOT AVAILABLE with GU4.		

CODE	DESCRIPTION	INVOICE	MSRP
GT4	3.73 Axle Ratio (4WD) *NOT AVAILABLE with M50, ZQ1.*	NC	NC
GU4	3.08 Axle Ratio (SL 2WD 2-Door) *NOT AVAILABLE with G80.*	NC	NC
GU6	3.42 Axle Ratio (SLS 2WD 2-Door/2WD 4-Door)	NC	NC
KA1	Driver's/Passenger's Heated Seats (SLT) *NOT AVAILABLE with ~~H.*	215	250
M30	Transmission: Electronic 4-Speed Automatic with Overdrive (SL 2-Door)	860	1000
M50	Transmission: 5-Speed Manual with Overdrive (SLS 2-Door) *REQUIRES GU6 and G80. NOT AVAILABLE with UK3, U1Z, UQ3, UP0, GT4.*	(860)	(1000)
N60	Wheels: 15" x 7" Aluminum (4) (SL 2WD 4-Door)	241	280
N90	Wheels: 15" x 7" Aluminum (4) (SL 4WD 4-Door)	241	280
NP8	Autotrac 2-Speed Active Transfer Case (4WD - SLS/SLE)	194	225
P16	Spare Tire and Wheel Carrier (4WD 2-Door) *Includes gray cover with GMC lettering. Tailgate mounted.*	137	159
PF2	Wheels: 15" x 7" Aluminum (4) (SLT 4WD 4-Door)	NC	NC
QBF	Tires: P235/70R15 AS BSW SBR (SL 4-Door) *Includes front, rear and full size spare. NOT AVAILABLE with QBG, QCA, QEB.*	165	192
QBG	Tires: P235/70R15 AS WOL SBR (SL 4-Door) *Includes front, rear and full size spare. NOT AVAILABLE with QCA, QEB.*	280	325
QBG	Tires: P235/70R15 AS WOL SBR (All Except SL 4-Door) *Includes front, rear and full size spare. NOT AVAILABLE with ZBF, QEB, ZEB, ZM6, QCE, QCA, ZQ1.*	114	133
QCA	Tires: P205/75R15 AS WOL SBR (SL 2WD 4-Door) *Includes front, rear and full size spare. NOT AVAILABLE with QBG.*	104	121
QCA	Tires: P205/75R15 AS WOL SBR (2WD SLE/SLT) *Includes front, rear and full size spare. NOT AVAILABLE with QCE, QBG.*	(61)	(71)
QCE	Tires: P205/75R15 AS BSW SBR (SLS/SLT) *Includes front, rear and full size spare. NOT AVAILABLE with QBG, QCA, QEB.*	(165)	(192)
QEB	Tires: P235/75R15 AT WOL SBR (SL 4WD 4-Door) *NOT AVAILABLE with QBG.*	310	360
QEB	Tires: P235/75R15 AT WOL SBR (All Except SL 4-Door) *REQUIRES P16. NOT AVAILABLE with QBG, ZBF, ZBG, ZAA, QCE, ZQ1.*	144	168
RYJ	Retractable Cargo Cover (SLS 4WD) *REQUIRES P16.*	59	69
U1Z	6 Disc CD Changer (SLS/SLE/SLT) *Located in console under center armrest. REQUIRES UL0. NOT AVAILABLE with UP0, M50.*	340	395
UA1	690-CCA HD Delco Freedom Battery	48	56
UK3	Steering Wheel Radio Controls (SLS/SLE/SLT) *NOT AVAILABLE with M50.*	108	125
UL0	Radio: AM/FM Stereo with Cassette (SLE) *Includes digital clock, theft lock, speed sensitive volume, automatic tone control, auto reverse/music search cassette and enhanced performance 6 speaker system.*	69	80

CODE	DESCRIPTION	INVOICE	MSRP
UL0	Radio: AM/FM Stereo with Cassette (SLS) *Includes digital clock, theft lock, speed sensitive volume, automatic tone control, auto reverse/music search cassette and enhanced performance 6 speaker system. NOT AVAILABLE with UP0.*	(86)	(100)
UL5	Radio Delete (SL 2-Door)	(194)	(226)
UM6	Radio: AM/FM Stereo with Cassette (SL 4-Door) *Includes digital clock and 4 speakers.*	105	122
UN0	Radio: AM/FM Stereo with CD (SLT) *Includes digital clock, theft lock, speed sensitive volume, automatic tone control and enhanced performance 6 speaker system. NOT AVAILABLE with U1Z.*	86	100
UN0	Radio: AM/FM Stereo with CD (SLE) *Includes digital clock, theft lock, speed sensitive volume, automatic tone control and enhanced performance 6 speaker system. NOT AVAILABLE with U1Z, UL0.*	155	180
UP0	Radio: AM/FM Stereo with CD and Cassette (SLS) *Includes digital clock, speed sensitive volume, theft lock, automatic tone control, auto reverse/music search cassette and enhanced performance 8 speaker system. NOT AVAILABLE with UL0, U1Z, UQ3, M50.*	86	100
UQ3	Bose Premium Sound System (SLS/SLE/SLT) *REQUIRES UL0. NOT AVAILABLE with UP0, M50.*	426	495
V10	Cold Climate Package *Includes 690-CCA HD Delco freedom battery and engine block heater.*	77	89
V54	Roof Mounted Black Luggage Carrier (SL 4-Door)	108	126
Z82	HD Trailering Equipment *Includes 8-wire harness (7-wire with CHMSL wire), trailering hitch platform and heavy duty flasher. REQUIRES GU6 or GT4.*	181	210
Z85	Euro Ride Suspension Package (SL 4-Door) *Includes front and rear stabilizer bars, jounce bumpers and HD springs. REQUIRES QBG or QEB. NOT AVAILABLE with QCA.*	169	197
ZM5	Underbody Shield Package (4WD) *Includes sheilds/plates for: transfer case, front differential, steering linkage and fuel tank.*	108	126
ZM6	Off-Road Suspension Package (4WD 2-Door) *Includes front and rear urethane jounce bumpers, stabilizer bars, larger body mounts, upsized torsion bars and 46mm gas Bilstein shock absorbers. REQUIRES QEB. NOT AVAILABLE with QBG, ZBF, ZBG, ZAA.*	211	245
ZM8	Rear Window Convenience Package (SL) *Includes electric tailgate release, rear window defogger and wiper/washer.*	277	322
ZQ1	Smooth Ride Suspension Package (SLE/SLT) *Includes front and rear jounce bumpers, stabilizer bars and 32mm twin tube gas shocks. REQUIRES QCA or QCE. NOT AVAILABLE with QBG, QEB, GT4.*	(71)	(83)
ZQ3	Convenience Group (SL 2-Door) *Includes tilt steering and speed control.*	340	395
ZQ6	Power Convenience Group (SL 4-Door) *Includes power door locks, power windows and heated power exterior mirrors.*	611	710
ZQ6	Power Convenience Group (SL 2WD 2-Door) *Includes power door locks, power windows and heated power exterior mirrors.*	460	535

CODE	DESCRIPTION	INVOICE	MSRP
ZQ6	Power Convenience Package (SL 4WD 2-Door) *Includes power door locks, power windows and heated power exterior mirrors.*	460	535
ZW7	Luxury Ride Suspension Package (SL 4-Door) *Includes front and rear urethane jounce bumpers and front and rear stabilizer bars. REQUIRES QBG. NOT AVAILABLE with QCA, QEB.*	169	197
ZY2	Conventional Two-Tone Paint (SLE/SLT)	194	225

1999 SAFARI

1999 GMC Safari

What's New?

There are two new exterior paint and body-cladding colors, restyled wheels and outside mirrors, an overhead console and new optional integrated running boards. Additionally, all-wheel-drive Safari models get the new AutoTrac transfer case, and GM's OnStar communications system is now available.

Review

Choosing between a Chevrolet Astro and a GMC Safari is more a matter of image than necessity. Do you want to see Chevrolet's badge every time you approach? Or would it be viscerally satisfying to face those bold "GMC" block letters, with their implication – as brand managers hope – of upscale luxury?

In reality, tangible differences between the two are modest – a fact that's true of most Chevrolet and GMC cousins. Once you've decided that a rear-drive (or all-wheel-drive) General Motors midsize van is the rational choice, you'll likely be satisfied with either one.

Because of their traditional-type full-frame construction and standard rear-drive layout, Safaris are most adept at heavy hauling and burly trailer towing. This is one minivan that provides up to 5,500 pounds of trailering capacity and room for eight people. Not everyone will relish the truck-like ride over harsh surfaces, but it's not bad when the highway smoothes out. Don't expect top-notch fuel mileage, though.

Dual airbags are housed in an artfully styled dashboard, and antilock brakes are standard. For added safety and visibility, daytime running lights blaze the trail. Integrated child-safety seats are available for the center bench seat, and the sliding door has a child-safety lock. Rear-seat heat ducts direct warm air to rear passengers. Safari features GM's PassLock theft deterrent system and, for 1999, the OnStar mobile communications system is available.

One slick feature sure to be appreciated by the parents of teenagers is the middle seat radio option. The driver and front passenger can listen to Casey Kasem up front, or nothing at all, while Junior blasts the local alternative music station into his ears through headphones (a set of headphone jacks plugs into a separate radio unit in the center row). This option alone may be worth the savings in family therapy.

GM's 4300 Vortec V6 is standard, sending 190 horsepower to an electronically controlled four-speed automatic transmission. Long-life engine coolant and 100,000-mile spark plugs help keep maintenance costs to a minimum. This year brings the new AutoTrac transfer case on all-wheel-drive models, which automatically transfers power to the front axle when rear-wheel slippage is detected.

Safaris come in three trim levels, SL, SLE and SLT, with eight-passenger seating standard on all three. There's an FE2 touring suspension option that has stiffer shocks, a rear stabilizer bar and grabby Goodyear rubber for a firmer, more controlled ride. Instead of the typical minivan lift-up rear door, right- and left-hand rear load doors are standard on Safari, with "dutch" doors (a liftglass with split tailgate) optional.

Whether your choice is simple rear-drive or full-time all-wheel drive, Safaris can handle the muscular tasks that pose problems for most front-drive minivans and yet can transport up to eight people in comfort.

Safety Data

Side Airbag: *Not Available*
4-Wheel ABS: *Standard*
Driver Crash Test Grade: *Average*
Side Impact Crash Test Front: *Not Available*
Crash Offset: *Poor*
Integrated Child Seat(s): *Not Available*
Traction Control: *Not Available*
Passenger Crash Test Grade: *Average*
Side Impact Crash Test Rear: *Not Available*

Standard Equipment

SL RWD (4A): 4.3L V6 OHV SMPI 12-valve engine; 4-speed electronic overdrive automatic transmission with lock-up; 600-amp battery; engine oil cooler, HD radiator; 100-amp alternator; transmission oil cooler; rear wheel drive, 3.23 axle ratio; partial stainless steel exhaust; front independent suspension with anti-roll bar, front coil springs, rigid rear axle suspension with rear leaf springs; power re-circulating ball steering with engine speed-sensing assist; front disc/rear drum brakes with 4 wheel antilock braking system; 25 gal. capacity fuel tank; front license plate bracket; 3 doors with sliding right rear passenger door, split swing-out rear cargo door; trailer harness; front and rear body-colored bumpers with rear step; monotone paint; sealed beam halogen headlamps with daytime running lights; additional exterior lights include center high mounted stop light; driver's and passenger's manual black folding outside mirrors; front and rear 15" x 6" painted steel wheels; P215/75SR15 BSW AS front and rear tires; underbody mounted compact steel spare wheel; air conditioning, rear heat ducts; AM/FM stereo with clock, seek-scan, 6 speakers, and fixed antenna; child safety rear door locks; 4 power accessory outlets; instrumentation display includes oil pressure gauge, water temp gauge, volt gauge, trip odometer; warning indicators include oil pressure, battery, lights on, key in ignition, low fuel; dual airbags; ignition disable; tinted windows, vented rear windows, fixed 1/4 vent windows; variable intermittent front windshield wipers; seating capacity of 8, front bucket seats with fixed headrests, driver's and passenger armrests's, driver's seat includes 4-way direction control with lumbar support, passenger's seat includes 4-way direction control with lumbar support; removable 2nd row bench seat with adjustable headrests; removable 3rd row full folding bench seat with adjustable headrests; front height adjustable seatbelts; cloth seats, cloth door trim insert, full cloth headliner, full carpet floor covering; interior lights include dome light; vanity mirrors, dual auxiliary visors; day-night rearview mirror; engine cover console with storage, locking glove box with light, front and rear cupholders, driver's and passenger's door bins; carpeted cargo floor, plastic trunk lid, cargo light; black grille, black side window moldings, black front windshield molding, black rear window molding and black door handles.

SL AWD (4A) (in addition to or instead of SL RWD (4A) equipment): Full-time 4 wheel drive, 3.42 axle ratio; front non-independent torsion suspension with anti-roll bar, front torsion springs and front torsion bar.

Base Prices

	Invoice	MSRP
TM11006-YC5 SL RWD (4A)	19019	21016
TL11006-YC5 SL AWD (4A)	21101	23316
Destination Charge:	595	595

Accessories

Code	Description	Invoice	MSRP
*22	Leather Seat Trim *REQUIRES 1SE.*	817	950
—	Custom Cloth Seat Trim *REQUIRES 1SA.*	NC	NC
1SA	Marketing Option Package 1SA *Includes vehicle with standard equipment.*	NC	NC
1SE	Marketing Option Package 1SE	4598	5346
	Manufacturer Discount	(688)	(800)
	Net Price *Includes SLT Decor package: panel doors, cargo convenience net, power convenience group: power windows, power door locks; convenience group: tilt steering column, speed control; color-keyed rubber floor mats, overhead console with electronics, front and rear reading lights, dual illuminated visor vanity mirrors, uplevel grille with chrome accents, composite headlamps, remote keyless entry: illuminated entry, remote trunk release with keyfob; roof mounted black luggage carrier, dual electric control exterior mirrors, deep tinted glass, special cloth seat trim, rear vented window, leather-wrapped steering wheel, brushed aluminum wheels, ETR AM/FM stereo with CD, seek-scan, clock radio and driver's power seat.*	3910	4546
1SE	Marketing Option Package 1SE	4623	5376
	Manufacturer Discount	(688)	(800)
	Net Price *Includes SLT Decor package: panel doors, cargo convenience net, power convenience group: power windows, power door locks; convenience group: tilt steering column, speed control; color-keyed rubber floor mats, overhead console with electronics, front and rear reading lights, dual illuminated visor vanity mirrors, uplevel grille with chrome accents, composite headlamps, remote keyless entry: illuminated entry, remote trunk release with keyfob; roof mounted black luggage carrier, dual electric control exterior mirrors, deep tinted glass, special cloth seat trim, rear vented window, leather-wrapped steering wheel, brushed aluminum wheels, ETR AM/FM stereo with CD, seek-scan, clock radio, driver's power seat and front seat passenger storage compartment. NOT AVAILABLE with AG2.*	3935	4576

CODE	DESCRIPTION	INVOICE	MSRP
1SV	**Marketing Option Package 1SV (RWD)**	2843	3306
	Manufacturer Discount	(1872)	(2177)
	Net Price	971	1129
	Includes SLE Decor package: panel doors, 8 passenger seating, seat package, custom cloth seat trim, rear vented window, wheels: styled chrome appearance, ETR AM/FM stereo with seek, scan and cassette, cargo convenience net, power convenience group: power windows, power door locks; convenience group: tilt steering column, speed control; color-keyed rubber floor mats, overhead console with electronic instrumentation display, front and rear reading lights, dual illuminated visor vanity mirrors, uplevel grille with chrome accents, composite headlamps, remote keyless entry, illuminated entry, remote trunk release with keyfob, roof mounted black luggage carrier, dual electric control exterior mirrors and deep tinted glass.		
1SV	**Marketing Option Package 1SV (AWD)**	2843	3306
	Manufacturer Discount	(2302)	(2677)
	Net Price	541	629
	Includes SLE Decor package: panel doors, 8 passenger seating, seat package, custom cloth seat trim, rear vented window, wheels: styled chrome appearance, ETR AM/FM stereo with seek, scan and cassette, cargo convenience net, power convenience group: power windows, power door locks; convenience group: tilt steering column, speed control; color-keyed rubber floor mats, overhead console with electronic instrumentation display, front and rear reading lights, dual illuminated visor vanity mirrors, uplevel grille with chrome accents, composite headlamps, remote keyless entry, illuminated entry, remote trunk release with keyfob, roof mounted black luggage carrier, dual electric control exterior mirrors and deep tinted glass.		
1SV	**Marketing Option Package 1SV (AWD)**	2869	3336
	Manufacturer Discount	(2302)	(2677)
	Net Price	567	659
	Includes SLE Decor package: panel doors, 8 passenger seating, seat package, custom cloth seat trim, rear vented window, wheels: styled chrome appearance, ETR AM/FM stereo with seek, scan and cassette, cargo convenience net, power convenience group: power windows, power door locks; convenience group: tilt steering column, speed control; color-keyed rubber floor mats, front seat passenger storage compartment, overhead console with electronic instrumentation display, front and rear reading lights, dual illuminated visor vanity mirrors, uplevel grille with chrome accents, composite headlamps, remote keyless entry, illuminated entry, remote trunk release with keyfob, roof mounted black luggage carrier, dual electric control exterior mirrors and deep tinted glass. NOT AVAILABLE with AG2.		
1SV	**Marketing Option Package 1SV (RWD)**	2869	3336
	Manufacturer Discount	(1872)	(2177)
	Net Price	997	1159
	Includes SLE Decor package: panel doors, 8 passenger seating, seat package, custom cloth seat trim, rear vented window, wheels: styled chrome appearance, ETR AM/FM stereo with seek, scan and cassette, cargo convenience net, power convenience group: power windows, power door locks; convenience group: tilt steering column, speed control; color-keyed rubber floor mats, front seat passenger storage compartment, overhead console with electronic instrumentation display, front and		

CODE	DESCRIPTION	INVOICE	MSRP
	rear reading lights, dual illuminated visor vanity mirrors, uplevel grille with chrome accents, composite headlamps, remote keyless entry, illuminated entry, remote trunk release with keyfob, roof mounted black luggage carrier, dual electric control exterior mirrors and deep tinted glass. NOT AVAILABLE with AG2.		
AG1	Driver's Power Seat *REQUIRES 1SV.*	206	240
AG2	Passenger's Power Seat *REQUIRES AG1. NOT AVAILABLE with 1SA, R6V.*	206	240
AJ1	Deep Tinted Glass *Excludes tinted glass on windshield, passenger and driver's doors. REQUIRES 1SA.*	249	290
AN0	Seat Package *Includes inboard/outboard armrests on driver and passenger seats and manually adjustable lumbar support. REQUIRES 1SA.*	144	168
AP9	Cargo Convenience Net *REQUIRES 1SA.*	26	30
AU0	Remote Keyless Entry *Includes 2 transmitters and remote trunk release with keyfob. REQUIRES 1SA.*	129	150
AU3	Power Door Locks *REQUIRES 1SA.*	192	223
B37	Color-Keyed Front & Rear Rubber Floor Mats *REQUIRES 1SA.*	59	69
B74	Bodyside Moldings with Bright Insert *REQUIRES 1SA.*	104	121
B94	Gold Appearance Package *Includes gold metallic stripe decal and gold port aluminum wheels. REQUIRES 1SE. NOT AVAILABLE with ZY2.*	NC	NC
BA8	Front Seat Passenger Storage Compartment *REQUIRES 1SA.*	26	30
BX2	Lower Body Side Cladding (AWD) *REQUIRES 1SA.*	301	350
BX2	Lower Body Side Cladding (AWD) *REQUIRES 1SA. NOT AVAILABLE with ZY2.*	190	221
C36	Auxiliary Rear Heater	176	205
C49	Electric Rear Window Defogger *REQUIRES E54.*	132	154
C69	Front and Rear Air Conditioning *Includes 105-amp altemator.*	450	523
C95	Reading Lamps *REQUIRES 1SA. NOT AVAILABLE with DK6, DK8.*	28	33
D48	Dual Electric Control Exterior Mirrors *Black below-eye-line type. REQUIRES 1SA, ZQ2.*	84	98
DK6	Overhead Console without Electronics *Includes two storage compartments, garage door opener compartment, dome lamp and dual illuminated visor vanity mirrors. REQUIRES 1SA. NOT AVAILABLE with DK8, C95, UG1.*	71	83

CODE	DESCRIPTION	INVOICE	MSRP
DK8	**Overhead Console with Electronics** *Includes two storage compartments, garage door opener compartment, dome lamp, reading lamps and dual illuminated visor vanity mirrors. REQUIRES 1SA. NOT AVAILABLE with DK6, C95.*	192	223
E54	**Dutch Doors** *Includes lower swing-out with liftgate and intermittent rear window wiper/washer. NOT AVAILABLE with 1SA.*	262	305
E54	**Dutch Doors** *Includes lower swing-out with liftgate and intermittent rear window wiper/washer. REQUIRES 1SA.*	313	364
G80	**Locking Rear Differential**	217	252
GT4	**3.73 Axle Ratio**	NC	NC
GU6	**3.42 Axle Ratio (RWD)**	NC	NC
NC7	**Federal Emission Override** *For vehicles that will be registered or leased in California, Connecticut, Washington D.C, Delaware, Massachusetts, Maryland, New Hampshire, New Jersey, New York, Pennsylvania, Rhode Island and Virginia but sold by dealers outside those states.*	NC	NC
NP5	**Leather Wrapped Steering Wheel** *REQUIRES 1SV.*	46	54
PA6	**Wheels: Styled Steel Painted Silver** *Includes four 15" x 6.5" wheels. REQUIRES 1SA. NOT AVAILABLE with PC2.*	79	92
PC2	**Wheels: Styled Chrome Appearance** *Includes four 15" x 6.5" wheels. REQUIRES 1SA. NOT AVAILABLE with PA6.*	292	340
PF3	**Wheels: Aluminum Brushed** *Includes four 15" x 6.5" wheels. REQUIRES 1SA. NOT AVAILABLE with PA6, PC2.*	314	365
PF3	**Wheels: Aluminum Brushed** *Includes four 15" x 6.5" wheels. REQUIRES 1SE.*	21	25
PF3	**Wheels: Aluminum Brushed** *Includes four 15" x 6.5" wheels. REQUIRES 1SV.*	235	273
QCM	**Tires: P215/75R15 AS WOL SBR**	76	88
TL1	**Uplevel Grille with Chrome Accents** *Includes body colored painted bumpers and composite headlamps. REQUIRES 1SA.*	129	150
UG1	**Homelink Transmitter** *Includes 3-channel universal garage door opener. REQUIRES DK8. NOT AVAILABLE with DK6.*	99	115
UK6	**Rear Seat Audio Controls with Jacks** *Does not include headphones. REQUIRES UL0 or UP0. NOT AVAILABLE with 1SA.*	108	125
UL0	**Radio: AM/FM Stereo with Cassette** *Includes digital clock, 4 coaxial front speakers, 4 extended range rear speakers, theft lock feature, speed volume control and automatic tone controls. NOT AVAILABLE with UP0, 1SA.*	264	307
UM6	**Radio: AM/FM Stereo with Cassette** *Includes digital clock, 4 coaxial front speakers and 4 extended range rear speakers. REQUIRES 1SA.*	126	147

CODE	DESCRIPTION	INVOICE	MSRP
UN0	**Radio: AM/FM Stereo with CD and Clock** *Includes 4 coaxial front speakers, 4 extended range rear speakers, theft lock feature, speed volume control and automatic tone controls. REQUIRES 1SE. NOT AVAILABLE with UK6, UL0, UP0.*	350	407
UP0	**Radio: AM/FM Stereo, CD and Cassette** *Includes digital clock, 4 coaxial front speakers, 4 extended range rear speakers, theft lock feature, speed volume control and automatic tone controls. REQUIRES 1SV. NOT AVAILABLE with UL0.*	436	507
V10	**Cold Climate Package** *Includes extra coolant protection and engine block heater.*	40	46
V54	**Roof Mounted Black Luggage Carrier** *REQUIRES 1SA.*	108	126
Z82	**HD Trailering Special Equipment** *Includes trailering hitch platform and 8-wire harness.*	266	309
ZP7	**7-Passenger Seating** *Includes front reclining buckets with adjustable up and down headrests, two middle reclining bucket seats, removable split-back reclining passenger bench, fold-down center console with convenience tray, two cup holders and seat package. REQUIRES 1SE.*	NC	NC
ZP7	**7-Passenger Seating** *Includes front reclining buckets with adjustable up and down headrests, two middle reclining bucket seats, removable split-back reclining passenger bench, fold-down center console with convenience tray, two cup holders and seat package. REQUIRES 1SV.*	273	318
ZP7	**7-Passenger Seating** *Includes front reclining buckets with adjustable up and down headrests, two middle reclining bucket seats, removable split-back reclining passenger bench, fold-down center console with convenience tray, two cup holders and seat package. REQUIRES 1SA.*	494	574
ZQ2	**Power Convenience Group** *Includes power windows and power door locks. REQUIRES 1SA.*	408	474
ZQ3	**Convenience Group** *Includes tilt steering column and speed control. REQUIRES 1SA.*	329	383
ZY2	**Two-Tone Paint with Lower Cladding** *NOT AVAILABLE with 1SA, B94, BX2.*	NC	NC

1999 SAVANA

1999 GMC Savana

What's New?

GMC's full-size van gets two new exterior colors, one new interior color and automatic transmission enhancements.

Review

Believe it or not, it had been 25 years since GM redesigned its full-size van lineup when the Savana arrived in small numbers for 1996. The GMC Rally Van and Vandura were introduced in 1971, and sold steadily until they were discontinued. Competition and safety regulations had forced GM to redo the big vans in 1996 — heck, since 1971 Ford had re-engineered the Club Wagon and Econoline twice! To distinguish the new design, GMC rebadged the van Savana.

Savana features flush glass and door handles, hidden door hinges, standard antilock brakes and dual airbags. Front foot and legroom is adequate, and front seats offer a wide range of travel. Rear heat ducts are standard, but for better warming (and cooling), an optional rear heating and air conditioning unit is available. Front air conditioning is standard. The center console contains two cupholders, an auxiliary power outlet and storage for items like CDs and cassettes. Savana is available in 135- and 155-inch wheelbases, three weight series (1500, 2500 or 3500) and two (base SL and luxury SLE) trim levels. There is a choice of side-entry doors as well: a sliding door or a pair of 60/40 hinged doors.

Inside the short-wheelbase Savana, you'll find 267 cubic feet of cargo area, while the extended version provides a whopping 317 cubic feet of volume with the rear seats removed. Up to 15 passengers can be seated within the longer van on as many as five bench seats. Rear hinged doors open 180 degrees for easy loading and do not conceal high-mounted taillights when opened. Gross vehicle weight ratings of up to 9,500 pounds are available on either wheelbase.

The base engine is a Vortec 4300 V6 making 200 horsepower. Optional motors include the GM family of V8's, ranging from the popular Vortec 5000 to the monster Vortec 7400. Also available is a robust 6.5-liter turbo-diesel V8 good for 195 horsepower and 430 stump-pulling foot-pounds of torque.

Automatic transmission refinements result in lower levels of vibration and noise. These refinements include a two-piece transmission case that provides powertrain stiffness, software that compares engine/vehicle operating parameters and sets precise transmission line pressure, a deep oil pan which aids durability and fluid life, and an electrically controlled converter clutch which increases fuel economy.

Two new exterior colors, Fernmist Green Metallic and Dark Bronzemist Metallic, and one new interior color, Medium Dark Pewter, are available for 1999. Like most products in showrooms these days, the Savana's styling is rounded and bulbous, with a front end that mimics the corporate look carried by most of GM's truck family. This design should wear well into the next century.

Safety Data

Side Airbag: *Not Available*
4-Wheel ABS: *Standard*
Driver Crash Test Grade: *Not Available*
Side Impact Crash Test Front: *Not Available*
Crash Offset: *Not Available*
Integrated Child Seat(s): *Not Available*
Traction Control: *Not Available*
Passenger Crash Test Grade: *Not Available*
Side Impact Crash Test Rear: *Not Available*

Standard Equipment

G1500 STANDARD PASSENGER VAN LD (4A): 4.3L V6 OHV SMPI 12-valve engine; 4-speed electronic overdrive automatic transmission with lock-up; 600-amp HD battery; 100-amp alternator; rear wheel drive, 3.42 axle ratio; stainless steel exhaust; front independent suspension with anti-roll bar, HD front coil springs, rigid rear axle suspension with HD rear leaf springs; power re-circulating ball steering with engine speed-sensing assist; front disc/rear drum brakes with 4 wheel antilock braking system; 31 gal capacity fuel tank; 3 doors, split swing-out right rear passenger door, split swing-out rear cargo door; front and rear argent bumpers with rear step; monotone paint; sealed beam halogen headlamps with daytime running lights; additional exterior lights include center high mounted stop light, underhood light; driver's and passenger's manual remote black folding outside mirrors; front and rear 15" x 7" silver styled steel wheels; P235/75SR15 BSW AS front and rear tires; underbody mounted full-size conventional steel spare wheel; air conditioning, rear heat ducts; AM/FM stereo with clock, seek-scan, 4 speakers, and fixed antenna; child safety rear door locks; 2 power accessory outlets; instrumentation display includes oil pressure gauge, water temp gauge, volt gauge, trip odometer; warning indicators include battery, lights on, key in ignition; dual airbags; ignition disable; tinted windows, vented rear windows, fixed 1/4 vent windows; variable intermittent front windshield wipers, vented rear window; seating capacity of 8, front bucket seats with fixed headrests, driver's seat includes 4-way direction control, passenger's seat includes 4-way direction control; removeable bench 2nd row seat with shoulder belts mounted outboard only; removeable 3rd row seat bench with shoulder belts mounted outboard only; front height adjustable seatbelts; vinyl seats, full cloth headliner, full vinyl floor covering; interior lights include dome light; day-night rearview mirror; engine cover console with storage, glove box, front cupholder, instrument panel covered bin, 2 seat back storage pockets, driver's and passenger's door bins; vinyl cargo floor, plastic trunk lid, cargo light; black grille, black side window moldings, black front windshield molding, black rear window molding and black door handles.

G2500/G3500 STANDARD PASSENGER VAN HD (4A) (in addition to or instead of G1500 STANDARD PASSENGER VAN LD (4A) equipment): 5.7L V8 OHV SMPI 16-valve engine; 124-amp alternator; 3.73 axle ratio; front and rear 16" x 6.5" silver styled steel wheels; seating capacity of 12, front bucket seats with fixed headrests, driver's seat includes 4-way direction control and passenger's seat includes 4-way direction control.

Base Prices

Code	Description	Invoice	MSRP
TG11406-R9S	G1500 Standard Passenger Van LD	20242	23134
TG21406-R9S	G2500 Standard Passenger Van HD	22430	25634
TG21706-R9S	G2500 Standard Extended Passenger Van HD	23217	26534

CODE	DESCRIPTION	INVOICE	MSRP
TG31406-R9S	G3500 Standard Passenger Van HD	22679	25923
TG31706-R9S	G3500 Standard Extended Passenger Van HD	23506	26868
	Destination Charge:	625	625

Accessories

CODE	DESCRIPTION	INVOICE	MSRP
~~G	**Custom Cloth Seat Trim** *Includes cloth door trim and inboard armrests on front seats.*	NC	NC
1SA	**Marketing Option Package 1SA** *Includes standard decor package equipment. REQUIRES R6G or C60.*	NC	NC
1SB	**Marketing Option Package 1SB** *Includes standard decor package, power convenience group: power door locks, power windows, convenience group: tilt steering and speed control. NOT AVAILABLE with 9J6.*	739	859
1SC	**Marketing Option Package 1SC** *Includes power convenience group: power door locks, power windows, convenience group: tilt steering, speed control, SLE Decor package: full floor carpeting: cargo space carpet, auxiliary lighting: reading lamps, custom cloth seat trim, front and rear chrome bumpers, gray grille with bright trim ring, composite halogen headlamps, lower bodyside moldings, trim rings and bright center hub caps and passenger's visor mirror.*	1423	1655
1SD	**Marketing Option Package 1SD (2500/3500 LWB)** *Includes SLE Decor package: full floor carpeting: cargo space carpet, auxiliary lighting: reading lamps, custom cloth seat trim, front and rear chrome bumpers, gray grille with bright trim ring, composite halogen headlamps, lower bodyside moldings, trim rings and bright center hub caps, passenger's visor mirror, front and rear air conditioning: rear heater, power convenience group: power door locks, power windows, convenience group: tilt steering, speed control, rear heater, dual illuminated visor vanity mirrors, remote keyless entry, LH/RH electric remote mirrors and deep tinted glass.*	2049	2383
1SD	**Marketing Option Package 1SD (2500/3500 SWB)** *Includes SLE Decor package: full floor carpeting: cargo space carpet, auxiliary lighting: reading lamps, custom cloth seat trim, front and rear chrome bumpers, gray grille with bright trim ring, composite halogen headlamps, lower bodyside moldings, trim rings and bright center hub caps, passenger's visor mirror, front and rear air conditioning: rear heater, power convenience group: power door locks, power windows, convenience group: tilt steering, speed control, rear heater, dual illuminated visor vanity mirrors, remote keyless entry, LH/RH electric remote mirrors and deep tinted glass. NOT AVAILABLE with C69.*	2741	3187
1SD	**Marketing Option Package 1SD (1500)** *Includes SLE Decor package: full floor carpeting: cargo space carpet, auxiliary lighting: reading lamps, custom cloth seat trim, front and rear chrome bumpers, gray grille with bright trim ring, composite halogen headlamps, lower bodyside moldings, trim rings and bright center hub caps, passenger's visor mirror, front and rear air conditioning: rear heater, power convenience group: power door locks, power windows, convenience group: tilt steering, speed control, rear heater, dual illuminated visor vanity mirrors, remote keyless entry and deep tinted glass.*	2789	3243

CODE	DESCRIPTION	INVOICE	MSRP
AG1	**6-Way Power Driver's Seat** *REQUIRES custom cloth seat trim.*	206	240
AG2	**6-Way Power Passenger's Seat** *REQUIRES AG1.*	206	240
AJ1	**Deep Tinted Glass** *Excludes windshield and driver and passenger windows.*	335	390
AU0	**Remote Keyless Entry** *Includes 2 transmitters.*	129	150
B30	**Full Floor Carpeting** *Includes front and rear mats and cargo space carpet.*	126	147
C36	**Rear Heater**	206	240
C69	**Front and Rear Air Conditioning (2500/3500 SWB)** *Includes rear heater.*	692	804
C69	**Front and Rear Air Conditioning (1500)** *Includes rear heater and 124-amp generator.*	740	860
C69	**Front and Rear Air Conditioning (2500 LWB)** *Includes rear heater.*	NC	NC
DE5	**LH/RH Electric Remote Mirrors** *Includes electric defoggers and right hand convex mirror. REQUIRES (C60 or C69). NOT AVAILABLE with R6G, YF2.*	97	113
DH6	**Dual Illuminated Visor Vanity Mirrors**	65	75
G80	**Locking Differential** *NOT AVAILABLE with GU6.*	217	252
GT4	**3.73 Axle Ratio (1500)** *REQUIRES C5Y or C6P. NOT AVAILABLE with L30.*	NC	NC
GT5	**4.10 Axle Ratio (2500)** *REQUIRES C6P. NOT AVAILABLE with L30.*	NC	NC
GU6	**3.42 Axle Ratio (3500)** *REQUIRES L29.*	NC	NC
KL5	**Conversion Ready Engine (N/A 1500)** *Includes internal modifications for operation of natural or propane gas. REQUIRES L31. NOT AVAILABLE with L65.*	108	125
KW2	**124-Amp Generator (1500)**	52	60
L29	**Engine: Vortec 7400 V8 SFI (3500)**	516	600
L30	**Engine: Vortec 5000 SFI V8 (1500)** *NOT AVAILABLE with GT4.*	426	495
L31	**Engine: Vortec 5700 SFI V8 (1500)** *REQUIRES C5Y or (1SA or 1SB).*	1028	1195
L65	**Engine: 6.5L V8 Turbo Diesel (2500/3500)** *Also includes glow plugs, integral two stage fuel filter and fuel and water separator with instrument panel warning light, dual batteries, engine oil cooler, HD radiator, extra sound insulation and engine block heater.*	2460	2860
MT1	**Transmission: 4-Speed Automatic with Overdrive (2500)** *REQUIRES (GT4 or GT5) and C6P. NOT AVAILABLE with L30.*	NC	NC
N83	**Wheels: Chrome Styled (1500)** *Includes standard steel spare and tire: full size spare. REQUIRES (1SA or 1SB).*	267	310

CODE	DESCRIPTION	INVOICE	MSRP
N83	Wheels: Chrome Styled (1500)	215	250
	Includes standard steel spare and tire: full size spare. REQUIRES (1SC or 1SD).		
N90	Wheels: Cast Aluminum (1500)	215	250
	Includes standard steel spare and tire: full size spare. REQUIRES (1SC or 1SD).		
N90	Wheels: Cast Aluminum (1500)	267	310
	Includes standard steel spare and tire: full size spare. REQUIRES (1SA or 1SB).		
NG1	Emissions	145	170
	Includes Connecticut, District of Columbia, Delaware, Massachusetts, Maryland, New Hampshire, New Jersey, New York, Pennsylvania, Rhode Island and Virginia. Automatically added to vehicles shipped to and/or sold to retailers in the applicable states. Out-of-state retailers must order on vehicles to be registered or leased in applicable states.		
NP5	Leather-Wrapped Steering Wheel	52	60
P06	Trim Rings and Bright Center Hub Caps	52	60
R6G	Air Conditioning Not Desired	NC	NC
TR9	Auxiliary Lighting	138	160
	Includes dome light, override switch, stepwell lamps and underhood lamp and reading lamps.		
U75	Power Radio Antenna	73	85
	NOT AVAILABLE with UL5.		
UL0	Radio: AM/ FM Stereo, Cassette, Automatic Tone Control	380	442
	Includes auto reverse cassette player with music search, digital clock and 4 front and 4 rear speakers and power radio antenna.		
UL0	Radio: AM/FM Stereo, Automatic Tone Control, Cassette	181	210
	Includes in-radio clock, auto reverse cassette player with music search, 4 front and 4 rear speakers.		
UL5	Radio Delete	(264)	(307)
UM6	Radio: AM/ FM Stereo with Cassette	126	147
	Includes digital clock, 2 front and 2 extended range rear speakers. NOT AVAILABLE with UL5.		
UN0	Radio: AM/ FM Stereo, Automatic Tone Control, CD	267	310
	Includes in-radio clock, 4 front and 4 rear speakers.		
UN0	Radio: AM/ FM Stereo, CD Player	466	542
	Includes automatic tone control, digital clock and 4 front and 4 rear speakers and power radio antenna.		
UP0	Radio: AM/ FM Stereo with Cassette, CD	552	642
	Includes automatic tone control, digital clock and 4 front and 4 rear speakers and power radio antenna.		
UP0	Radio: AM/ FM Stereo, Automatic Tone Control, CD, Cass.	353	410
	Includes in-radio clock, 4 front and 4 rear speakers.		
V10	Cold Climate Package	41	48
	Includes engine block heater. NOT AVAILABLE with L65.		
XHA	Tires: Front P235/75R15 AS BSW (1500)	NC	NC
	REQUIRES YHA and (ZHA or ZX9).		
XHB	Tires: Front P235/75R15 AS WSW (1500)	89	104
	REQUIRES YHB and (ZHB or ZX9).		

CODE	DESCRIPTION	INVOICE	MSRP
XHB	Tires: Front P235/75R15 AS WSW (1500) *REQUIRES YHB and ZHB or YHB and ZHB or ZX9.*	34	40
XHF	Tires: Front LT225/75R16E AS BSW (2500) *REQUIRES YHF and ZHF or YHF and (ZHF or ZX9). NOT AVAILABLE with L30.*	NC	NC
XHM	Tires: Front P235/75R15 AS WOL (1500) *REQUIRES YHM and ZHM or YHM and ZHM or ZX9.*	43	50
XHM	Tires: Front P235/75R15 AS WOL (1500) *REQUIRES YHM and ZHM or ZX9.*	98	114
YA2	Sliding Side Door	NC	NC
YF5	California Emissions *Automatically added to vehicles shipped to and/or sold to retailers in California. Out-of-state retailers must order on vehicles to be registered or leased in California. REQUIRES (1SA or 1SB) or (L30 or L31 or L65).*	145	170
YF5	California Emissions *Automatically added to vehicles shipped to and/or sold to retailers in California. Out-of-state retailers must order on vehicles to be registered or leased in California.*	145	170
YHA	Tires: Rear P235/75R15 AS BSW (1500) *REQUIRES ZHA or ZX9.*	NC	NC
YHB	Tires: Rear P235/75R15 AS WSW (1500) *REQUIRES ZHB or ZX9.*	34	40
YHB	Tires: Rear P235/75R15 AS WSW (1500) *REQUIRES ZHB or ZX9.*	89	104
YHF	Tires: Rear LT225/75R16E AS BSW (2500) *REQUIRES ZHF or ZX9. NOT AVAILABLE with L30.*	NC	NC
YHM	Tires: Rear P235/75R15 AS WOL (1500) *REQUIRES ZHM or ZX9.*	98	114
YHM	Tires: Rear P235/75R15 AS WOL (1500) *REQUIRES ZHM or ZX9.*	43	50
Z82	HD Trailering Equipment *Includes trailering hitch platform and 8-wire harness.*	267	310
ZHA	Tire: Spare P235/75R15 AS BSW (1500)	NC	NC
ZHB	Tire: Spare P235/75R15 AS WSW (1500)	17	20
ZHB	Tire: Spare P235/75R15 AS WSW (1500)	45	52
ZHF	Tire: Spare LT225/75R16E AS BSW (2500) *NOT AVAILABLE with L30.*	NC	NC
ZHM	Tire: Spare P235/75R15 AS OWL (1500)	22	25
ZHM	Tire: Spare P235/75R15 AS WOL (1500)	49	57
ZP3	15 Passenger Seating (3500 LWB) *Includes 2 front high-back buckets, three 3 passenger bench seats, and one 4 passenger bench seat.*	319	371
ZP5	5 Passenger Seating (1500) *Includes two front high-back bucket seats and one rear 3-passenger bench seat.*	(319)	(371)
ZP8	8 Passenger Seating (2500 SWB/3500 SWB) *Includes two high back bucket seats and one 3 passenger bench seat.*	(319)	(371)
ZQ2	Power Convenience Group *Includes power door locks and power windows.*	408	474

CODE	DESCRIPTION	INVOICE	MSRP
ZQ3	Convenience Group *Includes tilt steering and speed control.*	331	385
ZX9	Spare Tire Delete (1500) *Also deletes hoist, jack, and tools.*	(95)	(110)
ZX9	Spare Tire Delete (2500) *Also deletes hoist, jack, and tools. NOT AVAILABLE with ZHF.*	(216)	(252)
ZX9	Spare Tire Delete (3500) *Also deletes hoist, jack, and tools.*	(256)	(298)

1999 SIERRA

1999 GMC Sierra

What's New?

Finally, the decade-old, full-size GMC pickup based on the C/K gets a complete redesign from the ground-up. Major structural, power, braking and interior enhancements characterize the all-new Sierra. Styling is evolutionary rather than revolutionary, both inside and out.

Review

Thanks to the myriad of improvements to the basic platform, the all-new GMC Sierra will impress most people who are in the market for a full-size pickup. At first glance, it appears GMC has launched an all-new model that remains as true to its roots as it does its brand image.

See, back in 1996, GMC decided to create a new image for itself by positioning the company as the premium truck division. Since then, GMC has been refinishing several of its existing rough-and-tough vehicles with a bit of powder and polish. It only stands to reason that the company would enhance the Sierra pickup for 1999, too. But this time, they started from scratch. Carrying over certain styling elements, like the ruby red GMC logo and the large centerport grille, was important to designers, but it was equally important to branch out with stiffer, lighter frames, larger engines and roomier cabs.

The '99 Sierras employ a new, three-piece frame construction and each piece of the frame serves a unique function, from protecting the engine and suspension to accommodating various trailer hitches. The result is a frame that absorbs 35 percent more energy than its predecessor, reduces vibrations, has better crash test results and is not as susceptible to corrosion.

Designers obviously thought that GMC's best-selling truck deserved several first-class engine choices, and we agree. Although the carryover Vortec 4.3-liter V6 is still standard on the trucks, the Sierras can also be equipped with three new powerful V8s. The Vortec 4800 V8 replaces the Vortec 5000, and makes 255 horsepower. There's also a 5.3-liter V8 with 270 ponies. Like the 4800, the 5300 engine displays a long, fairly flat torque curve for sustained hauling performance. And finally, you can buy a 6.0-liter V8 with 300 horsepower. These three new gasoline engines are based on the 5.7-liter LS1 engine in the Corvette but use cast iron blocks and all three produce between 10 and 25 more horsepower than the engines they replace. A 6.5-liter turbo-diesel V8 that offers 215 horsepower and a whopping 440 foot-pounds of torque will be available after the first of the year.

Each truck is available with a five-speed manual or four-speed automatic transmission. As usual, there is a variety of configurations to choose from, including regular or extended cabs, short bed or long bed, three trim levels and many options, as well as rear- or four-wheel-drive versions. But executives at GMC point out that they are now designing vehicles geared more toward on-road purposes. If you want a dirt-crunching, rock-hopping vehicle made by GM, Chevy is the place to shop.

Conservatively restyled, Sierras get bigger chrome bumpers and a meaner stance. Headlights are larger and offer 15 percent more forward lighting and 120 percent more left-side lighting without increasing the glare. Four-wheel antilock disc brakes are standard.

Inside the larger greenhouse is a mildly revamped interior, with a center armrest storage area that is large enough for a laptop computer-or a six pack of soda, depending on your priorities. Reduced-force airbags have been installed and the passenger gets an airbag on/off option. The glove compartment has separate sections so your sunglasses don't get lost under your maps, the foldout cupholders are large with space for a mug handle, and there are a total of three power outlets up front. All seatbelts are seat-mounted for convenience and the SLT trim level gets you an armrest that doubles as a writing tray.

Extended cabs have an amazing amount of room-38.4 inches of headroom and 33.7 inches of legroom-for backseat passengers. And, designers installed child-size seatbelt adjusters, two rear cupholders and two headrests for back seat riders. A larger third door allows for easy passenger access as well as quick cargo loading. Somehow, GMC did not make a four-door available this year.

There are far too many upgrades to the new Sierra to list here, but suffice it to say that nearly every area of functionality has been studied and improved. Overall, Sierra seems to be a much more capable truck than its predecessor, and a much more worthy competitor to its Ford and Dodge rivals. But because GMC is set on segmenting itself as the premium truck division that caters to upscale truck buyers, prepare yourself for price creep to start forcing less-affluent young cowboy types to shop elsewhere.

1999 SIERRA 1500

Safety Data

Side Airbag: *Not Available*
4-Wheel ABS: *Standard*
Driver Crash Test Grade: *Not Available*
Side Impact Crash Test Front: *Not Available*
Crash Offset: *Not Available*
Integrated Child Seat(s): *Not Available*
Traction Control: *Not Available*
Passenger Crash Test Grade: *Not Available*
Side Impact Crash Test Rear: *Not Available*

Standard Equipment

SL 2WD REGULAR CAB SB/LB (5M): 4.3L V6 OHV SMPI 12-valve engine; 5-speed overdrive manual transmission; 600-amp HD battery with run down protection; engine oil cooler; 105-amp alternator; rear wheel drive, 3.08 axle ratio; stainless steel exhaust; front independent suspension with anti-roll bar, front coil springs, rigid rear axle suspension with rear leaf springs; power rack-and-pinion steering with vehicle speed-sensing assist; 4 wheel disc brakes with 4 wheel antilock braking system;

26 gal (34 gal - LB) capacity fuel tank; trailer harness; front chrome bumper with black rub strip, rear argent bumper with black rub strip, rear tow hooks, rear step; monotone paint; aero-composite halogen auto on headlamps with daytime running lights; additional exterior lights include center high mounted stop light, pickup cargo box light, underhood light; driver's and passenger's manual black folding outside mirrors; front and rear 16" x 7" silver styled steel wheels; P235/75SR16 BSW AS front and rear tires; underbody mounted full-size conventional steel spare wheel; AM/FM stereo with clock, seek-scan, 2 speakers, and fixed antenna; 3 power accessory outlets, retained accessory power; instrumentation display includes tachometer, oil pressure gauge, water temp gauge, volt gauge, trip odometer; warning indicators include oil pressure, water temp, battery, low oil level, low coolant, lights on, key in ignition, low fuel, low washer fluid, door ajar, service interval; driver's side airbag, passenger's side cancelable airbag; ignition disable; tinted windows; variable intermittent front windshield wipers; seating capacity of 3, 40-20-40 split-bench front seat with adjustable headrests, center armrest with storage, driver's seat includes 4-way direction control with lumbar support, passenger's seat includes 4-way direction control with lumbar support; premium cloth seats, full cloth headliner, full carpet floor covering with rubber floor mats, cabback insulator; interior lights include dome light, front reading lights, illuminated entry; sport steering wheel with tilt adjustment; passenger's side vanity mirror; day-night rearview mirror; glove box with light, front cupholder, 2 seat back storage pockets, driver's and passenger's door bins; black grille, black side window moldings, black front windshield molding, black rear window molding and black door handles.

SL 2WD EXTENDED CAB SB/LB (4A) (in addition to or instead of SL 2WD REGULAR CAB SB/LB (5M) equipment): 4.8L V8 OHV SMPI 16-valve engine; 4-speed electronic overdrive automatic transmission with lock-up; driver selectable program transmission, transmission oil cooler; 3.42 axle ratio; rear heat ducts; AM/FM stereo with clock, seek-scan, 4 speakers, and fixed antenna; vented rear windows; seating capacity of 6, passenger's seat includes 4-way direction control with lumbar support and easy entry; full folding rear bench seat with adjustable headrests.

SLE 2WD REGULAR CAB SB/LB (5M) (in addition to or instead of SL 2WD REGULAR CAB SB/LB (5M) equipment): Front and rear chrome bumpers with front body-colored rub strip; chrome bodyside molding; driver's and passenger's power remote chrome folding outside mirrors; air conditioning, air filter; AM/FM stereo with clock, seek-scan, single CD, 6 performance speakers, automatic equalizer, theft deterrent, and fixed antenna; cruise control; power door locks with 2 stage unlock, remote keyless entry; ignition disable, panic alarm, security system; power front windows with driver's 1-touch down; interior lights include 2 door curb lights; leather-wrapped sport steering wheel with tilt adjustment and chrome grille.

SLE 2WD EXTENDED CAB SB/LB (4A) (in addition to or instead of SLE 2WD REGULAR CAB SB/LB (5M) equipment): 4.8L V8 OHV SMPI 16-valve engine; 4-speed electronic overdrive automatic transmission with lock-up; driver selectable program transmission, transmission oil cooler; 3.42 axle ratio; rear heat ducts; vented rear windows; seating capacity of 6, passenger's seat includes 4-way direction control with lumbar support and easy entry; full folding rear bench seat with adjustable headrests; mini overhead console with storage and front and rear cupholders.

SL 4WD REGULAR CAB SB/LB (5M) (in addition to or instead of SL 2WD REGULAR CAB SB/LB (5M): equipment): Part-time 4 wheel drive, auto locking hub control with manual shift, 3.73 axle ratio; front independent torsion suspension with anti-roll bar, front torsion springs, front torsion bar; power re-circulating ball steering with vehicle speed-sensing assist; 26 gal capacity fuel tank and front and rear 16" x 6.5" silver styled steel wheels.

SL 4WD EXTENDED CAB SB/LB (4A) (in addition to or instead of SL 4WD REGULAR CAB SB/LB (5M) equipment): 4.8L V8 OHV SMPI 16-valve engine; 4-speed electronic overdrive automatic transmission with lock-up; driver selectable program transmission, transmission oil cooler; rear heat ducts; AM/FM stereo with clock, seek-scan, 4 speakers, and fixed antenna; vented rear windows; seating capacity of 6, passenger's seat includes 4-way direction control with lumbar support and easy entry and full folding rear bench seat with adjustable rear headrest.

CODE	DESCRIPTION	INVOICE	MSRP

SLE 4WD REGULAR CAB SB/LB (5M) (in addition to or instead of SL 4WD REGULAR CAB SB/LB (5M) equipment): Front and rear 16" x 6.5" chrome styled steel wheels; front and rear chrome bumpers with front body-colored rub strip; chrome bodyside molding; driver's and passenger's power remote chrome folding outside mirrors; air conditioning, air filter; AM/FM stereo with clock, seek-scan, single CD, 6 performance speakers, automatic equalizer, theft deterrent, and fixed antenna; cruise control; power door locks with 2 stage unlock, remote keyless entry; ignition disable, panic alarm, security system; power front windows with driver's 1-touch down; interior lights include 2 door curb lights; leather-wrapped sport steering wheel with tilt adjustment and chrome grille.

SLE 4WD EXTENDED CAB SB/LB (4A) (in addition to or instead of SLE 4WD REGULAR CAB SB/LB (5M) equipment): 4.8L V8 OHV SMPI 16-valve engine; 4-speed electronic overdrive automatic transmission with lock-up; driver selectable program transmission, transmission oil cooler; rear heat ducts; vented rear windows; seating capacity of 6, passenger's seat includes 4-way direction control with lumbar support and easy entry; full folding rear bench seat with adjustable rear headrest; mini overhead console with storage and front and rear cupholders.

Base Prices

CODE	DESCRIPTION	INVOICE	MSRP
TC15703-R9S	SL 2WD Regular Cab SB (5M)	14439	15955
TC15903-R9S	SL 2WD Regular Cab LB (5M)	14711	16255
TK15703-R9S	SL 4WD Regular Cab SB (5M)	17244	19032
TK15903-R9S	SL 4WD Regular Cab LB (5M)	17495	19332
TC15703-YE9	SLE 2WD Regular Cab SB (5M)	17266	19733
TC15903-YE9	SLE 2WD Regular Cab LB (5M)	17529	20033
TK15703-YE9	SLE 4WD Regular Cab SB (5M)	19946	22795
TK15903-YE9	SLE 4WD Regular Cab LB (5M)	20208	23095
TC15753-R9S	SL 2WD Extended Cab SB (4A)	19838	21920
TC15953-R9S	SL 2WD Extended Cab LB (4A)	20109	22220
TK15753-R9S	SL 4WD Extended Cab SB (4A)	22609	24982
TK15953-R9S	SL 4WD Extended Cab LB (4A)	22880	25282
TC15753-YE9	SLE 2WD Extended Cab SB (4A)	21147	24168
TC15953-YE9	SLE 2WD Extended Cab LB (4A)	21410	24468
TK15753-YE9	SLE 4WD Extended Cab SB (4A)	23826	27230
TK15953-YE9	SLE 4WD Extended Cab LB (4A)	24089	27530
Destination Charge:		640	640

Accessories

CODE	DESCRIPTION	INVOICE	MSRP
~~2	Leather Seat Trim (SLE) *Includes leather front seating surface and simulated leather rear seating surface. REQUIRES 1SD.*	NC	NC
~~V	Vinyl Seat Trim (SL) *Includes fixed center seat section, deletes standard seat recliners, lumbar support, adjustable head restraints, center fold-down armrest, seatback storage pockets and full floor carpeting.*	NC	NC
1SA	Preferred Equipment Group 1SA (SL) *Includes vehicle with standard equipment. NOT AVAILABLE with PY2, R6S.*	NC	NC
1SA	Preferred Equipment Group 1SA (SL) *Includes vehicle with standard equipment. NOT AVAILABLE with PY2, R6S.*	NC	NC

CODE	DESCRIPTION	INVOICE	MSRP
1SB	**Preferred Equipment Group 1SB (SL)** *Includes argent-painted cast aluminum wheels, non-matching spare wheel, chrome grille surround, chromed rear step bumper with step pad and black bodyside moldings.*	538	625
1SC	**Preferred Equipment Group 1SC (SLE)** *Includes vehicle with standard equipment.*	NC	NC
1SD	**Preferred Equipment Group 1SD (SLE 2WD)** *Includes SLT Decor Group: 6-way power driver's/passenger's seats, electrochromic inside rearview mirror, 8 point compass, polished cast aluminum wheels and HD suspension package.*	1557	1810
1SD	**Preferred Equipment Group 1SD (SLE 4WD)** *Includes SLT Decor Group: 6-way power driver's/passenger's seats, electrochromic inside rearview mirror, 8 point compass, polished cast aluminum wheels, HD suspension package and autotrac active transfer case.*	1879	2185
A28	**Sliding Rear Window** *NOT AVAILABLE with C49.*	108	125
A95	**High Back Reclining Bucket Seats (Reg Cab)** *Includes inboard armrests, manual driver/passenger lumbar, overhead console, adjustable headrests and seatback storage pockets and floor console.*	258	300
A95	**High Back Reclining Bucket Seats (X-Cab)** *Includes inboard armrests, manual driver/passenger lumbar, overhead console, adjustable headrests, seatback storage pockets and forward-folding driver seat and floor console.*	323	375
A95	**High Back Reclining Bucket Seats (SLE X-Cab)** *Includes inboard armrests, manual driver/passenger lumbar, overhead console, adjustable headrests and seatback storage pockets and floor console. REQUIRES 1SD.*	232	270
AJ1	**Deep Tinted Solar Ray Glass (X-Cab)**	92	107
AJ1	**Deep Tinted Solar Ray Glass (Reg Cab)** *REQUIRES A28 or C49.*	43	50
AU3	**Power Door Locks (SL)** *REQUIRES R6R or R6S.*	139	162
C49	**Electric Rear Window Defogger** *REQUIRES C60. NOT AVAILABLE with A28.*	153	175
C60	**Air Conditioning (SL)** *Includes micron air filtration.*	722	825
DD7	**Electrochromic Inside Rearview Mirror (SLE)** *Includes 8 point compass.*	125	145
DF2	**Camper Type Mirrors (SL)** *Retractable with wide field of vision. Shipped loose for dealer installation.*	52	60
DF2	**Camper Type Mirrors (SLE)** *Retractable with wide field of vision. Shipped loose for dealer installation. REQUIRES YE9 or R9L. NOT AVAILABLE with DL8.*	(33)	(38)
DL8	**Power Heated/Electrochromic Fold-Away Mirrors (SLE)** *REQUIRES C49. NOT AVAILABLE with DF2.*	36	42
G80	**Locking Differential** *Includes premium carbon fiber friction plates. REQUIRES GT4 or GU6.*	249	285

CODE	DESCRIPTION	INVOICE	MSRP
GT4	3.73 Axle Ratio (2WD)	NC	NC
GT5	4.10 Axle Ratio (4WD) *REQUIRES LM7 or LR4.*	NC	NC
GU6	3.42 Axle Ratio (Reg Cab) *NOT AVAILABLE with LM7.*	NC	NC
K05	Engine Block Heater	30	35
K34	Cruise Control (SL) *REQUIRES R6R or R6S.*	206	240
K47	High Capacity Air Cleaner	22	25
KNP	HD Auxiliary Transmission Cooler *REQUIRES M30.*	82	95
LM7	Engine: Vortec 5300 SFI V8 (X-Cab)	602	700
LM7	Engine: Vortec 5300 SFI V8 (Reg Cab) *REQUIRES M30 and GT4 or M30.*	1114	1295
LR4	Engine: Vortec 4800 SFI V8 (Reg Cab) *REQUIRES GT4.*	512	595
M30	Transmission: 4-Speed Automatic with OD (Reg Cab) *Includes tow/haul mode selector and transmission oil cooler.*	856	995
NP8	Autotrac Active Transfer Case (SLE 4WD)	323	375
NZZ	Skid Plate Package (4WD) *Includes front differential and transfer case shields.*	82	95
PF4	Wheels: Bright Machined Cast Aluminum (SLE) *NOT AVAILABLE with QC3.*	77	90
PF9	Wheels: Argent-Painted Cast Aluminum (SL) *Includes non-matching spare wheel . NOT AVAILABLE with PY2.*	267	310
PY2	Wheels: Chrome-Plated Steel (SL) *Includes chrome center cap.*	267	310
PY2	Wheels: Chrome-Plated Steel (SL) *Includes chrome center cap. REQUIRES 1SB. NOT AVAILABLE with PF9, 1SA.*	NC	NC
QBN	Tires: LT245/75R16C On/Off Road BSW (4WD) *REQUIRES Z85 or Z71. NOT AVAILABLE with Z83.*	138	161
QBX	Tires: LT245/75R16C On/Off Road OWL (4WD) *REQUIRES Z85 or Z71. NOT AVAILABLE with Z83.*	245	286
QC3	Wheels: Polished Cast Aluminum (SLE) *NOT AVAILABLE with PF4.*	77	90
QCC	Tires: P255/70R16 AS BSW (2WD) *REQUIRES Z85 or ZX3. NOT AVAILABLE with Z83.*	146	170
QCJ	Tires: P255/70R16 AS WOL (2WD) *REQUIRES Z85 or ZX3. NOT AVAILABLE with Z83.*	254	295
QGA	Tires: P245/75R16 BSW AT (4WD) *NOT AVAILABLE with Z71.*	90	105
QGB	Tires: P245/75R16 AT WOL (4WD) *NOT AVAILABLE with Z71.*	198	230
QGC	Tires: P265/75R16 AT BSW (4WD) *REQUIRES (Z85 and PF9) or Z71. NOT AVAILABLE with Z83.*	206	240

CODE	DESCRIPTION	INVOICE	MSRP
QGD	Tires: P265/75R16 AT WOL (4WD) *REQUIRES (Z85 and PF9) or Z71 or Z85 and (QC3 or PF4). NOT AVAILABLE with Z83.*	314	365
QNG	Tires: P235/75R16 AS WOL (SLE 2WD) *REQUIRES 1SC. NOT AVAILABLE with Z85, Z82, ZX3.*	108	125
QNL	Tires: P245/75R16 AS OWL (4WD) *NOT AVAILABLE with Z71.*	108	125
R6R	Commercial Group (Reg Cab) *Includes 40/20/40 seats and transmission oil cooler. NOT AVAILABLE with ~~2.*	808	940
R6R	Commercial Group (Reg Cab) *Includes 40/20/40 seats and transmission oil cooler. REQUIRES ~~V.*	566	658
R6R	Commercial Group (X-Cab) *Includes 40/20/40 seats and vinyl floor covering. REQUIRES ~~V.*	(320)	(372)
R6R	Commercial Group (X-Cab) *Includes 40/20/40 seats and vinyl floor covering. NOT AVAILABLE with ~~2.*	(77)	(90)
R6S	Convenience Group (Reg Cab) *Includes cruise control, ETR AM/FM stereo with cassette, power door locks and air conditioning. REQUIRES 1SB. NOT AVAILABLE with 1SA.*	1222	1397
R6S	Convenience Group (X-Cab) *Includes cruise control, ETR AM/FM stereo with cassette, power door locks and air conditioning. REQUIRES 1SB. NOT AVAILABLE with 1SA.*	1205	1377
R6T	Convenience Plus Group (SLE 2WD) *Includes 6-way power driver's/passenger's seats, electrochromic inside rearview mirror and 8 point compass. REQUIRES 1SC.*	538	625
R6T	Convenience Plus Group (SLE 4WD) *Includes 6-way power driver's/passenger's seats, electrochromic inside rearview mirror, 8 point compass and Autotrac active transfer case. REQUIRES 1SC.*	860	1000
R6U	Comfort Group (SLE) *Includes high-back reclining heated bucket seats and floor console. REQUIRES 1SD.*	678	775
T96	Fog Lamps (SLE) *REQUIRES LM7 or LR4.*	120	140
UL5	Radio Delete (SL) *Includes stowage tray. Base speaker system and antenna remain. NOT AVAILABLE with UM6.*	(215)	(250)
UM6	Radio: AM/FM Stereo with Cassette (Reg Cab) *Includes digital clock and 4 speakers. NOT AVAILABLE with UL5.*	146	170
UM6	Radio: AM/FM Stereo with Cassette (X-Cab) *Includes digital clock. NOT AVAILABLE with UL5.*	129	150
UP0	Radio: AM/FM Stereo with CD and Cassette (SLE) *Includes digital clock, automatic tone control, search and repeat, theft lock, speed compensated volume and enhanced performance speaker system. REQUIRES R6U.*	86	100
UV8	Cellular Phone Provisions *Includes wiring for remote mircrophone and cellular phone.*	43	50
UY2	Camper and Fifth Wheel Wiring Provisions *Includes 8-lead trailering wire harness. REQUIRES (LM7 or LR4) and M30 and Z82.*	22	25

CODE	DESCRIPTION	INVOICE	MSRP
VB3	**Chromed Rear Step Bumper with Step Pad (SL)** *NOT AVAILABLE with VF7.*	86	100
VF7	**Rear Bumper Delete (SLE)** *Vehicles registered in certain states must have a rear bumper to be operated on their roads. Consult your local laws. Deletes standard bumper and locking system for spare tire. NOT AVAILABLE with Z82.*	(172)	(200)
VF7	**Rear Bumper Delete (SL)** *Vehicles registered in certain states must have a rear bumper to be operated on their roads. Consult your local laws. Deletes standard bumper and locking system for spare tire. NOT AVAILABLE with Z82, VB3.*	(86)	(100)
VYU	**Snow Plow Prep Package (4WD SB)** *Includes 10-amp power for rear backup light/roof-mounted emergency light, high airflow front bumper, forward lamp wiring harness, access hold with grommet, mounting location for snow plow controls and 130-amp alternator. REQUIRES MG5 or Z82.*	163	190
VYU	**Snow Plow Prep Package (4WD SB)** *Includes 10-amp power for rear backup light/roof-mounted emergency light, high airflow front bumper, forward lamp wiring harness, access hold with grommet, mounting location for snow plow controls, 130-amp alternator and HD auxiliary transmission cooler. REQUIRES M30.*	245	285
Z71	**Off-Road Package (SLE 4WD Reg Cab)** *Includes high pressure 46mm Monroe gas shocks, off-road jounce bumpers, stabilizer bars and high capacity air cleaner. REQUIRES LM7 or LR4. NOT AVAILABLE with QGA, QGB, QNL, Z85.*	302	345
Z71	**Off-Road Package (SLE 4WD X-Cab)** *Includes high pressure 46mm Monroe gas shocks, off-road jounce bumpers, stabilizer bars and high capacity air cleaner. REQUIRES 1SD. NOT AVAILABLE with QGA, QGB, QNL, Z85.*	172	200
Z82	**HD Trailering Special Equipment** *Includes 8-lead trailering wire harness and HD auxiliary transmission cooler. REQUIRES M30. NOT AVAILABLE with VF7, QNG, Z83.*	245	285
Z83	**Smooth Ride Suspension Package (SLE)** *Includes twintube 32mm shocks. REQUIRES 1SD. NOT AVAILABLE with QCC, QCJ, Z82, QBN, QBX, QGC, QGD.*	NC	NC
Z85	**HD Suspension Package** *Includes monotube Monroe 36mm shocks. NOT AVAILABLE with QNG, ZX3, Z71.*	82	95
ZX3	**Ride Control (SLE 2WD)** *Includes DeCarbon 46mm shocks and 2-position electronic control for shock setting (solid/smooth or handling/trailering). REQUIRES 1SD. NOT AVAILABLE with Z85.*	280	325
ZX3	**Ride Control (SLE 2WD)** *Includes DeCarbon 46mm shocks and 2-position electronic control for shock setting (solid/smooth or handling/trailering). REQUIRES LM7 or LR4. NOT AVAILABLE with QNG, Z85.*	361	420
ZY2	**Two Tone Paint Application (SLE)**	197	225

1999 SIERRA 2500

Safety Data

Side Airbag: *Not Available*
4-Wheel ABS: *Standard*
Driver Crash Test Grade: *Not Available*
Side Impact Crash Test Front: *Not Available*
Crash Offset: *Not Available*
Integrated Child Seat(s): *Not Available*
Traction Control: *Not Available*
Passenger Crash Test Grade: *Not Available*
Side Impact Crash Test Rear: *Not Available*

Standard Equipment

SL 2WD REGULAR CAB LB HD (5M): 6.0L V8 OHV SMPI 16-valve engine; 5-speed overdrive manual transmission; 600-amp HD battery with run down protection; engine oil cooler; 105-amp alternator; rear wheel drive, 3.73 axle ratio; stainless steel exhaust; front independent suspension with anti-roll bar, front coil springs, rigid rear axle suspension with rear leaf springs; power re-circulating ball steering with vehicle speed-sensing assist; 4 wheel disc brakes with 4 wheel antilock braking system; 34 gal capacity fuel tank; trailer harness; front and rear black rub strips, front chrome bumper, rear argent bumper, rear tow hooks, rear step; monotone paint; aero-composite halogen auto on headlamps with daytime running lights; additional exterior lights include center high mounted stop light, pickup cargo box light, underhood light; driver's and passenger's manual black folding outside mirrors; front and rear 16" x 6.5" silver styled steel wheels; LT245/75SR16 BSW AS front and rear tires; underbody mounted full-size conventional steel spare wheel; AM/FM stereo with clock, seek-scan, 2 speakers, and fixed antenna; 3 power accessory outlets, retained accessory power; instrumentation display includes tachometer, oil pressure gauge, water temp gauge, volt gauge, trip odometer; warning indicators include oil pressure, water temp, battery, low oil level, low coolant, lights on, key in ignition, low fuel, low washer fluid, door ajar, service interval; driver's side airbag, passenger's side cancelable airbag; ignition disable; tinted windows; variable intermittent front windshield wipers; seating capacity of 3, 40-20-40 split-bench front seat with adjustable headrests, center armrest with storage, driver's seat includes 4-way direction control with lumbar support, passenger's seat includes 4-way direction control with lumbar support; premium cloth seats, full cloth headliner, full carpet floor covering with rubber floor mats, cabback insulator; interior lights include dome light, front reading lights, illuminated entry; sport steering wheel with tilt adjustment; passenger's side vanity mirror; day-night rearview mirror; glove box with light, front cupholder, 2 seat back storage pockets, driver's and passenger's door bins; black grille, black side window moldings, black front windshield molding, black rear window molding and black door handles.

SL 2WD REGULAR CAB LB LD (4A) (in addition to or instead of SL 2WD REGULAR CAB LB HD (5M) equipment): 5.3L V8 OHV SMPI 16-valve engine; 4-speed electronic overdrive automatic transmission with lock-up and transmission oil cooler.

SL 2WD EXTENDED CAB SB HD (4A) (in addition to or instead of SL 2WD REGULAR CAB LB HD (5M) equipment): Four-speed electronic overdrive automatic transmission with lock-up; HD transmission oil cooler; 3.42 axle ratio; 26 gal capacity fuel tank; rear heat ducts; AM/FM stereo with clock, seek-scan, 4 speakers, and fixed antenna; vented rear windows; seating capacity of 6, 40-20-40 split-bench front seat with adjustable headrests and full folding rear bench seat with adjustable headrests.

SL 2WD EXTENDED CAB LB HD (4A) (in addition to or instead of SL 2WD EXTENDED CAB SB HD (4A) equipment): 3.73 axle ratio and chrome bodyside molding.

SLE 2WD REGULAR CAB LB HD (5M) (in addition to or instead of SL 2WD REGULAR CAB LB HD (5M) equipment): Front chrome bumper with body-colored rub strip, rear chrome bumper with black rub strip; chrome bodyside molding; driver's and passenger's power remote black folding outside mirrors; air conditioning, air filter; AM/FM stereo with clock, seek-scan, single CD, 6 performance speakers, automatic equalizer, theft deterrent, and fixed antenna; cruise control; power door locks with

2 stage unlock, remote keyless entry; ignition disable, panic alarm, security system; power front windows with driver's 1-touch down; cloth door trim insert; interior lights include 2 door curb lights; leather-wrapped sport steering wheel with tilt adjustment and chrome grille.

SLE 2WD REGULAR CAB LB LD (4A) (in addition to or instead of SLE 2WD REGULAR CAB LB HD (5M) equipment): 5.3L V8 OHV SMPI 16-valve engine; 4-speed electronic overdrive automatic transmission with lock-up and transmission oil cooler.

SLE 2WD EXTENDED CAB SB HD (4A) (in addition to or instead of SLE 2WD REGULAR CAB LB LD (5M) equipment): Four-speed electronic overdrive automatic transmission with lock-up; HD transmission oil cooler; 3.42 axle ratio; 26 gal capacity fuel tank; rear heat ducts; vented rear windows; seating capacity of 6, 40-20-40 split-bench front seat with adjustable headrests; full folding rear bench seat with adjustable headrests; mini overhead console with storage and front and rear cupholders.

SLE 2WD EXTENDED CAB LB HD (4A) (in addition to or instead of SLE 2WD EXTENDED CAB SB HD (4A) equipment): 3.73 axle ratio and colored bodyside moldings.

SL 4WD REGULAR CAB LB HD (5M) (in addition to or instead of SL 2WD REGULAR CAB LB HD (5M) equipment): Part-time 4 wheel drive, auto locking hub control with manual shift; front independent torsion suspension with anti-roll bar, front torsion springs, front torsion bar and black fender flares.

SL 4WD EXTENDED CAB SB/LB HD (4A) (in addition to or instead of SL 2WD EXTENDED CAB SB/LB HD (4A) equipment): Part-time 4 wheel drive, auto locking hub control with manual shift; front independent torsion suspension with anti-roll bar, front torsion springs, front torsion bar and black fender flares.

SLE 4WD REGULAR CAB LB HD (5M) (in addition to or instead of SLE 2WD REGULAR CAB LB HD (5M) equipment): Part-time 4 wheel drive, auto locking hub control with manual shift; front independent torsion suspension with anti-roll bar, front torsion springs, front torsion bar and black fender flares.

SLE 4WD EXTENDED CAB SB/LB HD (4A) (in addition to or instead of SLE 2WD EXTENDED CAB SB/LB HD (4A) equipment): Part-time 4 wheel drive, auto locking hub control with manual shift; front independent torsion suspension with anti-roll bar, front torsion springs, front torsion bar and black fender flares.

Base Prices

Code	Description	Invoice	MSRP
TC25903	SL 2WD Regular Cab LB LD (4A)	18162	20756
TC25903-C6P-R9S	SL 2WD Regular Cab LB HD (5M)	18029	20605
TC25753-R9S	SL 2WD Extended Cab SB HD (4A)	20419	23336
TC25953-R9S	SL 2WD Extended Cab LB HD (4A)	21420	24480
TK25903-R9S	SL 4WD Regular Cab LB HD	20709	23667
TK25753-R9S	SL 4WD Extended Cab SB HD (4A)	23837	27242
TK25953-R9S	SL 4WD Extended Cab LB HD (4A)	24099	27542
TC25903-YE9	SLE 2WD Regular Cab LB LD (4A)	20159	23039
TC25903-C6P-YE9	SLE 2WD Regular Cab LB HD (5M)	20027	22888
TC25753-YE9	SLE 2WD Extended Cab SB HD (4A)	22386	25584
TC25953-YE9	SLE 2WD Extended Cab LB HD (4A)	23387	26728
TK25903-YE9	SLE 4WD Regular Cab LB HD (4A)	22706	25950

SIERRA 2500 GMC

CODE	DESCRIPTION	INVOICE	MSRP
TK25753-YE9	SLE 4WD Extended Cab SB HD (4A)	25804	29490
TK25953-YE9	SLE 4WD Extended Cab LB HD (4A)	26066	29790
Destination Charge:		640	640

Accessories

CODE	DESCRIPTION	INVOICE	MSRP
~~V	Vinyl Seat Trim (SL) *NOT AVAILABLE with R6R.*	NC	NC
1SA	Preferred Equipment Group 1SA (SL) *Includes SL decor package. NOT AVAILABLE with PY2, R6S.*	NC	NC
1SB	Preferred Equipment Group 1SB (SL) *Includes SL decor package, 16" x 7" argent painted wheels, chrome center caps, chrome grille surround, chromed rear step bumper with step pad and exterior moldings.*	323	375
1SC	Preferred Equipment Group 1SC (SLE) *Includes SLE Decor package standard equipment.*	NC	NC
1SD	Preferred Equipment Group 1SD (SLE 2WD X-Cab) *Includes SLT Decor package: ultrasoft leather seat trim, chrome-plated steel wheels, ETR AM/FM stereo with CD and seek-scan, 40/20/40 reclining split bench seat, 6-way power driver's/passenger's seats, electrochromic mirror, 8 point auto calibrating compass, firm ride suspension and active transfer case.*	1479	1720
1SD	Preferred Equipment Group 1SD (SLE 4WD X-Cab) *Includes SLT Decor package: ultrasoft leather seat trim, chrome-plated steel wheels, ETR AM/FM stereo with CD and seek-scan, 40/20/40 reclining split bench seat, 6-way power driver's/passenger's seats, electrochromic mirror, 8 point auto calibrating compass, firm ride suspension and active transfer case.*	1802	2095
A28	Sliding Rear Window *NOT AVAILABLE with C49.*	108	125
A95	Front Reclining Bucket Seats (SLE Reg Cab) *Includes inboard armrests, dual adjustable headrests, manual lumbar and storage pockets behind seats and floor console. NOT AVAILABLE with R6U or 1SD.*	258	300
A95	Front Reclining Bucket Seats (SLE X-Cab) *Includes inboard armrests, dual adjustable headrests, manual lumbar, storage pockets behind seats and forward falling seat and floor console. NOT AVAILABLE with R6U or 1SD.*	323	375
AG2	6-Way Power Driver's/Passenger's Seats (X-Cab)	413	480
AJ1	Deep Tinted Glass (X-Cab) *Includes tinted rear and rear quarter windows. Includes light tinted rear window with (C49) Electric Rear Window Defogger.*	92	107
AJ1	Deep Tinted Glass (Reg Cab) *Includes rear window tint only. Includes light tinted rear window with (C49) Electric Rear Window Defogger. REQUIRES A28 or C49.*	43	50
AU3	Power Door Locks (SL) *REQUIRES R6R or R6S.*	139	162
C49	Electric Rear Window Defogger *REQUIRES C60. NOT AVAILABLE with A28.*	151	175

CODE	DESCRIPTION	INVOICE	MSRP
C60	**Air Conditioning (SL)** *Includes micron air filtration.*	710	825
DD7	**Electrochromic Mirror (SLE)** *Includes auto-dimming rear view mirror and 8 point auto calibrating compass. REQUIRES 1SD.*	125	145
DF2	**Camper Type Extendable Mirrors (SLE)** *Includes manually controlled 7.5"H x 10.5"W black mirrors with adjustable arm feature to provide field of vision for vehicles to 96" wide. Dual segment mirror on driver's side provides enhanced wide angle capacity. NOT AVAILABLE with DL8. REQUIRES 1SC or 1SD.*	(33)	(38)
DF2	**Camper Type Extendable Mirrors (SL)** *Includes manually controlled 7.5"H x 10.5"W black mirrors with adjustable arm feature to provide field of vision for vehicles to 96" wide. Dual segment mirror on driver's side provides enhanced wide angle capacity.*	52	60
DL8	**Power Heated External Mirrors with Chrome Cap** *REQUIRES C49. NOT AVAILABLE with DF2.*	36	42
G80	**Locking Differential** *Includes premium carbon fiber friction plates. REQUIRES GT4 or GT5.*	245	285
GT4	**3.73 Axle Ratio** *Includes air-to-oil cooler. NOT AVAILABLE with GT5.*	NC	NC
GT5	**4.10 Axle Ratio** *REQUIRES LQ4. NOT AVAILABLE with GT4.*	NC	NC
K05	**Engine Block Heater**	30	35
K34	**Cruise Control (SL)** *REQUIRES R6R or R6S.*	206	240
K47	**High Capacity Air Cleaner**	22	25
KC4	**Engine Oil Cooling (4WD)** *REQUIRES LQ4.*	116	135
KNP	**HD Auxiliary Transmission Cooler** *NOT AVAILABLE with MW3.*	82	95
LQ4	**Engine: Vortec 6000 V8 SFI (2WD - LD Reg Cab/SB X-Cab)** *Includes high capacity air cleaner. REQUIRES MT1 or MW3. NOT AVAILABLE with Z82.*	430	500
MT1	**Transmission: 4-Speed Automatic with Overdrive (HD Reg Cab)** *Includes electronic control, tow/haul mode selector, transmission temperature gauge and HD auxiliary transmission cooler.*	856	995
MT1	**Transmission: 4-Speed Automatic with Overdrive (All Except HD Reg Cab)** *Includes electronic control, tow/haul mode selector, transmission temperature gauge and HD auxiliary transmission cooler.*	NC	NC
MW3	**Transmission: 5-Speed Manual (All Except HD Reg Cab)** *NOT AVAILABLE with KNP, NP8, UPO.*	(856)	(995)
NP8	**Active Transfer Case (SLE 4WD)** *REQUIRES MT1. NOT AVAILABLE with MW3.*	323	375
NZZ	**Off-Road Skid Plates (4WD)** *Includes differential and transfer case shields.*	82	95
P03	**Chrome Center Caps (SL)**	52	60

CODE	DESCRIPTION	INVOICE	MSRP
PY0	Wheels: Forged Polished Aluminum *Includes non-matching spare wheel.*	77	90
PY2	Wheels: Chrome-Plated Steel (4) (SL) *REQUIRES 1SB. NOT AVAILABLE with 1SA.*	267	310
QIW	Tires: LT245/75R16E AT BSW (4WD HD)	47	55
QIW	Tires: LT245/75R16E AT BSW (LD) *NOT AVAILABLE with QIZ.*	241	280
QIZ	Tires: LT245/75R16E AS BSW (LD) *NOT AVAILABLE with QIW.*	194	225
R6R	Commercial Group (Reg Cab) *Includes 40/20/40 seats and vinyl floor covering. NOT AVAILABLE with ~~V.*	(47)	(55)
R6R	Commercial Group (X-Cab) *Includes vinyl 40/20/40 seats with fixed center seat section. Deletes the following: standard seat recliners, lumbar support, adjustable head restraints, center fold-down armrest, full floor carpeting and seatback storage pockets.*	(319)	(372)
R6R	Commercial Group (X-Cab) *Includes 40/20/40 seats and vinyl floor covering. NOT AVAILABLE with ~~V.*	(77)	(90)
R6R	Commercial Group (Reg Cab) *Includes vinyl 40/20/40 seats with fixed center seat section. Deletes the following: standard seat recliners, lumbar support, adjustable head restraints, center fold-down armrest, full floor carpeting and seatback storage pockets.*	(290)	(337)
R6S	Convenience Group (Reg Cab) *Includes cruise control, ETR AM/FM stereo with cassette and seek-scan, power door locks and air conditioning. REQUIRES 1SB.*	1201	1397
R6S	Convenience Group (X-Cab) *Includes cruise control, ETR AM/FM stereo with cassette and seek-scan, power door locks and air conditioning. REQUIRES 1SB. NOT AVAILABLE with 1SA.*	1201	1397
R6T	Convenience Plus Group (2WD) *Includes 6-way power driver's/passenger's seats, electrochromic mirror and 8 point auto calibrating compass.*	538	625
R6T	Convenience Plus Group (4WD) *Includes 6-way power driver's/passenger's seats, electrochromic mirror, 8 point auto calibrating compass and active transfer case.*	860	1000
R6U	Comfort Group (SLE X-Cab) *Includes full feature high back bucket seats, floor console, overhead console and 6-way power driver's/passenger's seats. REQUIRES 1SD. NOT AVAILABLE with A95.*	683	775
T96	Front Fog Lamps (SLE)	120	140
TP2	600 CCA Auxiliary HD Battery	116	135
UL5	Radio Delete (SL) *Includes front fender hole plugs and instrument panel storage bin. NOT AVAILABLE with UM6.*	(215)	(250)
UM6	Radio: AM/FM Stereo with Cassette (Reg Cab) *Includes digital clock and 4 speakers. NOT AVAILABLE with UL5.*	146	170
UM6	Radio: AM/FM Stereo with Cassette (X-Cab) *Includes digital clock and 4 speakers. NOT AVAILABLE with UL5.*	129	150

CODE	DESCRIPTION	INVOICE	MSRP
UP0	**Radio: AM/FM Stereo with CD and Cassette (SL)** *Includes digital clock, automatic tone control, selective tone control, search and repeat, theft lock, speed sensitive volume, auto reverse and music search cassette player with enhanced performance 6 speaker system. REQUIRES A95 or R6U. NOT AVAILABLE with MW3.*	86	100
UV8	**Cellular Phone Provisions** *Includes wiring for remote microphone jumper harness and cellular phone jumper harness.*	43	50
UY2	**Camper and Fifth Wheel Wiring Provisions** *Provides an additional 8-wire harness with 7-pin connector and separate CHMSL connector located at rear and tied to vehicle frame. REQUIRES Z82. NOT AVAILABLE with VF7, VYU.*	22	25
VB3	**Chromed Rear Step Bumper with Step Pad (SL)** *Includes rub strip. NOT AVAILABLE with VF7.*	86	100
VF7	**Rear Bumper Delete (SLE)** *Vehicles registered in certain states must have a rear bumper to be operated on their roads. Consult your local laws. NOT AVAILABLE with Z82, VYU, UY2.*	(172)	(200)
VF7	**Rear Bumper Delete (SL)** *Vehicles registered in certain states must have a rear bumper to be operated on their roads. Consult your local laws. NOT AVAILABLE with Z82, VB3, VYU, UY2.*	(86)	(100)
VYU	**Snow Plow Prep Package (4WD)** *Includes 10-amp power for rear backup light/roof-mounted emergency light, high airflow front bumper, forward lamp wiring harness, access hole with grommet and mounting location for snow plow controls and 130-amp alternator. REQUIRES Z82. NOT AVAILABLE with VF7.*	163	190
VYU	**Snow Plow Prep Package (4WD)** *Includes 10-amp power for rear backup light/roof-mounted emergency light, high airflow front bumper, forward lamp wiring harness, access hole with grommet and mounting location for snow plow controls, 130-amp alternator and engine oil cooling. NOT AVAILABLE with Z82, UY2.*	280	325
Z82	**HD Trailering Special Equipment (2WD - LD Reg Cab/X-Cab SB)** *Includes an electric trailer brake wire harness with mounting provisions, an 8-wire harness with fully independent with fused trailering circuits with 7-way sealed connector, IP jumper wiring harness for electric trailer brake controller (shipped loose) and a 1-way sealed connector for the CHMSL and trailer hitch platform. NOT AVAILABLE with VF7, LQ4.*	245	285
Z82	**HD Trailering Special Equipment (All Except 2WD - LD Reg Cab/X-Cab SB)** *Includes an electric trailer brake wire harness with mounting provisions, an 8-wire harness with fully independent with fused trailering circuits with 7-way sealed connector, IP jumper wiring harness for electric trailer brake controller (shipped loose) and a 1-way sealed connector for the CHMSL and engine oil cooling. NOT AVAILABLE with VF7, VYU.*	280	325
Z85	**Firm Ride Suspension** *Includes monotube 36mm shocks. REQUIRES QIW or QIZ.*	82	95
ZY2	**Two Tone Paint Application (SLE)**	194	225

1999 SIERRA CLASSIC

1999 GMC Sierra Classic

What's New?

Mechanical upgrades include new internal components and seals for automatic transmissions, improved cooling system and starter motor durability, and three new exterior paint colors. With an all-new Sierra in showrooms, changes to this outgoing model are limited to a few new colors.

Review

After a power infusion last year to the entire lineup of GMC truck engines, the Sierra becomes the Sierra Classic to distinguish the old model from the all-new Sierra in showrooms this model year.

Every Sierra Classic gasoline engine benefits from Vortec technology, which provides healthy power and torque ratings. For example, the standard 5000 V8 makes an ample 230 horsepower, but the optional 5700 V8 is a more satisfying powerplant. Also available is a big block 7400 V8, and regular- and heavy-duty turbo diesels sporting 6.5 liters of displacement. Power speaks volumes in the pickup truck market, and having competitive horsepower numbers goes a long way toward selling the consumer on these aging pickups. All Sierra Classics come standard with four-wheel antilock brakes.

Creature comforts aren't forgotten in the Sierra Classic. Manufacturers have been constantly trying to make their trucks more car-like, so GM has made rear-seat heating ducts standard on the extended cab. Shoulder belts are height-adjustable to fit a variety of physiques, and upholstery choices include leather. Heck, you'd hardly know this was a truck, especially with the passenger car tires that give some versions of the Sierra Classic a nicer ride and quieter driving environment.

While the side access panel option available on some 1500-series extended cab Sierra Classics makes loading cargo into the rear of the cab much easier, there is no four-door extended cab model like those Ford and Dodge offer for '99.

Improvements for 1999 are limited to some mechanical upgrades and a few new exterior colors. An all-new Sierra hit the showrooms in late-1998 as a 1999 model, so revisions this year on the previous-generation truck are understandably minimal.

Although Chevrolet's own C/K Series garners the greatest amount of publicity, GMC's equivalents are pretty strong sellers themselves. Sierras, in fact, account for close to half of GMC output. Americans continue to clamor for burly pickups, whether for their macho image or for real down-and-dirty work.

Whether you choose a light-duty two-wheel-drive (C1500) or the massive four-wheel-drive K3500 on a 155.5-inch wheelbase, GMC gives both Chevrolet and its Ford/Dodge rivals a "Classic" run for their money.

1999 SIERRA CLASSIC 1500

Safety Data

Side Airbag: *Not Available*
4-Wheel ABS: *Standard*
Driver Crash Test Grade: *Good*
Side Impact Crash Test Front: *Not Available*
Crash Offset: *Not Available*
Integrated Child Seat(s): *Not Available*
Traction Control: *Not Available*
Passenger Crash Test Grade: *Average*
Side Impact Crash Test Rear: *Not Available*

Standard Equipment

C1500 SLE EXTENDED CAB SHORTBED: 5.0L V8 OHV SMPI 16-valve engine; 4-speed electronic overdrive automatic transmission with lock-up; 600-amp HD battery; 100-amp alternator; rear wheel drive, 3.42 axle ratio; stainless steel exhaust; front independent suspension with anti-roll bar, front coil springs, rigid rear axle suspension with rear leaf springs; power re-circulating ball steering with engine speed-sensing assist; front disc/rear drum brakes with 4 wheel antilock braking system; 25 gal capacity fuel tank; 3rd door access; trailer harness; regular pickup box; front and rear chrome bumpers with black rub strip, front chrome bumper insert, rear step; black bodyside molding with chrome bodyside insert, chrome wheel well molding; monotone paint; aero-composite halogen headlamps with daytime running lights; additional exterior lights include center high mounted stop light, pickup cargo box light, underhood light; driver and passenger power remote black folding outside mirrors; front and rear 15" x 7" painted styled steel wheels with hub wheel covers and trim rings; P235/75SR15 BSW AS front and rear tires; underbody mounted full-size conventional steel spare wheel; air conditioning; AM/FM stereo with clock, seek-scan, cassette, 4 speakers, and fixed antenna; cruise control; power door locks; 3 power accessory outlets; instrumentation display includes tachometer, oil pressure gauge, water temp gauge, volt gauge, trip odometer; warning indicators include battery, lights on, key in ignition, door ajar; driver's side airbag, passenger's side cancellable airbag; ignition disable; tinted windows, power front windows with driver 1-touch down, vented rear windows; variable intermittent front windshield wipers; seating capacity of 6, 60-40 split-bench front seat with adjustable headrests, center armrest with storage, driver's seat includes 4-way direction control with power lumbar support and easy entry, passenger's seat includes 4-way direction control with power lumbar support and easy entry; full folding rear bench seat with adjustable rear headrest; front height adjustable seatbelts; premium cloth seats, cloth door trim insert, full cloth headliner, full carpet floor covering with rubber floor mats, cabback insulator; interior lights include dome light, front reading lights, 2 door curb lights; leather-wrapped sport steering wheel with tilt adjustment; passenger side vanity mirror; day-night rearview mirror; glove box with light, front cupholder, 2 seat back storage pockets, driver and passenger door bins; chrome grille, black side window moldings, black front windshield molding, black rear window molding and black door handles.

K1500 SLE EXTENDED CAB SHORTBED (in addition to or instead of C1500 SLE EXTENDED CAB SHORTBED equipment): Part-time 4 wheel drive, auto locking hub control and manual shift, 3.42 axle ratio; front independent torsion suspension with anti-roll bar, front torsion springs, front torsion bar, rigid rear axle suspension with rear leaf springs; front and rear chrome bumpers with black rub strip, front chrome bumper insert, rear tow hooks, rear step bumper; front and rear 16" x 6.5" painted styled steel wheels with hub wheel covers and trim rings.

CODE	DESCRIPTION	INVOICE	MSRP

Base Prices

TC10753-YE9	C1500 SLE X-Cab Shortbed (4A)	19946	22796
TK10753-YE9	K1500 SLE X-Cab Shortbed (4A)	22703	25946
Destination Charge:		625	625

Accessories

CODE	DESCRIPTION	INVOICE	MSRP
1SC	Marketing Option Package 1SC *Includes vehicle with standard equipment.*	NC	NC
1SG	Image Package 1SG *Includes 3.42 axle ratio, engine oil cooler, AM/FM stereo with seek, scan, automatic tone control, CD and cassette; electrochromic mirror with 8 point compass, reclining high back bucket seats, floor console, overhead console, 6-way power driver's seat, remote keyless entry and deep tinted solar ray glass.*	1442	1677
1SH	Trailering Package 1SH *Includes HD trailering equipment: trailer hitch platform, HD front and rear shock absorbers, 3.73 axle ratio: water to oil cooler, locking differential, AM/FM stereo with seek, scan, automatic tone control, cassette, 6-way power driver's seat, remote keyless entry and deep tinted solar ray glass.*	1305	1518
1SK	Off-Road Package 1SK (K1500 X-cab) *Includes GVWR: 6,600 lbs, On/Off Road Chassis equipment: off-road skid plates, 46 mm Bilstein shocks, HD chassis equipment, 3.42 axle ratio, locking differential, high capacity air cleaner, engine oil cooler, 16" x 7" aluminum wheels, AM/FM stereo with seek, scan, automatic tone control and cassette; sliding rear window and deep tinted solar ray glass.*	1345	1564
A28	Sliding Rear Window	99	115
A95	Reclining High Back Bucket Seats *Includes inboard armrests, dual adjustable headrests, power lumbars, storage pockets behind seats and easy entry feature, floor console and overhead console.*	232	270
AE7	60/40 Reclining Split-Bench Seat *Includes easy entry feature and center fold down storage armrest with coin holder, map strap, writing board, power lumbars and storage pockets behind seats. REQUIRES (1SG) Image Package 1SG.*	NC	NC
AG9	6-Way Power Driver's Seat	206	240
AJ1	Deep Tinted Solar Ray Glass *Excludes tinted glass on windshield, driver and passenger windows. Includes light tinted rear window. REQUIRES (C49).*	62	72
AJ1	Deep Tinted Solar Ray Glass *Excludes tinted glass on windshield, driver and passenger windows.*	92	107
AU0	Remote Keyless Entry *Includes 2 transmitters.*	129	150
BZY	Bedliner	194	225
C49	Electric Rear Window Defogger	132	154
C5S	GVWR: 6,600 Lbs (K1500 X-cab) *REQUIRES (F44) HD chassis equipment.*	NC	NC
DD7	Electrochromic Mirror *Includes light-sensitive rearview mirror and 8 point compass.*	125	145

CODE	DESCRIPTION	INVOICE	MSRP
DF2	Stainless Steel Camper Type Mirrors *7.5" width x 10.5" height. Includes adjustable area feature to provide field of vision for vehicles to 96" wide. Shipped loose for dealer installation.*	(39)	(45)
EF1	Rear Bumper Delete *Vehicles registered in certain states must have a rear bumper to be operated on their roads. Consult your local laws.*	(172)	(200)
F44	HD Chassis Equipment (K1500 X-cab)	198	230
F51	HD Front and Rear Shock Absorbers	34	40
F60	HD Front Springs (K1500 X-cab)	54	63
FG5	46 mm Bilstein Shocks (K1500 X-cab)	194	225
G80	Locking Differential *NOT AVAILABLE with (GU4) 3.08 axle ratio.*	217	252
GT4	3.73 Axle Ratio *Includes water to oil cooler. NOT AVAILABLE with (KC4) engine oil cooler.*	116	135
GU4	3.08 Axle Ratio (K1500 X-cab) *REQUIRES (L31) engine.*	NC	NC
K47	High Capacity Air Cleaner	22	25
KC4	Engine Oil Cooler	116	135
KNP	HD Auxiliary Transmission Cooler *REQUIRES (L31) engine. NOT AVAILABLE with (GU4) 3.08 axle ratio.*	83	96
L31	Engine: Vortec 5.7L V8 SFI	602	700
N83	Wheels: 15" x 7" Chrome (C1500 X-cab) *NOT AVAILABLE with (L31).*	215	250
N90	Wheels: 15" x 7" Aluminum (K1500 X-cab)	292	340
NC7	Federal Emission Override *For vehicles that will be registered or leased in California, Connecticut, Washington D.C, Delaware, Massachusetts, Maryland, New Hampshire, New Jersey, New York, Pennsylvania, Rhode Island and Virginia but sold by retailers outside those states. REQUIRES (YF5) California Emissions.*	NC	NC
NZZ	Off-Road Skid Plates (K1500 X-cab) *Includes differential and transfer case shields.*	82	95
PF4	Wheels: 16" x 7" Aluminum (K1500 X-cab)	292	340
TP2	600 CCA Auxiliary HD Battery	115	134
UL0	Radio: AM/FM Stereo, Automatic Tone Control and Cassette (K1500 X-cab) *Includes digital clock, electronically tuned AM/FM stereo with speed sensitive volume, theft lock, auto reverse with music search cassette and enhanced performance 6 speaker system.*	77	90
UN0	Radio: AM/FM Stereo, Automatic Tone Control and CD (C1500 X-cab) *Includes digital clock, electronically tuned AM/FM stereo with speed sensitive volume and theft lock with enhanced performance 6 speaker system.*	163	190
UP0	Radio: AM/FM Stereo, Automatic Tone Control, CD and Cass (C1500 X-cab) *Includes digital clock, electronically tuned AM/FM stereo with speed sensitive volume, theft lock, auto reverse with music search cassette and enhanced performance 6 speaker system.*	249	290
V10	Cold Climate Package *Includes engine block heater.*	28	33
V76	Tow Hooks (C1500 X-cab)	33	38

CODE	DESCRIPTION	INVOICE	MSRP
XFN	Tires: Front P235/75R15 AS WOL (C1500 X-cab) *REQUIRES (YFN) tires: rear P235/75R15 AS WOL and (ZFN) tire: spare P235/75R15 AS WOL.*	43	50
XGC	Tires: Front P265/75R16 AT BSW (K1500 X-cab) *REQUIRES (L31 or GT4) and YGC and ZGC and PF4.*	46	54
XGD	Tires: Front P265/75R16 AT WOL (K1500 X-cab) *REQUIRES (L31 or GT4) and YGD and ZGD and PF4.*	89	104
YF5	California Emissions *Automatically added to vehicles shipped to and/or sold to retailers in California. Out-of-state retailers must order on vehicles to be registered or leased in California.*	146	170
YFN	Tires: Rear P235/75R15 AS WOL (C1500 X-cab) *REQUIRES (ZFN) tire: dpare P235/75R15 AS WOL.*	43	50
YGC	Tires: Rear P265/75R16 AT BSW (K1500 X-cab) *REQUIRES (L31 or GT4) and PF4 and ZGC.*	46	54
YGD	Tires: Rear P265/75R16 AT WOL (K1500 X-cab) *REQUIRES (L31 or GT4) and PF4 and ZGD.*	89	104
Z71	On/Off Road Chassis Equipment (K1500 X-cab) *Includes off road skid plates and 46 mm Bilstein shocks. REQUIRES (XGC) tires or (XGD) tires.*	232	270
Z82	HD Trailering Equipment *Includes trailer hitch platform, HD front and rear shock absorbers. REQUIRES (L31 and KC4) or KC4. NOT AVAILABLE with FG5.*	175	204
Z82	HD Trailering Equipment (K1500 X-cab) *Includes trailer hitch platform. REQUIRES (KC4) engine oil cooler.*	141	164
ZFN	Tire: Spare P235/75R15 AS WOL (C1500 X-cab)	22	25
ZGC	Tire: Spare P265/75R16 AT BSW (K1500 X-cab) *REQUIRES ((L31) engine or (GT4) 3.73 axle ratio) and (PF4) wheels.*	23	27
ZGD	Tire: Spare P265/75R16 AT WOL (K1500 X-cab) *REQUIRES ((L31) engine or (GT4) 3.73 axle ratio) and (PF4) wheels.*	45	52
ZY2	Conventional Two-Tone Paint	163	190

1999 SIERRA CLASSIC 2500

Safety Data

Side Airbag: *Not Available*
Integrated Child Seat(s): *Not Available*
4-Wheel ABS: *Standard*
Traction Control: *Not Available*
Driver Crash Test Grade: *Good*
Passenger Crash Test Grade: *Average*
Side Impact Crash Test Front: *Not Available*
Side Impact Crash Test Rear: *Not Available*
Crash Offset: *Not Available*

Standard Equipment

SL 2WD REGULAR CAB (5M): 5.7L V8 OHV SMPI 16-valve engine; 5-speed overdrive manual transmission; 600-amp HD battery; engine oil cooler; 100-amp alternator; rear wheel drive, 3.73 axle ratio; stainless steel exhaust; front independent suspension with anti-roll bar, front coil springs, rigid rear axle suspension with rear leaf springs; power re-circulating ball steering with vehicle speed-sensing assist; front disc/rear drum brakes with 4 wheel antilock braking system; 34 gal capacity fuel tank; trailer harness; front chrome bumper, rear black bumper with rear step; monotone paint; sealed beam halogen headlamps with daytime running lights; additional exterior lights include center high mounted stop light, pickup cargo box light, underhood light; driver's and passenger's manual black folding outside mirrors; front and rear 16" x 6.5" painted styled steel wheels; LT245/75SR16 BSW AS front and rear tires; underbody mounted full-size conventional steel spare wheel; AM/FM stereo with clock, seek-scan, 4 speakers, and fixed antenna; 3 power accessory outlets; instrumentation display includes tachometer, oil pressure gauge, water temp gauge, volt gauge, trip odometer; warning indicators include battery, lights on, key in ignition, door ajar; ignition disable; tinted windows; variable intermittent front windshield wipers; seating capacity of 3, bench front seat with adjustable headrests, driver's seat includes 2-way direction control, passenger's seat includes 2-way direction control; front height adjustable seatbelts; vinyl seats, full cloth headliner, full vinyl floor covering, cabback insulator; interior lights include dome light, front reading lights; sport steering wheel; passenger's side vanity mirror; day-night rearview mirror; glove box with light, front cupholder, dashboard storage, driver's and passenger's door bins; black grille, black side window moldings, black front windshield molding, black rear window molding and black door handles.

SL 2WD EXTENDED CAB (5M) (in addition to or instead of SL 2WD REGULAR CAB (5M) equipment): Rear heat ducts; vented rear windows; seating capacity of 6, 60-40 split-bench front seat with adjustable headrests, driver's seat includes 4-way direction control with easy entry, passenger's seat includes 4-way direction control with easy entry and full folding rear bench seat with adjustable headrests.

SL 2WD CREW CAB SB (4A) (in addition to or instead of SL 2WD EXTENDED CAB (5M) equipment): Four-speed electronic overdrive automatic transmission with lock-up; transmission oil cooler; 26 gal capacity fuel tank; front chrome bumper with black rub strip, chrome bumper insert, rear black bumper, rear step; manual rear windows; bench front seat with adjustable headrests, driver's seat includes 2-way direction control, passenger's seat includes 2-way direction control; reclining rear bench seat with adjustable headrests; dashboard storage and rear door bins.

SL 4WD EXTENDED CAB (5M) (in addition to or instead of SL 2WD EXTENDED CAB (5M) equipment): Engine oil cooler; part-time 4 wheel drive, auto locking hub control with manual shift, 3.73 axle ratio; front independent torsion suspension with anti-roll bar, front torsion springs, front torsion bar; 25 gal capacity fuel tank; rear tow hooks and black fender flares.

SL 4WD CREW CAB SB (4A) (in addition to or instead of SL 2WD CREW CAB (4A) equipment): Engine oil cooler; part-time 4 wheel drive, auto locking hub control with manual shift, 3.73 axle ratio; front independent torsion suspension with anti-roll bar, front torsion springs, front torsion bar; 25 gal capacity fuel tank; rear tow hooks, black fender flares and child safety rear door locks.

HD SL 4WD REGULAR CAB (5M) (in addition to or instead of SL 4WD EXTENDED CAB (5M) equipment): Seating capacity of 3, bench front seat with adjustable headrests, driver's seat includes 2-way direction control and passenger's seat includes 2-way direction control.

HD SL 4WD EXTENDED CAB (5M) (in addition to or instead of HD SL 4WD REGULAR CAB (5M) equipment): Vented rear windows; seating capacity of 6, 60-40 split-bench front seat with adjustable headrests, driver's seat includes 4-way direction control with easy entry, passenger's seat includes 4-way direction control with easy entry; full folding rear bench seat with adjustable headrests.

Base Prices

CODE	DESCRIPTION	INVOICE	MSRP
TC20903	SL 2WD Regular Cab (5M)	16789	19188
TC20953	SL 2WD Extended Cab (5M)	18192	20792
TC20743-R9S	SL 2WD Crew Cab SB (4A)	20275	23172
TK20903	HD SL 4WD Regular Cab (5M)	19199	21943

CODE	DESCRIPTION	INVOICE	MSRP
TK20753-R9S	SL 4WD Extended Cab (5M)	20910	23898
TK20953	HD SL 4WD Extended Cab (4A)	21021	24025
TK20743-R9S	SL 4WD Crew Cab SB (4A)	23052	26346
Destination Charge:		640	640

Accessories

CODE	DESCRIPTION	INVOICE	MSRP
—	Cloth Seat Trim	NC	NC
—	Custom Cloth Seat Trim	NC	NC
	Includes seatback storage pockets, driver's and passenger's power lumbar and center fold down storage armrest. REQUIRES 1SC or 1SH.		
1SA	Marketing Option Package 1SA	NC	NC
	Includes SL decor package. REQUIRES YG6.		
1SB	Marketing Option Package 1SB (All Except Crew Cab)	1150	1337
	Manufacturer Discount	(430)	(500)
	Net Price	720	837
	Includes SL decor package, air conditioning, ETR AM/FM stereo with cassette and convenience group: tilt steering, cruise control and power door locks.		
1SB	Marketing Option Package 1SB (Crew Cab)	692	805
	Includes SL decor package and air conditioning. NOT AVAILABLE with YG6.		
1SC	Marketing Option Package 1SC (Crew Cab)	1150	1337
	Includes SL decor package, air conditioning, convenience group: tilt steering, cruise control, power door locks and ETR AM/FM stereo with cassette.		
1SC	Marketing Option Package 1SC (Crew Cab)	3156	3670
	Includes SLE Decor package: chrome rear step bumper with rub strip, dual power remote mirrors, trim rings, bright center hub caps, deluxe front appearance package: color keyed grille, composite halogen headlamps, 2 door curb/courtesy lights; air conditioning, convenience group: tilt steering, cruise control, power door locks and ETR AM/FM stereo with cassette.		
1SC	Marketing Option Package 1SC (All Except Crew Cab)	2611	3036
	Manufacturer Discount	(645)	(750)
	Net Price	1966	2286
	Includes SLE Decor package: air conditioning, ETR AM/FM stereo with cassette and seek/scan, convenience group: tilt steering, cruise control, power door locks; chrome rear step bumper with rub strip, dual power remote mirrors, trim rings and bright center hub caps, deluxe front appearance package: color keyed grille, composite halogen headlamps and 2 door curb/courtesy lights. NOT AVAILABLE with ZQ3.		
1SD	Marketing Option Package 1SD (X-Cab)	3884	4516
	Manufacturer Discount	(645)	(750)
	Net Price	3239	3766
	Includes SLT Decor package: air conditioning, convenience group: tilt steering, cruise control, power door locks; dual power remote mirrors, chrome rear step bumper with rub strip, deluxe front appearance package: color keyed grille, composite halogen headlamps, trim rings and bright center hub caps; 2 door curb/courtesy lights, power windows with driver's side express down, ETR AM/FM stereo with cassette, remote keyless entry system, 60/40 reclining split-bench seat, 6-way power driver's seat, ultra soft leather seat trim and seatback storage pockets.		

CODE	DESCRIPTION	INVOICE	MSRP
1SD	**Marketing Option Package 1SD (Reg Cab)**	3827	4450
	Manufacturer Discount	(645)	(750)
	Net Price	3182	3700
	Includes SLT Decor package: air conditioning, convenience group: tilt steering, cruise control, power door locks; dual power remote mirrors, chrome rear step bumper with rub strip, deluxe front appearance package: color keyed grille, composite halogen headlamps, trim rings and bright center hub caps; 2 door curb/courtesy lights, power windows with driver's side express down, ETR AM/FM stereo with cassette, remote keyless entry system, 60/40 reclining split-bench seat, 6-way power driver's seat, ultra soft leather seat trim and seatback storage pockets.		
1SD	**Marketing Option Package 1SD (Crew Cab)**	4601	5350
	Includes SLT Decor package: air conditioning, convenience group: tilt steering, cruise control, power door locks; dual power remote mirrors, chrome rear step bumper with rub strip, deluxe front appearance package: color keyed grille, composite halogen headlamps, trim rings and bright center hub caps; 2 door curb/courtesy lights, power windows with driver's side express down, ETR AM/FM stereo with cassette, remote keyless entry system, 60/40 reclining split-bench seat, 6-way power driver's seat, ultra soft leather seat trim and seatback storage pockets.		
1SH	**Marketing Option Package 1SH (2WD Reg Cab/4WD Reg & X-Cab)**	3983	4631
	Manufacturer Discount	(645)	(750)
	Net Price	3338	3881
	Includes SLE Decor package: air conditioning, ETR AM/FM stereo with cassette and seek/scan, convenience group: tilt steering, cruise control, power door locks; chrome rear step bumper with rub strip, dual power remote mirrors, trim rings and bright center hub caps, deluxe front appearance package: color keyed grille, composite halogen headlamps, 2 door curb/courtesy lights, engine: Vortec 7400 V8 HD, transmission: 4 speed automatic with overdrive, HD transmission oil cooler and PRNDL in instrument panel. NOT AVAILABLE with AE7.		
1SH	**Marketing Option Package 1SH (2WD Reg Cab/4WD Reg & X-Cab)**	5255	6111
	Manufacturer Discount	(645)	(750)
	Net Price	4610	5361
	Includes SLT Decor package: air conditioning, convenience group: tilt steering, cruise control, power door locks; dual power remote mirrors, chrome rear step bumper with rub strip, deluxe front appearance package: color keyed grille, composite halogen headlamps, trim rings and bright center hub caps; 2 door curb/courtesy lights, power windows with driver's side express down, ETR AM/FM stereo with cassette, remote keyless entry system, 60/40 reclining split-bench seat, 6-way power driver's seat, ultra soft leather seat trim, seatback storage pockets, engine: Vortec 7400 V8 HD, transmission: 4 speed automatic with overdrive, HD transmission oil cooler and PRNDL in instrument panel.		
1SR	**Marketing Option Package 1SR "Performax" (2WD Reg Cab)**	2421	2815
	Manufacturer Discount	(602)	(700)
	Net Price	1819	2115
	Includes SL decor package, air conditioning, convenience group: tilt steering, cruise control, power door locks, ETR AM/FM stereo with cassette, bright appearance package: deluxe front appearance package: color keyed grille, chrome deluxe front bumper with rub strip; chrome rear step bumper with rub strip, bright exterior		

CODE	DESCRIPTION	INVOICE	MSRP
	moldings, trim rings and bright center hub caps; engine: Vortec 5700 V8 SFI, transmission: 4-speed automatic with overdrive, HD transmission oil cooler and PRNDL in instrument panel.		
1SR	**Marketing Option Package 1SR "Performax" (4WD Reg Cab)**	2394	2784
	Manufacturer Discount	(602)	(700)
	Net Price	1792	2084
	Includes SL decor package, air conditioning, convenience group: tilt steering, cruise control, power door locks, ETR AM/FM stereo with cassette, bright appearance package: deluxe front appearance package: color keyed grille, chrome deluxe front bumper with rub strip; chrome rear step bumper with rub strip, bright exterior moldings, trim rings and bright center hub caps; engine: Vortec 5700 V8 SFI, transmission: 4 speed automatic with overdrive, HD transmission oil cooler and PRNDL in instrument panel.		
A28	**Sliding Rear Window**	99	115
	NOT AVAILABLE with C49.		
A95	**Front Reclining Bucket Seats (Reg Cab)**	332	386
A95	**Front Reclining Bucket Seats (X-Cab)**	364	423
	Includes 3-passenger adjustable split back rear bench seat and dual adjustable headrests and center console.		
AE7	**Reclining 60/40 Split Bench Seat (Crew Cab)**	86	100
	Includes 3-passenger adjustable split back rear bench seat. REQUIRES 1SC or 1SH.		
AE7	**Reclining 60/40 Split Bench Seat (Reg Cab)**	150	174
	REQUIRES 1SC or 1SH.		
AG9	**6-Way Power Driver's Seat**	206	240
	REQUIRES AE7 or A95.		
AJ1	**Deep Tinted Glass (Crew Cab)**	155	180
	Excludes tinted glass on windshield, driver's and front passenger's windows. Includes light tint glass rear window. REQUIRES C49.		
AJ1	**Deep Tinted Glass (Crew Cab)**	185	215
	Excludes tinted glass on windshield, driver's and front passenger's windows.		
AJ1	**Deep Tinted Glass (Reg Cab)**	30	35
	Excludes tinted glass on windshield, driver's and passenger's windows. REQUIRES 1SD or 1SH.		
AJ1	**Deep Tinted Glass (X-Cab)**	62	72
	Includes light tinted rear window and excludes tinted glass on windshield, driver's and passenger's windows. REQUIRES C49.		
AJ1	**Deep Tinted Glass (X-Cab)**	92	107
	Excludes tinted glass on windshield, driver's and front passenger's windows. REQUIRES 1SD or 1SH.		
AU0	**Remote Keyless Entry System**	129	150
	Includes two transmitters. REQUIRES 1SC or 1SH.		
AU3	**Power Door Locks (Crew Cab)**	192	223
AU3	**Power Door Locks (All Except Crew Cab)**	134	156
	NOT AVAILABLE with 9U0.		
B30	**Full Floor Color-Keyed Carpeting (Reg Cab)**	47	55
	Includes vinyl floor mats.		

CODE	DESCRIPTION	INVOICE	MSRP
B30	Full Floor Color-Keyed Carpeting (X-Cab) *Includes front and rear color-keyed mats.*	75	87
B30	Full Floor Color-Keyed Carpeting (X-Cab) *Includes front color-keyed mats. REQUIRES YG4.*	61	71
B85	Bright Exterior Moldings (4WD Reg Cab/4WD X-Cab) *Includes wheel opening moldings and body side moldings.*	65	76
B85	Bright Exterior Moldings (2WD Reg Cab/2WD X-Cab) *Includes wheel opening moldings and body side moldings.*	92	107
BG9	Color-Keyed Rubber Flooring (Reg Cab) *Replaces carpet and floor mats.*	(30)	(35)
BG9	Color-Keyed Rubber Flooring (X-Cab) *Replaces carpet and floor mats.*	(44)	(51)
BZY	Bedliner	194	225
C49	Electric Rear Window Defogger (Reg Cab/X-Cab)	132	154
C60	Air Conditioning *NOT AVAILABLE with YG6.*	692	805
DD7	Electrochromic Rearview Mirror (Reg Cab/X-Cab) *Includes 8 point compass.*	125	145
DF2	Camper Type Exterior Mirrors *7.5" x 10.5" stainless steel. Adjustable arm feature to provide field of vision for vehicles to 96" wide. REQUIRES 1SC, 1SD or 1SH.*	(39)	(45)
DF2	Camper Type Exterior Mirrors *7.5" x 10.5" stainless steel. Adjustable arm feature to provide field of vision for vehicles to 96" wide.*	46	53
EF1	Rear Bumper Delete *Vehicles registered in certain states must have a rear bumper to be operated on their roads. Consult your local laws. REQUIRES 1SC, 1SD or 1SH. NOT AVAILABLE with Z82.*	(172)	(200)
EF1	Rear Bumper Delete *Vehicles registered in certain states must have a rear bumper to be operated on their roads. Consult your local laws.*	(112)	(130)
F60	HD Front Springs	54	63
G80	Locking Rear Differential	217	252
GT5	4.10 Axle Ratio	NC	NC
K47	High Capacity Air Cleaner	22	25
KL5	Conversion Ready Engine (Reg Cab/X-Cab) *Internal modifications for operation of natural or propane gas. REQUIRES MT1.*	108	125
KL6	Natural Gas Provisions (Reg Cab/X-Cab) *Includes conversion ready engine. REQUIRES MT1.*	4988	5800
L29	Engine: Vortec 7400 V8 HD	516	600
L65	Engine: 6.5L V8 Turbo Diesel *Includes hydraulic brakes, extra sound insulation, glow plugs, integral two stage fuel filter, fuel and water separator with instrument panel warning light and fuel filter change signal.*	2460	2860
MT1	Transmission: 4-Speed Automatic with Overdrive (Reg Cab/X-Cab) *Includes HD transmission oil cooler.*	856	995

CODE	DESCRIPTION	INVOICE	MSRP
NP1	Electronic Shift Transfer Case (Reg Cab/X-Cab) *REQUIRES MT1.*	129	150
NZZ	Off-Road Skid Plates (4WD) *Includes differential and transfer case shields.*	82	95
P06	Trim Rings and Bright Center Hub Caps (Reg Cab/X-Cab)	52	60
R9Q	Bright Appearance Package (4WD Except Crew Cab) *Includes deluxe front appearance package: color keyed grille, chrome deluxe front bumper with rub strip; chrome rear step bumper with rub strip, bright exterior moldings, trim rings and bright center hub caps.*	389	452
R9Q	Bright Appearance Package (2WD Except Crew Cab) *Includes deluxe front appearance package: color keyed grille, chrome deluxe front bumper with rub strip; chrome rear step bumper with rub strip, bright exterior moldings, trim rings and bright center hub caps.*	416	483
R9R	Bright Appearance Group Discount (Reg Cab/X-cab) *REQUIRES R9Q. NOT AVAILABLE with 1SR.*	(172)	(200)
TP2	HD Auxiliary Battery *Delco Freedom with 600 cold cranking amps.*	115	134
U01	Roof Marker Lamps (5)	47	55
ULO	Radio: AM/FM Stereo with Cassette *Includes digital clock, speed sensitive volume, theft lock, automatic tone control, auto reverse, music search and an enhanced performance 6-speaker system. REQUIRES 1SC OR 1SH.*	77	90
UL5	Radio Delete *Includes front fender hole plugs and instrument panel storage bin.*	(247)	(287)
UM6	Radio: AM/FM Stereo with Cassette *Includes digital clock and 4 speakers. NOT AVAILABLE with UL5.*	126	147
UNO	Radio: AM/FM Stereo with CD *Includes digital clock, speed sensitive volume, theft lock and automatic tone control with enhanced performance 6-speaker system.*	163	190
UPO	Radio: AM/FM Stereo with CD and Cassette *Includes digital clock, speed sensitive volume, theft lock, seek and scan, automatic tone control, auto reverse and music search cassette with enhanced performance 6-speaker system. REQUIRES MT1.*	249	290
V10	Cold Climate Package *Includes special insulation.*	28	33
V22	Deluxe Front Appearance Package *Includes dual horns and color keyed grille.*	164	191
V76	Front Recovery Hooks	33	38
VB3	Chrome Rear Step Bumper with Rub Strip *Includes step pad.*	85	99
VG3	Chrome Front Bumper with Rub Strip (Reg Cab/X-Cab) *Includes black bumper guards with diesel engines.*	22	26
VYU	Snow Plow Prep Package (4WD Except Crew Cab) *Includes HD front springs and HD power steering cooler.*	101	118
XGK	Tires: Front LT245/75R16E AT BSW (4WD) *REQUIRES YGK and ZGK.*	19	23
YG4	Rear Seat Delete (X-Cab)	(374)	(435)

CODE	DESCRIPTION	INVOICE	MSRP
YG6	Air Conditioning Not Desired	NC	NC
YGK	Tires: Rear LT245/75R16-E BSW AT	19	23
Z81	Camper Equipment Package *Includes wiring harness and camper type exterior mirrors. REQUIRES L65.*	85	99
Z81	Camper Equipment Package *Includes wiring harness and camper type exterior mirrors.*	200	233
Z81	Camper Equipment Package *Includes wiring harness and camper type exterior mirrors. REQUIRES 1SC, 1SD or 1SH.*	116	135
Z81	Camper Equipment Package *Includes wiring harness and camper type exterior mirrors. REQUIRES L65 and 1SC, 1SD or 1SH.*	NC	NC
Z82	HD Trailering Equipment *Includes trailer hitch platform. NOT AVAILABLE with EF1.*	141	164
ZGK	Tire: Spare LT245/75R16-E AT BSW (2WD Except Crew Cab) *REQUIRES YGK.*	9	11
ZGK	Tire: Spare LT245/75R16E BSW AT (4WD Except Crew Cab) *REQUIRES YGK.*	9	11
ZQ3	Convenience Group *Includes tilt steering, power door locks and power windows.*	331	385

1999 SIERRA CLASSIC 3500

Safety Data

Side Airbag: *Not Available*
4-Wheel ABS: *Standard*
Driver Crash Test Grade: *Not Available*
Side Impact Crash Test Front: *Not Available*
Crash Offset: *Not Available*
Integrated Child Seat(s): *Not Available*
Traction Control: *Not Available*
Passenger Crash Test Grade: *Not Available*
Side Impact Crash Test Rear: *Not Available*

Standard Equipment

HD SL 2WD REGULAR CAB SRW (5M): 5.7L V8 OHV SMPI 16-valve engine; 5-speed overdrive manual transmission; 600-amp HD battery; engine oil cooler; 100-amp alternator; rear wheel drive, 4.1 axle ratio; stainless steel exhaust; front independent suspension with anti-roll bar, front coil springs, rigid rear axle suspension with rear leaf springs; power re-circulating ball steering with vehicle speed-sensing assist; front disc/rear drum brakes with 4 wheel antilock braking system; 34 gal capacity fuel tank; trailer harness; front chrome bumper, rear black bumper with rear step; monotone paint; sealed beam halogen headlamps with daytime running lights; additional exterior lights include center high mounted stop light, pickup cargo box light, underhood light; driver's and passenger's manual black folding outside mirrors; front and rear 16"x 6.5" painted styled steel wheels; LT245/75SR16 BSW AS front and rear tires; underbody mounted full-size conventional steel spare wheel; AM/FM stereo with clock, seek-scan, 4 speakers, and fixed antenna; 3 power accessory outlets; instrumentation display includes tachometer, oil pressure gauge, water temp gauge, volt gauge, trip odometer; warning indicators include battery, lights on, key in ignition, door ajar; ignition disable; tinted windows; variable intermittent front windshield wipers; seating capacity of 3, front bench seat with adjustable headrests, driver's seat includes 2-way direction control, passenger's seat includes 2-way direction control; front height adjustable seatbelts; vinyl seats, full cloth headliner, full vinyl floor covering, cabback insulator; interior lights include dome light, front reading lights; sport steering wheel; passenger side vanity mirror; day-night rearview mirror; glove box with light, front cupholder, dashboard storage, driver's and passenger's door bins; black grille, black side window moldings, black front windshield molding, black rear window molding and black door handles.

HD SL 2WD EXTENDED CAB DRW (5M) (in addition to or instead of HD SL 2WD REGULAR CAB SRW (5M) equipment): Front chrome bumper with black rub strip and chrome bumper insert; black bodyside molding with chrome bodyside insert, chrome wheel well molding; rear heat ducts, additional exterior lights include cab clearance lights; front and rear 16" x 6" painted steel wheels; vented rear windows; seating capacity of 6, 60-40 split-bench front seat with adjustable headrests, driver's seat includes 4-way direction control with easy entry, passenger's seat includes 4-way direction control with easy entry and full folding rear bench seat with adjustable headrests.

HD SL 2WD CREW CAB SRW (5M) (in addition to or instead of HD SL 2WD EXTENDED CAB DRW (5M) equipment): Manual rear windows; bench front seat with adjustable headrests, driver's seat includes 2-way direction control, passenger's seat includes 2-way direction control; reclining rear bench seat with adjustable headrests and rear door bins.

SL 2WD CREW CAB SB DRW (5M) (in addition to or instead of HD SL 2WD CREW CAB SRW (5M) equipment): 7.4L V8 OHV SMPI 16-valve engine and 26 gal capacity fuel tank.

HD SL 4WD REGULAR CAB SRW (5M) (in addition to or instead of HD SL 2WD REGULAR CAB SRW (5M)equipment): Part-time 4 wheel drive, auto locking hub control with manual shift; front independent torsion suspension with HD anti-roll bar, front torsion springs, front torsion bar; rear tow hooks and black fender flares.

HD SL 4WD EXTENDED CAB DRW (5M) (in addition to or instead of HD SL 4WD REGULAR CAB SRW (5M) equipment): Front chrome bumper with black rub strip and chrome bumper insert; black bodyside molding with chrome bodyside insert, chrome wheel well molding; rear heat ducts, additional exterior lights include cab clearance lights; front and rear 16" x 6" painted steel wheels; vented rear windows; seating capacity of 6, 60-40 split-bench front seat with adjustable headrests, driver's seat includes 4-way direction control with easy entry, passenger's seat includes 4-way direction control with easy entry and full folding rear bench seat with adjustable headrests.

HD SL 4WD CREW CAB SRW (5M) (in addition to or instead of HD SL 4WD EXTENDED CAB DRW (5M) equipment): Black fender flares; front and rear 16" x 6.5" painted styled steel wheels; child safety rear door locks; manual rear windows; bench front seat with adjustable headrests, driver's seat includes 2-way direction control, passenger's seat includes 2-way direction control; reclining rear bench seat with adjustable headrests and rear door bins.

SL 4WD CREW CAB SB DRW (5M) (in addition to or instead of HD SL 4WD CREW CAB SRW (5M) equipment): 7.4L V8 OHV SMPI 16-valve engine and 26 gal capacity fuel tank.

Base Prices

Code	Description	Invoice	MSRP
TC30903-E63	HD SL 2WD Regular Cab SRW (5M)	17312	19786
TC30953-E63	HD SL 2WD Extended Cab DRW (5M)	20311	23212
TC30943-E63	HD SL 2WD Crew Cab SRW (5M)	20051	22916
TC30743-R9S	SL 2WD Crew Cab SB DRW (5M)	21347	24396
TK30903-E63	HD SL 4WD Regular Cab SRW (5M)	19937	22786
TK30953-E63	HD SL 4WD Extended Cab DRW (5M)	22770	26023
TK30943-E63	HD SL 4WD Crew Cab SRW (5M)	22828	26090
TK30743-R9S	SL 4WD Crew Cab SB DRW (5M)	24124	27570
Destination Charge:		640	640

CODE	DESCRIPTION	INVOICE	MSRP
	Accessories		
—	Cloth Seat Trim	NC	NC
—	Custom Cloth Seat Trim	NC	NC
	Includes seatback storage pockets, driver's and passenger's power lumbar and center armrest with storage. REQUIRES 1SC or 1SK.		
1SA	**Marketing Option Package 1SA**	NC	NC
	Includes SL decor package. REQUIRES YG6.		
1SB	**Marketing Option Package 1SB (Crew Cab)**	692	805
	Includes SL decor package and air conditioning. NOT AVAILABLE with YG6.		
1SB	**Marketing Option Package 1SB (Reg Cab/X-Cab)**	1150	1337
	Manufacturer Discount	(430)	(500)
	Net Price	720	837
	Includes SL decor package, air conditioning, ETR AM/FM stereo with cassette, convenience package: tilt wheel and cruise control.		
1SC	**Marketing Option Package 1SC (Crew Cab)**	1150	1337
	Includes SL decor package, air conditioning, ETR AM/FM stereo with cassette, convenience package: tilt wheel and cruise control.		
1SC	**Marketing Option Package 1SC (Reg Cab/X-Cab)**	2611	3036
	Manufacturer Discount	(645)	(750)
	Net Price	1966	2286
	Includes air conditioning, ETR AM/FM stereo with cassette radio, convenience package: tilt wheel and cruise control; SLE Decor package: power door locks, door curb/courtesy lights, cloth door trim inserts, full color-keyed carpeting, leather-wrapped steering wheel, chrome rear step bumper with rub strip, deluxe front appearance package: composite halogen headlamps, color-keyed grille, dual power remote mirrors, bright trim rings and hub caps.		
1SC	**Marketing Option Package 1SC (Crew Cab)**	3156	3670
	Includes air conditioning, ETR AM/FM stereo with cassette radio, convenience package: tilt wheel and cruise control; SLE Decor package: power door locks, door curb/courtesy lights, cloth door trim inserts, full color-keyed carpeting, leather-wrapped steering wheel, chrome rear step bumper with rub strip, deluxe front appearance package: composite halogen headlamps, color-keyed grille, dual power remote mirrors, bright trim rings and hub caps.		
1SD	**Marketing Option Package 1SD (X-Cab)**	3884	4516
	Manufacturer Discount	(645)	(750)
	Net Price	3239	3766
	Includes ETR AM/FM stereo with cassette, air conditioning, convenience package: tilt wheel and cruise control; SLT Decor package: power door locks, door curb/courtesy lights, cloth door trim inserts, full color-keyed carpeting, leather-wrapped steering wheel, chrome rear step bumper with rub strip, deluxe front appearance package: composite halogen headlamps, color-keyed grille, dual power remote mirrors, bright trim rings and hub caps; remote keyless entry system, illuminated entry lights, 60/40 reclining split bench seat, 6-way power driver's seat, ultrasoft neutral leather seat trim, seatback storage pockets, center armrest with storage, driver's and passenger's power lumbar. REQUIRES MT1 or L29 or L65.		

CODE	DESCRIPTION	INVOICE	MSRP
1SD	**Marketing Option Package 1SD (Crew Cab)**	4601	5350
	Includes ETR AM/FM stereo with cassette, air conditioning, convenience package: tilt wheel and cruise control; SLT Decor package: power door locks, door curb/courtesy lights, cloth door trim inserts, full color-keyed carpeting, leather-wrapped steering wheel, chrome rear step bumper with rub strip, deluxe front appearance package: composite halogen headlamps, color-keyed grille, dual power remote mirrors, bright trim rings and hub caps; remote keyless entry system, illuminated entry lights, 60/40 reclining split bench seat, 6-way power driver's seat, ultrasoft neutral leather seat trim, seatback storage pockets, center armrest with storage, driver's and passenger's power lumbar. REQUIRES MT1 or L29 or L65.		
1SD	**Marketing Option Package 1SD (Reg Cab)**	3827	4450
	Manufacturer Discount	(645)	(750)
	Net Price	3182	3700
	Includes ETR AM/FM stereo with cassette, air conditioning, convenience package: tilt wheel and cruise control; SLT Decor package: power door locks, door curb/courtesy lights, cloth door trim inserts, full color-keyed carpeting, leather-wrapped steering wheel, chrome rear step bumper with rub strip, deluxe front appearance package: composite halogen headlamps, color-keyed grille, dual power remote mirrors, bright trim rings and hub caps; remote keyless entry system, illuminated entry lights, 60/40 reclining split bench seat, 6-way power driver's seat, ultrasoft neutral leather seat trim, seatback storage pockets, center armrest with storage, driver's and passenger's power lumbar. REQUIRES MT1 or L29 or L65.		
1SK	**Marketing Option Package 1SK (X-Cab)**	7199	8371
	Manufacturer Discount	(645)	(750)
	Net Price	6554	7621
	Includes GVWR: 10,000 lbs, engine: 6.5L V8 turbo diesel, dual batteries, HD radiator, engine oil cooler, engine block heater, extra sound insulation, transmission: 4-speed automatic with overdrive, PRNDL in instrument panel, dual rear wheels, 60/40 reclining split bench seat, air conditioning, convenience package: tilt wheel, cruise control, ETR AM/FM stereo with cassette, air conditioning, convenience package: tilt wheel and cruise control; SLT Decor package: power door locks, door curb/courtesy lights, cloth door trim inserts, full color-keyed carpeting, leather-wrapped steering wheel, chrome rear step bumper with rub strip, deluxe front appearance package: composite halogen headlamps, color-keyed grille, dual power remote mirrors, bright trim rings and hub caps; remote keyless entry system, illuminated entry lights, 60/40 reclining split bench seat, 6-way power driver's seat, ultrasoft neutral leather seat trim, seatback storage pockets, center armrest with storage, driver's and passenger's power lumbar. NOT AVAILABLE with KL5.		
1SK	**Marketing Option Package 1SK (Reg Cab)**	5926	6891
	Manufacturer Discount	(645)	(750)
	Net Price	5281	6141
	Includes GVWR: 10,000 lbs, engine: 6.5L V8 turbo diesel, dual batteries, HD radiator, engine oil cooler, engine block heater, extra sound insulation, transmission: 4-speed automatic with overdrive, PRNDL in instrument panel, dual rear wheels, 60/40 reclining split bench seat, air conditioning, ETR AM/FM stereo with cassette radio, convenience package: tilt wheel and cruise control; SLE Decor package: power door locks, door curb/courtesy lights, cloth door trim inserts, full color-keyed		

CODE	DESCRIPTION	INVOICE	MSRP
	carpeting, leather-wrapped steering wheel, chrome rear step bumper with rub strip, deluxe front appearance package: composite halogen headlamps, color-keyed grille, dual power remote mirrors, bright trim rings and hub caps.		
5V1	Carrier and Spare Wheel W/O Tire (Crew Cab DRW)	89	104
5V1	Carrier and Spare Wheel W/O Tire (Crew Cab SRW)	71	82
A28	Sliding Rear Window *NOT AVAILABLE with C49.*	99	115
A52	Front Bench Seat (Reg Cab) *Includes center fold down armrest with coin holder, map strap, writing board, power lumbar and storage pockets behind seats.*	NC	NC
A95	Front Reclining Bucket Seats (Reg Cab) *Includes inboard armrests, dual adjustable headrests, power lumbars and storage pocket behind seats and floor console. REQUIRES 1SC or 1SK.*	332	386
A95	Reclining High Back Bucket Seats (X-Cab) *Includes inboard armrests, dual adjustable headrests, power lumbar, easy entry feature, storage pockets behind seats and overhead console. REQUIRES 1SC or 1SK.*	232	270
A95	Reclining High Back Bucket Seats (Crew Cab) *Includes 3-passenger adjustable split back rear bench seat, inboard armrests, dual adjustable headrests, power lumbar, storage pockets behind seats and floor console.*	364	423
AE7	60/40 Reclining Split Bench Seat (Crew Cab) *Includes 3-passenger adjustable split back rear bench seat, center fold down storage armrest with coin holder, map strap and writing board, power lumbar and storage pockets behind seats. REQUIRES 1SC.*	86	100
AE7	60/40 Reclining Split Bench Seat (Reg Cab) *Includes center fold down storage armrests with coin holder, map strap and writing board, power lumbars and storage pockets behind seats. REQUIRES 1SC.*	150	174
AG9	6-Way Power Driver's Seat (X-Cab/Crew Cab) *REQUIRES 1SC and A95 or AE7.*	206	240
AJ1	Deep Tinted Glass (Crew Cab) *Includes light tinted rear window. Excludes tinted glass on windshield, driver's and passenger's windows. REQUIRES C49.*	155	180
AJ1	Deep Tinted Glass (X-Cab) *Excludes tinted glass on windshield, driver's and passenger's windows. NOT AVAILABLE with C49.*	92	107
AJ1	Deep Tinted Glass (X-Cab) *Excludes tinted glass on windshield, driver's and passenger's windows. Includes light tinted rear window. REQUIRES C49.*	62	72
AJ1	Deep Tinted Glass (Crew Cab) *Excludes tinted glass on windshield, driver's and passenger's windows.*	185	215
AJ1	Deep Tinted Glass (Reg Cab) *Excludes tinted glass on windshield, driver's and passenger's windows.*	30	35
AU0	Remote Keyless Entry System *Includes 2 transmitters and illuminated entry lights. NOT AVAILABLE with 1SA or 1SB.*	129	150
AU3	Power Door Locks (Reg Cab/X-Cab)	134	156
AU3	Power Door Locks (Crew Cab)	192	223

CODE	DESCRIPTION	INVOICE	MSRP
B30	Full Color-Keyed Carpeting (X-Cab) *Includes vinyl floor mats. REQUIRES 1SA or 1SB.*	75	87
B30	Full Color-Keyed Carpeting (X-Cab) *Includes front vinyl floor mats only. REQUIRES YG4.*	61	71
B30	Full Color-Keyed Carpeting (Reg Cab) *Includes vinyl floor mats.*	47	55
B85	Bright Bodyside and Wheel Opening Moldings (2WD Reg Cab)	92	107
B85	Bright Bodyside Moldings (4WD Reg Cab)	65	76
BG9	Color-Keyed Rubber Flooring (X-Cab) *Replaces carpet and floor mats. REQUIRES 1SC, 1SD or 1SK.*	(44)	(51)
BG9	Color-Keyed Rubber Flooring (Reg Cab) *Replaces carpet and floor mats. REQUIRES 1SC, 1SD or 1SK.*	(30)	(35)
BZY	Bedliner	194	225
C49	Electric Rear Window Defogger	151	175
C60	Air Conditioning *REQUIRES 1SA. NOT AVAILABLE with YG6.*	692	805
C6Y	GVWR: 9,600 Lbs (Crew Cab) *REQUIRES Z81.*	NC	NC
C7A	GVWR: 10,000 Lbs (Reg Cab/X-Cab) *REQUIRES R05.*	NC	NC
DD7	Electrochromic Rearview Mirror (Reg Cab/X-Cab) *Light sensitive mirror and 8-point compass. NOT AVAILABLE with 1SA.*	125	145
DF2	Camper Type Mirrors (Reg Cab/X-Cab) *7.5" x 10.5" stainless steel. Adjustable arm feature to provide field of vision for vehicles to 96" wide. REQUIRES 1SC, 1SD or 1SK.*	(39)	(45)
DF2	Camper Type Mirrors (Crew Cab) *7.5" x 10.5" stainless steel. Adjustable arm feature to provide field of vision for vehicles to 96" wide.*	46	53
EF1	Rear Bumper Delete *Vehicles registered in certain states MUST have a rear bumper to be operated on their roads. Consult your local laws. REQUIRES 1SC, 1SD or 1SK. NOT AVAILABLE with Z82.*	(172)	(200)
EF1	Rear Bumper Delete *Vehicles registered in certain states MUST have a rear bumper to be operated on their roads. Consult your local laws.*	(112)	(130)
F60	HD Front Springs (4WD)	54	63
G80	Locking Rear Differential	245	285
HC4	4.56 Axle Ratio	NC	NC
K47	High Capacity Air Cleaner	22	25
KL5	Conversion Ready Engine (Reg Cab/X-Cab) *Internal modifications for operation of natural or propane gas. REQUIRES MT1.*	108	125
L29	Engine: Vortec 7400 V8 SFI (Reg Cab/X-Cab)	516	600
L65	Engine: 6.5L V8 Turbo Diesel (Crew Cab DRW) *Includes hydraulic brakes, glow plugs, integral two stage fuel filter, fuel and water separator with instrument panel warning light, fuel filter change signal, HD radiator, engine oil cooler, engine block heater and extra sound insulation. REQUIRES MT1.*	1944	2260

CODE	DESCRIPTION	INVOICE	MSRP
L65	**Engine: 6.5L V8 Turbo Diesel (Reg Cab/X-Cab)** *Includes hydraulic brakes, glow plugs, integral two stage fuel filter, fuel and water separator with instrument panel warning light, fuel filter change signal, HD radiator, engine oil cooler, engine block heater and extra sound insulation. REQUIRES A52 (Reg Cab).*	2460	2860
MT1	**Transmission: 4-Speed Automatic with Overdrive**	856	995
NZZ	**Off-Road Skid Plates (4WD)** *Includes differential and transfer case shields.*	82	95
P06	**Bright Trim Rings and Hub Caps**	52	60
R05	**Dual Rear Wheels (Reg Cab)**	821	955
R9Q	**Bright Appearance Group (2WD Reg Cab)** *Includes deluxe front appearance package: composite halogen headlamps, color-keyed grille, chrome front bumper with rub strip; chrome rear step bumper with rub strip, bright bodyside and wheel opening moldings, bright trim rings and hub caps.*	415	483
R9Q	**Bright Appearance Group (4WD Reg Cab)** *Includes deluxe front appearance package: composite halogen headlamps, color-keyed grille, chrome front bumper with rub strip; chrome rear step bumper with rub strip, bright bodyside and wheel opening moldings, bright trim rings and hub caps.*	389	452
R9Q	**Bright Appearance Group (Reg Cab/X-Cab)** *Includes deluxe front appearance package: composite halogen headlamps, color-keyed grille, chrome front bumper with rub strip; chrome rear step bumper with rub strip, bright trim rings and hub caps. REQUIRES R05 (Reg Cab).*	323	376
R9R	**Bright Appearance Group Discount (Reg Cab/X-Cab)** *REQUIRES R9Q.*	(172)	(200)
TP2	**600 CCA Auxiliary HD Battery**	115	134
U01	**Roof Marker Lamps (5)**	47	55
UL0	**Radio: AM/FM Stereo with Cassette** *Includes clock, speed sensitive volume, theft lock, automatic tone control, auto reverse and music search cassette player and enhanced performance 6 speaker system.*	77	90
UL5	**Radio Delete** *Includes front fender hole plugs.*	(247)	(287)
UM6	**Radio: AM/FM Stereo with Cassette** *Includes seek and scan, digital clock and 4 speakers. NOT AVAILABLE with UL5.*	126	147
UN0	**Radio: AM/FM Stereo with CD** *Includes clock, speed sensitive volume, theft lock, automatic tone control and enhanced performance 6 speaker system. REQUIRES 1SC, 1SD or 1SK.*	163	190
UP0	**Radio: AM/FM Stereo with Cassette and CD** *Includes clock, speed sensitive volume, theft lock, automatic tone control, auto reverse and music search cassette player and enhanced performance 6-speaker system. REQUIRES MT1, 1SC, 1SD or 1SK.*	249	290
V10	**Cold Climate Package** *Includes engine block heater.*	28	33
V22	**Deluxe Front Appearance Package** *Includes dual horns and color-keyed grille.*	164	191
V76	**Recovery Hooks**	33	38

CODE	DESCRIPTION	INVOICE	MSRP
VB3	Chrome Rear Step Bumper with Rub Strip *REQUIRES VG3 (Reg Cab/X-Cab).*	85	99
VG3	Chrome Front Bumper with Rub Strip (Reg Cab/X-Cab) *Includes black bumper guards with diesel engine.*	22	26
VYU	Snow Plow Prep Package (4WD Reg Cab/4WD X-Cab) *Includes HD front springs and HD power steering.*	101	118
XGK	Tires: Front LT245/75R16E AT BSW (4WD)	19	23
XHP	Tires: Front LT225/75R16/D AS BSW (2WD Reg Cab/Crew Cab SRW)	(58)	(68)
XHR	Tires: Front LT225/75R16D AT BSW (4WD Reg Cab/Crew Cab SRW)	(40)	(46)
XHR	Tires: Front LT225/75R16D AT BSW (4WD X-Cab/Crew Cab DRW)	19	22
XYK	Tires: Front LT215/85R16D Highway BSW (2WD Reg Cab/Crew Cab SRW)	64	74
XYK	Tires: Front LT215/85R16D Highway BSW (2WD X-Cab/Crew Cab DRW)	122	142
XYL	Tires: Front LT215/85R16D AT BSW (4WD Reg Cab/Crew Cab SRW)	112	130
XYL	Tires: Front LT215/85R16D AT BSW (4WD X-Cab/Crew Cab DRW)	170	198
YG4	Rear Seat Delete (X-Cab)	(374)	(435)
YG6	Air Conditioning Not Desired	NC	NC
YGK	Tires: Rear LT245/75R16E BW On-Off Road (2WD)	19	23
YHP	Tires: Rear LT225/75R16/D BSW AS (2WD Reg Cab/Crew Cab SRW)	370	430
YHR	Tires: Rear LT225/75R16-D BSW AT (2WD X-Cab/Crew Cab DRW)	38	44
YHR	Tires: Rear LT225/75R16-D BSW AT (2WD Reg Cab/Crew Cab SRW)	408	474
YYK	Tires: Rear LT215/85R16/D Highway BSW (2WD X- Cab/Crew Cab DRW)	244	284
YYK	Tires: Rear LT215/85R16D Highway BSW (2WD Reg Cab/Crew Cab SRW)	614	714
YYL	Tires: Rear LT215/85R16D AT BSW (4WD X-Cab)	341	396
YYL	Tires: Rear LT215/85R16D AT BSW (4WD Reg Cab)	710	826
Z81	Camper Equipment Package *Includes wiring harness and camper type mirrors. REQUIRES 1SA or 1SB and L65.*	85	99
Z81	Camper Equipment Package *Includes wiring harness and 600-cca auxiliary HD battery. REQUIRES 1SA or 1SB.*	200	233
Z81	Camper Equipment Package *Includes wiring harness and camper type mirrors. REQUIRES 1SC, 1SD or 1SK and L65.*	NC	NC
Z81	Camper Equipment Package *Includes wiring harness and 600-cca auxiliary HD battery. REQUIRES 1SC or 1SD.*	116	135
Z82	HD Trailering Equipment *Includes trailer hitch platform.*	141	164
ZGK	Tire: Spare LT245/75R16E BW On-Off Road (2WD)	9	11
ZHP	Tire: Spare LT225/75R16/D BSW AS (2WD Reg Cab/Crew Cab SRW) *REQUIRES R05.*	(29)	(34)
ZHR	Tire: Spare LT225/75R16/D BSW AT (2WD Reg Cab/Crew Cab SRW) *REQUIRES R05.*	(20)	(23)
ZHR	Tire: Spare LT225/75R16/D BSW AT (2WD X-Cab/Crew Cab DRW)	9	11
ZQ3	Convenience Package *Includes tilt wheel and cruise control.*	331	385
ZYK	Tire: Spare LT215/85R16D Highway BSW (2WD X-Cab/Crew Cab DRW)	61	71
ZYK	Tire: Spare LT215/85R16D Highway BSW (2WD Reg Cab/Crew Cab SRW)	32	37
ZYL	Tire: Spare LT215/85R16D AT BSW (4WD Reg Cab/Crew Cab SRW)	56	65
ZYL	Tire: Spare LT215/85R16D AT BSW (4WD X-Cab/Crew Cab DRW)	85	99

1999 SONOMA

1999 GMC Sonoma

What's New?

The '99 Sonoma touts four new exterior colors, a new steering wheel with mini-module depowered airbag, and larger, more robust outside rearview mirrors, with the uplevel power mirror gaining a heated feature. AutoTrac, GM's electronic push-button two-speed transfer case, is now standard on four-wheel-drive models, and all Sonomas get a content theft alarm with remote keyless entry as well as a flash-to-pass headlamp feature for the smart stalk. Serious four-wheelers can now order composite skid plates.

Review

Looking for a way to distinguish the GMC Sonoma from the pedestrian Chevrolet S-10, marketers have decided to sell the Sonoma as a capable alternative to the traditional sporty coupe. With an aggressive look, available sport suspensions, a third-door extended cab, snazzy Sportside bed and a strong 4.3-liter V6 under the hood, it shouldn't be a hard sell.

Despite this new advertising image, Sonomas can be fitted to suit just about any requirement, from strict utility hauler to off-road bruiser. Choose from three wheelbases, three cabs, a short box or long box in Wideside or Sportside configuration and two- or four-wheel drive. Then, you still have to consider three trim levels (SL, SLS, SLE), three engines (a four-cylinder or two V6 choices), a manual or automatic shift, and no less than seven different suspension systems-three for 2WD and four for 4WD models. Whew!

GMC substantially improved the Sonoma inside and out last year, so minor revisions were on tap this time around. Four-wheel-drive models, which already have four-wheel disc brakes standard, now get GM's AutoTrac, an electronic two-speed transfer case that detects wheel slippage and automatically directs power to the axle with the most traction – all at the push of a button. Other minor upgrades, such as new colors, bigger outside mirrors and a content theft alarm with remote keyless entry, round out the changes for '99.

With the high-output, 180-horsepower Vortec 4300 V6 on tap, and the ZQ8 Sport Suspension package, the Sonoma performs as energetically as high-priced sports cars did a decade or so ago. By any definition, that's progress. The Sportside box and sharp, five-spoke alloys nicely complement the top powertrain and suspension, turning the Sonoma into a true factory sport truck. If off-roading is your thing, GMC offers the Highrider, sporting a reinforced frame (four inches wider, two inches taller) and beefed-up suspension riding on three-ply all-terrain tires. The GMC Sonoma can outperform Ford's Ranger on or off the pavement, but when it comes to interior fittings, Ford still has the General beat by a wide margin.

Inside, Sonomas and Chevrolet S-Series pickups are virtually identical, with a roomy cab and modern dash layout. Center stack controls are canted toward the driver for improved access. Unfortunately, the cloth trim and carpeting feel thin and plastic used for dash panels and switchgear still looks as though it was sourced from Fisher Price. On extended cab trucks, an optional left-side access panel makes loading passengers or cargo into the rear of the cab much easier, but choosing the three-door cab eliminates one of the rear foldout jump seats.

For our money, the Ford Ranger, Dodge Dakota and Toyota Tacoma come across as more refined vehicles than the Sonoma, and their sticker prices reflect this impression. But in the compact truck value-per-dollar equation, GMC just might best deliver all the goods you're seeking – especially if what you're after is a sporty little truck able to sprint like a sports car off the line and through the twisties.

Safety Data

Side Airbag: *Not Available*
4-Wheel ABS: *Standard*
Driver Crash Test Grade: *Poor*
Side Impact Crash Test Front: *Average*
Crash Offset: *Marginal*
Integrated Child Seat(s): *Not Available*
Traction Control: *Not Available*
Passenger Crash Test Grade: *Average*
Side Impact Crash Test Rear: *Not Available*

Standard Equipment

SL 2WD REGULAR CAB (5M): 2.2L I4 OHV SMPI 8-valve engine; 5-speed overdrive manual transmission; 525-amp battery with run down protection; 100-amp alternator; rear wheel drive, 3.73 axle ratio; stainless steel exhaust; comfort ride suspension, front independent suspension with antiroll bar, front coil springs, rigid rear axle suspension with rear leaf springs; power re-circulating ball steering; front disc/rear drum brakes with 4 wheel antilock braking system; 19 gal. capacity fuel tank; front license plate bracket; front and rear body-colored bumpers with rear step; monotone paint; aero-composite halogen fully automatic headlamps with daytime running lights, delay-off feature; additional exterior lights include center high mounted stop light, underhood light; driver's and passenger's manual black folding outside mirrors; front and rear 15" x 7" painted styled steel wheels; P205/75SR15 BSW AS front and rear tires; underbody mounted compact steel spare wheel; AM/FM stereo with clock, seek-scan, 4 speakers, and fixed antenna; 1 power accessory outlet, retained accessory power; instrumentation display includes oil pressure gauge, water temp gauge, volt gauge, trip odometer; warning indicators include battery, lights on, key in ignition; driver's side airbag, passenger's side cancelable airbag; ignition disable; tinted windows; variable intermittent front windshield wipers; seating capacity of 3, bench front seat with fixed headrests, driver's seat includes 2-way direction control, passenger's seat includes 2-way direction control; vinyl seats, vinyl door trim insert, full cloth headliner, full vinyl floor covering, cabback insulator; interior lights include dome light with fade; passenger's side vanity mirror; day-night rearview mirror; glove box with light, front cupholder, driver's and passenger's door bins; vinyl cargo floor, cargo concealed storage; colored grille, black side window moldings, black front windshield molding, black rear window molding and black door handles.

SLS 2WD REGULAR CAB (5M) (in addition to or instead of SL 2WD REGULAR CAB (5M) equipment): Front and rear colored bumpers with chrome bumper insert; colored bodyside molding with chrome bodyside insert; 3 power accessory outlets; seating capacity of 3, 60-40 split-bench front seat with fixed headrests, center armrest with storage, driver's seat includes 4-way direction control with lumbar support, passenger's seat includes 4-way direction control; premium cloth seats, cloth door trim insert, full carpet floor covering with rubber floor mats; interior lights include front reading lights, illuminated entry; dual illuminated vanity mirrors, dual auxiliary visors; carpeted cargo floor and chrome grille.

SLS 2WD EXTENDED CAB (5M) (in addition to or instead of SLS 2WD REGULAR CAB (5M) equipment): 4.1 axle ratio; HD ride suspension, HD front coil springs, HD front shocks, HD rear leaf springs, HD rear shocks; vented rear windows; seating capacity of 5, passenger's seat includes 4-way direction control with easy entry; 50-50 folding rear facing jump seats; rear console with storage, front and rear cupholders and 2 seat back storage pockets.

SL 4WD REGULAR CAB SB (5M) (in addition to or instead of SL 2WD REGULAR CAB (5M) equipment): 4.3L V6 OHV SMPI 12-valve engine; part-time 4 wheel drive, auto locking hub control with electronic shift, 3.08 axle ratio; front independent torsion suspension with antiroll bar, front torsion springs, front torsion bar; 4 wheel disc brakes with 4 wheel antilock braking system; front and rear body-colored bumpers and rear tow hooks.

SL 4WD REGULAR CAB LB (5M) (in addition to or instead of SL 4WD REGULAR CAB SB (5M) equipment): HD ride suspension, HD front torsion springs, HD front shocks, HD rear leaf springs and HD rear shocks.

SLS 4WD REGULAR CAB (5M) (in addition to or instead of SLS 2WD REGULAR CAB (5M) equipment): 4.3L V6 OHV SMPI 12-valve engine; part-time 4 wheel drive, auto locking hub control with electronic shift, 3.08 axle ratio; front independent torsion suspension with antiroll bar, front torsion springs, front torsion bar; 4 wheel disc brakes with 4 wheel antilock braking system and rear tow hooks.

SLS 4WD EXTENDED CAB (5M) (in addition to or instead of SLS 2WD EXTENDED CAB (5M) equipment): 4.3L V6 OHV SMPI 12-valve engine; part-time 4 wheel drive, auto locking hub control with electronic shift, 3.08 axle ratio; front independent torsion suspension with antiroll bar, front torsion springs, front torsion bar; 4 wheel disc brakes with 4 wheel antilock braking system and rear tow hooks.

Base Prices

CODE	DESCRIPTION	INVOICE	MSRP
TS10603-R9S-E63	SL 2WD Regular Cab SB (5M)	11533	12204
TS10803-R9S-E63	SL 2WD Regular Cab LB (5M)	12160	12868
TS10603-YC5-E63	SLS 2WD Regular Cab SB (5M)	12274	13562
TS10803-YC3-E63	SLS 2WD Regular Cab LB (5M)	12591	13913
TS10653-YC5-E63	SLS 2WD Extended Cab (5M)	14130	15613
TT10603-R9S-E63	SL 4WD Regular Cab SB (5M)	15826	16747
TT10803-R9S-E63	SL 4WD Regular Cab LB (5M)	16140	17079
TT10803-YC3-E63	SLS 4WD Regular Cab LB (5M)	16781	18542
TT10603-YC5-E63	SLS 4WD Regular Cab SB (5M)	16394	18115
TT10653-YC5-E63	SLS 4WD Extended Cab (5M)	18114	20015
Destination Charge:		520	520

Accessories

CODE	DESCRIPTION	INVOICE	MSRP
—	Custom Cloth Seat Trim (SL)	NC	NC
1SA	Marketing Option Package 1 (SL) *Includes vehicle with standard equipment. REQUIRES C60 or R6G.*	NC	NC
1SC	Marketing Option Package 2 (SLS 2WD Reg Cab) *Includes vehicle with standard equipment. REQUIRES (LF6 or L35) and (C60 or R6G). NOT AVAILABLE with ULO, AV5.*	(645)	(750)

CODE	DESCRIPTION	INVOICE	MSRP
1SD	**Marketing Option Package 1SD (SLS except 2WD Reg Cab)**	692	805
	Manufacturer Discount	(129)	(150)
	Net Price	563	655
	Includes air conditioning. NOT AVAILABLE with R6G, M30, ULO, AV5.		
1SE	**Super Spec Preferred Equipment Group (SLS 2WD Reg Cab SB)**	1583	1841
	Manufacturer Discount	(731)	(850)
	Net Price	852	991
	Includes SLS Decor package: GVWR: 4,200 lbs, smooth ride suspension package, engine: 2.2L SFI I4, transmission: 5-speed manual (std), 3.73 axle ratio, wheels: aluminum, tires: P205/75R15 AS BSW SBR, air conditioning, AM/FM stereo with seek, scan and CD, convenience group: tilt steering, speed control; 60/40 reclining split bench seat and tachometer. NOT AVAILABLE with A28, ANL, AV5, C5D, G80, GU4, GU6, L35, LF6, M50, NP5, QCA, R6G, R7R, ULO, UM6, UPO, Z85, ZCA, ZQ6, M30, V10.		
1SF	**Super Spec Preferred Equipment Group (SLS 2WD X-Cab)**	1837	2136
	Manufacturer Discount	(731)	(850)
	Net Price	1106	1286
	Includes SLS Decor package: P205/75R15 AS BSW SBR tires, air conditioning, convenience group: tilt steering, speed control; 60/40 reclining split bench seat, tachometer, GVWR: 4,600 lbs, HD suspension package, 4.10 axle ratio and third door side access panel with driver's side jump seat delete. NOT AVAILABLE with ULO, L35, LF6, M50, M30, GU6, G80, QCA, ZCA, AV5, R7R, V10, R6G, UM6, ZQ6, NP5, ANL, A28.		
1SG	**Super Spec Preferred Equipment Group (SLS 2WD X-Cab)**	3743	4352
	Manufacturer Discount	(645)	(750)
	Net Price	3098	3602
	Includes SLS Decor Package: GVWR: 4,600 lbs, HD suspension package, engine: Vortec 4300 V6 SFI, transmission: 4-speed automatic with overdrive, 3.42 axle ratio, P205/75R15 AS BSW SBR tires, air conditioning, convenience group: tilt steering, speed control; 60/40 reclining split bench seat, third door side access panel: driver's side jump seat delete and deep tinted glass. NOT AVAILABLE with UPO, LF6, L35, M50, M30, R7R, V10, R6G, UM6, ULO, NP5, A28.		
1SH	**Super Spec Preferred Equipment Group (SLS 4WD X-Cab)**	3076	3577
	Manufacturer Discount	(731)	(850)
	Net Price	2345	2727
	Includes SLS Decor package: HD suspension package: P235/70R15 AS BSW SBR tires, engine: Vortec 4300 V6 SFI, transmission: 4-speed automatic with overdrive, 3.42 axle ratio, air conditioning, AM/FM stereo with seek, scan and CD, convenience group: tilt steering, speed control; 60/40 reclining split bench seat: floor console delete, third door side access panel: driver's side jump seat delete, GVWR: 5,150 lbs and tachometer. NOT AVAILABLE with L35, QCA, ZCE, ZCA, ZR2, ZM5, V10, R6G, UM6, NP5, A28, ULO.		
1SJ	**Super Spec Preferred Equipment Group (SLS 4WD X-Cab)**	5534	6435
	Manufacturer Discount	(1161)	(1350)
	Net Price	4373	5085
	Includes SLS Decor package, transmission: 4-speed automatic with overdrive, locking differential, underbody shield package, third door side access panel: driver's side jump		

CODE	DESCRIPTION	INVOICE	MSRP
	seat delete, leather-wrapped steering wheel, tachometer, power convenience group: power door locks, power windows, dual exterior power remote mirrors; convenience group: tilt steering, speed control; air conditioning, AM/FM stereo with seek, scan and CD, engine: Vortec 4300 V6, tachometer, 3.73 axle ratio, high back reclining bucket seats, highrider suspension package: wheel opening flares, 31 x 10.5/15R AT BSW SBR tires and underbody shield package. NOT AVAILABLE with GU6, C6F, QCA, QEB, ZBF, ZCA, ZCE, Z85, R6G, ULO, UM6, ANL, A28.		
A28	**Sliding Rear Window**	103	120
	NOT AVAILABLE with 1SE, 1SF, 1SG, 1SH, 1SJ.		
AJ1	**Deep Tinted Glass (Reg Cab)**	64	75
	Includes rear window only.		
AJ1	**Deep Tinted Glass (X-Cab)**	99	115
	Includes rear window and rear quarter glass.		
AM6	**60/40 Reclining Split Bench Seat (4WD)**	(215)	(250)
	Includes floor console delete. REQUIRES M30. NOT AVAILABLE with ZR2, UPO, 1SJ.		
ANL	**Fog Lamps (All Except 4WD Reg Cab LB)**	99	115
	NOT AVAILABLE with 1SE, 1SF, ZR2, 1SJ.		
AV5	**Front Reclining Bucket Seats (2WD)**	250	291
	Includes cloth trim, folding seat backs, driver's manual lumbar adjuster and floor console. NOT AVAILABLE with 1SE, M50, LF6, L35, 1SF.		
AV5	**Front Reclining Bucket Seats (4WD)**	NC	NC
	Includes cloth trim, folding seat backs, driver's manual lumbar adjuster and floor console. NOT AVAILABLE with 1SE, M50, LF6, L35, 1SF.		
B30	**Color-Keyed Carpeting (SL)**	60	70
	Includes cargo space carpet.		
C3A	**GVWR: 4,400 Lbs (X-Cab)**	NC	NC
	Includes 2500 lbs. front and 2700 lbs. rear GAWR. NOT AVAILABLE with 1SV, QCA, ZCA, ZCE.		
C5A	**GVWR: 4,900 Lbs. (Reg Cab LB)**	NC	NC
	Includes 2500 lbs. front and 2700 lbs. rear GAWR. NOT AVAILABLE with R7R, M30, GT5.		
C5D	**GVWR: 4,600 Lbs**	NC	NC
	Includes 2500 lbs. front and 2700 lbs. rear GAWR. REQUIRES Z85. NOT AVAILABLE with ZQ8, 1SE.		
C60	**Air Conditioning**	692	805
	NOT AVAILABLE with R6G.		
C6F	**GVWR: 5,150 Lbs**	NC	NC
	Includes 2700 lbs. front and 2700 lbs. rear GAWR. REQUIRES Z85 and GU6. NOT AVAILABLE with ZR2, 1SJ.		
E24	**Third Door Side Access Panel (X-Cab)**	254	295
	Includes passenger side jump seat only and repositions rear speakers to doors and driver's side jump seat delete. Hinged door opens to rear of cab, located on drivers side of vehicle.		
G80	**Locking Differential**	232	270
	REQUIRES LF6 or L35. NOT AVAILABLE with GT5, R7R, M30, 1SE, 1SF.		

CODE	DESCRIPTION	INVOICE	MSRP
GT5	4.10 Axle Ratio (2WD)	NC	NC
	NOT AVAILABLE with LF6, L35, M50, GU4, GU6, G80, C5A.		
GU4	3.08 Axle Ratio (2WD X-Cab)	NC	NC
	REQUIRES LF6 or L35 or 1SG. NOT AVAILABLE with GT5, R7R, 1SE, M30.		
GU6	3.42 Axle Ratio (4WD Reg Cab)	NC	NC
	REQUIRES LF6 or G80 or 1SA or 1SC. NOT AVAILABLE with GT5, R7R, 1SE, M50, 1SF, ZR2, 1SJ.		
L35	Engine: Vortec 4300 V6 (4WD)	223	259
	Includes tachometer. REQUIRES G80. NOT AVAILABLE with 1SH.		
L35	Engine: Vortec 4300 V6 (2WD)	1160	1349
	Includes tachometer, transmission: 5-speed manual and 3.08 axle ratio. REQUIRES C5A or G80. NOT AVAILABLE with GT5, R7R, LF6, AV5, 1SF, 1SG.		
LF6	Engine: Vortec 4300 V6 SFI (2WD)	937	1090
	Includes transmission: 5-speed manual and 3.08 axle ratio. REQUIRES C5A. NOT AVAILABLE with 1SE, GT5, R7R, L35, AV5, 1SF, 1SG.		
M30	Transmission: 4-Speed Automatic with Overdrive	920	1070
	Includes brake/transmission shift interlock. NOT AVAILABLE with R7R, 1SE, 1SD, GU4, G80, C5A, 1SF.		
M50	Transmission: 5-Speed Manual	NC	NC
	REQUIRES LF6 or L35 or G80. NOT AVAILABLE with GT5, R7R, 1SE, AV5, GU6, 1SF, 1SG.		
N60	Wheels: Aluminum (SLS)	241	280
	NOT AVAILABLE with ZQ8.		
N60	Wheels: Aluminum (SL)	320	372
N90	Wheels: Aluminum (SL)	320	372
	NOT AVAILABLE with QEB.		
N90	Wheels: Aluminum (SLS)	241	280
	NOT AVAILABLE with ZR2, QEB.		
NP5	Leather-Wrapped Steering Wheel (SLS)	46	54
	NOT AVAILABLE with 1SE, 1SF, 1SG, 1SH.		
QCA	Tires: P205/75R15 AS WOL SBR (2WD)	104	121
	NOT AVAILABLE with ZQ8, ZCE, 1SE, C3A, 1SF, Z85, ZR2, ZBF, QEB, 1SH, 1SJ.		
QEB	Tires: P235/75R15 AT WOL SBR (4WD)	288	335
	Includes spare tire: full size temporary. NOT AVAILABLE with ZR2, ZCE, QCA, ZCA, ZBF, N90, Z85, 1SJ.		
QEB	Tires: P235/75R15 AT WOL SBR (4WD)	187	218
	NOT AVAILABLE with ZR2, ZCE, QCA, ZCA, ZBF, N90, 1SJ.		
R6G	Air Conditioning Not Desired	NC	NC
	NOT AVAILABLE with C60, 1SE, 1SD, 1SF, 1SG, 1SH, 1SJ.		
R7R	Powertrain Bonus Discount (SL SB)	(445)	(500)
	NOT AVAILABLE with LF6, L35, M50, M30, GU4, GU6, G80, ZQ8, 1SE.		
R7R	Powertrain Bonus Discount (SL LB)	(516)	(600)
	NOT AVAILABLE with LF6, L35, M50, M30, C5A, GU4, GU6, G80, 1SF, 1SG.		
U16	Tachometer	51	59

CODE	DESCRIPTION	INVOICE	MSRP
UL0	**Radio: AM/FM Stereo with Cassette** *Includes speed sensitive volume, theft lock, automatic tone control, auto reverse, music search cassette player with enhanced performance 6 speaker system and clock. REQUIRES 1SP. NOT AVAILABLE with UM6, UL5, 1SE, UN0, UP0, 1SF, 1SG, 1SH, 1SJ.*	174	202
UL5	**Radio Delete (SL)** *NOT AVAILABLE with UM6, UL0.*	(194)	(226)
UM6	**Radio: AM/FM Stereo with Cassette with Clock** *Includes 4 speakers. NOT AVAILABLE with UL0, UN0, UP0, 1SH, 1SJ.*	105	122
UN0	**Radio: AM/FM Stereo and CD (SLS Reg Cab)** *Includes speed sensitive volume, theft lock, automatic tone control and enhanced performance 6 speaker system. NOT AVAILABLE with UL0, UP0, UM6.*	260	302
UP0	**Radio: AM/FM Stereo with CD and Cassette (SLS)** *Includes speed sensitive volume, theft lock, seek-scan, automatic tone control, auto reverse and music search cassette player with enhanced performance 6 speaker system and clock. REQUIRES 1SG, 1SH or 1SJ. NOT AVAILABLE with 1SC, 1SD, 1SF, UL0, UM6, UN0.*	86	100
UP0	**Radio: AM/FM Stereo with CD and Cassette (SLS 2WD X-Cab)** *Includes speed sensitive volume, theft lock, seek-scan, automatic tone control, auto reverse, music search cassette player, enhanced performance 6 speaker system and clock. REQUIRES AV5. NOT AVAILABLE with 1SC, 1SD, UL0, UM6, UN0.*	174	202
UP0	**Radio: AM/FM Stereo with CD and Cassette (SLS)** *Includes speed sensitive volume, theft lock, seek-scan, automatic tone control, auto reverse and music search cassette player with enhanced performance 6 speaker system. REQUIRES M30 and AV5. NOT AVAILABLE with UM6, 1SE, UL0, UN0, 1SG.*	346	402
V10	**Cold Climate Package** *Includes engine block heater and HD battery. NOT AVAILABLE with 1SE, 1SF, 1SG, 1SH.*	77	89
VF7	**Rear Bumper Delete (SL)** *Includes non-impact and non-trailering panel.*	NC	NC
YC5	**SLE Decor Package (SLS)** *Includes manual driver's lumbar, bodyside moldings with bright insert, stripe delete and dual illuminated visor vanity mirrors. NOT AVAILABLE with 1SE, 1SF, 1SG, ZR2, 1SH, 1SJ.*	642	701
Z85	**HD Suspension Package (2WD SB)** *Includes HD rear springs, HD front and rear shocks and P235/70R15 AS BSW SBR tires. NOT AVAILABLE with ZQ8, 1SE.*	55	64
Z85	**HD Suspension Package (4WD SB/X-Cab)** *Includes HD rear springs, HD front and rear shocks and P235/70R15 AS BSW SBR tires. NOT AVAILABLE with ZR2, ZCE, QCA, ZCA, 1SJ.*	220	256
ZBF	**Tire: Spare P235/70R15 AS BSW SBR (4WD)** *REQUIRES Z85. NOT AVAILABLE with ZR2, ZCE, QCA, ZCA, QEB, 1SJ.*	82	95
ZCA	**Tire: Spare P205/75R15 AS WOL SBR (2WD)** *REQUIRES QCA. NOT AVAILABLE with ZQ8, ZCE, 1SE, C3A, 1SF, Z85, ZR2, ZBF, QEB, 1SH, 1SJ.*	82	95

CODE	DESCRIPTION	INVOICE	MSRP
ZCE	Tire: Spare P205/75R15 AS BSW SBR (2WD) *NOT AVAILABLE with ZQ8, QCA, ZCA, C3A, Z85, ZR2, ZBF, QEB, 1SH, 1SJ.*	82	95
ZM5	Underbody Shield Package (4WD) *Includes transfer case shield, front differential skid plates, fuel tank shield, and steering linkage shield. NOT AVAILABLE with 1SH.*	108	126
ZQ3	Convenience Group *Includes tilt steering and speed control.*	340	395
ZQ6	Power Convenience Group (SLS) *Includes power door locks, power windows and dual exterior power remote mirrors. NOT AVAILABLE with 1SE, 1SF.*	684	795
ZQ8	Sport Suspension Package (2WD Reg Cab SB/2WD X-Cab) *Includes HD front and rear stabilizer bars and 46mm DeCarbon front and rear shocks, special coil springs for reduced trim height, urethane jounce bumpers and tires: P235/55R16 AS BSW SBR. REQUIRES C3A and (LF6 or L35 or 1SG or 1SF). NOT AVAILABLE with N60, C5D, Z85, ZCE, QCA, ZCA, R7R, M30.*	632	735
ZR2	Highrider Suspension Package (4WD) *Includes 46mm Bilstein shocks, HD springs, and additional chassis enhancements for increased width/height, tires: 31 x 10.5/15R AT BSW SBR and underbody shield package. REQUIRES G80. NOT AVAILABLE with GU6, C6F, Z85, ZCE, QCA, ZCA, ZBF, QEB, N90, ANL, 1SH.*	1544	1795
ZY2	Conventional Two-Tone Paint (SLS SB)	194	225

1999 SUBURBAN

1999 GMC Suburban

What's New?

A couple of new colors are the only modifications to the Suburban.

Review

In some sections of the country, wise middle-class folks have been tooling around for several years in mile-long Suburbans, whether or not they have great need for all that expanse behind the driver's seat. These days, throughout the suburban reaches of Houston and Dallas, among other spots, the Chevrolet and GMC Suburban have become de facto status-flaunting vehicles, pushing prices beyond the reach of the common man.

Yes, those who formerly wheeled about town in a Cadillac, and wouldn't feel quite right in a pickup truck, appear to have twirled their affections toward the biggest passenger vehicles in the General Motors repertoire. Mechanically, you get the same layout in the smaller Yukon, but select a GMC Suburban and you get an available third-row seat and more cargo space. A 255-horsepower 5.7 liter V8 is standard. Or, with the 3/4-ton C/K 2500 series you can opt for the mammoth Vortec 7400 V8, whipping out 290 strutting horses and a mean 410 pound-feet of ground-tromping torque. Oh, there's also an optional turbo-diesel. Both the half- and 3/4-ton versions come with either two- or four-wheel drive, and all have four-wheel anti-lock braking.

Last year GMC introduced a new four- wheel drive system to the Suburban. Called Autotrac, it automatically shifts from 2WD to 4WD when wheel slippage is detected, just like Ford's Control-Trac system in the similarly gargantuan Expedition. This year, all that's new is fresh paint colors.

Buyers beware that GMC is preparing to introduce a completely new Suburban for the 2000 or 2001 model year. Based upon the rigid new Sierra pickup platform, the new 'Burban will be much improved inside and out. Wait for the new truck if you can.

Today's Suburban can seat up to nine occupants and tow as much as five tons, when properly equipped. For families that need plenty of room for youngsters, or for retirees who need loads of power to haul a travel trailer, a Suburban can make good sense. GMC is combating competition from Ford's new Expedition, but for heavy-duty use and maximum space, Chevrolet and GMC are still the only serious games in town for a mammoth "truck wagon."

Safety Data

Side Airbag: *Not Available*
4-Wheel ABS: *Standard*
Driver Crash Test Grade: *Good*
Side Impact Crash Test Front: *Not Available*
Crash Offset: *Not Available*
Integrated Child Seat(s): *Not Available*
Traction Control: *Not Available*
Passenger Crash Test Grade: *Good*
Side Impact Crash Test Rear: *Not Available*

Standard Equipment

1500 SL 2WD (4A): 5.7L V8 OHV SMPI 16-valve engine; 4-speed electronic overdrive automatic transmission with lock-up; 600-amp HD battery; 100-amp alternator; rear wheel drive, 3.42 axle ratio; stainless steel exhaust; front independent suspension with HD anti-roll bar, front coil springs, HD front shocks, rigid rear axle suspension with anti-roll bar, rear leaf springs, HD rear shocks; power re-circulating ball steering with engine speed-sensing assist; front disc/rear drum brakes with 4 wheel antilock braking system; 42 gal. capacity fuel tank; split swing-out rear cargo door; trailer harness; front and rear chrome bumpers with black rub strip, front chrome bumper insert, rear step; black bodyside molding with chrome bodyside insert, chrome wheel well molding; monotone paint; sealed beam halogen headlamps with daytime running lights; additional exterior lights include center high mounted stop light, underhood light; driver's and passenger's manual black folding outside mirrors; front and rear 15" x 7" painted styled steel wheels; P235/75SR15 BSW AS front and rear tires; inside mounted full-size conventional steel spare wheel; rear heat ducts; AM/FM stereo with clock, seek-scan, 4 speakers, and fixed antenna; power door locks, child safety rear door locks, power remote hatch/trunk release; 3 power accessory outlets; instrumentation display includes tachometer, oil pressure gauge, water temp gauge, volt gauge, trip odometer; warning indicators include battery, lights on, key in ignition, door ajar; dual airbags; ignition disable; tinted windows, manual rear windows, fixed 1/4 vent windows; variable intermittent front windshield wipers; seating capacity of 3, bench front seat with adjustable headrests, driver's seat includes 2-way direction control, passenger's seat includes 2-way direction control; front height adjustable seatbelts; vinyl seats, full cloth headliner, full vinyl floor covering;

interior lights include dome light with fade, front reading lights, illuminated entry; sport steering wheel; passenger's side vanity mirror; day-night rearview mirror; glove box with light, front cupholder, instrument panel bin, driver's and passenger's door bins, rear door bins; vinyl cargo floor, cargo tie downs, cargo light; colored grille, black side window moldings, black front windshield molding, black rear window molding and black door handles.

2500 SL 2WD (4A) (in addition to or instead of 1500 SL 2WD (4A) equipment): HD 4-speed electronic overdrive automatic transmission with lock-up, HD transmission oil cooler; 3.73 axle ratio; front and rear 16" x 6.5" painted styled steel wheels and carpeted cargo floor.

1500 SL 4WD (4A) (in addition to or instead of 1500 SL 2WD (4A) equipment): Part-time 4 wheel drive, auto locking hub control with electronic shift; front independent suspension front torsion springs and front torsion bar.

2500 SL 4WD (4A) (in addition to or instead of 1500 SL 4WD (4A) equipment): HD 4-speed electronic overdrive automatic transmission with lock-up, HD transmission oil cooler; 4.1 axle ratio, colored fender flares; front and rear 16" x 6.5" painted styled steel wheels; interior lights include front and rear reading lights and carpeted cargo floor.

Base Prices

Code	Description	Invoice	MSRP
TC10906-R9S	1500 SL 2WD (4A)	22522	25739
TC20906-R9S	2500 SL 2WD (4A)	23904	27323
TK10906-R9S	1500 SL 4WD (4A)	25147	28739
TK20906-R9S	2500 SL 4WD (4A)	26529	30323
Destination Charge:		685	685

Accessories

Code	Description	Invoice	MSRP
1SA	**Marketing Option Package 1SA** *Includes vehicle with standard equipment. REQUIRES C60 or C69 or YG6.*	NC	NC
1SB	**Marketing Option Package 1SB** *Includes SLE Decor package: convenience package: tilt wheel, speed control; interior lights, folding center and rear seats, rear cupholders, custom cloth seat trim, seatback storage pockets, leather-wrapped steering wheel, dual illuminated visor vanity mirrors, color keyed grille, composite halogen headlamps, black roof rack, electric remote outside mirrors, deep tinted glass, height adjustable front and rear seatbelts, electric rear window defogger, cloth door trim, carpet, front and rear air conditioning, auxiliary rear heater, front 60/40 reclining split bucket seat, 6-way power driver's seat, carpeted color-keyed floor mats, rear carpet floor mats, carpeted load floor mats, inside rearview light sensitive mirror, 8 point compass, remote keyless entry system with two key fobs and ETR AM/FM stereo with seek, scan and cassette. REQUIRES L65 (1500).*	6298	7323
1SB	**Marketing Option Package 1SB (1500)** *Includes SLE Decor package: convenience package: tilt wheel, speed control; interior lights, folding center and rear seats, rear cupholders, custom cloth seat trim, seatback storage pockets, leather-wrapped steering wheel, dual illuminated visor vanity mirrors, color keyed grille, composite halogen headlamps, black roof rack, electric remote outside mirrors, deep tinted glass, height adjustable front and rear seatbelts, electric rear window defogger, cloth door trim, carpet, front and rear air conditioning, auxiliary rear heater, front 60/40 reclining split bucket seat, 6-way power driver's*	6513	7573

CODE	DESCRIPTION	INVOICE	MSRP
	seat, carpeted color-keyed floor mats, rear carpet floor mats, carpeted load floor mats, inside rearview light sensitive mirror, 8 point compass, remote keyless entry system with two key fobs and ETR AM/FM stereo with seek, scan and cassette. NOT AVAILABLE with L65, QIZ, MT1, C3F, C5I.		
1SC	**Marketing Option Package 1SC**	8052	9363
	Includes SLT Decor package: convenience package: tilt wheel, speed control; interior lights, folding center and rear seats, rear cupholders, custom cloth seat trim, seatback storage pockets, leather-wrapped steering wheel, dual illuminated visor vanity mirrors, color keyed grille, composite halogen headlamps, black roof rack, electric remote outside mirrors, deep tinted glass, height adjustable front and rear seatbelts, electric rear window defogger, cloth door trim, carpet, front and rear air conditioning, auxiliary rear heater, front 60/40 reclining split bucket seat, 6-way power driver's seat, carpeted color-keyed floor mats, rear carpet floor mats, carpeted load floor mats, inside rearview light sensitive mirror, 8 point compass, remote keyless entry system with two key fobs; front high back reclining bucket seats with power lumbar, ultrasoft gray leather seat trim, roof console, floor console and ETR AM/FM stereo with seek, scan, CD and cassette.		
1SC	**Marketing Option Package 1SC (1500)**	8267	9613
	Includes SLT Decor package: convenience package: tilt wheel, speed control; interior lights, folding center and rear seats, rear cupholders, custom cloth seat trim, seatback storage pockets, leather-wrapped steering wheel, dual illuminated visor vanity mirrors, color keyed grille, composite halogen headlamps, black roof rack, electric remote outside mirrors, deep tinted glass, height adjustable front and rear seatbelts, electric rear window defogger, cloth door trim, carpet, front and rear air conditioning, auxiliary rear heater, front 60/40 reclining split bucket seat, 6-way power driver's seat, carpeted color-keyed floor mats, rear carpet floor mats, carpeted load floor mats, inside rearview light sensitive mirror, 8 point compass, remote keyless entry system with two key fobs; front high back reclining bucket seats with power lumbar, ultrasoft gray leather seat trim, roof console, floor console and ETR AM/FM stereo with seek, scan, CD and cassette.		
A95	**Reclining High Back Bucket Seats**	335	390
	Includes inboard armrests, dual adjustable headrests, storage pockets behind seats and power lumbar support. NOT AVAILABLE with YG4, 1SA.		
AE7	**Front 60/40 Reclining Split Bucket Seat**	86	100
	Includes center fold down armrest with coin holder, map strap, writing board, storage pockets behind seats, power lumbar support and overhead console delete. REQUIRES 1SC. NOT AVAILABLE with ZM9, YG4.		
AJ1	**Deep Tinted Glass**	262	305
	Excludes tinted glass on windshield, driver's and front passenger's windows. NOT AVAILABLE 1SB, 1SC.		
AS3	**Folding Center and Rear Seats**	1017	1182
	Includes center folding bench seat. NOT AVAILABLE with YG4, 1SB, 1SC.		
AT5	**Center Folding Bench Seat**	544	632
	Includes easy entry feature on passenger's side for access to rear seat/cargo area. NOT AVAILABLE with YG4, 1SB, 1SC.		
B71	**Wheel Flare Moldings (1500 4WD)**	155	180
	Deletes wheel opening moldings.		

CODE	DESCRIPTION	INVOICE	MSRP
BVE	Black Side Step Running Boards *NOT AVAILABLE with NZZ.*	280	325
C36	Auxiliary Rear Heater *Includes cloth rear quarter trim. REQUIRES 1SA.*	176	205
C3F	GVWR: 7,700 Lbs (1500 2WD) *REQUIRES MT1. NOT AVAILABLE with 1SB, 1SC, GT4, QHM, KC4, V10.*	NC	NC
C49	Electric Rear Window Defogger *REQUIRES 1SA.*	132	154
C5I	GVWR: 8,050 Lbs (1500 4WD) *REQUIRES MT1. NOT AVAILABLE with 1SB, 1SC, GT4, QGB, QBN, QBX, KC4, V10, F60.*	NC	NC
C60	Front Air Conditioning *NOT AVAILABLE with YG6.*	727	845
C69	Front and Rear Air Conditioning *Includes dual controls and rear overhead vents. NOT AVAILABLE with YG6.*	1200	1395
DF2	Camper Type Exterior Mirrors *7.5" X 10.5" stainless steel. Includes adjustable arm feature to provide field of vision for vehicles to 96' wide. REQUIRES 1SB or 1SC.*	(39)	(45)
DF2	Camper Type Exterior Mirrors *7.5" X 10.5" stainless steel. Includes adjustable arm feature to provide field of vision for vehicles to 96" wide. REQUIRES 1SA.*	46	53
F60	HD Front Springs (4WD) *NOT AVAILABLE with C5I.*	54	63
G80	Locking Rear Differential	217	252
GT4	3.73 Axle Ratio (2500) *Includes water to oil cooler. REQUIRES L29.*	NC	NC
GT4	3.73 Axle Ratio (1500) *Includes water to oil cooler. NOT AVAILABLE with L65, MT1, KC4, C3F, QIZ, C5I.*	116	135
GT5	4.10 Axle Ratio (2500)	NC	NC
K47	High Capacity Air Cleaner	22	25
KC4	Engine Oil Cooler (1500) *NOT AVAILABLE with GT4, MT1, C3F, L65, C5I.*	116	135
KNP	HD Auxiliary Transmission Oil Cooler (1500)	83	96
L29	Engine: 7.4L SFI V8 (2500) *REQUIRES F60. NOT AVAILABLE with TP3.*	516	600
L65	Engine: 6.5L V8 Turbo Diesel *Includes hydraulic brakes, glow plugs, integral two-stage fuel filter, fuel and water separator with instrument panel warning light, black front bumper guards, engine oil cooler, extra sound insulation and fuel filter change signal. REQUIRES F60 or MT1 and C3F and QIZ or C5I and QIW. NOT AVAILABLE with V10, TP3, QHM, KC4, QBN, QBX, QGB.*	2460	2860
MT1	Transmission: 4-Speed Automatic with Overdrive (1500) *Includes HD auxiliary transmission oil cooler. REQUIRES B71, L65. NOT AVAILABLE with 1SB, 1SC, GT4, QHM, KC4, V10, QBN, QBX, QGB.*	NC	NC
N90	Wheels: Cast Aluminum (1500 2WD) *Includes steel spare wheel. NOT AVAILABLE with L65, MT1, C3F, QIZ.*	267	310

CODE	DESCRIPTION	INVOICE	MSRP
NP8	Push Button Electronic Active Transfer Case (4WD) *REQUIRES ZQ3. NOT AVAILABLE with 1SA.*	NC	NC
NZZ	Off-Road Skid Plates (4WD) *Includes skid plates on front differential, transfer case and fuel tank. NOT AVAILABLE with BVE.*	202	235
P06	Trim Rings and Bright Center Hub Caps *Includes 4 bright metal trim rings. REQUIRES 1SA.*	52	60
PF4	Wheels: Aluminum (1500 4WD) *Includes steel spare wheel. NOT AVAILABLE with L65, QIZ, QIW, MT1, C5I.*	267	310
QBN	Tires: LT245/75R16C On/Off Road BSW SBR (1500 4WD) *NOT AVAILABLE with L65, MT1, C5I, QGB, QBX, QIZ, QIW.*	47	55
QBX	Tires: LT245/75R16C On/Off Road OWL SBR (1500 4WD) *NOT AVAILABLE with L65, MT1, C5I, QGB, QBN, QIZ, QIW.*	155	180
QGB	Tires: P245/75R16 AT WOL (1500 4WD) *NOT AVAILABLE with L65, MT1, C5I, QBN, QBX, QIZ, QIW.*	120	140
QHM	Tires: P235/75R15 AS WOL (1500 2WD) *NOT AVAILABLE with L65, MT1, C3F, QIZ.*	155	180
QIW	Tires: LT245/75R16E ON/OFF Road BSW SBR (2500 4WD)	47	55
QIW	Tires: LT245/75R16E ON/OFF Road BSW SBR (1500 4WD) *NOT AVAILABLE with QGB, QBN, QBX, QIZ.*	194	229
QIZ	Tires: LT245/75R/16E AS BSW (1500 4WD) *NOT AVAILABLE with GT4, QBX, QBN, QGB, QIW, 1SB, 1SC.*	146	174
QIZ	Tires: LT245/75R/16E AS BSW (2500) *NOT AVAILABLE with GT4, QHM, 1SB, 1SC.*	391	459
TP3	Dual 600- Amp Battery (4WD) *REQUIRES ZM9. NOT AVAILABLE with L29, L65.*	48	56
U01	Exterior Roof Marker Lamps (5)	47	55
UM6	Radio: AM/FM Stereo with Cassette *Includes digital clock and 4 speakers. REQUIRES 1SA.*	126	147
UN0	Radio: AM/FM Stereo with CD and Automatic Tone Control *Includes theft lock, digital clock, speed sensitive volume and enhanced performance 8 speaker system. REQUIRES 1SB.*	86	100
UP0	Radio: AM/FM Stereo with CD and Cassette *Includes theft lock, auto reverse/music search cassette, automatic tone control, digital clock, speed sensitive volume and enhanced performance 8 speaker system. REQUIRES 1SB. NOT AVAILABLE with UN0.*	172	200
V10	Cold Climate Package *NOT AVAILABLE with L65, MT1, C3F, C5I.*	28	33
V76	Front Recovery Hooks (2WD)	33	38
V96	Trailer Hitch Ball and Mount Provisions *Includes 2" chrome hitch ball. REQUIRES Z82.*	26	30
YG4	Rear Seat Delete *Deletes third seat and load floor mats. REQUIRES 1SC. NOT AVAILABLE with ZM9.*	(875)	(1018)
YG4	Rear Seat Delete *Deletes third seat and load floor mats. REQUIRES 1SB.*	(531)	(618)
YG4	Rear Seat Not Desired *REQUIRES 1SA. NOT AVAILABLE with AS3.*	NC	NC

CODE	DESCRIPTION	INVOICE	MSRP
YG6	**Air Conditioning Not Desired** *REQUIRES 1SA. NOT AVAILABLE with C60, C69.*	NC	NC
Z82	**HD Trailering Equipment** *Includes platform hitch and HD hazard flasher. REQUIRES GT5 or L29 or 1SA or 1SB or 1SC or KC4.*	184	214
ZM9	**Comfort & Security Convenience Package** *Includes heated driver's and passenger's seats, 6-way power passenger's seat, heated electrochromic exterior mirrors, Homelink programmable transmitter and gas preloaded shock absorbers. REQUIRES 1SC. NOT AVAILABLE with YG4, AE7.*	942	1095
ZP6	**Rear Window Equipment Package** *Includes rear window intermittent wiper/washer and electric rear window defogger. REQUIRES 1SA.*	240	279
ZQ3	**Convenience Package** *Includes tilt wheel and speed control. REQUIRES 1SA.*	329	383
ZY2	**Conventional Two-Tone Paint** *NOT AVAILABLE with 1SA.*	172	200

1999 YUKON

1999 GMC Yukon

What's New?

More new colors are added as Yukon cruises into 1999.

Review

Compact sport-utility vehicles get most of the attention nowadays, but for folks with big families – or scads of goods to lug around – they're just not spacious enough inside. GMC offers a solution to this problem with the Yukon, available only in a four-door body style.

At a glance, the four-door Yukon and larger Suburban look nearly identical, but a Yukon measures several inches shorter. Beneath the hood sits a Vortec 5700 V8, rated for 255 horsepower, powerful enough for any trip up a mountainside. From the driver's seat forward, space is massive in the Yukon. The two-wheel drive is capable of towing as much as 7,000 pounds, and Yukons seat up to six passengers.

On the Interstate, the Yukon rides nicely, but the wide body takes some getting used to if you're accustomed to compacts. Turning onto smaller roads, it suddenly feels more like a truck. Easy to control either way, this sizable machine is reasonably maneuverable, if driven with discretion. The V8 is strong, and the four-speed automatic transmission shifts neatly. Think about the "entry assist" running boards if your regular riders aren't so nimble. They help. So do the robust grab bars that ease entry into the rear seats.

In 1998, GMC introduced an optional automatic four-wheel drive system that shifts between 2WD and 4WD as conditions warrant. No longer is it necessary to push a button on the dashboard to actively engage four-wheel traction. For 1999, new colors have been added to the paint chart.

Because GMC targets customers with an average income of $114,000 a year, luxury conveniences are part of upscale Yukon packages. The typical prospect is a 48-year-old married man who is attracted to a vehicle's size and power. Those attributes the Yukon has in abundance, as does its little-different Chevy Tahoe counterpart. In the size race, the Yukon four-door fits squarely between the Jimmy compact and the big-bruiser Suburban wagons. Squint your eyes, in fact, and the difference between a Yukon and Suburban begins to evaporate, despite the latter's extra 20 inches of steel. Ford's Expedition is a bit larger than the Yukon, while the Dodge Durango is slightly smaller. Both of these competitors offer eight-passenger seating, which is not available on the Yukon.

With the introduction of the Ford Expedition a few years ago, GM lost its dominance of the full-size SUV market. Further complicating matters, the slightly larger, less expensive Expedition is derived from modern F-Series underpinnings. Until a redesigned Yukon arrives for the 2000 model year, it's anybody's game.

Safety Data

Side Airbag: *Not Available*
4-Wheel ABS: *Standard*
Driver Crash Test Grade: *Good*
Side Impact Crash Test Front: *Not Available*
Crash Offset: *Not Available*
Integrated Child Seat(s): *Not Available*
Traction Control: *Not Available*
Passenger Crash Test Grade: *Good*
Side Impact Crash Test Rear: *Not Available*

Standard Equipment

SLE 2WD: 5.7L V8 OHV SMPI 16-valve engine; four-speed electronic overdrive automatic transmission with lock-up; 600-amp battery; 100-amp alternator; rear wheel drive, 3.42 axle ratio; stainless steel exhaust; front independent suspension with anti-roll bar, front coil springs, front shocks, rear suspension with rear leaf springs, rear shocks; power re-circulating ball steering with engine speed-sensing assist; front disc/rear drum brakes with 4 wheel antilock braking system; 30 gal. capacity fuel tank; split swing-out rear cargo door; trailer harness; roof rack; front and rear chrome bumpers with black rub strip, chrome bumper insert, rear step bumper; black bodyside molding with chrome bodyside insert, chrome wheel well molding; monotone paint; aero-composite halogen headlamps with daytime running lights; additional exterior lights include center high mounted stop light, underhood light; driver and passenger power remote black folding outside mirrors; front and rear 15" x 7" silver alloy wheels; P235/75SR15 BSW AS front and rear tires; underbody mounted full-size temporary steel spare wheel; air conditioning, rear heat ducts; AM/FM stereo, clock, seek-scan, with cassette, eight performance speakers, automatic equalizer, theft deterrent, and fixed antenna; cruise control; power door locks, remote keyless entry, child safety rear door locks, power remote hatch/trunk release; three power accessory outlets; analog instrumentation display includes tachometer, oil pressure gauge, water temp gauge, volt gauge, compass, exterior temp, trip odometer; warning indicators include battery, lights on, key in ignition, door ajar; dual airbags; ignition disable; deep tinted windows, power front windows with driver 1-touch down, power rear windows, fixed 1/4 vent windows; variable intermittent

CODE	DESCRIPTION	INVOICE	MSRP

front windshield wipers, rear window defroster; seating capacity of 6, 60-40 split-bench front seat with adjustable headrests, center armrest with storage, driver's seat includes four-way power seat, eight-way direction control power lumbar support, passenger's seat includes four-way direction control power lumbar support; 60-40 folding rear split-bench seat with adjustable rear headrest, center armrest with storage; front and rear height adjustable seatbelts; premium cloth seats, cloth door trim insert, full cloth headliner, full carpet floor covering with carpeted floor mats; interior lights include dome light, front and rear reading lights, 4 door curb lights, illuminated entry; leather-wrapped sport steering wheel with tilt adjustment; dual illuminated vanity mirrors, dual auxiliary visors; auto-dimming day-night rearview mirror; glove box with light, front and rear cupholders, instrument panel bin, two seat back storage pockets, driver and passenger door bins; carpeted cargo floor, cargo cover, cargo net, cargo concealed storage; chrome grille, black side window moldings, black front windshield molding, black rear window molding, black door handles.

SLE 4WD (in addition to or instead of SLE 2WD): Part-time four-wheel drive, auto locking hub control and electronic shift; front torsion suspension, front torsion springs, front torsion bar; rear tow hooks; front and rear 16" x 6.5" wheels.

Base Prices

		Invoice	MSRP
TC10706-YE9	SLE 2WD	26284	30039
TK10706-YE9	SLE 4WD	28909	33039
Destination Charge:		650	650

Accessories

Code	Description	Invoice	MSRP
1SD	**Marketing Option Package 1SD** *Includes SLE decor package, 6-way power driver's seat, front carpet floor mats, rear carpet floor mats, carpeted load floor mats, inside rearview light sensitive mirror, remote keyless entry system. NOT AVAILABLE with AE7, ZM9.*	NC	NC
1SE	**Marketing Option Package 1SE** *Includes 6-way power driver's seat, front carpet floor mats, rear carpet floor mats, carpeted load floor mats, inside rearview light sensitive mirror, remote keyless entry system, SLT decor package, ultrasoft gray leather seat trim, front high back reclining bucket seats, roof console, floor console, front and rear air conditioning, AM/FM stereo with seek, scan, CD, cassette. NOT AVAILABLE with UNO.*	1838	2137
A95	**Front High Back Reclining Bucket Seats** *Includes inboard armrests, dual adjustable headrests, power lumbars, storage pockets behind seats, 3-passenger folding rear bench seat, roof console and floor console. NOT AVAILABLE with AE7.*	204	237
AE7	**60/40 Reclining Split Bench Seat** *Includes center fold down storage armrest with coin holder, map strap, writing board, power lumbars, storage pockets behind seats, 3-passenger folding rear bench seat, roof console delete, floor console delete. NOT AVAILABLE with 1SD, ZM9, A95.*	NC	NC
BVE	**Black Side Step Running Boards** *Shipped loose for dealer installation. NOT AVAILABLE with NZZ.*	280	325
C69	**Front and Rear Air Conditioning**	473	550
G80	**Locking Rear Differential**	216	252
GT4	**3.73 Axle Ratio** *Includes water to oil cooler. NOT AVAILABLE with KC4, Z82.*	116	135
K47	**High Capacity Air Cleaner**	22	25

CODE	DESCRIPTION	INVOICE	MSRP
KC4	Engine Oil Cooler *NOT AVAILABLE with GT4.*	116	135
KNP	HD Auxiliary Transmission Cooler	83	96
NZZ	Off Road Skid Plates (4WD) *Includes differential and transfer case shields. NOT AVAILABLE with BVE.*	90	105
QFN	Tires: P235/75R15 AS RWL SBR (2WD)	120	140
QGB	Tires: P245/75R16 AT WOL (2WD)	120	140
UNO	Radio: AM/FM Stereo with CD Player *Includes clock, theft lock, automatic tone control, speed sensitive volume and enhanced performance speaker system. NOT AVAILABLE with UPO.*	86	100
UPO	Radio: AM/FM Stereo with CD Player and Cassette *Includes clock, theft lock, automatic tone control, speed sensitive volume, auto reverse music search cassette and enhanced performance speaker system. NOT AVAILABLE with UNO.*	172	200
V10	Cold Climate Package *Includes engine block heater.*	28	33
V76	Tow Hooks (2WD)	33	38
YF5	California Emissions *Automatically added to vehicles shipped to and/or sold to retailers in California. Out-of-state retailers must order on vehicles to be registered or leased in California.*	146	170
Z82	HD Trailering Equipment *Includes trailering hitch platform and heavy duty hazard flasher. REQUIRES KC4. NOT AVAILABLE with GT4.*	184	214
ZM9	Luxury Convenience Package *Includes heated front seats, 6-way power front passenger seat, heated electrochromic exterior mirror, Homelink transmitter, 46 mm Bilstein shocks. REQUIRES A95. NOT AVAILABLE with AE7, 1SD.*	942	1095
ZY2	Conventional Two-Tone Paint	172	200

1999 YUKON DENALI

1999 GMC Yukon Denali

What's New?

General Motors brand managers came up with an idea to dress up the GMC Yukon, fill it full of luxury touches and give it a special name to toss their hat into the luxury SUV arena. Enter the 1999 GMC Yukon Denali, with loads of unique features and exclusive exterior paint colors – until, that is, GM decided to spin-off a clone for Cadillac called the Escalade.

Review

There's no secret as to why so many manufacturers have jumped into the luxury sport/utility segment with all four wheels. America seems to have an insatiable appetite for upscale SUVs right now, and gussied-up big utes that are derived from a company's bread-and-butter full-size pickup turn out to be the most profitable automotive product on the planet.

With GMC America's self-proclaimed premium truck brand, what could be more logical than to take the Chevy Tahoe/GMC Yukon, bolt-on a different face, toss in some special features, drape it in luxury and then market it as a upscale four-wheel-drive limo for the well-heeled?

Enter the 1999 GMC Yukon Denali (and its dolled-up sister, the Cadillac Escalade). Named after the Alaskan National Park that boasts the highest peak in North America, Denali is meant to take premium sport/utilities to a new high in distinct styling, luxury and content.

Exterior styling differs from the donor Yukon by the use of more distinct sheetmetal from the hoodline forward, plus a bold rectangular center-port grille. Reflector-optic halogen headlamps and recessed projector-beam fog lamps reside in a smoothed-out front fascia. Body-color cladding and integrated running boards spruce up the flanks, with textured body-color door handles, outside rearview mirrors and color-keyed rails on the flush roof rack completing the monotone look. Out back, a functional step bumper conceals a standard trailer hitch.

The Denali's interior features upper and lower consoles packed with storage cubbies and features such as reading lamps, cupholders, a rear power point and audio controls. Instrumentation is backlit in blue with white pointers and includes a tachometer. Luxury touches abound, with Zebrano wood trim, leather-trimmed front and rear heated seats, and a premium Bose sound system with six-CD changer and single-CD in-dash player. GM's OnStar mobile communications system is optional. Dual front next-generation airbags and keyless remote entry with an adjustable, shock-sensing anti-theft system are standard.

Powering all this opulence is a 5.7-liter pushrod V8 packing 255 horsepower. The Vortec 5700 puts its 330 foot-pounds of torque to the ground via a four-speed automatic transmission and the Auto Trac full-time four-wheel drive system. When activated, the AutoTrac transfer case will automatically shift from two-wheel drive to 4WD when it senses wheel slippage. Denali rides on unique six-spoke chromed aluminum wheels wearing Firestone 265/70R-16 touring tires designed especially for sport/utility applications on- and off-road in both wet and dry conditions.

Available in an array of unique exterior colors, the Denali provides a "look-at-me" driving experience around town and a king-of-the-road feel once you get out on the highway. Frankly, you expect a lot from a truck with a $43,000 price tag, and the Denali does have "new-toy" appeal. But understand that it is all riding atop a 10-year-old pickup truck design, with all the flaws inherent to its humble underpinnings, such as sloppy steering, numb brakes and unrefined ride. What's worse, use of standard GM interior plastics are simply not in keeping with Denali's price.

If you need to be the first one on your block with the latest the luxo-SUV world has to offer, there's no doubt the Denali is made for you. But if you happen to think, as we do, that the $5,000 or so price walk from an optioned-out GMC Yukon to the dolled-up Denali model is on the steep side, then maybe you should be shopping elsewhere. For our money, the Denali concept lost much of its luster when Cadillac literally thieved the whole vehicle from GMC to offer the Escalade. If GMC is truly meant to be the premium truck brand, that move confused things.

Safety Data

Side Airbag: *Not Available*
4-Wheel ABS: *Standard*
Driver Crash Test Grade: *Good*
Side Impact Crash Test Front: *Not Available*
Crash Offset: *Not Available*
Integrated Child Seat(s): *Not Available*
Traction Control: *Not Available*
Passenger Crash Test Grade: *Good*
Side Impact Crash Test Rear: *Not Available*

Standard Equipment

DENALI 4WD: 5.7L V8 OHV SMPI 16-valve engine; four-speed electronic overdrive automatic transmission with lock-up; 600-amp battery; engine oil cooler; 100-amp alternator; transmission oil cooler; limited slip differential, 3.73 axle ratio; stainless steel exhaust; front independent torsion suspension with anti-roll bar, front torsion springs, front torsion bar, rear suspension with rear leaf springs; power re-circulating ball steering with engine speed-sensing assist; front disc/rear drum brakes with four wheel antilock braking system; 30 gal. capacity fuel tank; front license plate bracket, running boards; split swing-out rear cargo door; trailer harness, trailer hitch; roof rack; front and rear body-colored bumpers with rear tow hooks, rear step bumper; body-colored bodyside cladding, body-colored fender flares; monotone paint; aero-composite halogen headlamps with daytime running lights; additional exterior lights include center high mounted stop light, underhood light; driver and passenger power remote body-colored heated folding outside mirrors; front and rear 16" x 7" chrome alloy wheels; P265/70SR16 BSW AT front and rear tires; underbody mounted full-size temporary steel spare wheel; air conditioning, rear air conditioning with separate controls, rear heat ducts; AM/FM stereo, clock, seek-scan, cassette, single CD, eight performance speakers, automatic equalizer, theft deterrent, and fixed antenna; cruise control; power door locks, remote keyless entry, child safety rear door locks, power remote hatch/trunk release; three power accessory outlets, garage door opener; analog instrumentation display includes tachometer, oil pressure gauge, water temp gauge, volt gauge, compass, exterior temp, trip odometer; warning indicators include battery, lights on, key in ignition, door ajar; dual airbags; ignition disable; deep tinted windows, power front windows with driver one-touch down, power rear windows, fixed 1/4 vent windows; variable intermittent front windshield wipers, rear window defroster; seating capacity of five, front bucket seats with heated driver and passenger seats and adjustable headrests, driver and passenger armrests, driver's seat includes four-way power seat, eight-way direction control, power lumbar support, passenger's seat includes four-way power seat, eight-way direction control, power lumbar support; 60-40 folding rear split-bench seat with adjustable rear headrest, center armrest with storage; front and rear height adjustable seatbelts; leather seats, cloth door trim insert, full cloth headliner, full carpet floor covering with carpeted

CODE	DESCRIPTION	INVOICE	MSRP

floor mats; interior lights include dome light, front and rear reading lights, four door curb lights, illuminated entry; leather-wrapped sport steering wheel with tilt adjustment; dual illuminated vanity mirrors, dual auxiliary visors; auto-dimming day-night rearview mirror; partial floor console, full overhead console with storage, glove box with light, front and rear cupholders, instrument panel bin, two seat back storage pockets, driver and passenger door bins; carpeted cargo floor, cargo cover, cargo net, cargo concealed storage; chrome grille, black side window moldings, black front windshield molding, black rear window molding, body-colored door handles.

Base Prices

CODE	DESCRIPTION	INVOICE	MSRP
TK10706	Denali 4WD	37603	42975
Destination Charge:		650	650

Accessories

CODE	DESCRIPTION	INVOICE	MSRP
1SF	Marketing Option Package 1SF *Includes HD trailering equipment, 3.73 axle ratio, Autotrac transfer case, locking rear differential, transmission oil cooler, 16" x 7" chrome cast aluminium wheels, P265/70R16 BW A/T tires, front and rear air conditioning, AM/FM stereo with seek, scan, CD, cassette, Luxury Convenience Package: front reclining bucket seats, console, six-way power driver's seat, six-way power passenger's seat, heated electrochromic exterior mirror, homelink transmitter, 46 mm Bilstein shocks, remote keyless entry, side step running boards, electric rear window defogger, deep tinted glass, solid paint, ultrasoft neutral leather seat trim.*	NC	NC

1999 CR-V

1999 Honda CR-V

What's New?

The CR-V gains 20 horsepower, bringing the total output to 146. Automatic transmission models have a revised column shifter with an overdrive switch. The power window buttons are illuminated, the spare tire cover has been upgraded, and the front passenger seat is equipped with an armrest. Since Honda has effectively addressed all of our previous gripes with this year's changes, we'll have to get more creative with our complaints.

Review

For years Honda has been selling a sport-utility vehicle that many consider a fraud. Forget that the Honda Passport is based on the rugged and capable Isuzu Rodeo. To Honda aficionados, it is not a real Honda. (Consider how the Porsche 914 fares in the eyes of diehard Porsche fanatics.) Thus, to many people, the CR-V is the first Honda sport-utility vehicle.

Built on the Civic platform, the CR-V successfully integrates familiar Honda components into a fresh new design. Honda's famous four-wheel double-wishbone suspension makes an appearance on the CR-V (the first-ever application of four-wheel double-wishbone technology on a sport-ute), as does the familiar four-speed automatic transmission, which now comes with an overdrive on/off switch. The 2.0-liter DOHC inline four-cylinder engine makes 146 horsepower and 133 foot-pounds of torque, up 20 horsepower from last year, thanks to intake and exhaust tuning along with an increased compression ratio.

The CR-V's Real Time four-wheel-drive system is a derivative of the unit that Honda initially offered on their Civic wagon. All 4WD models come with a five-speed manual transmission, while the four-speed automatic is optional. A front-wheel-drive model is offered, but it comes only with the automatic transmission. The result of using all of these car components is not surprising: the CR-V looks and feels like a car.

The CR-V's interior is instantly recognizable to anyone who has spent time in Honda's passenger cars. Functionality takes precedence over style in the CR-V's cabin, and the result is easy-to-read gauges, well-placed controls, and high-quality, if somewhat uninspired, interior materials. Fit and finish is equal to the highly acclaimed Accord. Cargo capacity is an impressive 67.2 cubic feet when the rear seats are folded. The CR-V offers comfortable chairs for its occupants, each of which has excellent visibility and the ability to recline when the trip grows long. For the first time this year, the front passenger also benefits from a left-side armrest, an item that was missing on previous models. Rear passengers will also enjoy cupholders, which are now mounted in the door panels.

Available in either LX or EX trim levels, the CR-V is surprisingly well-equipped even at the base LX trim level. Air conditioning with a filtration system is standard, as are power windows, power door locks, rear window wiper and defogger, AM/FM stereo with cassette, cruise control and a folding picnic table that doubles as a cargo area cover. Antilock brakes are available only on the EX model, which also comes with a CD player and alloy wheels.

The CR-V is not meant to replace hard-core recreational vehicles like the Jeep Wrangler or Toyota 4Runner. Instead, it is meant for the person who wants the functionality of a sport utility without having to pay an exorbitant sticker price and huge gas bills. The CR-V will get people to work and back in all but the worst weather, and to their favorite picnic area, assuming it's not on the Rubicon Trail. Best of all, this is a sport-utility vehicle that Honda lovers can finally call their own.

Safety Data

Side Airbag: *Not Available*
4-Wheel ABS: *Standard (EX); N/A (LX)*
Driver Crash Test Grade: *Good*
Side Impact Crash Test Front: *Excellent*
Crash Offset: *Poor*
Integrated Child Seat(s): *Not Available*
Traction Control: *Not Available*
Passenger Crash Test Grade: *Excellent*
Side Impact Crash Test Rear: *Excellent*

NOTE: In side impact crash testing, the CR-V rolled one-quarter of a turn onto its side.

Standard Equipment

LX FWD (4A): 2.0L I4 DOHC MPI 16-valve engine; 4-speed electronic overdrive automatic transmission; front wheel drive, 4.36 axle ratio; steel exhaust; front independent double wishbone suspension with anti-roll bar, front coil springs, rear independent double wishbone suspension with anti-roll bar, rear coil springs; power rack-and-pinion steering with engine speed-sensing assist; front disc/rear drum brakes; 15.3 gal. capacity fuel tank; rear mud flaps; conventional rear cargo door; front and rear black bumpers with rear step; black bodyside molding, rocker panel extensions, black wheel well molding; monotone paint; aero-composite halogen headlamps; additional exterior lights include center high mounted stop light; driver's and passenger's power remote black folding outside mirrors; front and rear 15" x 6" silver styled steel wheels; P205/70SR15 BSW AS front and rear tires; outside rear mounted full-size conventional steel spare wheel; air conditioning, air filter, rear heat ducts; AM/FM stereo with seek-scan, 4 speakers, and manual retractable antenna; cruise control with steering wheel controls; power door locks, child safety rear door locks, remote fuel release, power rear window remote release; 2 power accessory outlets, driver's foot rest; instrumentation display includes tachometer, water temp gauge, in-dash clock, trip odometer; warning indicators include oil pressure, battery, lights on, key in ignition, low fuel, trunk ajar; dual airbags; tinted windows, power front windows with driver's 1-touch down, power rear windows, fixed 1/4 vent windows; fixed interval front windshield wipers, flip-up rear window, fixed interval rear wiper, rear window defroster; seating capacity of 5, front bucket seats with adjustable headrests, driver's armrest, driver's seat includes 6-way direction control, passenger's seat includes 4-way direction control; 50-50 folding split-bench rear seat with reclining adjustable headrests, center armrest; front height adjustable seatbelts; cloth seats, vinyl door trim insert, full vinyl headliner, full carpet floor covering; interior lights include dome light, front reading lights; steering wheel with tilt adjustment; vanity mirrors; day-night rearview mirror; partial floor console, locking glove box, front and rear cupholders, instrument panel bin, 2 seat back storage pockets, driver's and passenger's door bins, rear door bins, front underseat tray; carpeted cargo floor, plastic trunk lid, cargo tie downs, cargo light, cargo concealed storage; black grille, black side window moldings, black front windshield molding, black rear window molding and black door handles.

LX AWD (5M) (in addition to or instead of LX FWD (4A) equipment): 5-speed overdrive manual transmission; full-time 4 wheel drive and 4.56 axle ratio.

CODE	DESCRIPTION	INVOICE	MSRP

EX AWD (5M) (in addition to or instead of LX AWD (5M) equipment): Front disc/rear drum brakes with 4 wheel antilock braking system; driver's and passenger's power remote body-colored folding outside mirrors; outside rear mounted full-size conventional alloy spare wheel; AM/FM stereo with seek-scan, single CD, 4 speakers, and manual retractable antenna; remote keyless entry and body-colored door handles.

Base Prices

RD284XPBW	LX FWD (4A)	16945	18550
RD174XPBW	LX AWD (5M)	17310	18945
RD176XEW	EX AWD (5M)	18679	20450
Destination Charge:		415	415

Accessories

—	California Emissions	85	100
—	Transmission: 4-Speed Automatic (AWD) *Includes floor console, 4.36 axle ratio and driver's armrest.*	730	800

1999 ODYSSEY

1999 Honda Odyssey

What's New?

Honda's latest masterpiece, the totally redesigned Odyssey, will finally give Chrysler's minivans a run for their money.

Review

Honda's first attempt at building a minivan came with the 1995 Odyssey – a smallish vehicle that drove like a car but couldn't fit the needs of most American minivan buyers. The Odyssey was misplaced in the minivan market, which favors a huge, comfortable amount of interior space and versatility to tight taxicab ambience and ease of parallel parking.

The new Odyssey can comfortably carry up to seven adult passengers, and it even has room under the seats for easy stowage of hockey sticks or skis. The suspension, engine, and every inch of sheetmetal are all-new, and the new Odyssey is related to the old Odyssey in name only - the car has been completely redesigned.

Starting with the engine, the Odyssey is powered by a 3.5-liter 24-valve VTEC V6, which produces up to 210 horsepower and 229 foot-pounds of torque, while achieving the environmentally friendly status of a low-emission vehicle. The V6 is based on the Accord's 3.0-liter engine but offers substantially more power, which helps to move a lot of extra girth.

The base model LX includes such standard fare as dual sliding doors, power windows (including power rear-vent windows), power locks, power mirrors, cruise control, a theft-deterrent system, two 12-volt power outlets, front and rear air conditioning, antilock brakes, and, of course, the 3.5-liter V6 engine. That price is actually $800 less than the previous-generation Odyssey LX, and severely undercuts similarly equipped long-wheelbase minivans from the competition.

The step-up EX model is exactly the same price as the previous Odyssey EX. The EX features such niceties as dual power sliding doors, body-colored door handles, a roof rack, keyless remote, an eight-way power driver's seat, alloy wheels, traction control, a CD player and steering wheel mounted radio controls. Plunking down the extra $3,000 for EX trim is worth it, just for the seats, which are infinitely more comfortable than the two-way manually adjustable seats of the LX. Leather seats are not available, so watch for an Acura version of the Odyssey sometime in the near future.

Sitting on a four-wheel independent suspension, a first in the minivan segment, the Odyssey is supported comfortably and it keeps the driver in touch with the road. Combined with the Odyssey's wide track, the suspension adds a nimble feel to this big car. Body roll around corners is well-damped for a vehicle of this height.

Takeoff from a stop is smooth, and gear changing is seamless, even at higher speeds. The front disc / rear drum brakes slow down the Odyssey smoothly and quickly for such a heavy car. All in all, it's a high-powered, smooth-shifting minivan that handles with confidence and doesn't make a powerful racket.

Instrument panel gauges are easy to read and the center controls are logically placed, and all controls are within easy reach. The cruise controls are mounted on the steering wheel, as are remote radio controls on the EX model. The EX is further enhanced with power door controls just left of the steering column. The interior abounds with cubbyholes and map pockets, and the nine cupholders are all functional, unlike some of the indentations other minivan makers are stamping onto seatbacks these days.

The most unique Odyssey feature continues to be its hideaway, or "magic" seat. With a minimum of effort and the use of one set of hands only, the rear seat can be folded out of sight and flush with the floor in a matter of seconds. The second row seats are convertible and can be used as separate captains chairs or as a bench.

A minivan would not be complete without safety features, and the Odyssey comes with its share. All seven passenger seating positions have headrests and three-point seatbelts, both firsts in the minivan market. An Electronic Brake Distribution system (EBD) is also standard. This system senses the placement and amount of cargo, and compensates for it during hard braking to avoid rear-wheel lockup.

The new Odyssey is a marvel of engineering and, if product excellence determines success, it will be the first hugely successful import minivan. Honda has expanded its horizons with the Odyssey, finally creating an epic worthy of the name.

Safety Data

Side Airbag: *Not Available*
4-Wheel ABS: *Standard*
Driver Crash Test Grade: *Excellent*
Side Impact Crash Test Front: *Excellent*
Crash Offset: *Good*
Integrated Child Seat(s): *Not Available*
Traction Control: *Standard (EX); N/A (LX)*
Passenger Crash Test Grade: *Excellent*
Side Impact Crash Test Rear: *Excellent*

Standard Equipment

LX (4A): 3.5L V6 SOHC SMPI with variable valve timing 24-valve engine, requires premium unleaded fuel; 4-speed electronic overdrive automatic transmission with lock-up; 72-amp battery; 130-amp alternator; front wheel drive, 3.94 axle ratio; steel exhaust; front independent strut suspension with anti-roll bar, front coil springs, rear independent double wishbone suspension with anti-roll bar, rear coil springs; power rack-and-pinion steering; front disc/rear drum brakes with 4 wheel antilock braking system; 20 gal. capacity fuel tank; front mud flaps; 4 doors with sliding left rear passenger door, sliding right rear passenger door, liftback rear cargo door; front and rear body-colored bumpers with rear step; black bodyside molding; monotone paint; aero-composite halogen headlamps; additional exterior lights include center high mounted stop light; driver's and passenger's power remote black folding outside mirrors; front and rear 16" x 6.5" steel wheels; P215/65TR16 BSW AS front and rear tires; inside mounted compact steel spare wheel; air conditioning, rear air conditioning with separate controls, air filter, rear heat ducts; AM/FM stereo with seek-scan, cassette, 4 speakers, and fixed antenna; cruise control with steering wheel controls; power door locks with 2 stage unlock, child safety rear door locks, remote fuel release; 2 power accessory outlets, driver's foot rest, retained accessory power; instrumentation display includes tachometer, water temp gauge, in-dash clock, trip odometer; warning indicators include oil pressure, battery, low oil level, lights on, key in ignition, low fuel, bulb failure, door ajar, trunk ajar, service interval; dual airbags; ignition disable; deep tinted windows, power front windows with driver's 1-touch down, fixed rear windows, power 1/4 vent windows; variable intermittent front windshield wipers, rear window wiper, rear window defroster; seating capacity of 7, front captain seats with adjustable headrests, driver's and passenger's armrests, driver's seat includes 4-way direction control, passenger's seat includes 4-way direction control; removable 50-50 folding bench 2nd row seat with reclining adjustable rear headrest; 3rd row full folding bench seat with adjustable headrests; front and rear height adjustable seatbelts with front pretensioners; cloth seats, cloth door trim insert, full vinyl headliner, full carpet floor covering; interior lights include dome light, front and rear reading lights, 2 door curb lights; steering wheel with tilt adjustment; dual illuminated vanity mirrors, dual auxiliary visors; day-night rearview mirror; partial floor console, mini overhead console with storage, glove box, front and rear cupholders, instrument panel bin, 1 seat back storage pocket; carpeted cargo floor, plastic trunk lid, cargo light, cargo concealed storage; chrome grille, black side window moldings, black front windshield molding, black rear window molding and black door handles.

EX (4A) (in addition to or instead of LX (4A) equipment): Traction control; front mud flaps, rear lip spoiler; roof rack; body-colored bodyside molding; aero-composite halogen auto off headlamps; driver's and passenger's power remote body-colored folding outside mirrors; air conditioning with climate control; AM/FM stereo with seek-scan, single CD, 6 speakers, and fixed antenna; radio steering wheel controls; remote keyless entry; power remote hatch/trunk release; garage door opener; ignition disable, panic alarm; driver's seat includes 6-way power seat with lumbar support; removable 50-50 folding captain's 2nd row seat with reclining adjustable headrests; auto-dimming day-night rearview mirror; 2 seat back storage pockets; cargo net and body-colored door handles.

Base Prices

Code	Description	Invoice	MSRP
RL184XEW	LX (4A)	20459	23000
RL186XPKW	EX (4A)	22947	25800
Destination Charge:		415	415

Accessories

Code	Description	Invoice	MSRP
—	Seats: 2nd Row Buckets (LX)	178	200

1999 PASSPORT

1999 Honda Passport

What's New?

Last year, the Passport and the identical Isuzu Rodeo were completely redesigned, so there are no new changes this year.

Review

Choices in the sub-$30,000 sport-utility class are numerous. Figuring out which truck best meets your needs almost always requires a compromise of some sort or another. The closest thing to perfect has been the Ford Explorer, and spectacular sales of this popular SUV prove that buyers find its combination of room, style and power the best in the segment.

The Explorer is a fine sport-ute, but there's another face in this neighborhood that deserves consideration. Meet the Honda Passport, which was completely redesigned a year ago. The new look is familiar yet contemporary and the Passport is one of the more ruggedly handsome SUVs available today.

Inside, the interior provides user-friendly ergonomics and plastic trim that feels surprisingly luxurious. Clamber aboard and head for the hills - it's easy with push-button 4WD and standard anti-lock brakes that thwart nature's attempts to impede your progress.

A unique hatchgate employs flip-up glass and a gate that swings from right to left. The full-size spare tire can be stored under the vehicle or on the hatchgate. Both LX and EX trim levels are offered with two- or four-wheel drive and come with a powerful 3.2-liter six-cylinder engine, with 205 horsepower to whisk you along with verve. EX is the upper-level trim, which adds a power moonroof, security system with remote entry, exterior-mounted spare tire, fog lights, leather-wrapped steering wheel, wood grain trim and map lights.

Problems with the new design are minimal. The location of the push-button 4WD switch is absurd, located directly next to the cruise control button where it could be activated accidentally. Off-road, the new Passport feels somewhat undersprung, but takes bumps and dips easily if speeds are kept down. Our final complaint is that there are no rear cupholders for the kiddies.

The new Passport is an excellent blend of old-fashioned truck toughness and modern day car-like convenience. If you're looking for a new $30,000 SUV, the Passport should be near the top of your shopping list. But so should the Ford Explorer, Dodge Durango and Toyota 4Runner.

Safety Data

Side Airbag: *Not Available*
4-Wheel ABS: *Standard*
Driver Crash Test Grade: *Average*
Side Impact Crash Test Front: *Excellent*
Crash Offset: *Not Available*
Integrated Child Seat(s): *Not Available*
Traction Control: *Not Available*
Passenger Crash Test Grade: *Good*
Side Impact Crash Test Rear: *Excellent*

NOTE: In side impact crash testing, the Passport rolled one-quarter of a turn onto its side.

Standard Equipment

LX 2WD (5M): 3.2L V6 DOHC SMPI 24-valve engine; 5-speed overdrive manual transmission; rear wheel drive, 4.1 axle ratio; steel exhaust; front independent double wishbone suspension with antiroll bar, front torsion springs, rigid rear axle suspension with rear coil springs; power rack-and-pinion steering with engine speed-sensing assist; front disc/rear drum brakes with 4 wheel antilock braking system; 21.1 gal. capacity fuel tank; skid plates; conventional rear cargo door; roof rack; front and rear body-colored bumpers with rear step; monotone paint; sealed beam halogen headlamps; additional exterior lights include center high mounted stop light; driver's and passenger's power remote black heated folding outside mirrors; front and rear 15" x 6" painted styled steel wheels; P235/75SR15 BSW M&S front and rear tires; inside under cargo mounted full-size temporary steel spare wheel; air conditioning; AM/FM stereo with seek-scan, cassette, 6 speakers, and fixed antenna; cruise control; power door locks, child safety rear door locks, power remote hatch/trunk release, power rear window remote release; 1 power accessory outlet; instrumentation display includes tachometer, water temp gauge, in-dash clock, trip odometer; warning indicators include water temp, battery, lights on, key in ignition, low fuel, trunk ajar; dual airbags; tinted windows, power front windows with driver's 1-touch down, power rear windows, fixed 1/4 vent windows; variable intermittent front windshield wipers, rear window defroster; seating capacity of 5, front bucket seats with adjustable headrests, center armrest with storage, driver's seat includes 4-way direction control, passenger's seat includes 4-way direction control; 60-40 folding rear bench seat with reclining adjustable headrests; front and rear height adjustable seatbelts; cloth seats, cloth door trim insert, full cloth headliner, full carpet floor covering; interior lights include dome light, 4 door curb lights; steering wheel with tilt adjustment; vanity mirrors; day-night rearview mirror; full floor console, locking glove box with light, front and rear cupholders, driver's and passenger's door bins; carpeted cargo floor, plastic trunk lid, cargo cover, cargo net, cargo tie downs, cargo light; black grille, black side window moldings, black front windshield molding, black rear window molding and black door handles.

EX 2WD (4A) (in addition to or instead of LX 2WD (5M) equipment): Four-speed electronic overdrive automatic transmission with lock-up and driver selectable program; 4.3 axle ratio; front power sliding and tilting glass sunroof with sunshade; additional exterior lights include front fog/driving lights; driver's and passenger's power remote body-colored heated folding outside mirrors; front and rear 16" x 7" silver alloy wheels; outside rear mounted full-size conventional steel spare wheel; remote keyless entry, child safety rear door locks, power remote hatch/trunk release, power rear window; panic alarm, security system; deep tinted windows; wood trim; interior lights include front reading lights; leather-wrapped steering wheel with tilt adjustment; dual illuminated vanity mirrors and body-colored door handles.

LX 4WD (5M) (in addition to or instead of LX 2WD (5M) equipment): Part-time 4 wheel drive, auto locking hub control with electronic shift; 4 wheel disc brakes with 4 wheel antilock braking system; front and rear mud flaps, skid plates; flip-up rear window and rear window wiper.

EX 4WD (4A) (in addition to or instead of EX 2WD (4A) equipment): Part-time 4 wheel drive, auto locking hub control with electronic shift, viscous limited slip differential; 4 wheel disc brakes with 4 wheel antilock braking system; flip-up rear window and rear window wiper.

CODE	DESCRIPTION	INVOICE	MSRP
	Base Prices		
9B214X2B1	LX 2WD (5M)	20268	22700
9B314X4B1	LX 4WD (5M)	22721	25450
9B226X2EA	EX 2WD (4A)	23658	26500
9B326X4EA	EX 4WD (4A)	25843	28950
Destination Charge:		415	415
	Accessories		
—	California Emissions	138	150
—	Leather Seat Trim (EX) *Includes leather door trim panels.*	892	1000
—	Transmission: 4-Speed Automatic (LX)	1026	1150
—	Wheel Package (LX 4WD) *Includes tailgate-mounted spare tire, 16" alloy wheels and P245/70R16 MS tires.*	357	400

1999.5 QX4

1999.5 Infiniti QX4

What's New?

Infiniti's luxury sport-ute receives new side airbags, different exterior colors and a revised four-wheel drive selector.

Review

In 1997, Infiniti released a luxury sport-utility vehicle based on the then-new Nissan Pathfinder. With little to differentiate the QX4 from the Pathfinder, other than a $10,000 price increase and a fancy-shmancy four-wheel drive system, many critics unleashed a torrent of criticism at the vehicle. The problem was not that people disliked the mechanics, driving style or appearance of this truck; they just couldn't get around the fact that the QX4 offered little, other than full-time 4WD and an impressive Infiniti warranty, to distinguish itself from the already-capable Pathfinder.

The critics might have cried foul, but the buying public seemed not to notice. The QX4 has been a strong seller for Infiniti, outpacing the optimistic projections that Infiniti had for this sport-ute. In its first year out, the QX4 received an award from J.D. Power and Associates in their initial quality study, ranking the QX4 the best compact sport-utility vehicle. Seems that those who did buy this truck were pretty darned happy with the purchase.

So what is it that people like about the QX4? Well, there is the full-time 4WD system that offers drivers the security of having maximum traction without having to change gear levers or control knobs. Called All-Mode 4WD, the system employs a wet multi-plate clutch in the center differential that shifts power between the front and rear wheels depending on road surface conditions. It does this by monitoring power distribution and wheel slippage via electronic sensors in the front and rear differentials, a throttle position sensor, and a transfer unit sensor in the antilock braking system. The unit ensures that the tires have traction by shifting up to 50 percent of the power to the front wheels if the rear wheels start to slip. This year's truck has an added 4-Lo position on the All-Mode selector dial and has deleted the 4-Lo from the transfer lever.

Another difference between the Pathfinder and QX4 is the treatment that the dealer is likely to give you when you attempt to buy one. Nissan dealers are like all car dealers: some are good, some are bad. Infiniti dealers, however, uniformly display style, grace and respect for their customers. For some, this alone is worth the extra money.

For 1999.5, Infiniti added a few more goodies to the QX4: side airbags with head and chest protection, a 12-volt outlet in the cargo area, UV cut glass and new halogen headlights with a multi-parabola reflector. Additionally, black rear privacy glass replaces the bronze and the following were added: automatic cut-off headlights, Infiniti Immobilizer System, five new paint colors and retained accessory power for the sunroof and windows.

Despite these benefits, the similarities between the QX4 and the Pathfinder keep us from highly recommending the Infiniti. Same basic shape. Same asthmatic 168-horsepower engine. Same interior materials. Is a great four-wheel drive system and decent treatment at the dealership worth the price of admission to the Infiniti club? Nah. Give us the Pathfinder SE, the extra $6K, and send us to Hawaii for a vacation.

Safety Data

Side Airbag: *Standard*
4-Wheel ABS: *Standard*
Driver Crash Test Grade: *Average*
Side Impact Crash Test Front: *Not Available*
Crash Offset: *Marginal*
Integrated Child Seat(s): *Not Available*
Traction Control: *Not Available*
Passenger Crash Test Grade: *Average*
Side Impact Crash Test Rear: *Not Available*

Standard Equipment

QX4 (4A): 3.3L V6 SOHC SMPI 12-valve engine; 4-speed electronic overdrive automatic transmission with lock-up; 90-amp alternator; transmission oil cooler; part-time 4 wheel drive, auto locking hub control with electronic shift, 4.64 axle ratio; stainless steel exhaust; front independent strut suspension with anti-roll bar, front coil springs, rigid rear axle multi-link suspension with anti-roll bar, rear coil springs; power rack-and-pinion steering with vehicle speed-sensing assist; front disc/rear drum brakes with 4 wheel antilock braking system; 21.1 gal. capacity fuel tank; front license plate bracket, front and rear mud flaps, running boards, skid plates; liftback rear cargo door; roof rack; front and rear body-colored bumpers with front and rear tow hooks, rear step; body-colored bodyside cladding, body-colored fender flares; monotone paint; aero-composite halogen auto off headlamps; additional exterior lights include front fog/ driving lights, center high mounted stop light; driver's and passenger's power remote body-colored heated folding outside mirrors; front and rear 16" x 7" silver alloy wheels; P245/70SR16 BSW AS front and rear tires; underbody mounted full-size conventional alloy spare wheel; air conditioning with climate control, rear heat ducts; premium AM/FM stereo with clock, seek-scan, cassette, single CD, 6 premium speakers, theft deterrent, and power retractable diversity antenna; cruise control with steering wheel controls; power door locks with 2 stage unlock, remote keyless entry, child safety rear door locks, power remote hatch/trunk release, remote fuel release, power rear window remote release; 3 power accessory outlets, driver's foot rest, retained accessory power, garage door opener; instrumentation display includes tachometer, water temp gauge, compass, exterior temp, trip odometer; warning indicators include oil pressure, water temp, battery, lights on, key in ignition, low fuel, low washer fluid, bulb failure, door ajar; dual airbags, seat mounted side airbags; ignition disable, panic alarm, security system; deep tinted windows, power front windows with driver's 1-touch down, power rear windows, fixed 1/ 4 vent windows; variable intermittent front windshield wipers, flip-up rear window, fixed interval rear wiper, rear window defroster; seating capacity of 5, front bucket seats with adjustable headrests, center armrest with storage, driver's seat includes 6-way power seat with lumbar support, passenger's seat includes 4-way power seat; 60-40 folding rear bench seat with reclining adjustable headrests, center armrest; front height adjustable seatbelts; leather seats, leatherette door trim insert, full cloth headliner, full carpet floor covering with carpeted floor mats, wood trim, leather-wrapped gear shift knob; interior lights include dome light, front and rear reading lights, illuminated entry; leather-wrapped steering wheel with tilt adjustment; dual illuminated vanity mirrors, dual auxiliary visors; auto-dimming day-night rearview mirror; full floor console, mini overhead console with storage, locking glove box, front and rear cupholders, 2 seat back storage pockets, driver's and passenger's door bins, rear door bins; carpeted cargo

CODE	DESCRIPTION	INVOICE	MSRP

floor, plastic trunk lid, cargo cover, cargo net, cargo tie downs, cargo light, cargo concealed storage; body-colored grille, black side window moldings, black front windshield molding, black rear window molding and body-colored door handles.

Base Prices

CODE	DESCRIPTION	INVOICE	MSRP
71119	QX4 (4A)	31976	35550
Destination Charge:		525	525

Accessories

CODE	DESCRIPTION	INVOICE	MSRP
E10	Two-Tone Paint	260	500
H70	Sunroof Preferred Package *Includes power tilt/slide sunroof, 6 disc CD autochanger and rear window wind deflector. NOT AVAILABLE with H71, S02.*	1123	1250
H71	Sunroof Preferred Package *Includes power tilt/slide sunroof, 6 disc CD autochanger and rear window wind deflector. NOT AVAILABLE with H70.*	1123	1250
H73	Power Tilt/Slide Sunroof *Includes sunshade.*	854	950
S02	Premium Sport Package *Includes Heated Seats Package: heated front seats with timer, HD battery and limited slip differential. REQUIRES (H70) Sunroof Preferred Package.*	628	700
W70	Towing Package *Includes hitch, harness and ball.*	292	390
X03	Heated Seats Package *Includes heated front seats with timer and HD battery. REQUIRES H70 or H73.*	359	400

1999 AMIGO

1999 Isuzu Amigo

What's New?

Two body styles are available – hardtop or softtop – and an automatic transmission is now offered with the V6 engine.

Review

1999 marks Amigo's second year back on the market after a three-year hiatus. Isuzu's small SUV convertible was reintroduced last year with a completely new façade and has done quite well.

Choices are plentiful when ordering an Amigo; consumers can choose between hardtop or softtop, two-wheel drive or four-wheel drive, four-cylinder or V6, and manual or automatic transmission.

Powering the base Amigo is a 2.2-liter, DOHC four-cylinder engine, which pumps out 130 horsepower and 144 foot-pounds of torque. The more powerful 3.2-liter V6 engine is the same one found under the hood of the Rodeo, and it makes 205 horsepower and 214 foot-pounds of torque. With the purchase of a V6 model, consumers can also opt for a four-speed automatic tranny.

Interestingly, four-wheel ABS and a manual moonroof come standard on the Amigo, but air conditioning and power door locks do not. All Amigos are available with a long list of options, however, including air conditioning, skid plates and big alloy wheels. A limited-slip differential can be had on four-wheel drive models and, for 1999, a hard-face spare tire cover is an option for trucks equipped with P245 tires and alloy wheels.

The capable Amigo seems to be holding its own against competitors such as the Chevrolet Tracker, Kia Sportage and Suzuki Vitara. Besides, we're suckers for the Jeep Wrangler convertible, and the Amigo looks like it was developed using the same recipe book.

Safety Data

Side Airbag: *Not Available*
4-Wheel ABS: *Standard*
Driver Crash Test Grade: *Not Available*
Side Impact Crash Test Front: *Not Available*
Crash Offset: *Poor*

Integrated Child Seat(s): *Not Available*
Traction Control: *Not Available*
Passenger Crash Test Grade: *Not Available*
Side Impact Crash Test Rear: *Not Available*

Standard Equipment

S 2.2L SOFT TOP 2WD (5M): 2.2L I4 DOHC SMPI 16-valve engine; 5-speed overdrive manual transmission; 600-amp battery; 100-amp alternator; rear wheel drive, 4.8 axle ratio; stainless steel exhaust; front independent double wishbone suspension with anti-roll bar, front torsion springs, front torsion bar, rigid rear axle multi-link suspension with anti-roll bar, rear coil springs; power rack-and-pinion steering with engine speed-sensing assist; front disc/rear drum brakes with 4 wheel antilock braking system; 17.7 gal. capacity fuel tank; front and rear mud flaps, skid plates; conventional rear cargo door; front manual pop-up glass sunroof with sunshade; manual convertible roof with roll-over protection; front and rear black bumpers with front and rear tow hooks, rear step; monotone paint; aero-composite halogen headlamps; additional exterior lights include center high mounted stop light; driver's and passenger's manual black folding outside mirrors; front and rear 15" x 6.5" silver styled steel wheels; P235/75SR15 BSW M&S front and rear tires; outside rear mounted full-size conventional steel spare wheel; AM/FM stereo with seek-scan, cassette, 4 speakers, and fixed antenna; 2 power accessory outlets, driver's foot rest; instrumentation display includes tachometer, water temp gauge, in-dash clock, trip odometer; warning indicators include oil pressure, battery, lights on, key in ignition, low fuel; dual airbags; tinted windows, fixed rear windows; fixed interval front windshield wipers; seating capacity of 5, front bucket seats with adjustable headrests, driver's seat includes 4-way direction control, passenger's seat includes 4-way direction control; full folding rear bench seat with adjustable headrests; front height adjustable seatbelts; cloth seats, cloth door trim insert, full cloth headliner, full carpet floor covering; interior lights include dome light, front reading lights; vanity mirrors; day-night rearview mirror; full floor console, locking glove box, front and rear cupholders, instrument panel bin, 1 seat back storage pocket, driver's and passenger's door bins; carpeted cargo floor, plastic trunk lid, cargo tie downs; body-colored grille, black side window moldings, black front windshield molding, black rear window molding and black door handles.

S 2.2L HARD TOP 2WD (5M) (in addition to or instead of S 2.2L SOFT TOP 2WD (5M) equipment): Front and rear manual pop-up glass sunroof with sunshade; fixed interval rear wiper, rear window defroster and cargo light.

S 3.2L V6 SOFT TOP 2WD (4A) (in addition to or instead of S 2.2L SOFT TOP 2WD (5M) equipment): 3.2L V6 DOHC SMPI 24-valve engine; 4-speed electronic overdrive automatic transmission with lock-up; 90-amp alternator; driver selectable program transmission; 4.3 axle ratio and steering wheel with tilt adjustment.

S 3.2L V6 HARD TOP 2WD (4A) (in addition to or instead of S 3.2L V6 SOFT TOP 2WD (4A) equipment): Front and rear manual pop-up glass sunroof with sunshade; fixed interval rear wiper, rear window defroster and cargo light.

S 2.2L SOFT TOP 4WD (5M) (in addition to or instead of S 2.2L SOFT TOP 2WD (5M) equipment): Part-time 4 wheel drive, auto locking hub control with electronic shift, limited slip differential, 4.8 axle ratio; 4 wheel disc brakes with 4 wheel antilock braking system.

S 3.2L V6 SOFT TOP 4WD (5M) (in addition to or instead S 3.2L V6 SOFT TOP 2WD (4A) equipment): Five-speed overdrive manual transmission; 90-amp alternator; part-time 4 wheel drive, auto locking hub control with electronic shift, limited slip differential and 4 wheel disc brakes with 4 wheel antilock braking system.

S 3.2L V6 HARD TOP 4WD (4A) (in addition to or instead of S 3.2L V6 HARD TOP 2WD (4A) equipment): Part-time 4 wheel drive, auto locking hub control with electronic shift, limited slip differential, 4.8 axle ratio; 4 wheel disc brakes with 4 wheel antilock braking system.

CODE	DESCRIPTION	INVOICE	MSRP

Base Prices

CODE	DESCRIPTION	INVOICE	MSRP
B15	S 2.2L Soft Top 2WD (5M)	14703	15810
E15	S 2.2L Hard Top 2WD (5M)	14703	15810
A14	S 3.2L V6 Soft Top 2WD (4A)	16334	17950
F14	S 3.2L V6 Hard Top 2WD (4A)	16334	17950
C15	S 2.2L Soft Top 4WD (5M)	17047	18330
D15	S 3.2L V6 Soft Top 4WD (5M)	17718	19470
G14	S 3.2L V6 Hard Top 4WD (4A)	18428	20250
Destination Charge:		495	495

Accessories

CODE	DESCRIPTION	INVOICE	MSRP
—	Transmission: 4-Speed Automatic with Overdrive (S V6 4WD Soft Top) *Includes driver selectable program.*	709	780
AT	Air Conditioning	836	950
BS2	Sport Side Step	278	355
CDA	Deluxe CD Player *Includes 4 speakers. NOT AVAILABLE with P7.*	390	500
CDC	6 Disc In-Dash CD Player (S V6) *REQUIRES P7.*	506	650
CDP	Premium CD Player (S V6) *Includes 6 speakers. REQUIRES P7.*	428	550
CMA	Cargo Mat	47	60
ENO	Cargo Convenience Net	20	25
FL	Fog Lamps (S V6 4WD) *REQUIRES P7 and M3.*	55	70
GRA	Brush Guard	233	298
ITA	Trailer Hitch	198	253
JAA	Carpeted Floor Mats	40	50
M3	Wheels: 16" Aluminum *Includes tires: P245/70R16.*	528	600
OVA	Fender Flares *REQUIRES M3.*	156	200
P20	Air Conditioning	836	950
P7	Preferred Equipment Package (S V6) *Includes power windows, power door locks, black power outside mirrors, remote keyless entry, security alarm, tilt steering column, variable intermittent wipers, AM/FM stereo with cassette, cargo convenience net, center armrest pad, courtesy lamp and carpeted floor mats.*	1821	2110
PBP	Granite Gray Paint Package (Hard Top) *REQUIRES M3.*	NC	NC
SCA	Center Armrest Pad	31	40
TLA	Tail Lamp Guards	66	84
XBX	Rear Storage Security Cover	140	180

1999 HOMBRE

1999 Isuzu Hombre

What's New?

Hombres receive additional exterior colors and a new bumper fascia. A three-door spacecab model is now available.

Review

The Hombre is Isuzu's entry in the compact-pickup market, built with sheetmetal stamped by General Motors and the basic mechanical and structural components of the Chevrolet S-10/GMC Sonoma twins. When it debuted in 1996, the Hombre came with two-wheel drive, a regular cab and a weak, 2.2-liter four-cylinder engine – not exactly the tough stuff truck buyers craved.

Isuzu introduced a spacecab extended-cab model, a 4.3-liter V6 engine and a four-speed automatic transmission in 1997. Last year, four-wheel drive became available. And for 1999, Hombres boast a change in bumper design and a third-door option. But while these small improvements are slowly accumulating, the Hombre pickup is not likely to take the world by storm just yet.

Built in the United States, Hombres are available in a variety of cab and powertrain configurations, ranging from a standard-cab, 2WD model with a 2.2-liter four-cylinder engine to a 4WD, 4.3-liter V6 spacecab model featuring an optional third door.

The regular-cab versions are available in S and XS trim levels, and options are few. S models are the workhorses, with vinyl floor covering and limited options that include air conditioning, stereo and rear step bumper. Hombre XS models are better equipped, offering custom cloth upholstery, carpeted floors and a tachometer.

Extended-cab models are offered in XS trim only and provide vinyl folding jump seats in the rear and easy-entry seats in the front. If ordered with the optional third door, the truck comes equipped with only one jump seat. Four-wheel antilock brakes and a theft-deterrent system are standard on all models, and 4WD Hombre buyers will enjoy standard alloy wheels. New colors to choose from this year include Indigo Blue, Meadow Green and Victory Red.

Isuzu hasn't been selling many pickups in the past several years. As personal-use pickup sales skyrocketed, the company stuck with basic trucks more suited for work than play. Only time will tell if the Hombre can change Isuzu's bleak forecast in this segment.

Safety Data

Side Airbag: *Not Available*
4-Wheel ABS: *Standard*
Driver Crash Test Grade: *Poor*
Side Impact Crash Test Front: *Average*
Crash Offset: *Marginal*
Integrated Child Seat(s): *Not Available*
Traction Control: *Not Available*
Passenger Crash Test Grade: *Average*
Side Impact Crash Test Rear: *Not Available*

Standard Equipment

S 2WD REGULAR CAB (5M): 2.2L I4 OHV SMPI 8-valve engine; 5-speed overdrive manual transmission; 525-amp battery with run down protection; 100-amp alternator; rear wheel drive, 3.73 axle ratio; stainless steel exhaust; front independent suspension with anti-roll bar, front coil springs, rigid rear axle suspension with rear leaf springs; power re-circulating ball steering; front disc/rear drum brakes with 4 wheel antilock braking system; 22.2 gal. capacity fuel tank; front black bumper; monotone paint; aero-composite halogen fully automatic headlamps with daytime running lights; additional exterior lights include center high mounted stop light, underhood light; driver's and passenger's manual black folding outside mirrors; front and rear 15" x 7" steel wheels; P205/75SR15 BSW AS front and rear tires; underbody mounted compact steel spare wheel; radio prep and fixed antenna; 1 power accessory outlet, retained accessory power; instrumentation display includes oil pressure gauge, water temp gauge, volt gauge, trip odometer; warning indicators include battery, lights on, key in ignition, low fuel; driver's side airbag, passenger's side cancelable airbag; tinted windows; variable intermittent front windshield wipers; seating capacity of 3, bench front seat with fixed headrests, driver's seat includes 2-way direction control, passenger's seat includes 2-way direction control; cloth seats, full cloth headliner, full vinyl floor covering, cabback insulator; interior lights include dome light; day-night rearview mirror; glove box with light, front cupholder, instrument panel bin, driver's and passenger's door bins; cargo concealed storage; black grille, black side window moldings, black front windshield molding, black rear window molding and black door handles.

XS 2WD REGULAR CAB (5M) (in addition to or instead of S 2WD REGULAR CAB (5M) equipment): Seating capacity of 3, 60-40 split-bench front seat with fixed headrests, center armrest with storage, driver's seat includes 4-way direction control, passenger's seat includes 4-way direction control and full carpet floor covering.

XS 2WD SPACE CAB (5M) (in addition to or instead of XS 2WD REGULAR CAB (5M) equipment): 4.1 axle ratio; rear black bumper with rear step; AM/FM stereo with clock, seek-scan, 4 speakers, and fixed antenna; 3 power accessory outlets, retained accessory power; ignition disable; vented rear windows; seating capacity of 5, 60-40 split-bench front seat with fixed headrests, center armrest with storage, passenger's seat includes 4-way direction control with easy entry; 50-50 folding side-facing rear jump seats; cloth door trim insert; interior lights include front reading lights; dual illuminated vanity mirrors, dual auxiliary visors and carpeted cargo floor.

XS V6 2WD SPACE CAB (4A) (in addition to or instead of XS 2WD SPACE CAB (5M) equipment): 4.3L V6 OHV SMPI 12-valve engine; 4-speed electronic overdrive automatic transmission with lock-up; 3.42 axle ratio and HD ride suspension.

S V6 4WD REGULAR CAB (5M) (in addition to or instead of XS 2WD REGULAR CAB (5M) equipment): 4.3L V6 OHV SMPI 12-valve engine; part-time 4 wheel drive, auto locking hub control with electronic shift, 3.42 axle ratio; HD ride suspension, front torsion springs, front torsion bar; 4 wheel disc brakes with 4 wheel antilock braking system; 18.5 gal. capacity fuel tank; underbody mounted full-size temporary steel spare wheel; 1 power accessory outlet and instrumentation display includes tachometer.

XS V6 4WD SPACE CAB (5M) (in addition to or instead of XS V6 2WD SPACE CAB (4A) equipment): 5-speed overdrive manual transmission; part-time 4 wheel drive, auto locking hub control with electronic

CODE	DESCRIPTION	INVOICE	MSRP

shift; front independent suspension with anti-roll bar, front torsion springs, front torsion bar; 4 wheel disc brakes with 4 wheel antilock braking system; 18.5 gal. capacity fuel tank; underbody mounted full-size temporary steel spare wheel and instrumentation display includes tachometer.

Base Prices

Code	Description	Invoice	MSRP
P15	S 2WD Regular Cab (5M)	10967	11545
P25	XS 2WD Regular Cab (5M)	11119	11955
P55	XS 2WD Space Cab (5M)	13528	15200
T35	S V6 4WD Regular Cab (5M)	15996	17200
P64	XS V6 2WD Space Cab (4A)	15504	17420
T65	XS V6 4WD Space Cab (5M)	17867	20075
Destination Charge:		495	495

Accessories

Code	Description	Invoice	MSRP
—	Transmission: 4 Speed Automatic (XS 2WD Reg Cab)	995	1070
—	Transmission: 4-Speed Automatic (XS 2WD X-Cab/XS V6 4WD X-Cab)	952	1070
	REQUIRES M1.		
—	Transmission: 4-Speed Automatic (S)	1017	1070
	REQUIRES P0.		
3DR	Driver's Side Third Door (X-Cab)	329	375
	Deletes 1 rear jumpseat.		
A1	Air Conditioning (Reg Cab)	735	835
	CFC free.		
C0	Convenience Package (XS X-Cab)	447	525
	Manufacturer Discount	(60)	(100)
	Net Price	387	425
	Includes tilt wheel and cruise control. REQUIRES 4A.		
F2	Radio: AM/FM with Clock and 4 Speakers (S 2WD)	207	235
F5	Radio: AM/FM Stereo with Cassette (S V6 4WD)	127	145
I2	Rear Step Bumper (Reg Cab)	53	60
JHG	Floor Mats (S V6 4WD)	26	30
M1	Wheels: Alloy (XS 2WD X-Cab)	246	280
P0	Performance Package (4-Cyl)	57	65
	Includes 29mm front stabilizer bar, stiffer and larger rear leaf springs, raised vehicle height by 20mm (2WD) and increased rear GAWR to 2700lbs (2WD) and increased GVWR to 5150 lbs (4WD).		
P1	Preferred Equipment Package P1 (XS 2WD Reg Cab)	1214	1429
	Manufacturer Discount	(145)	(286)
	Net Price	1069	1143
	Includes air conditioning, sliding rear window, AM/FM stereo with cassette and 4 speakers, tachometer and floor mats. REQUIRES P0.		
P10	Preferred Equipment Package P10 (XS V6 X-Cab 4WD)	964	1135
	Manufacturer Discount	(138)	(227)
	Net Price	826	908
	Includes air conditioning, sliding rear window, AM/FM stereo with cassette and 4 speakers and floor mats.		

CODE	DESCRIPTION	INVOICE	MSRP
P5	Power Package (V6 X-Cab)	636	750
	Manufacturer Discount	(44)	(100)
	Net Price	592	650
	Includes power windows, power door locks and heated power outside mirrors.		
P9	Preferred Equipment Package P9 (XS X-Cab 2WD)	1014	1194
	Manufacturer Discount	(145)	(239)
	Net Price	869	955
	Includes air conditioning, sliding rear window, AM/FM stereo with cassette and 4 speakers, tachometer and floor mats. REQUIRES P0.		

1999 OASIS

1999 Isuzu Oasis LS

What's New?

Only one trim level is available for 1999. Oasis has a new seating arrangement, interior and exterior refinements, and a couple of new colors.

Review

For several years, Honda had been purchasing Rodeo sport utilities from Isuzu and rebadging them as Honda Passports. A couple of years back, Honda also began selling an upscale version of the Isuzu Trooper as the Acura SLX, in order to capitalize on the booming luxury-SUV market.

To reciprocate these favors, Honda allows Isuzu to rebadge a Japanese-market sedan for sale across the Pacific and also donates the previous-style Odyssey minivan to fill a niche in Isuzu's U.S. lineup, called the Isuzu Oasis.

Powered by a strong 2.3-liter, 16-valve four-cylinder engine and featuring four conventional doors, the Oasis scores well in government crash tests and garners high customer satisfaction marks. The automatic transmission features a lockup torque converter and electronic grade-sensing system, which interprets throttle position to choose the optimum shift point and reduce hunting for gears when driving up or down hills. Antilock brakes and keyless entry are standard equipment.

For 1999, the Oasis is offered in one trim level only, with seating for six or seven. The six-passenger seating arrangement includes second-row captain's chairs, alloy wheels and a roof rack. With second-row seats removed and third-row seats folded down, Oasis provides 93.5 cubic feet of cargo space. This year, consumers can also choose from two new exterior colors: Clover Green Pearl or Crystal Silver Metallic.

Despite the distinct lack of V6 power, we think the Oasis offers solid value as a family wagon. It's roomy, attractive and well-equipped. Oasis offers an excellent warranty, proven Honda mechanicals and more versatility and cargo capacity than many competitors.

Safety Data

Side Airbag: *Not Available*
4-Wheel ABS: *Standard*
Driver Crash Test Grade: *Good*
Side Impact Crash Test Front: *Not Available*
Crash Offset: *Marginal*
Integrated Child Seat(s): *Not Available*
Traction Control: *Not Available*
Passenger Crash Test Grade: *Good*
Side Impact Crash Test Rear: *Not Available*

Standard Equipment

7-PASSENGER (4A): 2.3L I4 SOHC SMPI with variable valve timing 16-valve engine; 4-speed electronic overdrive automatic transmission with lock-up; 440-amp battery; 95-amp alternator; front wheel drive, 4.79 axle ratio; steel exhaust with chrome tip; front independent double wishbone suspension with anti-roll bar, front coil springs, rear independent double wishbone suspension with anti-roll bar, rear coil springs; power rack-and-pinion steering with engine speed-sensing assist; 4 wheel disc brakes with 4 wheel antilock braking system; 17.2 gal. capacity fuel tank; front and rear mud flaps, rear lip spoiler; 4 doors with conventional left rear passenger's door, conventional right rear passenger's door, liftback rear cargo door; front and rear body-colored bumpers with rear step; black bodyside molding, rocker panel extensions; monotone paint; aero-composite halogen headlamps; additional exterior lights include center high mounted stop light; driver's and passenger's power remote body-colored folding outside mirrors; front and rear 15" x 6" steel wheels; P205/65SR15 BSW AS front and rear tires; inside mounted compact steel spare wheel; air conditioning, rear air conditioning, rear heat ducts; AM/FM stereo with seek-scan, cassette, CD changer pre-wiring, in-dash CD pre-wiring, 4 speakers, and fixed antenna; cruise control with steering wheel controls; power door locks with 2 stage unlock, remote keyless entry, child safety rear door locks, power remote hatch/trunk release, remote fuel release; 1 power accessory outlet, driver's foot rest, retained accessory power; instrumentation display includes tachometer, water temp gauge, in-dash clock, trip odometer; warning indicators include battery, low oil level, lights on, key in ignition, low fuel, bulb failure, door ajar, trunk ajar, service interval; dual airbags; tinted windows, power front windows with driver's 1-touch down, power rear windows, fixed 1/4 vent windows; variable intermittent front windshield wipers, rear window wiper, rear window defroster; seating capacity of 7, front bucket seats with adjustable headrests, driver's and passenger's armrests, driver's seat includes 4-way direction control, passenger's seat includes 4-way direction control; 50-50 folding 2nd row bench seat with adjustable headrests, center armrest; 3rd row full folding bench seat with adjustable headrests; front height adjustable seatbelts; cloth seats, cloth door trim insert, full vinyl headliner, full carpet floor covering with carpeted floor mats; interior lights include dome light, front reading lights, 4 door curb lights; steering wheel with tilt adjustment; vanity mirrors, passenger's side illuminated; day-night rearview mirror; locking glove box, front and rear cupholders, instrument panel bin, 1 seat back storage pocket, driver's and passenger's door bins, rear door bins; carpeted cargo floor, plastic trunk lid, cargo light; chrome grille, black side window moldings, black front windshield molding, black rear window molding and body-colored door handles.

6-PASSENGER (4A) (in addition to or instead of 7-PASSENGER (4A) equipment): Front power sliding glass sunroof with sunshade; roof rack; body-colored bodyside molding, black wheel well molding; AM/FM stereo with seek-scan, cassette, CD changer pre-wiring, in-dash CD pre-wiring, 4 speakers, theft deterrent, and fixed antenna; seating capacity of 6 and removable 2nd row captain's seats with reclining adjustable headrests.

CODE	DESCRIPTION	INVOICE	MSRP
	Base Prices		
J54	S 7-Passenger (4A)	21548	23680
J64	S 6-Passenger (4A)	23296	25600
Destination Charge:		495	495
	Accessories		
CDD	In Dash CD Player	364	470
CDO	CD Changer	441	565
LRO	Roof Rack (7-Passenger)	179	230
RST	Rear Seat Tray (6-Passenger)	54	70

1999 RODEO

1999 Isuzu Rodeo

What's New?

Isuzu juggles minor standard and optional equipment for 1999, making items from last year's S V6 preferred equipment package standard on the LS, and last year's LS equipment standard on a new trim level called LSE.

Review

Choices in the compact sport-utility class are numerous. Figuring out which truck best meets your needs almost always requires a compromise of some sort or another. The closest thing to perfect in this price range has been the lower trim levels of the Ford Explorer, and spectacular sales of this popular SUV prove that buyers find its combination of room, style and power the best in the segment.

The Explorer is a fine sport-ute, but there's another face in this neighborhood that deserves consideration. Enter the Isuzu Rodeo, which was completely redesigned last year, adding modern styling, a user-friendly interior, more V6 power and extra passenger and cargo room.

The Rodeo's interior provides cupholders, excellent ergonomics, the industry's most perfectly designed steering wheel, and plastic trim that looks anything but cheap. Clamber aboard and head for the hills; it's easy to thwart nature's obstacles with push-button 4WD and standard antilock brakes.

Buyers can select a hatchback that lifts up from top to bottom or a hatchgate, which employs flip-up glass and a tailgate that swings from right to left. The full-size spare tire can be stored under the vehicle or on the hatchgate. Three trim levels are available: S, LS and LSE. The basic Rodeo has two-wheel drive and a weak 2.2-liter four-cylinder engine. Step up to the S V6 and a 205-horsepower, 3.2-liter unit whisks you along with verve.

At the top of the complaint list about the truck is the absurd location of the push-button 4WD switch, located directly next to the cruise control button, where it could be activated accidentally. Off-road, the new Isuzu feels somewhat undersprung, but takes bumps and dips easily if speeds are kept to a minimum. Front bucket seats are quite uncomfortable over the long haul, though rear seat riders enjoy a supportive bench seat and plenty of leg room. Finally, there are no rear cupholders for the kiddies.

For 1999, Isuzu added a gold trim package to the Rodeo LSE's option list and enhanced rear window defrosters with a timer. All V6 models receive a more powerful 90-amp alternator and a tilt steering wheel, while four-wheel drive versions get a limited-slip differential.

The Rodeo is an excellent blend of old-fashioned truck toughness and modern day car-like convenience. If you're looking for a new $30,000 SUV, this one should be on your shopping list.

Safety Data

Side Airbag: *Not Available*
4-Wheel ABS: *Standard*
Driver Crash Test Grade: *Average*
Side Impact Crash Test Front: *Excellent*
Crash Offset: *Not Available*
Integrated Child Seat(s): *Not Available*
Traction Control: *Not Available*
Passenger Crash Test Grade: *Good*
Side Impact Crash Test Rear: *Excellent*

NOTE: In side impact crash testing, the Rodeo rolled one-quarter turn onto its side.

Standard Equipment

S 2.2L 2WD (5M): 2.2L I4 DOHC SMPI 16-valve engine; 5-speed overdrive manual transmission; 600-amp battery; 100-amp alternator; rear wheel drive, 4.5 axle ratio; stainless steel exhaust; front independent double wishbone suspension with anti-roll bar, front torsion springs, front torsion bar, rigid rear axle multi-link suspension with anti-roll bar, rear coil springs; power rack-and-pinion steering with engine speed-sensing assist; front disc/rear drum brakes with 4 wheel antilock braking system; 21.1 gal capacity fuel tank; front and rear mud flaps, skid plates; conventional rear cargo door; front and rear black bumpers with front and rear tow hooks, rear step; monotone paint; aero-composite halogen headlamps; additional exterior lights include center high mounted stop light; driver's and passenger's manual black folding outside mirrors; front and rear 15" x 6.5" silver styled steel wheels; P235/75SR15 BSW M&S front and rear tires; underbody mounted full-size conventional steel spare wheel; AM/FM stereo with seek-scan, cassette, 4 speakers, and fixed antenna; child safety rear door locks; 2 power accessory outlets, driver's foot rest; instrumentation display includes tachometer, water temp gauge, in-dash clock, trip odometer; warning indicators include oil pressure, battery, lights on, key in ignition, low fuel, door ajar, trunk ajar; dual airbags; tinted windows, manual rear windows; fixed interval front windshield wipers, flip-up rear window, fixed interval rear wiper, rear window defroster; seating capacity of 5, front bucket seats with adjustable headrests, driver's seat includes 4-way direction control, passenger's seat includes 4-way direction control; 60-40 folding rear split-bench seat with adjustable headrests; front and rear height adjustable seatbelts; cloth seats, cloth door trim insert, full cloth headliner, full carpet floor covering; interior lights include dome light; driver's side vanity mirror; day-night rearview mirror; full floor console, locking glove box, front and rear cupholders, 1 seat back storage pocket, driver's and passenger's door bins; carpeted cargo floor, plastic trunk lid, cargo tie downs, cargo light; body-colored grille, black side window moldings, black front windshield molding, black rear window molding and black door handles.

CODE	DESCRIPTION	INVOICE	MSRP

S 2WD (5M) (in addition to or instead of S 2.2L 2WD (5M) equipment): 3.2L V6 DOHC SMPI 24-valve engine; 90-amp alternator; 4.3 axle ratio; steering wheel with tilt adjustment.

LS 2WD (5M) (in addition to or instead of S 2WD (5M) equipment): Roof rack; front and rear body-colored bumpers; driver's and passenger's power remote black heated folding outside mirrors; air conditioning; AM/FM stereo with seek-scan, cassette, CD changer pre-wiring, in-dash CD pre-wiring, 6 speakers, and fixed antenna; cruise control; power door locks with 2 stage unlock, remote keyless entry, power remote hatch/trunk release; 3 power accessory outlets; panic alarm; power front windows with driver's 1-touch down, power rear windows; variable intermittent front windshield wipers; center armrest with storage; premium cloth seats; carpeted floor mats; interior lights include 4 door curb lights; cargo cover and cargo net.

LSE 2WD (4A) (in addition to or instead of LS 2WD (5M) equipment): Four-speed electronic overdrive automatic transmission with lock-up; driver selectable program transmission; front power sliding and tilting glass sunroof with sunshade; body-colored bodyside molding; additional exterior lights include front fog/driving lights; driver's and passenger's power remote body-colored heated folding outside mirrors; deep tinted windows; leather seats, leather door trim insert; wood trim; interior lights include front reading lights; leather-wrapped steering wheel with tilt adjustment; dual illuminated vanity mirrors; full floor console; 2 seat back storage pockets and body-colored door handles.

S 4WD (5M) (in addition to or instead of S 2WD (5M) equipment): Part-time 4 wheel drive, auto locking hub control with electronic shift, limited slip differential and 4 wheel disc brakes with 4 wheel antilock braking system.

LS 4WD (5M) (in addition to or instead of LS 2WD (5M) equipment): Part-time 4 wheel drive, auto locking hub control with electronic shift, limited slip differential, 4 wheel disc brakes with 4 wheel antilock braking system and underbody mounted full-size temporary steel spare wheel.

LSE 4WD (4A) (in addition to or instead of LSE 2WD (4A) equipment):): Part-time 4 wheel drive, auto locking hub control with electronic shift, limited slip differential, 4 wheel disc brakes with 4 wheel antilock braking system; front and rear 16" x 7" silver alloy wheels and outside rear mounted full-size conventional alloy spare wheel.

Base Prices

CODE	DESCRIPTION	INVOICE	MSRP
P45	S 2.2L 2WD (5M)	16907	18180
R45	S 2WD (5M)	18814	21140
R55	LS 2WD (5M)	20950	23540
R64	LSE 2WD (4A)	24912	28150
V45	S 4WD (5M)	21084	23690
V55	LS 4WD (5M)	23576	26490
V64	LSE 4WD (4A)	27126	30650
Destination Charge:		495	495

Accessories

CODE	DESCRIPTION	INVOICE	MSRP
—	Transmission: 4-Speed Automatic (V6 - S/LS) *Includes driver selectable program.*	890	1000
AR	Air Conditioning (S)	836	950
BST	Sport Side Step	278	355
CMC	Cargo Mat	47	60
ENN	Cargo Convenience Net (S)	20	25

CODE	DESCRIPTION	INVOICE	MSRP
FDC	6 Disc CD Changer In Dash (LS/LSE)	507	650
FLY	Premium CD Player (LS/LSE) *Includes 6 speakers.*	429	550
GPG	Gold Package (LSE) *Includes gold plated "Rodeo", "LSE" and "V6" badges and 16" gold accented wheels.*	312	400
GRG	Brush Guard	233	298
H2	Power Moonroof (LS) *Includes sunshade.*	616	700
H2V	Moon Roof Visor (LS/LSE)	56	71
JAH	Carpeted Floor Mats (S)	43	55
M2	Wheels: 16" Aluminum (LS 4WD/LSE 2WD) *Includes P245/70R16 tires and conventional spare tire.*	176	200
OM	Bodyside Molding (S/LS)	44	56
P21	Preferred Equipment Package #1 (S) *Includes air conditioning and aero roof rack.*	889	1010
R1	Outside Spare Mount and Cover (S/LS/LSE 2WD)	NC	NC
RBS	Running Boards	280	360
RCR	Cargo Organizer	68	86
RSP	Rear Roof Spoiler	77	98
SCO	Center Armrest Pad (S)	31	40
SP1	Wheels: 15" Aluminum (LS 2WD) *Includes conventional spare tire. NOT AVAILABLE with SP2.*	352	400
SP2	Wheels: 16" Aluminum (LS 2WD) *Includes P245/70R16 tires and conventional spare tire.NOT AVAILABLE with SP1.*	528	600
TLG	Tail Lamp Guards	66	84
TRP	Trailer Hitch	198	253
UCC	Retractable Cargo Cover (S)	70	90

1999 TROOPER

1999 Isuzu Trooper

What's New?

A gold trim package is added to the Trooper's option list and Torque on Demand is now standard with the automatic transmission.

Review

More than a decade ago, Isuzu introduced the first Trooper. It was a tough truck, sturdy and boxy in style, with two doors and a sparse interior. Powered by a four-cylinder engine, the original Trooper wasn't prepped to win any drag races, but the truck won fans for its off-road prowess and exceptional reliability. Soon, four-door models joined the lineup, and a GM-sourced V6 engine became available. As the sport-utility market grew, luxury amenities were added to the Trooper, but by the early Nineties, it was apparent that Isuzu needed to redesign the Trooper so that it could remain competitive against steadily improving competitors.

The Rodeo claimed the entry-level slot for Isuzu in 1991, so the Trooper was moved into the upscale category in 1992. Since then, continued refinements have given the Trooper one of the best blends of style, comfort and utility in its class. Dual airbags and four-wheel antilock brakes are standard equipment. Fold the rear seats, and a Trooper can carry 90 cubic feet of cargo, over 10 percent more than its rival, the Ford Explorer. Ground clearance measures an impressive 8.3 inches with the manual transmission, and rear seat passengers enjoy nearly as much rear legroom as what is found in a Mercedes S500 sedan.

A 3.5-liter, 24-valve DOHC V6 powers the Trooper, pumping out 215 horsepower and 230 foot-pounds of torque. Torque on Demand, Isuzu's traction system, which instantly directs more power to the front or rear wheels as needed, is now standard on a Trooper with an automatic transmission. With the system engaged, you get the on-road stability of all-wheel drive and off-road capability of part-time four-wheel drive.

Only one trim level is available: the S model, which can be equipped with performance and luxury package upgrades. With these enhancements you've got a comfortable, luxurious cruiser that you won't be afraid to take off-roading.

Many of you may have heard a rumor that the Trooper is dangerous and prone to going around corners on two wheels at moderate speeds. Forget it. Government agencies and private test facilities have debunked the myth. The Trooper is no more tippy than any other sport-utility vehicle on the market. However, keep the following in mind: any vehicle with a short wheelbase and a high center of gravity requires care when cornering or traversing rough terrain. The rules of physics necessarily dictate that such a vehicle is more prone to tipping than a longer wheelbase car or truck with a lower center of gravity.

The Trooper has always been one of our favorite trucks because it has loads of personality and off-road ability. As an alternative to the urban-friendly Ford Explorer XLT and Jeep Grand Cherokee Laredo, the Trooper makes little sense for most suburbanites whose idea of off-road driving is the dirt parking lot at the sweet corn stand. However, as an alternative to more expensive and competent SUVs like the Toyota Land Cruiser and Land Rover Discovery, the Trooper makes perfect sense.

Safety Data

Side Airbag: *Not Available*
4-Wheel ABS: *Standard*
Driver Crash Test Grade: *Average*
Side Impact Crash Test Front: *Not Available*
Crash Offset: *Not Available*
Integrated Child Seat(s): *Not Available*
Traction Control: *Not Available*
Passenger Crash Test Grade: *Average*
Side Impact Crash Test Rear: *Not Available*

Standard Equipment

S (5M): 3.5L V6 DOHC SMPI 24-valve engine; 5-speed overdrive manual transmission; HD battery; engine oil cooler; 75-amp alternator; part-time 4 wheel drive, auto locking hub control with electronic shift, 4.3 axle ratio; stainless steel exhaust; front independent double wishbone suspension with antiroll bar, front torsion springs, front torsion bar, rigid rear axle multilink suspension with antiroll bar, rear coil springs; power re-circulating ball steering with engine speed-sensing assist; 4 wheel disc brakes with 4 wheel antilock braking system; 22.5 gal. capacity fuel tank; front and rear mud flaps, skid plates; split swing-out rear cargo door; front and rear colored bumpers with front and rear tow hooks, rear step; colored bodyside cladding, rocker panel extensions, colored fender flares; monotone paint; aero-composite halogen headlamps; additional exterior lights include cornering lights, center high mounted stop light; driver's and passenger's power remote black heated folding outside mirrors; front and rear 16" x 7" silver alloy wheels; P245/70SR16 BSW M&S front and rear tires; outside rear mounted full-size conventional alloy spare wheel; air conditioning, rear heat ducts; AM/FM stereo with seek-scan, cassette, 6 speakers, and fixed antenna; cruise control; power door locks with 2 stage unlock, remote keyless entry, child safety rear door locks, remote fuel release; 1 power accessory outlet, driver's foot rest; instrumentation display includes tachometer, oil pressure gauge, water temp gauge, volt gauge, in-dash clock, trip odometer; warning indicators include oil pressure, water temp, battery, lights on, key in ignition, low fuel, door ajar, brake fluid; dual airbags; ignition disable, security system; tinted windows, power front windows with driver's 1-touch down, power rear windows, fixed 1/4 vent windows; fixed interval front windshield wipers, fixed interval rear wiper, rear window defroster; seating capacity of 5, front bucket seats with adjustable headrests, driver's seat includes 4-way direction control, passenger's seat includes 4-way direction control; 60-40 folding rear split-bench seat with adjustable headrests; front height adjustable seatbelts; cloth seats, cloth door trim insert, full cloth headliner, full carpet floor covering with carpeted floor mats; interior lights include dome light, 4 door curb lights; steering wheel with tilt adjustment; dual illuminated vanity mirrors; day-night rearview mirror; full floor console, locking glove box with light, front and rear cupholders, interior concealed storage, 2 seat back storage pockets, driver's and passenger's door bins; carpeted cargo floor, vinyl trunk lid, cargo cover, cargo net, cargo tie downs, cargo light, cargo concealed storage; chrome grille, body-colored side window moldings, black front windshield molding, black rear window molding and chrome door handles.

Base Prices

CODE	DESCRIPTION	INVOICE	MSRP
L45	S (5M)	23984	27100
Destination Charge:		495	495

CODE	DESCRIPTION	INVOICE	MSRP
	Accessories		
—	Transmission: 4-Speed Automatic	1372	1550
BSK	Black Side Step	265	340
BSP	Polished Side Step	296	380
CDQ	Compact Disc Player	428	550
CDT	6-Disc In-Dash CD Player	506	650
CMX	Cargo Mat	72	92
DBV	Running Boards	265	340
E1	Leather Heated Power Driver's and Passenger's Seats	1980	2250
GPK	Gold Package *REQUIRES K5.*	312	400
H3	Power Moonroof with Sunshade *REQUIRES K5.*	968	1100
HP	Hood Protector	55	70
K10	M74 Luxury Package *Includes power moonroof with sunshade, leather seat surfaces, leather-wrapped gearshift knob, heated power driver and passenger seats, woodgrain trim, multimeter and two-tone paint with bright exterior trim. REQUIRES K5.*	3569	4300
K5	M64 Performance Package *Includes leather-wrapped steering wheel, dual map lights, dual power folding heated mirrors, tinted privacy glass, 6-disc in-dash CD player, diversity antenna, monotone paint with bright trim, variable intermittent wiper/washer, 4-way driver's/ passenger's seats, body colored front and rear bumpers, bodyside moldings, time delay touch roof lamp, rear passenger foot rest, cargo floor rails (4) and fog lamps.*	1162	1400
M9	Multimeter *REQUIRES K5.*	176	200
RCX	Cargo Organizer	40	50
TRT	Trailer Hitch	198	253
WTA	Woodgrain Trim *REQUIRES K5.*	484	550
YSK	Ski Rack	229	293

1999 VEHICROSS

1999 Isuzu VehiCROSS

What's New?

Isuzu imports its unique-looking, award-winning SUV to the U.S. in 1999.

Review

Isuzu's VehiCROSS began as an innovative concept vehicle that garnered loads of attention back in 1993 and then entered limited production for the Japanese market. Because of its excellent reception in Japan, the continued popularity of sport-utility vehicles here in the States, and the company's need for an image vehicle in the U.S., Isuzu decided to bring the VehiCROSS across the pond this year.

Powered by a 215-horsepower, 3.5-liter, direct-injection, DOHC V6, the VehiCROSS comes with a four-speed automatic transmission with winter and power modes. It also boasts technical innovations like an advanced Torque-On-Demand (TOD) four-wheel-drive system, limited slip differential and four-wheel ABS. Isuzu's TOD system (the same one found on the Trooper) senses driving conditions and adjusts the torque balance between the front and rear wheels, changing from 100-percent rear drive to 50/50 four-wheel drive in a matter of milliseconds.

Isuzu's front double-wishbone torsion bar and rear four-link coil suspension are enhanced by an industry first: a 6061-T8 extruded aluminum shock absorber with attached expansion chamber, which makes for greater endurance and superior shock cooling. On rough roads, the truck's 16-inch alloy wheels and modified P245/70R16 steel-belted radial tires are stopped by 11-inch ventilated front and 12.3-inch ventilated rear disc brakes.

The truck's capabilities as a trailblazer seem solid, but what most people first notice about the vehicle is its unconventional, techno-styling. The VehiCROSS has an expansive windshield, composite bumpers, underbody moldings, roof-end spoiler, integrated headlamps with marker lights, and unpainted polypropylene covering the lower section of the truck's body. An Isuzu spokesperson said that the truck is meant to appeal to consumers who "want to be different." We'd have to agree.

Inside, the vehicle seats four and provides a sports car atmosphere complete with red and black leather-trimmed seating. With tinted glass, leather-wrapped tilt steering wheel, and collapsible, heated side mirrors, the VehiCROSS mixes ruggedness with luxury. Features include a matte-black panel inset in the hood to reduce glare, roof rail system, aircraft-type fuel filler door, and a side-hinged tailgate that carries the spare tire securely inside the cargo door.

CODE	DESCRIPTION	INVOICE	MSRP

The $995 special edition "Ironman" option, available only in white, gets you leather-trimmed front seats embossed with the "Ironman Triathlon" label, a special hood insert and a few more decals on the tailgate and beneath the C-pillar. Isuzu plans to make 20 percent of its 1999 VehiCROSS production units Ironman editions.

Available in only three colors-Ebony Black, Astral Silver Metallic and Victory White-Isuzu believes the VehiCROSS is in a category all its own. Not quite a mini-sport-ute or a big SUV, the 1999 VehiCROSS is a contemporary vehicle that isn't quite like any other. Whether you want to buy one or not, this truck will be hard to miss.

Safety Data

Side Airbag: *Not Available*
4-Wheel ABS: *Standard*
Driver Crash Test Grade: *Not Available*
Side Impact Crash Test Front: *Not Available*
Crash Offset: *Not Available*
Integrated Child Seat(s): *Not Available*
Traction Control: *Not Available*
Passenger Crash Test Grade: *Not Available*
Side Impact Crash Test Rear: *Not Available*

Standard Equipment

VehiCROSS: 3.5L V6 DOHC SMPI 24-valve engine; 4-speed electronic overdrive automatic transmission with lock-up; HD battery; engine oil cooler; 75-amp alternator; driver selectable program transmission; part-time 4 wheel drive, auto locking hub control with electronic shift, limited slip differential, 4.3 axle ratio; stainless steel exhaust; front independent double wishbone suspension with anti-roll bar, front torsion springs, front torsion bar, rigid rear axle multi-link suspension with anti-roll bar, rear coil springs; power re-circulating ball steering with engine speed-sensing assist; 4 wheel disc brakes with 4 wheel antilock braking system; 22.5 gal. capacity fuel tank; rear wing spoiler, skid plates; conventional rear cargo door; front and rear black bumpers with front and rear tow hooks, rear step; black bodyside cladding, black fender flares; monotone paint; aero-composite halogen headlamps; additional exterior lights include front fog/driving lights, center high mounted stop light; driver's and passenger's power remote black heated folding outside mirrors; front and rear 16" x 7" chrome alloy wheels; P245/70SR16 BSW M&S front and rear tires; outside rear mounted full-size conventional alloy spare wheel; air conditioning, rear heat ducts; AM/FM stereo with seek-scan, cassette, 6 speakers, and integrated roof antenna; cruise control; power door locks with 2 stage unlock, remote keyless entry, child safety rear door locks; 1 power accessory outlet, driver's foot rest; instrumentation display includes tachometer, oil pressure gauge, water temp gauge, volt gauge, in-dash clock, trip odometer; warning indicators include oil pressure, water temp, battery, lights on, key in ignition, low fuel, door ajar, brake fluid; dual airbags; ignition disable, security system; tinted windows, power front windows with driver's 1-touch down, fixed rear windows, fixed 1/4 vent windows; fixed interval front windshield wipers, rear window defroster; seating capacity of 4, front sports seats with adjustable headrests, center armrest, driver's seat includes 4-way direction control, passenger's seat includes 4-way direction control; 50-50 folding rear bench seat with reclining adjustable headrests; front height adjustable seatbelts; leather seats, full cloth headliner, full carpet floor covering with carpeted floor mats, leather-wrapped gear shift knob; interior lights include dome light; leather-wrapped steering wheel with tilt adjustment; dual illuminated vanity mirrors; day-night rearview mirror; full floor console, locking glove box with light, front cupholder, 2 seat back storage pockets; carpeted cargo floor, plastic trunk lid, cargo net, cargo light; black grille, black side window moldings, black front windshield molding, black rear window molding and black door handles.

Base Prices

X74	VehiCROSS	25577	28900
Destination Charge:		695	695

CODE	DESCRIPTION	INVOICE	MSRP
	Accessories		
HTV	Roof Rack	229	293
RCV	Cargo Mat *NOT AVAILABLE with VIM.*	72	92
VIM	Ironman Package *Includes cargo mat, "Ironman Triathalon" decals on the hood, c-pillar and tailgate, "Ironman Triathalon" embossed leather seats and "Ironman Triathalon" floor mats and roof rack. NOT AVAILABLE with RCV.*	876	995

1999 CHEROKEE

1999 Jeep Cherokee

What's New?

The Cherokee Sport gets a revised front fascia including body-colored grille and bumpers. New exterior colors include Forest Green and Desert Sand, to match the most common Cherokee surroundings.

Review

Some things never change, and the Jeep Cherokee is one of those mainstays. Unlike its posh-and bigger-Grand Cherokee brother, which keeps adding comforts and graceful touches, the ever-practical, affordable Cherokee simply keeps on rolling, looking little different now than when it was first introduced in 1984.

Utilitarian and upright it is, but with a compelling personality that even the Grand Cherokee lacks. Four adults fit inside the Cherokee in reasonable comfort, with adequate headroom. Rear legroom is lacking, due to a short seat, and a narrow door constricts entry to the rear. Worth noting is the fact that the rear bench folds but doesn't offer a split, meaning you can't haul a toddler and a treadmill simultaneously.

Relatively comfortable on the road, the compact Cherokee is capable of strutting its stuff when the going gets rough. Acceleration is brisk with the 4.0-liter, inline six-cylinder engine, courtesy of 190 horsepower and 225 foot-pounds of torque. We highly recommend this upgrade if you select the SE model, which comes with a measly 2.5-liter four-cylinder that pumps out 65 fewer horses. The Cherokee's 4.0-liter engine puts the "sport" into sport utility.

The Cherokee is offered in three trim levels: SE, Sport and Classic. SE and Sport models can have two or four doors, while the step-up Classic edition is four-door only. All are available with either two- or four-wheel drive. Command-Trac part-time four-wheel drive allows shift-on-the-fly operation. Selec-Trac is Jeep's full-time four-wheel drive system, and is not available on the SE. A Limited package on the Classic offers upgrades to Selec-Trac, leather seats, an overhead console, power accessories and "Limited" badging.

Standard gear includes power steering, tinted glass and power front disc brakes. Four-wheel antilock braking is optional (six-cylinder only), as are power windows and door locks, keyless entry system, cruise control, air conditioning and leather seats. Seat heaters are available for the first time this year on the Limited package.

CODE	DESCRIPTION	INVOICE	MSRP

Despite its age, the compact Jeep sport-utility remains a sensible choice in its field, more capable than most SUVs of heading into the woods at a moment's notice. What more can anyone ask of a moderately priced on/off-roader?

Safety Data

Side Airbag: *Not Available*
4-Wheel ABS: *Optional*
Driver Crash Test Grade: *Average*
Side Impact Crash Test Front: *Average*
Crash Offset: *Marginal*
Integrated Child Seat(s): *Not Available*
Traction Control: *Not Available*
Passenger Crash Test Grade: *Average*
Side Impact Crash Test Rear: *Excellent*

Standard Equipment

SE 2-DR 2WD (5M): 2.5L I4 OHV SPI 8-valve engine; 5-speed overdrive manual transmission; 500-amp battery; 117-amp HD alternator; rear wheel drive, 4.1 axle ratio; stainless steel exhaust; front non-independent suspension with anti-roll bar, front coil springs, rigid rear axle suspension with anti-roll bar, rear leaf springs; power rack-and-pinion steering; front disc/rear drum brakes; 20 gal capacity fuel tank; liftback rear cargo door; front and rear black bumpers with black front rub strip, rear step; black fender flares; monotone paint; sealed beam halogen headlamps; additional exterior lights include center high mounted stop light; driver's and passenger's manual black folding outside mirrors; front and rear 15" x 7" silver styled steel wheels; P215/75SR15 BSW AS front and rear tires; inside mounted compact steel spare wheel; AM/FM stereo with clock, seek-scan, 2 speakers, and fixed antenna; 2 power accessory outlets; instrumentation display includes trip odometer; warning indicators include oil pressure, water temp warning, battery, lights on, key in ignition, trunk ajar; dual airbags; tinted windows, fixed rear windows; variable intermittent front windshield wipers; seating capacity of 5, front bucket seats with fixed headrests, center armrest with storage, driver's seat includes 4-way direction control, passenger's seat includes 4-way direction control; removable full folding rear bench seat; vinyl seats, vinyl door trim insert, full cloth headliner, full carpet floor covering, deluxe sound insulation; interior lights include dome light; day-night rearview mirror; full floor console, locking glove box with light, front cupholder, instrument panel bin; carpeted cargo floor, vinyl trunk lid, cargo tie downs; black grille, black side window moldings, black front windshield molding, black rear window molding and black door handles.

SE 4-DR 2WD (5M) (in addition to or instead of SE 2-DR 2WD (5M) equipment): Child safety rear door locks; tinted windows, manual rear windows and fixed 1/4 vent windows.

SE 2-DR 4WD (5M) (in addition to or instead of SE 2-DR 2WD (5M) equipment): Part-time 4 wheel drive, auto locking hub control with manual shift and rigid rear axle multi-link suspension with anti-roll bar.

SE 4-DR 4WD (5M) (in addition to or instead of SE 2-DR 4WD (5M) equipment): Child safety rear door locks; tinted windows, manual rear windows and fixed 1/4 vent windows.

SPORT 2-DR 2WD (5M) (in addition to or instead of SE 2-DR 2WD (5M) equipment): 4.0L I6 OHV SMPI 12-valve engine; 3.07 axle ratio; black bodyside molding; monotone paint with badging; AM/FM stereo with clock, seek-scan, cassette, 4 speakers, and fixed antenna; instrumentation display includes tachometer, oil pressure gauge, water temp gauge, volt gauge; warning indicators include low fuel; cloth seats and cargo light.

SPORT 4-DR 2WD (5M) (in addition to or instead of SPORT 2-DR 2WD (5M) equipment): Child safety rear door locks; manual rear windows and fixed 1/4 vent windows.

CODE	DESCRIPTION	INVOICE	MSRP

SPORT 2-DR 4WD (5M) (in addition to or instead of SPORT 2-DR 2WD (5M) equipment): Part-time 4 wheel drive, auto locking hub control with manual shift; rear rigid axle multi-link suspension with anti-roll bar.

SPORT 4-DR 4WD (5M) (in addition to or instead of SPORT 2-DR 4WD (5M) equipment): Child safety rear door locks; manual rear windows and fixed 1/4 vent windows.

CLASSIC 4-DR 2WD (4A) (in addition to or instead of SPORT 4-DR 2WD (5M) equipment): Four-speed electronic overdrive automatic transmission with lock-up; 3.55 axle ratio; roof rack; front and rear body-colored bumpers with body-colored front rub strip; body-colored bodyside molding, body-colored fender flares; driver's and passenger's power remote black folding outside mirrors; rear heat ducts; variable intermittent front windshield wipers, fixed interval rear wiper; premium cloth seats; carpeted floor mats and body-colored grille.

CLASSIC 4-DR 4WD (4A) (in addition to or instead of CLASSIC 4-DR 2WD (4A) equipment): Part-time 4 wheel drive, auto locking hub control with manual shift and rigid rear axle multi-link suspension with anti-roll bar and rear leaf springs.

Base Prices

CODE	DESCRIPTION	INVOICE	MSRP
XJTL72	SE 2-Dr 2WD (5M)	15086	16050
XJTL74	SE 4-Dr 2WD (5M)	16052	17090
XJJL72	SE 2-Dr 4WD (5M)	16484	17565
XJJL74	SE 4-Dr 4WD (5M)	17446	18600
XJTL72	Sport 2-Dr 2WD (5M)	17002	18775
XJTL74	Sport 4-Dr 2WD (5M)	17933	19810
XJJL72	Sport 2-Dr 4WD (5M)	18351	20285
XJJL74	Sport 4-Dr 4WD (5M)	19282	21320
XJTL74	Classic 4-Dr 2WD (4A)	19166	21155
XJJL74	Classic 4-Dr 4WD (4A)	20470	22670
Destination Charge:		525	525

Accessories

CODE	DESCRIPTION	INVOICE	MSRP
22A	Quick Order Package 22A (SE 2WD)	NC	NC
	Includes vehicle with standard equipment. REQUIRES EPE and DGA and 4XA.		
22B	Quick Order Package 22B (SE 2WD)	1084	1275
	Manufacturer Discount	(1084)	(1275)
	Net Price	NC	NC
	Includes air conditioning, power folding mirrors, premium cloth highback bucket seats and rear window wiper/washer. REQUIRES EPE and DGA.		
23A	Quick Order Package 23A (SE)	NC	NC
	Includes vehicle with standard equipment. REQUIRES 4XA and EPE.		
23B	Quick Order Package 23B (SE)	1084	1275
	Manufacturer Discount	(1084)	(1275)
	Net Price	NC	NC
	Includes air conditioning, power folding mirrors, premium cloth highback bucket seats and rear window wiper/washer. REQUIRES EPE.		

CODE	DESCRIPTION	INVOICE	MSRP
25A	Quick Order Package 25A (SE)	NC	NC
	Includes vehicle with standard equipment. REQUIRES 4XA and ERH.		
25B	Quick Order Package 25B (SE)	1084	1275
	Manufacturer Discount	(1084)	(1275)
	Net Price	NC	NC
	Includes power folding mirrors, premium cloth highback bucket seats and rear window wiper/washer. REQUIRES ERH.		
25D	Quick Order Package 25D (Sport)	NC	NC
	Includes vehicle with standard equipment. REQUIRES (HAA or 4XA) and ERH and DDQ.		
25J	Quick Order Package 25J (Sport 4-Door)	1993	2345
	Manufacturer Discount	(1993)	(2345)
	Net Price	NC	NC
	Includes front and rear floor mats, power folding mirrors, power equipment group: remote keyless entry, power door locks, power windows; roof rack and tilt steering column. REQUIRES ERH and DDQ.		
25J	Quick Order Package 25J (Sport 2-Door)	1845	2170
	Manufacturer Discount	(1845)	(2170)
	Net Price	NC	NC
	Includes front and rear floor mats, power folding mirrors, power equipment group: remote keyless entry, power door locks, power windows; roof rack, tilt steering column and leather wrapped steering wheel. REQUIRES ERH and DDQ.		
26A	Quick Order Package 26A (SE)	NC	NC
	Includes vehicle with standard equipment. REQUIRES 4XA and ERH and DGB.		
26B	Quick Order Package 26B (SE)	1084	1275
	Manufacturer Discount	(1084)	(1275)
	Net Price	NC	NC
	Includes air conditioning, power folding mirrors, premium cloth highback bucket seats and rear window wiper/washer. REQUIRES ERH and DGB.		
26D	Quick Order Package 26D (Sport)	NC	NC
	Includes vehicle with standard equipment. REQUIRES (HAA or 4XA) and ERH and DGB.		
26H	Quick Order Package 26H (Classic 2WD)	3217	3785
	Manufacturer Discount	(1683)	(1980)
	Net Price	1534	1805
	Includes Limited Decor Group: front door Cherokee Limited badge, cargo compartment cover, woodgrain instrument panel bezel, premium vinyl door trim with map pocket, dual upper body paint stripe, tires: P225/70R15 Eagle GA AS BSW, wheels: 15"x 7" luxury aluminum, power equipment group: remote keyless entry, power door locks, power folding mirrors, power windows; premium leather low back buckets and tilt steering column. REQUIRES ERH and DGB.		
26H	Quick Order Package 26H (Classic 4WD)	3732	4390
	Manufacturer Discount	(1683)	(1980)
	Net Price	2049	2410
	Includes Limited Decor Group: front door Cherokee Limited badge, Selec-Trac full Time 4WD system, cargo compartment cover, woodgrain instrument panel bezel, premium vinyl door trim with map pocket, dual upper body paint stripe, tires: P225/70R15		

CODE	DESCRIPTION	INVOICE	MSRP
	Eagle GA AS BSW, wheels: 15"x 7" luxury aluminum, power equipment group: remote keyless entry, power door locks, power folding mirrors, power windows; premium leather low back buckets and tilt steering column. REQUIRES ERH and DGB.		
26J	Quick Order Package 26J (Sport 2-Door)	1845	2170
	Manufacturer Discount	(1845)	(2170)
	Net Price	NC	NC
	Includes front and rear floor mats, power folding mirrors, power equipment group: remote keyless entry, power door locks, power windows; roof rack, tilt steering column and leather wrapped steering wheel. REQUIRES ERH and DGB.		
26J	Quick Order Package 26J (Sport 4-Door)	1993	2345
	Manufacturer Discount	(1993)	(2345)
	Net Price	NC	NC
	Includes front and rear floor mats, power folding mirrors, power equipment group: remote keyless entry, power door locks, power windows; roof rack and tilt steering column. REQUIRES ERH and DGB.		
26S	Quick Order Package 26S (Classic)	1551	1825
	Manufacturer Discount	(1551)	(1825)
	Net Price	NC	NC
	Includes power equipment group: remote keyless entry, power door locks, power folding mirrors, power windows and tilt steering column. REQUIRES ERH and DGB.		
26X	Quick Order Package 26X (Classic)	NC	NC
	Includes Classic Decor Group. REQUIRES (HAA or 4XA) and ERH and DGB.		
4XA	Air Conditioning Bypass	NC	NC
ADA	Light Group	136	160
	Includes courtesy lamps, underhood light, front map/dome lights and illuminated visor vanity mirrors. REQUIRES RAS or RAZ.		
ADL	Skid Plate Group (4WD)	123	145
	Includes skid plates for fuel tank, transfer case and front suspension.		
AHT	Trailer Tow Group	310	365
	Includes HD engine cooler. REQUIRES ERH.		
AHT	Trailer Tow Group (SE 2-Dr 2WD/Sport 2-Dr 2WD)	276	325
	Includes HD engine cooler. REQUIRES TBB and DGB.		
AHT	Trailer Tow Group (4WD)	208	245
	Includes HD engine cooler. REQUIRES AWE and DGB.		
AWE	Up Country Suspension Package (Sport 4WD)	684	805
	Includes P225/75 R15 Wrangler RT/S A/T tires, HD engine cooler, skid plate group, tire: full size spare, delete rear stabilizer bar suspension, HD suspension and tow hooks. REQUIRES WJW.		
AWE	Up Country Suspension Package (SE 4WD)	876	1030
	Includes trac-lok differential, HD engine cooler, skid plate group, tire: full size spare, delete rear stabilizer bar suspension, HD suspension, tires: P225/75R15 Wrangler RT/S AT and tow hooks.		
AWE	Up Country Suspension Package (Sport 4WD/Classic 4WD)	718	845
	Includes P225/75 R15 Wrangler RT/S A/T tires, HD engine cooler, skid plate group, tire: full size spare, delete rear stabilizer bar suspension, HD suspension and tow hooks. REQUIRES WJW and ERH and DGB. NOT AVAILABLE with 26H.		

CODE	DESCRIPTION	INVOICE	MSRP
AWE	Up Country Suspension Package (Sport 4WD) *Includes P225/75 R15 Wrangler RT/S A/T tires, HD engine cooler, skid plate group, tire: full size spare, delete rear stabilizer bar suspension, HD suspension and tow hooks. REQUIRES ERH.*	663	780
AWE	Up Country Suspension Package (Sport 4WD) *Includes P225/75 R15 Wrangler RT/S A/T tires, HD engine cooler, skid plate group, tire: full size spare, delete rear stabilizer bar suspension, HD suspension and tow hooks.*	629	740
AWE	Up Country Suspension Package (SE 4WD) *Includes trac-lok differential, HD engine cooler, skid plate group, tire: full size spare, delete rear stabilizer bar suspension, HD suspension, tires: P225/75R15 Wrangler RT/S AT and tow hooks. REQUIRES DGB and ERH.*	910	1070
AWH	Power Equipment Group (Sport 4-Door) *Includes power folding mirrors, power door locks and power windows. REQUIRES ADA and JHB.*	684	805
AWH	Power Equipment Group (Classic 4-Door) *Includes remote keyless entry, power door locks, power folding mirrors and power windows. REQUIRES ADA.*	574	675
AWH	Power Equipment Group (Sport 2-Door) *Includes power folding mirrors, power door locks and power windows. REQUIRES ADA and JHB.*	536	630
AWS	Smoker's Group *Includes front and rear ash receiver and cigar lighter.*	17	20
BGK	4-Wheel Antilock Brakes *REQUIRES ERH.*	510	600
CLE	Front and Rear Floor Mats (All Except Classic)	43	50
CSA	Spare Tire Cover (SE)	43	50
CSC	Cargo Compartment Cover	64	75
CUN	Overhead Console (All Except SE) *REQUIRES ADA.*	200	235
DDQ	Transmission: 5-Speed Manual (All Except Classic)	NC	NC
DGA	Transmission: 3-Speed Automatic (SE 2WD)	531	625
DGB	Transmission: 4-Speed Automatic (All Except Classic) *Includes 3.55 axle ratio.*	803	945
DGB	Transmission: 4-Speed Automatic (Classic)	NC	NC
DHP	Selec-Trac Full Time 4WD System (Sport 4WD) *Includes full size spare tire. REQUIRES DGB.*	459	540
DHP	Selec-Trac Full Time 4WD System (Sport 4WD/Classic 4WD) *Includes full size spare tire. REQUIRES AWE.*	336	395
DHP	Selec-Trac Full Time 4WD System (Classic 4WD)	514	605
DL	Premium Leather Low Back Buckets (Classic)	NC	NC
DSA	Trac-Lok Differential	242	285
EPE	Engine: 2.5L 4-Cylinder SMPI (SE)	NC	NC
ERH	Engine: 4.0L Power-Tech I6 (SE) *Includes 3.07 axle ratio.*	846	995
ERH	Engine: 4.0L Power-Tech I6 (All Except SE)	NC	NC

CODE	DESCRIPTION	INVOICE	MSRP
GTS	Power Heated Foldaway Mirrors *REQUIRES AWH.*	38	45
GTS	Power Heated Foldaway Mirrors	149	175
GTZ	Power Folding Mirrors (All Except Classic)	111	130
GXX	Sentry Key Theft Deterrent System	64	75
HAA	Air Conditioning (All Except Classic)	723	850
JHB	Rear Window Wiper/Washer (All Except Classic)	128	150
JPM	Heated Front Seats (Classic)	468	550
JPS	6-Way Power Driver's Seat (All Except SE) *REQUIRES AWH. NOT AVAILABLE with 26H.*	255	300
LNJ	Fog Lamps (All Except SE) *REQUIRES JHB.*	94	110
M5	Premium Cloth Highback Bucket Seats (SE)	123	145
MWG	Roof Rack (All Except Classic)	119	140
NAE	California Emissions *Automatically coded.*	NC	NC
NBN	Northeastern States Emissions *Includes Connecticut, Delaware, Maryland, New Hampshire, New Jersey, Pennsylvania, Rhode Island, Virginia and District of Columbia. Also available in border states of these states. Not available in Massachusetts or New York.*	NC	NC
NHK	Engine Block Heater	34	40
NHM	Speed Control *REQUIRES SCG. NOT AVAILABLE with 26H.*	213	250
RAS	Radio: AM/FM Stereo with Cassette (SE)	255	300
RAZ	Radio: AM/FM Stereo with CD, Cassette and EQ (SE)	604	710
RAZ	Radio: AM/FM Stereo with CD, Cassette and EQ (All Except SE)	349	410
RCG	6 Premium Infinity Speakers *REQUIRES RAZ.*	298	350
SCG	Leather Wrapped Steering Wheel (All Except Classic)	43	50
SUA	Tilt Steering Column	119	140
TBB	Tire: Full Size Spare (All Except Classic 4WD) *Includes matching spare wheel. REQUIRES WJU or WJW.*	179	210
TBB	Tire: Full Size Spare (All Except SE) *Includes matching spare wheel.*	123	145
TBB	Tire: Full Size Spare (SE) *Includes matching spare wheel.*	64	75
TBB	Tire: Full Size Spare (SE) *Includes matching spare wheel. REQUIRES TRL.*	102	120
TRL	Tires: P225/75R15 Wrangler RT/S AT (SE)	268	315
WJU	Wheels: 15" x 7" Ecco Cast Aluminum (Sport) *REQUIRES PTD. NOT AVAILABLE with WJW.*	208	245
WJW	Wheels: 15" x 7" Ecco Cast Aluminum (Sport) *NOT AVAILABLE with WJU.*	208	245
WJW	Wheels: 15" x 7" Ecco Cast Aluminum (SE)	374	440
YCF	Border State Emissions (California)	NC	NC

1999 GRAND CHEROKEE

1999 Jeep Grand Cherokee

What's New?

The new-for-99 Grand Cherokee contains only 127 carryover parts from the current model, and gets a new powertrain, rear suspension, braking and steering systems, 4WD system, interior and exterior styling.

Review

After a man vacationing in Utah snapped an unofficial spy photo of the redesigned Grand Cherokee and posted it on his website last summer, hype over the much-anticipated remodeled Jeep escalated. Why? The photo showed a sleek, beefy sport-utility vehicle worthy of the Grand Cherokee nameplate.

Receiving its first redesign since its introduction, designers treaded a fine line between incorporating new devices and retaining the traditional components that make a Jeep a Jeep. Signature items like the vertical slot grille and trapezoidal wheel openings remain, but are altered just enough to change the total look of the vehicle. The truck gets a toothier, raked grille that is less angular than the previous model, a steeply angled windshield, an arced roof and stretched wheel arches. Using the same 105.9-inch wheelbase from the Jeeps of old, engineers made the truck longer, higher and wider than before. We are happy to hear that step-in height is reduced by an inch while the driver seat gains an inch in height for those commanding views sport-utility connoisseurs love.

Inside the truck, you'll find an extra inch of headroom in front and an extra .5 inch in the rear, along with 1.2 more cubic feet of cargo room. Thankfully, the spare tire is relocated to beneath the floor of the cargo area. Jeep public relations executives are also clamoring about a "new level of luxury" and improved ergonomics inside the vehicle.

The 1999 Grand Cherokee will be offered with two new engines, but only one will be available in North America: the 4.7-liter V8 Power-Tech engine, which produces 235 hp at 4800 rpm. Replacing the current 5.2-liter engine, this SOHC, 16-valve Power-Tech V8 makes 295 foot-pounds of torque at 3200 rpm and provides better fuel economy than its predecessor. The other engine available for North American consumers is the old 4.0-liter inline six-cylinder, which has been refined for more power and lower emissions.

Other improvements to the truck include standard all-wheel antilock brakes and full-time 4WD. The new braking system has electronic brake distribution capability, which makes for a quieter, less pulsing and more balanced braking experience. Possessing the largest brake rotors in the sport-utility segment, the Grand Cherokee meets or exceeds requirements for passenger vehicles, which are stricter than those for light trucks. The Quadra-Drive four-wheel drive system has never been used in a sport-ute-until now. The system keeps the vehicle moving even if only one wheel has traction.

While Jeep boasts about its testing of the Grand Cherokee's off-road capability on the Rubicon Trail, these sport-utes are rarely taken far from modern asphalt, making the on-road ride far more important to the suburbanites who will buy the vehicle. Recognizing that truth, a new automatic transmission has been introduced that will increase initial acceleration and provide smoother shifting between gears. Steering ability has also been enhanced and the new Grand Cherokee has a turning radius that is one foot tighter than the older model. The three-link rear suspension offers a smooth, car-like ride and reduces body lean, while the new hydroformed tubular control arms are five times as stiff as the previous design.

With all this, we are anticipating ride and handling like what you'd find in a luxury sedan. We are certain that the interior improvements will contribute to the high-end feel of the truck, and the snazzy exterior styling speaks for itself.

Safety Data

Side Airbag: *Not Available*
4-Wheel ABS: *Standard*
Driver Crash Test Grade: *Not Available*
Side Impact Crash Test Front: *Good*
Crash Offset: *Not Available*
Integrated Child Seat(s): *Not Available*
Traction Control: *Not Available*
Passenger Crash Test Grade: *Not Available*
Side Impact Crash Test Rear: *Excellent*

Standard Equipment

LAREDO 2WD (4A): 4.0L I6 OHV SMPI 12-valve engine; 4-speed electronic overdrive automatic transmission with lock-up; 600-amp HD battery with run down protection; 136-amp HD alternator; rear wheel drive, 3.55 axle ratio; stainless steel exhaust; front non-independent suspension with anti-roll bar, front coil springs, rigid rear axle suspension with anti-roll bar, rear coil springs; power re-circulating ball steering; 4 wheel disc brakes with 4 wheel antilock braking system; 20.5 gal capacity fuel tank; liftback rear cargo door; roof rack; front and rear black bumpers with rear step; black bodyside cladding; monotone paint; aero-composite halogen headlamps; additional exterior lights include center high mounted stop light, underhood light; driver's and passenger's power remote black folding outside mirrors; front and rear 16" x 7" silver alloy wheels; P225/75SR16 BSW AS front and rear tires; inside under cargo mounted compact steel spare wheel; air conditioning, rear heat ducts; AM/FM stereo with clock, seek-scan, cassette, 6 speakers, and fixed antenna; cruise control with steering wheel controls; power door locks, remote keyless entry, ignition disable, child safety rear door locks, power remote hatch/trunk release; 2 power accessory outlets, driver's foot rest, retained accessory power; instrumentation display includes tachometer, oil pressure gauge, water temp gauge, volt gauge, trip odometer; warning indicators include oil pressure, water temp warning, battery, lights on, key in ignition, low fuel; dual airbags; panic alarm; tinted windows, power front windows with driver's 1-touch down, power rear windows, fixed 1/4 vent windows; variable intermittent front windshield wipers, flip-up rear window, fixed interval rear wiper, rear window defroster; seating capacity of 5, front bucket seats with adjustable headrests, center armrest with storage, driver's seat includes 4-way direction control, passenger's seat includes 4-way direction control; removable 60-40 folding rear bench seat with adjustable rear headrest; front and rear height adjustable seatbelts; cloth seats, vinyl door trim insert, full cloth headliner, full carpet floor covering, deluxe sound insulation; interior lights include dome light with fade, front reading lights, illuminated entry; steering wheel with tilt adjustment; vanity mirrors; day-night rearview mirror; full floor console, locking glove box with light, front and rear cupholders, driver's and passenger's door bins; carpeted cargo floor, carpeted trunk lid, cargo tie downs, cargo light; chrome grille, black side window moldings, black front windshield molding, black rear window molding and black door handles.

CODE	DESCRIPTION	INVOICE	MSRP

LAREDO 4WD (4A) (in addition to or instead of LAREDO 2WD (4A) equipment): Selec-Trac full-time 4 wheel drive, auto locking hub control and manual shift; power rack-and-pinion steering.

LIMITED 2WD (4A) (in addition to or instead of LAREDO 2WD (4A) equipment): Front and rear body-colored bumpers with rear step; body-colored bodyside cladding; monotone paint with bodyside accent stripe; aero-composite halogen fully automatic headlamps; additional exterior lights include front fog/driving lights; driver's and passenger's power remote body-colored heated folding outside mirrors; inside mounted compact steel spare wheel; dual zone front air conditioning with climate control; premium AM stereo/FM stereo with clock, seek-scan, cassette, single CD, 8 premium speakers, amplifier, graphic equalizer, and fixed antenna, radio steering wheel controls; garage door opener; instrumentation display includes compass, exterior temp, systems monitor, trip computer; warning indicators include low washer fluid, bulb failure, door ajar, trunk ajar, service interval; panic alarm, security system; deep tinted windows, driver's seat includes 6-way power seat with power lumbar support, passenger's seat includes 6-way power seat with power lumbar support; leather seats; carpeted floor mats, deluxe sound insulation, wood trim; memory on driver's seat with 2 memory setting(s) includes settings for exterior mirrors; interior lights include front and rear reading lights, 2 door curb lights; leather-wrapped steering wheel with tilt adjustment; dual illuminated vanity mirrors, dual auxiliary visors; auto-dimming day-night rearview mirror; mini overhead console; cargo cover, cargo net and body-colored grille.

LIMITED 4WD (4A) (in addition to or instead of LIMITED 2WD (4A) equipment): Quadra-Trac II on-demand 4 wheel drive; power rack-and-pinion steering and inside mounted compact alloy spare wheel.

Base Prices

Code	Description	Invoice	MSRP
WJTL74	Laredo 2WD (4A)	23571	25995
WJJL74	Laredo 4WD (4A)	25339	27965
WJTL74	Limited 2WD (4A)	28644	31760
WJJL74	Limited 4WD (4A)	30817	34190
Destination Charge:		525	525

Accessories

Code	Description	Invoice	MSRP
26D	**Quick Order Package 26D (Laredo)**	NC	NC
	Includes vehicle with standard equipment. REQUIRES ERH.		
26E	**Quick Order Package 26E (Laredo)**	880	1035
	Manufacturer Discount	(425)	(500)
	Net Price	455	535
	Includes mini overhead console, deep tinted sunscreen glass, protection group: cargo net and cover, front and rear floor mats and tires: P225/75R16 OWL AS. REQUIRES ERH.		
26F	**Quick Order Package 26F (Laredo)**	2631	3095
	Manufacturer Discount	(680)	(800)
	Net Price	1951	2295
	Includes mini overhead console, deep tinted sunscreen glass, luxury group: automatic headlamps, 6-way power seats, illuminated visor vanity mirrors, power heated fold-away mirrors; protection group: cargo net and cover, front and rear floor mats; AM/FM stereo with CD, cassette, EQ and Infinity speaker system, security alarm: sentry key theft deterrent system; leather-wrapped steering wheel and tires: P225/75R16 OWL AS. REQUIRES ERH.		

CODE	DESCRIPTION	INVOICE	MSRP
26G	Quick Order Package 26G (Limited)	NC	NC
	Includes vehicle with standard equipment. REQUIRES ERH.		
26K	Quick Order Package 26K (Limited)	893	1050
	Includes 10-way heated power seats with memory and power sunroof. REQUIRES ERH.		
28E	Quick Order Package 28E (Laredo 4WD)	880	1035
	Manufacturer Discount	(425)	(500)
	Net Price	455	535
	Includes mini overhead console, deep tinted sunscreen glass, protection group: cargo net and cover, front and rear floor mats and tires: P225/75R16 OWL AS. REQUIRES EVA.		
28F	Quick Order Package 28F (Laredo 4WD)	2631	3095
	Manufacturer Discount	(680)	(800)
	Net Price	1951	2295
	Includes mini overhead console, deep tinted sunscreen glass, luxury group: automatic headlamps, 6-way power seats, illuminated visor vanity mirrors, power heated fold-away mirrors; protection group: cargo net and cover, front and rear floor mats; AM/FM stereo with CD, cassette, EQ and Infinity speaker system, security alarm: sentry key theft deterrent system; leather-wrapped steering wheel and tires: P225/75R16 OWL AS. REQUIRES EVA.		
28G	Quick Order Package 28G (Limited 4WD)	NC	NC
	Includes vehicle with standard equipment. REQUIRES EVA.		
28K	Quick Order Package 28K (Limited 4WD)	893	1050
	Includes 10-way heated power seats with memory and power sunroof. REQUIRES EVA.		
ADB	Protection Group (Laredo)	170	200
	Includes cargo net and cover, front and rear floor mats. REQUIRES 26D.		
ADE	Cold Weather Group (Limited 4WD)	213	250
	Includes 10-way heated power seats with memory. REQUIRES 26G.		
ADE	Cold Weather Group (Laredo 4WD)	255	300
	Includes power heated fold-away mirrors and 10-way heated power seats. REQUIRES AFF. NOT AVAILABLE with 26D.		
ADL	Skid Plate Group (4WD)	170	200
	Includes skid plate package: front suspension, fuel tank and transfer case and front tow hooks.		
AFF	Luxury Group (Laredo)	638	750
	Includes automatic headlamps, auto day/night rear view mirror and 6-way power seats. REQUIRES ATA or (RAZ and RCE). NOT AVAILABLE with 26D.		
AHC	Trailer Tow Prep Group	89	105
	Includes class III trailering, mechanical cooling fan, trailer tow wiring assembly and 3.73 axle ratio. NOT AVAILABLE with AHT or EVA.		
AHT	Trailer Tow Group	306	360
	Includes 5000-lb maximum trailer weight, 750-lb maximum tongue weight, frame mounted receiver hitch, 7 way round wiring connector, 7 way round to 4 way flat plug adapter and plastic receiver cover. NOT AVAILABLE with AHC or EVA .		

CODE	DESCRIPTION	INVOICE	MSRP
AHX	Trailer Tow Group IV (4WD) *Includes maximum trailering weight (6500 lb), power steering cooler and trailer hitch receiver. REQUIRES EVA.*	217	255
ATA	Radio: AM/FM Stereo with Cass., CD Chgr. and Infinity Speakers (Laredo) *Includes 8 Infinity speakers, covered cargo storage and 10 disc CD changer.*	888	1045
ATA	Radio: AM/FM Stereo with Cass., CD Chgr. and Infinity Speakers (Limited) *Includes 8 Infinity speakers, covered cargo storage and 10 disc CD changer.*	255	300
AWB	Quadra Drive 4WD System (Laredo 4WD) *Includes vari-lock progressive axles and Quadra Trac II on demand 4WD system.*	846	995
AWB	Quadra Drive 4WD System (4WD) *Includes vari-lock progressive axles. NOT AVAILABLE with DHP.*	468	550
AWE	Up Country Suspension Group (4WD) *Includes skid plate group: skid plate package: front suspension, fuel tank and transfer case; front tow hooks full size spare tire, matching spare 5th wheel, HD suspension and tires: P245/70R16 SL OWL AT. NOT AVAILABLE with 26D.*	489	575
AWS	Smoker's Group *Includes cigarette lighter.*	NC	NC
DGB	Transmission: 4-Speed Automatic	NC	NC
DHF	Quadra Trac II On Demand 4WD System (Laredo 4WD)	378	445
DHP	Selec-Trac Full Time 4WD System (Limited 4WD)	NC	NC
DSA	Trac-Lok Differential Axle *REQUIRES ERH.*	242	285
ERH	Engine: 4.0L Power-Tech I6	NC	NC
EVA	Engine: 4.7L Power-Tech OHC V8 (Limited 4WD)	910	1070
EVA	Engine: 4.7L Power-Tech OHC V8 (Laredo 4WD)	990	1165
FL	Leather Low Back Bucket Seats (Laredo) *Includes 10-way power seats and map pockets. REQUIRES AFF. NOT AVAILABLE with 26D.*	493	580
GEG	Deep Tinted Sunscreen Glass (Laredo)	234	275
GTM	Power Heated Fold-Away Mirrors (Laredo) *NOT AVAILABLE with 26D.*	43	50
GWA	Power Sunroof *NOT AVAILABLE with 26D.*	680	800
LNJ	Fog Lamps (Laredo) *NOT AVAILABLE with 26D.*	102	120
LSA	Security Alarm (Laredo) *NOT AVAILABLE with 26D.*	128	150
NAE	CA/MA/NY Emissions *Automatically coded. NOT AVAILABLE with YCF.*	NC	NC
NBN	Northeastern States Emissions *Covers the following states: KY, ME, MA, NY, NC, OH, TN, VT or WV.*	NC	NC
NHK	Engine Block Heater	34	40
PUL	Sienna Tinted Pearl Coat	170	200
RAZ	Radio: AM/FM Stereo with CD, Cassette and EQ (Laredo) *Includes 4 speakers.*	285	335
RCE	Infinity Speaker System (Laredo) *Includes 8 speakers. NOT AVAILABLE with 26D.*	349	410

CODE	DESCRIPTION	INVOICE	MSRP
TBW	Tire: Full Size Spare *Includes wheel: spare matching 5th wheel.*	136	160
TTB	Tires: P245/70R 16 SL OWL AT (All Except Limited 4WD)	NC	NC
TTB	Tires: P245/70R 16 SL OWL AT (Laredo 2WD) *REQUIRES 26E or 26F.*	157	185
TTB	Tires: P245/70R 16 SL OWL AT (Laredo 2WD) *REQUIRES 26D.*	370	435
YCF	Border State Emissions (California) *NOT AVAILABLE with NAE.*	NC	NC

1999 WRANGLER

1999 Jeep Wrangler

What's New?

The Wrangler's interior finally enters the '90s with rotary HVAC controls, replacing the old slider control system. The hard or soft top is available in Dark Tan, and new colors decorate both the exterior and the interior.

Review

The Wrangler is the off-road icon. Originally built for military use, the original Jeep has retained its Spartan utility while slowly evolving into a practical means of transportation. The Wrangler is still the drive-me-hard-through-the-slop beast of yesterday, with a few appreciated improvements for the daily commute.

Jeep Wranglers have long been the standard for those valiant explorers who truly wish to go where no one has gone before. The go-anywhere ability of the Wrangler has been improved by the Quadra-Coil suspension which allows an additional seven inches of articulation over the old leaf spring set-up; thus resulting in increased approach and departure angles. The Quadra-Coil suspension, along with improved shocks and tires, also greatly improve the Wrangler's on-road manners.

Available in SE, Sport and Sahara trim levels, the Wrangler fits into several budgets. Our favorite model is the Sport, which comes with the powerful 4.0-liter engine yet retains no-nonsense utility; nicely equipped, the Sport comes in at under $20,000. The SE is for people who don't mind a lack of power or available ABS, and the Sahara is for anyone who can't live without leather and a quality sound system. Nobody, however, will mistake this vehicle for a smooth-running family sedan; the Wrangler is very much a truck thanks to its high step-in height and abundant wind and road noise. A five-speed manual transmission remains standard and a three-speed automatic is available for those who don't plan on any serious off-roading.

For 1999, Jeep has decided to give the Wrangler some additional user-friendliness by tossing out the sliding heater controls and replacing them with twist knobs. A revised frame makes the Wrangler 16 lbs. lighter than before, and a passenger-side airbag cutoff switch, introduced in May of 1998, continues to offer value for anyone who must tote children up front.

Over the past few years, Jeep has done a great job improving the Wrangler. Gone are some of the nagging complaints we had about safety, wind noise and engine roar; what remains is a solid truck with hard-core capabilities and rugged good looks. This is obviously not the truck for everybody, but those willing to put up with a cloth interior and a little road noise will be rewarded with an amazingly fun and extremely useful vehicle.

Safety Data

Side Airbag: *Not Available*
4-Wheel ABS: *Optional (Sport/Sahara); N/A (SE)*
Driver Crash Test Grade: *Good*
Side Impact Crash Test Front: *Not Available*
Crash Offset: *Acceptable*
Integrated Child Seat(s): *Not Available*
Traction Control: *Not Available*
Passenger Crash Test Grade: *Good*
Side Impact Crash Test Rear: *Not Available*

Standard Equipment

SE (5M): 2.5L I-4 OHV SPI 8-valve engine; 5-speed overdrive manual transmission; 500-amp battery; 81-amp alternator; part-time 4 wheel drive, auto locking hub control with manual shift, 4.11 axle ratio; stainless steel exhaust; front non-independent suspension with anti-roll bar, front coil springs, rear non-independent suspension with anti-roll bar, rear coil springs; power rack-and-pinion steering; front disc/rear drum brakes; 15 gal capacity fuel tank; skid plates; tailgate rear cargo door; manual convertible roof with roll-over protection; front and rear black bumpers; black fender flares; monotone paint with bodyside accent stripe; sealed beam halogen headlamps; additional exterior lights include center high mounted stop light; driver's and passenger's manual black folding outside mirrors; front and rear 15" x 6" silver styled steel wheels; P205/75SR15 BSW AT front and rear tires; outside rear mounted compact steel spare wheel; fixed antenna; 1 power accessory outlet; instrumentation display includes tachometer, oil pressure gauge, water temp gauge, volt gauge, trip odometer; warning indicators include battery, key in ignition, low fuel; dual airbags; tinted windows, manual rear windows; fixed interval front windshield wipers; seating capacity of 2, front bucket seats with fixed headrests, driver's seat includes 4-way direction control, passenger's seat includes 4-way direction control with easy entry; front height adjustable seatbelts; vinyl seats, front carpet floor covering; day-night rearview mirror; partial floor console, locking glove box, front cupholder, dashboard storage, driver's and passenger's door bins; cargo tie downs; body-colored grille, black front windshield molding and black door handles.

SPORT (5M) (in addition to or instead of SE (5M) equipment): 4.0L I6 OHV SMPI 12-valve engine; 3.07 axle ratio; front and rear 15" x 7" silver steel wheels; AM/FM stereo with clock, seek-scan, 2 speakers, and fixed antenna; removable full folding rear bench seat and full carpet floor covering.

SAHARA (5M) (in addition to or instead of SPORT (5M) equipment): 600-amp HD battery; 117-amp HD alternator; 19 gal capacity fuel tank; running boards, skid plates; rear tow hooks; body-colored fender flares; additional exterior lights include front fog/driving lights, underhood light; AM/FM stereo with clock, seek-scan, cassette, 4 speakers, and fixed antenna; variable intermittent front windshield wipers; driver seat's includes 4-way direction control with easy entry; premium cloth seats, carpeted floor mats; interior lights include dome light; leather-wrapped steering wheel with tilt adjustment; full floor console, 2 seat back storage pockets and driver's and passenger's door bins.

Base Prices

Code	Description	Invoice	MSRP
TJJL77	SE (5M)	13756	14345
TJJL77	Sport (5M)	16171	17905
TJJL77	Sahara (5M)	18134	20135
Destination Charge:		525	525

Accessories

22A **Quick Order Package 22A (SE)** ..... NC NC
Includes vehicle with standard equipment. REQUIRES (HAA or 4XA) and EPE and DGA. NOT AVAILABLE with DSA, RAS, AAX, DDQ, K5.

22N **Quick Order Package 22N (SE)** 735 865
Includes AM/FM stereo with 2 speakers and vinyl high-back bucket seats. REQUIRES (HAA or 4XA) and EPE and DGA. NOT AVAILABLE with DSA, RAS, DDQ.

23A **Quick Order Package 23A (SE)** ..... NC NC
Includes vehicle with standard equipment. REQUIRES (HAA or 4XA) and EPE and DDQ. NOT AVAILABLE with RAS, AAX, DGA, K5.

23N **Quick Order Package 23N (SE)** 735 865
Includes AM/FM stereo with 2 speakers and vinyl high-back bucket seats. REQUIRES (HAA or 4XA) and EPE and DDQ. NOT AVAILABLE with RAS, DGA.

24C **Quick Order Package 24C (Sport)** ..... NC NC
Includes vehicle with standard equipment. REQUIRES (HAA or 4XA) and ERH and DGA. NOT AVAILABLE with TRN, DDQ.

24D **Quick Order Package 24D (Sport)** 404 475
Includes convenience group: full length floor console, underhood lamp, courtesy lamps; 19 gallon fuel tank, tilt steering column and intermittent wipers. REQUIRES (HAA or 4XA) and ERH and DGA. NOT AVAILABLE with AAS, TMW, DDQ.

24G **Quick Order Package 24G (Sahara)** ..... NC NC
Includes Sahara decor group. REQUIRES (HAA or 4XA) and ERH and DGA. NOT AVAILABLE with DDQ.

25C **Quick Order Package 25C (Sport)** ..... NC NC
Includes vehicle with standard equipment. REQUIRES (HAA or 4XA) and ERH and DDQ. NOT AVAILABLE with DGA, TRN.

25D **Quick Order Package 25D (Sport)** 404 475
Includes convenience group: full length floor console, underhood lamp, courtesy lamps; 19 gallon fuel tank, tilt steering column and intermittent wipers. REQUIRES (HAA or 4XA) and ERH and DDQ. NOT AVAILABLE with DGA, AAS, TMW.

25G **Quick Order Package 25G (Sahara)** ..... NC NC
Includes Sahara decor group. REQUIRES (HAA or 4XA) and ERH and DDQ. NOT AVAILABLE with DGA.

CODE	DESCRIPTION	INVOICE	MSRP
4XA	Air Conditioning Bypass *NOT AVAILABLE with HAA.*	NC	NC
6**	Hardtop (SE/Sport) *REQUIRES 22A or 23A or 22N or 23N.*	642	755
6**	Hardtop (Sahara) *REQUIRES 24G or 25G.*	986	1160
AAS	30" Tire and Wheel Group (Sport) *Includes 15" Wrangler GSA AT OWL tires, 15" x 8" aluminum wheels and full size spare tire with matching wheel. Deletes standard spare tire cover. NOT AVAILABLE with TMW, TRN, CSA, WJ1, 24D, 25D.*	667	785
AAS	30" Tire and Wheel Group (Sahara) *Includes 15" Wrangler GSA AT OWL tires, 15" x 8" aluminum wheels and full size spare tire with matching wheel. Deletes standard spare tire cover.*	306	360
AAS	30" Tire and Wheel Group (Sport) *Includes 15" Wrangler GSA AT OWL tires, 15" x 8" aluminum wheels and full size spare tire with matching wheel. Deletes standard spare tire cover. NOT AVAILABLE with TMW, TRN, CSA, WJ1, 24C, 25C.*	570	670
AAX	Sound Group (SE) *Includes rear sportbar with full padding and 4 speakers with sound bar. NOT AVAILABLE with RAS, 22N, 23N.*	455	535
AAX	Sound Group (SE) *Includes AM/FM stereo and rear sportbar with full padding and 4 speakers with sound bar. NOT AVAILABLE with RAS, 22A, 23A.*	225	265
ADC	Convenience Group (SE/Sport) *Includes full length floor console, under dash courtesy lamps and underhood lamp.*	140	165
ADH	HD Electrical Group (SE/Sport) *Includes HD 117-amp alternator and HD 600-amp maintenace free battery.*	115	135
AEM	Dual Top Group with Matching Colors (SE/Sport) *Includes hardtop with tinted glass on rear quarter and liftgate, rear cargo lamp and rear window wiper/washer and easy folding soft top with soft windows and full metal doors with roll-up windows.*	1186	1395
AEM	Dual Top Group with Matching Colors (Sahara) *Includes hardtop with tinted glass on rear quarter and liftgate, rear cargo lamp and rear window wiper/washer and easy folding soft top with soft windows and full metal doors with roll-up windows.*	1530	1800
BGK	4-Wheel Antilock Brakes (Sport/Sahara) *REQUIRES DSA. NOT AVAILABLE with DRK.*	510	600
CLC	Front Floor Mats (SE/Sport)	26	30
CSA	Spare Tire Cover (SE/Sport) *NOT AVAILABLE with AAS.*	43	50
DDQ	Transmission: 5-Speed Manual *NOT AVAILABLE with 22A, 22N, 24C, 24D, 24G.*	NC	NC
DGA	Transmission: 3-Speed Automatic *NOT AVAILABLE with 23A, 23N, 25C, 25D, 25G.*	531	625
DME	3.73 Axle Ratio (Sport/Sahara)	NC	NC
DRK	Dana 44 Rear Axle (Sport/Sahara) *REQUIRES TBB or DDQ. NOT AVAILABLE with BGK.*	506	595

CODE	DESCRIPTION	INVOICE	MSRP
DSA	Rear Axle Trac-Lok Differential *REQUIRES TBB and DDQ. NOT AVAILABLE with 22A, 22N.*	242	285
EPE	Engine: 2.5L I4 MPI (SE)	NC	NC
ERH	Engine: 4.0L I6 MPI (Sport/Sahara)	NC	NC
GCD	Hard Top Deep Tint Glass *Includes rear quarter windows and liftgate and rear window defroster.*	344	405
GCF	Full Metal Doors with Roll-Up Windows	106	125
GFA	Rear Window Defroster *REQUIRES ADH or HAA.*	140	165
GXX	Sentry Key Theft Deterrent System *Includes 2 keys.*	64	75
HAA	Air Conditioning *NOT AVAILABLE with 4XA.*	761	895
J6	Vinyl High-Back Bucket Seats (SE) *Includes rear seat. NOT AVAILABLE with K5.*	506	595
JKC	Add-A-Trunk with Lockable Storage *REQUIRES J6 or K5.*	106	125
K5	Cloth High-Back Bucket Seats (SE/Sport) *Includes rear seat. NOT AVAILABLE with J6, 22A, 23A.*	128	150
K5	Cloth High-Back Bucket Seats (SE) *Includes rear seat. NOT AVAILABLE with J6, 22N, 23N.*	633	745
LNJ	Fog Lamps (Sport) *REQUIRES HAA or ADH.*	102	120
MRJ	Bodyside Steps (SE/Sport)	64	75
NAE	California Emissions *Automatically coded. NOT AVAILABLE with YCF.*	NC	NC
NBN	Northeastern States Emissions *NOT AVAILABLE with YCF.*	NC	NC
NHK	Engine Block Heater	30	35
NHM	Speed Control (Sahara) *Includes leather-wrapped steering wheel.*	213	250
NHM	Speed Control (SE/Sport) *Includes leather-wrapped steering wheel.*	255	300
RAL	Radio: AM/FM Stereo with 2 Speakers (SE) *NOT AVAILABLE with RAS.*	230	270
RAS	Radio: AM/FM Stereo with Cassette (SE) *Includes 4 speakers. NOT AVAILABLE with AAX, RAL, 23A, 22A.*	378	445
RAS	Radio: AM/FM Stereo with Cassette (SE) *Includes 4 speakers. NOT AVAILABLE with AAX, RAL, 23N, 22N.*	608	715
RAS	Radio: AM/FM Stereo with Cassette (Sport) *Includes clock and 4 speakers with sound bar.*	361	425
RCD	4 Speakers with Sound Bar (Sport)	208	245
SCG	Leather-Wrapped Steering Wheel (SE/Sport)	43	50
SDU	High Pressure Gas Charged Shocks *REQUIRES TMW or TRN.*	77	90
SUA	Tilt Steering Column (SE/Sport) *Includes intermittent wipers.*	166	195

CODE	DESCRIPTION	INVOICE	MSRP
TBB	Tire: Full Size Spare (Sahara) *Includes matching spare wheel.*	183	215
TBB	Tire: Full Size Spare (SE/Sport) *Includes matching spare wheel.*	98	115
TMW	Tires: P215/75R15 AT OWL (Sport) *NOT AVAILABLE with TRN, AAS, 24D, 25D.*	200	235
TMW	Tires: P215/75R15 AT OWL (Sport) *NOT AVAILABLE with TRN, AAS, 24C, 25C.*	102	120
TMW	Tires: P215/75R15 AT OWL (SE) *Includes full size spare tire and matching wheel. NOT AVAILABLE with TRN.*	238	280
TRN	Tires: P225/75R15 AT OWL (Sport) *Includes full size spare. NOT AVAILABLE with TMW, AAS, 24C, 25C.*	264	310
TRN	Tires: P225/75R15 AT OWL (Sport) *Includes full size spare. NOT AVAILABLE with TMW, AAS, 24D, 25D.*	361	425
TRN	Tires: P225/75R15 Wrangler AT OWL (SE) *Includes full size spare tire and matching wheel. NOT AVAILABLE with TMW.*	400	470
WJ1	Wheels: 15" x 7" Grizzly Aluminum (Sport) *Includes full size spare tire and matching wheel. REQUIRES TMW or TRN. NOT AVAILABLE with AAS.*	225	265
WJ1	Wheels: 15" x 7" Grizzly Aluminum (SE) *REQUIRES TMW or TRN. NOT AVAILABLE with WJ5.*	421	495
WJ5	Wheels: 15" x 7" Full-Face Steel (SE) *Includes full size spare tire and matching wheel. REQUIRES TMW or TRN. NOT AVAILABLE with WJ1.*	196	230
XEA	Tow Hooks (2 Front) (SE/Sport)	34	40
YCF	Border State Emissions (California) *NOT AVAILABLE with NAE, NBN.*	NC	NC

1999 SPORTAGE

1999 Kia Sportage

What's New?

A new two-door convertible model joins the four-door Sportage in 1999. The convertible comes in either a 4x2 layout with automatic transmission or a 4x4 layout with five-speed manual transmission. It also boasts dual front airbags and a driver's side front knee bag.

Review

Part owned by Ford and Mazda before Hyundai acquired the company, Kia relies heavily on resources from all three automakers as it struggles to its feet in a tough marketplace. The Sportage is the product of collaboration between Kia, Ford, Mazda and suspension-tuning guru Lotus. Designed from the start as a sport utility, the Sportage sports tough ladder frame construction, shift-on-the-fly four-wheel drive, and a Mazda-based 2.0-liter engine that makes 130 horsepower and 127 pound-feet of torque.

Two trim levels are available: base and EX. Base models are well-trimmed, including power windows, split-folding rear seats, a remote fuel door release, power mirrors, a rear defroster and air conditioning. Optional equipment includes four-wheel antilock brakes, leather interior, cruise control and an automatic transmission.

A wide variety of colors are available on the Sportage models, a few of which appear to have originated from the minds of the folks currently in charge of painting Hot Wheels cars. The look is rugged yet cute; perfect for family duty in the 'burbs. Off-road, we found the Sportage confidence inspiring, but it didn't feel as tight as a Toyota RAV4 or Honda CR-V.

For most owners, that won't matter. Few SUVs actually leave the pavement, and on the pavement is where the Sportage shines. Lotus engineers worked wonders here, and the Sportage is stable and comfortable. In the four-door model, the seating position is high and upright, visibility is outstanding, and the layout of the dashboard and controls makes the Sportage easy to manipulate. Rear seat riders enjoy lots of room and support, afforded by "stadium style" elevated seating. The convertible offers an easy-folding soft-top and a full-size spare tire mounted in an outside carrier. From the driver's seat, the Sportage looks and feels much more substantial than its low price would lead you to believe.

For young families and active singles looking to get into a sport-ute without getting into financial servitude, the Sportage is worth a look.

Safety Data

Side Airbag: *Not Available*
4-Wheel ABS: *Optional*
Driver Crash Test Grade: *Average*
Side Impact Crash Test Front: *Not Available*
Crash Offset: *Marginal*
Integrated Child Seat(s): *Not Available*
Traction Control: *Not Available*
Passenger Crash Test Grade: *Average*
Side Impact Crash Test Rear: *Not Available*

Standard Equipment

2-DOOR 2WD CONVERTIBLE (4A): 2.0L I-4 DOHC MPI 16-valve engine; 4-speed electronic overdrive automatic transmission with lock-up; 48-amp battery; 70-amp alternator; rear wheel drive, 4.78 axle ratio; partial stainless steel exhaust; front independent double wishbone suspension with anti-roll bar, front coil springs, rigid rear axle multi-link suspension with anti-roll bar, rear coil springs; power re-circulating ball steering with engine speed-sensing assist; front disc/rear drum brakes with rear wheel antilock braking system; 14 gal capacity fuel tank; liftback rear cargo door; manual convertible roof with roll-over protection; front and rear body-colored bumpers with rear tow hooks; monotone paint; aero-composite halogen headlamps; additional exterior lights include center high mounted stop light; driver's and passenger's power remote black folding outside mirrors; front and rear 15" x 6" silver styled steel wheels; P205/75SR15 BSW AS front and rear tires; outside rear-mounted full-size conventional steel spare wheel; power door locks, remote fuel release; 1 power accessory outlet; instrumentation display includes tachometer, water temp gauge, in-dash clock, trip odometer; warning indicators include low fuel; dual airbags; driver's knee airbag; security system; tinted windows, power front windows fixed 1/4 vent windows; fixed interval front windshield wipers; seating capacity of 5, front bucket seats with adjustable headrests, center armrest with storage, driver's seat includes 4-way direction control with lumbar support, passenger's seat includes 4-way direction control; 50-50 folding rear bench seat with fixed rear headrest; front height adjustable seatbelts; cloth seats, cloth door trim insert, full cloth headliner, full carpet floor covering; interior lights include dome light; day-night rearview mirror; full floor console, glove box, front cupholder, instrument panel bin, driver's and front passenger's door bins; carpeted cargo floor, plastic trunk lid; body-colored grille, chrome side window moldings, black front windshield molding, black rear window molding and black door handles.

BASE 4-DOOR 2WD (5M) (in addition to or instead of 2-DOOR 2WD CONVERTIBLE (4A) equipment): Five-speed overdrive manual transmission; 15.8 gal capacity fuel tank; child safety rear door locks and rear garment hook.

EX 4-DOOR 2WD (5M) (in addition to or instead of BASE 4-DOOR 2WD (5M) equipment): Roof rack; body-colored bodyside cladding, rocker panel extensions; two-tone paint; front and rear 15" x 6" silver styled alloy wheels; alloy spare wheel; air conditioning; AM/FM stereo, seek-scan, single CD player, 6 speakers and manual retractable antenna; cruise control; deep tinted windows; rear window wiper; wood trim; passenger side vanity mirror; chrome door handles.

2-DOOR 4WD CONVERTIBLE (5M) (in addition to or instead of 2-DOOR 2WD CONVERTIBLE (4A) equipment): 5-speed overdrive manual transmission; part-time 4 wheel drive, auto locking hub control with manual shift, 4.78 axle ratio; manual convertible roof with convertible hard top.

BASE 4-DOOR 4WD (5M) (in addition to or instead of BASE 4-DOOR 2WD (5M) equipment): Part-time 4 wheel drive, auto locking hub control and manual shift; front and rear 15" x 6" silver styled alloy wheels and alloy spare wheel.

EX 4-DOOR 4WD (5M) (in addition to or instead of EX 4-DOOR 2WD (5M) equipment): Part-time 4 wheel drive, auto locking hub control and manual shift.

SPORTAGE

CODE	DESCRIPTION	INVOICE	MSRP
	Base Prices		
42212	Base 2WD Convertible (4A)	12724	13995
42411	Base 4WD Convertible (5M)	13058	14495
42221	Base 4-Door 2WD (5M)	13441	14795
42421	Base 4-Door 4WD (5M)	14670	16295
42241	EX 4-Door 2WD (5M)	15680	17395
42441	EX 4-Door 4WD (5M)	16600	18595
Destination Charge:		450	450
	Accessories		
AB	Antilock Brakes	410	490
AC	Air Conditioning (Base/Convertible)	745	900
AW	Alloy Wheels (Base 2WD/Convertible)	274	340
CD	Radio: AM/FM Stereo with CD (Base/Convertible)	375	475
CF	Carpeted Floor Mats	45	69
CM	Carpeted Floor Mat Set (4-Door)	83	119
CP	Cruise Package (Convertible)	200	250
	Includes cruise control and variable intermittent wipers.		
CT	Cargo Tray (4-Door)	40	67
GP	Graphics Package (Convertible)	61	92
LE	Leather Package (EX)	760	900
	Includes leather seats, leather door panel inserts, leather-wrapped steering wheel and leather-wrapped gear shift handle.		
RM	Radio: AM/FM Stereo with Cassette (Base/Convertible)	250	320
RR	Roof Rack (Base 4-Door)	150	195
RW	Rear Window Wiper (Base 4-Door)	100	125
SG	Sport Appearance Graphic (Base 4-Door)	60	95
SP	Rear Spoiler (4-Door)	143	189

1999 DISCOVERY SERIES II

1999 Land Rover Discovery Series II

What's New?

The release of the 1999 Discovery Series II brings the first engineering redesign since the vehicle's European introduction 11 years ago. Traction Control, Active Cornering Enhancement and Hill Descent Control will be standard features.

Review

It may look the same, but don't be fooled—the 1999 Land Rover Discovery Series II is all-new and ready to flaunt it. Like the Discoveries of yesteryear, this new version exhibits excellent off-road prowess and distinctive, hardy styling, but also adds new performance features that promise a more capable on-road driving experience.

Introduced to the U.S. in April 1994, Discoveries are best known as vigorous off-road warriors bejeweled with the snob appeal of the Land Rover marque. For 1999, Land Rover is offering an interim Discovery SD model until later in the model year when the Series II will become available.

The Series II enters its next stage of development with improvements in performance and design. With 85 percent of the truck's parts brand-new, the Discovery Series II is 6.5 inches longer and 3.8 inches wider than the first Discovery. Furthermore, this is the first sport-utility vehicle to be equipped with Active Cornering Enhancement (ACE), which uses a hydraulic system to control body roll on turns, and Hill Descent Control (HDC), a driver-activated feature which supplements traditional braking when descending steep, slippery slopes in extreme conditions.

Other new features for the 1999 Series II include a self-leveling suspension, traction control, forward-facing rear jump seats, a taller windshield, an improved shift lever, more ergonomic exterior door handles, raised rear light clusters and Optikool glass that reduces ultraviolet rays by 31 percent and heat transmission by 76 percent. The rear door-mounted spare tire has been lowered by one inch to improve rearward visibility and new paint colors include Java Black, Niagara Gray, Blenheim Silver and Kinversand.

Just one body style is available: a five-door wagon with permanent four-wheel drive and a new, standard adaptive automatic transmission that adjusts to different driving styles. There is only one trim level available as well. Beneath the vehicle's hood is a new generation of the 4.0-liter, 182-horsepower V8 engine that powered last year's model. This V8 makes 18 foot-pounds more torque than the engine in the 1998 Discovery, at a lower rpm. This powerplant is rated for only 13 mpg in the city and 16 mpg for highway driving, though, and that's with a light foot. The previous model exhibited gear noise and other aural annoyances, but Land Rover claims to have dramatically reduced noise, vibration and harshness (NVH) levels in the new truck. The Series II's stance is wider than last year's Discovery by 2.1 inches at the front and 2.9 inches at the rear, making for a smoother on-road feel, and the self-leveling suspension benefits off-roaders by allowing the driver to raise or lower the rear of the truck by 1.6 inches.

Inside the Series II, both front and backseat passengers sit high for a superior view. Seating can be expanded to seven, in the form of forward-facing, stowable rear jump seats. This Discovery boasts 5.7 cubic feet more storage space than the previous vehicle and only a handful of options are available. The driver and front passenger receive adjustable lumbar support and enjoy the benefits of dual-temperature control air conditioning as well as a full-size glovebox and four cupholders.

Legendary off-road capabilities help make the aluminum-bodied Discovery Series II an attractive choice in this segment, augmented by safety equipment like ABS and traction control. With competitors releasing new hybrid sport-utes faster than horses can race the Kentucky Derby, Land Rover remains true to its original industry mission—building a go-anywhere, do-anything vehicle. The Series II will undoubtedly live up to that reputation, but with the new suspension, powertrain and handling features available on the truck, urban driving may become a bit more enjoyable as well.

Safety Data

Side Airbag: *Not Available*
4-Wheel ABS: *Standard*
Driver Crash Test Grade: *Not Available*
Side Impact Crash Test Front: *Not Available*
Crash Offset: *Not Available*
Integrated Child Seat(s): *Not Available*
Traction Control: *Standard*
Passenger Crash Test Grade: *Not Available*
Side Impact Crash Test Rear: *Not Available*

Standard Equipment

SERIES II (4A): 4.0L V8 OHV SMPI 16-valve engine, requires premium unleaded fuel; 4-speed electronic overdrive automatic transmission with lock-up; 590-amp battery; engine oil cooler, HD radiator, HD starter; 130-amp alternator; driver selectable program transmission, transmission oil cooler; full-time 4 wheel drive, traction control, 3.54 axle ratio; steel exhaust; HD ride suspension, front non-independent suspension with anti-roll bar, front coil springs, rigid rear axle multi-link suspension with anti-roll bar, rear coil springs; power re-circulating ball steering; 4 wheel disc brakes with 4 wheel antilock braking system; 24.6 gal. capacity fuel tank; rear mud flaps; conventional rear cargo door; class III trailering, trailer harness, trailer hitch; roof rack; front colored bumper with black rub strip, rear black bumper, front and rear tow hooks, rear step; rocker panel extensions, black fender flares; monotone paint; aero-composite halogen headlamps with washer, delay-off feature; additional exterior lights include center high mounted stop light; driver's and passenger's power remote black heated folding outside mirrors; front and rear 16" x 8" silver alloy wheels; P255/65HR16 BSW M&S front and rear tires; outside rear mounted full-size conventional alloy spare wheel; dual zone front air conditioning, rear heat ducts; premium AM/FM stereo with seek-scan, cassette, 6 premium speakers, and window grid diversity antenna, radio steering wheel controls; cruise control with steering wheel controls; power door locks with 2 stage unlock, remote keyless entry, child safety rear door locks, remote fuel release; 1 power accessory outlet, driver's foot rest, retained accessory power, garage door opener; instrumentation display includes tachometer, water temp gauge, in-dash clock, exterior temp, trip odometer; warning indicators include oil pressure, water temp, battery, low oil level, low coolant, lights on, key in ignition, low fuel; dual airbags; ignition disable, security system; deep tinted windows, power front windows with driver's and passenger's 1-touch down, power rear windows, fixed 1/4 vent windows; variable intermittent front windshield wipers, variable intermittent rear wiper, rear window defroster; seating capacity of 5, front bucket seats with fixed headrests, center armrest with storage, driver's seat includes 4-way direction control with lumbar support, passenger's seat includes 4-way direction control with lumbar support; 60-40 folding rear split-bench seat with adjustable headrests, center armrest; seatbelts with front pretensioners; cloth seats, cloth door trim insert, full cloth headliner, full carpet floor covering; interior lights include dome light with fade, front reading lights, 4 door curb

CODE	DESCRIPTION	INVOICE	MSRP

lights; leather-wrapped steering wheel with tilt adjustment; dual illuminated vanity mirrors; auto-dimming day-night rearview mirror; full floor console, mini overhead console glove box, front and rear cupholders, 2 seat back storage pockets, driver's and passenger's door bins; carpeted cargo floor, plastic trunk lid, cargo cover, cargo net, cargo light; black grille, black side window moldings, black front windshield molding, black rear window molding and black door handles.

Base Prices

CODE	DESCRIPTION	INVOICE	MSRP
SD	Series II AWD	30394	34150
Destination Charge:		625	625

Accessories

CODE	DESCRIPTION	INVOICE	MSRP
—	California Emissions	100	100
—	Java Black Paint	250	300
CCP	Cold Climate Package *Includes heated front seats and heated windshield.*	445	500
CD	6 Disc CD Changer	525	625
LJ	Lightstone Paint *REQUIRES LTHR.*	400	500
LTHR	Leather Interior	1735	1950
PPK	Performance Package *Includes active cornering enhancement (ACE), 18" alloy wheels and tires: P255/ 55HR18.*	2581	2900
RAC	Rear Air Conditioning *REQUIRES RSP.*	668	750
RSP	Rear Seat Package *Includes forward facing rear seat, rear step and self leveling rear suspension.*	1588	1750
SLS	Self Leveling Rear Suspension	668	750
SUN	Power Sun Roofs (2)	1335	1500

1999 RX 300

1999 Lexus RX 300

What's New?

The RX 300 is an all-new SUV from Lexus designed to compete against the Infiniti QX4, Mercedes-Benz ML 320 and the Jeep Grand Cherokee Limited.

Review

Lexus, like most manufacturers these days, is jumping on the sedan/sport-utility hybrid bandwagon with the all-new RX 300. Touted as a "new breed of SUV," the RX 300 is supposed to offer the style, versatility, and poor-weather traction of an all-wheel drive SUV without the compromise in ride, fuel economy, or ease of entry/exit associated with most SUVs.

Lexus is smart to get into this segment while the gettin's good. Consumers who want all the luxury of a high-end sedan along with the security and beefiness of a truck are buying these vehicles faster than the manufacturers can produce them.

Powering the RX 300 is a 3.0-liter 24-valve V6 that makes 220 horsepower and 222 pound-feet of torque. Lexus' trademark Variable Valve Timing with intelligence (VVTi) is used to create 80 percent of the engine's torque at 1,600 rpm. It also enhances fuel economy and reduces emissions.

For buyers living in mild climates, the RX 300 can be had in front-wheel drive, which improves both performance and gas mileage. To add to the front-wheel drive model's capability in less than perfect weather, electronic traction control is optional. Full-time four-wheel drive is also available with a viscous center coupling that directs torque to the wheels with the most traction whenever slippage occurs.

In keeping with its Lexus nameplate, the RX offers numerous luxury features like a dash-mounted liquid crystal display for relaying climate control and trip computer information. A standard 190-watt Pioneer system can be upgraded to an optional 230-watt Nakamichi sound system for audiophiles who like to scare the wild life while slogging though the wilderness.

With its long list of luxury and safety features Lexus is able to offer a lot of car (or is that truck?) for not a lot of money. While we wouldn't recommend the RX to anyone with serious off-road aspirations, it fulfills its intended mission of giving semi-affluent buyers an SUV that won't offend the other country club members.

Safety Data

Side Airbag: *Standard*
4-Wheel ABS: *Standard*
Driver Crash Test Grade: *Not Available*
Side Impact Crash Test Front: *Not Available*
Crash Offset: *Not Available*
Integrated Child Seat(s): *Not Available*
Traction Control: *Optional (FWD); N/A (4WD)*
Passenger Crash Test Grade: *Not Available*
Side Impact Crash Test Rear: *Not Available*

Standard Equipment

RX 300 FWD (4A): 3.0L V6 DOHC SMPI 24-valve engine with variable valve timing; 4-speed electronic automatic transmission with lock-up and driver selectable program; 65-amp battery; 80-amp alternator; front wheel drive, 3.08 axle ratio; stainless steel exhaust; front independent strut suspension with anti-roll bar, front coil springs, rear independent strut suspension with anti-roll bar, rear coil springs; power rack-and-pinion steering; 4 wheel disc brakes with 4 wheel antilock braking system; 17.2 gal capacity fuel tank; body-colored front and rear mud flaps; liftback rear cargo door; front and rear colored bumpers with rear step; body-colored bodyside cladding; monotone paint; aero-composite halogen fully automatic headlamps with daytime running lights, delay-off feature; additional exterior lights include front fog/driving lights, center high mounted stop light; driver and passenger power remote body-colored folding outside mirrors; front and rear 16" x 6.5" silver alloy wheels; P225/70SR16 BSW M&S front and rear tires; inside under cargo mounted full-size temporary steel spare wheel; air conditioning with climate control, rear heat ducts; AM/FM stereo with seek-scan, cassette, CD changer pre-wiring, pre-wiring in-dash CD, 7 speakers, amplifier, automatic equalizer, theft deterrent, and power retractable diversity antenna; cruise control; power door locks with 2 stage unlock, remote keyless entry, child safety rear door locks, power remote hatch/trunk release, remote fuel release; cell phone pre-wiring, 3 power accessory outlets, driver's foot rest, retained accessory power; instrumentation display includes tachometer, water temp gauge, in-dash clock, exterior temp, trip computer, trip odometer; warning indicators include oil pressure, battery, lights on, key in ignition, low fuel, low washer fluid, bulb failure, door ajar; dual airbags, seat mounted side airbag; ignition disable, panic alarm, security system; deep tinted windows, power front windows with front and rear 1-touch down power rear windows, fixed 1/4 vent windows; variable intermittent front windshield wipers, fixed interval rear wiper, rear window defroster; seating capacity of 5, front bucket seats with adjustable headrests, driver and passenger armrests, driver's seat includes 6-way power seat with, power lumbar support, passenger's seat includes 4-way power seat; 60-40 folding rear split-bench seat with reclining adjustable rear headrest, center armrest; front height adjustable seatbelts with front pretensioners; premium cloth seats, cloth door trim insert, full cloth headliner, full carpet floor covering, wood trim, leather gear shift knob; interior lights include dome light, front reading lights, 4 door curb lights, illuminated entry; leather-wrapped steering wheel with tilt adjustment; dual illuminated vanity mirrors, dual auxiliary visors; day-night rearview mirror; partial floor console, mini overhead console with storage, locking glove box with light, front and rear cupholders, instrument panel bin, 2 seat back storage pockets, driver and passenger door bins, rear door bins; carpeted cargo floor, carpeted trunk lid, cargo cover, cargo light, cargo concealed storage; chrome grille, black side window moldings, black front windshield molding, black rear window molding and body-colored door handles.

RX 300 AWD (4A) (in addition to or instead of RX 300 FWD (4A)): Full-time 4 wheel drive, 3.29 axle ratio.

CODE	DESCRIPTION	INVOICE	MSRP
	Base Prices		
9420	RX 300 FWD	27799	32005
9424	RX 300 AWD	29015	33405
Destination Charge:		795	795
	Accessories		
—	Limited Package *Includes leather trim, driver's seat memory, programmable garage door opener and air filtration system.*	1456	1820
9410	California Emissions	NC	NC
9414	New York Emissions	NC	NC
DC	Radio: 6-Disc CD Changer *Includes in-dash mounting.*	864	1080
HH	Heated Front Seats *REQUIRES Premium Package.*	352	440
LA	Leather Trim Package	1024	1280
LD	Torsen Rear Limited Slip Differential (4WD)	312	390
NK	Radio: Nakamichi Premium with 6-CD Changer	1277	1630
PM	Premium Package *Includes leather trim, driver's seat memory, electrochromic inside and outside heated mirrors, programmable garage door opener and air filtration system.*	1536	1920
SR	Power Tilt/Slide Moonroof	800	1000
TN	Traction Control System (FWD)	240	300

1999 NAVIGATOR

1999 Lincoln Navigator

What's New?

Into its second year, Lincoln's Navigator enters 1999 with more power, adjustable pedals, speed-sensitive stereo volume, and a hands-free cellular phone. Also, the optional third row seat is mounted on rollers this year for easy installation and removal.

Review

Based on Ford's hot-selling Expedition, the Navigator is the first truck ever sold by Lincoln. Second in size only to the Chevrolet/GMC Suburban, Lincoln differentiates the Navigator from its Ford-based brethren with a massive chrome grille, additional body cladding, and a host of luxury items. With a list of standard features like load leveling air suspension, power heated outside mirrors, and second row climate/audio controls, this is one SUV that won't let you forget it's a Lincoln.

Last year's 5.4-liter 16-valve V8 will be replaced mid-year by a more powerful In-Tech 5.4-liter engine. With DOHC 32-valve technology, horsepower jumps from 230 to 300 and maximum torque increases from 325 to 360 foot-pounds.

Four-wheel drive models come with Lincoln's adjustable Control Trac 4WD system that can be set in one of three positions by turning a dash-mounted knob. In A4WD mode, the system uses only the rear wheels unless slippage is detected; in which case it applies power to the front wheels until rear-wheel traction is regained. In 4H mode, power to the front wheels is constantly engaged which is ideal for snow, ice, and shallow mud or sand at normal speeds. Finally, in 4L mode, engine torque is multiplied by a factor of 2.64 for climbing up steep grades or out of deep snow.

Option changes for 1999 include an Alpine audio system, a hands-free cellular phone, and heated front seats. As an eight passenger SUV with limo-like luxury, it's hard to call the Navigator a truck, even with the Kenworth-like chrome grille. And with a base price approaching 40 grand (more if you want four-wheel drive), the Navigator is no bargain when compared to the Expedition. But with an advanced four-wheel drive system, optional skid plates, and 300 horses under the hood, it can certainly take you places no previous Lincoln ever could.

Safety Data

Side Airbag: *Not Available*
4-Wheel ABS: *Standard*
Driver Crash Test Grade: *Good*
Side Impact Crash Test Front: *Not Available*
Crash Offset: *Not Available*
Integrated Child Seat(s): *Not Available*
Traction Control: *Not Available*
Passenger Crash Test Grade: *Good*
Side Impact Crash Test Rear: *Not Available*

Standard Equipment

2WD (4A): 5.4L V8 SOHC SMPI 16-valve engine; 4-speed electronic overdrive automatic transmission with lock-up; 72-amp battery with run down protection; engine oil cooler; 130-amp alternator; transmission oil cooler; rear wheel drive, limited slip differential, 3.73 axle ratio; stainless steel exhaust; auto-leveling suspension, front independent suspension with anti-roll bar, front coil springs, rigid rear axle multi-link suspension with anti-roll bar, rear coil springs; power re-circulating ball steering with vehicle speed-sensing assist; 4 wheel disc brakes with 4 wheel antilock braking system; 30 gal capacity fuel tank; running boards; liftback rear cargo door; HD class III trailering, trailer harness, trailer hitch; roof rack; front and rear body-colored bumpers with front body-colored rub strip, rear step; body-colored bodyside cladding, body-colored wheel well molding, body-colored fender flares; monotone paint; aero-composite halogen fully automatic headlamps with delay-off feature; additional exterior lights include front fog/driving lights, center high mounted stop light, underhood light; heated driver's and passenger's power remote body-colored folding outside mirrors; front and rear 16" x 7" silver alloy wheels; P245/75SR16 BSW AS front and rear tires; underbody mounted full-size temporary steel spare wheel; air conditioning with climate control, rear air conditioning, rear heat ducts; premium AM/FM stereo with seek-scan, cassette, 4 speakers, and fixed antenna, radio steering wheel controls, rear audio controls; cruise control with steering wheel controls; power door locks, remote keyless entry, child safety rear door locks, power remote hatch/trunk release; 3 power accessory outlets, driver's foot rest, retained accessory power; instrumentation display includes tachometer, oil pressure gauge, water temp gauge, volt gauge, in-dash clock, compass, exterior temp, trip computer, trip odometer; warning indicators include oil pressure, water temp warning, battery, low oil level, lights on, key in ignition, low fuel, low washer fluid, door ajar, trunk ajar; dual airbags; ignition disable, panic alarm; deep tinted windows, power front windows with driver's 1-touch down, power rear windows, power 1/4 vent windows; variable intermittent front windshield wipers, flip-up rear window, fixed interval rear wiper, rear window defroster; seating capacity of 7, front bucket seats with adjustable headrests, center armrest with storage, driver's seat includes 4-way power seat with 8-way direction control and lumbar support, passenger's seat includes 4-way power seat with 8-way direction control and lumbar support; 2nd row reclining bucket seats with adjustable headrests, center armrest with storage; removable 3rd row full folding bench seat; front and rear height adjustable seatbelts; leather seats, leatherette door trim, full cloth headliner, full carpet floor covering with carpeted floor mats, wood trim; memory on driver's seat with 3 memory setting(s) includes settings for exterior mirrors; interior lights include dome light, front and rear reading lights, 2 door curb lights, illuminated entry; steering wheel with tilt adjustment; dual illuminated vanity mirrors, dual auxiliary visors; auto-dimming day-night rearview mirror; full floor console, full overhead console with storage, rear console with storage, glove box with light, front and rear cupholders, instrument panel covered bin, 2 seat back storage pockets, driver's and passenger's door bins, rear door bins; carpeted cargo floor, carpeted trunk lid, cargo net, cargo tie downs, cargo light; chrome grille, black side window moldings, black front windshield molding, black rear window molding and chrome door handles.

4WD (4A) (in addition to or instead of 2WD (4A) equipment): Part-time 4 wheel drive, auto locking hub control with electronic shift; front independent torsion suspension with anti-roll bar, front torsion springs, front torsion bar, and rear tow hooks.

CODE	DESCRIPTION	INVOICE	MSRP

Base Prices

CODE	DESCRIPTION	INVOICE	MSRP
U27	2WD (4A)	35476	40660
U28	4WD (4A)	38578	44310
Destination Charge:		640	640

Accessories

CODE	DESCRIPTION	INVOICE	MSRP
17P	Power Adjustable Pedals *Includes 3-setting memory function. Option is integrated with the seat and mirror memory function and allows movement of the brake and accelerator pedals allowing for custom pedal placement. NOTE: Standard equipment after 12/7/98 production.*	158	185
21S	2nd Row Leather 60/40 Bench Seat *Includes removable 3rd row bench seat with rollers and fold flat feature and rear console delete.*	NC	NC
413	Skid Plate Package (4WD) *Includes fuel tank, transfer case and front differential/suspension protection package.*	89	105
41H	Engine Block Heater	30	35
43M	Power Moonroof *Includes mini overhead console and universal garage door opener. NOT AVAILABLE with 575.*	1407	1655
516	Portable Cellular Telephone *Includes hands free function and is located in front floor console. REQUIRES 91P.*	553	650
575	Auxiliary Climate Control *Increases heater capacity. Recommended for cold climates. NOT AVAILABLE with 43M.*	599	705
64B	Wheels: 17" x 7.5" Styled Chrome Steel (4WD) *NOT AVAILABLE with T47.*	298	350
64H	Wheels: 17" x 7.5" Cast Aluminum (4WD) *NOT AVAILABLE with T47, 64B.*	298	350
90H	Heated Front Passenger Seats	247	290
916	Radio: Alpine Audio System *Includes cassette, 7 premium speakers, delayed accessory feature, subwoofer and speed compensated volume control.*	484	570
91P	6-Disc CD Changer *Located in front floor console.*	506	595
T47	Tires: P245/75R16 OWL All-Season	111	130
T5P	Tires: P255/75R17 OWL All-Terrain (4WD) *REQUIRES 64B. NOT AVAILABLE with T47.*	259	305
XH6	Limited Slip Differential (2WD) *NOTE: Standard equipment after 12/7/98 production.*	217	255

1999 B-SERIES PICKUP

1999 Mazda B-Series Pickup

What's New?

The B-Series now comes with a four-door option called the Cab Plus 4. Option packages have been consolidated and simplified this year to reduce buyer confusion. A class III frame-mounted hitch receiver is available with V6 applications.

Review

As a mechanical clone to the Ford Ranger, Mazda's compact B-Series comes in a wide range of configurations to suit the ever-expanding truck buyers' needs. Styling was updated in '98 and the B-Series is one of the best-looking trucks available today. We're particularly fond of the flareside bed design with Cab Plus 4 seating. The rear seats easily fold up and out of the way to allow for increased cargo carrying and the rear doors make entry/egress a breeze. In this world of do-all vehicles, why anyone would buy a truck with only two doors is beyond comprehension.

Besides offering convenience and style, the B-Series has great on-road characteristics, courtesy of its short-long arm independent front suspension and rack-and-pinion steering. The advanced shift-on-the-fly, four-wheel drive system features pulse vacuum hub-lock technology, allowing the driver to engage four-wheel drive at speeds up to 70 mph. No stopping or backing up is required when shifting into or out of 4-Lo. This less expensive and complex system improves fuel economy and reduces maintenance requirements.

Available in SX or SE trim, the B-Series can be equipped with engines ranging from a 2.5-liter inline four to a 4.0-liter V6. Either a five-speed automatic or five-speed manual transmission is available with the larger V6 engine. Select one of the option groups and goodies like 16-inch aluminum wheels, color-keyed bumpers and fog lamps will make your already attractive pickup a real boulevard cruiser.

With a rugged design, solid good looks and an excellent warranty, Mazda has done truck buyers right with its newest B-Series. If you're in the market for a fun and practical pickup, give these trucks a close look.

Safety Data

Side Airbag: *Not Available*
4-Wheel ABS: *Optional (B4000 4WD); N/A (B2500/B3000)*
Driver Crash Test Grade: *Good*
Side Impact Crash Test Front: *Excellent*
Crash Offset: *Acceptable*
Integrated Child Seat(s): *Not Available*
Traction Control: *Not Available*
Passenger Crash Test Grade: *Good*
Side Impact Crash Test Rear: *Not Available*

Standard Equipment

B2500 SX 2WD REGULAR CAB (5M): 2.5L I4 SOHC MPI 8-valve engine; 5-speed overdrive manual transmission; 58-amp battery; 95-amp alternator; rear wheel drive, 3.45 axle ratio; steel exhaust; front independent double wishbone suspension with anti-roll bar, front coil springs, rigid rear axle suspension with rear leaf springs; power rack-and-pinion steering; front disc/rear drum brakes with rear wheel antilock braking system; 17 gal capacity fuel tank; front and rear mud flaps; front and rear black bumpers with rear step; monotone paint; aero-composite halogen headlamps; additional exterior lights include center high mounted stop light; driver's and passenger's manual black folding outside mirrors; front and rear 14" x 6" silver styled steel wheels; P205/70SR14 BSW AS front and rear tires; underbody mounted full-size conventional steel spare wheel; AM/FM stereo with clock, seek-scan, 4 speakers, and fixed antenna; 2 power accessory outlets, driver's foot rest; instrumentation display includes oil pressure gauge, water temp gauge, volt gauge, trip odometer; warning indicators include oil pressure, battery, lights on, key in ignition, door ajar; driver's side airbag, passenger's side cancelable airbag; tinted windows; variable intermittent front windshield wipers; seating capacity of 3, bench front seat with fixed headrests, driver's seat includes 2-way direction control, passenger's seat includes 2-way direction control; front height adjustable seatbelts; vinyl seats, full cloth headliner, full vinyl floor covering; interior lights include dome light, illuminated entry; day-night rearview mirror; glove box with light, instrument panel bin; black grille, black side window moldings, black front windshield molding, black rear window molding and black door handles.

B2500 SE 2WD REGULAR CAB (5M) (in addition to or instead of B2500 SX 2WD REGULAR CAB (5M) equipment): 3.73 axle ratio; front and rear chrome bumpers with black rub strip; chrome bodyside molding; monotone paint with bodyside accent stripe; additional exterior lights include pickup cargo box light; front and rear 15" x 6" silver alloy wheels; AM/FM stereo with clock, seek-scan, single CD, 4 speakers, and fixed antenna; instrumentation display includes tachometer; seating capacity of 3, 60-40 split-bench front seat with fixed headrests, center armrest with storage, driver's seat includes 4-way direction control, passenger's seat includes 4-way direction control; cloth seats, vinyl door trim insert; interior lights include front reading lights; partial floor console and driver's and passenger's door bins.

B2500 SE 2WD CAB PLUS/CAB PLUS 4 (5M) (in addition to or instead of B2500 SE 2WD REGULAR CAB (5M) equipment): 20.5 gal capacity fuel tank; tinted windows, fixed rear windows; seating capacity of 5, 60-40 split-bench front seat with fixed headrests, center armrest with storage, driver's seat includes 4-way direction control with easy entry, passenger's seat includes 4-way direction control with easy entry; 50-50 folding side facing rear jump seats; rear access doors (Cab Plus 4); leather-wrapped gear shift knob; passenger side vanity mirror; carpeted cargo floor, cargo net; chrome grille and chrome side window moldings.

B3000 SE 2WD CAB PLUS/CAB PLUS 4 (5M) (in addition to or instead of B2500 SE 2WD CAB PLUS/CAB PLUS 4 (5M) equipment): 3.0L V6 OHV MPI 24-valve engine; 3.73 axle ratio; P225/70SR15 BSW AS front and rear tires, ignition disable and front height adjustable seatbelts.

CODE	DESCRIPTION	INVOICE	MSRP

B3000 SE 4WD REGULAR CAB (5M) (in addition to or instead of B2500 SE 2WD REGULAR CAB (5M) equipment): 3.0L V6 OHV MPI 24-valve engine; 72-amp battery; part-time 4 wheel drive, auto locking hub control with electronic shift, 3.27 axle ratio; front independent double wishbone suspension with anti-roll bar, front torsion springs, front torsion bar; 17 gal capacity fuel tank; skid plates; rear tow hooks; black fender flares; seating capacity of 3, bench front seat with fixed headrests, driver's seat includes 2-way direction control, passenger's seat includes 2-way direction control; full vinyl floor covering; vinyl cargo floor, cargo tie downs, chrome grille and black side window moldings.

B3000 SE 4WD CAB PLUS/CAB PLUS 4 (5M) (in addition to or instead of B3000 SE 4WD REGULAR CAB (5M) equipment): 72-amp battery with run down protection; 20.5 gal capacity fuel tank; fixed rear windows; seating capacity of 5, 60-40 split-bench front seat with fixed headrests, center armrest with storage, driver's seat includes 4-way direction control with easy entry, passenger's seat includes 4-way direction control with easy entry; 50-50 folding side facing rear jump seats; rear access doors (Cab Plus 4); full carpet floor covering, cabback insulator; passenger side vanity mirror; partial floor console; carpeted cargo floor, cargo net and chrome side window moldings.

B4000 SE 2WD REGULAR CAB (5M) (in addition to or instead of B3000 SE 4WD REGULAR CAB (5M) equipment): 4.0L V6 OHV MPI 24-valve engine; 58-amp battery; rear wheel drive; front independent double wishbone suspension with anti-roll bar, front coil springs; additional exterior lights include front fog/driving lights; premium AM/FM stereo with clock, seek-scan, cassette, single CD, 4 speakers, and fixed antenna; cruise control with steering wheel controls; sliding rear window; carpeted floor mats, leather-wrapped steering wheel with tilt adjustment and bedliner.

B4000 SE 2WD CAB PLUS/CAB PLUS 4 (4A) (in addition to or instead of B4000 SE 2WD REGULAR CAB (5M) equipment): Four-speed electronic overdrive automatic transmission with lock-up; 72-amp battery with run down protection; 3.08 axle ratio; 20.5 gal capacity fuel tank; vented rear windows; seating capacity of 5, 60-40 split-bench front seat with fixed headrests, center armrest with storage, driver's seat includes 4-way direction control with easy entry, passenger's seat includes 4-way direction control with easy entry; 50-50 folding side facing rear jump seats; rear access doors (Cab Plus 4), 2 seat back storage pockets and cargo net.

B4000 SE 2WD CAB PLUS/CAB PLUS 4 (5M) (in addition to or instead of B4000 SE 4WD CAB PLUS/CAB PLUS 4 (4A) equipment): 72-amp battery with run down protection; part-time 4 wheel drive, auto locking hub control with electronic shift, 3.27 axle ratio; front independent double wishbone suspension with anti-roll bar, front torsion springs, front torsion bar; skid plates; rear tow hooks; black fender flares; driver's and passenger's power remote black folding outside mirrors; power door locks, remote keyless entry; power front windows with driver's 1-touch down.

Base Prices

CODE	DESCRIPTION	INVOICE	MSRP
B25SSX2P	B2500 SX 2WD Regular Cab (5M)	10568	11285
B25SSE2P	B2500 SE 2WD Regular Cab (5M)	12359	13660
B25CSE2P	B2500 SE 2WD Cab Plus (5M)	14216	15715
B2500M5	B2500 SE 2WD Cab Plus 4 (5M)	14812	16375
B30CSE2P	B3000 SE 2WD Cab Plus (5M)	14735	16290
B30002SEM5	B3000 SE 2WD Cab Plus 4 (5M)	15331	16950
B3XSSEXP	B3000 SE 4WD Regular Cab (5M)	15868	17550
B3XCSEXP	B3000 SE 4WD Cab Plus (5M)	17363	19205
B30004SEM5	B3000 SE 4WD Cab Plus 4 (5M)	17958	19865
B4000SERCM5	B4000 SE 2WD Regular Cab (5M)	14876	16450

CODE	DESCRIPTION	INVOICE	MSRP
B40CSESA	B4000 SE 2WD Cab Plus (4A)	17751	19635
B40002SECA	B4000 SE 2WD Cab Plus 4 (4A)	18346	20295
B4XCSEXP	B4000 SE 4WD Cab Plus (5M)	19550	21630
B40004SECPM5	B4000 SE 4WD Cab Plus 4 (5M)	20146	22290
Destination Charge:		510	510

Accessories

CODE	DESCRIPTION	INVOICE	MSRP
1CP	Convenience Package (X-Cab Except Cab Plus 4 & B4000) *Includes tilt steering wheel, cruise control, sliding rear window, bedliner and floor mats.*	574	700
1PO	Power Package (SE Except B4000) *Includes power windows, power door locks, dual power mirrors and remote keyless entry.*	439	535
1TC	Traction Package (B4000 4WD) *Includes 4-wheel antilock brakes and limited slip differential.*	492	600
AC1	Air Conditioning (SE)	NC	NC
AC1	Air Conditioning (SX)	660	805
AT1	Transmission: 4-Speed Automatic (B2500/B3000)	898	1095
AT1	Transmission: 5-Speed Automatic (B4000)	927	1130

1999 M-CLASS

1999 Mercedes-Benz ML430

What's New?

Mercedes expands its M-Class with the addition of the more powerful and luxurious ML430 and gives the 320 more standard equipment.

Review

Despite increased sales during the last several years, the good people at Mercedes recognized a gaping hole that had existed in their lineup since 1993. That was the last year that Mercedes offered any sort of AWD vehicle, and, for the 1994 model year, the cancellation of their 4Matic sedans and wagons left them vulnerable to attacks from Audi, Subaru and Volvo. Recognizing this weakness, Mercedes introduced the ML320 sport-utility vehicle in 1997. This year, Mercedes adds a more powerful, all-new sport-ute, the ML430, to the lineup.

The ML320 was designed from the ground up as a unique Mercedes, capable of taking people off road or through poor weather without sacrificing the luxury, safety or performance that Mercedes' shoppers have come to expect. This year, the 320 gets Electronic Stability Program (ESP), Brake Assist, BabySmart and the Homelink programmable garage door opener as standard equipment, with the MSRP rising only $1,000.

For an extra $9,000, the ML430 continues in this tradition, but gives occupants a more stately, refined interior and V8 performance. In addition to the standard equipment offered on the 320, the 430 includes standard leather-trimmed seating, burled walnut interior trim, heated eight-way power seats, an automatic dimming rearview mirror, lockable safety box, trip computer and privacy glass. The exterior of the new vehicle is unique, with body-colored bumpers, rocker panels, rub strips, rearview mirror housings, and 275/55R17 tires mounted on seven-spoke, 17-inch alloy wheels.

These trucks combine many technologies that have heretofore been exclusively car or exclusively truck. Using a frame boxed at both ends, M-Class has the sort of torsional rigidity that is necessary for serious off-road maneuvers. To this truck-tough frame, Mercedes has attached a four-wheel independent double-wishbone suspension. The result is a fantastic on-road ride that enables the vehicles to hustle through the slalom at the same impressive speed as the E320 sedan. Off-road capability is certainly adequate, but putting these trucks up against something like a Land Rover Discovery will teach them a lesson in humility.

Mercedes SUVs have all of the touches we expect of vehicles carrying the three-pointed star on their hoods. Interior materials, except for the plastic on the dashboard, are first rate. The seats are comfortable for all-day driving, there are multiple cupholders for front and rear passengers, the stereo sounds great, and the secondary controls are devoid of the confusing pictographs that have adorned many of M-B's previous efforts.

Compared to trucks like the GMC Yukon Denali and Jeep Grand Cherokee Limited, the M-Class is easily the superior choice for all but the most demanding of off-road challenges. On-road, these American contenders can't touch Mercedes' Teutonic trailblazers. If your vehicle purchase is leading you to the four-wheel drive neck of the woods, ignoring the Mercedes-Benz M-Class is the biggest mistake you could make.

Safety Data

Side Airbag: *Standard*
4-Wheel ABS: *Standard*
Driver Crash Test Grade: *Not Available*
Side Impact Crash Test Front: *Not Available*
Crash Offset: *Not Available*
Integrated Child Seat(s): *Not Available*
Traction Control: *Standard*
Passenger Crash Test Grade: *Not Available*
Side Impact Crash Test Rear: *Not Available*

Standard Equipment

ML320 (5A): 3.2L V6 SOHC SMPI 18-valve engine, requires premium unleaded fuel; 5-speed electronic overdrive automatic transmission with lock-up; engine oil cooler; full-time 4 wheel drive, traction control, 3.69 axle ratio; front independent double wishbone suspension with anti-roll bar, front torsion springs, front torsion bar, rear independent double wishbone suspension with anti-roll bar, rear coil springs; power rack-and-pinion steering; 4 wheel disc brakes with 4 wheel antilock braking system; 19 gal capacity fuel tank; liftback rear cargo door; roof rack; front and rear black bumpers; black bodyside molding, rocker panel extensions; monotone paint; aero-composite halogen headlamps with delay-off feature; additional exterior lights include center high mounted stop light; driver and passenger power remote black heated folding outside mirrors; front and rear 16" x 8" silver alloy wheels; P255/65TR16 BSW M&S front and rear tires; inside under cargo mounted compact steel spare wheel; air conditioning, air filter, rear heat ducts; AM/FM stereo with seek-scan, cassette, CD changer pre-wiring, in-dash CD pre-wiring, 4 speakers, amplifier, theft deterrent, and window grid diversity antenna; cruise control; power door locks with 2 stage unlock, remote keyless entry, child safety rear door locks, fuel filler door included with power doors, power remote hatch/trunk release, power remote fuel release; cell phone pre-wiring, 3 power accessory outlets, driver foot rest, retained accessory power, garage door opener; instrumentation display includes tachometer, water temp gauge, in-dash clock, systems monitor, trip odometer; warning indicators include water temp warning, battery, low oil level, low coolant, lights on, key in ignition, low fuel, low washer fluid, bulb failure, brake fluid; dual airbags, door mounted side airbags; ignition disable, panic alarm, security system; tinted windows, power front windows with driver and passenger 1-touch down, power rear windows, fixed 1/4 vent windows; variable intermittent front windshield wipers, fixed interval rear wiper, rear window defroster; seating capacity of 5, front bucket seats with adjustable tilt headrests, center armrest with storage, driver's seat includes 6-way direction control, passenger's seat includes 6-way direction control; folding rear split-bench seat with tilting rear headrest; front and rear height adjustable seatbelts; cloth seats, leatherette door trim insert, full cloth headliner, full carpet floor covering with carpeted floor mats; interior lights include dome light with fade, front and rear reading lights, illuminated entry; steering wheel with tilt adjustment; dual illuminated vanity mirrors; day-night rearview mirror; full floor console, glove box, front and rear cupholders, instrument panel bin, driver and passenger door bins, rear door bins; carpeted cargo floor, plastic trunk lid, cargo cover, cargo tie downs, cargo light; black grille, black side window moldings, black front windshield molding, black rear window molding and black door handles.

CODE	DESCRIPTION	INVOICE	MSRP

ML430 (5A) (in addition to or instead of ML320 (5A) equipment): 4.3L V8 SOHC SMPI 24-valve engine, requires premium unleaded fuel; automatic ride control; front body-colored bumper with body-colored rub strip, rear body-colored bumper; body-colored bodyside molding, rocker panel extensions; driver and passenger power remote body-colored heated folding outside mirrors; front and rear 17" x 8.5" silver alloy wheels; instrumentation display includes exterior temp, trip computer; deep tinted windows; heated leather driver and front passenger seats , center armrest with storage, driver's seat includes 6-way power seat, passenger's seat includes 6-way power seat; wood trim, leather-wrapped gear shift knob; leather-wrapped steering wheel with tilt adjustment and auto-dimming day-night rearview mirror.

Base Prices

CODE	DESCRIPTION	INVOICE	MSRP
ML320	ML320 (5A)	30410	34950
ML430	ML430 (5A)	38060	43750
Destination Charge:		595	595

Accessories

CODE	DESCRIPTION	INVOICE	MSRP
—	Metallic Paint	413	475
136	Option Package M1 (ML320) *Includes leather trim on seats, leather-wrapped shift knob, leather-wrapped steering wheel, rear privacy glass on rear doors, auto dimming rearview mirror, lockable safe box, 8-way power heated front seats, digital trip computer and burled walnut wood trim. REQUIRES 414 or 417.*	2566	2950
137	Option Package M4 *Includes front brush guard, dual stainless steel side runners, molded front and rear mud flaps. REQUIRES 414 or 417.*	1388	1595
258	Bose Premium Sound System *Includes integrated 6-disc CD changer. REQUIRES 136 on ML320.*	913	1050
414	Power Tilt/Sliding Sunroof with Tinted Glass *NOT AVAILABLE with 417.*	953	1095
417	Power Skyview Top *NOT AVAILABLE with 414.*	2084	2395

1999 MOUNTAINEER

1999 Mercury Mountaineer

What's New?

For '99 the Mountaineer gets optional rear load leveling and a reverse parking aid. It also receives a new seat design.

Review

The Explorer-based Mountaineer changes little for '99. Marketed as an upscale SUV for women and families, the Mountaineer receives new safety features in the form of optional side airbags and an optional reverse parking aid that warns of impending collision with an audible beep. Braking has also improved this year with a larger brake booster and upgraded rear-brake calipers. The rear load leveling option will ensure that your Mountaineer doesn't sag even when pulling a heavy load.

The engine lineup remains the same in '99 with the 4.0-liter SOHC V6 making five more horsepower than in '98 (for a total of 210) and the 5.0-liter V8 maintaining its 215 peak horsepower. Transmission choices still include a five-speed automatic for the V6 and a four-speed automatic with the V8. For those living in cold-weather climates, or for those who actually intend to make use of the vehicle's off-road capabilities, there is a full-time all-wheel drive model available and a four-wheel drive model that features an SOHC V6 and Control Trac four-wheel drive.

The Mountaineer has been a hit at Lincoln-Mercury dealers. Like the Explorer it is based on, the Mountaineer has plenty of space for hauling people and their stuff through the suburban jungle. The Mercury SUV's abundant standard features list provides a great deal of comfort, and the strong engine choices are a bonus when passing at freeway speeds.

If you like the Explorer but don't want to see your own vehicle every 10 minutes while driving, the Mountaineer offers a unique alternative.

Safety Data

Side Airbag: *Optional*
4-Wheel ABS: *Standard*
Driver Crash Test Grade: *Good*
Side Impact Crash Test Front: *Excellent*
Crash Offset: *Acceptable*
Integrated Child Seat(s): *Not Available*
Traction Control: *Not Available*
Passenger Crash Test Grade: *Good*
Side Impact Crash Test Rear: *Excellent*

CODE	DESCRIPTION	INVOICE	MSRP

Standard Equipment

2WD (5A): 4.0L V6 SOHC SMPI 12-valve engine; 5-speed electronic overdrive automatic transmission; 72-amp battery with run down protection; engine oil cooler, HD radiator; 95-amp alternator; rear wheel drive, 3.55 axle ratio; front independent suspension with anti-roll bar, front coil springs, front torsion bar, HD front shocks, rigid rear axle suspension with anti-roll bar, rear leaf springs, HD rear shocks; power rack-and-pinion steering; 4 wheel disc brakes with 4 wheel antilock braking system; 21 gal capacity fuel tank; running boards; liftback rear cargo door; roof rack; front and rear body-colored bumpers with body-colored rub strip, rear step bumper; body-colored bodyside molding; two-tone paint; aero-composite halogen headlamps; additional exterior lights include front fog/driving lights, center high mounted stop light; driver's and passenger's power remote black folding outside mirrors; front and rear 15" x 7" silver alloy wheels; P225/70SR15 BSW AS front and rear tires; underbody mounted full-size temporary steel spare wheel; air conditioning, rear heat ducts; AM/FM stereo with clock, seek-scan, cassette, 4 speakers, and fixed antenna; cruise control with steering wheel controls; power door locks, child safety rear door locks; 2 power accessory outlets, retained accessory power; instrumentation display includes tachometer, oil pressure gauge, water temp gauge, volt gauge, trip odometer; warning indicators include oil pressure, battery, lights on, key in ignition; dual airbags; ignition disable; deep tinted windows, power front windows with driver's 1-touch down, power rear windows; variable intermittent front windshield wipers, flip-up rear window, fixed interval rear wiper, rear window defroster; seating capacity of 5, front bucket seats with fixed headrests, center armrest with storage, driver's seat includes 4-way direction control, passenger's seat includes 4-way direction control; 60-40 folding rear bench seat with adjustable rear headrest; front height adjustable seatbelts; premium cloth seats, vinyl door trim insert, full cloth headliner, full carpet floor covering with carpeted floor mats, deluxe sound insulation; interior lights include dome light with fade, front reading lights, 2 door curb lights, illuminated entry; leather-wrapped steering wheel with tilt adjustment; dual illuminated vanity mirrors; day-night rearview mirror; full floor console, glove box with light, front and rear cupholders, driver's and passenger's door bins; carpeted cargo floor, plastic trunk lid, cargo cover, cargo tie downs, cargo light; chrome grille, black side window moldings, black front windshield molding, black rear window molding and body-colored door handles.

4WD (5A) (in addition to or instead of 2WD (5A) equipment): Part-time 4 wheel drive, auto locking hub control and electronic shift and 3.55 axle ratio.

AWD (4A) (in addition to or instead of 4WD (5A) equipment): 5.0L V8 OHV SMPI 16-valve engine; 4-speed electronic overdrive automatic transmission with lock-up; full-time 4 wheel drive and 3.73 axle ratio.

Base Prices

CODE	DESCRIPTION	INVOICE	MSRP
U52	2WD (5A)	24536	27160
U54	4WD (5A)	26296	29160
U55	AWD (4A)	26706	29625
Destination Charge:		525	525

Accessories

CODE	DESCRIPTION	INVOICE	MSRP
21A	Side Air Bags *REQUIRES 66A.*	332	390
41H	Engine Block Heater	30	35
439	Power Moonroof *Includes sunshade, one touch open. Deletes overhead storage and 2nd row map/ dome light. REQUIRES 66A.*	680	800

CODE	DESCRIPTION	INVOICE	MSRP
44U	**Transmission: 4-Speed Automatic with Overdrive** *REQUIRES 99P.*	NC	NC
558	**Appearance Package** *Includes 15" bright chrome wheels and tone-on tone paint or two-tone paint. REQUIRES 66A.*	421	495
573	**Air Conditioning with Automatic Temp Control** *Includes steering wheel audio controls and message center. REQUIRES 916 and 66A.*	502	590
66A	**Convenience Group** *Includes cloth sport bucket seats, remote keyless entry with panic button, electronics package: driver's door keypad, puddle lamps on outside mirrors and auto-lock and re-lock system; premium AM/FM stereo with CD and cassette, electrochromic rear view mirror, automatic on/off headlamps, overhead console: outside temperature and compass display; 2nd row map/dome light, high series floor console: rear heater/air conditioning with controls and rear audio controls.*	1016	1195
66B	**Luxury Group** *Includes leather sport bucket seats with 6-way power driver's seat and dual manual lumbar supports, remote keyless entry, appearance package: tone-on tone paint or two-tone paint and 15" bright chrome wheels; Ford Mach audio system: AM/FM stereo with cassette, single CD, 7 premium speakers with 8" subwoofer, 290-watts peak power, and personal audio system. REQUIRES 66A.*	1186	1395
67H	**Home Link System** *With Travel Note digital memo recorder.*	182	215
68L	**Rear Load Leveling (All Except 2WD)** *REQUIRES 66A and F.*	277	325
76R	**Reverse Sensing System** *REQUIRES 66A.*	208	245
87K	**Skid Plates (All Except 2WD)** *Includes transfer case and fuel tank plates.*	89	105
916	**Radio: Ford MACH Audio System** *Includes AM/FM stereo, cassette, single CD player, 7 premium speakers with 8" subwoofer, 290 watts peak power and personal audio system. REQUIRES 66A.*	374	440
91P	**6-Disc CD Changer** *REQUIRES 66A.*	314	370
99P	**Engine: 5.0L OHV (2WD)** *Includes V8 fender badges, 3.73 limited slip axle and trailer tow group. REQUIRES 44U.*	395	465
F	**Leather Sport Bucket Seats** *Includes 6-way power driver and passenger seats and dual manual lumbar supports. REQUIRES 66A.*	808	950
T7R	**Tires: P235/75R15 AT OWL (All Except AWD)**	196	230
XD4	**3.73 Limited Slip Axle (All Except AWD)** *Includes trailer tow group.*	302	355
Z	**Cloth Sport Bucket Seats** *Includes 6-way power driver seat and dual manual lumbar supports.*	511	600

1999 VILLAGER

1999 Mercury Villager

What's New?

The Mercury Villager is completely redesigned for '99. Improvements range from a more powerful engine to a larger interior to a second sliding door on the driver's side. New styling features include larger headlights and a distinctive front grille. Inside, ergonomic glitches have been addressed with easier to reach controls and an innovative storage shelf located behind the third seat.

Review

Mercury has answered the ever-increasing demands of the modern minivan buyer with an all-new Villager for 1999. Improvements start under the hood with a new V6 that has increased in size from 3.0 to 3.3 liters. Horsepower is a robust 170 (up 16 from last year) with torque topping out at 200 foot-pounds (49 foot-pounds higher than last year's model). Lightweight pistons, a newly tuned upper air intake, and a more advanced ignition system combine to make this engine quieter and more reliable than in previous models.

Suspension components have also been tweaked with a revised front strut design and a new single-leaf rear spring system for a smoother, more controlled ride. Combined with a new antilock brake system and second-generation air bags for driver and front passenger, the Villager is prepared to duke it out on the mean streets of America.

Inside, Mercury has performed a complete makeover with new radio and climate controls, an easier to read instrument panel, and even better cupholders. The rear cargo area now features a storage shelf that can be repositioned for stacking soft and hard items. Seating is also improved, with more legroom for second and third row passengers and a versatile in-track system for easy adjustment or removal of the third row seat. A new climate control system uses under seat ducting to keep rear passengers warm or cool and an optional audio system can be ordered to let front and rear passengers enjoy separate music selections.

With more power, a driver's side sliding door, and improved creature comforts, the all-new Villager enters '99 ready for battle in the minivan arena.

Safety Data

Side Airbag: *Not Available*
4-Wheel ABS: *Optional*
Driver Crash Test Grade: *Not Available*
Side Impact Crash Test Front: *Not Available*
Crash Offset: *Poor*
Integrated Child Seat(s): *Optional*
Traction Control: *Not Available*
Passenger Crash Test Grade: *Not Available*
Side Impact Crash Test Rear: *Not Available*

Standard Equipment

BASE (4A): 3.3L V6 SOHC SMPI 24-valve engine; 4-speed electronic overdrive automatic transmission with lock-up; 60-amp battery with run down protection; HD radiator; 125-amp alternator; front wheel drive, 3.86 axle ratio; partial stainless steel exhaust; front independent strut suspension with anti-roll bar, front coil springs, rear non-independent suspension with rear leaf springs; power rack-and-pinion steering; front disc/rear drum brakes; 20 gal capacity fuel tank; sliding left rear passenger door, sliding right rear passenger door, liftback rear cargo door; roof rack; front and rear body-colored bumpers; body-colored bodyside molding; monotone paint; aero-composite halogen headlamps; additional exterior lights include cornering lights, center high mounted stop light; driver's and passenger's power remote black folding outside mirrors; front and rear 15" x 5.5" steel wheels; P215/70SR15 BSW AS front and rear tires; underbody mounted compact steel spare wheel; air conditioning, rear heat ducts; AM/FM stereo with clock, seek-scan, cassette, 4 speakers, and fixed antenna; cruise control with steering wheel controls; power door locks, child safety rear door locks, remote fuel release; 3 power accessory outlets, retained accessory power; instrumentation display includes tachometer, water temp gauge, trip odometer; warning indicators include water temp warning, battery, lights on, key in ignition, low fuel, low washer fluid, door ajar; dual airbags; tinted windows, power front windows with driver's 1-touch down, vented rear windows, manual 1/4 vent windows; variable intermittent front windshield wipers, fixed interval rear wiper, rear window defroster; seating capacity of 7, front captain seats with adjustable headrests, driver's and passenger's armrests, driver's seat includes 4-way direction control, passenger's seat includes 4-way direction control; removable full folding 2nd row bench seat with adjustable rear headrest; 3rd row removable full folding bench seat with adjustable 3rd row headrest; front height adjustable seatbelts; cloth seats, cloth door trim insert, full cloth headliner, full carpet floor covering with carpeted floor mats; interior lights include dome light; steering wheel with tilt adjustment; vanity mirrors; day-night rearview mirror; glove box with light, front and rear cupholders, instrument panel covered bin, dashboard storage, interior concealed storage, driver's and passenger's door bins, front underseat tray; carpeted cargo floor, cargo net, cargo light; chrome grille, black side window moldings, black front windshield molding, black rear window molding and body-colored door handles.

ESTATE (4A) (in addition to or instead of BASE (4A) equipment): Touring ride suspension; body-colored bodyside molding with colored bodyside insert; two-tone paint; aero-composite halogen fully automatic headlamps with delay-off feature; driver's and passenger's power remote black heated folding outside mirrors; front and rear 16" x 6" painted alloy wheels; premium AM/FM stereo with clock, seek-scan, cassette, 4 speakers, and fixed antenna, radio steering wheel controls; removable full folding captain 2nd row seat with reclining adjustable rear headrest; leather-wrapped steering wheel with tilt adjustment; dual illuminated vanity mirrors and 2 seat back storage pockets.

SPORT (4A) (in addition to or instead of ESTATE (4A) equipment): Two-tone paint with badging.

CODE	DESCRIPTION	INVOICE	MSRP

Base Prices

CODE	DESCRIPTION	INVOICE	MSRP
V11	Base (4A)	20250	22415
V11	Estate (4A)	22538	25015
V11	Sport (4A)	22538	25015
Destination Charge:		580	580

Accessories

CODE	DESCRIPTION	INVOICE	MSRP
15A	Electronic Instrument Cluster (All Except Base) *Includes outside temperature reading, digital speedometer, odometer, dual trip odometers, analog tachometer, trip computer with instantaneous fuel economy, average fuel economy and distance-to-empty. REQUIRES 573 and 58K.*	208	245
21A	7-Passenger Seating with 2nd Row Bench (All Except Base)	NC	NC
41H	Engine Block Heater	30	35
439	Power Moonroof (All Except Base) *Includes sliding sunshade and fixed air deflector. REQUIRES 76B and 66A. NOT AVAILABLE with 21A.*	659	775
534	Trailer Tow Prep Package *Includes trailering weight (3500 lb), trailer tow module and jumper harness and full size spare tire.*	213	250
573	Electronic Automatic Temperature Control (All Except Base) *Controls cabin temperature at desired preset temperature. REQUIRES 76B.*	153	180
586	Radio: Premium AM/FM Stereo with Cassette (Base)	263	310
58K	Radio: Supersound AM/FM with Cassette and CD (All Except Base) *Includes 7 speakers, partitioned audio and 6 disc CD changer.*	735	865
60L	Luxury Group (All Except Base) *Includes garage opener/electronic voice note recorder, leather seating surfaces, memory seats, memory mirrors and 4-way power passenger's seat. REQUIRES 76B and 66A.*	846	995
63B	Smoker's Package *Includes front and 2nd row right hand ashtray and cigar lighter.*	13	15
64A	Wheels: 15" 5-Spoke Aluminum (Base) *NOT AVAILABLE with 64J.*	336	395
64J	Wheels: 15" Deluxe Aluminum (Base) *NOT AVAILABLE with 64A.*	336	395
66A	Convenience Group *Includes light group: overhead map lights, overhead console; power vent windows, remote keyless entry system: panic alarm and illuminated entry. One compartment in overhead console is deleted when (439) power moonroof is ordered. REQUIRES 76B.*	421	495
67B	Antilock Braking System	502	590
76B	Comfort Group *Includes auxiliary A/C with rear audio controls, 72-amp battery, particulate air filter, privacy glass and 6-way power driver's seat.*	846	995
87C	Two Integrated Child Seats *REQUIRES 21A.*	204	240

CODE	DESCRIPTION	INVOICE	MSRP
904	Anti-Theft Security System *Includes blinking security light. Detects forced entry. REQUIRES 66A.*	85	100
91P	6-Disc CD Changer	314	370
952	Two-Tone Paint (Base)	251	295

1999 MONTERO

1999 Mitsubishi Montero

What's New?

Following substantial updates for 1998, Mitsubishi leaves well enough alone for 1999 and drops the price more than $2,000 in an effort to increase sales.

Review

Marketed since 1983, Mitsubishi's Montero sport-utility ranks as an old-timer in its field, though the current four-door version has only been around since '92. Once a quirky and low-priced alternative to domestic SUVs, the Montero has moved steadily upscale over the years. Today, this monster is tall, narrow, and space inefficient, though seven passengers can be accommodated in a pinch.

Active Trac four-wheel-drive can be shifted "on the fly," or set up to operate all the time. A power sunroof is available with the Luxury Package, but it opens over the rear seat leaving front passengers stuck in the shade. Monteros can tow as much as 5,000 pounds. A variable shock-absorber system has three settings: hard, medium, and soft.

Despite the fact that the Montero is powered by a 3.5-liter V6 making 200 horsepower, this beast is slow off the line, provides little steering feel, and rolls significantly in turns. All this adds up to a mediocre urban driving experience. However, visibility is fantastic, the driver's seat is quite comfortable, and there's a rugged weekend-warrior interior atmosphere complete with haphazardly placed controls. Makes sense, since this vehicle serves duty as military transport in other regions of the world.

Basically, the Montero is an interesting blend of gee-whiz gadgetry, luxurious conveniences, go-anywhere capability, and unique styling. Buyers considering other sport utility vehicles will want to drop by the Mitsubishi dealer and consider this one as well — particularly if they're interested in standing apart from the crowd.

Safety Data

Side Airbag: *Not Available*
4-Wheel ABS: *Standard*
Integrated Child Seat(s): *Not Available*
Traction Control: *Not Available*

CODE	DESCRIPTION	INVOICE	MSRP

Driver Crash Test Grade: *Not Available*
Passenger Crash Test Grade: *Not Available*
Side Impact Crash Test Front: *Not Available*
Side Impact Crash Test Rear: *Not Available*
Crash Offset: *Acceptable*

Standard Equipment

MONTERO: 3.5L V-6 SOHC MPI 24-valve engine; 4-speed electronic overdrive automatic transmission with lock-up; engine oil cooler; 75-amp alternator; driver selectable program transmission; transmission oil cooler; part-time 4 wheel drive, auto locking hub control and manual shift, 4.27 axle ratio; stainless steel exhaust; front independent double wishbone suspension with anti-roll bar, front torsion springs, front torsion bar, front shocks, rear multi-link suspension with anti-roll bar, rear coil springs, rear shocks; power re-circulating ball steering; 4 wheel disc brakes with 4 wheel anti-lock braking system; 24.3 gal capacity fuel tank; body-colored front and rear mud flaps, running boards, skid plates; conventional rear cargo door; front and rear chrome bumpers with body-colored rub strip, front and rear tow hooks; rear step; two-tone paint; aero-composite halogen headlamps; additional exterior lights include front fog/driving lights, center high mounted stop light; driver and passenger power remote black folding outside mirrors; front and rear 15" x 7" silver alloy wheels; P265/70SR15 BSW M&S front and rear tires; outside rear mounted full-size conventional steel spare wheel; air conditioning, rear heat ducts; AM/FM stereo with cassette, seek-scan, 6 speakers, theft deterrent, and power retractable diversity antenna; cruise control; power door locks, child safety rear door locks, remote fuel release; 3 power accessory outlets; analog instrumentation display includes tachometer, oil pressure gauge, water temp gauge, volt gauge, in-dash clock, compass, exterior temp, trip odometer; warning indicators include oil pressure, battery, low fuel, low washer fluid, door ajar, service interval; dual airbags; deep tinted windows, power front windows with driver 1-touch down, power rear windows, fixed 1/4 vent windows; variable intermittent front windshield wipers, fixed interval rear wiper; rear window defroster; seating capacity of 7, front bucket seats with adjustable headrests, center armrest with storage, driver's seat includes 4-way direction control; passenger's seat includes 4-way direction control; 2nd row seat with reclining adjustable rear headrest; 3rd row seat 50-50 folding split-bench with adjustable 3rd row headrest; front height adjustable seatbelts; cloth seats, cloth door trim insert, full cloth headliner, full carpet floor covering; interior lights include dome light, front and rear reading lights, 2 door curb lights; leather-wrapped sport steering wheel with tilt adjustment; vanity mirrors; day-night rearview mirror; full floor console, locking glove box, front and rear cupholders, 2 seat back storage pockets, driver and passenger door bins, front underseat tray; carpeted cargo floor, plastic trunk lid, cargo tie downs, cargo light; black grille, black side window moldings, black front windshield molding, black rear window molding, black door handles.

Base Prices

MP45B	Montero (4A)	27916	31370
Destination Charge:		445	445

Accessories

—	Destination Surcharge: Alaska	120	120
C3	Single-Disc CD Player	299	399
HI	Trailer Hitch with Harness	164	252
P2	Luxury Package *Includes Infinity premium AM/FM cassette stereo with 8 speakers and amplifier, leather seat trim, power sunroof, power driver's seat.*	2285	2826
P3	Cold Weather Package *Includes heated front seats, heated mirrors, locking rear differential, headlamp washers.*	635	774

CODE	DESCRIPTION	INVOICE	MSRP
P4	Premium Package	910	1110
	Includes adjustable shocks, sport suspension, chrome-plated alloy wheels.		
P5	Value Package	1467	2320
	Manufacturer Discount	(500)	(1200)
	Net Price	967	1120
	Includes floor mats, Cargo Storage Kit: cargo net, cargo cover, cargo mat; roof rack, 10-disc CD changer, wood interior trim, security system with keyless entry and alarm, wheel locks.		

1999 MONTERO SPORT

1999 Mitsubishi Montero Sport

What's New?

A new Limited model joins the Montero Sport lineup and with it comes a powerful new V6 engine.

Review

Mitsubishi was in the vanguard at the beginning of the sport-utility boom. Way back in 1989, when the Explorer was yet to be introduced and the Grand Cherokee was little more than scribbles in a designer's notebook, the Montero had already evolved into a wonderfully practical four-door design that offered excellent utility and go-anywhere capability. As the years passed, however, the Montero moved further and further up-market as Mitsubishi lavished additional equipment and expensive gee-whiz components on its only sport-ute. Today, the Montero's price starts above $31,000.

Realizing that they were losing sales because of this high price, Mitsubishi penned a newly-shaped truck, placed it on a proven platform and came up with a not-very-original name for a smaller, less-expensive SUV in 1997 – the Montero Sport. The Sport shares a frame with the larger Montero, which is good news for those seeking off-road capability, but it is shorter overall due to decreased front and rear overhangs. The Montero Sport's cabin holds five passengers instead of seven but the Sport's cargo space actually surpasses that of the full-size Montero.

This year, the Montero Sport is available in four trim levels: ES, LS, XLS and the all-new Limited. Each trim level comes with two- or four-wheel drive except the ES, which is only available as a 2WD model. The ES is powered by a four-cylinder 134-horsepower engine, but not many people opt for this value leader due to its weak engine and sparse equipment. Recently, the most popular model has been the LS 4WD automatic. This year, the LS also gets alloy wheels, black fender flares, side steps, cruise control, AM/FM/CD audio system, and power windows, door locks and mirrors as standard equipment. This truck, as well as the XLS model, includes a 3.0-liter SOHC V6 engine. Be sure to check out the acceleration, though; we were disappointed by this V6's lack of oomph.

The new Limited trim level promises to please many and includes the 3.5-liter SOHC 24-valve V6 engine that also powers the larger Montero. Other standard features on the Limited include a unique chrome grille and front bumper with integrated fog lamps, integrated side steps, leather seat trim, antilock brakes, power windows/door locks/sunroof, Infinity premium sound system and a security system with remote keyless entry. The Limited 4WD version adds a locking rear differential, rear heaters, heated outside mirrors and multimeter with compass, exterior thermometer and an oil pressure gauge/voltmeter.

Available in 1999 on all Montero Sports is a new automatic transmission, new rear bumper design, new roof rack design, and three new colors: Cambridge Red Pearl (replaces Phoenix Red), New Zealand Green Pearl (replaces Belgium Green Pearl and Ozark Green Metallic), and Royal Blue Pearl.

Safety Data

Side Airbag: *Not Available*
4-Wheel ABS: *Std. (LS 4WD/XLS 4WD/LTD); N/A (ES/LS 2WD/XLS 2WD)*
Driver Crash Test Grade: *Average*
Side Impact Crash Test Front: *Not Available*
Crash Offset: *Not Available*
Integrated Child Seat(s): *Not Available*
Traction Control: *Not Available*
Passenger Crash Test Grade: *Average*
Side Impact Crash Test Rear: *Not Available*

Standard Equipment

ES 2WD (5M): 2.4L I4 SOHC MPI 16-valve engine; 5-speed overdrive manual transmission; 60-amp alternator; rear wheel drive, 4.22 axle ratio; stainless steel exhaust; front independent suspension with anti-roll bar, front torsion springs, front torsion bar, rigid rear axle suspension with anti-roll bar, rear leaf springs; power re-circulating ball steering; front disc/rear drum brakes; 19.5 gal capacity fuel tank; front and rear mud flaps, skid plates; tailgate rear cargo door; front and rear body-colored bumpers with front and rear tow hooks, rear step; monotone paint; aero-composite halogen headlamps; additional exterior lights include center high mounted stop light; driver's and passenger's manual black folding outside mirrors; front and rear 15" x 6" silver styled steel wheels; P235/75SR15 BSW M&S front and rear tires; underbody mounted full-size conventional steel spare wheel; AM/FM stereo with clock, seek-scan, single CD, 4 speakers, and fixed antenna; remote fuel release; 2 power accessory outlets, driver's foot rest; instrumentation display includes tachometer, water temp gauge, trip odometer; warning indicators include oil pressure, battery, lights on, key in ignition, door ajar, brake fluid; dual airbags; tinted windows, manual rear windows, fixed 1/4 vent windows; fixed interval front windshield wipers, flip-up rear window, rear window wiper, rear window defroster; seating capacity of 5, front bucket seats with adjustable headrests, center armrest with storage, driver's seat includes 6-way direction control, passenger's seat includes 4-way direction control; full folding rear bench seat with reclining adjustable rear headrest, center armrest with storage; front height adjustable seatbelts; cloth seats, cloth door trim insert, full cloth headliner, full carpet floor covering; interior lights include dome light, front reading lights, 2 door curb lights; steering wheel with tilt adjustment; vanity mirrors; day-night rearview mirror; full floor console, full overhead console with storage, locking glove box, front cupholder, 2 seat back storage pockets, driver's and passenger's door bins; carpeted cargo floor, plastic trunk lid, cargo tie downs, cargo light, cargo concealed storage; black grille, black side window moldings, black front windshield molding, black rear window molding and black door handles.

LS 2WD (4A) (in addition to or instead of ES 2WD (5M) equipment): 3.0L V6 SOHC MPI 24-valve engine; 4-speed electronic overdrive automatic transmission with lock-up; 85-amp alternator; transmission oil cooler; running boards; body-colored fender flares; driver's and passenger's power remote black folding outside mirrors; air conditioning; AM/FM stereo with clock, seek-scan, cassette, single CD, 6 speakers, and fixed antenna; deep tinted windows, power front windows with driver 1-touch down, power rear windows; variable intermittent front windshield wipers; 60-40 reclining and folding rear bench seat with adjustable rear headrest; front and rear cupholders, interior concealed storage and cargo net.

LS 4WD (5M) (in addition to or instead of LS 2WD (4A) equipment): 5-speed overdrive manual transmission; part-time 4 wheel drive, auto locking hub control with manual shift, 4.27 axle ratio and 4 wheel disc brakes with 4 wheel antilock braking system.

XLS 2WD (4A) (in addition to or instead of LS 2WD (4A) equipment): 4.64 axle ratio; front power sliding and tilting glass sunroof with sunshade; two-tone paint; front and rear 15" x 7" silver alloy wheels; AM/FM stereo with clock, seek-scan, cassette, CD changer pre-wiring, in-dash CD pre-wiring, 6 speakers, theft deterrent, and power retractable antenna; cruise control; power door locks, remote keyless entry; security system; leather-wrapped steering wheel with tilt adjustment; dual illuminated vanity mirrors; mini overhead console and chrome grille.

XLS 4WD (4A) (in addition to or instead of XLS 2WD (4A) equipment): Part-time 4 wheel drive, auto locking hub control with manual shift; 4 wheel disc brakes with 4 wheel antilock braking system; underbody mounted full-size conventional alloy spare wheel.

LTD 2WD (4A) (in addition to or instead of XLS 2WD (4A) equipment): 3.5L V6 SOHC MPI 24-valve engine; front disc/rear drum brakes with 4 wheel antilock braking system; additional exterior lights include front fog/driving lights, front power sliding and tilting glass sunroof with sunshade; Infinity AM/FM stereo with clock, seek-scan, cassette, CD changer pre-wiring, in-dash CD pre-wiring, 8 premium speakers, amplifier, theft deterrent, and power retractable antenna; leather seats and leatherette door trim insert.

LTD 4WD (4A) (in addition to or instead of LTD 2WD (4A) equipment): Part-time 4 wheel drive, auto locking hub control with manual shift; 4 wheel disc brakes with 4 wheel antilock braking system; underbody mounted full-size conventional alloy spare wheel.

Base Prices

Code	Description	Invoice	MSRP
MT45B	ES 2WD (5M)	17023	18310
MT45D	LS 2WD (4A)	22452	24950
MT45F	LS 4WD (5M)	23514	26130
MT45G	XLS 2WD (4A)	24270	26970
MT45K	XLS 4WD (4A)	26004	28900
MT45P	LTD 2WD (4A)	27212	30240
MT45X	LTD 4WD (4A)	29367	32630
Destination Charge:		445	445

CODE	DESCRIPTION	INVOICE	MSRP
	Accessories		
—	California Emissions	70	70
—	Transmission: 4-Speed Automatic (LS 4WD)	773	860
AC	Air Conditioning (ES) *NOT AVAILABLE with P3.*	750	915
C3	Single Disc CD Player (XLS/LTD)	299	399
C4	10 Disc CD Changer (XLS/LTD)	399	599
FG	Fog Lights (ES/LS/XLS)	140	200
HI	Trailer Hitch with Harness	164	252
KC	Cargo Kit (ES) *Includes floor mats, cargo cover and cargo net. NOT AVAILABLE with P3.*	131	200
P3	Preferred Package (ES) *Includes air conditioning, roof rack, fender flares, mudguards, cargo cover, cargo net, floor mats and side steps.*	1470	2184
P6	Luxury Package (XLS) *Includes Infinity AM/FM stereo with cassette and 8 speakers and power sliding sunroof.*	1000	1220
RD	Rear Deflector	95	145
SE	Security System (LS) *Includes keyless entry.*	224	345

1999 FRONTIER

1999 Nissan Frontier

What's New?

Two new King Cab models debut with a powerful V6 engine under the hood, and new standard and optional equipment is available.

Review

Nissan has been selling trucks in this country for 40 years. In 1998, they decided to redesign the pickup and for the first time ever, gave it a name – the Frontier. Building upon the success of the Frontier and dismissing last year's main gripe about the truck, Nissan has placed the 3.3-liter V6 engine that currently powers the Pathfinder into its King Cab lineup. The new engine produces 170 horsepower at 4,800 rpm and 200 foot-pounds of torque at 2,800 rpm. If it's got the optional automatic transmission mated to it, the truck is able to tow 5,000 pounds of gear. The broad, flat torque curve delivers extra power for off-roading and towing.

Frontiers range from the entry-level, two-wheel drive XE Regular Cab to the top-of-the-line four-wheel drive, King Cab SE V6. There are seven Frontier models available for 1999. XE or SE trim levels can be configured with Regular or King Cabs, and five-speed manual or four-speed automatic transmissions. The new V6 engine is not available on the Regular Cab models; these trucks are powered by a 2.4-liter, 16-valve, four-cylinder DOHC engine that makes an adequate but uninspiring 143 horsepower.

For 1999, consumers can get an optional limited-slip rear differential on 4WD V6 models. Automatic locking hubs, which allow the driver to switch into four-wheel drive at speeds up to 50 mph, are standard. Bucket seats are available on Regular Cab models, and a redesigned center console comes standard on the SE King Cab but is optional on the XE King Cab. A new body-colored trim package comes standard on all SE V6 Frontiers. There are no changes to the Frontier 2WD models this year.

Inside, the Frontier has a user-friendly layout. Standard amenities range from cup holders and adjustable seatbelts to a coin holder and LCD odometer display. The Frontier's spacious interior continues to please for 1999, making long trips in the truck more enjoyable.

The truck's bed is still the largest available in its class. Measuring 17.1 inches deep, the Frontier's pickup box can be partitioned horizontally and vertically – perfect for keeping loads separate and secure.

The 1999 Frontier provides comfort, practical utility and, finally, plenty of power when the V6 is ordered. If you're in the market for a compact pickup, be sure to check this one out.

Safety Data

Side Airbag: *Not Available*
4-Wheel ABS: *Standard (4WD); N/A (2WD)*
Driver Crash Test Grade: *Average*
Side Impact Crash Test Front: *Good*
Crash Offset: *Poor*
Integrated Child Seat(s): *Not Available*
Traction Control: *Not Available*
Passenger Crash Test Grade: *Good*
Side Impact Crash Test Rear: *Not Available*

Standard Equipment

XE 2WD REGULAR CAB (5M): 2.4L I4 DOHC SMPI 16-valve engine; 5-speed overdrive manual transmission; 490-amp battery; 70-amp alternator; rear wheel drive, 3.55 axle ratio; steel exhaust; front independent double wishbone suspension with anti-roll bar, front torsion springs, front torsion bar, rigid rear axle suspension with rear leaf springs; manual re-circulating ball steering; front disc/rear drum brakes with rear wheel antilock braking system; 15.9 gal capacity fuel tank; front and rear mud flaps, skid plates; regular pickup box; front and rear black bumpers; monotone paint; sealed beam halogen headlamps; additional exterior lights include center high mounted stop light; driver's manual black folding outside mirror; front and rear 14" x 5" silver styled steel wheels; P195/75SR14 BSW AS front and rear tires; underbody mounted compact steel spare wheel; 1 power accessory outlet, driver's foot rest; instrumentation display includes water temp gauge, trip odometer; warning indicators include oil pressure, battery, lights on, key in ignition, brake fluid; driver's side airbag, passenger's side cancelable airbag; tinted windows; fixed interval front windshield wipers; seating capacity of 3, bench front seat with fixed headrests, driver's seat includes 2-way direction control, passenger's seat includes 2-way direction control; front height adjustable seatbelts; vinyl seats, full cloth headliner, full vinyl floor covering; interior lights include dome light; day-night rearview mirror; glove box, front cupholder, instrument panel bin; black grille, black side window moldings, black front windshield molding, black rear window molding and black door handles.

XE 2WD KING CAB (5M) (in addition to or instead of XE 2WD REGULAR CAB (5M) equipment): 3.7 axle ratio; power re-circulating ball steering; front and rear black bumpers with rear step; driver's and passenger's manual black folding outside mirrors; front and rear 15" x 6" silver styled steel wheels; tinted windows, vented rear windows; seating capacity of 5, 60-40 split-bench front seat with adjustable headrests, center armrest with storage, driver's seat includes 4-way direction control, passenger's seat includes 4-way direction control with easy entry; 50-50 folding rear side facing jump seats; premium cloth seats, cloth door trim insert, full carpet floor covering and driver's and passenger's door bins.

SE 2WD KING CAB (5M) (in addition to or instead of XE 2WD KING CAB (5M) equipment): Front and rear chrome bumpers with rear step; black fender flares; additional exterior lights include front fog/driving lights; driver's and passenger's manual body-colored folding outside mirrors; air conditioning; AM/FM stereo with clock, seek-scan, cassette, 4 speakers, and fixed antenna; 2 power accessory outlets; instrumentation display includes tachometer; warning indicators include low fuel; deep tinted windows; variable intermittent front windshield wipers, sliding rear window; seating capacity of 4, front sports seats with adjustable headrests; interior lights include front reading lights; steering wheel with tilt adjustment; passenger's side vanity mirror; partial floor console and chrome grille.

XE 4WD REGULAR CAB (5M) (in addition to or instead of XE 2WD REGULAR CAB (5M) equipment): Part-time 4 wheel drive, manual locking hub control with manual shift, 3.89 axle ratio; front disc/rear drum brakes with 4 wheel antilock braking system; black fender flares; front and rear 15" x 7" silver styled steel wheels; underbody mounted full-size conventional steel spare wheel; cloth seats, cloth door trim insert; full carpet floor covering and cabback insulator.

XE 4WD KING CAB (5M) (in addition to or instead of XE 4WD REGULAR CAB (5M) equipment): 4.38 axle ratio; tinted windows, fixed rear windows; seating capacity of 5, 60-40 split-bench front seat with adjustable headrests, center armrest with storage, driver's seat includes 4-way direction control, passenger's seat includes 4-way direction control with easy entry; 50-50 folding rear side facing jump seats and premium cloth seats.

XE V6 4WD KING CAB (5M) (in addition to or instead of XE 4WD KING CAB (5M) equipment): 3.3L V6 SOHC SMPI 12-valve engine; 19.4 gal capacity fuel tank; seating capacity of 4, front bucket seats with adjustable headrests and partial floor console.

SE V6 4WD KING CAB (5M) (in addition to or instead of XE V6 4WD KING CAB (5M) equipment): Front and rear mud flaps, running boards, skid plates; front and rear chrome bumpers with rear tow hooks, rear step; body-colored fender flares; monotone paint with badging; additional exterior lights include front fog/driving lights, center high mounted stop light, pickup cargo box light; driver's and passenger's manual body-colored folding outside mirrors; air conditioning; AM/FM stereo with clock, seek-scan, cassette, 4 speakers, and fixed antenna; 2 power accessory outlets; instrumentation display includes tachometer; warning indicators include low fuel; deep tinted windows, vented rear windows; variable intermittent front windshield wipers, sliding rear window; front sports seats with adjustable headrests; premium cloth seats; interior lights include front reading lights; steering wheel with tilt adjustment; passenger side vanity mirror and chrome grille.

Base Prices

Code	Description	Invoice	MSRP
33559	XE 2WD Regular Cab (5M)	10806	11490
53559	XE 2WD King Cab (5M)	12546	13490
53259	SE 2WD King Cab (5M)	13785	14990
33759	XE 4WD Regular Cab (5M)	14871	15990
53759	XE 4WD King Cab (5M)	15899	17290
63759	XE V6 4WD King Cab (5M)	16819	18290
63659	SE V6 4WD King Cab (5M)	18355	20190
Destination Charge:		520	520

Accessories

Code	Description	Invoice	MSRP
—	Transmission: 4-Speed Automatic (SE V6 4WD X-Cab)	955	1050
—	Transmission: 4-Speed Automatic (XE 2WD Reg Cab)	988	1050
—	Transmission: 4-Speed Automatic (XE 2WD X-Cab)	977	1050
—	Transmission: 4-Speed Automatic (XE V6 4WD X-Cab)	966	1050
—	Transmission: 4-Speed Automatic (SE 2WD X-Cab)	965	1050
A01	Air Conditioning (XE 2WD Reg Cab)	825	950
B10	Limited Slip Differential (SE V6 4WD X-Cab)	173	200
F05	Power Package (XE X-Cab) *Includes power windows, power door locks, power mirrors, vehicle security system and remote keyless entry. REQUIRES V01 (XE 2WD/4WD X-Cab), G02, J02, N05. NOT AVAILABLE with P04, W01.*	676	780

CODE	DESCRIPTION	INVOICE	MSRP
F05	Power Package (SE) *Includes power windows, power door locks, power mirrors, vehicle security system, remote keyless entry and cruise control.*	849	980
G02	Value Truck Package (XE 4WD Reg Cab) *Includes air conditioning, chrome bumper and grille, deluxe AM/FM stereo with cassette, 15" alloy wheels and sliding rear window. NOT AVAILABLE with W01.*	747	794
G02	Value Truck Package (XE 2WD X-Cab) *Includes air conditioning, chrome bumper and grille, deluxe AM/FM stereo with cassette, 15" alloy wheels, sliding rear window, cargo lamp and privacy glass. NOT AVAILABLE with P04, W01.*	893	949
G02	Value Truck Package (XE 4WD X-Cab) *Includes air conditioning, chrome bumper and grille, deluxe AM/FM with cassette, 15" alloy wheels, sliding rear window, cargo lamp and privacy glass. NOT AVAILABLE with P04, W01.*	893	949
G03	Value Truck Package (XE 2WD Reg Cab) *Includes air conditioning, chrome bumper and grille, and deluxe AM/FM stereo with cassette and 4 speakers. NOT AVAILABLE with S01.*	516	549
H92	Single Disc CD Player (All Except SE 2WD/XE 4WD X-Cab)	310	469
H93	3 Disc CD Player (All Except SE 2WD/XE 4WD X-Cab)	412	559
J02	Sport Package (XE 2WD & 4WD X-Cab/XE V6 4WD X-Cab) *Includes flip-up sunroof and premium audio with subwoofer. REQUIRES G02, V01 and T08 (XE V6 4WD X-Cab). NOT AVAILABLE with P04, W01.*	650	749
J03	Sport Package (SE) *Includes flip-up sunroof and premium audio with subwoofer. REQUIRES F05.*	650	749
J92	Fender Flares/Splash Guards (XE 2WD Models) *NOT AVAILABLE with V01, V02.*	167	219
L92	Floor Mats	43	59
M94	Under Rail Bedliner (All Except XE Reg Cab 2WD & 4WD)	141	299
M95	Over Rail Bedliner (All Except XE Reg Cab 2WD & 4WD)	141	299
M96	Under Rail Bedliner (XE Reg Cab 2WD & 4WD)	141	299
M97	Over Rail Bedliner (XE Reg Cab 2WD & 4WD)	141	299
N05	Comfort Package (All 2WD Except SE) *Includes auxiliary 12-volt outlet, cruise control, low fuel warning light, variable intermittent windshield wipers and passenger's vanity mirror. REQUIRES G03 or G02. NOT AVAILABLE with S01, P04.*	346	399
N05	Comfort Package (All 4WD Except SE) *Includes auxiliary 12-volt power outlet, cruise control, low fuel warning light, variable intermittent windshield wipers and passenger's vanity mirror. REQUIRES G02. NOT AVAILABLE with W01, P04.*	346	399
P04	Popular Equipment Package (XE 2WD X-Cab/XE 4WD) *Includes air conditioning, chrome bumpers and grille and deluxe AM/FM stereo with cassette. NOT AVAILABLE with any other package.*	1213	1399
S01	Chrome and Audio Package (XE 2WD Reg Cab) *Includes chrome bumpers and grille and deluxe AM/FM stereo with cassette and 4 speakers. NOT AVAILABLE with G03, N05, V01, V02, W01.*	390	449

CODE	DESCRIPTION	INVOICE	MSRP
T08	Off-Road Package (XE V6 4WD X-Cab) *Includes off road decal, tailgate finisher, limited slip differential and tachometer. REQUIRES G02. NOT AVAILABLE with P04, W01.*	488	525
V01	Sport Value Package (XE 4WD Reg Cab) *Includes bodyside graphics, tailgate finisher and tachometer. REQUIRES G02. NOT AVAILABLE with V02, W01.*	429	495
V01	Sport Value Package (XE 2WD X-Cab) *Includes passenger assist grip, tailgate finisher, tachometer, bodyside graphics and fender flares. REQUIRES G02. NOT AVAILABLE with V02, P04, W01.*	329	380
V01	Sport Value Package (XE 2WD Reg Cab) *Includes passenger assist grip, tailgate finisher, tachometer, fender flares and bodyside graphics. REQUIRES G03. NOT AVAILABLE with*	519	599
V01	Sport Value Package (XE 4WD X-Cab) *Includes tailgate finisher, tachometer and bodyside graphics. REQUIRES G02. NOT AVAILABLE with V02, P04, W01.*	230	265
V02	Sport Value Package W/O Graphics (XE 2WD Reg Cab) *Includes passenger assist grip, tailgate finisher, tachometer and fender flares. REQUIRES G03. NOT AVAILABLE with V01, S01.*	519	599
V02	Sport Value Package W/O Graphics (XE 2WD X-Cab) *Includes passenger assist grip, tailgate finisher, tachometer and fender flares. REQUIRES G02. NOT AVAILABLE with V01, P04, W01.*	329	380
V02	Sport Value Package W/O Graphics (XE 4WD Reg Cab) *Includes tailgate finisher and tachometer. REQUIRES G02. NOT AVAILABLE with V01, W01.*	429	495
V02	Sport Value Package W/O Graphics (XE 4WD X-Cab) *Includes tailgate finisher and tachometer. REQUIRES G02. NOT AVAILABLE with V01, P04, W01.*	230	265
W01	Appearance Package (XE 4WD X-Cab) *Includes 15" alloy wheels, sliding rear window, cargo lamp and privacy glass. NOT AVAILABLE with any other packages.*	564	650
W01	Appearance Package (XE 2WD & 4WD Reg Cab) *Includes sliding rear window. REQUIRES G03. NOT AVAILABLE with S01, G02, N05, P04, V01, V02.*	343	395
W01	Appearance Package (XE 2WD X-Cab) *Includes 15" alloy wheels, sliding rear window, cargo lamp and privacy glass. NOT AVAILABLE with any other packages.*	564	650

1999.5 PATHFINDER

1999.5 Nissan Pathfinder

What's New?

Aggressive front and rear styling, more horsepower, and a new SE Limited model are available to buyers of the 1999.5 Pathfinder.

Review

The Pathfinder sports one of the friendliest interiors of any SUV that we've tested in recent years. Ample passenger space fore and aft, a large cargo area with convenient tie-down hooks, standard dual air bags, a killer sound system, comfortable seats and a great view are just a few of the reasons we like this truck so much.

A few things we don't like, however, are the narrow rear doors and tubular running boards. This poorly planned combination means that passengers exiting from the rear of the truck will undoubtedly have their pants dirtied by the ineffectual running board as they try to squeeze through the small door.

With Nissan's 1996 Pathfinder redesign came a more sophisticated, aerodynamic look and a gutsier version of their 3.3-liter SOHC V6 engine. Though not the engine of choice for speed freaks, it moves the Pathfinder along highways and two-track roads with ease. Speaking of two-track roads, the Nissan lost none of its sporting personality when it acquired its much-heralded car-like ride. Just ask our editor-in-chief, who took the Pathfinder on a day-long jaunt along the Continental Divide and managed to squeeze the truck through some nasty Jeep trails without scratching the paint.

On sale in the winter of 1999 is the 1999.5 Pathfinder, which boasts aggressive front and rear styling (including a new tailgate and taillights), more interior appointments (including different fabric and an upgraded stereo), improved power (now makes 170 hp and 200 foot-pounds of torque) and new color choices. The SE Limited trim level is completely new for the midyear release and features exclusive exterior treatments and a titanium-colored instrument panel. Sixteen-inch alloy wheels are also now standard on all trim levels and several modifications have been made to reduce noise, vibration and harshness.

The Nissan Pathfinder gives a competent on- and off-road ride, while surrounding its passengers in surprising comfort and luxury. If you require a rugged yet sophisticated vehicle for hauling your tribe around town and over the hills, the Pathfinder deserves your attention.

Safety Data

Side Airbag: *Optional (LE/SE); N/A (XE)*
4-Wheel ABS: *Standard*
Driver Crash Test Grade: *Average*
Side Impact Crash Test Front: *Not Available*
Crash Offset: *Not Available*
Integrated Child Seat(s): *Not Available*
Traction Control: *Not Available*
Passenger Crash Test Grade: *Average*
Side Impact Crash Test Rear: *Not Available*

Standard Equipment

XE 2WD (4A): 3.3L V6 SOHC SMPI 12-valve engine; 4-speed electronic overdrive automatic transmission with lock-up; 90-amp alternator; rear wheel drive, 4.36 axle ratio; stainless steel exhaust; front independent strut suspension with anti-roll bar, HD front coil springs, rigid rear axle multi-link suspension with anti-roll bar, rear coil springs; power rack-and-pinion steering; front disc/rear drum brakes with 4 wheel antilock braking system; 21 gal. capacity fuel tank; front and rear mud flaps, skid plates; liftback rear cargo door; roof rack; front and rear black bumpers with chrome bumper insert, rear step; monotone paint; aero-composite halogen headlamps; additional exterior lights include center high mounted stop light; driver's and passenger's manual black folding outside mirrors; front and rear 16" x 6.5" chrome alloy wheels; P245/70SR16 BSW M&S front and rear tires; underbody mounted full-size temporary steel spare wheel; air conditioning; AM/FM stereo with seek-scan, single CD, 6 speakers, and fixed diversity antenna; child safety rear door locks, remote fuel release; 2 power accessory outlets, driver's foot rest, retained accessory power; instrumentation display includes tachometer, water temp gauge, in-dash clock, trip odometer; warning indicators include oil pressure, water temp, battery, lights on, key in ignition, low fuel, low washer fluid, door ajar; dual airbags; ignition disable; deep tinted windows, manual rear windows, fixed 1/4 vent windows; variable intermittent front windshield wipers, flip-up rear window, fixed interval rear wiper, rear window defroster; seating capacity of 5, front bucket seats with adjustable headrests, center armrest with storage, driver's seat includes 4-way direction control, passenger's seat includes 4-way direction control; 60-40 folding rear bench seat with reclining adjustable headrests; front height adjustable seatbelts with front pretensioners; cloth seats, cloth door trim insert, full cloth headliner, full carpet floor covering; interior lights include dome light, front reading lights; steering wheel with tilt adjustment; passenger's side vanity mirror; day-night rearview mirror; full floor console, mini overhead console with storage, locking glove box with light, front and rear cupholders, 1 seat back storage pocket, driver's and passenger's door bins, rear door bins; carpeted cargo floor, plastic trunk lid, cargo tie downs, cargo light, cargo concealed storage; body-colored grille, black side window moldings, black front windshield molding, black rear window molding and black door handles.

SE 2WD (5M) (in addition to or instead of XE 2WD (4A) equipment): 5-speed overdrive manual transmission; 4.64 axle ratio; step rails; front and rear tow hooks; black fender flares; driver's and passenger's power remote black heated folding outside mirrors; titanium-tinted SE Limited badging; front and rear 16" x 7" titanium-tinted alloy wheels; P255/65SR16 BSW M&S front and rear tires; cruise control with steering wheel controls; power door locks with 2 stage unlock, remote keyless entry; panic alarm, security system; power front windows with driver's 1-touch down, power rear windows; driver's seat includes 6-way direction control with lumbar support, rear center armrest; rubber floor mats; leather-wrapped steering wheel with tilt adjustment; cargo cover and titanium-tinted grille.

LE 2WD (4A) (in addition to or instead of SE 2WD (5M) equipment): 4-speed electronic overdrive automatic transmission with lock-up; transmission oil cooler; body-colored front and rear mud flaps; front and rear body-colored bumpers with chrome bumper insert; body-colored bodyside cladding, body-colored fender flares; titanium-tinted running boards, monotone paint with bodyside accent stripe; additional exterior lights include front fog/driving lights; driver's and passenger's power remote body-colored heated folding outside mirrors; front and rear 16" x 7" painted alloy wheels; outside rear mounted full-size temporary steel spare wheel; air conditioning with climate control; Bose AM/FM stereo with seek-scan, cassette, single CD, 6 premium speakers, and power retractable diversity antenna; garage door opener; instrumentation display includes compass, exterior temp; wood trim, leather-wrapped gear shift knob; dual illuminated vanity mirrors, dual auxiliary visors; cargo net and titanium-tinted grille with chrome surround.

XE 4WD (4A) (in addition to or instead of XE 2WD (4A) equipment): Part-time 4 wheel drive and auto locking hub control with manual shift.

SE 4WD (5M) (in addition to or instead of SE 2WD (5M) equipment): Part-time 4 wheel drive and auto locking hub control with manual shift.

LE 4WD (4A) (in addition to or instead of LE 2WD (4A) equipment): Part-time 4 wheel drive and auto locking hub control with manual shift.

Base Prices

CODE	DESCRIPTION	INVOICE	MSRP
19219	XE 2WD (4A)	23909	26299
19459	SE 2WD (5M)	24774	27249
19319	LE 2WD (4A)	26646	29199
19619	XE 4WD (4A)	25728	28298
19759	SE 4WD (5M)	26592	29249
19819	LE 4WD (4A)	28364	31199
Destination Charge:		520	520

Accessories

CODE	DESCRIPTION	INVOICE	MSRP
—	Transmission: 4-Speed Automatic (SE)	910	1000
B10	Limited Slip Rear Differential (SE/LE 4WD) *REQUIRES J03.*	216	249
F92	Floor Mats (XE/LE)	58	79
G02	Popular Package (XE) *Includes large door armrests, power door locks, vehicle security system, remote keyless entry, cruise control, retractable cargo area cover, cargo net, power heated mirrors, leather-wrapped steering wheel and leather-wrapped shift knob.*	1085	1250
G03	Popular Package (SE) *Includes Bose AM/FM stereo with CD and cassette, power antenna, cargo net, halogen fog lights and rear window deflector.*	693	799
J03	Sunroof Package (LE) *Includes power tilt and slide glass sunroof.*	779	899
J03	Sunroof Package (SE) *Includes power tilt and slide glass sunroof, dual driver's side sunvisors, integrated homelink transmitter, digital compass and outside temperature display and dual illuminated visor vanity mirrors. REQUIRES G03.*	953	1099
P92	Tow Hitch III	284	389
R94	Body Color Side Moldings	79	99
T09	Off-Road Package (SE 2WD) *Includes titanium-tinted outside spare tire carrier and outside spare tire carrier ajar dashboard light. REQUIRES J03.*	346	399
T09	Off-Road Package (SE 4WD) *Includes limited slip rear differential, titanium-tinted outside spare tire carrier and outside spare tire carrier ajar dashboard light.*	519	599

CODE	DESCRIPTION	INVOICE	MSRP
W94	Gold Badging (XE)	123	389
W97	Gold Badging (LE)	123	389
X03	Leather Package (SE/LE - 2WD) *Includes simulated leather door trim, leather seating surfaces, power driver's and passenger's seats, leather-wrapped shift knob and side airbags. REQUIRES J03 and 4AT (SE).*	1560	1799
X03	Leather Package (SE/LE - 4WD) *Includes simulated leather door trim, leather-wrapped transfer case knob, leather seating surfaces, heated front seats, power driver's and passenger seats, leather-wrapped shift knob and side airbags. REQUIRES J03 and 4AT (SE).*	1734	1999

1999 QUEST

1999 Nissan Quest

What's New?

Nissan redesigns its minivan for 1999 and adds a new SE trim level, standard driver-side sliding rear door and a more powerful engine.

Review

Nissan's minivan factory is now cranking out a whole new Quest. For 1999, the minivan has been completely redesigned, both inside and out. The van's exterior is larger than before, with 4.6 more inches in length and 1.2 more inches in width. These new dimensions provide an extra 9.6 cubic feet of cargo volume for a total of 135.6 cubic feet. Stylistically, the Quest's front end is rounded with a chrome-ringed grille and new multiparabola headlights with crystalline lenses. A standard driver's side rear sliding door debuts on the van, making entry and exit easier for the kiddies.

Under the hood is a new 3.3-liter, 170-horsepower V6 engine that makes 200 foot-pounds of torque. This engine replaces the old 3.0-liter V6 and is mated to a four-speed automatic transmission that changes gears neatly, without a hint of harshness due to electronic controls. Antilock brakes are now standard on all Quest models and the suspension has been enhanced to improve the van's already smooth, quiet, sedan-like ride.

This year, the minivan is available in three flavors: value-oriented GXE, new sporty SE with larger 16-inch alloy wheels and a rear stabilizer bar, and luxurious GLE trim, featuring leather seating and the Quest Trac flexible seating system. Versatile passenger space is the Quest's stock in trade, and for 1999, a third-row limousine seating option is available.

With seven-passenger Quest Trac Flexible Seating, you can get 24 different combinations with the bench seat and 66 with the second-row captains chairs. Second-row seats can fold down into a table, or be removed completely. The third-row seat also folds into a table, folds further for more cargo space, or slides forward on integrated tracks-all the way to the driver's seat. Storage compartments now total 31 and cupholders will hold 13 drinks throughout. To enhance storage even more, Nissan added an optional multi-adjustable Quest Smart Shelf with mesh net located behind the third row.

The Quest's dashboard gets a facelift for 1999 with the audio unit moved above the climate controls for easier access. An automatic headlight on/off switch can be set to sense the onset of darkness and automatically turn the headlights on. Visibility is great, too, from upright but comfortable seating that's tempting for a long trek. Gauges are small, but acceptable, and controls are pleasing to operate.

Distinctive in shape and enjoyable on the road, Quests are solidly assembled and perform admirably. Except for the upright seating position, it's easy to forget that you're inside a minivan.

Safety Data

Side Airbag: *Not Available*
4-Wheel ABS: *Standard*
Driver Crash Test Grade: *Not Available*
Side Impact Crash Test Front: *Not Available*
Crash Offset: *Poor*
Integrated Child Seat(s): *Optional (GXE); N/A (SE/GLE)*
Traction Control: *Not Available*
Passenger Crash Test Grade: *Not Available*
Side Impact Crash Test Rear: *Not Available*

Standard Equipment

GXE (4A): 3.3L V6 SOHC SMPI 12-valve engine; 4-speed electronic overdrive automatic transmission with lock-up; battery with run down protection; front wheel drive; steel exhaust; front independent strut suspension with anti-roll bar, front coil springs, rear non-independent suspension with rear leaf springs; power rack-and-pinion steering; front disc/rear drum brakes with 4 wheel antilock braking system; 20.1 gal. capacity fuel tank; 4 doors with sliding left rear passenger's door and sliding right rear passenger's door, liftback rear cargo door; roof rack; front and rear body-colored bumpers with rear step; body-colored bodyside molding; monotone paint; aero-composite halogen headlamps; additional exterior lights include cornering lights, center high mounted stop light; driver's and passenger's manual black heated folding outside mirrors; front and rear 15" x 5.5" steel wheels; P215/70SR15 BSW AS front and rear tires; underbody mounted full-size temporary steel spare wheel; air conditioning, rear heat ducts; AM/FM stereo with clock, seek-scan, cassette, 4 speakers, and fixed antenna; cruise control with steering wheel controls; power door locks with 2 stage unlock, remote keyless entry, child safety rear door locks, remote fuel release; 1 power accessory outlet, driver's foot rest, retained accessory power; instrumentation display includes tachometer, water temp gauge, trip odometer; warning indicators include oil pressure, battery, lights on, key in ignition, low fuel, low washer fluid, door ajar, brake fluid; dual airbags; panic alarm, security system; deep tinted windows, power front windows with driver's 1-touch down, vented rear windows, manual 1/4 vent windows; variable intermittent front windshield wipers, fixed interval rear wiper, rear window defroster; seating capacity of 7, front bucket seats with adjustable headrests, driver's and passenger's armrests, driver's seat includes 4-way direction control, passenger's seat includes 4-way direction control; removable full folding 2nd row bench seat with adjustable headrests; 3rd row full folding bench seat with adjustable headrests; front height adjustable seatbelts; cloth seats, cloth door trim insert, full cloth headliner, full carpet floor covering with carpeted floor mats; interior lights include dome light with fade, 2 door curb lights, illuminated entry; steering wheel with tilt adjustment; dual illuminated vanity mirrors; day-night rearview mirror; locking glove box with light, front and rear cupholders, instrument panel covered bin, 1 seat back storage pocket, driver's and passenger's door bins, front underseat tray; carpeted cargo floor, plastic trunk lid, cargo light; chrome grille, black side window moldings, black front windshield molding, black rear window molding and body-colored door handles.

SE (4A) (in addition to or instead of GXE (4A) equipment): HD battery with run down protection; sport ride suspension; rear non-independent suspension with anti-roll bar; driver's and passenger's power remote black heated folding outside mirrors; front and rear 16" x 6" silver alloy wheels; rear air conditioning with separate controls, air filter; radio steering wheel controls with rear controls; 2 power accessory outlets; removable 2nd row reclining captain's seat with adjustable headrests; interior lights include front and rear reading lights; leather-wrapped steering wheel with tilt adjustment; mini overhead console with storage and body-colored grille.

GLE (4A) (in addition to or instead of SE (4A) equipment): Aero-composite halogen fully automatic headlamps with delay-off feature; front and rear 15" x 6" steel wheels; underbody mounted full-size conventional steel spare wheel; air conditioning with climate control; garage door opener; power 1/4 vent windows; front premium bucket seats with adjustable headrests; driver's seat includes 6-way power seat with lumbar support, passenger's seat includes 4-way power seat; leather seats, leatherette door trim insert; memory on driver's seat with 2 memory setting(s) includes settings for exterior mirrors and chrome grille.

Base Prices

Code	Description	Invoice	MSRP
10319	GXE (4A)	20145	22159
10419	SE (4A)	21478	23899
10519	GLE (4A)	23635	26299
Destination Charge:		520	520

Accessories

Code	Description	Invoice	MSRP
E10	Two-Tone Paint (SE/GLE)	259	299
F05	SE Convenience Package (SE) *Includes multi-adjustable Quest Smart Shelf, 6-way power driver's seat, power flip-out rear quarter windows, flip-up rear hatch glass and homelink universal tramsmitter.*	693	799
H08	GXE Audio Upgrade Package (GXE) *Includes 6 disc CD autochanger. REQUIRES N07.*	372	429
H08	SE Audio Upgrade Package (SE) *Includes 6 disc CD autochanger, premium AM/FM stereo with cassette and CD. REQUIRES J01 and F05.*	571	659
H94	6 Disc CD Autochanger (GXE/SE)	594	809
J01	Sunroof Package (SE/GLE) *Includes power sliding glass sunroof and rear window wind deflector. REQUIRES F05.*	779	899
J92	Splash Guards *NOT AVAILABLE with J01.*	63	89
K06	Integrated Child Safety Seat (GXE) *REQUIRES N07.*	199	229
N07	GXE Comfort Plus Package (GXE) *Includes multi-adjustable Quest Smart Shelf, rear air conditioning, rear audio controls, 12-volt DC power outlet, HD battery and replaceable in-cabin microfilter.*	563	649
P95	Fog Lamps (SE) *REQUIRES F05.*	275	379

CODE	DESCRIPTION	INVOICE	MSRP
P96	Fog Lamps *NOT AVAILABLE with F05.*	271	369
R09	GLE Popular Package (GLE) *Includes multi-adjustable Quest Smart Shelf, premium AM/FM stereo with cassette and CD, conventional spare tire and trailer wiring harness.*	433	500
T04	Towing Package (GXE/SE) *Includes conventional spare tire and trailer wiring harness. REQUIRES N07 and H08.*	146	169
W92	Tow Hitch I *NOT AVAILABLE with T04, R09.*	305	419
W93	Tow Hitch II *REQUIRES T04 or R09.*	202	289
X03	SE Leather Trim Package (SE) *Includes leather seating surfaces, memory driver's seat and driver seatback map pocket. REQUIRES F05.*	1300	1499

1999 BRAVADA

1999 Oldsmobile Bravada

What's New?

In the wake of last year's restyle, Bravada sees feature refinements for '99. The driver-side airbag has been redesigned into a mini-module to permit a clearer view of the instruments, while the turn signal stalk now provides a flash-to-pass feature. A telltale warning lamp has been added to alert the driver when the tailgate lift glass is ajar. And an anti-theft alarm system is now standard. There's also an option package that combines a driver-side memory seat and a power passenger-side seat, as well as sound system upgrades across the board.

Review

After a one year hiatus, the Oldsmobile Bravada returned for the 1996 model year, based on the same platform that serves as the basis for the Chevrolet Blazer and the GMC Jimmy. We said we doubted Oldsmobile would find many buyers for the Bravada, partly because of myriad choices in the luxo-SUV market, and partly because we didn't think the Bravada was worth the price of admission over similarly equipped Chevy Blazers and GMC Jimmys. Sales didn't meet expectations that first year, but nearly doubled during 1997. Still, Oldsmobile would like to be moving twice as many Bravadas. So last year, Bravada got a freshening both inside and out.

The Bravada should do well for 1999 because it's a nice truck. No tacky fender flares and no dopey, two-tone paint schemes here. The interior is swathed in leather and offers one of the most comfortable driver seats we've encountered in an SUV. The sound system is outstanding. Controls are easy to see and use (though they still look and feel somewhat cheap). Bravada's SmartTrak all-wheel drive system makes finding grip in a variety of road conditions carefree. Best of all, this is one speedy, fun-to-drive truck that can easily swallow a full-size dryer. Truly, the Bravada is what a luxury compact sport/utility is all about.

As an upscale Oldsmobile, the Bravada comes loaded with nearly every conceivable option. That's a good thing, too, with the quickly expanding luxury sport/ute arena overflowing with entries, even from Lincoln and Infiniti – makers not known for building truck products. But this may not be your best choice to go bounding down a dusty trail. Oldsmobile makes no bones about designing Bravada to be an on-road SUV.

Is the Bravada worth the price of admission over the Blazer and the Jimmy? Well, the front seats and the SmartTrak all-wheel drive system are exclusive to the Olds, but otherwise not much differentiates the Bravada from its corporate twins. In fact, most of the standard equipment on the Bravada is available on the Chevy or the GMC, with an end result that is less expensive than the Oldsmobile.

Few options are available on the Bravada. Buyers can order a 5000-pound towing package, an engine block heater, a Bose premium sound system, a six-disc CD changer located in the console, redundant radio and climate controls for the steering wheel, heated seats, white-letter 235/70R-15 all-season tires, a power sunroof, and the obligatory gold trim package. Cloth seats are a no-charge replacement for the standard leather hides. A new option package puts together five features: the optional tires and heavy-duty towing package, plus a driver-side memory seat, power passenger seat, and electrochromic outside rearview mirrors (inside electrochromic rearview mirror is standard).

Styling is pretty much identical to the Chevy Blazer and GMC Jimmy. The Bravada gets a unique grille and headlamp treatment, bumper trim and body cladding. The overall effect distances the Olds far enough away from its corporate siblings to make it look and feel unique in a world populated by look-alike Jeep Grand Cherokees and Ford Explorers. A 4.3-liter Vortec V6 engine that makes 190 horsepower propels the Bravada's four wheels. Though strong, we find the V6 a strange choice when the Jeep and the Ford can be equipped with a V8 engine. The Explorer-based Mercury Mountaineer also has all-wheel drive, like the Bravada, along with V8 power. Four-wheel disc brakes provide very good stopping ability, though we could do without the mushy feel to the brake pedal.

The original Bravada, which competed in a market populated by few luxury-oriented SUVs, never sold very well. It was based on aging technology, and buyers saw through the first-generation Bravada quicker than they did the ill-fated Cadillac Cimarron. Oldsmobile has come up with quite an enticing package with the second-generation Bravada. However, the luxury/ute market is becoming saturated with a number of very good trucks, which will inevitably push down demand for any particular model. We also think that aging, affluent Boomers are going to tire of climbing in and out of these things, depositing their aching legs and backs into the seats of the Cadillacs, BMWs and Acuras that they're currently trading like baseball cards for the more rugged, SUV image.

Safety Data

Side Airbag: *Not Available*
4-Wheel ABS: *Standard*
Driver Crash Test Grade: *Average*
Side Impact Crash Test Front: *Excellent*
Crash Offset: *Poor*
Integrated Child Seat(s): *Not Available*
Traction Control: *Not Available*
Passenger Crash Test Grade: *Good*
Side Impact Crash Test Rear: *Excellent*

Standard Equipment

BRAVADA (4A): 4.3L V6 OHV SMPI 12-valve engine; 4-speed electronic overdrive automatic transmission with lock-up; 100-amp battery with run down protection; engine oil cooler; 525-amp alternator; full-time 4 wheel drive, limited slip differential, 3.73 axle ratio; stainless steel exhaust; front independent suspension with anti-roll bar, front torsion springs, front torsion bar, rigid rear axle suspension with anti-roll bar, rear leaf springs; power re-circulating ball steering with vehicle speed-sensing assist; 4 wheel disc brakes with 4 wheel antilock braking system; 18 gal capacity fuel tank; front license plate bracket; liftback rear cargo door; roof rack; front and rear body-colored bumpers with rear tow hooks, rear step; body-colored bodyside cladding, rocker panel extensions, body-colored wheel well molding; monotone paint with bodyside accent stripe; aero-composite halogen fully automatic headlamps with daytime running lights, delay-off feature; additional exterior lights include front fog/driving lights, center high mounted stop light, underhood light; driver's and passenger's power remote black heated folding outside mirrors; front and rear 15" x 7" silver alloy wheels; P235/70SR15 BSW AS front and rear tires; underbody mounted full-size temporary steel spare wheel; air conditioning with climate control, rear heat ducts; AM/FM stereo with clock, seek-scan, cassette, single CD, 6 speakers, graphic equalizer, and fixed antenna; cruise control; power door locks with 2 stage unlock, remote keyless entry, child safety rear door locks, power remote hatch/trunk release; 3 power accessory outlets, retained accessory power, garage door opener; instrumentation display includes tachometer, oil pressure gauge, water temp gauge, volt gauge, compass, exterior temp, trip computer, trip odometer; warning indicators include battery, lights on, key in ignition, trunk ajar; dual airbags; ignition disable, panic alarm, security system; deep tinted windows, power front windows with driver's 1-touch down, power rear windows, fixed 1/4 vent windows; variable intermittent front windshield wipers, flip-up rear window, fixed interval rear wiper, rear window defroster; seating capacity of 5, front bucket seats with adjustable tilt headrests, center armrest with storage, driver's seat includes 6-way power seat with power lumbar support, passenger's seat includes 4-way direction control with power lumbar support; 60-40 folding rear split-bench seat with adjustable rear headrest; leather seats, leatherette door trim insert, full cloth headliner, full carpet floor covering with carpeted floor mats, leather-wrapped gear shift knob; interior lights include dome light, front and rear reading lights, illuminated entry; leather-wrapped steering wheel with tilt adjustment; dual illuminated vanity mirrors; auto-dimming day-night rearview mirror; partial floor console, full overhead console with storage, glove box with light, front cupholder, 2 seat back storage pockets, driver's and passenger's door bins, rear door bins; carpeted cargo floor, carpeted trunk lid, cargo cover, cargo net, cargo tie downs, cargo light, cargo concealed storage; body-colored grille, black side window moldings, black front windshield molding, black rear window molding and black door handles.

Base Prices

Code	Description	Invoice	MSRP
V06TV-R7A	Base	28184	31143
Destination Charge:		525	525

Accessories

Code	Description	Invoice	MSRP
1SA	**Option Package 1SA**	NC	NC
	Includes vehicle with standard equipment.		
AG0	**Driver's Seat Memory Control**	73	85
AH8	**Passenger's Power Seat Adjuster**	215	250
	Eight-way power including power recliner.		
B94	**Gold Package**	151	175
	Includes gold emblems on vehicle, wheels and a gold accent stripe.		
CF5	**Electric Sliding Glass Astroroof**	645	750
	Includes gray tint, sunshade, compass/temperature display and garage door opener transmitter.		
DD0	**Electrochromic Heated Driver's Mirror**	66	77
K05	**Engine Block Heater**	28	33
KA1	**Heated Driver's and Passenger's Seats**	215	250
QBG	**Tires: P235/70R15 AS WOL SBR**	116	135
	Use of chains is not recommended with these tires.		
R9B	**Convenience Package**	49	757
	Includes passenger's power seat adjuster, driver's seat memory control, HD trailer towing package, electrochromic heated driver's mirror and P235/70R15 AS WOL SBR tires. NOT AVAILABLE with R9D.		
R9E	**Platinum Edition Package**	808	939
	Manufacturer Discount	(602)	(700)
	Net Price	206	239
	Includes eight way power passenger's seat, memory for driver's seat, heavy duty towing package: weight-distributing platform hitch, heavy-duty flasher, eight-wire		

CODE	DESCRIPTION	INVOICE	MSRP
	electrical harness, engine oil cooler; P235/70R15 WOL tires, pewter colored lower body cladding and Platinum Edition decals. NOT AVAILABLE with B94 or R9B.		
UTF	Radio: Bose AM/FM Stereo with CD	426	495
	Includes seek-scan, auto-reverse cassette, digital clock and six-speaker Bose sound system powered by a six-channel amplifier.		
U1Z	6 Disc CD Changer	340	395
	Console-mounted.		
UK3	Steering Wheel Radio Controls	108	125
Z82	HD Trailer Towing Package	181	210
	Includes weight-distributing platform hitch, heavy-duty flasher and eight-wire electrical harness (engine oil cooler included with engine). Towing capacity is 5,000 pounds.		

1999 SILHOUETTE

1999 Oldsmobile Silhouette

What's New?

Olds is headlining its Premiere Edition, a loaded-up model that debuted in mid-'98 with a standard integrated video entertainment system in back. But other news for 1999 includes a horsepower and torque increase for Silhouette's 3.4-liter V6, plus the addition of a theft-deterrent system and heated outside rearview mirrors as standard equipment. And if four new exterior colors (Sky, Ruby, Silvermist and Cypress) weren't enough, then consider the availability of a new Gold Package (but only if you must).

Review

After years of unsuccessfully peddling a huge four-wheeled version of the plastic Dustbuster found in your hall closet, Oldsmobile went back to the drawing board and introduced a fresh, conservative, steel-bodied, fun-to-drive minivan to market in 1997. Did we actually say "fun to drive?"

Yes. Available in four trim levels and three bodystyles, the Silhouette is indeed one minivan today's consumers need to consider.

Just why is this Oldsmobile so good? Because you name the convenience, and Olds has thought of it. Want a sliding driver-side door? You can get one here. Wish that passenger-side sliding door was power operated? Oldsmobile has you covered. Want leather? A CD player? Separate audio controls for rear passengers? Traction control? A powerful V6? How about easy to unload seats that can be configured in a variety of ways? It's all here, depending on the bodystyle and trim level you select. There's even a TV/VCP for rear seat passengers to enjoy.

Silhouette is available in four flavors (all with dual sliding doors standard): GS rides on the regular wheelbase while GL and GLS get the extended length (120-inch) wheelbase as does the Premiere Edition, which is actually a gussied-up GLS with touring suspension and rear-mounted air inflator. All Silhouettes are front-wheel drive, powered by a 185-horsepower 3.4-liter V6 (up five ponies from '98) mated to an electronically controlled four-speed automatic transmission. Dual airbags, side airbags, antilock brakes and fog lamps are standard, and for '99 GM adds heated outside mirrors and its PASSKEY III anti-theft system.

GS models (with a 112-inch wheelbase) come with air-conditioning, tilt steering wheel, cruise control, power seats, windows and door locks, power passenger-side door, keyless entry, overhead console and dual lighted visor vanity mirrors. (Rear wiper, rooftop luggage carrier, deep-tint glass and AM/FM stereo cassette are standard on all models.) Options include traction control, alloy wheels, integrated child seats, leather upholstery, CD player and eight-passenger seating.

The GL model gets you the longer, 120-inch wheelbase, but costs you the power seats and passenger-side door, remote entry, overhead console and vanity mirrors. If you need the long wheelbase with all the bells and whistles, then go for the GLS, which adds a touring suspension package, traction control, 15-inch alloy wheels, rear A/C, heat and audio controls, leather seating and steering-wheel mounted radio controls to the GS standard equipment roster.

A new model appeared in the spring of 1998. Called the Premiere Edition, it comes with nearly every goodie standard, including a combination television and video cassette player for rear seat passengers. The only available options on the Premiere Edition are a towing package, OnStar communications, an engine block heater and a new gold package.

We've driven the Silhouette and came away quite impressed. These well-equipped minivans are smooth and powerful. Thanks to excellent road feel provided by precise steering and easily modulated brakes, they are actually fun to drive – which can't be said about some of today's best-selling makes. Our complaints are limited to uncomfortable rear seating and a noticeable amount of cheap-looking plastic inside the cabin.

As you've probably guessed, we like the Oldsmobile Silhouette, and find its exterior styling to be the most attractive of GM's trio of sister minivans.

Safety Data

Side Airbag: *Standard*

4-Wheel ABS: *Standard*

Driver Crash Test Grade: *Good*
Side Impact Crash Test Front: *Excellent*
Crash Offset: *Poor*

Integrated Child Seat(s): *Optional (GL/GS); Not Available (GLS/ Premiere)*

Traction Control: *Standard (GLS/Premiere); Optional (GL/GS)*

Passenger Crash Test Grade: *Average*
Side Impact Crash Test Rear: *Excellent*

Standard Equipment

GL EXTENDED (4A): 3.4L V6 OHV SMPI 12-valve engine; 4-speed electronic overdrive automatic transmission with lock-up; 600-amp battery with run down protection; 105-amp alternator; front wheel drive, 3.29 axle ratio; stainless steel exhaust; front independent strut suspension with anti-roll bar, front coil springs, rear non-independent suspension with rear coil springs; power rack-and-pinion steering; front disc/rear drum brakes with 4 wheel antilock braking system; 25 gal capacity fuel tank; body-colored front and rear mud flaps, side impact bars; roof rack; front and rear body-colored bumpers with rear step; body-colored bodyside molding, rocker panel extensions; aero-composite halogen headlamps with daytime running lights; additional exterior lights include front fog/driving lights, center high mounted stop light, underhood light; driver's and passenger's power remote black heated folding outside mirrors; front and rear 15" x 6" steel wheels; P205/70SR15 BSW AS tires; underbody mounted compact steel spare wheel; air conditioning, air filter; AM/FM stereo with clock, seek-scan, cassette, 4 speakers, automatic equalizer, and window grid antenna; cruise control; power door locks with 2 stage unlock, child safety rear door locks; 3 power accessory outlets; instrumentation display includes tachometer, water temp gauge, trip odometer; warning indicators include battery, low oil level, low coolant, lights on, key in ignition; dual airbags, seat mounted side airbags; deep tinted windows, power front windows with driver's 1-touch down, power rear windows, power 1/4 vent windows; variable intermittent front windshield wipers, fixed interval rear wiper, rear window defroster; seating capacity of 7, front bucket seats with adjustable headrests, driver's and passenger's armrests, driver's and passenger's seat includes 4-way direction control with lumbar support; removable 2nd row 60-40 folding split-bench seat with adjustable rear headrests; 3rd row removable 50-50 folding split-bench seat; front height adjustable seatbelts; cloth seats, cloth door trim insert, full carpet with carpeted floor mats; interior lights include dome light, front and rear reading lights, illuminated entry; steering wheel with tilt adjustment; day-night rearview mirror; mini overhead console; locking glove box with light, front and rear cupholders, instrument panel covered bin, dashboard storage, 2 seat back storage pockets, driver's and passenger's door bins, front underseat tray; carpeted cargo floor, plastic trunk lid, cargo net, cargo light; body-colored grille, black moldings, and body-colored door handles.

GS (4A) (in addition to or instead of GL EXTENDED (4A) equipment): 20 gal capacity fuel tank; power sliding right rear passenger's door; trip computer; remote keyless entry; ignition disable, panic alarm, security system; driver's and passenger's seat includes 6-way power seat with 8-way direction control and lumbar support; full overhead console with storage and driver information center and dual illuminated vanity mirrors.

GLS EXTENDED (4A) (in addition to or instead of GL EXTENDED (4A) equipment): Traction control; touring ride suspension with auto-leveling; 25 gal capacity fuel tank; rear air conditioning with separate controls, air filter, rear heat ducts, rear heater; radio steering wheel controls, rear audio controls; power remote hatch/trunk release; instrumentation display includes compass, exterior temp; seating capacity of 6, front bucket seats with adjustable headrests, driver's and passenger's armrests; removable 2nd row captain's seats with adjustable rear headrests; leather seats, leatherette door trim insert; interior lights include illuminated entry and leather-wrapped steering wheel with tilt adjustment.

PREMIERE EDITION EXTENDED (4A) (in addition to or instead of GLS EXTENDED (4A) equipment): AM/FM stereo with clock, seek-scan, cassette, single CD, 4 speakers, automatic equalizer, and window grid antenna; rear seat video cassette player, rear seat overhead fold-down LCD color monitor, six headphones with individual volume control, input jack for video games or camcorder.

Base Prices

Code	Description	Invoice	MSRP
3UN16	GS 4-Door (4A)	22525	24890
3UM16	GL 4-Door Ext. (4A)	22182	24510
3UM16	GLS 4-Door Ext. (4A)	25507	28185
3UM16	Premiere Edition 4-Door Ext. (4A)	28146	31100
Destination Charge:		580	580

CODE	DESCRIPTION	INVOICE	MSRP
	Accessories		
—	Cloth Seat Trim (Premiere Edition)	NC	NC
1SA	Option Package 1SA (GL) *Includes vehicle with standard equipment.*	NC	NC
1SB	Option Package 1SB (GS) *Includes vehicle with standard equipment.*	NC	NC
1SC	Option Package 1SC (GLS) *Includes vehicle with standard equipment.*	NC	NC
1SD	Option Package 1SD (Premiere Edition) *Includes vehicle with standard equipment.*	NC	NC
ABD	Captain's Chairs (Second Row) (GL/GS)	254	295
AG9	6-Way Power Driver's/Passenger's Seats (GL)	495	575
AN2	Integrated Child Safety Seat (GL/GS)	108	125
AN5	Dual Integrated Child Safety Seats (GL/GS)	194	225
DK6	Overhead Extended Console (GL) *Includes storage for sunglasses and garage door opener, compass, outdoor temperature and driver's information center.*	151	175
E58	Power Sliding Passenger's Right Side Door (GL) *REQUIRES UA6.*	387	450
FE3	Touring Suspension Group (GL/GS) *Package includes an air inflation kit and automatic level control.*	232	270
K05	Engine Block Heater	17	20
NW9	Traction Control (GL/GS) *Full function engine and brakes.*	168	195
PH3	Wheels: 15" Aluminum (GL/GS)	254	295
R8P	Convenience Package (GL) *Includes rear air conditioning and heater and rear seat audio controls.*	464	540
R8Q	Personal Convenience Package (GL) *Includes captain's chairs (second row), 6-way power driver's/passenger's seats, Delco ETR AM/FM stereo with CD and cassette, keyless remote entry system, remote trunk release, panic alarm and illuminated entry.*	1122	1305
R8U	Personal Attention Package (GS) *Includes captain's chairs (second row), custom leather seat trim, touch control (audio controls) leather-wrapped steering wheel, rear seat audio controls and Delco ETR AM/FM stereo with CD and cassette.*	1428	1660
UA6	Keyless Remote Entry System (GL) *Includes key-chain transmitter with panic alarm and illuminated entry.*	202	235
UK3	Touch Control Steering Wheel (GS) *Controls on steering wheel for radio functions.*	108	125
UK6	Rear Seat Audio Controls (GL/GS) *Provides choice of music source and includes headphones and volume control.*	77	90
UN0	Radio: Delco AM/FM Stereo with CD (GL/GS/GLS) *Includes automatic tone control, seek and scan, digital display clock and coaxial speaker system.*	86	100

CODE	DESCRIPTION	INVOICE	MSRP
UN7	Radio: Delco AM/FM Stereo with CD and Cassette (GL/GS/GLS) *Includes CD, auto-reverse cassette, seek and scan, automatic tone control, digital display clock and coaxial speaker system. NOT AVAILABLE with UNO.*	172	200
V92	Trailer Towing Package (GL/GS/GLS) *3500 lbs. capacity, heavy-duty radiator, engine oil cooler and 5-wire trailer wiring harness.*	305	355
V92	Trailer Towing Package (Premiere Edition) *3500 lbs. capacity, heavy-duty radiator, engine oil cooler and 5-wire trailer wiring harness.*	73	85
WJ7	Custom Leather Seat Trim (GS) *REQUIRES ABD.*	817	950
Y11	Gold Graphics Package *Includes gold emblems and wheel accents.*	129	150
ZP8	Eight Passenger Seating (GL/GS) *Includes three reclining bucket seats in second row, and three passenger 50/50 divided bench seat in third row.*	241	280

1999 GRAND VOYAGER / VOYAGER

1999 Plymouth Voyager

What's New?

SE trim levels get body-colored door and liftgate handles, as well as a body-colored front grille. All models add a cargo net between the front seats, and the new exterior color this year is Light Cypress Green.

Review

Chrysler Corporation is the minivan champion. They pioneered the concept of a seven-passenger box-on-wheels way back in 1984, and have dominated this market ever since.

In the past, Plymouth renderings of Chrysler's popular front-drive minivans have been virtual clones of the Dodge Caravan. In engineering and design, that's also true of this latest iteration. In an assertive marketing move, however, Plymouth is pushing value pricing, aiming squarely at entry-level buyers who are shopping for their first minivans. Plymouth offers two short-wheelbase Voyagers: the base model and the step-up SE. SE models get a standard 3.3-liter engine, good for an additional eight horsepower and 36 foot-pounds of torque over the base engine. The longer wheelbase Grand Voyager is also offered in SE trim. You may opt for the "Expresso" graphics and gizmo package for either Voyager or Grand Voyager, which includes a handy remote keyless entry.

A 2.4-liter four-cylinder engine is standard on base models, but these sizable vans benefit from a little extra oomph when the V6 is selected. Acceleration with the 3.3-liter, 158-horsepower engine is pretty strong from startup, but sometimes unimpressive when merging onto an expressway. Automatic transmission shifts are neat and smooth. Engine and tire sounds are virtually absent.

Though tautly suspended, the ride is seldom harsh or jarring, unless you get onto truly rough surfaces. Even then, the seven-passenger minivan behaves itself well. Light steering wheel response makes handling even more car-like than in the past. Visibility is great, courtesy of more glass and a reduced-height cowl.

So, how does Plymouth improve on this package for 1999? By keeping the price low and the value high. As for physical differences, SE trim on both Voyager and Grand Voyager receives an appearance upgrade: the door handles and grille are body colored instead of black.

CODE	DESCRIPTION	INVOICE	MSRP

This minivan exhibits not a hint of looseness, squeaks or rattles, feeling tight all over. Newly revised minivans from Honda, Ford and GM are the strongest challengers, but the Voyager holds its own when it comes to value.

Safety Data

Side Airbag: *Not Available*
4-Wheel ABS: *Optional (Base); Standard (SE)*
Driver Crash Test Grade: *Average*
Side Impact Crash Test Front: *Excellent*
Crash Offset: *Poor*
Integrated Child Seat(s): *Optional*
Traction Control: *Not Available*
Passenger Crash Test Grade: *Average*
Side Impact Crash Test Rear: *Average*

Standard Equipment

BASE VOYAGER [3A]: 2.4L DOHC 16-valve SMPI four-cylinder engine, 3-speed automatic transmission, 3.19 axle ratio, front wheel drive, power rack and pinion steering, power front disc/rear drum brakes, strut-type front suspension with gas-charged shocks, coil springs, assymetrical lower control arms and link-type stabilizer bar; single-leaf spring rear suspension with tubular beam axle, track bar and gas-charged shocks; 14" steel wheels with full wheel covers, P205/75R14 AS BSW tires, compact spare tire, tinted glass, bodyside molding, variable intermittent windshield wipers, rear window wiper/washer, dual manual exterior mirrors, dual front airbags, 5-passenger seating, AM/FM stereo with digital clock and 4 speakers, gauges include fuel, coolant temp., trip odometer; warning indicators include low fuel, low washer fluid, check engine, liftgate ajar, door ajar, low voltage, seat belt unfastened; message center warnings for airbags, ABS, engine temp., oil pressure; chimes for headlights-on, key-in-ignition; dashboard storage bin, rear seatback grocery bag hooks, ful carpeting, front and rear dome lighting, cargo light, courtesy lights, map lights, liftgate flood lighting, dual front and rear accessory power outlets, visor mirrors.

BASE GRAND VOYAGER [4A] (in addition to or instead of BASE VOYAGER [3A] equipment): 3.3L FFV V6 engine, 4-speed electronically-controlled automatic transmission, 2.98 axle ratio, dual sliding side doors, 7-passenger seating.

VOYAGER/GRAND VOYAGER SE [4A] (in addition to or instead of BASE GRAND VOYAGER [4A] equipment): Four-wheel antilock brakes, 3.62 axle ratio, 15" steel wheels with full wheel covers, P215/65R15 AS BSW tires, wide bodyside molding, liftgate molding, dual power exterior mirrors, air conditioning with rear climate controls, rear window defroster, windshield wiper de-icer, tachometer, tilt steering wheel, cruise control, AM/FM stereo with cassette player and 4 speakers, rear floor silencer, front seat cargo net, underseat locking storage bin, rear cargo net, rear passenger assist strap.

Base Prices

CODE	DESCRIPTION	INVOICE	MSRP
NSHL52	Voyager Base (3A)	16374	18005
NSHH52	Voyager SE (4A)	19784	21880
NSHL53	Grand Voyager Base (4A)	19168	21140
NSHH53	Grand Voyager SE (4A)	20695	22875
Destination Charge:		580	580

Accessories

CODE	DESCRIPTION	INVOICE	MSRP
2*B	SE Quick Order Package B (SE/Grand SE) *Includes vehicle with standard equipment.*	NC	NC

CODE	DESCRIPTION	INVOICE	MSRP
2*D	SE Quick Order Package D (SE/Grand SE)	854	1005
	Manufacturer Discount	(255)	(300)
	Net Price	599	705
	Includes power door locks, power windows, power quarter vent windows, floor mats, illuminated visor vanity mirrors, deluxe insulation, light group: ashtray light, glovebox light, illuminated ignition ring.		
2*E	Expresso Quick Order Package E (SE/Grand SE)	1598	1880
	Manufacturer Discount	(412)	(485)
	Net Price	1186	1395
	Includes Expresso Group: dark tinted glass, AM/FM stereo with CD, special wheel covers; power door locks, power windows, power quarter vent windows, floor mats, illuminated visor vanity mirrors, deluxe insulation, light roup: ashtray light, glovebox light, illuminated ignition ring.		
2*L	SE Quick Order Package L (SE/Grand SE)	2061	2425
	Manufacturer Discount	(340)	(400)
	Net Price	1721	2025
	Includes power door locks, power windows, power quarter vent windows, floor mats, illuminated visor vanity mirrors, deluxe insulation, light group: ashtray light, glovebox light, illuminated ignition ring; overhead console with trip computer, 8-way power adjustable driver's seat with manual lumbar, deluxe quad bucket seating, premium cloth upholstery, reading lights.		
2*N	Expresso Quick Order Package N (SE/Grand SE)	2805	3300
	Manufacturer Discount	(497)	(585)
	Net Price	2308	2715
	Includes Expresso Group: dark tinted glass, AM/FM stereo with CD, special wheel covers; power door locks, power windows, power quarter vent windows, floor mats, illuminated visor vanity mirrors, deluxe insulation, light roup: ashtray light, glovebox light, illuminated ignition ring; overhead console with trip computer, 8-way power adjustable driver's seat with manual lumbar, deluxe quad bucket seating, premium cloth upholstery, reading lights.		
2*S	Base Quick Order Package S (Base/Grand Base)	NC	NC
	Includes vehicle with standard equipment.		
2*T	Base Quick Order Package T (Grand Base)	765	900
	Manufacturer Discount	(646)	(760)
	Net Price	119	140
	Includes air conditioning, front seat cargo net, rear floor silencer, locking underseat storage bin.		
2*T	Base Quick Order Package T (Base)	1084	1275
	Manufacturer Discount	(646)	(760)
	Net Price	438	515
	Includes air conditioning, front seat cargo net, rear floor silencer, 7-passenger seating, locking underseat storage bin.		
4XA	Air Conditioning Bypass (Base/Base Grand)	NC	NC
	*REQUIRES 2*S.*		
4XN	Rear Air Conditioning Bypass (Grand SE)	NC	NC
AAA	Climate Group 2	383	450
	*Includes air conditioning, deep tinted glass. NOT AVAILABLE with 2*E or 2*N.*		

CODE	DESCRIPTION	INVOICE	MSRP
AAB	Climate Group 3 (Grand SE) *Includes rear air conditioning, rear heater, dual-zone temperature control, overhead console with trip computer. REQUIRES 2*E. NOT AVAILABLE with AHT.*	642	755
AAB	Climate Group 3 (Grand SE) *Includes rear air conditioning, rear heater, dual-zone temperature control, overhead console with trip computer, deep tinted glass. REQUIRES 2*D and AHT.*	969	1140
AAB	Climate Group 3 (Grand SE) *Includes rear air conditioning, rear heater, dual-zone temperature control, overhead console with trip computer, deep tinted glass. REQUIRES 2*D. NOT AVAILABLE with AHT.*	1024	1205
AAB	Climate Group 3 (Grand SE) *Includes rear air conditioning, rear heater, dual-zone temperature control, deep tinted glass. REQUIRES 2*L and AHT.*	803	945
AAB	Climate Group 3 (Grand SE) *Includes rear air conditioning, rear heater, dual-zone temperature control, deep tinted glass. REQUIRES 2*L. NOT AVAILABLE with AHT.*	859	1010
AAB	Climate Group 3 (Grand SE) *Includes rear air conditioning, rear heater, dual-zone temperature control, overhead console with trip computer. REQUIRES 2*E and AHT.*	587	690
AAB	Climate Group 3 (Grand SE) *Includes rear air conditioning, rear heater, dual-zone temperature control, overhead console with trip computer, deep tinted glass.*	1020	1200
AAB	Climate Group 3 (Grand SE) *Includes rear air conditioning, rear heater, dual-zone temperature control. REQUIRES 2*N. NOT AVAILABLE with AHT.*	476	560
AAB	Climate Group 3 (Grand SE) *Includes rear air conditioning, rear heater, dual-zone temperature control. REQUIRES 2*N and AHT.*	421	495
AAC	Convenience Group 1 (Base/Base Grand) *Includes power exterior mirrors, cruise control, tilt steering wheel.*	370	435
AAE	Convenience Group 2 (Base/Base Grand) *Includes power exterior mirrors, cruise control, tilt steering wheel power door locks. REQUIRES 2*T.*	638	750
AAE	Convenience Group 2 (SE/Grand SE) *Includes power exterior mirrors, cruise control, tilt steering wheel power door locks. REQUIRES 2*B.*	268	315
AAF	Convenience Group 3 (SE/Grand SE) *Includes power exterior mirrors, cruise control, tilt steering wheel power door locks, power windows, power rear quarter vent windows.*	582	685
AAG	Convenience Group 4 (SE/Grand SE) *Includes remote keyless entry, illuminated entry and headlight-off delay feature. NOT AVAILABLE with 2*B.*	204	240
AAH	Convenience Group 5 (SE/Grand SE) *Includes remote keyless entry, illuminated entry, headlight-off delay feature, security alarm. NOT AVAILABLE with 2*B.*	332	390
AAP	Loading Group (SE/Grand SE) *Includes heavy-duty suspension and fullsize spare.*	153	180

CODE	DESCRIPTION	INVOICE	MSRP
AHT	Trailer Tow Group (Grand SE) *Includes heavy-duty suspension, heavy-duty transmission oil cooler, heavy-duty brakes, fullsize spare tire, 600-amp battery, 125-amp alternator, wiring harness. NOT AVAILABLE with 2*B.*	357	420
AWS	Smoker's Group *Includes cigar lighter and three ashtrays.*	17	20
BGF	Antilock Brakes (Base/Base Grand)	480	565
CLE	Floor Mats (SE/Grand SE) *REQUIRES 2*B.*	77	90
CYE	Seating: 7-Passenger (Base) *REQUIRES 2*S.*	319	375
CYK	Seating: 7-Passenger with Integrated Child Seats (Base/Base Grand) *REQUIRES CYE on Base. NOT AVAILABLE with 2*S.*	200	235
CYR	Seating: 7-Passenger Deluxe with Integrated Child Seats (SE/Grand SE) *REQUIRES 2*D or 2*E.*	191	225
CYS	Seating: 7-Passenger Quad Bucket Group (SE/Grand SE) *Includes premium cloth upholstery. REQUIRES 2*D or 2*E.*	570	670
CYT	Seating: 7-Psgr. Quad Bucket Group with Int. Child Seats (SE/Grand SE) *Includes premium cloth upholstery. REQUIRES 2*L or 2*N.*	106	125
CYT	Seating: 7-Psgr. Quad Bucket Group with Int. Child Seats (SE/Grand SE) *Includes premium cloth upholstery. REQUIRES 2*D or 2*E.*	676	795
DGB	Transmission: 4-Speed Automatic (Base) *NOT AVAILABLE with EDZ.*	170	200
EDZ	Engine: 2.4L DOHC I4 (Base) *REQUIRES 2*T.*	(438)	(515)
EFA	Engine: 3.0L V6 (Base)	655	770
EGA	Engine: 3.3L V6 (Base) *REQUIRES 2*T and NAE.*	825	970
EGH	Engine: 3.8L V6 (SE/Grand SE) *REQUIRES 2*N.*	285	335
EGM	Engine: 3.3L FFV V6 (Base) *NOT AVAILABLE with NAE.*	825	970
GFA	Rear Window Defroster (Base/Base Grand) *REQUIRES AAA or AAC or AAE. NOT AVAILABLE with 2*S.*	196	230
GFA	Rear Window Defroster (Base/Base Grand) *NOT AVAILABLE with AAA, AAC, AAE.*	166	195
GKD	Sliding Door: Left Side (Base)	506	595
HAA	Climate Group 1 (Base/Base Grand) *Includes air conditioning. REQUIRES 2*S.*	731	860
MDA	Front License Plate Bracket	NC	NC
MWG	Luggage Rack *NOT AVAILABLE with 2*S.*	166	195
NAE	Emissions: California *NOT AVAILABLE with EFA, EGM.*	NC	NC
NBN	Emissions: Northeastern States	NC	NC
NHK	Engine Block Heater	30	35

CODE	DESCRIPTION	INVOICE	MSRP
RAS	Radio: AM/FM with Cassette (Base/Base Grand) *REQUIRES 2*T.*	153	180
RAZ	Radio: Uplevel AM/FM with Cassette and CD (SE/Grand SE) *Includes equalizer. NOT AVAILABLE with 2*E or 2*N.*	276	325
RAZ	Radio: Uplevel AM/FM with Cassette and CD (SE/Grand SE) *Includes equalizer. REQUIRES 2*E or 2*N.*	153	180
RBR	Radio: AM/FM with CD (Base/Base Grand) *REQUIRES 2*T.*	276	325
RCE	Radio: Infinity Speaker System (SE/Grand SE) *Includes 10 Infinity loudspeakers and 200-watt amplifier. REQUIRES RAZ. NOT AVAILABLE with 2*B.*	336	395
SER	Load Leveling Suspension (Grand SE) *NOT AVAILABLE with 2*B.*	247	290
TBB	Spare Tire: Fullsize *NOT AVAILABLE with 2*S, AWA, AAP, AHT.*	94	110
WJB	Aluminum Wheels (SE/Grand SE) *NOT AVAILABLE with 2*E or 2*N.*	353	415
WJB	Aluminum Wheels (SE/Grand SE) *REQUIRES 2*E or 2*N.*	225	265
YCF	Emissions: Border States	NC	NC

1999 MONTANA

1999 Pontiac Montana

What's New?

After a ground-up redesign in 1997, the entire line gets a name change this year, from Trans Sport to Montana (the name pulled from '98's sporty trim package). Regular-wheelbase models come with one or two sliding doors, while extended wheelbase vans get two only with a right-side power sliding door option. Side-impact airbags are standard, as are 15-inch 215-70R white-letter puncture sealant tires. New two-tone paint jobs are available and four new exterior colors are offered, as are options for front-row leather seats and an overhead video system. Better still, a special sport performance package adds cast aluminum wheels, traction control and a specially tuned sport suspension for soccer dads (and moms) who are sport sedan wannabees.

Review

The difference is like night and day. Pontiac's Montana is so much better than the previous version that there is really no comparison. So forget about the bullet-nosed, plastic-bodied, Dustbuster Trans Sport of yesteryear. Pontiac is rewriting Chrysler's book on minivans.

For starters, the Montana features a standard 3.4-liter, 185-horsepower V6 (up five ponies from last year), which tops the 180 horses that Chrysler offers with its top-of-the-line optional motor. Like Chrysler, Pontiac offers driver-side sliding doors on both wheelbase sizes, but Montana adds a power option for the passenger-side door on extended wheelbase models. And Pontiac's minivan can accommodate eight-passenger seating, while Chrysler and Ford models cannot. Yes, Chrysler vans do feature roll-away bench seats, but they're heavy suckers to unload. Montana can be equipped with modular seats that weigh just 38 pounds each and are relatively easy to remove.

In the safety column, dual front and side airbags are standard, as are antilock brakes and daytime running lights that operate the parking lamps rather than the headlights. Puncture-sealant type tires and a rear window defogger are standard this year, while traction control remains optional, though it must be ordered with the automatic load leveling suspension.

The Montana performed well during federal head-on crash runs and meets current side impact standards, too. Take note, however, that it fared poorly in offset crash testing conducted by the Insurance Institute for Highway Safety (there are no federal standards governing offset crashworthiness).

The sliding door on the right side of the 120-inch wheelbase van can be equipped to open automatically with the push of a button. The ventilation system features a replaceable pollen filter, which is good news for allergy sufferers. Optional rear audio controls allow rear passengers to listen to a CD, cassette or stereo via headphones while front passengers listen to their choice of any of the three mediums simultaneously.

New this year is a sport performance and handling package that offers upgraded tires on sporty alloy wheels, a luggage rack, saddlebag storage and a sport-tuned suspension featuring automatic load leveling and traction control. Who says minivans have to be boring?

Around town, Montana feels downright spunky, with good throttle response and car-like handling. Braking is excellent for a 4,000-pound vehicle. Visibility is uncompromised, thanks in part to the huge exterior mirrors that eliminate blind spots. Front seats are quite comfortable, and most controls are easy to see and use. If it weren't for the expansive windshield and high driving position, drivers might not realize the Montana was a minivan.

Product planners claim that the Montana bridges the gap between sport/utility and minivan. While we think it takes more than body-cladding, white-letter tires, alloy wheels, fog lights and traction control to match an SUV when it comes to capability, we understand what Pontiac is doing. It's tough to stand above the crowd today amid a slew of new and improved minivan models, and a sporty, SUV-fighter theme is unique among them (but not to station wagons, right Subaru?). Give Pontiac credit for sticking with the division's performance brand image here. Montana does blur the line between minivan and sport/utility in terms of styling – but don't worry, nobody will mistake this Pontiac for a Jeep Grand Cherokee.

The Montana is well-packaged and versatile. It isn't perfect, however. If you opt for the modular seats, understand that they provide little in the way of thigh and leg support. When sitting in one of the rear chairs for an extended period, adult passengers will grow uncomfortable quickly. While the automatic sliding door is great, it doesn't behave exactly like an elevator door. Designed to reverse direction when it determines that an object is blocking its closure path, it needs a stern reminder that you are in its way. Teach children that they are strong enough to push the door back, and not to be afraid of getting squished if the door doesn't stop immediately. Other flaws include difficult-to-reach center console storage, lack of a power lock switch in the cargo area and excessive amounts of cheap-looking plastic inside.

Basically, we like Montana for its array of standard and optional features, sporty yet functional image and surprising fun-to-drive demeanor. So long as adult passengers drive or ride shotgun, Pontiac's people mover makes perfect sense.

Safety Data

Side Airbag: *Standard*
4-Wheel ABS: *Standard*
Driver Crash Test Grade: *Good*
Side Impact Crash Test Front: *Excellent*
Crash Offset: *Poor*
Integrated Child Seat(s): *Optional*
Traction Control: *Optional*
Passenger Crash Test Grade: *Average*
Side Impact Crash Test Rear: *Excellent*

Standard Equipment

3-DOOR STANDARD LENGTH (4A): 3.4L V6 OHV SMPI 12-valve engine; 4-speed electronic overdrive automatic transmission with lock-up; 600-amp battery with run down protection; 105-amp alternator; front wheel drive, 3.29 axle ratio; stainless steel exhaust; front independent strut suspension with anti-roll bar, front coil springs, rear non-independent suspension with anti-roll bar, rear coil springs; power rack-and-pinion steering with vehicle speed-sensing assist; front disc/rear drum brakes with 4 wheel antilock braking system; 20 gal capacity fuel tank; 3 doors with sliding right rear passenger door, liftback rear cargo door; front and rear body-colored bumpers with rear step; body-colored bodyside molding, body-colored bodyside cladding, rocker panel extensions; monotone paint; aero-composite halogen fully automatic headlamps with daytime running lights; additional exterior lights include front fog/driving lights, center high mounted stop light, underhood light; driver's and passenger's power remote black heated folding outside mirrors; front

CODE	DESCRIPTION	INVOICE	MSRP

and rear 15" x 6" steel wheels; P205/70TR15 BSW self-sealing AS front and rear tires; inside under cargo mounted compact steel spare wheel; air conditioning, air filter; AM/FM stereo with clock, seek-scan, 4 speakers, and window grid antenna; power door locks, child safety rear door locks, power remote hatch/trunk release; 2 power accessory outlets, driver's foot rest; instrumentation display includes tachometer, water temp gauge, volt gauge, trip odometer; warning indicators include oil pressure, water temp warning, battery, low oil level, low coolant, lights on, key in ignition, low fuel, door ajar; dual airbags, seat mounted side airbags; ignition disable; tinted windows, vented rear windows, manual 1/4 vent windows; variable intermittent front windshield wipers, fixed interval rear wiper, rear window defroster; seating capacity of 7, front bucket seats with adjustable tilt headrests, driver's and passenger's armrests, driver's seat includes 6-way direction control with lumbar support and easy entry, passenger's seat includes 4-way direction control with lumbar support; removable full folding 2nd row bench seat with adjustable rear headrests; removable 3rd row full folding bench seat with adjustable headrests; front height adjustable seatbelts with pretensioners; cloth seats, leatherette door trim insert, full cloth headliner, full carpet floor covering with carpeted floor mats; interior lights include dome light with fade, front reading lights; sport steering wheel with tilt adjustment; vanity mirrors; auto-dimming day-night rearview mirror; mini overhead console, engine cover, console with storage, locking glove box with light, front and rear cupholders, instrument panel covered bin, interior concealed storage, 2 seat back storage pockets, driver's and passenger's door bins, rear door bins, front underseat tray; carpeted cargo floor, plastic trunk lid, cargo light; body-colored grille, black side window moldings, black front windshield molding, black rear window molding and body-colored door handles.

4-DOOR STANDARD LENGTH (4A) (in addition to or instead of 3-DOOR STANDARD LENGTH (4A) equipment): Cruise control; removable 60-40 folding split-bench 2nd row seat with adjustable headrests; removable 3rd row 50-50 folding split-bench seat with adjustable headrests and cargo net.

4-DOOR EXTENDED LENGTH (4A) (in addition to or instead of 4-DOOR STANDARD LENGTH (4A) equipment): 25 gal capacity fuel tank.

Base Prices

2UN06	3-Door Passenger Van (4A)	19299	21325
2UN16	4-Door Passenger Van (4A)	20752	22930
2UM16	4-Door Extended Passenger Van (4A)	21657	23930
Destination Charge:		580	580

Accessories

—	Montana Vision (Extended) *Includes fold down liquid crystal dispay (LCD) monitor, video cassette player, remote control, video game input, six headphone outlets located in the 2nd and 3rd rows and storage for up to four video cassette tapes. REQUIRES (1SC or 1SD) and UM1.*	2310	2595
142	Leather Seat Surfaces *Includes leather-wrapped steering wheel with steering wheel mounted radio controls. REQUIRES AG1.*	939	1055
1SA	Option Package 1SA (3-Dr) *Includes vehicle with standard equipment.*	NC	NC
1SB	Option Package 1SB (4-Dr) *Includes vehicle with standard equipment.*	NC	NC
1SB	Option Package 1SB (3-Dr) *Includes convenience net, cruise control and AM/FM stereo with cassette.*	236	265

CODE	DESCRIPTION	INVOICE	MSRP
1SC	**Option Package 1SC (4-Dr)** *Includes convenience net, cruise control, AM/FM stereo with cassette, deep tinted glass, remote keyless entry, power windows with driver's express down, power rear quarter vent windows and perimeter lighting.*	690	775
1SC	**Option Package 1SC (3-Dr)** *Includes convenience net, cruise control, AM/FM stereo with cassette, deep tinted glass, remote keyless entry, power windows with driver express down, power rear quarter vent windows and perimeter lighting.*	979	1100
1SD	**Option Package 1SD (3-Dr)** *Includes convenience net, cruise control, AM/FM stereo with cassette, deep tinted glass, remote keyless entry, power windows with driver express down, power rear quarter vent windows, perimeter lighting, illuminated visor vanity mirrors, overhead console, 6-way power driver's seat and luggage rack.*	1611	1810
1SD	**Option Package 1SD (4-Dr)** *Includes convenience net, cruise control, AM/FM stereo with cassette, deep tinted glass, remote keyless entry, power windows with driver express down, power rear quarter vent windows, perimeter lighting, illuminated visor vanity mirrors, overhead console, 6-way power driver's seat and luggage rack.*	1322	1485
A31	**Power Windows with Driver's Express Down** *Includes power rear quarter vent windows. NOT AVAILABLE with 1SA.*	289	325
ABD	**7-Passenger Seating with 2nd Row Captains** *Includes 50/50 modular third row split bench.*	263	295
AG1	**6-Way Power Driver's Seat**	240	270
AG9	**6-Way Power Driver's/Passenger's Seats**	512	575
AG9	**6-Way Power Passenger's Seat** *REQUIRES 1SD.*	271	305
AJ1	**Deep Tinted Glass**	245	275
AN2	**Integrated Child Safety Seat** *Available in gray or neutral only. REQUIRES ZP8.*	111	125
AU0	**Remote Keyless Entry** *NOT AVAILABLE with 1SA.*	156	175
B4U	**Sport Performance and Handling Package (4-Dr)** *Includes 15" aluminum wheels, P215/70R15 RWOL touring tires, traction control, saddle bag storage and automatic level control suspension. REQUIRES 1SD.*	828	930
B4U	**Sport Performance and Handling Package (4-Dr)** *Includes 15" aluminum wheels, P215/70R15 RWOL touring tires, traction control, saddle bag storage and automatic level control suspension. REQUIRES 1SC.*	983	1105
C34	**Front and Rear Air Conditioning (Extended)** *NOT AVAILABLE with 1SB.*	401	450
D84	**Two Tone Paint** *W/light taupe metallic lower and available interiors. NOT AVAILABLE with ZY7.*	111	125
DK6	**Overhead Console** *REQUIRES AU0.*	156	175
E58	**Power Sliding Door** *Includes panic alarm. REQUIRES AU0 and A31. NOT AVAILABLE with 1SA.*	401	450
G67	**Automatic Level Control** *Includes saddle bag storage. NOT AVAILABLE with 1SA.*	178	200

CODE	DESCRIPTION	INVOICE	MSRP
K05	Engine Block Heater	31	35
NW9	Traction Control *REQUIRES G67. NOT AVAILABLE with 1SA.*	174	195
PH3	Wheels: 15" Aluminum *Silver painted.*	249	280
U1C	Radio: AM/FM Stereo with CD *Includes 4 speakers.*	89	100
UA6	Theft Deterrent System *REQUIRES AUO.*	53	60
UK3	Leather-Wrapped Steering Wheel *Includes steering wheel mounted radio controls. NOT AVAILABLE with 1SA.*	165	185
UM1	Radio: AM/FM Stereo with Cassette and EQ *Includes dual playback remote compact disc and extended range coaxial speakers. REQUIRES 142.*	325	365
UM1	Radio: AM/FM Stereo with Cassette, CD and EQ *Includes rear seat audio controls with jacks and extended range coaxial speakers.*	490	550
UN6	Radio: AM/FM Stereo with Cassette (3-Dr) *Includes 4 speakers.*	174	195
UP3	Radio: AM/FM Stereo with CD and EQ *Includes leather-wrapped steering wheel with steering wheel mounted radio controls, rear seat audio controls with jacks and extended range coaxial speakers.*	401	450
UP3	Radio: AM/FM Stereo with CD and EQ *Includes rear seat audio controls with jacks and extended range coaxial speakers. REQUIRES 142.*	236	265
UZ5	Extended Range Coaxial Speakers	45	50
V54	Luggage Rack	156	175
V92	Trailer Provisions (3,500 Lbs) *Includes engine oil cooler and wiring provisions. Does not include hitch. REQUIRES G67 and B4U.*	134	150
XPU	Tires: P215/70R15 Touring Blackwall *Self-sealing.*	NC	NC
ZP8	8 Passenger Seating *Includes 3 modular second row buckets and 50/50 modular third row split bench.*	249	280
ZY7	Two-Tone Paint *With charcoal metallic lower and available interiors. NOT AVAILABLE with D84.*	111	125

1999 FORESTER

1999 Subaru Forester

What's New?

This year, Forester's engine makes more torque and the automatic transmission has been improved. L and S models have longer lists of standard equipment and two new colors are available.

Review

What do you do when sport-utility buyers won't drive home in your all-wheel drive station wagon, which is dressed up like an SUV, because it looks too 'wagony'? If you're gutsy like Subaru, you put a taller, more squared-off body on your wagon chassis, and call it good. The new Forester is a Subaru parts bin exercise, and since the parts bin is rather small at Fuji Heavy Industries, which owns the upstart all-wheel drive automaker, the car is cobbled together from a mixture of Impreza and Legacy bits.

Based on the rally-proven Impreza platform, the Forester uses the same AWD system found in other Subaru models. The 2.5-liter boxer engine comes from the Legacy Outback, and makes 165 horsepower in the Forester. Torque has been increased for 1999, earning a Stage II designation for this motor. Forester has more power than its primary competitors, though Suzuki's new Grand Vitara V6 has closed the gap.

Also, thanks to its hunkered-down stance, low center of gravity and car-based foundation, the Forester handles better than the Chevrolet Tracker, Honda CR-V, Suzuki Grand Vitara and Toyota RAV4. The trade-off is lower ground clearance and less capable off-road ability, but you weren't going to go too far off the beaten path anyway, were you? (Wink, wink, nudge, nudge, know-what-I-mean?)

Inside is room for four adults, with a rear center position marked off for a fifth rider in a pinch. Cargo space is equivalent to what you'd find in the RAV4 or Tracker, and storage room abounds.

Three Forester models are available: the base, the mid-level L and the high-end S. Air conditioning, roof rack, rear defogger, tachometer, power windows, tilt steering, rear wiper/washer, and an 80-watt cassette stereo are standard on the base model. The L adds antilock brakes, power door locks and cosmetic goodies. This year, the L's standard equipment list has been expanded to include power exterior mirrors. With a base price barely over $20,000 when destination charges are included, the L is Subaru's volume seller. The uplevel S gets a toothy chrome grille, alloy wheels, bigger tires, rear disc brakes, cruise control and upgraded interior trimmings.

New to the S for 1999 is a standard All Weather Package that includes heated seats and exterior mirrors, as well as a windshield wiper de-icer. Remote keyless entry and leather is optional on the L and S. Other Forester options include CD player, alloy wheels, cruise control, trailer hitch and a variety of cosmetic upgrades. All Foresters can be painted in two new colors: Silverthorn Metallic and Aspen White.

While we are partial to the Impreza Outback Sport and Legacy Outback models, the Forester will attract buyers who want an inexpensive, functional, all-wheel drive vehicle that looks like a truck and drives like a car. As long as Subaru can keep a lid on pricing, the Forester should pick up right where the Outback wagons leave off

Safety Data

Side Airbag: *Not Available*
4-Wheel ABS: *N/A (Base); Std. (L/S)*
Driver Crash Test Grade: *Good*
Side Impact Crash Test Front: *Not Available*
Crash Offset: *Good*
Integrated Child Seat(s): *Not Available*
Traction Control: *Not Available*
Passenger Crash Test Grade: *Good*
Side Impact Crash Test Rear: *Not Available*

Standard Equipment

BASE (5M): 2.5L H4 DOHC SMPI 16-valve engine; 5-speed overdrive manual transmission; 520-amp battery; 85-amp alternator; full-time 4 wheel drive, 4.44 axle ratio; HD ride suspension, front independent strut suspension with anti-roll bar, front coil springs, rear independent strut suspension with anti-roll bar, rear coil springs; power rack-and-pinion steering with engine speed-sensing assist; front disc/rear drum brakes; 15.9 gal capacity fuel tank; liftback rear cargo door; trailer harness; roof rack; front and rear body-colored bumpers; body-colored bodyside cladding, rocker panel extensions; two-tone paint; aero-composite halogen auto off headlamps; additional exterior lights include front fog/driving lights, center high mounted stop light; driver and passenger manual black folding outside mirrors; front and rear 15" x 6" silver styled steel wheels; P205/70SR15 OWL AS front and rear tires; inside under cargo mounted full-size conventional steel spare wheel; air conditioning, rear heat ducts; AM/FM stereo with clock, seek-scan, cassette, 4 speakers, and fixed antenna; child safety rear door locks; 2 power accessory outlets, driver foot rest; instrumentation display includes tachometer, water temp gauge, trip odometer; warning indicators include oil pressure, battery, key in ignition, low fuel, door ajar, trunk ajar; dual airbags; tinted windows, power front windows with driver's 1-touch down, power rear windows, fixed 1/4 vent windows; fixed interval front windshield wipers, rear window wiper, rear window defroster; seating capacity of 5, front bucket seats with adjustable headrests, driver's seat includes 6-way direction control with lumbar support, passenger's seat includes 4-way direction control; 55-45 folding rear bench seat with reclining adjustable rear headrest; front height adjustable seatbelts; cloth seats, cloth door trim insert, full cloth headliner, full carpet floor covering; interior lights include dome light, front reading lights; steering wheel with tilt adjustment; day-night rearview mirror; full floor console, mini overhead console with storage, locking glove box with light, front and rear cupholders, instrument panel bin, driver's and passenger's door bins; carpeted cargo floor, plastic trunk lid, cargo tie downs, cargo light, cargo concealed storage; black grille, black side window moldings, black front windshield molding, black rear window molding and black door handles.

L (5M) (in addition to or instead of BASE (5M) equipment): Front disc/rear drum brakes with 4 wheel antilock braking system; front and rear mud flaps; front and rear body-colored bumpers with rear step; driver and passenger power remote black folding outside mirrors and carpeted floor mats.

CODE	DESCRIPTION	INVOICE	MSRP

S (5M) (in addition to or instead of L (5M) equipment): 4 wheel disc brakes with 4 wheel antilock braking system; power remote black driver's folding heated outside mirror; front and rear 16" x 6.5" silver alloy wheels; window grid antenna; cruise control; fixed interval heated front windshield wipers, rear window wiper, rear window defroster; heated front bucket seats with adjustable headrests, center armrest with storage; vanity mirrors; 2 seat back storage pockets and chrome grille.

Base Prices

CODE	DESCRIPTION	INVOICE	MSRP
XCA	Base (5M)	17641	18695
XCB	L (5M)	18234	19995
XCD	S (5M)	20416	22495
Destination Charge:		495	495

Accessories

CODE	DESCRIPTION	INVOICE	MSRP
—	Roof Visor	78	120
—	Transmission: 4-Speed Automatic (L/S)	719	800
BWB	Gray Carpet Floor Covers (Base)	49	75
CXC	Cruise Control - A/T (L)	221	340
CXD	Cruise Control - M/T (Base/L)	221	340
DWA	Upgraded Speakers	127	195
DWB	Subwoofer/Amplifier	202	310
DXB	Tweeter Kit (Pair)	65	100
EWB	CD Player	315	420
EWC	CD Auto Changer *Includes CD controller and multi-purpose tray.*	517	689
HWA	Alloy Wheels (Base/L) *Includes attachment set: 15" aluminum wheel valve and 15" aluminum wheel cap.*	447	595
IWC	Leather-Wrapped Shift Knob - M/T	30	45
IWD	Leather-Wrapped Shift Knob - A/T (Base/L)	49	75
IWE	Beige Leather Seats (L/S)	975	1295
IWF	Gray Leather Seats (L/S)	975	1295
IWG	Woodgrain Trim Kit - A/T (L/S)	130	199
IWH	Woodgrain Trim Kit - M/T (L/S)	130	199
KWA	Air Filter *Includes air filter cover.*	56	85
KWB	Beige Armrest Extension (L/S)	58	89
KWC	Gray Armrest Extension	58	89
LWB	Custom Tail Pipe Cover	26	39
LWC	Rear Window Dust Deflector	72	110
LWD	Splash Guards (Base)	64	98
LWG	Trailer Hitch	192	295
MSV	Wheel Locks	18	34
MWA	Rear Cargo Net	27	41
MWD	Rear Cargo Tray (Base)	47	73
NWC	Gauge Pack (L/S) *Includes beige gauge pack housing.*	296	395

CODE	DESCRIPTION	INVOICE	MSRP
NWD	Gauge Pack *Includes gray gauge pack housing.*	296	395
NWE	Dual Power Outlet Socket (Base/L)	58	88
OWA	Beige Luggage Compartment Cover (L/S)	80	122
OWB	Gray Luggage Compartment Cover	80	122
PWD	Side Underguard Bar	228	350
PWE	Brush Guard	282	375
PWF	Bumper Cover (Base)	40	61
RWA	Keyless Entry System (L/S)	146	225
RWB	Security System Upgrade Kit (L/S)	82	125
TVB	Rear Differential Protector	104	159

1999 GRAND VITARA

1999 Suzuki Grand Vitara

What's New?

The Grand Vitara is a completely new design from Suzuki. Based on the slightly smaller Vitara, the Grand Vitara offers plenty of passenger room and a standard V6 engine.

Review

In creating the Grand Vitara, Suzuki has "raised the bar" by offering a standard V6 engine in the mini sport-ute class. This all-new, 2.5-liter V6 makes 155 horsepower and 160 pound-feet of torque. Even more impressive is that this maximum torque figure is reached at a relatively low 4,000 rpm, providing drivers with plenty of go-power even under real-world conditions. Harnessing those 155 horses is either a five-speed manual or four-speed automatic.

A monster engine isn't all that the Grand Vitara has to offer. Suzuki wanted to take expectations in the small sport-utility segment to the next level. This meant including a long list of standard features like air conditioning, power windows, keyless entry and daytime running lights.

Styling is another area where the Grand Vitara has gone its own way. The use of flush-surface design techniques has reduced the variance between windows and body panels to almost nil, cutting wind noise and creating a dramatic look. A chrome grille, body-side cladding, and an available two-tone paint scheme accent the overall wedge shape of the Grand Vitara.

Underneath the skin is an all-new chassis featuring a steel ladder box frame. A five-link coil spring suspension in back and independent MacPherson strut coil springs up front are designed to deal with on- or off-road activity. Power-assisted rack-and-pinion steering is standard, as are 16-inch wheels with 235/65R-16 all-season tires.

The Grand Vitara is available in either two- or four-wheel drive configurations, each with two trim levels. Upgraded models (JS+ and JLX+) come standard with ABS and alloy wheels.

The enthusiasm with which Suzuki has re-entered the mini-SUV class shows how serious the company is about attracting customers. With the only six-cylinder currently available to "cute-ute" buyers, the strategy will probably work.

Safety Data

Side Airbag: *Not Available*
4-Wheel ABS: *Standard (+); N/A (JS/JLX)*
Driver Crash Test Grade: *Not Available*
Side Impact Crash Test Front: *Not Available*
Crash Offset: *Acceptable*
Integrated Child Seat(s): *Not Available*
Traction Control: *Not Available*
Passenger Crash Test Grade: *Not Available*
Side Impact Crash Test Rear: *Not Available*

Standard Equipment

JS 2WD (5M): 2.5L V6 DOHC MPI 24-valve engine; 5-speed overdrive manual transmission; rear wheel drive, 4.3 axle ratio; partial stainless steel exhaust; front independent strut suspension with anti-roll bar, front coil springs, rigid rear axle multi-link suspension with rear coil springs; power rack-and-pinion steering; front disc/rear drum brakes; 17.4 gal. capacity fuel tank; skid plates; conventional rear cargo door; roof rack; front and rear body-colored bumpers with front and rear tow hooks, rear step; body-colored bodyside cladding, rocker panel extensions, body-colored fender flares; monotone paint; aero-composite halogen auto on headlamps with daytime running lights; additional exterior lights include center high mounted stop light; driver's and passenger's power remote body-colored folding outside mirrors; front and rear 16" x 7" silver styled steel wheels; P235/60SR16 BSW AS front and rear tires; outside rear mounted full-size conventional steel spare wheel; air conditioning, air filter, rear heat ducts; premium AM/FM stereo with clock, seek-scan, cassette, 4 speakers, and fixed antenna; cruise control; power door locks, remote keyless entry, child safety rear door locks, remote fuel release; 2 power accessory outlets; instrumentation display includes tachometer, water temp gauge, trip odometer; warning indicators include oil pressure, water temp warning, battery, key in ignition, low fuel; dual airbags; tinted windows, power front windows with driver's 1-touch down, power rear windows, fixed 1/4 vent windows; variable intermittent front windshield wipers, rear window wiper, rear window defroster; seating capacity of 5, front bucket seats with adjustable headrests, driver's seat includes 4-way direction control, passenger's seat includes 4-way direction control; 50-50 folding rear bench seat with adjustable rear headrest; front height adjustable seatbelts with front pretensioners; cloth seats, cloth door trim insert, full headliner, full carpet floor covering; interior lights include dome light, front reading lights; sport steering wheel with tilt adjustment; dual auxiliary visors, passenger's side vanity mirror; day-night rearview mirror; full floor console, locking glove box, front cupholder, 2 seat back storage pockets, driver's and passenger's door bins, rear door bins, front underseat tray; carpeted cargo floor, plastic trunk lid, cargo tie downs, cargo light; chrome grille, black side window moldings, black front windshield molding, black rear window molding and black door handles.

JS+ 2WD (5M) (in addition to or instead of JS 2WD (5M) equipment): Front disc/rear drum brakes with 4 wheel antilock braking system and front and rear 16" x 7" 5-spoke aluminum alloy wheels.

JLX 4WD (5M) (in addition to or instead of JS 2WD (5M) equipment): Part-time 4 wheel drive with auto locking hub control and manual shift.

JLX+ 4WD (5M) (in addition to or instead of JLX 4WD (5M) equipment): Front disc/rear drum brakes with 4 wheel antilock braking system and front and rear 16" x 7" 5-spoke aluminum alloy wheels.

Base Prices

CODE	DESCRIPTION	INVOICE	MSRP
LFN86FX	JS 2WD (5M)	16559	17999
LFN86TX	JS+ 2WD (5M)	17479	18999

CODE	DESCRIPTION	INVOICE	MSRP
LJN86FX	JLX 4WD (5M)	17479	18999
LJN86TX	JLX+ 4WD (5M)	18399	19999
Destination Charge:		430	430

Accessories

—	Transmission: 4-Speed Automatic *Includes driving mode switch (Power/Normal.).*	920	1000

1999 VITARA

1999 Suzuki Vitara

What's New?

The Vitara is an all-new model that replaces the Sidekick as Suzuki's entry into the mini SUV class.

Review

Watching the mini SUV class become increasingly crowded with entries from Toyota (RAV4), Honda (CR-V) and Kia (Sportage), Suzuki decided it was time to stir things up with a completely new mini-ute to replace the aging Sidekick.

The all-new Vitara enters this arena with bold styling, a rigid chassis and advanced suspension components. Available as either a two-door convertible or a four-door model, this new Suzuki boasts a long list of standard features plus several luxury options.

The two-door, soft-top Vitara comes standard with a 1.6-liter, 16-valve engine that makes 97 horsepower and 103 pound-feet of torque. An optional all-aluminum, 2.0-liter engine can be ordered which bumps horsepower to 127 and maximum torque to 134. The four-door Vitara comes standard with the larger engine, which uses a Direct Drive Valvetrain (DDV) for increased throttle response and lower fuel consumption.

Both the convertible and four-door models can be ordered in two- or four-wheel drive. An independent MacPherson strut front suspension and five-link coil spring rear suspension is used throughout the Vitara line and all models come with a five-speed manual transmission, an Alpine AM/FM/cassette sound system, dual airbags, and daytime running lights. Options include air conditioning, alloy wheels, power windows, and a four-speed automatic. Surprisingly, ABS is not available.

With it's creative look, powerful engine, and roomy interior, the Vitara offers a competition package that may take a bite out of RAV4 and CR-V sales.

Safety Data

Side Airbag: *Not Available*
4-Wheel ABS: *Not Available*
Driver Crash Test Grade: *Not Available*
Side Impact Crash Test Front: *Not Available*
Crash Offset: *Acceptable*
Integrated Child Seat(s): *Not Available*
Traction Control: *Not Available*
Passenger Crash Test Grade: *Not Available*
Side Impact Crash Test Rear: *Not Available*

Standard Equipment

2-DOOR JS 1.6 CONVERTIBLE 2WD (5M): 1.6L I4 SOHC MPI 16-valve engine; 5-speed overdrive manual transmission; 390-amp battery; 60-amp alternator; rear wheel drive, 5.13 axle ratio; partial stainless steel exhaust; front independent strut suspension with anti-roll bar, front coil springs, rigid rear axle multi-link suspension with rear coil springs; power rack-and-pinion steering; front disc/rear drum brakes; 14.8 gal. capacity fuel tank; conventional rear cargo door; manual convertible roof with roll-over protection; front and rear body-colored bumpers with front and rear tow hooks, rear step; monotone paint; aero-composite halogen auto on headlamps with daytime running lights; additional exterior lights include center high mounted stop light; driver's and passenger's manual black folding outside mirrors; front and rear 15" x 5.5" silver styled steel wheels; P195/75SR15 BSW AS front and rear tires; outside rear mounted full-size conventional steel spare wheel; premium AM/FM stereo with clock, seek-scan, cassette, 2 speakers, and manual retractable antenna; 1 power accessory outlet; instrumentation display includes tachometer, water temp gauge, trip odometer; warning indicators include oil pressure, water temp, battery, key in ignition, low fuel; dual airbags; tinted windows; variable intermittent front windshield wipers; seating capacity of 4, front bucket seats with adjustable headrests, driver's seat includes 4-way direction control with easy entry, passenger's seat includes 4-way direction control with easy entry; full folding rear bench seat; front height adjustable seatbelts with front pretensioners; cloth seats, full carpet floor covering; interior lights include dome light, front reading lights; sport steering wheel with tilt adjustment; dual auxiliary visors, passenger's side vanity mirror; day-night rearview mirror; full floor console, glove box, front cupholder, 2 seat back storage pockets, driver's and passenger's door bins; carpeted cargo floor, plastic trunk lid; body-colored grille, black side window moldings, black front windshield molding and black door handles.

2-DOOR JS 2.0 2WD CONVERTIBLE (5M) (in addition to or instead 2-DOOR JS 1.6 CONVERTIBLE 2WD (5M) equipment): 2.0L I4 DOHC MPI 16-valve engine; 550-amp battery; 70-amp alternator; 4.63 axle ratio; driver's and passenger's power remote black folding outside mirrors; front and rear 16" x 6.5" silver styled steel wheels; P215/65SR16 BSW AS front and rear tires; tinted windows, power front windows and 50-50 folding rear bench seat.

4-DOOR JS 2WD (5M) (in addition to or instead of 2-DOOR JS 2.0 CONVERTIBLE 2WD (5M) equipment): 17.4 gal. capacity fuel tank; roof rack; body-colored bodyside molding; driver's and passenger's manual body-colored folding outside mirrors; rear heat ducts; premium AM/FM stereo with clock, seek-scan, cassette, 4 speakers, and manual retractable antenna; child safety rear door locks; tinted windows, manual rear windows, fixed 1/4 vent windows; variable intermittent front windshield wipers, rear window wiper, rear window defroster; seating capacity of 5, front sports seats with adjustable headrests, driver's seat includes 4-way direction control, passenger's seat includes 4-way direction control; 50-50 folding rear bench seat with adjustable headrests; cloth door trim insert, full headliner; locking glove box and cargo light.

4-DOOR JS+ 2WD (5M) (in addition to or instead of 4-DOOR JS 2WD (5M) equipment): Driver's and passenger's power remote body-colored folding outside mirrors; air conditioning; cruise control; power door locks, remote keyless entry, power front windows and power rear windows.

2-DOOR JX 1.6 4WD CONVERTIBLE (5M) (in addition to or instead 2-DOOR JS 1.6 CONVERTIBLE 2WD (5M) equipment): Part-time 4 wheel drive, auto locking hub control with manual shift; skid plates and P205/75SR15 BSW AS front and rear tires.

2-DOOR JX 2.0 4WD CONVERTIBLE (5M) (in addition to or instead of 2-DOOR JS 2.0 4WD CONVERTIBLE (5M) equipment): Part-time 4 wheel drive, auto locking hub control with manual shift.

4-DOOR JX 4WD (5M) (in addition to or instead of 4-DOOR JS 2WD (5M) equipment): Part-time 4 wheel drive, auto locking hub control with manual shift.

4-DOOR JX+ 4WD (5M) (in addition to or instead of 4-DOOR JX+ 4WD (5M) equipment): Part-time 4 wheel drive, auto locking hub control with manual shift.

Base Prices

CODE	DESCRIPTION	INVOICE	MSRP
FME66CX	JS 1.6 Convertible 2WD (5M)	12959	13499
FME83FX	JS 2.0 Convertible 2WD (5M)	13727	14299
LLN83CX	JS 4-Door 2WD (5M)	14475	15399
LLN83FX	JS+ 4-Door 2WD (5M)	15415	16399
FGE66CX	JX 1.6 Convertible 4WD (5M)	14381	15299
FGE83FX	JX 2.0 Convertible 4WD (5M)	15133	16099
LKN83CX	JX 4-Door 4WD (5M)	15639	16999
LKN83FX	JX+ 4-Door 4WD (5M)	16559	17999
Destination Charge:		420	420

Accessories

CODE	DESCRIPTION	INVOICE	MSRP
—	Transmission: 4 Speed Automatic (Convertible - JS/JX) *Includes power/normal driving mode switch.*	940	1000
—	Transmission: 4-Speed Automatic (4-Door - JX/JX+) *Includes power/normal driving mode switch.*	920	1000
—	Transmission: 4-Speed Automatic (4-Door - JS/JS+) *Includes power/normal driving mode switch.*	960	1000

CODE	DESCRIPTION	INVOICE	MSRP

1999 4RUNNER

1999 Toyota 4Runner

What's New?

The 4Runner receives a number of upgrades this year, starting with a new and improved four-wheel drive system equipped with a center differential and featuring a full-time 4WD mode in addition to the current two-high, four-high and four-low modes. New exterior features include a front bumper redesign, multi-reflector headlamps, and an enhanced sport package with fender flares and a hood scoop on the SR5 model. Inside, a new center console/cupholder design will improve beverage-carrying capacity of the 4Runner and an automatic climate control system will be featured on the Limited models.

Review

In 1996, Toyota separated this high-volume SUV from its pickup truck roots. Thus, the current 4Runner shares little with the Tacoma pickup. As a result, engineers have created a refined vehicle without sacrificing tough off-road ability. Generous suspension travel and tread width provide capable off-road ability, ride and handling. The interior is quite roomy, thanks to a wheelbase that is two inches longer than the previous version. A low floor and wide doors make getting into and out of the 4Runner less of an exercise in contortionism than those riding in Jeep Cherokees or Nissan Pathfinders are likely to experience.

Two engines are available on the 4Runner: a 2.7-liter inline four cylinder that makes 150 horsepower at 4800 rpm and 177 foot-pounds of torque at 4000 rpm; and a 3.4-liter V6, producing 183 horsepower at 4800 rpm and 217 foot-pounds of torque at 3600 rpm. In fact, the 2.7-liter four is nearly as powerful as the base engine found in the Ford Explorer XL.

Needless to say, all of this adds up to a competitive sport-ute. Safety isn't ignored in the 4Runner, either, which sports dual airbags and standard antilock brakes on V6 models. (Antilock brakes are optional on four-cylinder models.)

Overall, the 4Runner is a nice truck which provides the sophistication that we have come to expect from Toyota products with the overall ruggedness more often associated with Jeeps. Prices are high, however, landing the 4Runner Limited right smack dab in Mercedes-Benz ML320, and Jeep Grand Cherokee Limited territory. The competition in this segment is getting fierce and there are plenty of good choices for your money, definitely something worth considering when shelling out such a large chunk of change.

Safety Data

Side Airbag: *Not Available*
Integrated Child Seat(s): *Not Available*
4-Wheel ABS: *Optional (4-Cyl), Standard (V6)*
Traction Control: *Not Available*
Driver Crash Test Grade: *Good*
Passenger Crash Test Grade: *Excellent*
Side Impact Crash Test Front: *Excellent*
Side Impact Crash Test Rear: *Excellent*
Crash Offset: *Acceptable*

Standard Equipment

BASE 2WD (5M) : 2.7L I4 DOHC MPI 16-valve engine; 5-speed overdrive manual transmission; engine oil cooler; rear wheel drive, 3.73 axle ratio; stainless steel exhaust; front independent double wishbone suspension with anti-roll bar, front coil springs, rigid rear axle multi-link suspension with anti-roll bar, rear coil springs; power rack-and-pinion steering with engine speed-sensing assist; front disc/rear drum brakes; 18.5 gal capacity fuel tank; front and rear mud flaps, skid plates; liftback rear cargo door; front and rear black bumpers with rear tow hooks and rear step; monotone paint; aero-composite halogen headlamps; additional exterior lights include center high mounted stop light; driver's and passenger's manual black folding outside mirrors; front and rear 15" x 7" silver styled steel wheels; P225/75SR15 BSW M&S front and rear tires; underbody mounted full-size conventional steel spare wheel; AM/FM stereo with seek-scan, cassette, 4 speakers, and fixed antenna; child safety rear door locks, remote fuel release; 2 power accessory outlets, driver's foot rest; instrumentation display includes tachometer, water temp gauge, trip odometer; warning indicators include oil pressure, battery, lights on, key in ignition, low fuel, door ajar, trunk ajar; dual airbags; tinted windows, manual rear windows, fixed 1/4 vent windows; fixed interval front windshield wipers, power rear window; seating capacity of 5, front bucket seats with adjustable headrests, center armrest with storage, driver's seat includes 4-way direction control, passenger's seat includes 4-way direction control; 50-50 folding rear bench seat with adjustable rear headrest; front height adjustable seatbelts; cloth seats, cloth door trim insert, full cloth headliner, full carpet floor covering; interior lights include dome light; passenger side vanity mirror; day-night rearview mirror; full floor console, locking glove box, front and rear cupholders, instrument panel bin, 2 seat back storage pockets, driver's and passenger's door bins, rear door bins; carpeted cargo floor, plastic trunk lid, cargo tie downs, cargo light; black grille, black side window moldings, black front windshield molding, black rear window molding and black door handles.

BASE 4WD (5M) (in addition to or instead of BASE 2WD (5M) equipment): Part-time 4 wheel drive, auto locking hub control with manual shift and 4.1 axle ratio.

SR5 V6 2WD (4A) (in addition to or instead of BASE 2WD (5M) equipment): 3.4L V6 DOHC SMPI 24-valve engine; 4-speed electronic overdrive automatic transmission with lock-up; front disc/rear drum brakes with 4 wheel antilock braking system; front and rear chrome bumpers with rear tow hooks and rear step; driver's and passenger's power remote body-colored folding outside mirrors; power retractable antenna; instrumentation display includes in-dash clock; deep tinted windows; variable intermittent front windshield wipers, power rear tailgate window, fixed interval rear wiper, rear window defroster; interior lights include front reading lights; steering wheel with tilt adjustment; locking glove box with light and chrome grille.

SR5 V6 4WD (5M) (in addition to or instead of SR5 V6 2WD (4A) equipment): Five-speed overdrive manual transmission; part-time 4 wheel drive, auto locking hub control with manual shift and 3.91 axle ratio.

LIMITED V6 2WD (4A) (in addition to or instead of SR5 V6 2WD (4A) equipment): 4.1 axle ratio; front and rear mud flaps, running boards, skid plates; body-colored bodyside insert, colored bodyside cladding, body-colored fender flares; two-tone paint; front and rear 16" x 7" silver alloy wheels, P265/70R 16 BSW M&S front and rear tires; underbody mounted full-size temporary steel spare wheel; air conditioning; premium AM/FM stereo with seek-scan, single CD, 6 speakers, graphic equalizer, theft deterrent, and power retractable diversity antenna; cruise control; retained accessory power; power front windows with driver's 1-touch down, power rear windows; front sports seats with adjustable tilt headrests, center armrest with storage, driver's seat includes 6-way power seat with power lumbar support, passenger's seat includes 4-way power seat; leather seats, leather door trim insert; wood trim; leather-wrapped steering wheel with tilt adjustment and passenger side illuminated vanity mirror.

LIMITED V6 4WD (4A) (in addition to or instead of LIMITED V6 2WD (4A) equipment): HD battery; engine oil cooler, HD starter; part-time 4 wheel drive, auto locking hub control with manual shift and 4.1 axle ratio.

Base Prices

CODE	DESCRIPTION	INVOICE	MSRP
8641	Base 2WD (5M)	18365	20978
8657	Base 4WD (5M)	20256	23138
8642	SR5 V6 2WD (4A)	22165	25318
8665	SR5 V6 4WD (5M)	23171	26468
8648	Limited V6 2WD (4A)	29152	33298
8668	Limited V6 4WD (4A)	31227	35668
Destination Charge:		420	420

Accessories

CODE	DESCRIPTION	INVOICE	MSRP
—	Southeast Toyota Administrative Fee *REQUIRED on models purchased in the following states: Alabama, Florida, Georgia, North Carolina and South Carolina.*	325	325
—	Southeast Toyota Destination Charge *REQUIRED on models purchased in the following states: Alabama, Florida, Georgia, North Carolina and South Carolina.*	55	55
—	Transmission: 4-Speed Automatic (SR5 4WD)	788	900
—	Transmission: 4-Speed Automatic (Base 2WD) *Includes 3.91 axle ratio.*	788	900
—	Transmission: 4-Speed Automatic (Base 4WD)	788	900
AA	Wheels: 16" Aluminum with Rear Differential Lock (SR5 4WD) *Includes P265/70R16 MS BSW tires, large wheel arch moldings and 4.30 rear differential.*	1065	1320
AB	Antilock Braking System (Base) *Includes 4 wheel ABS.*	507	590
AC	Air Conditioning (All Except Limited)	788	985
AK	4Runner Graphic (All Except Limited)	47	79
AW	Wheels: 16" Aluminum (All Except Limited 4WD) *Includes P265/60R16 tires, 13" brakes, large chrome wheel arch molding and 4.30 rear differential. REQUIRES AB.*	784	980
AY	Wheels: 15" Aluminum (All Except Limited) *Includes P225/75R15 tires.*	292	365
BM	Body Side Molding	89	139
BN	Black Pearl Emblems (Base)	137	206
BN	Black Pearl Emblems (All Except Base)	139	209
C1	Cargo Mat	43	72

CODE	DESCRIPTION	INVOICE	MSRP
C7	Discount Convenience Package *Includes rear window deflector, roof rack, towing hitch receiver and cargo mat.*	427	669
C9	Exterior Package (All Except Limited) *Includes chrome running boards and fender flares.*	510	845
CD	Tonneau Cover (All Except Limited)	72	90
CE	Radio: Premium AM/FM Stereo with Cassette (SR5) *Includes 6 speakers and power diversity antenna.*	257	335
CF	Carpeted Floor Mats (4 Piece Set) (All Except Limited)	50	83
CK	All Weather Guard Package (All Except Limited) *Includes HD battery, HD starter, HD windshield wiper motor, and large window wiper reservoir. REQUIRES RH or GH.*	59	70
CL	Cruise Control (Base)	200	250
CR	Chrome Running Boards (All Except Limited)	284	470
DC	Radio: Premium AM/FM Stereo 3-In-1 Combo (SR5) *Includes AM/FM stereo with cassette, CD player, 6 speakers and power diversity antenna.*	467	615
DC	Radio: Premium AM/FM Stereo 3-In-1 Combo (Limited) *Includes AM/FM stereo with cassette, CD player, 6 speakers and power diversity antenna.*	135	180
DD	Rear Window Deflector	71	118
DH	Towing Hitch Receiver	215	305
DL	Rear Differential Lock (4WD)	281	340
DR	Roof Rack	165	275
DU	Walnut Wood Dash (All Except Limited)	405	610
DV	Radio: Premium AM/FM Stereo with CD (SR5) *Includes 6 speakers and power diversity antenna.*	332	435
EL	Elite Package (All Except Limited) *Includes carpeted floor mats (4 piece set), walnut wood dash and gold package.*	599	899
ET	Black Elite Package (All Except Limited) *Includes black pearl emblems, carpeted floor mats (4 piece set) and walnut wood dash.*	581	889
FN	Fender Flares (All Except Limited 4WD)	226	375
FO	Chrome Brushguard/Grilleguard	455	760
FP	Black Brushguard/Grilleguard	385	645
FS	Sport Seat Package (SR5) *Includes cloth door trim and leather-wrapped steering wheel.*	332	415
GH	Upgrade Value Package #1 (Base) *Includes tilt steering wheel, variable intermittent windshield wipers, digital clock, intermittent rear window wiper, rear defroster, map lights, air conditioning, power package: power windows with 1-touch down, power door locks, power mirrors, passenger illuminated visor vanity mirror, power antenna, digital clock, keyless entry, power mirrors (black); cruise control and carpet floor mats.*	2356	2618
GI	Upgrade Value Package #2 (SR5) *Includes cruise control, power mirrors, passenger illuminated visor vanity mirror, keyless entry, premium AM/FM stereo with cassette, power diversity antenna and carpet floor mats.*	1425	1583

CODE	DESCRIPTION	INVOICE	MSRP
GJ	Upgrade Value Package #3 (SR5) *Includes upgrade value package #2: cruise control, power mirrors, passenger illuminated visor vanity mirror, keyless entry, premium AM/FM stereo with cassette, power diversity antenna and carpet floor mats; sport seat package: 6-way manual sport seat, leather-wrapped steering wheel and 15" aluminum wheels.*	2037	2263
GK	Upgrade Value Package #4 (SR5) *Includes upgrade value package #2: cruise control, power mirrors, passenger illuminated visor vanity mirror, keyless entry, premium AM/FM stereo with cassette, power diversity antenna and carpet floor mats, sport seat package: 6-way manual sport seat, leather-wrapped steering wheel, 16" aluminum wheels, P265/70R16 tires, large wheel arch molding, 13" brakes and 4.1 rear differential.*	2397	2663
GL	Upgrade Value Package #5 (Limited) *Includes power tilt & slide moonroof, premium 3-in-1 combo radio and 6 speakers.*	445	495
GN	Cargo Net	27	42
GP	Gold Package (All Except Limited)	149	224
GP	Gold Package (Limited)	215	323
GU	Upgrade Value Package #6 (SR5) *Includes upgrade value package #4: cruise control, power mirrors, passenger illuminated visor vanity mirror, keyless entry, premium AM/FM stereo with cassette, power diversity antenna, carpet floor mats, sport seat package: 6-way manual sport seat and leather-wrapped steering wheel; 16" aluminum wheels, P265/70R16 tires, large wheel arch molding, 13" brakes and 4.1 rear differential.*	2703	3003
HP	Hood Protector	55	89
KE	Keyless Entry System *REQUIRES PO.*	149	229
LA	Leather Package (SR5) *Includes 6-way leather trimmed sport seat, leather-wrapped steering wheel and leather door trim.*	1000	1250
LF	Fog Lights	155	260
LJ	Fog Lights For Grilleguard	115	190
P3	Toyota 3 Disc CD Changer	449	641
P4	Auto Reverse Cassette Deck *REQUIRES DV. NOT AVAILABLE with DC.*	162	231
P5	Compact Disc Deck	235	335
P9	6 Disc CD Autochanger	385	550
PG	Privacy Glass (Base) *Gray window glass on rear doors, rear quarter panels and back window.*	248	310
PN	Anti-Theft Device (SR5) *Anti-theft system and immobilizer. REQUIRES GI or GJ or GK or PO.*	256	320
PO	Power Package (Base) *Includes power windows with driver's 1-touch down, power door locks, power mirrors, passenger illuminated visor vanity mirror, power antenna, digital clock and keyless entry.*	1028	1285
PO	Power Package (SR5) *Includes power door locks and digital clock, power mirrors, passenger illuminated visor vanity mirror, power antenna and keyless entry.*	540	675
RB	Black Running Boards (All Except Limited)	209	345

CODE	DESCRIPTION	INVOICE	MSRP
RH	Rear Heater *Rear heating unit and rear console box with dual cupholders.*	136	170
RW	Intermittent Rear Window Wiper (Base) *Includes rear window defogger. NOT AVAILABLE with GH.*	308	385
SD	Sunroof Wind Deflector (SR5/Limited)	33	55
SP	Sport Package (SR5) *Includes hood scoop, 13" brakes, 5-spoke aluminum wheels, 4.10 rear differential, sport seat package: 6-way manual sport seat, leather-wrapped steering wheel; fog lamps, color keyed bumpers, color keyed grille and black fender flares.*	1116	1395
SR	Power Moonroof (SR5/Limited) *NOT AVAILABLE with DC.*	652	815
SV	Wheels: 16" Steel (Base) *Includes 13" brakes and 4.30 rear differential. REQUIRES AB.*	480	600
SX	Sport Package with Rear Differential Lock (SR5 4WD) *Includes sport package: P265/70R16 MS BSW tires, 5-spoke aluminum wheels, sport seat package: 6-way manual sport seat, leather-wrapped steering wheel; fog lamps, color keyed bumpers, color keyed grille, black fender flares and 4.30 rear differential.*	1397	1735
TW	Tilt Steering Wheel (Base) *Includes variable intermittent windshield wipers.*	209	245
V1	V.I.P. S1000 Base Security System (Base)	99	149
V3	V.I.P. RS3000 Deluxe Security System *REQUIRES PO.*	249	399
WL	Alloy Wheel Locks *REQUIRES AY or AW or SP or AA or SX.*	31	52
WS	Steel Wheel Locks (All Except Limited)	31	52

NOTE: Toyotas sold in Alabama, Florida, Georgia, North Carolina and South Carolina may be equipped with option packages not listed in this guide. You can expect to haggle 25% off the window sticker price of these packages.

1999 LAND CRUISER

1999 Toyota Land Cruiser

What's New?

The Land Cruiser was reintroduced in '98 with major upgrades. As such, it enters '99 completely unchanged.

Review

Back in 1958, Toyota brought a truck named BJ to U.S. shores, called it a Land Cruiser, and sold it in droves. Now into its 5th generation, Toyota's popular sport-utility vehicle features a 4.7-liter 32-valve DOHC V8 engine. This makes it the first Toyota to be powered by a V8. The engine produces 230 horsepower, 18 more than the last generation's six-cylinder engine, and 320 foot-pounds of torque, an increase of 45 over the '97 model. Toyota executives say that the new Land Cruiser is "larger, stronger and heavier" than the previous generation truck; it is also supposed to produce lower emissions, be more fuel efficient than its predecessor and offer increased luxury options.

The redesigned chassis and suspension resulted in a 50 percent increase in structural rigidity, making the SUV more comfortable, more durable and less noisy. Inside the Land Cruiser, you'll find more room in both length and width, larger door openings, more cup holders, an overhead console featuring three storage compartments and an eyeglass holder/garage door opener compartment. There are also front and rear door pockets and separate compartments for first aid and tool kits.

Other luxury options include power moonroof, leather seats, roof rack, locking differential and a third seat. Stylistically, Toyota has thrown out their old color options save Black, and offers this year's vehicle in Natural White, River Rock Green Metallic, Champagne Pearl, Mahogany Pearl, Desert Bronze, Imperial Jade Mica and Atlantis Blue Mica.

It seems the newest version of the Land Cruiser is expanding its reputation as a luxury sport-utility vehicle in all areas, and this year, it's got the power to prove it.

Safety Data

Side Airbag: *Not Available*
4-Wheel ABS: *Standard*
Driver Crash Test Grade: *Not Available*
Integrated Child Seat(s): *Not Available*
Traction Control: *Not Available*
Passenger Crash Test Grade: *Not Available*

CODE	DESCRIPTION	INVOICE	MSRP

Side Impact Crash Test Front: *Not Available* Side Impact Crash Test Rear: *Not Available*
Crash Offset: *Not Available*

Standard Equipment

LAND CRUISER (4A): 4.7L 32-valve DOHC V8 engine, 4-speed automatic overdrive transmission, full-time four-wheel drive, power four-wheel disc brakes with load sensing proportioning valve, antilock brakes, power rack and pinon steering, front double wishbone independent suspension with lower torsion bar, rigid rear full-floating axle suspension with control arms, stabilizer bar and four-link coil springs, locking center differential, 16" silver alloy wheels, P275/70R16 tires, front and rear tow hooks, fender flares, front and rear mud guards, chrome grille, chrome front bumper, color-keyed body trim, color-keyed exterior mirrors, color-keyed door handles, auto-off headlights with daytime running, tinted glass, power heated exterior mirrors, variable intermittent windshield wipers, rear window intermittent wiper, rear window defogger, dual front airbags, three-point seatbelts, AM/FM stereo with cassette, CD, digital clock, engine immobilizer, cloth front bucket seats with power reclining and adjustable headrests, power windows, power door locks, air conditioning with climate control, front and rear heaters, tilt steering wheel, cruise control, passenger's illuminated visor vanity mirror, full floor carpet, gauge cluster with tachometer, fuel, coolant temp., oil pressure, voltmeter, and trip meter, three 12-volt power outlets, remote fuel door opener, remote trunk/hatch release, front and rear cupholders, overhead console with storage, door pockets, tool kit, first aid kit.

Base Prices

Code	Description	Invoice	MSRP
6156	Base Land Cruiser (4A)	39973	46478
Destination Charge:		420	420

Accessories

Code	Description	Invoice	MSRP
—	Southeast Toyota Administrative Fee *REQUIRED on models purchased in the following states: Alabama, Florida, Georgia, North Carolina and South Carolina.*	325	325
—	Southeast Toyota Destination Charge *REQUIRED on models purchased in the following states: Alabama, Florida, Georgia, North Carolina and South Carolina.*	55	55
AC	Rear Air Conditioning *Includes automatic climate control. REQUIRES TH.*	456	570
DL	Locking Rear Differential	355	430
LA	Leather Trim Package *Includes leather seat trim and leather door panel inserts. REQUIRES TH.*	1456	1820
SR	Power Moonroof *Includes overhead console and jam protection.*	924	1155
TH	Third Seat *Includes split-folding and removable third seat, child lock on trunk/hatch door, three-point third row seatbelts, power swing-out quarter windows, ashtray, passenger assist grips, and cupholders.*	936	1135

NOTE: Toyotas sold in Alabama, Florida, Georgia, North Carolina and South Carolina may be equipped with option packages not listed in this guide. You can expect to haggle 25% off the window sticker price of these packages.

1999 RAV4

1999 Toyota RAV4

What's New?

Toyota promises minor upgrades for it's mini-SUV in '99. Leather seats and color-keyed body cladding are now available as part or the "L Special Edition" package. Color-keyed mirrors and door handles can also be had this year and the spare tire is now a full-size steel wheel with a soft cover.

Review

The mini-SUV business continues to grow with more manufacturers jumping into the fray every year. Largely comprised of car-based AWD vehicles, this new market will gain even more entrants soon as Ford, Land Rover, and Mercedes introduce small trucklets to the US. One of the early players in the game was Toyota, which recognized this potential boom early on and jumped into the action in 1996 with the RAV4.

A 2.0-liter, 120-horsepower engine hooked to either a five-speed manual or four-speed automatic transmission powers the front or all four wheels of the different RAV4 models. All-wheel drive versions use powertrain components from the now-defunct Celica All-Trac. Four-wheel antilock brakes are optional on all 4-door RAV4s. Minimum ground clearance is 7.5 inches on the four-door models; two-door RAV4s get .2 additional inches of clearance.

The RAV4 is an adequate around town driver, handling more like the car from which its platform is derived then a traditional SUV. Power is on the low side, however; the 120-horsepower engine works hard to drag this mini-ute up even small hills. The interior is not a bad place to spend time, offering fairly comfortable seating for four adults in the four-door models. The cargo area of the four-door is larger than one would expect, too, offering more room behind the rear seat than a Ford Crown Victoria. Two-door models are fine for singles or couples without children. The rear seat is tiny, and less than 10 cubic feet of cargo volume is available with the back seat up. On the plus side, Toyota does offer the RAV4 in convertible form while Honda's CR-V only comes with a hardtop.

We are fond of the RAV4, but there are a number of choices in this growing segment and we can't help but think that the more refined and powerful Honda CR-V might offer shoppers more of what they are looking for in a small truck – power, utility, and value.

Safety Data

Side Airbag: *Not Available*
4-Wheel ABS: *Optional (4-Door); N/A (2-Door)*
Driver Crash Test Grade: *Good*
Side Impact Crash Test Front: *Excellent*
Crash Offset: *Marginal*
Integrated Child Seat(s): *Not Available*
Traction Control: *Not Available*
Passenger Crash Test Grade: *Good*
Side Impact Crash Test Rear: *Excellent*

Standard Equipment

2-DOOR CONVERTIBLE FWD (5M): 2.0L I4 DOHC SMPI 16-valve engine; 5-speed overdrive manual transmission; front wheel drive, 4.56 axle ratio; stainless steel exhaust; front independent strut suspension with anti-roll bar, front coil springs, rear independent double wishbone suspension with rear coil springs; power rack-and-pinion steering with engine speed-sensing assist; front disc/rear drum brakes; 15.3 gal capacity fuel tank; conventional rear cargo door; front manual pop-up glass sunroof; manual convertible roof; front and rear black bumpers with rear tow hooks; black bodyside cladding; monotone paint; aero-composite halogen headlamps; additional exterior lights include center high mounted stop light; driver's and passenger's manual black folding outside mirrors; front and rear 16" x 6" silver styled steel wheels; P215/70SR16 BSW AS front and rear tires; outside rear mounted full-size conventional steel spare wheel; remote fuel release; 1 power accessory outlet, driver's foot rest; instrumentation display includes tachometer, water temp gauge, in-dash clock, trip odometer; warning indicators include oil pressure, battery, lights on, key in ignition, low fuel, door ajar; dual airbags; tinted windows; fixed interval front windshield wipers; seating capacity of 4, front bucket seats with adjustable headrests, driver's seat includes 4-way direction control, passenger's seat includes 4-way direction control with easy entry; 50-50 folding rear bench seat with reclining adjustable rear headrest; front pretensioner seatbelts; cloth seats, cloth door trim insert, full cloth headliner, full carpet floor covering; interior lights include dome light, front reading lights; passenger side vanity mirror; day-night rearview mirror; full floor console, glove box, front and rear cupholders, instrument panel bin, driver's and passenger's door bins; carpeted cargo floor, plastic trunk lid, cargo light; black grille, black side window moldings, black front windshield molding, black rear window molding and black door handles.

2-DOOR CONVERTIBLE AWD (5M) (in addition to or instead of 2-DOOR SOFTTOP FWD (5M) equipment): Full-time 4 wheel drive, auto locking hub control and manual shift, 4.93 axle ratio and skid plates.

4-DOOR FWD (5M) (in addition to or instead of 2-DOOR SOFTTOP FWD (5M) equipment): Driver selectable program transmission; child safety rear door locks; 2 power accessory outlets; tinted windows, manual rear windows, fixed 1/4 vent windows; fixed interval rear wiper, rear window defroster; seating capacity of 5; passenger seat includes 4-way direction control; front height adjustable seatbelts with front pretensioners; steering wheel with tilt adjustment; front cupholder and 2 seat back storage pockets.

4-DOOR AWD (5M) (in addition to or instead of 4-DOOR (5M) equipment): Full-time 4 wheel drive, auto locking hub control and manual shift, 4.93 axle ratio and skid plates.

Base Prices

Code	Description	Invoice	MSRP
4415	2-Door Convertible FWD (5M)	14290	15678
4417	4-Door FWD (5M)	14919	16368
4425	2-Door Convertible AWD (5M)	15312	17088
4427	4-Door AWD (5M)	15930	17778
Destination Charge:		420	420

CODE	DESCRIPTION	INVOICE	MSRP

Accessories

CODE	DESCRIPTION	INVOICE	MSRP
—	Southeast Toyota Administrative Fee *REQUIRED on models purchased in the following states: Alabama, Florida, Georgia, North Carolina and South Carolina.*	275	275
—	Southeast Toyota Destination Charge *REQUIRED on models purchased in the following states: Alabama, Florida, Georgia, North Carolina and South Carolina.*	55	55
—	Transmission: 4-Speed Automatic (AWD) *Includes 4.40 axle ratio.*	940	1050
—	Transmission: 4-Speed Automatic (FWD) *Includes 3.18 axle ratio.*	958	1050
AB	Antilock Brake System (4-Door)	539	630
AC	Air Conditioner	788	985
AL	Wheels: Aluminum with Overfenders (4-Door AWD) *Includes fender flares and tires: P235/60R16.*	864	1080
AW	Wheels: Aluminum	392	490
CK	All Weather Guard Package *Includes HD washer tank, HD starter and rear heater ducts.*	59	70
CL	Cruise Control	200	250
EV	Radio: CD Combo with 4 Speakers *NOT AVAILABLE with EX.*	338	450
EX	Radio: Deluxe Cassette with 4 Speakers *NOT AVAILABLE with EV.*	263	350
LD	Limited Slip Differential (4-Door AWD)	322	390
PG	Privacy Glass (4-Door)	248	310
SR	Power Moonroof (4-Door)	652	815
UT	Upgrade Package (4-Door) *Includes cloth front and rear headrests, power door locks and power mirrors. REQUIRES EV or EX.*	752	940
VK	Value Pkg. #2 (4-Door) *Includes cloth front and rear headrests, ETR AM/FM stereo CD combo with 4 speakers, cruise control, power windows, power door locks, power mirrors and carpeted floor mats.*	1523	1692
VL	Value Pkg. #5 with Special Edition and Leather (4-Door) *Includes vinyl headrests, ETR AM/FM stereo CD combo with 4 speakers, cruise control, power windows, power door locks, color-keyed power mirrors, color-keyed door handles, color-keyed cladding, color keyed bumpers, privacy glass, Bradley alloy wheels, steel spare wheel, leather seating surfaces and carpeted floor mats.*	2591	2879
VP	Value Pkg. #1 (4-Door) *Includes cloth front and rear headrests, ETR AM/FM stereo CD combo with 4 speakers, cruise control, power windows, power door locks, power mirrors and carpeted floor mats.*	1433	1592
VQ	Value Pkg. #3 with EX and Special Edition (4-Door) *Includes cloth front and rear headrests, ETR AM/FM stereo CD combo with 4 speakers, cruise control, power windows, power door locks, color-keyed power*	1934	2149

CODE	DESCRIPTION	INVOICE	MSRP
	mirrors, color-keyed door handles, color-keyed cladding, color keyed bumpers, privacy glass, Bradley alloy wheels, steel spare wheel and carpeted floor mats.		
VR	**Value Pkg. #4 with EV and Special Edition (4-Door)**	2024	2249
	Includes cloth front and rear headrests, ETR AM/FM stereo CD combo with 4 speakers, cruise control, power windows, power door locks, color-keyed power mirrors, color-keyed door handles, color-keyed cladding, color keyed bumpers, privacy glass, Bradley alloy wheels, steel spare wheel and carpeted floor mats.		

NOTE: Toyotas sold in Alabama, Florida, Georgia, North Carolina and South Carolina may be equipped with option packages not listed in this guide. You can expect to haggle 25% off the window sticker price of these packages.

1999 SIENNA

1999 Toyota Sienna

What's New?

Entering its second full model year of production at Toyota's Kentucky plant, the Sienna minivan gets a right side power sliding door. An engine immobilizer system has been added to the keyless-entry security system and all Siennas will be equipped with daytime running lights. Selected models have a full size spare tire and Woodland Pearl replaces Classic Green Pearl as an exterior color option.

Review

Toyota's new minivan sits in sharp contrast to the one it replaces. Whereas the Previa was a study in minivan abnormalities, with rear-wheel drive, a midship-mounted supercharged engine, and a shape that looked like the droid escape pod from the first Star Wars movie, the Sienna is a model of suburban respectability.

That doesn't, however, mean that this minivan is boring. Resting under the hood is a powerful, 3.0-liter V6 engine that was stolen from the Camry parts bin. The engine isn't the only piece of equipment pilfered from the Camry; the Sienna rides on a stretched and modified Camry platform and uses much of the Camry's interior switchgear. Appropriately referred to internally at Toyota as "The Camry of minivans," we can only assume that the company expects this creation to be as popular as their hot-selling sedan.

In order to harness the 194 horses at work under the hood, engineers put antilock brakes at all four wheels of every Sienna. Other safety equipment includes dual airbags, side-impact protection that meets future federal standards and seatbelt pretensioners for both front seats. Last year the Insurance Institute for Highway Safety conducted an offset crash test of the Sienna and called it "the best performing vehicle in the history of the test."

Interestingly, Toyota was able to talk rivals General Motors and Chrysler into lending a hand on the Sienna's manufacturing process. Not used to making such a large vehicle, Toyota had questions about how to deal with the interior assembly of this van which has well over 130 cubic feet of cargo space.

In the end, General Motors and Chrysler may be sorry that they offered to help Toyota figure out some of its manufacturing logistics. Toyota has been able to successfully capture the midsize sedan market with its excellent Camry. If this truly is "The Camry of minivans," GM and Chrysler better watch out.

Safety Data

Side Airbag: *Not Available*
4-Wheel ABS: *Standard*
Driver Crash Test Grade: *Excellent*
Side Impact Crash Test Front: *Good*
Crash Offset: *Good*
Integrated Child Seat(s): *Optional*
Traction Control: *Not Available*
Passenger Crash Test Grade: *Excellent*
Side Impact Crash Test Rear: *Excellent*

Standard Equipment

CE (4A): 3.0L V6 DOHC SMPI 24-valve engine; 4-speed electronic overdrive automatic transmission with lock-up; HD battery with run down protection; HD alternator; front wheel drive; stainless steel exhaust; front independent strut suspension with anti-roll bar, front coil springs, rear semi-independent torsion suspension with rear coil springs; power rack-and-pinion steering with engine speed-sensing assist; front disc/rear drum brakes with 4 wheel antilock braking system; 20.9 gal capacity fuel tank; 3 doors with sliding right rear passenger door, liftback rear cargo door; front and rear body-colored bumpers; body-colored bodyside cladding; monotone paint; aero-composite halogen headlamps; additional exterior lights include center high mounted stop light; driver's and passenger's manual remote black folding outside mirrors; front and rear 15" x 6" steel wheels; P205/70SR15 BSW AS front and rear tires; inside under cargo mounted compact steel spare wheel; air conditioning, rear heat ducts; AM/FM stereo with seek-scan, cassette, 4 speakers, and fixed antenna; child safety rear door locks, remote hatch/trunk release, remote fuel release; 2 power accessory outlets, driver's foot rest; instrumentation display includes water temp gauge, in-dash clock, trip odometer; warning indicators include oil pressure, battery, key in ignition, low fuel, low washer fluid, door ajar; dual airbags; tinted windows, manual rear windows, manual 1/4 vent windows; variable intermittent front windshield wipers, fixed interval rear wiper; seating capacity of 7, front bucket seats with adjustable headrests, driver's and passenger's armrests, driver's seat includes 6-way direction control, passenger's seat includes 4-way direction control; removable 2nd row bench seat with reclining adjustable rear headrest; 3rd row removable 50-50 folding split-bench seat with reclining adjustable 3rd row headrest; front height adjustable seatbelts with front pretensioners; cloth seats, cloth door trim insert, full cloth headliner, full carpet floor covering; interior lights include dome light, rear reading lights; steering wheel with tilt adjustment; vanity mirrors, dual auxiliary visors; day-night rearview mirror; mini overhead console with storage, locking glove box with light, front and rear cupholders, instrument panel bin, 1 seat back storage pocket, driver's and passenger's door bins, front underseat tray; vinyl cargo floor, plastic trunk lid, cargo light; body-colored grille, black side window moldings, black front windshield molding, black rear window molding and body-colored door handles.

LE (4A) (in addition to or instead of CE (4A) equipment): Four doors with sliding left rear passenger door, sliding right rear passenger door; driver's and passenger's power remote black folding outside mirrors; rear air conditioning with separate controls; rear heater; cruise control; retained accessory power; instrumentation display includes tachometer; deep tinted windows, power front windows with driver's 1-touch down, power 1/4 vent windows; rear window defroster; premium cloth seats; interior lights include front and rear reading lights; dual illuminated vanity mirrors, dual auxiliary visors and 2 seat back storage pockets.

XLE (4A) (in addition to or instead of LE (4A) equipment): Roof rack; aero-composite halogen auto off headlamps; driver's and passenger's power remote black heated folding outside mirrors; inside under cargo mounted full-size temporary steel spare wheel; premium AM/FM stereo with seek-scan, single CD, 6 speakers, and fixed diversity antenna; power door locks with 2 stage unlock, remote keyless entry; security system; front captain seats with adjustable headrests, driver's seat includes 6-way power seat; removable 2nd row captain seat with reclining adjustable rear headrest, seatbelt mounted on seat; full carpet floor covering with carpeted floor mats; leather-wrapped steering wheel with tilt adjustment; carpeted cargo floor and carpeted trunk lid.

Base Prices

Code	Description	Invoice	MSRP
5322	CE 4-Door (4A)	19050	21508
5324	CE 5-Door (4A)	19839	22398
5334	LE 5-Door (4A)	21394	24438
5344	XLE 5-Door (4A)	23265	26574
Destination Charge:		420	420

Accessories

Code	Description	Invoice	MSRP
—	Southeast Toyota Administrative Fee *REQUIRED on models purchased in the following states: Alabama, Florida, Georgia, North Carolina and South Carolina.*	325	325
—	Southeast Toyota Destination Fee *REQUIRED on models purchased in the following states: Alabama, Florida, Georgia, North Carolina and South Carolina.*	55	55
AJ	Right Side Power Sliding Door (LE/XLE)	316	395
AW	Wheels: Aluminum (LE) *Includes full size spare tire and P215/65R15 tires(5).*	380	475
BN	Black Pearl Emblems	99	149
CF	Floor and Cargo Carpeted Mats (CE)	96	160
DH	Towing Hitch Receiver	200	290
DR	Roof Rack (All Except XLE)	176	220
DU	Burlwood Wood Dash *Includes 10 piece set.*	305	459
EF	Rear Bumper Protector	33	50
EH	Heated Mirrors (LE)	24	30
EH	Heated Power Mirrors (CE)	152	190
EM	Power Mirrors (CE)	128	160
GN	Cargo Net	27	42
GP	Gold Appearance Package	109	164
HE	Package #10 (XLE) *Includes power moonroof.*	1020	1275

CODE	DESCRIPTION	INVOICE	MSRP
HF	Package #11 (XLE) *Includes leather package: leather seat trim, leather-wrapped steering wheel and 6-way power driver's seat.*	1444	1805
HV	Package #12 (CE 4-Door) *Includes privacy glass, power windows, power door locks, cruise control, power rear quarter vent windows, carpeted floor and cargo mats.*	770	856
HV	Package #12 (CE 5-Door) *Includes privacy glass, rear window defogger, power windows, power door locks, cruise control, power rear quarter vent windows, carpeted floor and cargo mats and heated mirrors.*	1171	1301
HX	Package #13 (CE 4-Door) *Includes privacy glass, rear window defogger, power windows, power door locks, power mirrors, cruise control, power rear quarter vent windows, carpeted floor and cargo mats.*	1144	1271
HX	Package #13 (CE 5-Door) *Includes privacy glass, power windows, power door locks, power mirrors, cruise control, power rear quarter vent windows, carpeted floor and cargo mats.*	743	826
KE	Keyless Entry System (All Except XLE)	149	229
KS	Child Restraint Seat (All Except XLE)	200	250
LA	Leather Package (XLE) *Includes leather seat trim.*	1128	1410
P3	Toyota 3 Disc CD Changer (CE)	449	641
P4	Auto Reverse Cassette Deck (All Except XLE)	162	231
P5	CD Deck (CE)	235	335
PN	Anti-Theft Device (LE) *Includes anti-theft system and engine immobilizer.*	432	540
RB	Running Boards (LE) *Painted.*	365	595
RB	Running Boards (CE) *Includes molded color - dark gray.*	290	480
RF	Rear Spoiler	170	284
SD	Sunroof Wind Deflector (LE)	33	55
SK	Center Console Box	80	135
SR	Power Moonroof (XLE) *Includes power tilt and slide glass with sunshade.*	704	880
TF	Tires: Full Size Spare (CE)	68	85
TO	Towing Package (All Except CE 4-Door) *Includes trailering weight (3500 lb) and dual air conditioning. REQUIRES TF.*	504	630
TO	Towing Package (CE 4-Door) *Includes trailering weight (3500 lb). REQUIRES TF.*	128	160
UH	Package #1 (CE 4-Door) *Includes dual air conditioning, rear window defogger, power windows, power door locks and cruise control. REQUIRES EH.*	1256	1570
UH	Package #1 (CE 5-Door) *Includes rear window defogger, power windows, power door locks and cruise control. REQUIRES EH.*	900	1125

CODE	DESCRIPTION	INVOICE	MSRP
UL	Package #2 (CE 5-Door) *Includes privacy glass, power windows, power door locks, cruise control and power rear quarter vent windows. REQUIRES EH.*	1204	1505
UL	Package #2 (CE 4-Door) *Includes privacy glass, rear window defogger, power windows, power door locks, cruise control and power rear quarter vent windows.*	1560	1950
UN	Package #4 (LE) *Includes privacy glass, power rear quarter vent windows and cloth captain's chairs.*	244	271
UO	Package #3 (CE 5-Door) *Includes privacy glass, rear window defogger, power windows, power door locks, cruise control and power rear quarter vent windows. REQUIRES (EH and TF) or TF.*	1332	1665
UO	Package #3 (CE 4-Door) *Includes privacy glass, dual air conditioning, rear window defogger, power windows, power door locks, cruise control and power rear quarter vent windows. REQUIRES (EH and TF) or TF.*	1688	2110
UP	Package #5 (LE) *Includes privacy glass and power rear quarter vent windows.*	341	440
UR	Package #6 (LE) *Includes cloth captain's chairs.*	712	890
UU	Package #7 (LE) *Includes privacy glass, power rear quarter vent windows, cloth captain's chairs, anti-theft device and power sliding door.*	1625	2045
V1	V.I.P. S1000 Base Security System (CE 4-Door)	99	149
V3	V.I.P. RS3000 Deluxe Security System (All Except XLE)	249	399
WL	Alloy Wheel Locks (CE 5-Door/LE)	32	53
WS	Steel Wheel Locks (CE)	31	52
XE	Package #9 (XLE) *Includes leather package: leather seat trim, leather-wrapped steering wheel, 6-way power driver's seat and power moonroof.*	2148	2685

NOTE: Toyotas sold in Alabama, Florida, Georgia, North Carolina and South Carolina may be equipped with option packages not listed in this guide. You can expect to haggle 25% off the window sticker price of these packages.

1999 TACOMA

1999 Toyota Tacoma

What's New?

Toyota adds new front seat belt pretensioners and force limiters. Newly optional on Xtra Cab models is an AM/FM four-speaker CD audio system while 4x4s get 15" x 7" inch steel wheels. The PreRunner adds a regular cab option to its model mix. Natural White, Imperial Jade Mica and Horizon Blue Metallic replace White, Copper Canyon Mica, Evergreen Pearl, and Cool Steel Metallic as color options.

Review

Toyota's sixth-generation compact pickup debuted as a 1995.5 model with an actual model name: Tacoma. It's supposed to suggest the rugged outdoors, as well as strength and adventure. Toyota aimed for aggressive styling, inside and out. A freshening of the front end occurred on both the two- and four-wheel drive models during the last two model years. Swoopy fenders, a larger bumper, aero-style headlamps and a new grille set this truck apart from its forebears. Tacomas sport an excellent selection of interior fittings. Regular and extended cab bodies are available, with either two- or four-wheel drive. Any of three potent engines go under the hood.

Two-wheel drive Tacomas get a 2.4-liter four-cylinder base engine, rated at 142-horsepower. Tacoma 4x4s earn a 150-horspower, 2.7-liter four. Toyota claims that its four-cylinder engines are comparable to V6s from competitors. If those won't suffice, however, consider the V6 option: a DOHC, 24-valve unit that whips out 190 horses and 220 foot-pounds of torque. With V6 power, borrowed from the now defunct T100, this compact pickup can tow up to 5,000 pounds and soundly trounce most factory sport trucks in the stoplight dragrace.

All Tacomas have front coil springs instead of the former torsion bars, but 4x4s feature longer suspension travel to improve ride/handling qualities. Manual-shift trucks feature reverse-gear synchronization to reduce gear noise when shifting into reverse. Four-wheel antilock braking is optional on all Tacomas, and all pickups contain dual airbags with a shut-off switch for the passenger's side. In top-of-the-line Limited pickups, a One-Touch Hi-Four switch is available for easy, pushbutton engagement of four-wheel drive.

The PreRunner model is set to attract truck buyers who desire, but cannot afford, a 4WD truck, 4WD truck owners who don't use their 4WD as often as they expected, and 2WD truck buyers who take their vehicle off-road. Historically, a "pre-runner" is a truck that pre-runs an off-road race course. Toyota's

PreRunner has benefited from considerable suspension tuning and development work with Toyota Motorsports desert racing truck program to produce a 2WD vehicle with 4WD capabilities.

Toyota hopes to attract buyers with the style and image of its Tacoma. We like the Tacoma, but question the value it represents. Most of these Toyota trucks don't come cheap. Guess that's the price you pay for the peace of mind a Toyota provides.

Safety Data

Side Airbag: *Not Available*
4-Wheel ABS: *Optional*
Driver Crash Test Grade: *Good*
Side Impact Crash Test Front: *Not Available*
Crash Offset: *Acceptable*
Integrated Child Seat(s): *Not Available*
Traction Control: *Not Available*
Passenger Crash Test Grade: *Good*
Side Impact Crash Test Rear: *Not Available*

Standard Equipment

BASE 2WD REGULAR CAB (5M): 2.4L I4 DOHC MPI 16-valve engine; 5-speed overdrive manual transmission; HD battery; rear wheel drive, 3.42 axle ratio; stainless steel exhaust; front independent double wishbone suspension with anti-roll bar, front coil springs, rigid rear axle suspension with rear leaf springs; manual rack-and-pinion steering; front disc/rear drum brakes; 15.1 gal capacity fuel tank; front black bumper; monotone paint; aero-composite halogen headlamps; additional exterior lights include center high mounted stop light; driver's and passenger's manual black folding outside mirrors, passenger's convex outside mirror; front and rear 14" x 5" steel wheels; P195/75SR14 BSW AS front and rear tires; underbody mounted full-size conventional steel spare wheel; fuel filler door; 3 power accessory outlets, driver's foot rest; instrumentation display includes water temp gauge; warning indicators include battery, lights on, key in ignition, low washer fluid; driver's side airbag, passenger's side cancelable airbag; tinted windows; seating capacity of 3, bench front seat with fixed headrests, driver's seat includes 2-way direction control, passenger's seat includes 2-way direction control; front height adjustable seatbelts; cloth seats, cloth door trim insert, full vinyl headliner, full carpet floor covering; interior lights include dome light; day-night rearview mirror; glove box, front cupholder, instrument panel bin, driver's and passenger's door bins; black grille, black side window moldings, black front windshield molding, black rear window molding and black door handles.

PRERUNNER 2WD REGULAR CAB (4A) (in addition to or instead of BASE 2WD REGULAR CAB (5M) equipment): 2.7L I4 DOHC MPI 16-valve engine; 4-speed electronic overdrive automatic transmission with lock-up; 4.3 axle ratio; power rack-and-pinion steering; 18 gal capacity fuel tank; front black bumper, rear chrome bumper with rear step; front and rear 15" x 6" steel wheels; tinted windows; sliding rear window; cab-back insulator; vanity mirrors and interior concealed storage.

BASE 2WD XTRACAB (5M) (in addition to or instead of BASE 2WD REGULAR CAB (5M) equipment): Front and rear black bumpers with rear step; front and rear 14" x 6" steel wheels; tinted windows, vented rear windows; seating capacity of 5, 60-40 split-bench front seat with adjustable headrests, driver's seat includes 4-way direction control, passenger's seat includes 4-way direction control with easy entry; 50-50 folding rear jump seat; cab-back insulator; interior concealed storage and carpeted cargo floor.

PRERUNNER 2WD XTRACAB (4A) (in addition to or instead of PRERUNNER 2WD REGULAR CAB (4A) equipment): Air conditioning, vented rear windows; AM/FM stereo with seek-scan, cassette, 4 speakers, and fixed antenna; seating capacity of 5, passenger's seat includes 4-way direction control with easy entry; 50-50 folding rear jump seat; front and rear cupholders and carpeted cargo floor.

BASE V6 2WD XTRACAB (5M) (in addition to or instead of BASE 2WD XTRACAB (5M) equipment): 3.4L V6 DOHC SMPI 24-valve engine; 3.15 axle ratio and power rack-and-pinion steering.

CODE	DESCRIPTION	INVOICE	MSRP

PRERUNNER V6 2WD XTRACAB (4A) (in addition to or instead of PRERUNNER 2WD XTRACAB (4A) equipment): 3.4L V6 DOHC SMPI 24-valve engine and 4.1 axle ratio.

BASE 4WD REGULAR CAB (5M) (in addition to or instead of BASE 2WD REGULAR CAB (5M) equipment): 2.7L I4 DOHC MPI 16-valve engine; part-time 4 wheel drive, manual locking hub control with manual shift, 3.42 axle ratio; power rack-and-pinion steering; 18 gal capacity fuel tank; front and rear mud flaps, skid plates; front and rear black bumpers with rear tow hooks, rear step; front and rear 15" x 6" silver styled steel wheels and warning indicators include oil pressure.

BASE 4WD XTRACAB (5M) (in addition to or instead of BASE 4WD REGULAR CAB (5M) equipment): Vented rear windows; seating capacity of 5, 60-40 split-bench front seat with adjustable headrests, driver's seat includes 4-way direction control, passenger's seat includes 4-way direction control with easy entry; 50-50 folding rear jump seat; front and rear cupholders and carpeted cargo floor.

BASE V6 4WD XTRACAB (5M) (in addition to or instead of BASE 4WD XTRACAB (5M) equipment): 3.4L V6 DOHC SMPI 24-valve engine and engine oil cooler.

LIMITED V6 4WD XTRACAB (5-speed) (in addition to or instead of BASE V6 4WD XTRACAB (5M) equipment): Front and rear chrome bumpers with rear tow hooks; chrome wheel well molding; driver's and passenger's manual chrome folding outside mirrors; front and rear 15" x 7" silver alloy wheels; cruise control; instrumentation display includes tachometer, in-dash clock, trip odometer; warning indicators include low fuel, power front windows with driver's 1-touch down; variable intermittent front windshield wipers, sliding rear window; seating capacity of 4, front sports seats with adjustable headrests, driver's seat includes 6-way direction control with lumbar support; premium cloth seats, interior lights include front reading lights; steering wheel with tilt adjustment; passenger side vanity mirror; partial floor console, glove box with light; chrome grille and chrome door handles.

Base Prices

CODE	DESCRIPTION	INVOICE	MSRP
7103	Base 2WD Regular Cab (5M)	11640	12698
7503	Base 4WD Regular Cab (5M)	15761	17588
7132	PreRunner 2WD Regular Cab (4A)	13401	14768
7162	PreRunner 2WD Xtracab (4A)	15978	17608
7164	PreRunner V6 2WD Xtracab (4A)	16827	18538
7113	Base 2WD Xtracab (5M)	13475	14868
7513	Base 4WD Xtracab (5M)	17059	19038
7153	Base V6 2WD Xtracab (5M)	14690	16208
7553	Base V6 4WD Xtracab (5M)	18036	20128
7557	Limited V6 4WD Xtracab (5M)	22122	24688
Destination Charge:		420	420

Accessories

CODE	DESCRIPTION	INVOICE	MSRP
—	Southeast Toyota Administrative Fee (4WD)	275	275
—	Southeast Toyota Administrative Fee (2WD) *REQUIRED on models purchased in the following states: Alabama, Florida, Georgia, North Carolina and South Carolina.*	250	250
—	Southeast Toyota Destination Charge (4WD) *REQUIRED on models purchased in the following states: Alabama, Florida, Georgia, North Carolina and South Carolina.*	55	55

CODE	DESCRIPTION	INVOICE	MSRP
—	Southeast Toyota Destination Charge (2WD) *REQUIRED on models purchased in the following states: Alabama, Florida, Georgia, North Carolina and South Carolina.*	(45)	(45)
—	Transmission: 4-Speed Automatic (Base 4WD Reg Cab)	805	900
—	Transmission: 4-Speed Automatic (Base 4WD X-Cab)	805	900
—	Transmission: 4-Speed Automatic (Base 2WD Reg Cab)	659	720
—	Transmission: 4-Speed Automatic (Limited)	805	900
—	Transmission: 4-Speed Automatic (Base V6 4WD X-Cab)	805	900
—	Transmission: 4-Speed Automatic (Base V6 2WD X-Cab)	805	900
—	Transmission: 4-Speed Automatic (Base 2WD X-Cab)	659	720
AA	Wheels: 15" Aluminum (PreRunner) *Includes 265/75R15 tires and wheel arch moldings. NOT AVAILABLE with ST.*	756	945
AB	4-Wheel Antilock Braking System	507	590
AC	Air Conditioning (All Except Pre-Runner X-Cab)	788	985
AL	Wheels: Aluminum (Base 4WD)	324	405
AW	Wheels: Aluminum (Base 2WD X-Cab)	296	370
AW	Wheels: Aluminum (Base Reg Cab 2WD) *NOT AVAILABLE with TU.*	440	550
BL	Over Rail Bedliner	160	299
BM	Body Side Molding	53	85
BT	Tonneau Cover	200	300
BU	Cloth Bucket Seats (Base 2WD X-Cab) *Includes center console box.*	52	65
BU	Cloth Bucket Seats (PreRunner X-Cab) *Includes center console box.*	60	75
BU	Cloth Bucket Seats (Base 2WD Regular Cab) *Includes cloth headrests and center console box.*	244	305
BU	Cloth Bucket Seats (PreRunner Reg Cab) *Includes cloth headrests and center console box.*	252	315
CF	Carpeted Floor Mats (4 Piece Set) (X-Cab)	40	68
CH	Chrome Package (Base 4WD/PreRunner) *Includes chrome front bumper, chrome grille, chrome door handles and chrome plated rear bumper.*	200	250
CH	Chrome Package (Base 2WD Reg Cab) *Includes chrome front bumper, chrome grille, chrome door handles and chrome plated rear bumper.*	320	400
CK	All Weather Guard Package *Includes HD starter, HD windshield wiper motor and rain channeled windshield molding.*	63	75
CL	Cruise Control (All Except Limited)	200	250
CQ	Convenience Package (All Except Limited) *Includes tilt steering wheel, variable intermittent wipers, cruise control, tachometer, dual digital tripmeter, digital clock and lighting package.*	565	690
CT	Carpeted Floor Mats (2 Piece Set) (Base Reg Cab)	31	51
DH	Towing Hitch Receiver	200	285
DL	Rear Differential Lock (PreRunner V6/V6 4WD/4-cyl 4WD 5M) *REQUIRES CQ or TA or SX or FD.*	281	340

CODE	DESCRIPTION	INVOICE	MSRP
DQ	**Digital Clock**	50	82
EB	**Deluxe Painted Rear Bumper (Base)**	128	215
EC	**Deluxe Chrome Rear Bumper (Base)**	173	290
EU	**Radio: AM/FM Stereo with Cassette (All Except PreRunner X-Cab)** *Includes 2 speakers and antenna. NOT AVAILABLE with RA.*	278	370
EV	**Radio: CD Combo with 4 Speakers (Base X-Cab)** *Includes antenna.*	510	680
EX	**Radio: Deluxe Cassette with 4 Speakers (Base X-Cab)** *Includes antenna.*	435	580
FB	**High 4 Selector Switch (Limited)**	111	135
FD	**4-Wheel Demand (Base 4WD)**	198	240
FT	**Preferred Equipment Package #1 (PreRunner V6)** *Includes wheels: styled steel: tires: 265/75R15: wheel arch moldings and over rail bedliner.*	576	770
FV	**Preferred Equipment Package #2 (PreRunner V6)** *Includes wheels: styled steel: tires: 265/75R15: wheel arch moldings and under rail bedliner.*	576	770
FX	**Preferred Equipment Package #3 (PreRunner V6)** *Includes TRD off-road package: 15" aluminum wheels, 31x10.5R15 tires, wheel arch moldings, tachometer, black overfenders, off-road suspension, rear differential lock, badging; dual digital tripmeter and over rail bedliner.*	1481	1890
FY	**Preferred Equipment Package #4 (PreRunner V6)** *Includes TRD off-road package: 15" aluminum wheels, 31x10.5R15 tires, wheel arch moldings, tachometer, black overfenders, off-road suspension, rear differential lock, badging; dual digital tripmeter and under rail bedliner.*	1481	1890
GN	**Cargo Net**	27	42
HP	**Hood Protector**	55	89
IX	**SR5 Color-keyed Package (Base 2WD X-Cab)** *Includes SR5 badging, power steering, sliding rear window: gray privacy glass, sunvisor with mirror and pocket; deluxe ETR stereo with cassette and 4 speakers, air conditioning, color keyed package: color-keyed front bumper, color keyed grille and chrome plated rear bumper.*	855	950
IX	**SR5 Color-keyed Package (Base V6 2WD X-Cab)** *Includes SR5 badging, power steering, sliding rear window: gray privacy glass, sunvisor with mirror and pocket; deluxe ETR stereo with cassette and 4 speakers, air conditioning, color keyed package: color-keyed front bumper, color keyed grille and chrome plated rear bumper.*	661	735
IX	**SR5 Color-keyed Package (Base 4WD X-Cab)** *Includes SR5 badging, sliding rear window: gray privacy glass, sunvisor with mirror and pocket; deluxe ETR stereo with cassette and 4 speakers, air conditioning, color keyed package: color-keyed front bumper, color keyed grille and chrome plated rear bumper. REQUIRES PX.*	391	435
KE	**Keyless Entry System** *REQUIRES PO.*	149	239
KP	**Color Keyed Package (All Except 2WD Reg Cab)** *Includes color keyed valance, color keyed grille and chrome plated rear bumper. REQUIRES PX.*	140	175

CODE	DESCRIPTION	INVOICE	MSRP
KP	**Color Keyed Package (Base 2WD Reg Cab)** *Includes color keyed valance, color keyed grille and chrome plated rear bumper. REQUIRES PQ and PX.*	260	325
LB	**Tonneau Cover and Under The Rail Bedliner**	370	623
LU	**Under Rail Bedliner**	160	299
LX	**SR5 Chrome Package (Base V6 2WD X-Cab)** *Includes SR5 badging, sliding rear window: gray privacy glass, sunvisor with mirror and pocket; deluxe ETR stereo with cassette and 4 speakers, air conditioning, chrome package: chrome front bumper, chrome grille, chrome door handles and chrome plated rear bumper.*	729	810
LX	**SR5 Chrome Package (Base 4WD X-Cab)** *Includes SR5 badging, sliding rear window: gray privacy glass, sunvisor with mirror and pocket; deluxe ETR stereo with cassette and 4 speakers, air conditioning, chrome package: chrome front bumper, chrome grille, chrome door handles and chrome plated rear bumper.*	459	510
LX	**SR5 Chrome Package (Base 2WD X-Cab)** *Includes SR5 badging, power steering, sliding rear window: gray privacy glass, sunvisor with mirror and pocket; deluxe ETR stereo with cassette and 4 speakers, air conditioning, chrome package: chrome front bumper, chrome grille, chrome door handles and chrome plated rear bumper.*	877	975
MF	**Mud Guards**	30	50
OF	**TRD Offroad Package (PreRunner X-Cab)** *Includes 15" aluminum wheels, 31x10.5R15 tires, wheel arch moldings, tachometer, dual digital tripmeter, black overfenders, off-road suspension and badging.*	1056	1320
OF	**TRD Offroad Package (Base 4WD X-Cab)** *Includes 15" aluminum wheels, 31x10.5R15 tires, wheel arch moldings, tachometer, dual digital tripmeter, black overfenders, off-road suspension, badging and rear differential lock. REQUIRES FD. NOT AVAILABLE with automatic transmission.*	1337	1660
OF	**TRD Offroad Package (Limited)** *Includes 31x10.5R15 tires, wheel arch moldings, black overfenders, off-road suspension and badging.*	357	435
OF	**TRD Offroad Package (PreRunner V6 X-Cab)** *Includes 15" aluminum wheels, 31x10.5R15 tires, wheel arch moldings, tachometer, dual digital tripmeter, black overfenders, off-road suspension, badging and rear differential lock.*	1281	1590
PO	**Power Package (All Except Limited)** *Includes power windows and power door locks. REQUIRES CL or CQ.*	376	470
PQ	**Value Edition Package (Base 2WD Reg Cab)** *Includes power steering, black rear bumper, ETR AM/FM stereo with cassette and carpeted floor mats.*	256	285
PS	**Power Steering (2WD 4-Cyl)**	269	315
PV	**Value Edition Plus Package (PreRunner Reg Cab)** *Includes ETR AM/FM stereo with cassette, air conditioning and carpeted floor mats.*	499	555

CODE	DESCRIPTION	INVOICE	MSRP
PV	**Value Edition Plus Package (Base 4WD Reg Cab)** *Includes ETR AM/FM stereo with cassette, air conditioning and carpeted floor mats. NOT AVAILABLE with RA.*	184	205
PX	**Metallic Paint** *Requires metallic exterior color.*	NC	NC
PY	**Value Edition Plus Package (Base 2WD Reg Cab)** *Includes power steering, ETR AM/FM stereo with cassette, air conditioning, chrome package: chrome front bumper, chrome grille, chrome door handles, chrome plated rear bumper and carpeted floor mats.*	783	870
QY	**Value Edition Plus Color-keyed Package (Base 2WD Reg Cab)** *Includes power steering, ETR AM/FM stereo with cassette, air conditioning, color keyed package: color-keyed front bumper, color keyed grille, chrome plated rear bumper and carpeted floor mats. REQUIRES PX.*	760	845
RA	**Radio: AM/FM Stereo with 2 Speakers (Base Reg Cab)** *Includes antenna.*	203	270
RB	**Running Boards**	244	400
SE	**Special Edition Package (PreRunner X-Cab)** *Includes chrome package: chrome front bumper, chrome grille, chrome door handles, chrome plated rear bumper; sliding rear window, gray privacy glass, deluxe ETR stereo with cassette and 4 speakers, sunvisor with mirror and pocket.*	NC	NC
SN	**Special Edition Color-keyed Package (PreRunner X-Cab)** *Includes color keyed package: color-keyed front bumper, color keyed grille, chrome plated rear bumper; sliding rear window, gray privacy glass, deluxe ETR stereo with cassette and 4 speakers, sunvisor with mirror and pocket.*	NC	NC
SR	**Manual Pop-Up Sunroof (X-Cab/PreRunner X-Cab)**	312	390
ST	**Wheels: Styled Steel (All Except Base 2WD)** *Includes 265/75R15 tires and wheel arch moldings.*	376	470
SX	**Sport Package (PreRunner Reg Cab)** *Includes 15" aluminum wheels, 265/75R15 tires, wheel arch moldings, chrome package: chrome front bumper, chrome grille, chrome door handles, chrome plated rear bumper; sunvisor with mirror and pocket, sliding rear window, gray privacy glass, cloth bucket seats and center console box. NOT AVAILABLE with ST.*	603	670
SX	**Sport Package (Base 4WD Reg Cab)** *Includes 15" aluminum wheels, 265/75R15 tires, wheel arch moldings, chrome package: chrome front bumper, chrome grille, chrome door handles, chrome plated rear bumper; sunvisor with mirror and pocket, sliding rear window, gray privacy glass, cloth bucket seats and center console box. REQUIRES PV or EU.*	423	470
TA	**Tachometer (All Except Limited)** *Includes dual digital tripmeter.*	76	95
TU	**Tires: 215/70R14 (Base 2WD Reg Cab)** *NOT AVAILABLE with AW.*	144	180
TW	**Tilt Steering Wheel (All Except Limited)** *Includes variable intermittent wipers.*	209	245
V3	**V.I.P. RS3000 Deluxe Security System**	249	399
VI	**V.I.P. S1000 Base Security System**	99	159

CODE	DESCRIPTION	INVOICE	MSRP
VK	SR5 Value Color-keyed Package with CD (Base V6 2WD X-Cab) *Includes SR5 badging, power steering, sliding rear window, gray privacy glass, sunvisor with mirror and pocket, ETR stereo with CD and 4 speakers, air conditioning, color keyed package: color-keyed front bumper, color keyed grille and chrome plated rear bumper. REQUIRES PX.*	751	835
VK	SR5 Value Color-keyed Package with CD (Base 4WD X-Cab) *Includes SR5 badging, power steering, sliding rear window, gray privacy glass, sunvisor with mirror and pocket, ETR stereo with CD and 4 speakers, air conditioning, color keyed package: color-keyed front bumper, color keyed grille and chrome plated rear bumper. REQUIRES PX.*	481	535
VK	SR5 Value Color-keyed Package with CD (Base 2WD X-Cab) *Includes SR5 badging, power steering, sliding rear window, gray privacy glass, sunvisor with mirror and pocket, ETR stereo with CD and 4 speakers, air conditioning, color keyed package: color-keyed front bumper, color keyed grille and chrome plated rear bumper. REQUIRES PX.*	945	1050
VP	SR5 Value Chrome Package with CD (Base V6 2WD X-Cab) *Includes SR5 badging, power steering, sliding rear window, gray privacy glass, sunvisor with mirror and pocket, ETR stereo with CD and 4 speakers, air conditioning, chrome package: chrome front bumper, chrome grille, chrome door handles and chrome plated rear bumper.*	819	910
VP	SR5 Value Chrome Package with CD (Base 2WD X-Cab) *Includes SR5 badging, power steering, sliding rear window, gray privacy glass, sunvisor with mirror and pocket, ETR stereo with CD and 4 speakers, air conditioning, chrome package: chrome front bumper, chrome grille, chrome door handles and chrome plated rear bumper.*	967	1075
VP	SR5 Value Chrome Package with CD (Base 4WD X-Cab) *Includes SR5 badging, power steering, sliding rear window, gray privacy glass, sunvisor with mirror and pocket, ETR stereo with CD and 4 speakers, air conditioning, chrome package: chrome front bumper, chrome grille, chrome door handles and chrome plated rear bumper.*	549	610
VX	Value Chrome Package with CD (PreRunner X-Cab) *Includes chrome package: chrome front bumper, chrome grille, chrome door handles, chrome plated rear bumper; sliding rear window, gray privacy glass, deluxe ETR stereo with CD and 4 speakers, sunvisor with mirror and pocket.*	NC	NC
VZ	Value Color-keyed Package with CD (PreRunner X-Cab) *Includes sliding rear window, gray privacy glass, deluxe ETR stereo with CD and 4 speakers, sunvisor with mirror and pocket and color keyed package: color-keyed front bumper, color keyed grille and chrome plated rear bumper.*	NC	NC
WI	Spare Tire Security Lock	30	49
WL	Alloy Wheel Locks	31	52
WR	Sliding Rear Window (X-Cab Except Limited) *Includes gray privacy glass.*	228	285
WR	Sliding Rear Window (Reg Cab)	128	160
WS	Steel Wheel Locks	31	52

NOTE: Toyotas sold in AL, FL, GA, NC and SC may be equipped with option packages not listed in this guide. You can expect to haggle 25% off the window sticker price of these packages.

2000 TUNDRA

2000 Toyota Tundra

What's New?

This is an all-new, full-size pickup truck designed to compete with the Ford F-150, Chevrolet Silverado 1500, GMC Sierra 1500 and Dodge Ram 1500. It features an optional V8 engine and can be ordered in a two or four-door, extended-cab configuration.

Review

As the maker of America's best-selling automobile (the Camry), if must have been frustrating for Toyota to learn that trucks are now outselling cars in this country. Especially since the closest thing to a full-size pickup truck previously offered by Toyota was the anemic and poorly received T100.

With the introduction of the Tundra in spring of 1999, as a 2000 model, Toyota has finally crafted a full-fledged, maximum-sized pickup, capable of running with the big dogs. Topping its pedigree is an optional 4.7-liter, I-Force V8 engine lifted directly from the Land Cruiser/LX 470 sport utility twins. This powerplant makes 245 horsepower and 315 foot-pounds of torque and can be mated to either a four-speed automatic or five-speed manual transmission. Payload capacity is 2,000 pounds and towing capacities for the V8 start at 5,000 pounds (it goes up to 7,000 pounds with an optional tow package). A 3.4-liter V6, making 190 horsepower and 220 foot-pounds of torque, is standard on base model Tundras.

Toyota has also met the demand of current truck buyers when it comes to configuration. The Tundra is available in regular and extended-cab versions. The latter with two rear-facing doors for easier rear-seat access (which, by the way, is what Toyota calls its four door Tundra layout: Access). Unfortunately, regular-cab versions come in longbed form only while Access cab models come only as shortbeds.

Inside, the Tundra feels a bit more compact than its American counterparts, but not uncomfortably so for front-seat passengers. Rear seating is another matter, with legroom at a premium for anyone of average height. With the exception of rear seating, the Tundra cabin is an excellent place to spend the day. It offers a quiet ride that surpasses competing trucks, as well as many cars. Options like leather seating and a 10-disc CD changer further contribute to the Tundra's relaxing internal environment.

We wish Toyota offered more variety in areas like configuration and option packages, and an increase in rear-seat legroom would help the Tundra better compete with the extended cab models from GM, Ford and Dodge. Still, the very fact that a V8-powered, full-size pickup can now be had with a Toyota nameplate on it means a whole new set of rules for America's truck buyer.

Safety Data

Side Airbag: *Not Available*
4-Wheel ABS: *Optional*
Driver Crash Test Grade: *Not Available*
Side Impact Crash Test Front: *Not Available*
Crash Offset: *Not Available*
Integrated Child Seat(s): *Not Available*
Traction Control: *Not Available*
Passenger Crash Test Grade: *Not Available*
Side Impact Crash Test Rear: *Not Available*

Standard Equipment

BASE 2WD REGULAR CAB (5M) : 3.4L V6 DOHC SMPI 24-valve engine; 5-speed overdrive manual transmission; rear wheel drive; regular pickup box; driver's and passenger's manual black outside mirrors; 2 power accessory outlets; driver side airbag, passenger side cancelable airbag; tinted windows; fixed interval front windshield wipers; bench front seat; seatbelts with front pretensioners; vinyl seats, with rubber floor mats; front cupholder.

SR5 2WD ACCESS CAB (5M) (in addition to or instead of BASE 2WD REGULAR CAB (5M) equipment): Front and rear mud flaps; air conditioning; variable intermittent front windshield wipers; 60-40 folding rear split-bench seat with adjustable rear headrest, center armrest; steering wheel with tilt adjustment.

SR5 4WD REGULAR CAB (5M) (in addition to or instead of SR5 2WD ACCESS CAB (5M) equipment): Part-time 4 wheel drive.

SR5 V8 2WD ACCESS CAB (4A) (in addition to or instead of SR5 4WD REGULAR CAB (5M) equipment): 4.7L V8 DOHC SMPI 32-valve engine; 4-speed electronic overdrive automatic transmission with lock-up; rear wheel drive; cruise control; 60-40 folding rear split-bench seat with adjustable rear headrest and center armrest.

SR5 V8 4WD REGULAR CAB (4A) (in addition to or instead of SR5 V8 2WD ACCESS CAB (4A) equipment): Part-time 4 wheel drive; 60-40 split-bench front seat.

SR5 4WD ACCESS CAB (5M) (in addition to or instead of SR5 4WD REGULAR CAB (5M) equipment): Front captain seats; 60-40 folding rear split-bench seat with adjustable rear headrest and center armrest.

LIMITED V8 2WD ACCESS CAB (4A) (in addition to or instead of SR5 4WD ACCESS CAB (5M) equipment): 4.7L V8 DOHC SMPI 32-valve engine; 4-speed electronic overdrive automatic transmission with lock-up; rear wheel drive; additional exterior lights include front fog/driving lights; driver's and passenger's power remote chrome outside mirrors; cruise control; deep tinted windows, power front windows; variable intermittent front windshield wipers sliding rear window; bench front seat; dual auxiliary visors.

SR5 V8 4WD ACCESS CAB (4A) (in addition to or instead of SR5 V8 4WD REGULAR CAB (4A) equipment): 60-40 folding rear split-bench seat with adjustable rear headrest, center armrest.

LIMITED V8 4WD ACCESS CAB (4A) (in addition to or instead of LTD V8 2WD ACCESS CAB (4A) equipment): Part-time 4 wheel drive; front and rear mud flaps; front and rear 16" diameter alloy wheels; 60-40 split-bench front seat.

Base Prices

Code	Description	Invoice	MSRP
7711	Base 2WD Regular Cab (5M)	13359	14995
7811	SR5 4WD Regular Cab (5M)	17992	20195
7818	SR5 V8 4WD Regular Cab (4A)	20232	22710

CODE	DESCRIPTION	INVOICE	MSRP
7721	SR5 2WD Access Cab (5M)	17974	20175
7728	SR5 V8 2WD Access Cab (4A)	19822	22250
7821	SR5 4WD Access Cab (5M)	20825	23375
7828	SR5 V8 4WD Access Cab (4A)	22794	25585
7738	Limited V8 2WD Access Cab (4A)	21822	24495
7838	Limited V8 4WD Access Cab (4A)	24794	27830
Destination Charge:		420	420

Accessories

CODE	DESCRIPTION	INVOICE	MSRP
4AT	Transmission: 4-Speed Automatic (SR5 2WD X-Cab)	682	765
4AT	Transmission: 4-Speed Automatic (SR5 4WD X-Cab)	735	825
4AT	Transmission: 4-Speed Automatic (SR5 2WD Reg Cab)	801	900
4AT	Transmission: 4-Speed Automatic (Base Reg Cab)	747	840
AA	Wheels: 16" Aluminum (SR5) *Includes 5-spoke cast aluminum wheels, front and rear contoured mudguards, wheel ornament and black overfenders. NOT AVAILABLE with AL, AY, ST, SV, LO, OF.*	584	730
AB	Antilock Brake System *Includes 4-wheel ABS and daytime running lights. NOT AVAILABLE with LO.*	539	630
AC	Air Conditioner (Base Reg Cab)	788	985
AL	Wheels: 16" Aluminum (4WD/SR5 2WD) *Includes 1-piece 5 spoke cast aluminum wheels, wheel ornament and chrome-lined wheel arch molding. NOT AVAILABLE with AA, AY, ST, SV, LO, OF.*	480	600
AY	Wheels: 16" Aluminum (4WD/SR5 2WD) *Includes P245/70R16 tires. NOT AVAILABLE with AA, AL, ST, SV, LO, OF.*	304	380
CB	Painted Bumper (Base Reg Cab)	120	150
CC	Cloth Captain's Chairs (Limited) *Includes power driver's seat. NOT AVAILABLE with LA.*	316	395
CC	Cloth Captain's Chairs (SR5 2WD/SR5 - 4WD X-Cab/4WD Reg Cab V8) *REQUIRES 4AT. NOT AVAILABLE with LO.*	60	75
CC	Cloth Captain's Chairs (SR5 4WD Reg Cab) *REQUIRES 4AT. NOT AVAILABLE with SB.*	244	305
CK	All Weather Guard Package *Includes anti-chip paint, heavy duty starter and heavy duty heater. REQUIRES MG.*	59	70
CQ	Convenience Package (SR5 V6 X-Cab) *Includes lighting package, power door locks, driver and passenger double sunvisor, chrome power mirrors, sliding rear window with privacy glass and cruise control.*	1048	1310
CQ	Convenience Package (SR5 V8) *Includes lighting package, power door locks, driver and passenger double sunvisor, chrome power mirrors and sliding rear window with privacy glass. NOT AVAILABLE with LO.*	848	1060
DO	Delete Package (Base Reg Cab) *Includes vinyl floor mats and vinyl seats.*	(72)	(90)
DZ	Radio: Deluxe 3-In-1 Combo (SR5 4WD Reg Cab) *Includes AM/FM stereo, cassette, CD player and 4 speakers.*	75	100

CODE	DESCRIPTION	INVOICE	MSRP
DZ	Radio: Deluxe 3-In-1 Combo (SR5 2WD X-Cab) *Includes AM/FM stereo; cassette, CD player and 4 speakers. NOT AVAILABLE with LO.*	188	250
EJ	Radio: Premium 3-In-1 with CD Changer (Limited) *Includes AM/FM stereo, cassette, CD player, 6 disc in-dash CD changer, 6 speakers and power amplifier.*	150	200
FW	Full Wheel Covers (Base Reg Cab)	80	100
LA	Leather Package (Limited) *Includes leather captain's chairs with power driver's seat and synthetic wood trim. NOT AVAILABLE with CC.*	1136	1420
LF	Front Fog Lamps (All Except Limited) *NOT AVAILABLE with LO.*	80	100
LO	Payload Package (SR5 2WD V8) *Includes increased payload to 2,011 lbs and tires: P245/70R16. NOT AVAILABLE with AA, AB, AL, AY, CC, CQ, DZ, LF, ST, SV.*	364	455
MG	Black Mudguards (Base Reg Cab)	48	60
OF	Off Road Package (SR5 4WD X-Cab) *Includes front and rear contoured mudguards, wheel ornament, front fog lamps, black overfenders, tires: BF Goodrich P265/70, Bilstein shocks and off-road tuned suspension. NOT AVAILABLE with AA, AL, AY, ST, SV.*	740	925
OF	Off Road Package (Limited 4WD) *Includes front and rear contoured mudguards, wheel ornament, front fog lamps, black overfenders, tires: BF Goodrich P265/70, Bilstein shocks and off-road tuned suspension.*	76	95
SB	40/60 Split Bench Seat (SR5 4WD Reg Cab) *REQUIRES 4AT. NOT AVAILABLE with CC.*	184	230
ST	Wheels: 16" Styled Steel (SR5) *Includes wheel ornament and chrome-lined wheel arch molding. NOT AVAILABLE with AA, AL, AY, SV, LO, OF.*	176	220
SV	Wheels: Styled Steel (SR5 X-Cab) *Includes wheel ornament, front and rear contoured mudguards and black overfenders. NOT AVAILABLE with AA, AL, AY, ST, LO, OF.*	280	350
TW	Tilt Steering Wheel (Base Reg Cab) *Includes variable intermittent wipers with timer.*	171	200
TX	Two-Tone Paint (Limited)	292	365
WR	Sliding Rear Window (Base Reg Cab)	128	160

NOTE: Toyotas sold in Alabama, Florida, Georgia, North Carolina and South Carolina may be equipped with option packages not listed in this guide. You can expect to haggle 25% off the window sticker price of these packages.

1999 EUROVAN

1999 Volkswagen EuroVan

What's New?

After a five-year hiatus, the funky EuroVan passenger van returns to the U.S. with a six-cylinder engine, structural improvements and new safety features.

Review

Despite, or perhaps because of, myriad shortcomings, the Volkswagen Vanagon and its successor, the EuroVan, became people-mover cult favorites. Last marketed to Americans in non-RV guise in 1993, the EuroVan returns for 1999 with several improvements designed to make the oddball entry more palatable to American tastes.

The most obvious change to the 1999 model is the inclusion of a 140-horsepower VR6 six-cylinder engine. This motor, making 177 foot-pounds of torque at 3,200, allows the EuroVan to get out of its own way - finally! Charged with motivating more than two tons of steel, plastic and glass, the new EuroVan is still no drag strip performer, but we'll take what we can get. With this new engine, the EuroVan can tow a 4,400-pound trailer and haul nearly 1,000 pounds of cargo.

Engineers have also strengthened the EuroVan's body, reinforced the floor panels and stiffened the B and C pillars. Additional sound insulation cuts unwanted road and engine noise from filtering into the cabin.

Two trim levels are available: GLS and Multivan (MV). Order a GLS and you get seating for seven forward-facing passengers. The MV also seats seven, but two riders are looking out the back window and the third-row bench converts into a bed. An optional Weekender package is available on the MV and should prove quite popular. It includes a pop-up roof with a two-person bed, a small refrigerator, swiveling captain's chairs, side sliding windows with screens and an additional battery.

Standard equipment includes dual front airbags, daytime running lights, power windows and locks, air conditioning with pollen filtration, cruise, cassette stereo, heated washer nozzles, rear wiper with defroster, power mirrors and an automatic transmission. A sliding sunroof is available as long as you don't opt for the Weekender package, and GLS buyers can get leather trim with heated front seats.

EuroVans are covered by a five-year/50,000-mile powertrain warranty, and all scheduled maintenance for the first two years is free. Pull the seats out and the GLS is capable of moving

150 cubic feet of stuff. While some might find the price prohibitively high, many of you have been waiting patiently for this day. As George Costanza exclaimed on his way to the Hamptons, "Let's get nuts!"

Safety Data

Side Airbag: *Not Available*
4-Wheel ABS: *Standard*
Driver Crash Test Grade: *Not Available*
Side Impact Crash Test Front: *Not Available*
Crash Offset: *Not Available*
Integrated Child Seat(s): *Not Available*
Traction Control: *Standard*
Passenger Crash Test Grade: *Not Available*
Side Impact Crash Test Rear: *Not Available*

Standard Equipment

GLS (4A): 2.8L V6 SOHC SMPI 12-valve engine; 4-speed electronic overdrive automatic transmission with lock-up; 92-amp battery; 90-amp alternator; front wheel drive, traction control, 4.61 axle ratio; front independent double wishbone suspension with anti-roll bar, front torsion springs, front torsion bar, rear independent suspension with rear coil springs; power rack-and-pinion steering; 4 wheel disc brakes with 4 wheel antilock braking system; 21.1 gal capacity fuel tank; front license plate bracket; 3 doors with sliding right rear passenger door, liftback rear cargo door; front and rear body-colored bumpers; monotone paint; sealed beam halogen headlamps with daytime running lights; additional exterior lights include front fog/driving lights, center high mounted stop light; driver's and passenger's heated power remote body-colored folding outside mirrors; front and rear 15" x 6" silver alloy wheels; P205/65SR15 BSW AS front and rear tires; inside under cargo mounted full-size conventional steel spare wheel; air conditioning with climate control, rear air conditioning with separate controls, air filter, rear heat ducts; premium AM/FM stereo with seek-scan, cassette, 6 speakers, theft deterrent, and manual retractable antenna; cruise control; power door locks, remote keyless entry, child safety rear door locks; 2 power accessory outlets, driver's foot rest; instrumentation display includes tachometer, water temp gauge, in-dash clock, trip odometer; warning indicators include oil pressure, water temp warning, battery, lights on, key in ignition, low fuel; dual airbags; tinted windows, power front windows with driver's and passenger's 1-touch down, sliding rear windows; fixed interval front windshield wipers with heated jets, fixed interval rear wiper, rear window defroster; seating capacity of 7, front bucket seats with adjustable tilt headrests, driver's and passenger's armrests, driver's seat includes 4-way direction control, passenger's seat includes 4-way direction control; full folding bench 2nd row seat with center pass-thru armrest; 3rd row removable full folding bench seat with tilt headrests; front height-adjustable seatbelts with front pretensioners; cloth seats, cloth door trim insert, full vinyl headliner, full carpet floor covering; interior lights include dome light, front reading lights; dual illuminated vanity mirrors; day-night rearview mirror; locking glove box, front and rear cupholders, dashboard storage, 2 seat back storage pockets, driver's and passenger's door bins; carpeted cargo floor, plastic trunk lid, cargo cover, cargo tie downs, cargo light; body-colored grille, black side window moldings, black front windshield molding, black rear window molding and black door handles.

MV (4A) (in addition to or instead of GLS (4A) equipment): Three power accessory outlets; removable 3rd row full folding bench seat convertabed with reclining adjustable 3rd row headrest and interior lights include rear reading lights.

Base Prices

Code	Description	Invoice	MSRP
7DC2L3	GLS (4A)	27519	30650
7DCML3	MV (4A)	28858	32150
Destination Charge:		590	590

CODE	DESCRIPTION	INVOICE	MSRP
	Accessories		
3EF	Power Glass Sunroof *NOT AVAILABLE with W2B.*	873	1000
4A3	Heated Front Seats	349	400
BOW	Emissions: California	98	100
CMP	Metallic Paint: Pearl Clearcoat	241	275
NEV	Emissions: Northeastern States	98	100
W28	Weekender Package (MV) *Includes pop-up roof with 2-person bed, air conditioning, window screens, refrigerator, second battery, 120-amp alternator and window curtains.*	3051	3495

Specifications and EPA Mileage Ratings

New Trucks

Contents

1999 Suzuki Grand Vitara

SPECIFICATIONS & EPA MILEAGE RATINGS	EPA Hwy (mpg) - Auto	EPA City (mpg) - Auto	EPA Hwy (mpg) - Manual	EPA City (mpg) - Manual	Towing Capacity	Fuel Capacity	Torque @ RPM	Horsepower @ RPM	Displacement (liters)	Number of Cylinders	Maximum Payload (lbs.)	Max Cargo Capacity (cu ft.)	Maximum Seating	Rear Leg Room (in.)	Front Leg Room (in.)	Rear Head Room (in.)	Front Head Room (in.)	Wheelbase (in.)	Curb Weight (lbs.)	Height (in.)	Width (in.)	Length (in.)	Turning Circle (in.)	Braking Dist. (60-0/ft)	Acceleration (0-60/sec)
ACURA																									
SLX	19	15	NA	NA	5000	22.5	230@ 3000	215@ 5400	3.5	6	895	90.2	5	39.1	40.8	37.8	39.4	108.7	4615	72.2	72.2	187	38.1	145	9.9
CADILLAC																									
Escalade	16	12	NA	NA	6500	30	330@ 2800	255@ 4600	5.7	8	1423	118.2	5	36.4	41.7	38.9	39.9	117.5	5867	79	78.8	201.2	40.7	151	10.1
CHEVROLET																									
Astro RWD Passenger	21	16	NA	NA	5500	25	250@ 2800	190@ 4400	4.3	6	1763	170	8	36.5	41.6	37.9	39.2	111.2	4187	76	77.5	189.8	39.5	150	9.9
Astro AWD Passenger	19	15	NA	NA	5000	25	250@ 2800	190@ 4400	4.3	6	1649	170	8	36.5	41.6	37.9	39.2	111.2	4397	76	77.5	189.8	40.5	148	11.5
Blazer 2WD 2-Door	21	16	23	17	3500	19	250@ 2800	190@ 4400	4.3	6	950	67	5	35.6	42.4	38.3	39.6	100.5	3536	64.9	67.8	176.8	34.8	147	9
Blazer 4WD 2-Door	20	16	18	15	3500	19	250@ 2800	190@ 4400	4.3	6	1025	67	5	35.6	42.4	38.3	39.6	100.5	3418	67.8	67.8	176.8	35.2	160	9.8
Blazer 2WD 4-Door	21	16	NA	NA	3500	18	250@ 2800	190@ 4400	4.3	6	1196	74	6	36.3	42.4	38.3	39.5	107	3692	64.3	67.8	183.3	36.6	154	9.6

SPECIFICATIONS & EPA MILEAGE RATINGS

SPECIFICATIONS & EPA MILEAGE RATINGS	Blazer 4WD 4-Door	C/K1500 C1500 X-cab SB	C/K1500 K1500 X-cab SB	C/K2500 2WD Reg Cab LB	C/K2500 2WD X-Cab LB	C/K2500 2WD Crew Cab SB	C/K2500 HD 4WD Reg Cab LB	C/K2500 HD 4WD X-Cab SB	C/K2500 HD 4WD X-Cab LB	C/K2500 4WD Crew Cab SB
Acceleration (0-60/sec)	9.3	9.5	NA	NA	NA	NA	NA	NA	NA	NA
Braking Dist. (60-0/ft)	150	148	NA	NA	NA	NA	NA	NA	NA	NA
Turning Circle (in.)	39.5	46.6	47.6	43.7	50.2	NA	44.7	47.6	52.2	NA
Length (in.)	183.3	217.5	217.9	213.4	237.4	231.8	213.4	218.5	237.4	231.8
Width (in.)	67.8	76.8	76.8	76.8	76.8	76.8	76.8	76.8	76.8	76.8
Height (in.)	64.2	70.6	72.6	71.2	72.6	73.9	76	74	74	74.5
Curb Weight (lbs.)	4023	4173	4566	4737	5107	NA	5165	5217	5470	NA
Wheelbase (in.)	107	141.5	141.5	131.5	155.5	154.5	131.5	141.5	155.5	154.5
Front Head Room (in.)	39.5	39.9	39.9	39.9	39.9	39.9	39.9	39.9	39.9	39.9
Rear Head Room (in.)	38.3	37.5	37.5	NA	37.5	40.8	NA	37.5	37.5	40.8
Front Leg Room (in.)	42.4	41.7	41.7	41.7	41.7	41.7	41.7	41.7	41.7	41.7
Rear Leg Room (in.)	36.3	34.8	34.8	NA	34.8	37.9	NA	34.8	34.8	37.9
Maximum Seating	6	6	6	3	6	6	3	6	6	6
Max Cargo Capacity (cu ft.)	74	NA	NA	69	69	56	69	56	69	56
Maximum Payload (lbs.)	1293	2027	1634	3516	3516	NA	3435	3383	3130	NA
Number of Cylinders	6	8	8	8	8	8	8	8	8	8
Displacement (liters)	4.3	5.0	5.0	5.7	5.7	5.7	5.7	5.7	5.7	5.7
Horsepower @ RPM	190@ 4400	230@ 4600	230@ 4600	255@ 4600	255@ 4600	255@ 4600	255@ 4600	255@ 4600	255@ 4600	255@ 4600
Torque @ RPM	250@ 2800	285@ 2800	285@ 2800	330@ 2800	330@ 2800	330@ 2800	330@ 2800	330@ 2800	330@ 2800	330@ 2800
Fuel Capacity	18	25	25	34	34	26	34	25	34	26
Towing Capacity	3500	5000	5000	8000	8000	8000	7500	7500	7500	7500
EPA City (mpg) - Manual	NA	15	13	15	14	15	13	13	13	13
EPA Hwy (mpg) - Manual	NA	20	18	19	19	19	18	18	18	18
EPA City (mpg) - Auto	16	15	14	15	15	15	13	13	13	13
EPA Hwy (mpg) - Auto	20	21	18	18	19	18	17	17	17	17

SPECIFICATIONS & EPA MILEAGE RATINGS

	C/K3500 2WD Reg Cab LB SRW	C/K3500 2WD X-Cab LB DRW	C/K3500 2WD Crew Cab SRW	C/K3500 4WD Reg Cab LB SRW	C/K3500 4WD X-Cab LB DRW	C/K3500 4WD Crew Cab LB SRW	C/K3500 4WD Crew Cab SB SRW	Express G1500 Passenger	Express G2500 Passenger	Express G2500 Psgr. Ext.
Acceleration (0-60/sec)	NA	NA	NA	NA	NA	NA	NA	9	NA	NA
Braking Dist. (60-0/ft)	NA	NA	NA	NA	NA	NA	NA	161	NA	NA
Turning Circle (in.)	43.4	50.5	53.8	45	52	55.8	55.8	45.1	47.4	53.4
Length (in.)	213.4	237.4	250.9	213.4	237.4	250.9	231.9	218.7	218.7	238.7
Width (in.)	76.8	94.3	76.8	76.8	94.3	76.8	76.8	79.2	79.2	79.2
Height (in.)	70	72.6	73.9	74	73.4	74.5	94.3	79.6	82.5	81.1
Curb Weight (lbs.)	4838	5427	5509	5229	5836	5893	5893	5075	5803	6008
Wheelbase (in.)	131.5	155.5	168.5	131.5	155.5	168.5	168.5	135	135	155
Front Head Room (in.)	39.9	39.9	39.9	39.9	39.9	39.9	39.9	40.6	40.6	40.6
Rear Head Room (in.)	NA	37.5	40.8	NA	37.5	40.8	40.8	39.2	39.2	39.2
Front Leg Room (in.)	41.7	41.7	41.7	41.7	41.7	41.7	41.7	41.2	41.2	41.2
Rear Leg Room (in.)	NA	34.8	37.9	NA	34.8	37.9	37.9	38.5	35.4	36.2
Maximum Seating	3	6	6	3	6	6	6	8	8	12
Max Cargo Capacity (cu ft.)	69	69	69	69	69	69	56	267.3	267.3	316.8
Maximum Payload (lbs.)	4171	4583	3499	3988	4184	3327	3334	2025	2798	2592
Number of Cylinders	8	8	8	8	8	8	8	6	8	8
Displacement (liters)	5.7	5.7	5.7	5.7	5.7	5.7	7.4	4.3	5.7	5.7
Horsepower @ RPM	255@ 4600	255@ 4600	255@ 4600	255@ 4600	255@ 4600	255@ 4600	290@ 4000	200@ 4400	245@ 4600	245@ 4600
Torque @ RPM	330@ 2800	330@ 2800	330@ 2800	330@ 2800	330@ 2800	330@ 2800	410@ 3200	250@ 2800	325@ 2800	325@ 2800
Fuel Capacity	34	34	34	34	34	34	26	31	31	31
Towing Capacity	7500	9000	7000	7000	7000	6500	10000	6000	8000	8000
EPA City (mpg) - Manual	NA	NA	NA	NA	NA	NA	NA	NA	NA	NA
EPA Hwy (mpg) - Manual	NA	NA	NA	NA	NA	NA	NA	NA	NA	NA
EPA City (mpg) - Auto	NA	NA	NA	NA	NA	NA	NA	15	13	13
EPA Hwy (mpg) - Auto	NA	NA	NA	NA	NA	NA	NA	19	18	18

SPECIFICATIONS & EPA MILEAGE RATINGS	EPA Hwy (mpg) - Auto	EPA City (mpg) - Auto	EPA Hwy (mpg) - Manual	EPA City (mpg) - Manual	Towing Capacity	Fuel Capacity	Torque @ RPM	Horsepower @ RPM	Displacement (liters)	Number of Cylinders	Maximum Payload (lbs.)	Max Cargo Capacity (cu ft.)	Maximum Seating	Rear Leg Room (in.)	Front Leg Room (in.)	Rear Head Room (in.)	Front Head Room (in.)	Wheelbase (in.)	Curb Weight (lbs.)	Height (in.)	Width (in.)	Length (in.)	Turning Circle (in.)	Braking Dist. (60-0/ft)	Acceleration (0-60/sec)
Express G3500 Passenger	18	13	NA	NA	10000	31	325@ 2800	245@ 4600	5.7	8	3563	267.3	8	35.4	41.2	39.2	40.6	135	5937	83.9	79.2	218.7	47.5	NA	NA
Express G3500 Psgr. Ext.	18	13	NA	NA	10000	31	325@ 2800	245@ 4600	5.7	8	3358	316.8	15	36.2	41.2	39.2	40.6	155	6142	82.5	79.2	238.7	53.5	NA	NA
S10 2WD Reg Cab SB	22	17	29	23	2000	19	140@ 3600	120@ 5000	2.2	4	1212	39	3	NA	42.4	NA	39.5	108.3	3029	63.2	67.9	190.1	36.9	148	12.3
S10 2WD Reg Cab LB	22	17	29	23	2000	19	140@ 3600	120@ 5000	2.2	4	1533	48	3	NA	42.4	NA	39.5	117.9	3204	62.9	67.9	206.1	39.8	148	12.3
S10 2WD X-Cab SB	26	19	29	23	2000	19	140@ 3600	120@ 5000	2.2	4	1158	39	5	NA	42.4	NA	39.6	122.9	3053	62.7	67.9	204.7	41.3	148	12.3
S10 4WD Reg Cab SB	21	16	21	17	3500	19	240@ 2800	180@ 4400	4.3	6	1094	39	3	NA	42.4	NA	39.5	108.3	3556	63.4	67.9	190.1	37.3	154	9
S10 4WD Reg Cab LB	21	16	21	17	3500	19	240@ 2800	180@ 4400	4.3	6	1531	48	3	NA	42.4	NA	39.5	117.9	3641	65	67.9	206.1	40.2	154	9
S10 4WD X-Cab	21	16	21	17	3500	19	240@ 2800	180@ 4400	4.3	6	900	39	4	NA	42.4	NA	39.6	122.9	3754	62.7	67.9	204.7	41.6	154	9
Silverado 1500 2WD Reg Cab SB V6	23	17	20	16	5000	26	260@ 2800	200@ 4600	4.3	6	2177	57	3	NA	41.3	NA	41	119	3923	71.2	78.5	203.3	40	NA	NA
Silverado 1500 2WD Reg Cab LB V6	23	17	20	16	5000	34	260@ 2800	200@ 4600	4.3	6	2368	71	3	NA	41.3	NA	41	133	4023	71	78.5	222.2	43.6	NA	NA

SPECIFICATIONS & EPA MILEAGE RATINGS	EPA Hwy (mpg) - Auto	EPA City (mpg) - Auto	EPA Hwy (mpg) - Manual	EPA City (mpg) - Manual	Towing Capacity	Fuel Capacity	Torque @ RPM	Horsepower @ RPM	Displacement (liters)	Number of Cylinders	Maximum Payload (lbs.)	Max Cargo Capacity (cu ft.)	Maximum Seating	Rear Leg Room (in.)	Front Leg Room (in.)	Rear Head Room (in.)	Front Head Room (in.)	Wheelbase (in.)	Curb Weight (lbs.)	Height (in.)	Width (in.)	Length (in.)	Turning Circle (in.)	Braking Dist. (60-0/ft)	Acceleration (0-60/sec)
Silverado 1500 4WD Reg Cab SB V6	20	16	18	15	4500	26	260@ 2800	200@ 4600	4.3	6	1852	57	3	NA	41.3	NA	41	119	4248	72.7	78.5	203.3	40.7	NA	NA
Silverado 1500 4WD Reg Cab LB V6	20	16	18	15	4500	34	260@ 2800	200@ 4600	4.3	6	2035	71	3	NA	41.3	NA	41	133	4365	72.7	78.5	222.2	44.5	NA	NA
Silverado 1500 2WD X-Cab SB V6	23	17	20	16	5000	26	260@ 2800	200@ 4600	4.3	6	1965	57	6	33.7	41.3	38.4	41	143.5	4235	71.2	78.5	227.6	46.6	NA	NA
Silverado 1500 2WD X-Cab SB V8	21	16	20	16	7000	34	285@ 4000	255@ 5200	4.8	8	1757	71	6	33.7	41.3	38.4	41	157.5	4442	71.2	78.5	246.7	50.4	NA	NA
Silverado 1500 4WD X-Cab SB V8	18	15	19	15	7500	26	285@ 4000	255@ 5200	4.8	8	1779	57	6	33.7	41.3	38.4	41	143.5	4621	72.7	78.5	227.6	47.3	NA	NA
Silverado 1500 4WD X-Cab LB V8	18	15	19	15	7500	34	285@ 4000	255@ 5200	4.8	8	1652	71	6	33.7	41.3	38.4	41	157.5	4748	72.7	78.5	246.7	51.1	NA	NA
Silverado 1500 LT 2WD X-Cab SB V8	20	16	NA	NA	8200	26	315@ 4000	270@ 5000	5.3	8	1965	57	5	33.7	41.3	38.4	41	143.5	4235	71.2	78.5	227.6	46.6	137	8.3
Silverado 1500 LT 2WD X-Cab LB V8	20	16	NA	NA	8200	34	315@ 4000	270@ 5000	5.3	8	1757	71	5	33.7	41.3	38.4	41	157.5	4442	71.2	78.5	246.7	50.4	137	8.9
Silverado 1500 LT 4WD X-Cab SB V8	18	15	NA	NA	8000	26	315@ 4000	270@ 5000	5.3	8	1779	57	5	33.7	41.3	38.4	41	143.5	4621	72.7	78.5	227.6	47.3	148	8.9
Silverado 1500 LT 4WD X-Cab LB V8	18	15	NA	NA	8000	34	315@ 4000	270@ 5000	5.3	8	1652	71	5	33.7	41.3	38.4	41	157.5	4748	72.7	78.5	246.7	51.1	148	8.9

SPECIFICATIONS & EPA MILEAGE RATINGS	Acceleration (0-60/sec)	Braking Dist. (60-0/ft)	Turning Circle (in.)	Length (in.)	Width (in.)	Height (in.)	Curb Weight (lbs.)	Wheelbase (in.)	Front Head Room (in.)	Rear Head Room (in.)	Front Leg Room (in.)	Rear Leg Room (in.)	Maximum Seating	Max Cargo Capacity (cu ft.)	Maximum Payload (lbs.)	Number of Cylinders	Displacement (liters)	Horsepower @ RPM	Torque @ RPM	Fuel Capacity	Towing Capacity	EPA City (mpg) - Manual	EPA Hwy (mpg) - Manual	EPA City (mpg) - Auto	EPA Hwy (mpg) - Auto
Silverado 2500 2WD Reg Cab LB 5.3	NA	NA	NA	222.2	78.5	73.7	4586	133	41	NA	41.3	NA	3	71	2614	8	5.3	270@ 5000	315@ 4000	34	8500	NA	NA	15	19
Silverado 2500 4WD Reg Cab LB 6.0	NA	NA	NA	222.2	78.5	74.5	5266	133	41	NA	41.3	NA	3	71	3334	8	6	300@ 4800	355@ 4000	34	10000	NA	NA	NA	NA
Silverado 2500 2WD X-Cab SB 5.3	NA	NA	NA	227.6	78.5	74	4766	143.5	41	38.4	41.3	33.7	6	57	2434	8	5.3	270@ 5000	315@ 4000	26	8500	NA	NA	15	19
Silverado 2500 2WD X-Cab LB 6.0	NA	NA	51.1	246.7	78.5	74.1	5485	157.5	41	38.4	41.3	33.7	6	71	1883	8	6	300@ 4800	355@ 4000	34	10500	NA	NA	12	16
Silverado 2500 4WD X-Cab SB 6.0	8.8	141	NA	227.6	78.5	74.4	5485	143.5	41	38.4	41.3	33.7	6	57	1716	8	6	300@ 4800	355@ 4000	26	10000	NA	NA	NA	NA
Silverado 2500 4WD X-Cab LB 6.0	8.8	141	51.1	246.7	78.5	74.5	5523	157.5	41	38.4	41.3	33.7	6	71	3077	8	6	300@ 4800	355@ 4000	34	10000	NA	NA	NA	NA
Suburban C1500	9.4	155	43.6	219.5	76.7	71.3	4825	131.5	39.9	38.9	41.3	36.4	9	150	1905	8	5.7	255@ 4600	330@ 2800	42	6500	NA	NA	14	18
Suburban K1500	10.3	156	44.6	219.5	76.7	71.3	5293	131.5	39.9	38.9	41.3	36.4	9	150	1836	8	5.7	255@ 4600	330@ 2800	42	6000	NA	NA	14	18
Suburban C2500	9.8	157	43.4	219.5	76.7	73.6	5249	131.5	39.9	38.9	41.3	36.4	9	150	3357	8	5.7	255@ 4600	330@ 2800	42	7516	NA	NA	NA	NA
Suburban K2500	10.4	164	45	219.5	76.7	74.6	5693	131.5	39.9	38.9	41.3	36.4	9	150	2914	8	5.7	255@ 4600	330@ 2800	42	7013	NA	NA	NA	NA

SPECIFICATIONS & EPA MILEAGE RATINGS

	Tahoe 2WD 2-door	Tahoe 4WD 2-door	Tahoe 2WD 4-door	Tahoe 4WD 4-door	Tracker 2WD Convertible	Tracker 4WD Convertible	Tracker 2WD 4-Door	Tracker 4WD 4-Door	Venture 3-Door	Venture 4-Door
Acceleration (0-60/sec)	7.8	8.5	8.8	9.5	NA	NA	NA	NA	9.8	10.2
Braking Dist. (60-0/ft)	148	150	149	161	NA	NA	NA	NA	141	141
Turning Circle (in.)	38	39	39.8	40.6	NA	NA	NA	NA	37.4	37.4
Length (in.)	188	188	199.6	199.6	148.8	148.8	159.8	159.8	186.9	186.9
Width (in.)	77.1	77.1	76.8	76.8	66.7	66.7	66.7	66.7	72	72
Height (in.)	71.4	72.8	72.8	75	66.5	66.5	66.5	66.5	67.4	67.4
Curb Weight (lbs.)	4632	4952	4423	4865	2596	2717	2860	2891	3671	3671
Wheelbase (in.)	111.5	111.5	117.5	117.5	86.6	86.6	97.6	97.6	112	112
Front Head Room (in.)	39.9	39.9	39.9	39.9	40.8	40.8	40.7	40.7	39.9	39.9
Rear Head Room (in.)	37.8	37.8	38.9	38.9	NA	NA	39.6	39.6	39.3	39.3
Front Leg Room (in.)	41.7	41.7	41.7	41.7	41.3	41.3	41.3	41.3	39.9	39.9
Rear Leg Room (in.)	36.4	36.4	36.4	36.7	35.9	35.9	35.9	35.9	36.9	36.9
Maximum Seating	5	5	6	6	4	4	5	5	7	7
Max Cargo Capacity (cu ft.)	99.4	99.4	118.2	118.2	10.2	10.2	20.2	20.2	127	127
Maximum Payload (lbs.)	1590	1396	1437	1534	NA	NA	NA	NA	1658	1612
Number of Cylinders	8	8	8	8	4	4	4	4	6	6
Displacement (liters)	5.7	5.7	5.7	5.7	1.6	1.6	2	2	3.4	3.4
Horsepower @ RPM	255@ 4600	255@ 4600	255@ 4600	255@ 4600	90@ 5600	90@ 5600	120@ 6000	120@ 6000	185@ 5200	185@ 5200
Torque @ RPM	330@ 2800	330@ 2800	330@ 2800	330@ 2800	100@ 4000	100@ 4000	122@ 3000	122@ 3000	210@ 4000	210@ 4000
Fuel Capacity	30	30	30	30	14.8	14.8	17.4	17.4	20	20
Towing Capacity	6012	6512	7013	6512	1000	1000	1500	1500	3500	3500
EPA City (mpg) - Manual	NA	NA	NA	NA	25	25	23	22	NA	NA
EPA Hwy (mpg) - Manual	NA	NA	NA	NA	28	28	25	25	NA	NA
EPA City (mpg) - Auto	15	13	15	15	23	23	24	23	18	18
EPA Hwy (mpg) - Auto	19	17	19	18	25	25	26	25	25	25

SPECIFICATIONS & EPA MILEAGE RATINGS	EPA Hwy (mpg) - Auto	EPA City (mpg) - Auto	EPA Hwy (mpg) - Manual	EPA City (mpg) - Manual	Towing Capacity	Fuel Capacity	Torque @ RPM	Horsepower @ RPM	Displacement (liters)	Number of Cylinders	Maximum Payload (lbs.)	Max Cargo Capacity (cu ft.)	Maximum Seating	Rear Leg Room (in.)	Front Leg Room (in.)	Rear Head Room (in.)	Front Head Room (in.)	Wheelbase (in.)	Curb Weight (lbs.)	Height (in.)	Width (in.)	Length (in.)	Turning Circle (in.)	Braking Dist. (60-0/ft)	Acceleration (0-60/sec)
Venture Extended 4-Door	25	18	NA	NA	3500	25	210@ 4000	185@ 5200	3.4	6	1457	156	7	36.9	39.9	39.3	39.9	120	3792	68.1	72	200.9	39.7	146	10.6
CHRYSLER																									
Town & Country SX FWD	24	18	NA	NA	2000	20	203@ 3250	158@ 4850	3.3	6	NA	143	7	36.6	41.2	40.1	39.8	113.3	3959	68.5	75	186.3	39.5	130	9.5
Town & Country LX FWD	24	18	NA	NA	2000	20	203@ 3250	158@ 4850	3.3	6	NA	169	7	39.6	41.2	40	39.8	119.3	4042	68.5	75	199.6	39.4	135	10.7
Town & Country LX AWD	23	16	NA	NA	2000	20	227@ 3100	180@ 4300	3.8	6	NA	169	7	39.6	41.2	40	39.8	119.3	4155	68.5	75	199.6	39.5	NA	NA
Town & Country Limited FWD	24	17	NA	NA	2000	20	227@ 3100	180@ 4300	3.8	6	NA	162	7	38.5	40.8	40	39.8	119.3	4224	68.5	75	199.6	39.4	135	9.9
Town & Country Limited AWD	24	17	NA	NA	2000	20	227@ 3100	180@ 4300	3.8	6	NA	162	7	38.5	40.8	40	39.8	119.3	4488	68.5	75	199.6	39.5	NA	NA
DODGE																									
Caravan Base	25	20	NA	NA	3500	20	167@ 4000	150@ 5200	2.4	4	NA	126.7	7	35.8	41.2	38.1	39.8	113.3	3517	68.5	76.8	186.3	37.6	146	10.8
Caravan SE/LE	24	18	NA	NA	3500	20	203@ 3250	158@ 4850	3.3	6	NA	126.7	7	35.8	41.2	38.1	39.8	113.3	3967	68.5	76.8	186.3	37.6	130	9.5

SPECIFICATIONS & EPA MILEAGE RATINGS	EPA Hwy (mpg) - Auto	EPA City (mpg) - Auto	EPA Hwy (mpg) - Manual	EPA City (mpg) - Manual	Towing Capacity	Fuel Capacity	Torque @ RPM	Horsepower @ RPM	Displacement (liters)	Number of Cylinders	Maximum Payload (lbs.)	Max Cargo Capacity (cu ft.)	Maximum Seating	Rear Leg Room (in.)	Front Leg Room (in.)	Rear Head Room (in.)	Front Head Room (in.)	Wheelbase (in.)	Curb Weight (lbs.)	Height (in.)	Width (in.)	Length (in.)	Turning Circle (in.)	Braking Dist. (60-0/ft)	Acceleration (0-60/sec)
Dakota Reg Cab 2WD SB	NA	NA	25	20	2000	15	145@ 3250	120@ 5200	2.5	4	1275	47	3	NA	41.9	NA	40	112	3335	65.2	71.5	196	36	152	8.3
Dakota Reg Cab 2WD LB	NA	NA	25	20	2000	15	145@ 3250	120@ 5200	2.5	4	1275	56	3	NA	41.9	NA	40	123.9	3396	65.2	71.5	214.5	39.4	152	8.3
Dakota Reg Cab 4WD SB	18	14	19	15	4100	15	225@ 3200	175@ 4800	3.9	6	1450	47	3	NA	41.9	NA	40	111.9	3808	67.9	71.5	196	35.8	157	8.8
Dakota X-Cab 2WD SB	NA	NA	25	20	2000	15	145@ 3250	120@ 5200	2.5	4	1275	47	6	32.1	41.9	38	40	131	3557	65.6	71.5	215	41.2	152	8.3
Dakota X-Cab 4WD SB	18	14	19	15	3800	15	225@ 3200	175@ 4800	3.9	6	1450	47	6	32.1	41.9	38	40	131	4022	68.1	71.5	215	41	157	8.8
Durango 2WD	19	14	NA	NA	4100	25	300@ 3200	230@ 4400	5.2	8	1656	88	8	35.4	41.9	40.6	39.8	115.7	4260	71	71.7	193.5	38.9	NA	NA
Durango 4WD	18	15	NA	NA	4100	25	300@ 3200	230@ 4400	5.2	8	1745	88	8	35.4	41.9	40.6	39.8	115.9	4689	72.5	71.7	193.5	38.9	146	9.3
Grand Caravan Basé/LE/SE FWD	24	18	NA	NA	3500	20	203@ 3250	158@ 4850	3.3	6	NA	169	7	39.6	41.2	40	39.8	119.3	3684	68.5	75.6	199.6	39.5	135	10.7
Grand Caravan ES FWD	22	15	NA	NA	3500	20	227@ 3100	180@ 4300	3.8	6	NA	169	7	39.6	41.2	40	39.8	119.3	4050	68.5	75.6	199.6	39.5	136	9.9
Grand Caravan ES/LE/SE AWD	22	15	NA	NA	3500	20	227@ 3100	180@ 4300	3.8	6	NA	169	7	39.6	41.2	40	39.8	119.3	4359	68.5	76.8	199.6	39.5	NA	NA

SPECIFICATIONS & EPA MILEAGE RATINGS

SPECIFICATIONS & EPA MILEAGE RATINGS	Ram 1500 2WD Reg Cab SB	Ram 1500 2WD Reg Cab LB	Ram 1500 4WD Reg Cab SB	Ram 1500 2WD X-Cab SB	Ram 1500 2WD X-Cab LB	Ram 1500 4WD Reg Cab LB	Ram 1500 4WD X-Cab SB	Ram 1500 4WD X-Cab LB	Ram 2500 2WD Reg Cab LB	Ram 2500 2WD Club Cab SB
Acceleration (0-60/sec)	12.1	12.1	8.7	9.5	9.5	8.7	9.5	9.5	NA	NA
Braking Dist. (60-0/ft)	149	149	160	153	153	160	153	153	NA	NA
Turning Circle (in.)	40.6	45.2	40.6	45.2	51.6	45.2	45.4	51.6	45.4	51.6
Length (in.)	199.9	220.1	204.1	224.2	244.1	224.1	224.2	244.1	224.1	224.2
Width (in.)	79.3	79.3	79.3	79.3	79.3	79.3	79.3	79.3	79.3	79.3
Height (in.)	72	72	75.4	71.6	72.7	75.4	74.6	76.9	72	71.6
Curb Weight (lbs.)	4021	4304	4567	4470	4658	4702	4778	4926	4378	4983
Wheelbase (in.)	118.7	134.7	118.7	138.7	154.7	134.7	138.7	154.7	134.7	138.7
Front Head Room (in.)	40.2	40.2	40.2	40.2	40.2	40.2	40.2	40.2	40.2	40.2
Rear Head Room (in.)	NA	NA	NA	39.4	39.4	NA	39.4	39.4	NA	39.4
Front Leg Room (in.)	41	41	41	41	41	41	41	41	41	41
Rear Leg Room (in.)	NA	NA	NA	33.2	33.2	NA	33.2	33.2	NA	33.2
Maximum Seating	3	3	3	6	6	3	6	6	3	6
Max Cargo Capacity (cu ft.)	56	72	56	56	72	72	56	72	72	56
Maximum Payload (lbs.)	2300	2125	1725	1655	1450	1560	1500	1325	3875	3575
Number of Cylinders	6	6	8	8	8	8	8	8	8	8
Displacement (liters)	3.9	3.9	5.2	5.2	5.2	5.2	5.2	5.2	5.9	5.9
Horsepower @ RPM	175@ 4800	175@ 4800	230@ 4400	230@ 4400	230@ 4400	230@ 4400	230@ 4400	230@ 4400	245@ 4000	245@ 4000
Torque @ RPM	230@ 3200	230@ 3200	300@ 3200	300@ 3200	300@ 3200	300@ 3200	300@ 3200	300@ 3200	335@ 3200	335@ 3200
Fuel Capacity	26	35	26	26	35	35	26	35	35	34
Towing Capacity	3600	3600	5200	3500	3500	5200	4800	4800	9100	9100
EPA City (mpg) - Manual	15	15	13	14	14	13	13	13	NA	NA
EPA Hwy (mpg) - Manual	21	21	18	19	19	18	18	18	NA	NA
EPA City (mpg) - Auto	15	15	13	13	13	13	13	13	NA	NA
EPA Hwy (mpg) - Auto	19	19	17	18	18	17	17	17	NA	NA

SPECIFICATIONS & EPA MILEAGE RATINGS	Ram 2500 2WD Club Cab LB	Ram 2500 2WD Quad Cab SB	Ram 2500 2WD Quad Cab LB	Ram 2500 4WD Reg Cab LB	Ram 2500 4WD Club Cab SB	Ram 2500 4WD Club Cab LB	Ram 2500 4WD Quad Cab SB	Ram 2500 4WD Quad Cab LB	Ram 3500 2WD Reg Cab DRW	Ram 3500 2WD Quad Cab DRW
Acceleration (0-60/sec)	NA	NA	NA	NA	NA	NA	NA	NA	NA	NA
Braking Dist. (60-0/ft)	NA	NA	NA	NA	NA	NA	NA	NA	NA	NA
Turning Circle (in.)	51.6	51.6	51.6	45.3	51.6	51.6	51.6	51.6	45.4	52.5
Length (in.)	244.1	224	244	224.1	224.2	244	224	244	224.1	244.1
Width (in.)	79.3	79.3	79.3	79.3	79.3	79.3	79.3	79.3	93.8	93.8
Height (in.)	72.7	71.6	7.3	75.4	71.6	72.7	71.6	72.7	72	72.7
Curb Weight (lbs.)	5103	4983	5103	4843	5211	5211	5211	5211	5392	5712
Wheelbase (in.)	154.7	138.7	154.7	134.7	138.7	154.7	138.7	154.7	134.7	154.7
Front Head Room (in.)	40.2	40.2	40.2	40.2	40.2	40.2	40.2	40.2	40.2	40.2
Rear Head Room (in.)	39.4	39.4	39.4	NA	39.4	39.4	39.4	39.4	NA	39.4
Front Leg Room (in.)	41	41	41	41	41	41	41	41	41	41
Rear Leg Room (in.)	33.2	33.2	33.2	NA	33.2	33.2	33.2	33.2	NA	33.2
Maximum Seating	6	6	6	3	6	6	6	6	3	6
Max Cargo Capacity (cu ft.)	72	56	72	72	56	72	56	72	72	72
Maximum Payload (lbs.)	3460	3495	3385	3565	3135	3035	3055	2955	5005	4755
Number of Cylinders	8	8	8	8	8	8	8	8	8	8
Displacement (liters)	5.9	5.9	5.9	5.9	5.9	5.9	5.9	5.9	5.9	5.9
Horsepower @ RPM	245@ 4000	245@ 4000	245@ 4000	245@ 4000	245@ 4000	245@ 4000	245@ 4000	245@ 4000	245@ 4000	245@ 4000
Torque @ RPM	335@ 3200	335@ 3200	335@ 3200	335@ 3200	335@ 3200	335@ 3200	335@ 3200	335@ 3200	345@ 3200	345@ 3200
Fuel Capacity	35	34	35	35	34	35	34	35	35	35
Towing Capacity	9100	9100	9100	8700	8700	8700	8700	8700	9600	9600
EPA City (mpg) - Manual	NA	NA	NA	NA	NA	NA	NA	NA	NA	NA
EPA Hwy (mpg) - Manual	NA	NA	NA	NA	NA	NA	NA	NA	NA	NA
EPA City (mpg) - Auto	NA	NA	NA	NA	NA	NA	NA	NA	NA	NA
EPA Hwy (mpg) - Auto	NA	NA	NA	NA	NA	NA	NA	NA	NA	NA

SPECIFICATIONS & EPA MILEAGE RATINGS	EPA Hwy (mpg) - Auto	EPA City (mpg) - Auto	EPA Hwy (mpg) - Manual	EPA City (mpg) - Manual	Towing Capacity	Fuel Capacity	Torque @ RPM	Horsepower @ RPM	Displacement (liters)	Number of Cylinders	Maximum Payload (lbs.)	Max Cargo Capacity (cu ft.)	Maximum Seating	Rear Leg Room (in.)	Front Leg Room (in.)	Rear Head Room (in.)	Front Head Room (in.)	Wheelbase (in.)	Curb Weight (lbs.)	Height (in.)	Width (in.)	Length (in.)	Turning Circle (in.)	Braking Dist. (60-0/ft)	Acceleration (0-60/sec)
Ram 3500 4WD Reg Cab DRW	NA	NA	NA	NA	9200	35	345@ 3200	245@ 4000	5.9	8	4610	72	3	NA	41	NA	40.2	134.7	5960	75.4	93.8	224.1	52.5	NA	NA
Ram 3500 4WD Quad Cab DRW	NA	NA	NA	NA	9200	35	345@ 3200	245@ 4000	5.9	8	4790	72	6	33.2	41	39.4	40.2	154.7	5940	76.9	93.8	244.1	52.5	NA	NA
Ram Wagon 1500	17	15	NA	NA	5700	32	230@ 3200	175@ 4800	3.9	6	2040	209	8	40.6	39	39.2	38.9	109.6	4245	79.6	78.8	192.6	39.4	165	9.8
Ram Wagon 2500	18	13	NA	NA	7700	36	300@ 3200	230@ 4400	5.2	8	2520	241	8	40.6	39	39.2	38.9	127.6	4290	80	78.8	208.5	46.2	NA	NA
Ram Wagon 3500	18	13	NA	NA	7900	36	300@ 3200	230@ 4400	5.2	8	3125	300	15	40.6	39	39.2	38.9	127.6	4645	83.6	78.8	234.5	52.4	NA	NA
FORD																									
Econoline E-150 Wagon	18	14	NA	NA	6900	35	250@ 2800	200@ 4800	4.2	6	NA	230	8	36.9	40	40.2	42.5	138	5087	80.9	79.3	211.9	46.7	162	11.1
Econoline E-350 Super Duty Wagon	NA	NA	NA	NA	NA	35	335@ 3000	235@ 4250	5.4	8	NA	230	12	36.9	40	40.2	42.5	138	5840	83.4	79.3	211.9	48	162	9.8
Econoline E-350 Super Duty Wagon	NA	NA	NA	NA	NA	35	335@ 3000	235@ 4250	5.4	8	NA	276	15	36.9	40	40.2	42.5	138	6174	84.1	79.3	231.9	48	162	9.8
Expedition 2WD	18	13	NA	NA	4000	26	293@ 3500	240@ 4750	4.6	8	1800	118	8	38.9	40.9	39.8	39.8	119.1	4808	74.3	78.6	204.6	40.4	NA	NA

SPECIFICATIONS & EPA MILEAGE RATINGS	EPA Hwy (mpg) - Auto	EPA City (mpg) - Auto	EPA Hwy (mpg) - Manual	EPA City (mpg) - Manual	Towing Capacity	Fuel Capacity	Torque @ RPM	Horsepower @ RPM	Displacement (liters)	Number of Cylinders	Maximum Payload (lbs.)	Max Cargo Capacity (cu ft.)	Maximum Seating	Rear Leg Room (in.)	Front Leg Room (in.)	Rear Head Room (in.)	Front Head Room (in.)	Wheelbase (in.)	Curb Weight (lbs.)	Height (in.)	Width (in.)	Length (in.)	Turning Circle (in.)	Braking Dist. (60-0/ft)	Acceleration (0-60/sec)
Expedition 4WD	16	12	NA	NA	4008	30	293@ 3500	240@ 4750	4.6	8	1800	118	8	38.9	40.9	39.8	39.8	119.1	5177	76.6	78.6	204.6	40.5	157	11.5
Explorer 2-Door OHV V6 2WD	21	16	23	18	2000	17.5	225@ 2750	160@ 4200	4	6	750	69	4	34.5	42.4	39.1	39.9	101.7	3675	67	70.2	180.8	34.6	140	9.5
Explorer 2-Door OHV V6 4WD	19	15	20	16	1799	17.5	225@ 2750	160@ 4200	4	6	750	69	4	34.5	42.4	39.1	39.9	101.7	3898	67	70.2	180.8	34.7	150	9.7
Explorer 4-Door OHV V6 2WD	19	14	23	18	1799	21	225@ 2750	160@ 4200	4	6	900	82	5	36.8	42.4	39.3	39.9	111.6	3819	67.7	70.2	190.7	37.3	148	9.5
Explorer 4-Door OHV V6 4WD	19	15	20	16	2800	21	225@ 2750	160@ 4200	4	6	900	82	5	36.8	42.4	39.3	39.9	111.6	4128	67.6	70.2	190.7	37.3	150	9.5
Explorer 4-Door OHC V6 2WD	20	16	NA	NA	4799	21	240@ 3250	210@ 5250	4	6	900	82	5	36.8	42.4	39.3	39.9	111.6	3819	67.7	70.2	190.7	37.3	129	8.5
Explorer 4-Door OHC V6 4WD	19	15	NA	NA	5600	21	240@ 3250	210@ 5250	4	6	900	82	5	36.8	42.4	39.3	39.9	111.6	4128	67.6	70.2	190.7	37.3	130	8.5
Explorer 4-Door V8 AWD	19	14	NA	NA	5600	21	288@ 3300	215@ 4200	5	8	900	82	5	36.8	42.4	39.3	39.9	111.6	4128	67.6	70.2	190.7	37.3	131	9.2
F-150 2WD Reg Cab SB V6	20	16	21	16	2300	25	255@ 3000	205@ 4750	4.2	6	1675	59	3	NA	40.9	NA	40.8	119.9	3850	72.7	78.4	205.6	40.5	152	10.3
F-150 2WD Reg Cab LB V6	20	16	21	16	2300	30	255@ 3000	205@ 4750	4.2	6	1555	73	3	NA	40.9	NA	40.8	138.5	3960	72.4	78.4	224.2	45.9	152	10.3

SPECIFICATIONS & EPA MILEAGE RATINGS

SPECIFICATIONS & EPA MILEAGE RATINGS	F-150 2WD X-Cab SB V6	F-150 2WD X-Cab LB V6	F-150 4WD Reg Cab SB V6	F-150 4WD Reg Cab LB V6	F-150 2WD Reg Cab LB V8	F-150 2WD Reg Cab SB V8	F-150 2WD X-Cab LB V8	F-150 2WD X-Cab SB V8	F-150 4WD Reg Cab LB V8	F-150 4WD Reg Cab SB V8
Acceleration (0-60/sec)	9.6	9.6	9.5	9.5	8.7	8.7	9.6	9.6	9.5	9.5
Braking Dist. (60-0/ft)	149	149	166	166	152	152	149	149	166	166
Turning Circle (in.)	45.9	51.3	40.5	45.9	45.9	40.5	51.3	45.9	45.9	40.5
Length (in.)	224.2	242.8	207.1	225.7	224.2	205.9	242.8	224.5	225.7	207.4
Width (in.)	78.4	78.4	79.5	79.5	78.4	79.1	78.4	79.1	79.5	79.5
Height (in.)	72.8	72.5	75.1	75.1	72.4	72.7	72.5	72.8	75.1	75.4
Curb Weight (lbs.)	4045	4200	4235	4339	3960	3929	4200	4203	4339	4310
Wheelbase (in.)	138.5	157.1	120.2	138.8	138.5	119.9	157.1	138.5	138.8	120.2
Front Head Room (in.)	40.8	40.8	40.8	40.8	40.8	40.8	40.8	40.8	40.8	40.8
Rear Head Room (in.)	37.8	37.8	NA	NA	NA	NA	37.8	37.8	NA	NA
Front Leg Room (in.)	40.9	40.9	40.9	40.9	40.9	40.9	40.9	40.9	40.9	40.9
Rear Leg Room (in.)	32.2	32.2	NA	NA	NA	NA	32.2	32.2	NA	NA
Maximum Seating	6	6	3	3	3	3	6	6	3	3
Max Cargo Capacity (cu ft.)	59	73	59	73	73	50	73	50	73	50
Maximum Payload (lbs.)	1780	1605	1700	1615	1930	2020	1575	1730	1785	1845
Number of Cylinders	6	6	6	6	8	8	8	8	8	8
Displacement (liters)	4.2	4.2	4.2	4.2	4.6	4.6	4.6	4.6	4.6	4.6
Horsepower @ RPM	205@ 4750	205@ 4750	205@ 4750	205@ 4750	220@ 4500	220@ 4500	220@ 4500	220@ 4500	220@ 4500	220@ 4500
Torque @ RPM	255@ 3000	255@ 3000	255@ 3000	255@ 3000	290@ 3250	290@ 3250	290@ 3250	290@ 3250	290@ 3250	290@ 3250
Fuel Capacity	25.1	30	24.5	30	30	25	30	25.1	30	24.5
Towing Capacity	2100	2100	1900	1900	2200	3300	3300	3300	1800	1800
EPA City (mpg) - Manual	16	16	15	15	14	14	14	14	14	14
EPA Hwy (mpg) - Manual	21	21	18	18	19	19	19	19	17	17
EPA City (mpg) - Auto	16	16	15	15	15	15	15	15	14	14
EPA Hwy (mpg) - Auto	20	20	18	18	19	19	19	19	17	17

SPECIFICATIONS & EPA MILEAGE RATINGS	EPA Hwy (mpg) - Auto	EPA City (mpg) - Auto	EPA Hwy (mpg) - Manual	EPA City (mpg) - Manual	Towing Capacity	Fuel Capacity	Torque @ RPM	Horsepower @ RPM	Displacement (liters)	Number of Cylinders	Maximum Payload (lbs.)	Max Cargo Capacity (cu ft.)	Maximum Seating	Rear Leg Room (in.)	Front Leg Room (in.)	Rear Head Room (in.)	Front Head Room (in.)	Wheelbase (in.)	Curb Weight (lbs.)	Height (in.)	Width (in.)	Length (in.)	Turning Circle (in.)	Braking Dist. (60-0/ft)	Acceleration (0-60/sec)
F-150 4WD X-Cab LB V8	17	14	17	14	3000	30	290@ 3250	220@ 4500	4.6	8	1440	73	6	32.2	40.9	37.8	40.8	157.4	4045	75.5	79.5	244.3	51.3	166	10.5
F-150 4WD X-Cab SB V8	17	14	17	14	3000	25.1	290@ 3250	220@ 4500	4.6	8	1610	50	6	32.2	40.9	37.8	40.8	138.8	4631	75.5	79.5	226	45.9	166	10.5
F-250 2WD Reg Cab	18	14	19	14	2600	30	290@ 3250	220@ 4500	4.6	8	2650	73	3	NA	40.9	NA	40.8	138.5	4300	73.8	78.4	220.8	45.9	NA	NA
F-250 2WD X-Cab	18	14	19	14	2500	25	290@ 3250	220@ 4500	4.6	8	2440	59	6	32.2	40.9	37.8	40.8	138.5	4364	72.6	78.4	220.8	45.9	NA	NA
F-250 4WD Reg Cab	16	13	17	13	2100	30	290@ 3250	220@ 4500	4.6	8	2510	73	3	NA	40.9	NA	40.8	138.8	4689	76.7	79.5	222.3	45.9	NA	NA
F-250 4WD X-Cab	16	13	17	13	2100	25	290@ 3250	220@ 4500	4.6	8	2435	59	6	32.2	40.9	37.8	40.8	138.8	4756	75.3	79.5	222.3	45.9	159	10.7
F-250 SuperDuty 2WD Reg Cab	NA	NA	NA	NA	9800	38	335@ 3000	235@ 4250	5.4	8	3840	78	3	NA	40.7	NA	41.3	137	4960	76.2	80	222.2	48.2	NA	NA
F-250 SuperDuty 4WD Reg Cab	NA	NA	NA	NA	9300	38	335@ 3000	235@ 4250	5.4	8	3360	78	3	NA	40.7	NA	41.3	137	5440	79.7	80	222.2	50.4	NA	NA
F-250 SuperDuty 2WD SuperCab	NA	NA	NA	NA	9400	29	335@ 3000	235@ 4250	5.4	8	3610	65	6	32.4	40.7	38.5	41.4	141.8	5190	76.6	80	227	49.6	NA	NA
F-250 SuperDuty 4WD SuperCab	NA	NA	NA	NA	9000	29	335@ 3000	235@ 4250	5.4	8	3160	65	6	32.4	40.7	38.5	41.4	141.8	5640	80.4	80	227	52	NA	NA

SPECIFICATIONS & EPA MILEAGE RATINGS	EPA Hwy (mpg) - Auto	EPA City (mpg) - Auto	EPA Hwy (mpg) - Manual	EPA City (mpg) - Manual	Towing Capacity	Fuel Capacity	Torque @ RPM	Horsepower @ RPM	Displacement (liters)	Number of Cylinders	Maximum Payload (lbs.)	Max Cargo Capacity (cu ft.)	Maximum Seating	Rear Leg Room (in.)	Front Leg Room (in.)	Rear Head Room (in.)	Front Head Room (in.)	Wheelbase (in.)	Curb Weight (lbs.)	Height (in.)	Width (in.)	Length (in.)	Turning Circle (in.)	Braking Dist. (60-0/ft)	Acceleration (0-60/sec)
F-250 SuperDuty 2WD Crew Cab	NA	NA	NA	NA	9100	29	335@ 3000	235@ 4250	5.4	8	3310	65	6	42.5	40.7	41	41.4	156.2	5490	77.2	80	241.4	53.7	NA	NA
F-250 SuperDuty 4WD Crew Cab	NA	NA	NA	NA	8700	29	335@ 3000	235@ 4250	5.4	8	2860	65	6	42.5	40.7	41	41.4	156.2	6000	80.8	80	241.4	56.6	NA	NA
F-350 2WD Reg Cab SRW	NA	NA	NA	NA	8300	38	335@ 3000	235@ 4250	5.4	8	4930	78	3	NA	40.7	NA	41.3	137	4970	76.3	80	222.2	48.2	NA	NA
F-350 4WD Reg Cab SRW	NA	NA	NA	NA	7800	38	335@ 3000	235@ 4250	5.4	8	4450	78	3	NA	40.7	NA	41.3	137	5450	80	80	222.2	50.4	NA	NA
F-350 2WD SuperCab SRW	NA	NA	NA	NA	7900	29	335@ 3000	235@ 4250	5.4	8	4700	65	6	32.4	40.7	38.5	41.4	141.8	5200	76.8	80	227	49.6	NA	NA
F-350 4WD SuperCab SRW	NA	NA	NA	NA	7500	38	335@ 3000	235@ 4250	5.4	8	4160	78	6	32.4	40.7	38.5	41.4	158	5650	80.3	80	243.2	57.2	NA	NA
F-350 2WD Crew Cab SRW	NA	NA	NA	NA	7600	29	335@ 3000	235@ 4250	5.4	8	4400	65	6	42.5	40.7	41	41.4	156	5500	77	80	241.4	53.8	NA	NA
F-350 4WD Crew Cab SRW	NA	NA	NA	NA	7200	29	335@ 3000	235@ 4250	5.4	8	3950	65	6	42.5	40.7	41	41.4	156	5950	81.2	80	241.4	56.6	NA	NA
F-350 4WD Crew Cab SRW LB	NA	NA	NA	NA	7200	38	335@ 3000	235@ 4250	5.4	8	3860	78	6	42.5	40.7	41	41.4	172	5950	81.3	80	257.6	61.6	NA	NA
F-350 2WD Reg Cab DRW	NA	NA	NA	NA	NA	38	335@ 3000	235@ 4250	5.4	8	5970	NA	3	NA	40.7	NA	41.3	137	5230	NA	80	222.2	NA	NA	NA

SPECIFICATIONS & EPA MILEAGE RATINGS	F-350 4WD Reg Cab DRW	F-350 2WD SuperCab DRW	F-350 4WD SuperCab DRW	F-350 2WD Crew Cab DRW	F-350 4WD Crew Cab DRW	Ranger 2WD Reg Cab SB	Ranger 2WD Reg Cab LB	Ranger 4WD Reg Cab SB	Ranger 4WD Reg Cab LB	Ranger 2WD SuperCab SB
Acceleration (0-60/sec)	NA	NA	NA	NA	NA	10.6	10.6	10.4	12	10.6
Braking Dist. (60-0/ft)	NA	NA	NA	NA	NA	161	161	150	152	161
Turning Circle (in.)	NA	NA	NA	NA	NA	36.7	36.7	37.4	37.4	38.1
Length (in.)	243.2	243.2	243.2	241.4	241.4	187.5	200.7	187.5	200.7	202.9
Width (in.)	80	80	80	80	80	69.4	69.4	69.4	69.4	69.4
Height (in.)	NA	NA	NA	NA	NA	63.9	63.8	67.4	67.4	64.1
Curb Weight (lbs.)	5710	5500	5900	5760	6200	3030	3086	3445	3505	3210
Wheelbase (in.)	158	158	158	156.2	156.2	111.6	117.5	111.6	117.5	125.7
Front Head Room (in.)	41.1	41.4	41.3	41.4	41.4	39.2	39.2	39.2	39.2	39.2
Rear Head Room (in.)	38.5	38.5	NA	41	41	NA	NA	NA	NA	NA
Front Leg Room (in.)	40.7	40.7	40.7	40.7	40.7	42.4	42.4	42.4	42.4	42.4
Rear Leg Room (in.)	32.4	32.4	NA	42.5	42.5	NA	NA	NA	NA	NA
Maximum Seating	6	6	3	6	6	3	3	3	3	5
Max Cargo Capacity (cu ft.)	NA	NA	NA	NA	NA	37	43	37	43	37
Maximum Payload (lbs.)	5650	5650	5300	5400	4910	1260	1260	1260	1260	1260
Number of Cylinders	8	8	8	10	10	4	4	6	6	4
Displacement (liters)	5.4	5.4	5.4	6.8	6.8	2.5	2.5	3	3	2.5
Horsepower @ RPM	235@ 4250	235@ 4250	235@ 4250	275@ 4250	275@ 4250	119@ 4800	119@ 4800	152@ 4750	152@ 4750	119@ 4800
Torque @ RPM	335@ 3000	335@ 3000	335@ 3000	410@ 2750	410@ 2750	146@ 2400	146@ 2400	192@ 3750	192@ 3750	146@ 2400
Fuel Capacity	38	38	38	38	38	16.5	19.5	16.5	19.5	19.5
Towing Capacity	NA	NA	NA	NA	NA	1600	1600	2300	2300	1300
EPA City (mpg) - Manual	NA	NA	NA	NA	NA	23	23	18	18	23
EPA Hwy (mpg) - Manual	NA	NA	NA	NA	NA	27	27	24	24	27
EPA City (mpg) - Auto	NA	NA	NA	NA	NA	21	21	17	17	21
EPA Hwy (mpg) - Auto	NA	NA	NA	NA	NA	25	25	23	23	25

SPECIFICATIONS & EPA MILEAGE RATINGS

Model	Acceleration (0-60/sec)	Braking Dist. (60-0/ft)	Turning Circle (in.)	Length (in.)	Width (in.)	Height (in.)	Curb Weight (lbs.)	Wheelbase (in.)	Front Head Room (in.)	Rear Head Room (in.)	Front Leg Room (in.)	Rear Leg Room (in.)	Maximum Seating	Max Cargo Capacity (cu ft.)	Maximum Payload (lbs.)	Number of Cylinders	Displacement (liters)	Horsepower @ RPM	Torque @ RPM	Fuel Capacity	Towing Capacity	EPA City (mpg) - Manual	EPA Hwy (mpg) - Manual	EPA City (mpg) - Auto	EPA Hwy (mpg) - Auto
Ranger 4WD SuperCab SB	10.4	150	39.4	202.9	69.4	67.5	3606	125.7	39.2	NA	42.4	NA	5	37	1260	6	3	152@ 4750	192@ 3750	19.5	2100	18	24	17	23
Windstar Base	10.9	139	NA	200.9	76.6	66.1	3761	120.7	39.3	41.1	40.7	36.8	7	146	1831	6	3	150@ 5000	172@ 3300	26	3500	NA	NA	17	24
Windstar LX/SE/SEL	9.7	139	NA	200.9	76.6	66.1	3890	120.7	39.3	41.1	40.7	36.8	7	146	1831	6	3.8	200@ 5000	225@ 3000	26	3500	NA	NA	17	24
GMC																									
C/K1500 2WD X-cab SB	9.4	146	46.6	218.5	76.8	70.4	4160	141.5	39.9	37.5	41.7	34.8	6	NA	2027	8	5.0	230@ 4600	285@ 2800	30	5000	15	20	15	21
C/K1500 4WD X-cab SB	NA	NA	47.6	217.9	76.8	72.6	4533	141.5	39.9	37.5	41.7	34.8	6	NA	1634	8	5.0	230@ 4600	285@ 2800	25	5000	13.	18	14	18
C/K2500 2WD Reg Cab	9.9	145	43.7	213.4	76.8	71.2	4737	131.5	40	NA	41.5	NA	3	69	3516	8	5.7	255@ 4600	330@ 2800	34	8000	14	19	15	19
C/K2500 2WD X-Cab	9.9	145	46.6	236.6	76.8	72.6	5084	155.5	40	38	41.5	28.7	6	69	3516	8	5.7	255@ 4600	330@ 2800	34	8000	14	19	15	19
C/K2500 2WD Crew Cab SB	NA	NA	NA	231.8	76.8	73.9	NA	154.5	40	40.8	41.5	37.9	6	56	NA	8	5.7	255@ 4600	330@ 2800	26	8000	NA	NA	NA	NA
C/K2500 HD 4WD Reg Cab	NA	NA	44.7	213.4	76.8	76	5165	131.5	40	NA	41.5	NA	3	69	3435	8	5.7	255@ 4600	330@ 2800	34	7500	14	19	15	19

SPECIFICATIONS & EPA MILEAGE RATINGS	EPA Hwy (mpg) - Auto	EPA City (mpg) - Auto	EPA Hwy (mpg) - Manual	EPA City (mpg) - Manual	Towing Capacity	Fuel Capacity	Torque @ RPM	Horsepower @ RPM	Displacement (liters)	Number of Cylinders	Maximum Payload (lbs.)	Max Cargo Capacity (cu ft.)	Maximum Seating	Rear Leg Room (in.)	Front Leg Room (in.)	Rear Head Room (in.)	Front Head Room (in.)	Wheelbase (in.)	Curb Weight (lbs.)	Height (in.)	Width (in.)	Length (in.)	Turning Circle (in.)	Braking Dist. (60-0/ft)	Acceleration (0-60/sec)
C/K2500 4WD X-Cab	19	15	19	14	7500	25	330@ 2800	255@ 4600	5.7	8	3383	56	6	28.7	41.5	38	40	141.5	5217	73.7	76.8	218.5	47.6	NA	NA
C/K2500 HD 4WD X-Cab	19	15	19	14	7500	34	330@ 2800	255@ 4600	5.7	8	3130	69	6	28.7	41.5	38	40	155.5	5470	74	76.8	237.4	52.2	NA	NA
C/K2500 4WD Crew Cab SB	NA	NA	NA	NA	7500	26	330@ 2800	255@ 4600	5.7	8	NA	56	6	37.9	41.5	40.8	40	154.5	NA	74.5	76.8	231.8	NA	NA	NA
C/K3500 HD 2WD Reg Cab SRW	19	15	19	14	7500	34	330@ 2800	255@ 4600	5.7	8	4171	69	3	NA	41.5	NA	40	131.5	4838	73.2	76.8	213.4	43.4	NA	NA
C/K3500 HD 2WD X-Cab DRW	19	15	19	14	9000	34	330@ 2800	245@ 4200	5.7	8	4583	69	6	28.7	41.5	38	40	155.5	5427	72.6	94.3	237.4	50.5	NA	NA
C/K3500 HD 2WD Crew Cab SRW	19	15	19	14	7000	34	330@ 2800	255@ 4600	5.7	8	3499	69	6	37.9	41.5	40.8	40	168.5	5509	73.9	76.8	250.9	53.8	NA	NA
C/K3500 2WD Crew Cab SB DRW	19	15	19	14	NA	26	410@ 3200	290@ 4000	7.4	8	3512	56	6	37.9	41.5	40.8	40	154.5	5509	73.9	94.3	231.9	53.8	NA	NA
C/K3500 HD 4WD Reg Cab SRW	17	13	18	13	7000	34	330@ 2800	255@ 4600	5.7	8	3988	69	3	NA	41.5	NA	39.9	131.5	5229	74	76.8	213.4	45	NA	NA
C/K3500 HD 4WD X-Cab DRW	17	13	18	13	7000	34	330@ 2800	255@ 4600	5.7	8	4184	69	6	28.7	41.5	38	40	155.5	5836	73.4	94.3	237.4	52	NA	NA
C/K3500 HD 4WD Crew Cab SRW	17	13	18	13	6500	34	330@ 2800	255@ 4600	5.7	8	3327	69	6	37.9	41.7	40.8	39.9	168.5	5893	74.5	76.8	250.9	55.8	NA	NA

SPECIFICATIONS & EPA MILEAGE RATINGS	EPA Hwy (mpg) - Auto	EPA City (mpg) - Auto	EPA Hwy (mpg) - Manual	EPA City (mpg) - Manual	Towing Capacity	Fuel Capacity	Torque @ RPM	Horsepower @ RPM	Displacement (liters)	Number of Cylinders	Maximum Payload (lbs.)	Max Cargo Capacity (cu ft.)	Maximum Seating	Rear Leg Room (in.)	Front Leg Room (in.)	Rear Head Room (in.)	Front Head Room (in.)	Wheelbase (in.)	Curb Weight (lbs.)	Height (in.)	Width (in.)	Length (in.)	Turning Circle (in.)	Braking Dist. (60-0/ft)	Acceleration (0-60/sec)
C/K 3500 4WD Crew Cab SB DRW	17	13	18	13	NA	26	410@ 3200	290@ 4000	7.4	8	3325	56	6	37.9	41.7	40.8	39.9	168.5	5893	94.3	76.8	231.9	55.8	NA	NA
Jimmy 2WD 2-Door	21	16	23	17	4500	19	250@ 2800	190@ 4400	4.3	6	932	67	5	35.6	42.4	38.3	39.5	100.5	3518	66	67.8	175	34.8	147	9
Jimmy 4WD 2-Door	20	16	18	15	4000	19	250@ 2800	190@ 4400	4.3	6	1002	67	5	35.6	42.4	38.3	39.5	100.5	3848	66.9	67.8	177.3	34.6	160	9.8
Jimmy 2WD 4-Door	21	16	NA	NA	4500	18	250@ 2800	190@ 4400	4.3	6	1329	74	5	36.3	42.4	38.1	39.5	107	3671	64.8	67.8	181.1	36.6	154	9.6
Jimmy 4WD 4-Door	20	16	NA	NA	4000	18	250@ 2800	190@ 4400	4.3	6	1301	74	5	36.3	42.4	38.1	39.5	107	4049	64.4	67.8	183.8	36.8	150	9.3
Safari Passenger RWD	20	16	NA	NA	5500	25	250@ 2800	190@ 4400	4.3	6	1763	170	8	36.5	41.6	37.9	39.2	111.2	4187	75	77.5	189.8	39.4	150	9.9
Safari Passenger AWD	19	15	NA	NA	5000	25	250@ 2800	190@ 4400	4.3	6	1672	170	8	36.5	41.6	37.9	39.2	111.2	4428	75	77.5	189.8	40.5	148	11.5
Savana G1500 Passenger LD	19	15	NA	NA	4000	31	250@ 2800	200@ 4400	4.3	6	1958	267	8	38.5	41.1	39	40.6	135	5070	81.4	79.2	218.8	45.2	161	9
Savana G2500 Pass HD	18	14	NA	NA	5500	31	330@ 2800	250@ 4600	5.7	8	2776	267	12	38.5	41.1	39	40.6	135	5717	82.7	79.2	218.8	47.4	NA	NA
Savana G2500 Ext Pass HD	18	14	NA	NA	5500	31	330@ 2800	250@ 4600	5.7	8	2555	317	12	38.5	41.1	39	40.6	155	5899	81.3	79.2	238.8	53.4	NA	NA

SPECIFICATIONS & EPA MILEAGE RATINGS

	Savana G3500 Passenger HD	Savana G3500 Ext Pass HD	Sierra 1500 2WD Reg Cab SB	Sierra 1500 2WD Reg Cab LB	Sierra 1500 4WD Reg Cab SB	Sierra 1500 4WD Reg Cab LB	Sierra 1500 2WD X-Cab SB	Sierra 1500 2WD X-Cab LB	Sierra 1500 4WD X-Cab SB	Sierra 1500 4WD X-Cab LB
Acceleration (0-60/sec)	NA	NA	NA	NA	NA	NA	NA	NA	8.9	8.9
Braking Dist. (60-0/ft)	NA	NA	NA	NA	NA	NA	NA	NA	148	148
Turning Circle (in.)	47.5	53.5	40	43.6	40.7	44.5	46.6	50.4	47.3	51.1
Length (in.)	218.8	238.8	203	221.9	203	221.9	227.5	246.4	227.5	246.4
Width (in.)	79.2	79.2	78.5	78.5	78.5	78.5	78.5	78.5	78.5	78.5
Height (in.)	81.3	82.1	71.2	71	73.8	73.7	71.2	70.8	72.7	72.7
Curb Weight (lbs.)	5905	6078	3923	4023	4248	4365	4235	4442	4621	4748
Wheelbase (in.)	135	155	119	133	119	133	143.5	157.5	143.5	157.5
Front Head Room (in.)	40.6	40.6	41	41	41	41	41	41	41	41
Rear Head Room (in.)	39	39	NA	NA	NA	NA	38.4	38.4	38.4	38.4
Front Leg Room (in.)	41.1	41.1	41.3	41.3	41.3	41.3	41.3	41.3	41.3	41.3
Rear Leg Room (in.)	38.5	38.5	NA	NA	NA	NA	33.7	33.7	33.7	33.7
Maximum Seating	15	12	3	3	3	3	6	6	6	6
Max Cargo Capacity (cu ft.)	267	317	57	71	57	71	57	71	57	71
Maximum Payload (lbs.)	3513	3294	2177	2368	1852	2035	1965	1757	1779	1652
Number of Cylinders	8	8	6	6	6	6	8	8	8	8
Displacement (liters)	5.7	5.7	4.3	4.3	4.3	4.3	4.8	4.8	4.8	4.8
Horsepower @ RPM	250@ 4600	250@ 4600	200@ 4600	200@ 4600	200@ 4600	200@ 4600	255@ 5200	255@ 5200	255@ 5200	255@ 5200
Torque @ RPM	330@ 2800	330@ 2800	260@ 2800	260@ 2800	260@ 2800	260@ 2800	285@ 4000	285@ 4000	285@ 4000	285@ 4000
Fuel Capacity	31	31	26	34	26	34	26	34	26	34
Towing Capacity	5500	5500	3500	3500	4000	4000	6000	6000	6500	6500
EPA City (mpg) - Manual	NA	NA	17	17	15	15	16	16	15	15
EPA Hwy (mpg) - Manual	NA	NA	23	23	18	18	20	20	19	19
EPA City (mpg) - Auto	14	14	16	16	16	16	16	16	15	15
EPA Hwy (mpg) - Auto	18	18	20	20	20	20	21	21	18	18

SPECIFICATIONS & EPA MILEAGE RATINGS

	Sierra 2500 2WD Reg Cab LB LD	Sierra 2500 2WD Reg Cab LB HD	Sierra 2500 2WD X-Cab SB HD	Sierra 2500 2WD X-Cab LB HD	Sierra 2500 4WD Reg Cab LB HD	Sierra 2500 4WD X-Cab SB HD	Sierra 2500 4WD X-Cab LB HD	Sonoma 2WD Reg Cab SB	Sonoma 2WD Reg Cab LB	Sonoma 2WD X-Cab
Acceleration (0-60/sec)	NA	NA	NA	NA	NA	8.8	8.8	12.3	12.3	NA
Braking Dist. (60-0/ft)	NA	NA	NA	NA	NA	141	141	148	148	NA
Turning Circle (in.)	NA	NA	NA	NA	NA	NA	NA	36.9	39.9	41.3
Length (in.)	222	222	227.6	246.5	222	227.6	246.7	190.6	206.6	205.3
Width (in.)	78.5	78.5	78.5	78.5	78.5	78.5	78.5	67.9	67.9	67.9
Height (in.)	73.7	73.7	74	74.1	74.2	74.4	74.5	63.2	65	63.3
Curb Weight (lbs.)	4586	4999	4766	5320	5266	5485	5523	3031	3058	3240
Wheelbase (in.)	133	133	143.5	157.5	133	143.5	157.5	108.3	117.9	122.9
Front Head Room (in.)	41	41	41	41	41	41	41	39.5	39.5	39.5
Rear Head Room (in.)	NA	NA	38.4	38.4	NA	38.4	38.4	NA	NA	NA
Front Leg Room (in.)	41.3	41.3	41.3	41.3	41.3	41.3	41.3	42.4	42.4	42.4
Rear Leg Room (in.)	NA	NA	33.7	33.7	NA	33.7	33.7	NA	NA	NA
Maximum Seating	3	3	6	6	3	6	6	3	3	5
Max Cargo Capacity (cu ft.)	71	71	57	71	71	57	71	39	48	39
Maximum Payload (lbs.)	2614	3601	2433	3280	3334	NA	NA	1171	1509	1168
Number of Cylinders	8	8	8	8	8	8	8	4	4	4
Displacement (liters)	5.3	6	5.3	6	6	6	6	2.2	2.2	2.2
Horsepower @ RPM	270@ 5000	300@ 4800	270@ 5000	300@ 4800	300@ 4800	300@ 4800	300@ 4800	120@ 5000	120@ 5000	120@ 5000
Torque @ RPM	315@ 4000	355@ 4000	315@ 4000	355@ 4000	355@ 4000	355@ 4000	355@ 4000	140@ 3600	140@ 3600	140@ 3600
Fuel Capacity	34	34	26	34	34	26	34	19	19	19
Towing Capacity	5000	5000	10500	5000	10000	10000	10000	2000	2000	2000
EPA City (mpg) - Manual	NA	NA	NA	NA	NA	NA	NA	23	23	23
EPA Hwy (mpg) - Manual	NA	NA	NA	NA	NA	NA	NA	29	29	29
EPA City (mpg) - Auto	15	12	15	12	NA	NA	NA	19	19	19
EPA Hwy (mpg) - Auto	19	16	19	16	NA	NA	NA	26	26	26

SPECIFICATIONS & EPA MILEAGE RATINGS	EPA Hwy (mpg) - Auto	EPA City (mpg) - Auto	EPA Hwy (mpg) - Manual	EPA City (mpg) - Manual	Towing Capacity	Fuel Capacity	Torque @ RPM	Horsepower @ RPM	Displacement (liters)	Number of Cylinders	Maximum Payload (lbs.)	Max Cargo Capacity (cu ft.)	Maximum Seating	Rear Leg Room (in.)	Front Leg Room (in.)	Rear Head Room (in.)	Front Head Room (in.)	Wheelbase (in.)	Curb Weight (lbs.)	Height (in.)	Width (in.)	Length (in.)	Turning Circle (in.)	Braking Dist. (60-0/ft)	Acceleration (0-60/sec)
Sonoma 4WD Reg Cab SB	21	16	21	17	5500	19	240@ 2800	180@ 4400	4.3	6	1094	39	3	NA	42.4	NA	39.5	108.3	3564	63.9	67.9	190.6	37.3	154	9
Sonoma 4WD Reg Cab LB	21	16	21	17	5500	19	240@ 2800	180@ 4400	4.3	6	1509	48	3	NA	42.4	NA	39.5	117.9	4053	65	67.9	206.6	40.1	154	9
Sonoma 4WD X-Cab	21	16	22	17	5500	19	240@ 2800	180@ 4400	4.3	6	896	39	4	NA	42.4	NA	39.5	122.9	3757	63.9	67.9	205.3	41.6	160	9.8
Suburban 1500 2WD	18	14	NA	NA	5500	42	330@ 2800	255@ 4600	5.7	8	1680	150	9	36.4	41.3	38.9	39.9	131.5	4769	71.3	76.7	219.5	43.7	157	10.3
Suburban 2500 2WD	NA	NA	NA	NA	6000	42	330@ 2800	255@ 4600	5.7	8	3357	150	9	36.4	41.3	38.9	39.9	131.5	5243	73.6	76.7	219.5	43.4	162	10.8
Suburban 1500 4WD	18	14	NA	NA	5000	42	330@ 2800	255@ 4600	5.7	8	2003	150	9	36.4	41.3	38.9	39.9	131.5	5226	73	76.7	219.5	47.8	NA	NA
Suburban 2500 4WD	NA	NA	NA	NA	7000	42	330@ 2800	255@ 4600	5.7	8	2913	150	9	36.4	41.3	38.9	39.9	131.5	5686	74.6	76.7	219.5	44.7	NA	NA
Yukon 2WD	19	15	NA	NA	6000	30	330@ 2800	255@ 4600	5.7	8	1629	118	6	36.2	41.7	38.9	39.9	117.5	4911	72.8	76.8	199.6	39	153	8.2
Yukon 4WD	19	15	NA	NA	5500	30	330@ 2800	255@ 4600	5.7	8	1423	118	6	36.2	41.7	38.9	39.9	117.5	5332	75	76.8	199.6	40.7	165	9.4
Yukon Denali	16	12	NA	NA	6500	30	330@ 2800	255@ 4600	5.7	8	1423	118.2	5	36.4	41.7	38.9	39.9	117.5	5867	79	78.8	201.2	40.7	151	9.9

SPECIFICATIONS & EPA MILEAGE RATINGS	EPA Hwy (mpg) - Auto	EPA City (mpg) - Auto	EPA Hwy (mpg) - Manual	EPA City (mpg) - Manual	Towing Capacity	Fuel Capacity	Torque @ RPM	Horsepower @ RPM	Displacement (liters)	Number of Cylinders	Maximum Payload (lbs.)	Max Cargo Capacity (cu ft.)	Maximum Seating	Rear Leg Room (in.)	Front Leg Room (in.)	Rear Head Room (in.)	Front Head Room (in.)	Wheelbase (in.)	Curb Weight (lbs.)	Height (in.)	Width (in.)	Length (in.)	Turning Circle (in.)	Braking Dist. (60-0/ft)	Acceleration (0-60/sec)
HONDA																									
CR-V FWD	25	22	NA	NA	1000	15.3	133@ 4500	146@ 6200	2	4	NA	67	5	36.7	41.5	39.2	40.5	103.2	3126	65.9	68.9	177.6	34.8	NA	NA
CR-V AWD	25	22	25	22	1000	15.3	133@ 4500	146@ 6200	2	4	NA	67	5	36.7	41.5	39.2	40.5	103.2	3164	65.9	68.9	177.6	34.8	141	9.9
Odyssey LX/EX	26	18	NA	NA	2000	20	229@ 4300	210@ 5200	3.5	6	NA	163	7	40	41	40	41.2	118.1	4288	69.7	75.6	201.2	37.7	146	9.5
Passport 2WD	20	16	20	18	4500	21.1	214@ 3000	205@ 5400	3.2	6	NA	81	5	35	42.1	38.3	38.9	106.4	3613	68.5	70.4	177.4	38.4	NA	NA
Passport 4WD	20	16	20	18	4500	21.1	214@ 3000	205@ 5400	3.2	6	NA	81	5	35	42.1	38.3	38.9	106.4	3860	68.5	70.4	177.4	38.4	156	9
INFINITI																									
QX4	19	15	NA	NA	5000	21.1	196@ 2800	168@ 4800	3.3	6	NA	85	5	31.8	41.7	37.5	39.5	106.3	4275	70.7	72.4	183.9	37.4	139	12
ISUZU																									
Amigo 2.2L 2WD	NA	NA	24	21	2500	17.7	144@ 4000	130@ 5200	2.2	4	1091	62	5	33.3	42.1	37.3	38.9	96.9	3359	66.6	70.4	167.8	35.4	NA	NA

SPECIFICATIONS & EPA MILEAGE RATINGS	Amigo V6 2WD	Amigo 2.2L 4WD	Amigo V6 4WD	Hombre 4-Cyl 2WD Reg Cab	Hombre 4-Cyl 2WD X-Cab	Hombre V6 4WD Reg Cab	Hombre V6 2WD X-Cab	Hombre V6 4WD X-Cab	Oasis S	Rodeo 2WD 4-Cyl
Acceleration (0-60/sec)	NA	12.2	8.2	12.3	NA	9	9.1	9.8	11.3	NA
Braking Dist. (60-0/ft)	NA	134	132	148	NA	154	156	160	140	NA
Turning Circle (in.)	35.4	35.4	35.4	37	41.3	37.3	41.3	41.6	37.6	38.4
Length (in.)	167.8	167.8	167.8	187.1	201.7	187.1	201.7	201.7	187.2	176.7
Width (in.)	70.4	70.4	70.4	67.9	67.9	67.9	67.9	67.9	70.6	70.4
Height (in.)	66.6	66.6	66.6	63.2	63.3	63.9	63.3	63.9	64.6	66.1
Curb Weight (lbs.)	3514	3583	3668	3024	3278	3583	3278	3583	3473	3471
Wheelbase (in.)	96.9	96.9	96.9	108.3	122.9	108.3	122.9	122.9	111.4	106.4
Front Head Room (in.)	38.9	38.9	38.9	39.5	39.6	39.5	39.6	39.6	40.1	38.9
Rear Head Room (in.)	37.3	37.3	37.3	NA	NA	NA	NA	NA	39.3	38.3
Front Leg Room (in.)	42.1	42.1	42.1	42.4	42.4	42.4	42.4	42.4	40.7	42.1
Rear Leg Room (in.)	33.3	33.3	33.3	NA	NA	NA	NA	NA	40.2	35
Maximum Seating	5	5	5	3	5	3	5	5	7	5
Max Cargo Capacity (cu ft.)	62	62	62	39	39	39	39	39	93	81
Maximum Payload (lbs.)	1136	1067	982	1176	1122	1067	1122	1067	1267	NA
Number of Cylinders	6	4	6	4	4	6	6	6	4	4
Displacement (liters)	3.2	2.2	3.2	2.2	2.2	4.3	4.3	4.3	2.3	2.2
Horsepower @ RPM	205@ 5400	130@ 5200	205@ 5400	120@ 5000	120@ 5000	180@ 4400	180@ 4400	180@ 4400	150@ 5600	130@ 5200
Torque @ RPM	214@ 3000	144@ 4000	214@ 3000	140@ 3600	140@ 3600	240@ 2800	240@ 2800	240@ 2800	152@ 4700	144@ 4000
Fuel Capacity	17.7	17.7	17.7	22.2	22.2	18.5	22.2	18.5	17.2	21.1
Towing Capacity	4500	2500	4500	2000	2000	5500	5500	5500	840	2500
EPA City (mpg) - Manual	NA	21	18	23	23	17	NA	17	NA	21
EPA Hwy (mpg) - Manual	NA	24	20	29	29	21	NA	21	NA	24
EPA City (mpg) - Auto	21	NA	18	19	19	16	19	16	21	NA
EPA Hwy (mpg) - Auto	24	NA	20	26	26	21	26	21	26	NA

SPECIFICATIONS & EPA MILEAGE RATINGS	EPA Hwy (mpg) - Auto	EPA City (mpg) - Auto	EPA Hwy (mpg) - Manual	EPA City (mpg) - Manual	Towing Capacity	Fuel Capacity	Torque @ RPM	Horsepower @ RPM	Displacement (liters)	Number of Cylinders	Maximum Payload (lbs.)	Max Cargo Capacity (cu ft.)	Maximum Seating	Rear Leg Room (in.)	Front Leg Room (in.)	Rear Head Room (in.)	Front Head Room (in.)	Wheelbase (in.)	Curb Weight (lbs.)	Height (in.)	Width (in.)	Length (in.)	Turning Circle (in.)	Braking Dist. (60-0/ft)	Acceleration (0-60/sec)
Rodeo 2WD V6	20	16	20	18	4500	21.1	214@ 3000	205@ 5400	3.2	6	NA	81	5	35	42.1	38.3	38.9	106.4	3651	68.5	70.4	176.7	38.4	NA	NA
Rodeo 4WD V6	NA	NA	20	16	4500	21.1	214@ 3000	205@ 5400	3.2	6	989	81	5	35	42.1	38.3	38.9	106.4	3863	68.5	70.4	176.7	38.4	156	9
Trooper	19	15	19	16	5000	22.5	230@ 3000	215@ 5400	3.5	6	980	90	5	39.1	40.8	39.8	39.8	108.7	4530	72.2	72.2	185.5	38.1	145	9.9
JEEP																									
Cherokee 2-Dr 2WD 4 Cyl	23	17	23	20	2000	20	150@ 3250	125@ 5400	2.5	4	1151	69	5	35	41.4	38	37.8	101.4	2979	63.8	69.4	167.5	35.8	NA	NA
Cherokee 4-Dr 2WD 4 Cyl	23	17	23	20	2000	20	150@ 3250	125@ 5400	2.5	4	1151	69	5	35	41.4	38	37.8	101.4	3032	63.8	69.4	167.5	35.8	NA	NA
Cherokee 2-Dr 4WD 4 Cyl	21	16	21	19	2000	20	150@ 3250	125@ 5400	2.5	4	1151	69	5	35	41.4	38	37.8	101.4	3125	63.8	69.4	167.5	35.8	145	12.2
Cherokee 4-Dr 4WD 4 Cyl	21	16	21	19	2000	20	150@ 3250	125@ 5400	2.5	4	1151	69	5	35	41.4	38	37.8	101.4	3181	63.9	69.4	167.5	35.8	145	12.2
Cherokee 2-Dr 2WD 6 Cyl	21	16	23	17	5000	20	225@ 3000	190@ 4600	4	6	1151	69	5	35	41.4	38	37.8	101.4	2979	63.8	69.4	167.5	35.8	NA	NA
Cherokee 4-Dr 2WD 6 Cyl	21	16	23	17	5000	20	225@ 3000	190@ 4600	4	6	1151	69	5	35	41.4	38	37.8	101.4	3032	63.8	69.4	167.5	35.8	NA	NA

SPECIFICATIONS & EPA MILEAGE RATINGS	EPA Hwy (mpg) - Auto	EPA City (mpg) - Auto	EPA Hwy (mpg) - Manual	EPA City (mpg) - Manual	Towing Capacity	Fuel Capacity	Torque @ RPM	Horsepower @ RPM	Displacement (liters)	Number of Cylinders	Maximum Payload (lbs.)	Max Cargo Capacity (cu ft.)	Maximum Seating	Rear Leg Room (in.)	Front Leg Room (in.)	Rear Head Room (in.)	Front Head Room (in.)	Wheelbase (in.)	Curb Weight (lbs.)	Height (in.)	Width (in.)	Length (in.)	Turning Circle (in.)	Braking Dist. (60-0/ft)	Acceleration (0-60/sec)
Cherokee 2-Dr 4WD 6 Cyl	20	15	20	17	5000	20	225@ 3000	190@ 4600	4	6	1151	69	5	35	41.4	38	37.8	101.4	3125	63.8	69.4	167.5	35.8	145	8.4
Cherokee 4-Dr 4WD 6 Cyl	20	15	20	17	5000	20	225@ 3000	190@ 4600	4	6	1151	69	5	35	41.4	38	37.8	101.4	3181	63.9	69.4	167.5	35.8	128	9.1
Grand Cherokee 2WD	21	16	NA	NA	5000	20.5	230@ 3000	195@ 4600	4	6	1150	72	5	35.3	41.4	39.5	39.7	105.9	3880	69.4	72.3	181.5	37.5	NA	NA
Grand Cherokee 4WD	21	16	NA	NA	5000	20.5	230@ 3000	195@ 4600	4	6	1150	72	5	35.3	41.4	39.5	39.7	105.9	4130	69.4	72.3	181.5	37.5	NA	NA
Wrangler SE	19	17	21	19	2000	19	140@ 3500	120@ 5400	2.5	4	800	55	4	34.9	41.1	40.6	42.3	93.4	3045	70.9	66.7	152	33.6	144	10.6
Wrangler Sport/Sahara	18	15	21	17	2000	19	222@ 2800	181@ 4600	4	6	800	55	4	34.9	41.1	40.6	42.3	93.4	3247	70.9	66.7	152	33.6	144	9
KIA																									
Sportage 2WD Conv	23	19	NA	NA	2000	14	127@ 4000	130@ 5500	2	4	838	39	5	31	41.3	38.2	39.6	92.9	3108	65	68.1	156.4	32.2	NA	NA
Sportage 4WD Conv	NA	NA	23	19	2000	14	127@ 4000	130@ 5500	2	4	838	39	5	31	41.3	38.2	39.6	92.9	3230	65	68.1	156.4	32.2	NA	NA
Sportage 4-Door 2WD	23	19	23	19	2000	15.8	127@ 4000	130@ 5500	2	4	860	55.4	5	31.1	44.5	37.8	39.6	104.3	3186	65	68.1	170.3	34.8	NA	NA

SPECIFICATIONS & EPA MILEAGE RATINGS	EPA Hwy (mpg) - Auto	EPA City (mpg) - Auto	EPA Hwy (mpg) - Manual	EPA City (mpg) - Manual	Towing Capacity	Fuel Capacity	Torque @ RPM	Horsepower @ RPM	Displacement (liters)	Number of Cylinders	Maximum Payload (lbs.)	Max Cargo Capacity (cu ft.)	Maximum Seating	Rear Leg Room (in.)	Front Leg Room (in.)	Rear Head Room (in.)	Front Head Room (in.)	Wheelbase (in.)	Curb Weight (lbs.)	Height (in.)	Width (in.)	Length (in.)	Turning Circle (in.)	Braking Dist. (60-0/ft)	Acceleration (0-60/sec)
Sportage 4-Door 4WD	23	19	23	19	2000	15.8	127@ 4000	130@ 5500	2	4	860	55.4	5	31.1	44.5	37.8	39.6	104.3	3352	65	68.1	170.3	34.8	170	12.1
LAND ROVER																									
Discovery Series II AWD	17	14	NA	NA	1650	23.4	233@ 3000	182@ 4750	4	8	1554	70	5	36.3	43.2	39.2	37.4	100	4465	77.4	70.6	178.7	39.4	NA	NA
LEXUS																									
RX300 FWD	24	19	NA	NA	3500	17.2	222@ 4400	220@ 5800	3	6	1258	39.8	5	36.4	41.3	37.2	39.5	103	3789	65.7	71.5	180.1	40	129	8.5
RX300 AWD	22	18	NA	NA	3500	17.2	222@ 4400	220@ 5800	3	6	1050	39.8	5	36.4	40.7	39.2	39.5	103	4037	65.7	71.5	180.1	24	129	8.7
LINCOLN																									
Navigator 2WD	17	13	NA	NA	8850	30	355@ 2750	300@ 5000	5.4	8	1800	116	7	39.7	41	39.8	39.8	119	5174	75.2	79.9	204.8	NA	149	9.9
Navigator 4WD	16	12	NA	NA	8700	30	355@ 2750	300@ 500	5.4	8	1600	116	7	39.7	41	39.8	39.8	119	5583	76.7	79.9	204.8	NA	158	10.3

SPECIFICATIONS & EPA MILEAGE RATINGS	EPA Hwy (mpg) - Auto	EPA City (mpg) - Auto	EPA Hwy (mpg) - Manual	EPA City (mpg) - Manual	Towing Capacity	Fuel Capacity	Torque @ RPM	Horsepower @ RPM	Displacement (liters)	Number of Cylinders	Maximum Payload (lbs.)	Max Cargo Capacity (cu ft.)	Maximum Seating	Rear Leg Room (in.)	Front Leg Room (in.)	Rear Head Room (in.)	Front Head Room (in.)	Wheelbase (in.)	Curb Weight (lbs.)	Height (in.)	Width (in.)	Length (in.)	Turning Circle (in.)	Braking Dist. (60-0/ft)	Acceleration (0-60/sec)
MAZDA																									
B2500 B2500 2WD Reg Cab	25	21	27	23	1380	17	146@ 3000	119@ 5000	2.5	4	1260	NA	3	NA	42.4	NA	39.2	111.6	3025	64.9	69.4	187.5	36.4	NA	NA
B2500 B2500 2WD X-Cab	25	21	27	23	1380	20.5	146@ 3000	119@ 5000	2.5	4	1260	NA	5	40.3	42.2	35.6	39.2	125.7	3355	64.7	69.4	202.9	41.6	NA	NA
B3000 B3000 2WD X-Cab	23	17	24	18	2500	20.5	185@ 3750	150@ 5000	3	6	1620	NA	5	40.3	42.2	35.6	39.2	125.7	3355	64.7	67.4	202.9	41.6	161	10.6
B3000 B3000 4WD Reg Cab	20	16	22	17	2380	17	185@ 3750	150@ 5000	3	6	1260	NA	3	NA	42.4	NA	39.2	111.6	3433	67.5	70.3	187.7	37	152	12
B3000 B3000 4WD X-Cab	20	16	22	17	2200	20.5	185@ 3750	150@ 5000	3	6	1260	NA	5	40.3	42.2	35.6	39.2	125.8	3625	67.5	70.3	201.7	41.6	152	12
B4000 B4000 2WD Reg Cab	22	16	23	18	3420	17	225@ 3000	160@ 4200	4	6	1260	NA	3	NA	42.4	NA	39.2	111.6	3025	64.9	69.4	187.5	36.4	151	8.3
B4000 B4000 2WD X-Cab	22	16	23	18	3420	20.5	225@ 3000	160@ 4200	4	6	1620	NA	5	40.3	42.2	35.6	39.2	125.7	3355	64.7	69.4	202.9	41.6	141	9.3
B4000 B4000 4WD X-Cab	20	16	20	16	3180	20.5	225@ 3000	160@ 4200	4	6	1500	NA	5	40.3	42.2	35.6	39.2	125.9	3625	67.5	70.3	201.7	41.6	150	9.5

SPECIFICATIONS & EPA MILEAGE RATINGS	EPA Hwy (mpg) - Auto	EPA City (mpg) - Auto	EPA Hwy (mpg) - Manual	EPA City (mpg) - Manual	Towing Capacity	Fuel Capacity	Torque @ RPM	Horsepower @ RPM	Displacement (liters)	Number of Cylinders	Maximum Payload (lbs.)	Max Cargo Capacity (cu ft.)	Maximum Seating	Rear Leg Room (in.)	Front Leg Room (in.)	Rear Head Room (in.)	Front Head Room (in.)	Wheelbase (in.)	Curb Weight (lbs.)	Height (in.)	Width (in.)	Length (in.)	Turning Circle (in.)	Braking Dist. (60-0/ft)	Acceleration (0-60/sec)
MERCEDES-BENZ																									
ML-Class ML320	21	17	NA	NA	5000	19	233@ 3000	215@ 5500	3.2	6	1684	85	5	38	44.3	39.7	39.8	111	4237	69.9	72.2	180.6	37.1	139	9
ML-Class ML430	18	15	NA	NA	5000	19	295@ 3000	268@ 5750	4.3	8	1684	85	5	38	44.3	39.7	39.8	111	4237	69.9	72.2	180.6	37.1	137	8.2
MERCURY																									
Mountaineer 2WD	20	15	NA	NA	4500	21	240@ 3250	210@ 5250	4	6	NA	80	5	35.8	42.4	39.3	39.9	111.6	4161	70.5	70.2	190.1	37.3	148	8.9
Mountaineer 4WD	19	15	NA	NA	4860	21	240@ 3250	210@ 5250	4	6	NA	80	5	35.8	42.4	39.3	39.9	111.6	4396	70.3	70.2	190.1	37.3	135	9
Mountaineer AWD	18	14	NA	NA	6400	21	288@ 3300	215@ 4200	5	8	NA	80	5	35.8	42.4	39.3	39.9	111.6	4396	70.3	70.2	190.1	37.3	154	9.2
Villager Base/Estate/Sport	24	17	NA	NA	2000	20	200@ 2800	170@ 4800	3.3	6	1290	136	7	36.4	39.9	39.9	39.7	112.2	3854	70.1	74.9	194.7	39.9	NA	NA
MITSUBISHI																									
Montero	19	16	NA	NA	5000	24.3	228@ 3500	200@ 5000	3.5	6	5840	67	7	37.6	40.3	40	40.9	107.3	4431	74.8	69.9	186.6	38.7	138	10.5

SPECIFICATIONS & EPA MILEAGE RATINGS	EPA Hwy (mpg) - Auto	EPA City (mpg) - Auto	EPA Hwy (mpg) - Manual	EPA City (mpg) - Manual	Towing Capacity	Fuel Capacity	Torque @ RPM	Horsepower @ RPM	Displacement (liters)	Number of Cylinders	Maximum Payload (lbs.)	Max Cargo Capacity (cu ft.)	Maximum Seating	Rear Leg Room (in.)	Front Leg Room (in.)	Rear Head Room (in.)	Front Head Room (in.)	Wheelbase (in.)	Curb Weight (lbs.)	Height (in.)	Width (in.)	Length (in.)	Turning Circle (in.)	Braking Dist. (60-0/ft)	Acceleration (0-60/sec)
Montero Sport ES	NA	NA	25	22	2300	19.5	148@ 2750	132@ 5500	2.4	4	1230	79.3	5	33.5	42.8	37.3	38.9	107.3	3500	65.6	66.7	178.3	40.7	143	12.3
Montero Sport LS/XLS 2WD	22	19	NA	NA	5000	19.5	188@ 4000	173@ 5250	3	6	1245	79.3	5	33.5	42.8	37.3	38.9	107.3	3755	65.6	66.7	178.3	40.7	NA	NA
Montero Sport LS/XLS 4WD	21	18	20	17	5000	19.5	188@ 4000	173@ 5250	3	6	1370	79.3	5	33.5	42.8	37.3	38.9	107.3	3980	65.6	66.7	178.3	40.7	143	11.2
Montero Sport LTD 2WD	20	17	NA	NA	5000	19.5	228@ 3500	200@ 5000	3.5	6	1045	79.3	5	33.5	42.8	37.3	38.9	107.3	3955	66.2	69.9	178.3	41	NA	NA
Montero Sport LTD 4WD	20	16	NA	NA	5000	19.5	228@ 3500	200@ 5000	3.5	6	1205	79.3	5	33.5	42.8	37.3	38.9	107.3	4145	66.2	69.9	178.3	41	NA	NA
NISSAN																									
Frontier 4-Cyl 2WD Reg Cab	24	20	26	22	3500	15.9	154@ 4000	143@ 5200	2.4	4	1400	46	3	NA	40.9	NA	39.3	104.3	2911	62.8	66.5	184.3	33.4	153	11.5
Frontier 4-Cyl 2WD X-Cab	24	20	26	22	3500	15.9	154@ 4000	143@ 5200	2.4	4	1330	44	4	NA	41.4	NA	39.3	116.1	3217	62.6	66.5	196.1	36.8	148	11.6
Frontier 4-Cyl 4WD Reg Cab	NA	NA	21	18	3500	15.9	154@ 4000	143@ 5200	2.4	4	1400	46	3	NA	40.9	NA	39.3	104.3	3554	66.1	71.9	184.3	35.5	148	11.6
Frontier 4-Cyl 4WD X-Cab	NA	NA	21	18	3500	15.9	154@ 4000	143@ 5200	2.4	4	1400	44	5	NA	41.4	NA	39.3	116.1	3599	65.9	71.9	196.1	39	153	11.5

SPECIFICATIONS & EPA MILEAGE RATINGS	EPA Hwy (mpg) - Auto	EPA City (mpg) - Auto	EPA Hwy (mpg) - Manual	EPA City (mpg) - Manual	Towing Capacity	Fuel Capacity	Torque @ RPM	Horsepower @ RPM	Displacement (liters)	Number of Cylinders	Maximum Payload (lbs.)	Max Cargo Capacity (cu ft.)	Maximum Seating	Rear Leg Room (in.)	Front Leg Room (in.)	Rear Head Room (in.)	Front Head Room (in.)	Wheelbase (in.)	Curb Weight (lbs.)	Height (in.)	Width (in.)	Length (in.)	Turning Circle (in.)	Braking Dist. (60-0/ft)	Acceleration (0-60/sec)
Frontier SE V6 4WD X-Cab	19	15	19	16	5000	19.4	200@ 2800	170@ 4800	3.3	6	1200	44	4	NA	41.4	NA	39.3	116.1	3726	65.9	71.9	196.1	39	138	11.2
Pathfinder 2WD	NA	NA	NA	NA	3500	21	200@ 2800	170@ 4800	3.3	6	1175	85	5	31.8	41.7	37.5	39.5	106.3	NA	67.9	72.4	178.3	35.4	NA	NA
Pathfinder 4WD	NA	NA	NA	NA	3500	21	200@ 2800	170@ 4800	3.3	6	1165	85	5	31.8	41.7	37.5	39.5	106.3	4050	67.9	72.4	178.3	42	NA	NA
Quest GXE/SE/GLE	24	17	NA	NA	3500	20.1	200@ 2800	170@ 4800	3.3	6	NA	125	7	36.4	39.9	39.9	38.1	112.2	3986	67.3	74.9	194.8	NA	NA	NA
OLDSMOBILE																									
Bravada	21	16	NA	NA	5000	18	250@ 2800	190@ 4400	4.3	6	1257	74.2	5	36.3	42.4	38.2	39.6	107	4049	64.4	67.8	183.7	39.5	147	9.9
Silhouette Regular	25	18	NA	NA	2000	20	210@ 4000	185@ 5200	3.4	6	1543	133	7	36.9	39.9	39.3	39.9	112	3721	67.4	72.2	187.4	37.4	146	9.8
Silhouette Extended	25	18	NA	NA	2000	25	210@ 4000	185@ 5200	3.4	6	1409	156	7	39	39.9	39.3	39.9	120	3948	68.1	72.2	201.4	39.7	146	9.8
PLYMOUTH																									
Grand Voyager Base	24	18	NA	NA	3500	20	203@ 3250	158@ 4850	3.3	6	NA	147.7	7	39.8	40.6	38.5	39.8	119.3	3683	68.5	76.8	199.6	39.5	136	11.2

SPECIFICATIONS & EPA MILEAGE RATINGS	EPA Hwy (mpg) - Auto	EPA City (mpg) - Auto	EPA Hwy (mpg) - Manual	EPA City (mpg) - Manual	Towing Capacity	Fuel Capacity	Torque @ RPM	Horsepower @ RPM	Displacement (liters)	Number of Cylinders	Maximum Payload (lbs.)	Max Cargo Capacity (cu ft.)	Maximum Seating	Rear Leg Room (in.)	Front Leg Room (in.)	Rear Head Room (in.)	Front Head Room (in.)	Wheelbase (in.)	Curb Weight (lbs.)	Height (in.)	Width (in.)	Length (in.)	Turning Circle (in.)	Braking Dist. (60-0/ft)	Acceleration (0-60/sec)
Grand Voyager SE	24	18	NA	NA	3500	20	203@ 3250	158@ 4850	3.3	6	NA	147.7	7	39.8	40.6	38.5	39.8	119.3	3812	68.5	76.8	199.6	39.5	136	11.2
Voyager Base	26	20	NA	NA	3500	20	167@ 4000	150@ 5200	2.4	4	NA	126.7	7	35.8	40.6	38.1	39.8	113.3	3516	68.5	76.8	186.3	37.6	146	12.1
Voyager SE	26	20	NA	NA	3500	20	203@ 3250	158@ 4850	3.3	6	NA	126.7	7	35.8	40.6	38.1	39.8	113.3	3711	68.5	76.8	186.3	37.6	146	10.8
PONTIAC																									
Montana Regular	25	18	NA	NA	3500	20	210@ 4000	185@ 5200	3.4	6	1655	130	7	36.9	39.9	39.3	39.9	112	3702	72.7	67.4	187.3	38.6	141	9.8
Montana Extended	25	18	NA	NA	3500	25	210@ 4000	185@ 5200	3.4	6	1437	155	7	39	39.9	39.3	39.9	120	3920	72.7	68.1	201.3	40.6	146	10.5
SUBARU																									
Forester Base/L/S	26	21	27	21	2000	15.9	162@ 4000	165@ 5600	2.5	4	1075	65	5	33.4	43	39.6	40.6	99.4	3058	62.8	68.3	175.2	35.4	133	9.3
SUZUKI																									
Grand Vitara 2WD	21	19	22	19	1500	17.4	160@ 4000	155@ 6500	2.5	6	926	45	5	35.9	41.4	39.6	39.9	97.6	3064	68	70.1	164.6	34.8	145	9.4

SPECIFICATIONS & EPA MILEAGE RATINGS	EPA Hwy (mpg) - Auto	EPA City (mpg) - Auto	EPA Hwy (mpg) - Manual	EPA City (mpg) - Manual	Towing Capacity	Fuel Capacity	Torque @ RPM	Horsepower @ RPM	Displacement (liters)	Number of Cylinders	Maximum Payload (lbs.)	Max Cargo Capacity (cu ft.)	Maximum Seating	Rear Leg Room (in.)	Front Leg Room (in.)	Rear Head Room (in.)	Front Head Room (in.)	Wheelbase (in.)	Curb Weight (lbs.)	Height (in.)	Width (in.)	Length (in.)	Turning Circle (in.)	Braking Dist. (60-0/ft)	Acceleration (0-60/sec)
Grand Vitara 4WD	20	18	21	19	1500	17.4	160@ 4000	155@ 6500	2.5	6	926	45	5	35.9	41.4	39.6	39.9	97.6	3197	68.5	70.1	164.6	34.8	145	9.4
Vitara 1.6 Conv. 2WD	27	25	28	25	1000	14.8	103@ 4000	97@ 5200	1.6	4	772	34	4	35.9	41.4	39.5	40.9	86.6	2601	65.7	67.3	152	31.6	NA	NA
Vitara 2.0 Conv. 2WD	25	23	24	22	1000	14.8	134@ 3000	127@ 6000	2	4	793	34	4	35.9	41.4	39.5	40.9	86.6	2690	66.1	67.3	152	31.6	NA	NA
Vitara 4-Door 2WD	25	23	25	22	1500	17.4	134@ 3000	127@ 6000	2	4	948	45	5	35.9	41.4	39.6	39.9	97.6	2866	68	67.3	163	34.8	NA	NA
Vitara 1.6 Conv. 4WD	27	24	27	25	1000	14.8	103@ 4000	97@ 5200	1.6	4	760	34	4	35.9	41.4	39.5	40.9	86.6	2723	66.5	67.3	152	34.8	NA	NA
Vitara 2.0 Conv. 4WD	25	23	24	22	1000	14.8	134@ 3000	127@ 6000	2	4	782	34	4	35.9	41.4	39.5	40.9	86.6	2811	66.5	67.3	152	34.8	NA	NA
Vitara 4-Door 4WD	25	23	25	22	1500	17.4	134@ 3000	127@ 6000	2	4	937	45	5	35.9	41.4	39.6	39.9	97.6	2987	68.5	67.3	163	34.8	NA	NA
TOYOTA																									
4Runner 4-Cyl 2WD	24	20	23	19	3500	18.5	177@ 4000	150@ 4800	2.7	4	1810	80	5	34.9	43.1	38.7	39.2	105.3	3440	67.5	66.5	178.7	37.4	NA	NA
4Runner 4-Cyl 4WD	22	18	21	16	3500	18.5	177@ 4000	150@ 4800	2.7	4	1515	80	5	34.9	43.1	38.7	39.2	105.3	3690	67.5	66.5	178.7	37.4	136	NA

SPECIFICATIONS & EPA MILEAGE RATINGS

	4Runner V6 4WD	4Runner V6 2WD	4Runner V6 4WD Limited	RAV4 2-Door Convertible FWD	RAV4 4-Door FWD	RAV4 2-Door Convertible AWD	RAV4 4-Door AWD	Sienna CE/LE/XLE	Tacoma 4-Cyl Reg Cab 2WD	Tacoma 4-Cyl Reg Cab 4WD
Acceleration (0-60/sec)	9.6	9.1	9.6	NA	10.5	NA	10.5	9.3	8.1	NA
Braking Dist. (60-0/ft)	138	136	138	NA	149	NA	149	134	136	NA
Turning Circle (in.)	37.4	37.4	37.4	33.5	36	33.5	36	40	35.4	34.4
Length (in.)	178.7	178.7	178.7	147.6	163.8	147.6	163.8	193.5	178.7	178.7
Width (in.)	66.5	70.9	70.9	66.7	66.7	66.7	66.7	73.4	66.5	66.5
Height (in.)	67.5	69.3	69.3	65.2	65.4	65.2	65.4	67.3	62	67.7
Curb Weight (lbs.)	3850	3610	3940	2546	2668	2723	2789	3825	2580	3360
Wheelbase (in.)	105.3	105.3	105.3	86.6	94.9	86.6	94.9	114.2	103.3	103.3
Front Head Room (in.)	39.2	39.2	39.2	39.3	40.3	39.3	40.3	40.6	38.2	38.2
Rear Head Room (in.)	38.7	38.7	38.7	38.6	39	38.6	39	40.7	NA	NA
Front Leg Room (in.)	43.1	43.1	43.1	39.5	39.5	39.5	39.5	41.9	41.7	41.7
Rear Leg Room (in.)	34.9	34.9	34.9	33.9	33.9	33.9	33.9	36.5	NA	NA
Maximum Seating	5	5	5	4	5	4	5	7	3	3
Max Cargo Capacity (cu ft.)	80	80	80	35	58	35	58	131	44	44
Maximum Payload (lbs.)	1400	1640	1310	1004	1245	926	1157	NA	1664	1914
Number of Cylinders	6	6	6	4	4	4	4	6	4	4
Displacement (liters)	3.4	3.4	3.4	2	2	2	2	3	2.4	2.7
Horsepower @ RPM	183@ 4800	183@ 4800	183@ 4800	127@ 5400	127@ 5400	127@ 5400	127@ 5400	194@ 5200	142@ 5000	150@ 4800
Torque @ RPM	217@ 3600	217@ 3600	217@ 3600	132@ 4600	132@ 4600	132@ 4600	132@ 4600	209@ 4400	160@ 4000	177@ 4000
Fuel Capacity	18.5	18.5	18.5	15.3	15.3	15.3	15.3	20.9	15.1	18
Towing Capacity	5000	5000	5000	1500	1500	1500	1500	1000	3500	3500
EPA City (mpg) - Manual	17	NA	NA	24	24	22	22	NA	22	17
EPA Hwy (mpg) - Manual	21	NA	NA	28	28	26	26	NA	27	21
EPA City (mpg) - Auto	16	17	16	23	23	22	22	18	21	18
EPA Hwy (mpg) - Auto	19	21	19	28	28	26	26	24	24	21

SPECIFICATIONS & EPA MILEAGE RATINGS	EPA Hwy (mpg) - Auto	EPA City (mpg) - Auto	EPA Hwy (mpg) - Manual	EPA City (mpg) - Manual	Towing Capacity	Fuel Capacity	Torque @ RPM	Horsepower @ RPM	Displacement (liters)	Number of Cylinders	Maximum Payload (lbs.)	Max Cargo Capacity (cu ft.)	Maximum Seating	Rear Leg Room (in.)	Front Leg Room (in.)	Rear Head Room (in.)	Front Head Room (in.)	Wheelbase (in.)	Curb Weight (lbs.)	Height (in.)	Width (in.)	Length (in.)	Turning Circle (in.)	Braking Dist. (60-0/ft)	Acceleration (0-60/sec)
Tacoma PreRunner Reg Cab	21	18	NA	NA	3500	18	177@ 4000	150@ 4800	2.7	4	1729	44	5	NA	42.8	NA	38.4	121.9	3175	66.9	66.5	203.1	40	NA	NA
Tacoma PreRunner X-Cab	21	18	NA	NA	3500	18	177@ 4000	150@ 4800	2.7	4	1729	44	5	27.2	42.8	35.5	38.4	121.9	3175	66.9	66.5	203.1	40	NA	NA
Tacoma PreRunner V6 X-Cab	20	17	NA	NA	5000	18	220@ 3600	190@ 4800	3.4	6	1664	44	5	27.2	42.8	35.5	38.4	121.9	3175	66.9	66.5	203.1	40	143	9
Tacoma 4-Cyl X-Cab 2WD	24	21	27	22	3500	15.1	160@ 4000	142@ 5000	2.4	4	1752	44	5	27.2	42.8	35.5	38.4	121.9	2760	62.2	66.5	197.2	41.4	NA	NA
Tacoma 4-Cyl X-Cab 4WD	21	18	21	17	3500	18	177@ 4000	150@ 4800	2.7	4	1759	44	5	27.2	42.8	35.5	38.4	121.9	3390	67.7	66.5	202.1	40	NA	NA
Tacoma V6 X-Cab 2WD	23	19	23	19	5000	15.1	220@ 3600	190@ 4800	3.4	6	1602	44	5	27.2	42.8	35.5	38.4	121.9	2780	62.2	66.5	197.2	41.4	139	7.6
Tacoma V6 X-Cab 4WD	23	19	19	16	5000	18	220@ 3600	190@ 4800	3.4	6	1694	44	5	27.2	42.8	35.5	38.4	121.9	3425	67.7	66.5	202.1	40	148	9
Tundra V6 2WD Reg Cab	19	16	20	16	5250	26.4	220@ 3600	190@ 4800	3.4	6	1705	NA	3	NA	41.5	NA	40.3	128.8	3795	70.5	75.2	217.5	44.9	NA	NA
Tundra V6 2WD X-Cab	19	16	20	16	4950	26.4	220@ 3600	190@ 4800	3.4	6	1612	NA	6	29.6	41.5	37	40.3	128.8	4088	70.7	75.2	217.5	44.9	NA	NA
Tundra V6 4WD Reg Cab	18	16	18	16	5250	26.4	220@ 3600	190@ 4800	3.4	6	1377	NA	3	NA	41.5	NA	40.3	128.8	4123	71.1	75.2	217.5	44.3	NA	NA

SPECIFICATIONS & EPA MILEAGE RATINGS	EPA Hwy (mpg) - Auto	EPA City (mpg) - Auto	EPA Hwy (mpg) - Manual	EPA City (mpg) - Manual	Towing Capacity	Fuel Capacity	Torque @ RPM	Horsepower @ RPM	Displacement (liters)	Number of Cylinders	Maximum Payload (lbs.)	Max Cargo Capacity (cu ft.)	Maximum Seating	Rear Leg Room (in.)	Front Leg Room (in.)	Rear Head Room (in.)	Front Head Room (in.)	Wheelbase (in.)	Curb Weight (lbs.)	Height (in.)	Width (in.)	Length (in.)	Turning Circle (in.)	Braking Dist. (60-0/ft)	Acceleration (0-60/sec)
Tundra V8 2WD X-Cab	19	15	NA	NA	7200	26.4	315@ 3400	245@ 4800	4.7	8	1924	NA	6	29.6	41.5	37	40.3	128.8	4276	70.5	75.2	217.5	44.9	NA	NA
Tundra V8 4WD Reg Cab	17	14	NA	NA	7200	26.4	315@ 3400	245@ 4800	4.7	8	1879	NA	3	NA	41.5	NA	40.3	128.8	4321	71.1	75.2	217.5	44.3	NA	NA
Tundra V6 4WD X-Cab	18	16	18	16	5000	26.4	220@ 3600	190@ 4800	3.4	6	1680	NA	6	29.6	41.5	37	40.3	128.8	4320	71.5	75.2	217.5	44.3	NA	NA
Tundra V8 4WD X-Cab	17	14	NA	NA	7100	NA	315@ 3400	245@ 4800	4.7	8	1532	NA	6	29.6	41.5	37	40.3	128.8	4518	71.3	75.2	217.5	44.3	NA	NA
VOLKSWAGEN																									
EuroVan GLS/MV	20	15	NA	NA	1500	21.1	177@ 3200	140@ 4500	2.8	6	1380	19	7	28.3	37.8	41.3	39.3	115	4220	764	72.4	188.5	38.4	NA	NA

CRASH TEST DATA

In 1994, the National Highway and Traffic Safety Administration (NHTSA) changed the way they rate frontal crash test performances of the cars and trucks they run into a fixed barrier at 35 mph. Instead of the confusing numerical scale that had been in place for years, NHTSA decided to make the data more user-friendly for interested consumers by converting to a five star rating system. This system is just like the one used by the movie reviewer in your local paper and the lucky folks AAA employs to travel around the world eating and sleeping in the best restaurants and hotels. Boy, they've got it rough, don't they?

For frontal impact NHTSA crash tests, the scale is as follows:

1 Star	Better than a 45% chance of life-threatening injury
2 Stars	A 35-45% chance of life-threatening injury
3 Stars	A 20-35% chance of life-threatening injury
4 Stars	A 10-20% chance of life-threatening injury
5 Stars	Less than a 10% chance of life-threatening injury

Two years ago, NHTSA began testing side impact protection as well as frontal impact protection. For side impact testing, NHTSA runs a deformable barrier into the side of a car twice, once at the front passenger's level and once at the rear passenger's level. As with frontal impact testing, the side impact test is conducted at five mph above the federal standard, which means the deformable barrier hits the car at 38 mph.

For side impact NHTSA crash tests, the scale is as follows:

1 Star	Better than a 25% chance of life-threatening injury
2 Stars	A 21-25% chance of life-threatening injury
3 Stars	A 11-20% chance of life-threatening injury
4 Stars	A 6-10% chance of life-threatening injury
5 Stars	A 0-5% chance of life-threatening injury

The Insurance Institute for Highway Safety (IIHS) began conducting offset frontal crash tests in 1995. The offset test is conducted at 40 mph, and vehicles crash into a fixed barrier just like in the NHTSA testing, but only half of the front end of the vehicle contacts the barrier. The IIHS claims this test, at this speed, more accurately reflects the most deadly real-world crash situations. Offset crash tests do not conform to the scale listed above. Instead, the IIHS rates a vehicle good, acceptable, marginal or poor.

The IIHS also conducts bumper bashing tests. They run cars and trucks into barriers at five mph to see how much damage results, in terms of dollars. Front ends are smacked into flat and angled barriers, and they back vehicles into poles and angled barriers. Each vehicle is crashed four times; the lower the total cost for repair after all four tests, the better the vehicle scores.

Our scale for bumper bash tests, based on IIHS information, is as follows:

Good	up to $1000 damage
Acceptable	$1001 - $2000 damage
Marginal	$2001 - $3000 damage
Poor	$3001 damage and above

Following are the results of all crash testing conducted since 1994. All test results are applicable to the 1999 equivalent of the listed model, with one caveat. Most of the models tested before 1998 come equipped with de-powered airbags this year, and until the vehicle is re-tested by NHTSA, it is unknown how the presence of a de-powered airbag will affect occupant safety.

NHTSA Frontal Impact Crash Testing Results:

Acura Integra	Driver: 4 Stars	Passenger: 3 Stars
Acura SLX	Driver: 3 Stars	Passenger: 3 Stars
Audi A4	Driver: 4 Stars	Passenger: 5 Stars
Audi A8	Driver: 5 Stars	Passenger: 5 Stars
BMW 3-Series Coupe/Convertible	Driver: 4 Stars	Passenger: 4 Stars
Buick Century	Driver: 4 Stars	Passenger: 3 Stars
Buick LeSabre	Driver: 4 Stars	Passenger: 4 Stars
Cadillac DeVille	Driver: 4 Stars	Passenger: 4 Stars
Cadillac Escalade	Driver: 4 Stars	Passenger: 4 Stars
Cadillac Eldorado	Driver: 4 Stars	Passenger: 4 Stars
Chevrolet Astro	Driver: 3 Stars	Passenger: 3 Stars
Chevrolet Blazer	Driver: 3 Stars	Passenger: 4 Stars
Chevrolet C/K Pickup	Driver: 4 Stars	Passenger: 3 Stars
Chevrolet Camaro	Driver: 4 Stars	Passenger: 5 Stars
Chevrolet Cavalier Coupe	Driver: 3 Stars	Passenger: 4 Stars
Chevrolet Cavalier Sedan	Driver: 4 Stars	Passenger: 4 Stars
Chevrolet Lumina	Driver: 4 Stars	Passenger: 5 Stars
Chevrolet Malibu	Driver: 4 Stars	Passenger: 4 Stars
Chevrolet Metro	Driver: 4 Stars	Passenger: 4 Stars
Chevrolet Monte Carlo	Driver: 4 Stars	Passenger: 4 Stars
Chevrolet Prizm	Driver: 4 Stars	Passenger: 4 Stars
Chevrolet S-10 Pickup	Driver: 2 Stars	Passenger: 3 Stars
Chevrolet Suburban	Driver: 4 Stars	Passenger: 4 Stars

CRASH TEST DATA

Chevrolet Tahoe	Driver: 4 Stars	Passenger: 4 Stars
Chevrolet Venture	Driver: 4 Stars	Passenger: 3 Stars
Chrysler 300M	Driver: 4 Stars	Passenger: 4 Stars
Chrysler Cirrus	Driver: 3 Stars	Passenger: 4 Stars
Chrysler Concorde	Driver: 4 Stars	Passenger: 4 Stars
Chrysler LHS	Driver: 4 Stars	Passenger: 4 Stars
Chrysler Sebring Convertible	Driver: 4 Stars	Passenger: 4 Stars
Chrysler Sebring Coupe	Driver: 5 Stars	Passenger: 5 Stars
Chrysler Town & Country SX	Driver: 3 Stars	Passenger: 3 Stars
Chrysler Town & Country LX/LXi	Driver: 3 Stars	Passenger: 3 Stars
Dodge Avenger	Driver: 5 Stars	Passenger: 5 Stars
Dodge Caravan	Driver: 3 Stars	Passenger: 3 Stars
Dodge Dakota	Driver: 4 Stars	Passenger: 4 Stars
Dodge Durango	Driver: 2 Stars	Passenger: 3 Stars
Dodge Grand Caravan	Driver: 3 Stars	Passenger: 3 Stars
Dodge Intrepid	Driver: 4 Stars	Passenger: 4 Stars
Dodge Neon	Driver: 3 Stars	Passenger: 4 Stars
Dodge Ram Pickup	Driver: 4 Stars	Passenger: 4 Stars
Dodge Stratus	Driver: 3 Stars	Passenger: 4 Stars
Ford Contour	Driver: 5 Stars	Passenger: 4 Stars
Ford Crown Victoria	Driver: 5 Stars	Passenger: 5 Stars
Ford Econoline	Driver: 4 Stars	Passenger: 4 Stars
Ford Escort	Driver: 3 Stars	Passenger: 3 Stars
Ford Expedition	Driver: 4 Stars	Passenger: 4 Stars
Ford Explorer	Driver: 4 Stars	Passenger: 4 Stars
Ford F-150	Driver: 4 Stars	Passenger: 4 Stars
Ford Mustang	Driver: 4 Stars	Passenger: 4 Stars
Ford Ranger	Driver: 4 Stars	Passenger: 4 Stars
Ford Taurus	Driver: 5 Stars	Passenger: 5 Stars
Ford Windstar	Driver: 5 Stars	Passenger: 5 Stars
GMC Envoy/Jimmy	Driver: 3 Stars	Passenger: 4 Stars
GMC Safari	Driver: 3 Stars	Passenger: 3 Stars
GMC Sierra Classic	Driver: 4 Stars	Passenger: 3 Stars
GMC Sonoma	Driver: 2 Stars	Passenger: 3 Stars
GMC Suburban	Driver: 4 Stars	Passenger: 4 Stars
GMC Yukon/Yukon Denali	Driver: 4 Stars	Passenger: 4 Stars
Honda Accord	Driver: 4 Stars	Passenger: 4 Stars
Honda Civic Coupe	Driver: 4 Stars	Passenger: 4 Stars
Honda Civic Sedan	Driver: 4 Stars	Passenger: 4 Stars
Honda CR-V	Driver: 4 Stars	Passenger: 5 Stars
Honda Odyssey	Driver: 5 Stars	Passenger: 5 Stars
Honda Passport	Driver: 3 Stars	Passenger: 4 Stars
Hyundai Accent	Driver: 3 Stars	Passenger: 4 Stars
Hyundai Elantra	Driver: 3 Stars	Passenger: 3 Stars
Infiniti I30	Driver: 4 Stars	Passenger: 4 Stars
Infiniti QX4	Driver: 3 Stars	Passenger: 3 Stars

CRASH TEST DATA

Isuzu Oasis	Driver: 4 Stars	Passenger: 4 Stars
Isuzu Rodeo	Driver: 3 Stars	Passenger: 4 Stars
Isuzu Trooper	Driver: 3 Stars	Passenger: 3 Stars
Jeep Cherokee	Driver: 3 Stars	Passenger: 3 Stars
Jeep Wrangler	Driver: 4 Stars	Passenger: 4 Stars
Kia Sportage	Driver: 3 Stars	Passenger: 3 Stars
Land Rover Discovery	Driver: 3 Stars	Passenger: 3 Stars
Lexus ES300	Driver: 4 Stars	Passenger: 4 Stars
Lincoln Navigator	Driver: 4 Stars	Passenger: 4 Stars
Mazda 626	Driver: 4 Stars	Passenger: 5 Stars
Mazda B-Series	Driver: 4 Stars	Passenger: 4 Stars
Mazda Millenia	Driver: 4 Stars	Passenger: 5 Stars
Mazda Protégé	Driver: 4 Stars	Passenger: 4 Stars
Mercedes-Benz C-Class	Driver: 4 Stars	Passenger: 4 Stars
Mercury Grand Marquis	Driver: 5 Stars	Passenger: 5 Stars
Mercury Mountaineer	Driver: 4 Stars	Passenger: 4 Stars
Mercury Mystique	Driver: 5 Stars	Passenger: 4 Stars
Mercury Sable	Driver: 5 Stars	Passenger: 5 Stars
Mercury Tracer	Driver: 3 Stars	Passenger: 3 Stars
Mitsubishi Eclipse	Driver: 4 Stars	Passenger: 4 Stars
Mitsubishi Galant	Driver: 4 Stars	Passenger: 4 Stars
Mitsubishi Montero Sport	Driver: 3 Stars	Passenger: 3 Stars
Nissan Altima	Driver: 3 Stars	Passenger: 3 Stars
Nissan Frontier	Driver: 3 Stars	Passenger: 4 Stars
Nissan Maxima	Driver: 4 Stars	Passenger: 4 Stars
Nissan Pathfinder	Driver: 3 Stars	Passenger: 3 Stars
Nissan Sentra	Driver: 3 Stars	Passenger: 4 Stars
Oldsmobile 88	Driver: 5 Stars	Passenger: 3 Stars
Oldsmobile Alero	Driver: 4 Stars	Passenger: 4 Stars
Oldsmobile Aurora	Driver: 3 Stars	Passenger: 3 Stars
Oldsmobile Bravada	Driver: 3 Stars	Passenger: 4 Stars
Oldsmobile Cutlass	Driver: 4 Stars	Passenger: 4 Stars
Oldsmobile Intrigue	Driver: 4 Stars	Passenger: 3 Stars
Oldsmobile Regency	Driver: 5 Stars	Passenger: 3 Stars
Oldsmobile Silhouette	Driver: 4 Stars	Passenger: 3 Stars
Plymouth Breeze	Driver: 3 Stars	Passenger: 4 Stars
Plymouth Grand Voyager	Driver: 3 Stars	Passenger: 3 Stars
Plymouth Neon	Driver: 3 Stars	Passenger: 4 Stars
Plymouth Voyager	Driver: 3 Stars	Passenger: 3 Stars
Pontiac Bonneville	Driver: 5 Stars	Passenger: 3 Stars
Pontiac Firebird	Driver: 4 Stars	Passenger: 5 Stars
Pontiac Grand Am	Driver: 4 Stars	Passenger: 4 Stars
Pontiac Grand Prix	Driver: 4 Stars	Passenger: 4 Stars
Pontiac Montana	Driver: 4 Stars	Passenger: 3 Stars
Pontiac Sunfire Coupe	Driver: 3 Stars	Passenger: 4 Stars
Pontiac Sunfire Sedan	Driver: 4 Stars	Passenger: 4 Stars

Saab 9-3	Driver: 4 Stars	Passenger: 4 Stars
Saturn SL/SW	Driver: 5 Stars	Passenger: 5 Stars
Subaru Forester	Driver: 4 Stars	Passenger: 4 Stars
Subaru Impreza	Driver: 4 Stars	Passenger: 4 Stars
Subaru Legacy	Driver: 4 Stars	Passenger: 4 Stars
Suzuki Swift	Driver: 4 Stars	Passenger: 4 Stars
Toyota 4Runner	Driver: 4 Stars	Passenger: 5 Stars
Toyota Avalon	Driver: 4 Stars	Passenger: 5 Stars
Toyota Camry	Driver: 4 Stars	Passenger: 5 Stars
Toyota Corolla	Driver: 4 Stars	Passenger: 4 Stars
Toyota RAV4 4-door	Driver: 4 Stars	Passenger: 4 Stars
Toyota Sienna	Driver: 5 Stars	Passenger: 5 Stars
Toyota Tacoma	Driver: 4 Stars	Passenger: 4 Stars
Volkswagen New Beetle	Driver: 4 Stars	Passenger: 4 Stars
Volvo S70	Driver: 5 Stars	Passenger: 5 Stars

NHTSA Side Impact Crash Testing Results:

Buick Century	Front: 3 Stars	Rear: 3 Stars
Buick LeSabre	Front: 3 Stars	Rear: 3 Stars
Buick Regal	Front: 3 Stars	Rear: 3 Stars
Cadillac DeVille	Front: 4 Stars	Rear: 4 Stars
Chevrolet Blazer	Front: 5 Stars	Rear: 5 Stars
Chevrolet Camaro	Front: 3 Stars	Rear: 4 Stars
Chevrolet Cavalier Coupe	Front: 1 Star	Rear: 2 Stars
Chevrolet Cavalier Sedan	Front: 1 Star	Rear: 3 Stars
Chevrolet Lumina	Front: 4 Stars	Rear: 3 Stars
Chevrolet Malibu	Front: 1 Star	Rear: 3 Stars
Chevrolet Prizm	Front: 3 Stars	Rear: 3 Stars
Chevrolet Prizm (w/side airbag)	Front: 4 Stars	Rear: 3 Stars
Chevrolet S-10	Front: 3 Stars	Rear: Not Applicable
Chevrolet Venture	Front: 5 Stars	Rear: 5 Stars
Chrysler 300M	Front: 4 Stars	Rear: 3 Stars
Chrysler Cirrus	Front: 3 Stars	Rear: 2 Stars
Chrysler Concorde	Front: 4 Stars	Rear: 3 Stars
Chrysler LHS	Front: 4 Stars	Rear: 3 Stars
Chrysler Town & Country	Front: 5 Stars	Rear: 3 Stars
Dodge Caravan/Grand Caravan	Front: 5 Stars	Rear: 3 Stars
Dodge Dakota	Front: 5 Stars	Rear: Not Applicable
Dodge Intrepid	Front: 4 Stars	Rear: 3 Stars
Dodge Neon	Front: 2 Stars	Rear: 3 Stars
Dodge Stratus	Front: 3 Stars	Rear: 2 Stars
Ford Contour	Front: 3 Stars	Rear: 4 Stars
Ford Crown Victoria	Front: 4 Stars	Rear: 4 Stars
Ford Escort	Front: 3 Stars	Rear: 3 Stars
Ford Escort ZX2	Front: 1 Star	Rear: 4 Stars

CRASH TEST DATA

Vehicle	Front	Rear
Ford Explorer	Front: 5 Stars	Rear: 5 Stars
Ford F-150	Front: 4 Stars	Rear: Not Applicable
Ford Mustang	Front: 3 Stars	Rear: 3 Stars
Ford Ranger	Front: 5 Stars	Rear: Not Applicable
Ford Taurus	Front: 3 Stars	Rear: 3 Stars
Ford Windstar	Front: 5 Stars	Rear: 5 Stars
GMC Envoy/Jimmy	Front: 5 Stars	Rear: 5 Stars
GMC Sonoma	Front: 3 Stars	Rear: Not Applicable
Honda Accord Coupe	Front: 3 Stars	Rear: 4 Stars
Honda Accord Sedan	Front: 4 Stars	Rear: 4 Stars
Honda Civic Coupe	Front: 2 Stars	Rear: 3 Stars
Honda Civic Sedan	Front: 3 Stars	Rear: 3 Stars
Honda CR-V	Front: 5 Stars	Rear: 5 Stars
NOTE: Vehicle rolled one quarter turn in test.		
Honda Odyssey	Front: 5 Stars	Rear: 5 Stars
Honda Passport	Front: 5 Stars	Rear: 5 Stars
NOTE: Vehicle rolled one quarter turn in test.		
Infiniti I30	Front: 4 Stars	Rear: 3 Stars
Isuzu Hombre	Front: 3 Stars	Rear: Not Applicable
Isuzu Rodeo	Front: 5 Stars	Rear: 5 Stars
NOTE: Vehicle rolled one quarter turn in test.		
Jeep Cherokee	Front: 3 Stars	Rear: 5 Stars
Jeep Grand Cherokee	Front: 4 Stars	Rear: 5 Stars
Lexus ES300	Front: 5 Stars	Rear: 4 Stars
Lincoln Town Car	Front: 4 Stars	Rear: 4 Stars
Mazda 626	Front: 3 Stars	Rear: 3 Stars
Mazda B-Series	Front: 5 Stars	Rear: Not Applicable
Mercedes-Benz C-Class	Front: 3 Stars	Rear: 4 Stars
Mercury Grand Marquis	Front: 4 Stars	Rear: 4 Stars
Mercury Mountaineer	Front: 5 Stars	Rear: 5 Stars
Mercury Mystique	Front: 3 Stars	Rear: 4 Stars
Mercury Sable	Front: 3 Stars	Rear: 3 Stars
Mercury Tracer	Front: 3 Stars	Rear: 3 Stars
Mitsubishi Eclipse	Front: 1 Star	Rear: No Data
Mitsubishi Galant	Front: 5 Stars	Rear: 4 Stars
Nissan Altima	Front: 3 Stars	Rear: 3 Stars
Nissan Frontier	Front: 4 Stars	Rear: Not Applicable
Nissan Maxima	Front: 4 Stars	Rear: 3 Stars
Nissan Sentra	Front: 3 Stars	Rear: 3 Stars
Oldsmobile Alero Sedan	Front: 3 Stars	Rear: 3 Stars
Oldsmobile Bravada	Front: 5 Stars	Rear: 5 Stars
Oldsmobile Cutlass	Front: 1 Star	Rear: 3 Stars
Oldsmobile Intrigue	Front: 3 Stars	Rear: 1 Star
Oldsmobile Silhouette	Front: 5 Stars	Rear: 5 Stars
Plymouth Breeze	Front: 3 Stars	Rear: 2 Stars
Plymouth Grand Voyager/Voyager	Front: 5 Stars	Rear: 3 Stars

CRASH TEST DATA

Plymouth Neon	Front: 2 Stars	Rear: 3 Stars
Pontiac Bonneville	Front: 3 Stars	Rear: 2 Stars
Pontiac Firebird	Front: 3 Stars	Rear: 4 Stars
Pontiac Grand Am Sedan	Front: 3 Stars	Rear: 3 Stars
Pontiac Montana	Front: 5 Stars	Rear: 5 Stars
Pontiac Sunfire Coupe	Front: 1 Star	Rear: 2 Stars
Pontiac Sunfire Sedan	Front: 1 Star	Rear: 3 Stars
Saturn SL/SW	Front: 3 Stars	Rear: 3 Stars
Subaru Legacy	Front: 3 Stars	Rear: No Data
Toyota 4Runner	Front: 5 Stars	Rear: 5 Stars
Toyota Avalon	Front: 5 Stars	Rear: 4 Stars
Toyota Camry	Front: 3 Stars	Rear: 3 Stars
Toyota Corolla	Front: 3 Stars	Rear: 3 Stars
Toyota Corolla (w/side airbag)	Front: 4 Stars	Rear: 3 Stars
Toyota RAV4 4-door	Front: 5 Stars	Rear: 5 Stars
Toyota Sienna	Front: 4 Stars	Rear: 5 Stars
Volvo S70	Front: 4 Stars	Rear: No Data

IIHS Offset Impact Crash Testing Results:

BMW 5-series	Good
Buick Century	Acceptable
Buick Regal	Acceptable
Chevrolet Astro	Poor
Chevrolet Blazer	Poor
Chevrolet Cavalier	Poor
Chevrolet Lumina	Good
Chevrolet Prizm	Acceptable
Chevrolet S-10	Marginal
Chevrolet Tracker 4-door	Acceptable
Chevrolet Venture	Poor
Chrysler Cirrus	Poor
Chrysler Town & Country LX/LXi	Marginal
Dodge Dakota	Poor
Dodge Grand Caravan	Marginal
Dodge Neon	Marginal
Dodge Stratus	Poor
Ford Contour	Poor
Ford Escort	Acceptable
Ford Explorer	Acceptable
Ford Ranger	Acceptable
Ford Taurus	Good
Ford Windstar	Good
GMC Envoy/Jimmy	Poor
GMC Safari	Poor

CRASH TEST DATA

GMC Sonoma	Marginal
Honda Accord	Acceptable
Honda Civic	Acceptable
Honda CR-V	Marginal
Honda Odyssey	Good
Hyundai Elantra	Acceptable
Hyundai Sonata	Acceptable
Infiniti I30	Acceptable
Infiniti Q45	Marginal
Infiniti QX4	Marginal
Isuzu Amigo	Poor
Isuzu Hombre	Marginal
Isuzu Oasis	Marginal
Jeep Cherokee	Marginal
Jeep Wrangler	Acceptable
Kia Sephia	Poor
Kia Sportage 4-door	Marginal
Land Rover Discovery	Acceptable
Lexus LS400	Good
Lincoln Continental	Acceptable
Mazda B-Series Pickup	Acceptable
Mazda Millenia	Acceptable
Mazda Protege	Acceptable
Mercedes-Benz E-Class	Acceptable
Mercury Mountaineer	Acceptable
Mercury Mystique	Poor
Mercury Sable	Good
Mercury Tracer	Acceptable
Mercury Villager	Poor
Mitsubishi	Acceptable
Mitsubishi Mirage	Poor
Mitsubishi Montero	Acceptable
Nissan Frontier	Poor
Nissan Maxima	Acceptable
Nissan Pathfinder	Marginal
Nissan Quest	Poor
Nissan Sentra	Acceptable
Oldsmobile Bravada	Poor
Oldsmobile Intrigue	Acceptable
Oldsmobile Silhouette	Poor
Plymouth Breeze	Poor
Plymouth Neon	Marginal

Plymouth Grand Voyager	Marginal
Pontiac Grand Prix	Acceptable
Pontiac Sunfire	Poor
Pontiac Trans Sport	Poor
Saab 9-3	Acceptable
Saturn SL/SW	Acceptable
Subaru Forester	Good
Subaru Legacy	Acceptable
Suzuki Grand Vitara	Acceptable
Suzuki Vitara 4-door	Acceptable
Toyota 4Runner	Acceptable
Toyota Avalon	Acceptable
Toyota Camry	Good
Toyota Corolla	Acceptable
Toyota RAV4 4-door	Marginal
Toyota Sienna	Good
Toyota Tacoma	Acceptable
Volkswagen Cabrio	Poor
Volkswagen Golf	Acceptable
Volkswagen Jetta	Acceptable
Volkswagen New Beetle	Good
Volkswagen Passat	Good
Volvo S70	Good

IIHS Bumper Bash Crash Testing Results:

BMW 5-series	Poor
Cadillac Seville	Acceptable
Chevrolet Astro	Poor
Chevrolet Blazer	Poor
Chevrolet Cavalier	Acceptable
Chevrolet Lumina	Marginal
Chevrolet Prizm	Good
Chevrolet S-10	Marginal
Chevrolet Venture	Poor
Chrysler Cirrus	Marginal
Chrysler Town & Country LX/LXi	Poor
Dodge Dakota	Poor
Dodge Grand Caravan	Poor
Dodge Neon	Acceptable
Dodge Stratus	Marginal
Ford Contour	Poor
Ford Escort	Acceptable

CRASH TEST DATA

Ford Explorer	Poor
Ford Ranger	Marginal
Ford Taurus	Acceptable
Ford Windstar	Acceptable
GMC Envoy/Jimmy	Poor
GMC Safari	Poor
GMC Sonoma	Marginal
Honda Accord	Acceptable
Honda Civic	Acceptable
Honda CR-V	Poor
Honda Odyssey	Acceptable
Honda Passport	Poor
Hyundai Elantra	Acceptable
Hyundai Sonata	Marginal
Infiniti I30	Good
Infiniti Q45	Poor
Infiniti QX4	Poor
Isuzu Amigo	Poor
Isuzu Hombre	Marginal
Isuzu Oasis	Acceptable
Isuzu Rodeo	Poor
Jeep Cherokee	Poor
Jeep Grand Cherokee	Poor
Jeep Wrangler	Marginal
Kia Sephia	Marginal
Kia Sportage	Poor
Land Rover Discovery	Poor
Lexus LS400	Poor
Lincoln Continental	Acceptable
Mazda B-Series Pickup	Marginal
Mazda Millenia	Marginal
Mazda Protegé	Poor
Mercedes-Benz E-Class	Poor
Mercury Mountaineer	Poor
Mercury Mystique	Poor
Mercury Sable	Acceptable
Mercury Tracer	Acceptable
Mercury Villager	Marginal
Mitsubishi Galant	Acceptable
Mitsubishi Mirage	Marginal
Mitsubishi Montero	Poor
Nissan Frontier	Poor

CRASH TEST DATA

Nissan Maxima	Acceptable
Nissan Pathfinder	Poor
Nissan Sentra	Acceptable
Nissan Quest	Acceptable
Oldsmobile Bravada	Poor
Oldsmobile Silhouette	Poor
Plymouth Breeze	Marginal
Plymouth Neon	Acceptable
Plymouth Grand Voyager	Poor
Pontiac Grand Prix	Acceptable
Pontiac Sunfire	Acceptable
Pontiac Trans Sport	Poor
Saab 9-3	Acceptable
Saturn SL	Good
Subaru Forester	Marginal
Subaru Legacy	Acceptable
Toyota 4Runner	Poor
Toyota Avalon	Acceptable
Toyota Camry	Acceptable
Toyota Corolla	Good
Toyota RAV4	Poor
Toyota Sienna	Marginal
Toyota Tacoma	Poor
Volkswagen Golf	Acceptable
Volkswagen Jetta	Acceptable
Volkswagen New Beetle	Good
Volkswagen Passat	Good
Volvo S70	Good

WARRANTIES & ROADSIDE ASSISTANCE

All new vehicles sold in America come with at least two warranties, and many include roadside assistance. Described below are the major types of warranties and assistance provided to consumers:

Basic: Your basic warranty covers everything except items subject to wear and tear, such as oil filters, wiper blades, and the like. Tires and batteries often have their own warranty coverage, which will be outlined in your owner's manual. Emissions equipment is required to be covered for five years or 50,000 miles by the federal government.

Drivetrain: Drivetrain coverage takes care of most of the parts that make the car move, like the engine, transmission, drive axles and driveshaft. Like the basic warranty, parts subject to wear and tear like hoses and belts are not covered. However, most of the internal parts of the engine, such as the pistons and bearings, which are subject to wear and tear are covered by the drivetrain warranty. See your owner's manual or local dealer for specific coverage.

Rust or Corrosion: This warranty protects you from rust-through problems with the sheetmetal. Surface rust doesn't count. The rust must make a hole to be covered. Keep your car washed and waxed, and rust shouldn't be a problem.

Roadside Assistance: Most manufacturers provide a service that will rescue you if your car leaves you stranded, even if it's your fault. Lock yourself out of the car? Somebody will come and open it up. Run out of gas? Somebody will deliver some fuel. Flat tire? Somebody will change it for you. See your owner's manual for details, or ask the dealer about specifics.

Make	Basic (yrs/mi)	Drivetrain (yrs/mi)	Rust/Corrosion (yrs/mi)	Roadside Assistance (yrs/mi)
Acura	4/50,000	4/50,000	4/50,000	4/50,000
Audi	3/50,000	3/50,000	10/Unlimited	3/Unlimited
BMW	4/50,000	4/50,000	6/Unlimited	4/50,000
Buick	3/36,000	3/36,000	6/100,000	3/36,000

WARRANTIES & ROADSIDE ASSISTANCE

Make	Basic (yrs/mi)	Drivetrain (yrs/mi)	Rust/Corrosion (yrs/mi)	Roadside Assistance (yrs/mi)
Cadillac	4/50,000	4/50,000	6/100,000	4/50,000
Chevrolet	3/36,000	3/36,000	6/100,000	3/36,000
Chrysler	3/36,000	3/36,000	7/100,000	3/36,000
Daewoo	3/36,000	5/60,000	5/Unlimited	3/36,000
Dodge	3/36,000	3/36,000	7/100,000	3/36,000
Eagle	3/36,000	3/36,000	5/100,000	3/36,000
Ford	3/36,000	3/36,000	6/100,000	3/36,000
GMC	3/36,000	3/36,000	6/100,000	3/36,000
Honda	3/36,000	3/36,000	3/36,000	None Available
Hyundai	5/60,000	10/100,000	5/100,000	5/Unlimited
Infiniti	4/60,000	6/70,000	7/Unlimited	4/Unlimited
Isuzu	5/50,000	5/60,000	6/100,000	5/60,000
Kia	3/36,000	5/60,000	5/100,000	3/36,000
Jeep	3/36,000	3/36,000	7/100,000	3/36,000
Land Rover	4/50,000	4/50,000	6/Unlimited	4/50,000
Lexus	4/50,000	6/70,000	6/Unlimited	4/Unlimited
Lincoln	4/50,000	4/50,000	6/100,000	4/50,000
Mazda	3/50,000	3/50,000	3/50,000	3/50,000 (Millenia & MPV only)
Mercedes	4/50,000	4/50,000	4/50,000	Unlimited
Mercury	3/36,000	3/36,000	6/100,000	3/36,000
Mitsubishi	3/36,000	5/60,000	7/100,000	3/36,000
Nissan	3/36,000	5/60,000	5/60,000	None Available
Oldsmobile	3/36,000	3/36,000	6/100,000	3/36,000
Plymouth	3/36,000	3/36,000	7/100,000	3/36,000
Pontiac	3/36,000	3/36,000	6/100,000	3/36,000
Porsche	4/50,000	4/50,000	10/Unlimited	4/50,000
Saab	4/50,000	4/50,000	6/Unlimited	4/50,000
Saturn	3/36,000	3/36,000	6/100,000	3/36,000
Subaru	3/36,000	5/60,000	5/Unlimited	None Available
Suzuki	3/36,000	3/36,000	3/Unlimited	None Available
Toyota	3/36,000	5/60,000	5/Unlimited	None Available
Volkswagen	2/24,000	10/100,000	6/Unlimited	2/Unlimited
Volvo	4/50,000	4/50,000	8/Unlimited	4/50,000

** All data sourced directly from manufacturer customer assistance telephone operatives.*

DEALER HOLDBACKS

What is Dealer Holdback?

Dealer holdback is a percentage of the MSRP or invoice of a new vehicle that is paid to the dealer by the manufacturer to assist in the dealership's financing of the vehicle. It is almost always non-negotiable. However, by knowing about the holdback, you can use it as a negotiating tool. First, a little more background:

The total invoice cost of the car is due to the manufacturer, payable by the dealership, when the vehicle is ordered, not when it is sold. Since car dealerships (or any retail operation, for that matter) must have an inventory on hand, they must borrow money from the bank to pay for that inventory. The manufacturer pays for financing and maintenance for the first 90 days the vehicle is on the lot, in the form of a quarterly check called "holdback." After the first 90 days, the dealership dips into its own pocket, and into its own profit to finance the car. Fortunately, most cars don't stay on the lot for three full months.

This amount is "invisible" to the consumer because it does not appear on the dealer invoice (except in the case of Mitsubishi Motors, where the manufacturer allows dealers to charge the customer directly for the holdback.) Therefore, the dealer is guaranteed a profit even if they sell the vehicle to you at cost (if, that is, the car is sold within 90 days). Because of the holdback, the dealer can advertise a car at $1 over invoice and still make hundreds of dollars on the sale.

For example, let's say you're interested in a Ford with a Manufacturer's Suggested Retail Price (MSRP) of $20,500, including optional equipment and destination charge. Dealer invoice on this hypothetical Ford is $18,000, including optional equipment. The invoice includes a dealer holdback that, in the case of all Ford vehicles, amounts to 3% of the total MSRP. The $500 destination charge should not be included when figuring the holdback. So, on this particular Ford, the true dealer cost is actually $17,400, plus destination charges. Even if the dealer sells you the car for invoice, which is unlikely, he would still be making as much as $600 on the deal when his quarterly check arrived. That is profit to the dealer only; the sales staff doesn't see any of it.

So, if you offer the dealership 3% over invoice for this Ford, or $18,540 plus the destination charge, the dealer and the sales staff are making as much as $1,140 and you're still getting a good deal by paying $1,460 less than the MSRP. (Remember that this price doesn't include destination charges, advertising [if applicable], additional fees, tax, or license plates.)

However, the true "profit" of holdback money depends on how long the car has been on the lot. If our hypothetical Ford had been sitting there for 45 days before you bought it, the dealer's holdback profit is only half of what it could have been, or only $300, cutting total profit on the deal to $840.

Dealer holdback allows dealers to advertise big sales. Often, ads promise that your new car will cost you just "$1 over/under invoice!" Additionally, the dealer stands to reap further benefits if there is some sort of dealer incentive or customer rebate on the car. Generally, sale prices stipulate that all rebates and incentives go to the dealer. Using the example above, let's see what happens when there is a rebate.

Suppose the car described above has a $1,000 rebate in effect. You need to subtract that $1,000 rebate (remember, the dealer is keeping the rebate) from the dealer invoice of $18,000, which results in a new dealer invoice of just $17,000. Now, you must calculate a fair price. In this example, 3% of dealer invoice is $510, which means that the price you should try to buy the car for is $17,510, plus destination, advertising (if applicable), taxes, and fees. The dealer is still making as much as $1,110 and you're paying $2,490 less than the MSRP. Remember, the longer the car has been in the dealer's inventory, the less money the dealer is making.

Almost all dealerships consider holdback money sacred, and are unwilling to share any portion of it with the consumer. Don't push the issue. Your best strategy is to avoid mentioning that you know the holdback amount and what it is during negotiations. Mention holdback only if the dealer gives you some song-and-dance about not making any money at 3% over invoice.

So how can you truly benefit from this information? Well, if the dealership doesn't have that pretty green color you're interested in, and they can't find it at another dealership in the area, they have to order it directly from the manufacturer. If that's the case, make sure that they know that you know about the holdback. If a vehicle is special-ordered, holdback money is pure profit, and you will need to factor this into price negotiations.

Domestic manufacturers (Chrysler, Ford, and GM) generally offer dealers a holdback equaling 3% of the total sticker price, or MSRP, of the car. Import manufacturers (Honda, Nissan, Toyota, etc.) provide varying holdback amounts that are equal to a percentage of total MSRP, base MSRP, total invoice or base invoice.

If a holdback is off the:

- Total MSRP, consumers must include the MSRP price of all options before figuring the holdback.
- Base MSRP, consumers must figure the holdback before adding desired options.
- Total Invoice, consumers must include the invoice price of all options before figuring the holdback.
- Base Invoice, consumers must figure the holdback before adding desired options.

Following is a current list of makes and the amount of the 1999 dealer holdback.

Make	Holdback
Acura	3.5% of the Base MSRP
Audi	No Holdback
BMW	2% of the Base MSRP
Buick	3% of the Total MSRP
Cadillac	3% of the Total MSRP
Chevrolet	3% of the Total MSRP
Chrysler	3% of the Total MSRP
Daewoo	No Holdback
Dodge	3% of the Total MSRP
Eagle	3% of the Total MSRP
Ford	3% of the Total MSRP
GMC	3% of the Total MSRP
Honda	2% of the Base MSRP (except Prelude, which has no holdback.)
Hyundai	2% of the Total Invoice

DEALER HOLDBACKS

Make	Holdback
Infiniti	1% of the Base MSRP (holdback) + 2% of the Base Invoice (floorplanning allowance)
Isuzu	3% of the Total MSRP
Jeep	3% of the Total MSRP
Kia	No Holdback
Land Rover	No Holdback
Lexus	2% of the Base MSRP
Lincoln	3% of the Total MSRP
Mazda	2% of the Base MSRP
Mercedes-Benz	3% of the Total MSRP
Mercury	3% of the Total MSRP
Mitsubishi	2% of the Total MSRP
Nissan	2% + 1.5% of the Total Invoice (holdback + floorplanning allowance)
Oldsmobile	3% of the Total MSRP
Plymouth	3% of the Total MSRP
Pontiac	3% of the Total MSRP
Porsche	No Holdback
Saab	3% of the Base MSRP
Saturn	One-price sales. Customer pays MSRP.
Subaru	2% of the Total MSRP
Suzuki	2% of the Base MSRP
Toyota	2% of the Base Invoice (Amount may differ in Southeastern U.S.)
Volkswagen	2% of Total MSRP
Volvo	$300 Flat Amount

1999 Pontiac Montana

FREQUENTLY ASKED QUESTIONS

Edmund's® solicits e-mail from consumers who visit our website at http://www.edmund.com. Below are 22 commonly asked questions regarding new cars and the buying process.

---

1. How soon after a price increase does Edmund's® modify its data?

This depends on how soon our sources are notified. Sometimes, it's a matter of days; other times, it can take longer. Rest assured that we painstakingly attempt to maintain the most up-to-date pricing. If a dealer disputes the accuracy of our pricing, ask them to prove it by showing you the invoice so you can compare. If prices have indeed increased, the amount will not be substantial: the new figures should easily be within a few percentage points of those published in this guide.

2. Do factory orders cost more than buying from dealer stock?

All things considered equal, ordered vehicles cost no more than vehicles in dealer stock and, in some cases, may actually cost less. When you buy from dealer stock, you may have to settle for a vehicle with either more or less equipment or your second or third color choice. Moreover, the dealership pays interest on stocked vehicles at a predetermined monthly rate to the manufacturer. This interest is called floor plan, and is subsidized by the dealer holdback. When you factory order, you get exactly what you want, in the color you want, and the dealer should eliminate the floor plan cost. In most cases, the dealer passes the savings on to the customer, and the savings could amount to several hundred dollars.

The downside to ordering is that incentives and rebates are good only on the day of delivery, unless stated otherwise (in writing) by the dealer. If an incentive or rebate plan was in effect when the vehicle was ordered, but not in effect the day of delivery, the customer is usually not eligible for the incentive or rebate. If you order a vehicle, and the delivery date is very close to the expiration date of a rebate or incentive program, beware that the dealer may try to delay delivery until after the rebate or incentive has expired.

From a negotiation standpoint, dealers may be more likely to offer a better price on a vehicle in stock, particularly if the monthly floor plan payments have exceeded the holdback amount and are now chewing into the dealer's profit.

3. Can I order a car directly from the factory without going through a dealer?

No, you cannot. Direct factory ordering is a hoax concocted by Zeke and Butherus over their nightly Jim Beam pow-wow at Hic-a-Billies. Dealerships are franchisees of the manufacturer, and are protected as such.

4. Why is the car I'm looking at on the West Coast priced differently than what's listed in this guide?

California, Oregon, Washington and Idaho are the testing grounds for different pricing and option schemes. Because of the popularity of imported makes in this market, domestic manufacturers will often slash dealer profit margins and offer better-equipped cars at lower prices than those available in other parts of the country. This is why some dealer incentives and customer rebates do not apply on the West Coast, and why some option packages available in those states may not be listed in this guide.

5. When should a car be considered used?

Technically, a vehicle is considered used if it has been titled. However, some dealers can rack up hundreds or thousands of miles on a new car without titling it. In these cases, the ethical definition of a used car should include any car used for extensive demonstration or personal use by dealership staff members. The only miles a new car should have on the odometer when purchased are those put on during previous test drives by prospective buyers (at dealerships where demonstrators are not used), and any miles driven during a dealer trade, within a reasonable limit. If the new car you're considering has more than 300 miles on the odometer, you should question how the car accumulated so many miles, and request a discount for the excessive mileage. We think a discount amounting to a dime a mile is a fair charge for wear and tear inflicted by the dealership.

A car should not be considered used if it is a brand-new leftover from a previous model year. However, it should be discounted, because many manufacturers offer dealers incentives designed to help the dealer lower prices and clear out old stock.

6. Why doesn't Edmund's® list option prices for some makes and models?

Almost all Acura, Honda, and Suzuki options are dealer installed. Some manufacturers, like Nissan, Subaru, Toyota and Volvo, will offer both factory- and dealer-installed options. Pricing for these items can vary depending on region and dealer. Therefore, it is impossible for Edmund's® to list an accurate price for these items. Our experience shows that these items often carry a 100% mark up in dealer profit. We recommend that you avoid buying dealer-installed options if you can help it.

7. How can a dealer sell a new car for less than the invoice price Edmund's® publishes?

Auto manufacturers will often subsidize volume-sellers to keep sales and production up by offering car dealers hefty cash rewards for meeting monthly or quarterly sales goals. In other words, the dealer will take a slight loss on the car in anticipation of larger cash rewards if sales goals are met. It has been our experience that when a dealer sells a vehicle for less than invoice, the manufacturer is in one form or another always subsidizing the deal. In print ads, always look for phrases such as "all incentives and/or rebates assigned to dealer."

Also, since profit can be made on other parts of the deal, a dealer may be willing to take a loss on the price of the car in exchange for profit gleaned from a low-ball trade-in value, financing, rustproofing, an extended warranty, and aftermarket or dealer-installed accessories. We once met a Plymouth salesman who bragged that he sold a Neon Sport for invoice, but with the undervalued trade-in, high-interest financing and dealer-installed items factored into the deal, the buyer actually paid more than $20,000 for the car. Keep in mind that there is more to a good deal than a low price.

8. How much does an extended warranty cost the warranty company?

The cost of an extended warranty is based upon the degree of probability that any given vehicle will require repairs during the extended warranty period. Reliability records and repair cost information for a vehicle are evaluated to forecast potential future repair costs, and the extended warranty company will then charge a premium adequate enough to cover the potential cost of repairing the vehicle during the warranty period, while still making a profit. It is important to note that the cost of an extended warranty includes administrative costs for handling paperwork and claims, and insurance to guarantee that claims will be paid.

Extended warranty costs are based on averages, so the cost of applying an extended warranty to any given make and model of car can vary from consumer to consumer. Let's say you bought a $1,000 extended warranty for two identical Brand X vehicles: Car A and Car B. During the extended warranty period, Car A never breaks, so the extended warranty is never used. At the same time, Car B suffers bills amounting to $1,200 for transmission and valve problems. Profit on the warranty sold for Car A will counterbalance the loss suffered on Car B. Extended warranty companies sell thousands of warranties annually, and are able to make a profit when the actual loss experience is lower than the forecast potential for future repair. In other words, when sales exceed overhead the company makes money.

You can purchase an extended warranty several ways, and we recommend shopping around for the best price. Start with the warranty providers, such as Warranty Gold, and then compare to what the dealer can offer. The majority of the time, the dealer cannot beat your best price from a warranty provider because of the markup a dealer must charge to make a profit on the extended warranty offered. Also, when shopping extended warranties, be sure the policies are comparable in terms of deductible costs, covered parts and the amount of labor that will be paid for.

9. Why won't the dealer accept my offer of 3% over true dealer cost?

The dealer doesn't have to sell you a car. If demand for the model is high, if supplies are short, or if the dealer enjoys making a healthy profit, you won't be able to buy the car for a fair price. Don't argue the point, just find another dealer. If all the dealers you contact refuse to sell the car at this price, then your offer is too low, and you must start over at a higher value.

10. How do I figure a fair deal?

Use this formula: Dealer Invoice of car and options - Rebates/Incentives + 3% Fair Profit + Destination Charge + Advertising Fees + Tax = Fair Deal

11. Why should I pay advertising fees?

Most vehicles carry a legitimate advertising fee levied by either the manufacturer or by regional dealer groups. National or regional advertising fees, when charged, should not exceed one percent of the vehicle's MSRP. Because individual dealership advertising is a cost of doing business, you should never pay an advertising fee levied by the dealer rather than a regional dealer association or the manufacturer.

12. Can I negotiate the price of a new Saturn or Daewoo?

No, you cannot. All Saturn dealers post the same non-negotiable price for identical cars. This way, a buyer cannot shop down the street for a better deal, because the deal will be the same. You can, however, demand top dollar for your trade and/or a lower interest rate to lower the overall cost of the deal.

13. How can I find out what customer rebates or dealer incentives are currently available?

Rebates to customers are clearly announced in advertising. Incentives to dealers, commonly known as "back-end monies," are not. Edmund's® publishes current national and large regional rebate and incentive programs online at **http://www.edmunds.com**. Local rebate and incentive programs also exist on occasion, but Edmund's® doesn't have access to this information. Ask your dealer if the local automobile dealer association or advertising association is sponsoring any rebates or incentives in your area.

14. Why do some dealer incentives on specific models have a range of values?

Sometimes, the manufacturer will tell the dealer that he must sell a certain number of cars to qualify for an incentive. For example, let's say Nissan offered dealers an incentive of $100-1,000 on the Altima. This is a quota-based incentive. It means that to get the $100 per car, the dealer might have to sell 10 cars before a certain date. To get $500 per car, the dealer might have to sell 50 cars before a certain date. To get $1,000 per car, the dealer might have to sell 100 cars before a certain date. The more cars the dealer sells, the more money he makes, because quota-based rebates are retroactive.

With these types of quota-based incentives, you have leverage. With your sale, the dealer is one car closer to clearing the next hurdle and making more money. We recommend that you request half of the maximum quota-based incentive while negotiating your deal, unless the dealer or salesperson bungles and admits that your sale will put them into the next tier of incentive qualification. In this case, demand the maximum incentive.

15. When I use Edmund's® formula to calculate a lease, I get a payment that is substantially higher than what the dealer quoted me. Why is this?

The manufacturer subsidizes most nationally advertised leases. This means that the manufacturer gives the dealer incentive money to lower the capitalized cost (selling price) listed on the lease, or that the financing institution owned by the manufacturer has artificially inflated the residual value to lower the monthly payment, or both. Dealers may not inform you of these adjustments in the numbers.

Another problem with advertised lease payments seen in newspapers and on television is that consumers don't read the terms of the lease carefully. Sometimes, a substantial capitalized cost reduction (down payment) is required. Sometimes hefty deposits and other drive-off fees are involved. Mileage limits may be ridiculously low. Payments may be required for 39, 48 or 60 months rather than the conventional 24- or 36-month term. Read the fine print carefully!

Also, keep in mind that there are more than 250 different lending institutions across the country, and each one sets its own residual values for lease contracts. Don't be surprised if you go to three different dealers and get three different lease payments for the same vehicle over the same term.

16. Why are destination charges the same for every dealer around the country?

Auto manufacturers will average the cost to ship a car from the factory to the furthest dealership with the cost to ship a car from the factory to the closest dealership. Some manufacturers do this for each model, others average costs across an entire make. Sometimes, shipping costs to Hawaii and Alaska may be higher than the averaged amount for the contiguous 48 states.

17. Can I avoid paying the destination charge by picking up a car at the factory?

Currently, the only North American factories that allow customers to take delivery the minute a car rolls off the assembly line are the Corvette plant in Bowling Green, Ky., and the Dodge Viper plant in Detroit. Buyers who opt to travel to the Bluegrass or Great Lakes states to pick up their new Corvette or Viper still pay the dealer they bought it from the destination charge. We don't know if you can avoid paying destination charges on European models by ordering and taking delivery of a car in Europe, but that's an expensive proposition to avoid paying a few hundred bucks.

18. What is a carryover allowance?

At the beginning of a new model year, some manufacturers provide dealers with a carryover allowance in addition to the dealer holdback. The carryover allowance is applied to cars from the previous model year, and is designed to assist dealers in lowering prices and clearing out old stock. Currently, the only domestic automaker that gives its dealers a carryover allowance is Ford Motor Company. The amounts can vary, but they average five percent of the MSRP. General Motors and Chrysler target slow sellers with heavy incentives and rebates. Most import manufacturers subscribe to the incentive and rebate philosophy as well.

19. Should I buy rustproofing, fabric protection packages, paint sealant, and other dealer-installed items?

Of course not. Most new cars are covered against rust perforation for several years and up to 100,000 miles. Want to protect your fabric? Go to an auto parts store and buy a can or two of Scotchgard. New cars have clearcoat paint, which offers protection from the elements. A little elbow grease and a jar of carnauba wax will keep the finish protected and looking great. By investing a little time and effort into your automobile, you can save hundreds on these highly profitable dealer protection packages.

20. Who sets the residual value for a lease?

The financing institution that is handling the lease for the dealership sets the residual value, which can be affected by market forces and vehicle popularity. When shopping leases, it is important to shop different financing institutions for the highest residual value and the lowest interest rate.

21. I want to pay cash for my new car. Do I have an advantage?

Not necessarily. You must remember that no matter how you pay for your car, it's all cash to the dealer. In the old days when dealers carried your note, you could save money by paying cash because there was no risk to the dealer. Today, dealerships finance through one of several lending institutions (banks, credit unions, or the automaker's captive financing division) who pay them cash when the contract is presented. In fact, if dealerships do the financing on your behalf, they tend to make more money on your contract in the form of a reserve; anywhere from ½ to 1 point spread on the interest. For example, if the published rate is 8.75%, the lender to dealer rate may be discounted to 8%; the .75% is the reserve held by the dealer as additional profit. This may not sound like much, but it adds up to hundreds of thousands of dollars a year at larger dealerships. This is the reason you should always arrange financing before going to the dealership, and then ask the dealer if they can beat your pre-approved rate. In most cases, they cannot, because of the reserve.

Paying cash is an advantage if you suffer from poor credit or bankruptcy, because it allows you to avoid the higher interest rates charged on loans to people with past credit problems. The bottom line is that if you think you can invest your money at a higher return than the interest rate of the car, you could actually save money by not paying cash.

22. When is the best time to purchase a car from a dealer?

There's as much advice about when is the best time to visit a dealer as there are days in a year. Some say that Mondays are good because business is slower on Monday than on the weekend. Some say holidays like Thanksgiving are good for the same reason: nobody else will be there, and the sales team will be hungry for a sale. Others advise to go when it's raining or snowing; after all, who wants to look at a car and get wet? Then there's the advice that the end of the month is the best time because the dealership needs to make its "quota" of car sales and will be more willing to cut a deal. Still others advise not to buy a car until the end of the model year, or in slow months like August or December when people are busy thinking about going back to school or shopping for Christmas gifts rather than buying a new car.

Our advice is don't buy a car until you need one. That's usually the best time. By then you have saved enough for a substantial down payment, and you've had plenty of time to do your research for the lowest interest rate, and you know all the current incentives and rebates. There is no way to tell when is the best time to buy other than personal need.

If a dealer has already made his target sales for the month, you're not going to have any advantage by showing up on the 31st of the month. While there may be something to say for going to a dealership on a weekday near the end of the month on Thanksgiving at five o'clock during a raging blizzard, your best bet is to track incentives and rebates, don't buy hot new models, and do your research first.

1999.5 Nissan Pathfinder

LEASING TIPS

You've seen the ads: Mazda Miata for $199 a month. Nissan Altima for $269 a month. Jeep Grand Cherokee for $319 a month. GMC Yukon for $409 a month. Wow! You can't believe your eyes. Visions of shiny new golf clubs in your trunk, a big-screen TV in your living room and two weeks of prime vacationing in Vail release endorphins at twice the Surgeon General's recommended level.

But be careful, because you probably shouldn't believe your eyes when you read such banner ads, not until they're grazing over the fine print. See where it says "Capitalized Cost Reduction"? That's lease-speak for down payment. See where it says "30,000 miles over three-year term"? That's lease-speak for "You're going to the Safeway and back—and that's all folks." Want the car for zero down? That's gonna cost you. You drive someplace more than twice a month? That's gonna cost you, too.

Like most consumers, you want to know how to buy or lease the car of your choice for the best possible price. Buyers are attracted to leasing by low payments and the prospect of driving a new car every two or three years. Many people figure that a car payment is an unavoidable fact of budgetary life, and they might as well drive 'new' rather than 'old.' True, leasing is an attractive alternative, but there are some things you need to understand about leasing before jumping in feet first without a paddle. Whatever. You know what we mean.

1.) How to Lease

Never walk into a dealership and announce that you want to lease a car. Don't talk payment, either. Concentrate on finding a car you like, and know **before** you go into the dealership what you can afford. Lease payments are based on the capitalized cost, which is the selling price of the car. The residual value is the predicted value of the vehicle at the end of the lease term, and can be expressed as a percentage of the MSRP. Sometimes, the residual value is not the predicted value of the car at the end of the lease, but a number that allows the leasing company to lower the cost of the lease as much as possible without incurring excessive risk. A money factor, which is lease-speak for 'interest rate,' is also involved in the calculation of a lease payment. If the money factor is expressed as a percentage, convert the percentage to the money factor by dividing the number by 24 (yes, it's 24 regardless of the term of the lease). For example, a 7% (.07) interest rate converts to a .0029 money factor. Then, of course, there are associated taxes and fees that are added. Accept the fact that if the car you want to lease is not a popular model, your lease may be a bit higher than you anticipated.

Calculating an actual lease payment is nearly impossible, particularly when the lease is subsidized by the automaker, but you can arrive at a ball-park figure by using the following formula, which we will illustrate using a 1999 Mazda Miata as an example. Remember, if you put any money down, or trade in your old car, you must deduct this amount from the capitalized cost. This deduction is called the *capitalized cost reduction.* We recommend paying the destination charge, the acquisition fee, the security deposit, and any taxes up front rather than rolling them into the lease.

1999 Mazda Miata with leather package, A/C, ABS and floor mats	
MSRP	**$25,275**
Capitalized Cost (negotiated fair price)	**$22,548**
Destination Charge	**$450**
Acquisition Fee	**$450**
Security Deposit	**$450** (refunded at end of lease)
Capitalized Cost Reduction	**$900** (destination charge + acquisition fee)
Total Payment Due at Lease Signing	**$1,350** (security deposit + cap. reduction)
Residual Value after 3 years	(55% of MSRP in this example) $25,275 x .55 = **$13,901.25**
Term Depreciation	(Capitalized Cost - Residual Value) $22,548 - $13,901.25 = **$8,646.75**
Money Factor	(Interest Rate divided by 24) 7.5% divided by 24 = **.0031**
Monthly Lease Rate	(Capitalized Cost + Residual Value x .0031) ($22,548 + $13,901.25) x .0031 = **$112.99**
Monthly Depreciation	(Term Depreciation divided by Lease Term) $8,646.75 divided by 36 = **$240.78**
State Sales Tax	([Monthly Depreciation + Monthly Lease Rate] x Sales Tax Rate [6.5% in this ex.) $240.78 + $112.99 x .065 = **$23.00**
Monthly Payment	(Monthly Depreciation + Monthly Lease Rate + State Sales Tax) $240.78 + $112.99 + $23.00 = **$376.77**

Keep in mind that every vehicle will have a unique residual value, based on its popularity, its resale value and its reputation for reliability. Also remember that the above formula doesn't take the following into account: delivery and handling (D&H fees), documentation fees, the cost of license plates, city or county sales tax (if applicable in your part of the country), or trade-in values. The trade-in value and any cash down payment should be deducted from the capitalized cost before calculating the lease.

If you're upside down on your trade, which means the car is worth less than you owe on the loan, you'll need to add the difference between the balance due on the loan and the trade-in value to the capitalized cost.

The example we illustrated is a straightforward lease with no factory subsidy. This formula will not account for subsidized leases. Subsidized leases allow dealers to lower payments by artificially raising residual values or lowering the capitalized cost through dealer incentives. You can easily recognize a subsidized lease. Any nationally or regionally advertised lease is generally subsidized by the manufacturer to keep lease payments low. The $199 per month Mazda Miata and $319 per month Jeep Grand Cherokee are examples of subsidized leases.

Computing a lease payment can be frustrating. Ford Motor Company has developed special calculators for the sole purpose of computing lease payments because their method is not nearly as simplistic as the one above. However, a buyer interested in a Ford can use the formula to calculate a ballpark figure and find out whether or not the lease fits their budget. This figure can also be compared with similar calculations for competing models whose manufacturer may or may not be offering subsidized leases.

Actual lease payments are affected by negotiation of the sticker price on the vehicle, term of the lease, available incentives, residual values, and layers of financial wizardry that even sales managers can't interpret without divine intervention. Once you find a car you can afford, negotiate the sticker price and then explore leasing based on the negotiated price. Ask what the residual value is and subtract any rebates or incentives from the capitalized cost. Use the formula above to calculate a ballpark figure, and if the dealer balks at your conclusion, ask them to explain the error of your ways.

Your best bet when leasing is to choose a model with a subsidized lease. Payments are low, terms are simple to understand, and they are the only true bargain in the world of leasing.

2.) Low Payments

Low payments aren't a fallacy with leasing, when taken in proper context. For example, a Ford Ranger XLT SuperCab stickers for about $21,000, give or take. To lease for two years with no *capitalized cost reduction* (down payment); it'll cost you about $415 per month (plus tax). To lease for three years: about $360 per month (plus tax). Assume that a single payment of $900 was made up front to cover the acquisition fee and the security deposit. Generally, Ford allows 15,000 miles per year and charges 11 cents per mile for each one over the term limit. To buy that Ranger, financed for 24 months at 10% APR with no money down, you would pay about $967 per month (plus tax). For three years at 10%, the payment would be around $678 per month (plus tax). So you see, leasing is cheaper on a monthly basis when compared to financing *for the same term*.

There are two flaws here. First, 60-month financing is now the standard, and 72-month financing is becoming more popular. The Ranger will cost right around $446 per month (plus tax) for five years, at 10% APR with zero down, and still be worth a good chunk of change at the end of the loan if cared for properly. Second, ownership is far less restrictive, even if the bank holds the title until 2003. You can drive as far as you want, paint the thing glow-in-the-dark orange with magenta stripes, and spill coffee on the seats without sweating a big wear-and-tear bill down the road. Leasing for two years costs about $10,410 (assuming you get the entire security deposit back), and you don't own the truck at lease-end. Financing for two years costs about $23,210, but you own a truck worth about $13,650 when the payment book is empty (unless, of course, you've actually painted it orange with magenta stripes and spilled coffee all over the interior), which makes your actual cost a tad over $9,560. Is leasing cheaper? Monthly payments, when compared to financing over the same term, are lower. But in many cases, leasing is actually more expensive.

Let's compare the longer-term effects of leasing vs. buying, over the same term and under identical conditions. By leasing the Ranger in this example for two years, and then buying the truck for its $13,650 residual value with financing at a slightly higher interest rate than you would have paid new (interest rates rise as the vehicle gets older), you pay hundreds less than if you had financed for 60 months at a lower rate when the truck was new. Assume the interest rate for 36 months on a two-year-old truck is 12%. Payments for the loan would total about $455 per month, or just over $16,380 for the life of the loan. Added to the cost of the two-year lease, the $21,000 Ranger has cost you $26,390 (plus tax). Had you bought the Ranger outright, financing for 60 months at 10% interest, the Ranger would have cost $26,775 (plus tax).

In our hypothetical example, the lease customer comes out ahead by nearly $950 once the security deposit has been returned. But there are several factors that should be kept in mind. When leasing, tax is calculated on the payment; when buying, tax is calculated on the selling price of the truck. At a 6.5% sales tax rate, the Ranger costs the buyer using conventional 60-month financing $169.65 less in sales tax than the buyer who leases and then purchases the truck at the residual value. Other factors, like fluctuating interest rates, down payments, and contractual obligations can also affect the lease vs. loan scenario. Additionally, vehicle condition can have a tremendous affect on value. A few dents, dings or scratches could easily make a lease the more expensive proposition. When trying to determine if it is less expensive to lease and buy for the residual or finance outright, carefully weigh all the factors that can affect payments over the term of the lease or loan, including the way you drive and maintain a vehicle.

3.) Restrictions

Leasing severely restricts your use of a vehicle. Mileage allowances are limited, modifications to the vehicle can result in hefty fines at the end of the lease, and if the vehicle is not in top condition when it is returned, excessive wear-and-tear charges may be levied. Many dealers will be more lenient if you buy or lease another vehicle from them at the end of your term, but if you drop off the car and walk, prepare yourself for some lease-end misery.

Be sure to define these limitations at the beginning of the lease so that you know what you're getting yourself into. Find out what will be considered excessive in the wear-and-tear department and try to negotiate a higher mileage limit.

4.) Benefits

By leasing, you always get to drive a new vehicle every two or three years. This also means that, in most cases, the only time the car will be in the shop is for routine maintenance. And, as long as you lease only for the term of the original manufacturer's warranty, you're not liable for catastrophic repair bills. Additionally, leasing can allow a buyer to make that dream car fit the budget when conventional financing will not. Finally, and perhaps for some people this is the most important benefit, you're never again upside-down on a car loan, unless you try to end the lease early.

5.) Lease-end

Studies show that consumers generally like leases, right up until they end. The reason for their apprehension is rooted in the dark days of *open-end leasing*, when Joe Lessee was dealt a sucker punch by the lessor on the day Joe returned the car to the leasing agent. Back then, residual values were established at the beginning of the lease, but the lessee was responsible for the difference between the residual value and the fair market value at the end of the lease. The resulting lease-end charges maxxed out credit cards and dealers laughed all the way to the bank.

Leasing has evolved, and with today's *closed-end leases* (the only type of lease you should consider), the lease-end fees are quite minimal, unless the car has 100,000 miles on it, a busted-up grille and melted chocolate smeared into the upholstery. Dealers want you to buy or lease another car from them, and can be rather lenient regarding excess mileage and abnormal wear. After all, if they hit you with a bunch of trumped up charges you're not going to remain a loyal customer, are you?

Additionally, closed-end leasing establishes a set, non-negotiable residual value for the car in advance, at the beginning of the lease. Also, any fees or charges you may incur at the lease-end are spelled out in detail before you sign the lease. All the worry is removed by the existence of concrete figures.

LEASING TIPS

Another leasing benefit is the myriad of choices you have at the end of the term. Well, maybe not a myriad, but there are four, which is more than you have after two or three years of financing. They are:

* **Return the car to the dealer and walk away from it** after paying any applicable charges like a termination fee, wear-and-tear repairs, or excessive mileage bills. Of course, if you don't plan to buy or lease another car from the dealer, you may get hit for every minor thing, but those are the risks.

* **Buy the car** from the dealer for the residual value established at the beginning of the lease. If the car is in good shape, the residual value is probably lower than the true value of the car, making it a bargain, and many leasing companies will guarantee financing at the lowest interest rate available at the time your lease ends. If you've trashed the lease car, compare the lease-end wear-and-tear charges to the devaluation in worth the vehicle has suffered while in your care. You might be surprised to find that it's easier and less expensive to just give the car back and pay the fines.

* **Use any equity in the car as leverage in a new deal** with the dealer. Since residual values are generally set artificially high, the car is not likely to be worth more than the residual value at lease-end. However, a well-maintained, low mileage lease car might allow the dealer to knock up to a couple of thousand bucks off your next deal.

* **Sell the car yourself** and pay off the residual value, pocketing whatever profit you make.

Closed-end leasing is a win-win situation for everybody. The manufacturer sells more cars, the dealer sells more cars, and you get low payments and a new car every couple of years. However, it is important to stress that you never own the car and leasing can be quite restrictive. If you're a low mileage driver who maintains cars in perfect condition, don't like tying up capital in down payments and don't mind never-ending car payments, leasing is probably just right for you. If you're on the road all day every day, beat the stuffing out of your wheels, enjoy a 'customized' look or drive your cars until the wheels fall off, buy whatever it is you're considering, or plan to buy the leased car at the end of the term.

The Villager Tapes

By Special Agent Greg Anderson

photography courtesy of Ford Motor Company

PROS:
Much improved over the previous generation in both power and refinement.

CONS:
The Villager has excess gadgetry, and gadgetry has its price. And why not make the third-row seat removable?

While studying the driver's sun visor on the new Mercury Villager, Ron Howard's 1982 comedy film "Night Shift" suddenly came to mind. In case that logic doesn't follow, let us explain. Starring Henry Winkler, Michael Keaton and Shelly Long, "Night Shift" is the story of two morgue workers who become pimps by turning their somber office into a brothel. In it, Keaton plays a character named Bill Blazejowski, a self-described "idea man." Bill is always recording verbal notes into a tape recorder, for future reference. He records "business ideas, inventions, musicals." The ideas are random, the sort of fleeting thoughts that most people don't have the time to write down, such as: "This is Bill. Idea to eliminate garbage: edible paper." What does Billy Blaze from "Night Shift" have to do with the sun visor of our 1999 Mercury Villager Sport, you say? That's simple: they both carry tape recorders.

The Villager we tested was loaded with options, some of which were unlike anything we're used to finding in a minivan. Sure, lots of vehicles have six-disc CD changers, automatic temperature control systems, memory seats and keyless entry systems. Fewer have trip computers that display average mileage and miles-to-empty. And how many digital fuel gauges have you seen recently? Several cars or trucks nowadays are equipped with garage door openers located on the driver's sun visor, but our Villager Sport also came with its own built-in TravelNote digital voice message recorder. This device was handy for recording comments and complaints about the test car, and we barely had to take our eyes from the road to do so. As Billy Blaze would say: "You wonder why I carry this tape recorder? It's to tape things."

Note to self: Verbal recordings are a potential source of entertainment.

Minivans are among the most competitive class of vehicle in the American marketplace. Each year, these suburban people-movers come out with ingenious new features, extra safety equipment, more powerful engines, and more interior room in a manageable package. If it weren't for their slightly bloated, strictly utilitarian appearance, minivans would be sought after for more than just family transportation.

The Lincoln-Mercury division of Ford Motor Company partners with Nissan Motor Corp. The Quest and Villager twins are designed by Nissan and make use of a Nissan engine, but they're built at a Ford manufacturing plant in Ohio and sold under two nameplates. The Villager differs from the Nissan Quest only in name, a few interior pieces and some exterior badges.

From the driver's seat, the Villager is a study in futuristic automotive design, and, in this regard, it may be a few years ahead of its time. We're not talking about the placement of stereo or temperature controls, which are modern and completely intuitive. Our test vehicle came with the optional Electronic Instrument Cluster, which includes everything from an outside temperature reading to the aforementioned digital fuel gauge. The speedometer is located in the center of it all, showing the car's speed in a glowing green digital

readout that looks like the display on a police radar gun. A digital tachometer glows up and around the speedometer readout, and the effect — though high-tech — is surprisingly uncluttered and easy to read.

Note to self: Disco dash isn't as annoying as it seems at first. But why opt for it when the Sport model normally comes with unique white-faced gauges?

In order to remain competitive these days, minivan makers must pay close attention to the trends. This year, the Villager comes with dual sliding doors. Unfortunately, neither door is electrically powered, even on the top-level Sport trim. Well, at least the doors are there this year; maybe they're saving the power wiring for next year's update.

Derived from the same platform as the Nissan Maxima, the Villager is hampered by a relatively short 112.2-inch wheelbase. When compared to another recently redesigned Japanese competitor, the Honda Odyssey, the Villager suffers from size envy; both the Odyssey's wheelbase and overall length are six inches longer, making the interior much roomier. A parcel shelf is located behind the Villager's rear bench, which creates twice as much space for grocery storage. The shelf can hold up to 30 pounds.

The Villager Sport's second-row chairs (a bench unit on the base model) can be removed easily from either side of the van, but we had a difficult time removing the third-row bench seat. Try as we might, the stubborn legs simply would not release from the floor. Then we discovered that the legs were attached to rails, which allowed the seat to slide forward all the way to the front of the van, ending up just behind the front seats. This procedure creates an open space in the back of the vehicle, but it makes us think fondly of the Honda Odyssey's magic flip-and-fold seat. The Villager's available cargo space proved adequate for our needs, but it's not up to carrying a 4x8 sheet of plywood. Interior width is four feet, but available length is only 68 inches, or five feet, eight-inches long with the rear seat pushed forward.

Note to self: If we could take the third-row seat out completely, we'd have even more *space.*

Being the automotive journalists that we are, last year's 151-horsepower 3.0-liter engine could not satisfy our thirst for power. For 1999, the Villager receives a 3.3-liter V6, which provides 170 horsepower and 200 foot-pounds of torque. This is the same engine you'll find under the hoods of Nissan Pathfinder sport-utes and Frontier pickups, and it proved adequate in the performance department, mated to a four-speed automatic transmission. The down side is that when compared to the Honda Odyssey's 210-horsepower motor, the Villager comes up limping once again. Darn that Honda for creating such a solid benchmark.

The Villager's suspension has been revised up front, and, combined with new single-leaf springs in the rear, the Villager is blessed with a comfortable, balanced ride. Steering is stable, and the van tracks straight on highways. The turning diameter is 39.9 feet, which is two feet wider than — you guessed it — the Odyssey.

Note to self: With all the recent talk about corporate mergers involving Ford and Honda, Mercury might do well to just buy Honda and re-badge the Odyssey.

The Sport trim level offers similar equipment to Estate trim, but adds a silver-painted luggage rack and two-tone paint. The Sport and Estate versions further exceed base trim by a leather-wrapped tilt steering wheel with audio and cruise controls, a rear parcel shelf, powered and heated side mirrors, a rear stabilizer bar and 16-inch aluminum wheels.

Antilock brakes are optional equipment on all Villagers, once again making this vehicle fall short of the standard set so recently by Honda's similarly priced EX trim-level Odyssey. The value-packed Odyssey also gets a standard CD player and power seats, items that end up costing much more on the Villager. Because our test car topped out at a hair under $30,000 while lacking the cargo room available on minivans from several other manufacturers, we're left wondering how quickly Mercury and Nissan can design the next generation of the Villager/Quest duo. Maybe next time the targets will be more clearly defined.

Note to Mercury and Nissan: If you're serious about selling minivans, take a good look at Chrysler and Honda and copy what they've done right. Then give us powered sliding doors, ABS and side airbags, and take out the do-dads and electronic gizmos. Offer substance over hype. But leave the tape recorder in the sun visor, 'cause this thing's more fun than a telephone conversation with Monica Lewinsky.

Vehicle Tested: 1999 Mercury Villager Sport
Base Price of Test Vehicle: $25,595 *(including destination charge)*
Options on Test Vehicle: *Electronic Instrument Cluster (includes outside temperature reading, digital speedometer, odometer, dual trip odometers, analog tachometer, trip computer with instantaneous fuel economy, average fuel economy and distance-to-empty), Electronic Automatic Temperature Control, Supersound AM/FM Radio with Cassette and CD (includes seven speakers, partitioned audio and six-disc CD changer), Luxury Group (includes garage opener/electronic voice note recorder, leather seating surfaces, memory seats, memory mirrors and four-way power passenger's seat), Smoker's Package (includes front- and second-row right-hand ashtray and cigar lighter), Convenience Group (includes light group: overhead map lights, overhead console; power vent windows, remote keyless entry system: panic alarm and illuminated entry), Antilock Braking System, Comfort Group (includes auxiliary A/C with rear audio controls, 72-amp battery, particulate air filter, privacy glass and six-way power driver's seat).*
Price of Test Vehicle: $29,975 *(including destination charge)*

STEP-BY-STEP COST WORKSHEET

MAKE: EXTERIOR COLOR:

MODEL: INTERIOR COLOR:

TRIM LEVEL: ENGINE SIZE/TYPE:

ITEMS	INVOICE
Basic Vehicle Price:	
Optional Equipment:	
1.	
2.	
3.	
4.	
5.	
6.	
7.	
8.	
9.	
10.	
11.	
12.	
13.	
14.	
15.	
TOTAL	
SUBTRACT Holdback Amount (if ordering car)	
SUBTRACT Rebates and/or Incentives	
ADD 3% Fair Profit	
ADD Destination Charge	
ADD Advertising Fees (1% of MSRP maximum)	
ADD Documentation and D&H fees ($100 maximum)	
SUBTRACT Trade-In Value or Cash Down Payment	
or	
ADD Difference Between Trade Value and Loan Balance	
FINAL Price for Purchase or Capitalized Cost for Lease	
ADD Sales Taxes (and Registration fees, if applicable in your region)	
TOTAL COST	

Automobile Manufacturers

Customer Assistance Numbers

Acura	1-800-382-2238
Audi	1-800-822-2834
BMW	1-800-831-1117
Buick	1-800-521-7300
Cadillac	1-800-458-8006
Chevrolet	1-800-222-1020
Chrysler	1-800-992-1997
Daewoo	1-888-643-2396
Dodge	1-800-992-1997
Ford	1-800-392-3673
GMC	1-800-462-8782
Honda	1-800-999-1009
Hyundai	1-800-633-5151
Infiniti	1-800-662-6200
Isuzu	1-800-255-6727
Jeep	1-800-992-1997
Kia	1-800-333-4542
Land Rover	1-800-637-6837
Lexus	1-800-255-3987
Lincoln	1-800-392-3673
Mazda	1-800-222-5500
Mercedes-Benz	1-800-222-0100
Mercury	1-800-392-3673
Mitsubishi	1-800-222-0037
Nissan	1-800-647-7261
Oldsmobile	1-800-442-6537
Plymouth	1-800-992-1997
Pontiac	1-800-762-2737
Porsche	1-800-545-8039
Saab	1-800-955-9007
Saturn	1-800-553-6000
Subaru	1-800-782-2783
Suzuki	1-800-934-0934
Toyota	1-800-331-4331
Volkswagen	1-800-822-8987
Volvo	1-800-458-1552

Notes

Notes

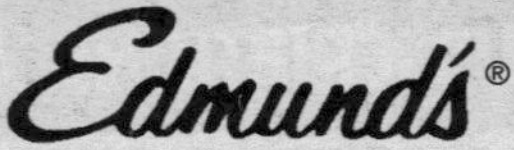

BUYER'S GUIDES SCHEDULED RELEASE DATES FOR 1999/2000*

VOL. 33/34		RELEASE DATE	COVER DATE
U3303	USED CARS & TRUCKS:Prices & Ratings	JUL 99	FALL 99
N3303	NEW CARS:Prices & Reviews[American & Import]	SEPT 99	FALL 99
S3303	NEW TRUCKS:Prices & Reviews[American & Import]	SEPT 99	FALL 99
U3304	USED CARS & TRUCKS:Prices & Ratings	OCT 99	WINTER 99
N3304	NEW CARS:Prices & Reviews[American & Import]	DEC 99	WINTER 00
S3304	NEW TRUCKS:Prices & Reviews[American & Import]	DEC 99	WINTER 00
U3401	USED CARS & TRUCKS:Prices & Ratings	JAN 00	SPRING 00
N3401	NEW CARS:Prices & Reviews[American & Import]	MAR 00	SPRING 00
S3401	NEW TRUCKS:Prices & Reviews[American & Import]	MAR 00	SPRING 00
U3402	USED CARS & TRUCKS:Prices & Ratings	APR 00	SUMMER 00
N3402	NEW CARS:Prices & Reviews[American & Import]	JUN 00	SUMMER 00
S3402	NEW TRUCKS:Prices & Reviews[American & Import]	JUN 00	SUMMER 00

**Subject to Change*